Feel

Feel: Robbie Williams

by Chris Heath

EBURY PRESS

First published in Great Britain in 2004

10 9 8 7 6 5 4 3 2 1

First published by
Ebury Press
Random House, 20 Vauxhall Bridge Road, London SW1V 2SA

Random House Australia (Pty) Limited
20 Alfred Street, Milsons Point, Sydney, New South Wales 2061, Australia

Random House New Zealand Limited
18 Poland Road, Glenfield, Auckland 10, New Zealand

Random House South Africa (Pty) Limited
Endulini, 5A Jubilee Road, Parktown 2193, South Africa

The Random House Group Limited Reg. No. 954009

www.randomhouse.co.uk
www.robbiewilliams.com

A CIP catalogue record for this book is available from the British Library.

Cover and packaging design by Dave Breen
Interior by seagulls

Printed and bound in Great Britain by Clays Ltd, of St. Ives Plc

ISBN 0 091 90495 1

Papers used by Ebury Press are natural, recyclable products made from wood grown in sustainable forests.

Before

1

'*Yeah, I'm a star, but I'll fade,*' he sings. '*If you ain't sticking your knives in me, you will be eventually.*'

'One more,' says Guy Chambers, his principal songwriting partner, producer and musical director.

August 2002. Late afternoon. Robbie Williams is in the vocal booth at Record Plant studios, a rectangular building on an unassuming Hollywood side street, singing a new song called 'Monsoon'. Like many of his songs, it is a thick stew of insecurity, honesty, immodesty and self-deprecation.

He starts again. '*I've sung some songs that were lame,*' he begins. '*I've slept with girls on the game.*'

Apart from the vocals, this new album is mostly finished. Rob came to Los Angeles at the beginning of this year and stayed because he discovered he was happier here. He had just released the *Swing When You're Winning* album, his fourth in five years, and finished a tour that had left him exhausted and miserable. To those around him, he announced that he was having the next year off. He knew he deserved it, and he knew he needed it. That didn't necessarily mean he knew what to do with it.

In the end, he has found himself making another record. His daily routine is to come down from his house in the Hollywood Hills for a few hours before dusk, listen to the latest mixes, make suggestions, and sing.

'I think the middle eight shouldn't be as hard,' Guy tells him.

'But it sounds great,' argues Rob.

'It'd be nice to have colour in the middle,' Guy persists.

'OK,' says Rob. 'Let's have it beige.'

Guy rolls his eyes.

Rob tries 'Monsoon' again, getting into it a little more now, playing air guitar as he sings. When he reaches the chorus, he lifts his shirt to show his nipples. There are nine people in the control room. Some are involved in making the record in various ways; some are simply there. I have just spent four days driving from Oklahoma City – Rob seems fascinated, and a little bewildered, that someone would want to be alone with their thoughts for that long – to be here. To watch and listen, to catch up with what has been happening in his life and to write a few words about it. I had bumped into him by chance this January at the Sunset Marquis hotel, where he was living while he decided whether Los Angeles was the place he wanted to be; the most recent of a series of occasional but friendly encounters over the years. I presume it was that chance meeting that prompted his invitation to be here now.

I imagine I'll be around for about a week. Maybe ten days.

* * *

Back in January, after we stumble upon each other on the patio of the Sunset Marquis, he invites me up to his villa to play backgammon. He thrashes me as we chat. It's good to see him, but he seems antsy and unsettled. When a girl he's been momentarily seeing telephones the room, he pretends to be his best friend Jonathan Wilkes (who is also in town, but out), says that Robbie is not here right now, and takes a message for himself that he will probably never return.

Between rolls of the dice, he sketches out his predicament as he sees it. Though in truth he is deeply proud of the swing record that has just come out, today he speaks as though he had been counting on it being a failure. As though it had been his foolproof way to torpedo his career, lighten his burdens and take the pressure off himself. And now his ploy is backfiring. The album, considered enough of a gamble by his record company that they had refused to accept it as a full Robbie Williams album for contractual purposes, is now on its way to becoming his most successful album yet. He should be feeling triumphant, but instead he feels as though he has just scored another in a series of own goals.

After a while, I have to go and work, but I see him later in the hotel bar, the Whiskey: not drinking, but where the drinking people are. He now has a huge blue tattoo down his right forearm, MOTHER. Because he loves his mother, but also because he needed a different kind of pain this evening, to take his mind off his mind. He has relied on this breather from work to help him feel better, but so far he doesn't – he feels worse, and now he has all the time in the world for those feelings to confront him. He has been sober for over a year, but now he feels the closest he has been to breaking his sobriety.

As it gets late, he sits with some people he doesn't know, chatting, and then realises what it is in their manner that he recognises so well. They are coming up on ecstasy. He calls them on it and discovers he is right. And they have plenty more, with them in the bar, right here, and are happy to share.

Go on. Treat yourself. Have one.

He is so tempted, but he forces himself to bed instead.

A few days after that, he returns to the tattoo parlour. He likes the way MOTHER looks and he wants something to balance it on the opposite forearm. He asks for six other letters, pushed together to offer balance: ILOVEU.

* * *

In the studio, they abandon 'Monsoon' for now and move on to something else. 'Me and My Monkey' is a long, lunatic, narrative song about the adventures of a man and his monkey sidekick; written in Bangkok and set in Las Vegas. For reasons that the song does not explain and its singer may not even know, the monkey, who habitually wears dungarees and rollerblades, leads the narrator into a perilous world of guns, pimps, gambling and simian prostitution. At the end of the song the story is unresolved. Rob acts out the dialogue as he sings it, standing on the scooter he is forever riding round the studio.

'Do you like that, Dad?' he asks. Today his father, in Los Angeles to visit his son, is amongst the control room crowd. Until a couple of weeks ago, they hadn't spoken in well over a year.

'I think that's incredible,' replies his father, Pete Conway. (It is his father's name that is the assumed one, not Rob's. His father was born Peter Williams; 'Pete Conway', which he lives and works under, is the name he took when he became a professional comedian. Someone else was already trying to entertain people under the name Peter Williams.)

'We wrote that, we did,' says Rob, mock pride disguising real pride.

Guy persuades him to do the vocal again. Back in the booth he says, 'Turn my vocal right up ... turn the light off ... let's get some vibe in here ... '

Guy fiddles with the switches and the lights go down in the control room.

'Not the light off in there, you tool,' comes Rob's voice. 'In here.'

'I couldn't find them,' Guy explains.

'But what a marvellous tool you are,' continues Rob in an affected posh voice. 'If you were a tool, you'd be a Black & Decker workbench ... '

The lights eventually go off around Rob, and he sings the song again, in the dark. After the line 'the monkey was high' he does a loud snorting noise.

'I find it disturbing not being able to see you,' says Guy. 'You're probably naked with a hard-on.' This is not baseless speculation. Rob has already been naked for quite a few vocal performances while making this album. For one of them – a cover of the Lynyrd Skynyrd song 'Simple Man' that has since been discarded – he wore a Superman costume.

'It's very liberating, singing naked,' says Rob to Guy. Pause. 'By Louise Nurding.'

'Who's Louise Nurding?' mutters Guy.

Rob doesn't bother to explain. Instead, he and Guy have a reasonably heated argument of a kind you don't hear every day, about the voices in which a monkey and a baboon pimp might actually speak. Rob lights a cigarette and, as the match flares, he is briefly lit up in the vocal booth. He's not naked.

Today is the first time I have heard these songs. Before he leaves, Rob announces that he wants me to hear one more. It is called 'Cursed' and is about a departed friend, though he doesn't explain that today. As the track plays, he sits me in Guy's chair at the recording desk, props himself on the desk, facing me, and leans forward to sing the sad, angry words from inches away, directly into my ear, spraying slightly as he does so.

* * *

When you are wealthy and famous and easily unsettled, it is easy to find a house but more difficult to find a home. The first house Rob rented in Los Angeles belonged to Dan Aykroyd. His stay was not a success. For one thing, the press and paparazzi found him there right away, and they couldn't be kept at a distance because, unlike many of Los Angeles' finer properties, this one wasn't in a gated community where only the homeowners and their guests are allowed to enter. There were other problems, too.

He was told that this house was where Aykroyd wrote *Ghostbusters*; the library and video collection were crammed with stuff about UFOs and the supernatural. Rob says he knew the house was already occupied the day he moved in, but the contract had been signed. So he decided to speak to the ghosts, and to offer them a truce. 'I sat on the edge of the bed,' he explains, 'and I said, "Hi, my name's Rob and I'm from England, and I'm here for three months, and I know you're there but I want you to know that I'm a bit scared of you, and I'm here just trying to get my life together and I hope you don't mind, but I'll be in your space and I know you'll be in mine, but if you just don't come through because it'll scare me. Thank you." And it *felt* like they'd heard and they'd acknowledged it.'

But one night he came back home to find all the windows and doors wide open. He waited in the driveway while the house was searched. Nobody there, nothing touched. Another night, Sid, his pet wolf, who was sleeping in a crate by his bed, seemed uncharacteristically restless. Rob assumed Sid wanted to pee, so at about four in the morning he walked him down the back stairs, into the kitchen and out of the door, but all Sid seemed to want was to play, so he took Sid back upstairs, closing all the doors as he went. Suddenly Sid darted away. Rob found him in the kitchen, shaking, on the other side of a closed door he couldn't have opened or shut.

Other guests heard unexplained voices at night. One day, out and about in Los Angeles, he bumped into The Who's drummer, Zak Starkey, who used to live there with his father Ringo.

'I heard you're in the old place,' he said to Rob. 'Seen the kids, yet?'

'What?'

'There's two kids in the garden,' Zak told him, 'and there's an old lady in the house.'

Rob never saw the woman, or the kids, but he did experience his bedroom going cold – 'like all the air was taken out the room' – when the Mamas & Papas' 'California Dreaming' came on the TV as part of a commercial for a sixties compilation. And by then, he thought he knew exactly why that was. He'd been told that this was also the house in which Mama Cass ate her final sandwich.

Never mind that houses sometimes collect stories that don't belong to them. (Mama Cass actually died in London, in another ill-fated property, the same flat where Keith Moon overdosed.) Rob had seen enough and felt enough. He decided to move out.

When the removal men came, he says that they went into the house once and refused to continue the job. Their reason: 'The old lady sat in the chair.'

* * *

'Have you met Pompey?' he asks me, as the two of them prepare to leave the recording studio. 'Pompey does the beating up.'

Pompey is a gentle-faced man who grew up in Portsmouth, hence the name. He is Rob's principal 24-hour bodyguard, in charge of all his security arrangements, but their relationship is much deeper than that. He is an ex-marine and will sometimes launch into extraordinary, demented tales of military life.

He will regularly announce, usually when some combination of tension and levity is in the air, 'Security isn't a dirty word.' Pause. '*Crevice* is a dirty word … '

Rob takes me up to his home, to the house he bought in the wake of the rental fiasco. The house where he says that he's happier than he's been for many years. This property used to belong to Clint Black, the country singer. 'Not my mat,' Rob says on the way in, pointing to the BEWARE OF UNSTABLE DOG doormat. He shows me the garden, the pool, the view over the valley. When he first moved in, he would wake up, open the curtains, stretch out his arms … and immediately the voice inside his head would start. *You don't deserve this*, it would say. *And it's all going to be taken away from you anyway*. And he'd look out and see the man taking the leaves out of the pool (in his head it would start: *How much does he get paid?*) and see the woman doing his laundry (*How much does she get paid?*) and the panic would rise inside him.

'If it is my lot that this all gets taken away from me then there's something I need to learn from it,' he says. 'But also, if this stays with me for the rest of my life, then there's something I need to learn from that too.'

He goes into the kitchen and lies on the floor, on his back. His three dogs – Sid, Rudy and Sammy – surround him, licking and nuzzling.

Then he stands up and walks into the hall, and presses a button.

'Look,' he says. A door opens. 'I've got a lift,' he says, grinning.

Sometimes he takes it up the one floor to the hallway outside his bedroom. It doesn't save much time. But, in its own small way, it can be a great thing to have your own lift, and to know and appreciate the pointless joy to be had from using it.

* * *

Rob and his father slip into what appears to be an ongoing joke-telling competition. This is the mode in which they seem most comfortable together.

'I get all my timing wrong when he's here,' Rob complains. He's still happy to act as the straight man for his father, when required.

'I tried that Chinese thing with needles,' his father says this afternoon.

'What?' says Rob. Setting it up. 'Acupuncture?'

'No,' says his father. 'Heroin.'

They head for the table tennis table, set up in the garage, next to the E-type Jag. The two of them are extraordinarily competitive, even as they play for service. Rob takes a lead in the first game, then his father draws level at 10–10. ('Tens,' he mutters, father serving.) Rob pulls 18–16 ahead, then his father wins three points in a row. 18–19. Then two points for Rob. 20–19. And then, one more point, just touching the end of the table, unplayable.

'Right,' says his father.

'You in for the battle now?' says Rob. 'Let me unload.'

He takes his Silk Cut from out of his pocket and assumes the position. In the next game, Rob is soon 5–10 down. Then 7–13. At 8–17 he goes for all-out attack, with little result. 'Bollocks,' he shouts, missing a shot for 10–20. Then, on the brink, a glimmer of hope. 'No!' shouts his father, missing to make it 14–20. Then, two points later – 'Yes, that's the one,' says his father – it's over. 15–21.

One game all.

'Last one,' announces Rob.

This time, it's even more intense. Rob is 10–6 up, then again it levels at 10–10. But Rob pulls away again and wins 21–12.

'Played, Rob,' says his father. They hug.

Then his father turns to me, grins, and points out that he has won the previous two matches. Rob laughs.

'We used to play it when he was younger,' Pete tells me. 'We used to play everything, really.'

* * *

When I arrive at the recording studio the next day, Josie Cliff is on the phone, hiring a film crew to shoot some footage of Rob here later this week. 'Basically he's a UK recording artist, very well known in Europe, sold about 20 million records,' she patiently explains. Josie is the member of his management team who is always with him. Because he has moved to Los Angeles, so has she. She is largely responsible for running his life: everything from managing his diary, hiring and firing his staff and finding his houses to packing his clothes for trips and responding to his immediate need for food or coffee or a cigarette. (Sometimes outsiders who first see her in action in these last roles underestimate her importance and influence. They soon learn.)

Rob appears from a room down the corridor. He has just been watching 20 minutes of camcorder footage Guy has brought in, filmed on an early solo tour in 1998, when he was in a bad way.

'It's really disturbing,' he says.

'Good times, bad times,' sighs Guy, nonchalantly.

'I know how much pain I was in,' says Rob.

'Is it depressing?' David Enthoven asks.

'It is for me,' says Rob. 'A state of alpha depression.'

David Enthoven is one of the two heads of his management company, IE Music – the one who travels with Rob when he tours and who visits more often at times like these, when he is recording or making a video or working in some other way, while his partner, Tim Clark, takes care of business in their London office. David now goes next door to watch the same footage.

'It reminded me of all the pain,' he says when he returns. 'It really actually quite disturbed me.'

'See, Guy?' says Rob accusingly. '*You* find it funny.' He is genuinely annoyed that his past suffering is being treated as entertainment. If he chooses to treat it so himself, that is his prerogative; it doesn't give others the same licence.

'There was a lot of pain, wasn't there, Robert?' says David.

He just nods.

* * *

You could fill a book trying to detail the ways in which his successes and triumphs have been interwoven with misery and despair, and the ways in which each has triggered, fired, and sometimes become part of the other. Never mind the ways in which a combination of all these has also become part of the show Robbie Williams offers as public entertainment.

The basic history, which may hide more than it reveals, is that by the time he parted with Take That in early 1995 he was already a heavy drinker and regular drug-user. After starting what nearly never became his solo career with an aimless year-long bender, he first went to rehab the day after he finished recording the vocals for his first solo album, *Life Thru A Lens*, in 1997. For several more years, he struggled to stay sober and to find a way of living that suited sobriety. Recently, perhaps, he has found one. Twenty months ago, he stopped again, and so far he has not faltered.

One evening, by his pool, I ask him about that last day, and he says that he was on the way to a work meeting in London. He'd been trying not to drink, and it was too hard, and in his head he cracked. He made a clear and conscious decision to give in to his worst instincts, to become a lush. He thought it through. Why did it have to be so bad? He had enough money to drink himself to death if he wanted to. And, failing that, he could just become one of those gentlemen with rosy cheeks, heavy padding and a bulbous nose.

It was only after he had reconciled himself with this future that another voice in his head spoke up.

'Hang on … ' it said.

Maybe he could just try one more of those meetings.

* * *

Rob smokes maybe three packs of Silk Cut a day. 'I'm really good at it,' he says wryly. 'I can't get through ten minutes without a fucking cigarette.' He wants to give up. He hates the idea that some kid would take it up because they've seen him sit down halfway through his live show, desperate for a fag, and light up. (Which is what he has always done during his live shows. He loves that bit. He can stop running around for a moment.)

He's vowed to give up when he's 30, and he mentions this often. He wonders how his voice will change.

He forever tries to flip cigarettes up with his fingers and catch them in his mouth, even when no one's watching.

This time, I'm watching.

One try. Second try. (Now he sees me.) Third try … and in.

'Back of the fucking net,' he mutters.

2

Another day at his house, in the early afternoon. Rob is still asleep. Pompey takes his cereal up on a tray while I sit with his father in the kitchen, drinking coffee, nibbling bits of melon. Outside, a man goes round the lawn, raking up pieces of dog poo. Beyond him is the pool. Beyond that, under a clean blue sky, the Los Angeles valley stretches north.

'I'm in Torquay next week,' his father says.

He was a policeman, then worked in an electronics factory and started doing stand-up in the evenings. When Rob was born, he and Rob's mother, Jan, ran a pub, but it didn't suit him, and after a while he left both the pub and Jan. While Rob was growing up, Pete's most regular jobs were at holiday camps around the coast where Rob would stay with him over the summer holidays.

Rob appears and says he wants to go down to the nearest shops to rent *Sexy Beast* for his dad to see, and to get coffee. A few of us are gathered by now: Pete, Pompey, his A&R man Chris Briggs, myself. On the way there, he plays Dusty Springfield's *Dusty In Memphis*.

We sit outside Starbucks. This is where he bumped into Mike Myers and his wife a while back and sat with them for an hour or so. 'It was lovely,' he says. 'You can't do that in Notting Hill.' The other day, he spotted Brian Wilson in the deli.

Chris Briggs mentions that he's going to learn to swim.

'Remember the first time you dived in?' his father asks Rob.

'Cornwall,' nods Rob.

His father reminisces about the time he sent Rob out for milk and the paper. 'Two hours later I was a bit concerned he wasn't back.' Eventually his son returned. 'He said, "See that little stone – I've kicked it all the way there and all the way back".'

'Very important,' says Rob.

When I ask him about it later he says he remembers it all – the day, the walk, the stone – perfectly.

'It's called obsession,' he says.

* * *

Rob's favourite book as a child was *The Adventures of the Wishing Chair.*

'It's a magic chair that takes kids to places. I used to wish that there was a magic door I could walk through, from my house, so that I could walk through into wherever my dad was on the holiday camps.'

So you used to wish that there were a magic door from where you were to the world of light entertainment?

'Yeah,' he nods, playing along. 'And now I've created that door. Whichever door I happen to walk through, there is light entertainment on the other side.'

* * *

Back up at the house, we sit in the garden for a while, and then Rob asks me whether I want to come with him to look at a property up the road. There is an open house today, and he fancies having a look, if only to be nosey about what other homes on this estate are like.

We take the black Jaguar. He has no driving licence. He has never taken his test, partly because he has never got around to it, partly because he worries he wouldn't be a very good driver, and partly because he can't bear the thought of someone sitting there and passing judgement on him. But within the gated community, the roads are private and he is allowed to drive. Once we're in the car, he doesn't make much effort to find the open house – we never do find it – but we start talking, and he keeps driving, and for the next hour and a half that's all we do. We loop over and over around the same seven or eight streets that make up the estate, sometimes fast, sometimes slow. Sometimes he accelerates swiftly just so he has a reason to brake.

We haven't really discussed anything in much depth since I arrived in town a few days ago, but he seems comfortable talking like this. He explains how much better his life is here in Los Angeles. 'For about six years I've known that for me to establish any kind of life without being under the microscope, I'd have to leave England,' he explains. 'And I haven't wanted to, and it made me cry. I always used to think about the park that I used to go to when I was a kid, the walks we'd go on with the dogs, the picnics at Buxton ... all these great things that I couldn't do any more. And I knew that I'd have to leave "my England", which is the phrase that was in my head. England, as far as I can see it, is a nation at the moment governed by gossip and governed by what celebrity does on a day-to-day basis. And, you know, I want to be a pop star when I go onstage, I want to be a pop star when I do my promotion, I don't want to be a pop star when I get out of my bed and go and get a coffee or some milk from round the corner and have it be on the fucking *News At Ten*.'

He knows it's hard for people to understand what the relentless attentions of the paparazzi can do to someone like him.

'When you're on 24-hour watch with the paparazzi, you wake up in the morning and there's maybe five carfuls parked outside your house, every fucking day, and they follow you everywhere, all day,' he describes. 'After five years of it, it can grind you down. It's really important you separate yourself from your tabloid entity or your television entity. And when you can't, because they're in your life, the chatter in your head increases even more and you take everything so personally because you really think they're writing about *you*.'

He read an interview with *The Simpsons'* creator, Matt Groening, where he was asked, 'What's the worst thing that could possibly happen in your life?' and Matt Groening answered, 'That my deepest fears about myself are true.' Living in England, with the ceaseless barrage it brought, that was how Rob felt: that perhaps his deepest fears about himself were true. 'Somewhere along the line, my head learned to say "No, you're shit",' he says. 'Somewhere along the line I became everything that was written about me that was grotesque and evil.' He'd rather not offer a full list of these fears – not yet, anyway – because they're still there somewhere. 'Everything I'm doing, I play devil's advocate,' he says. 'And the devil normally wins.'

But over here, in Los Angeles, nearly everything has seemed better. Just the fact that he lives on a private road, and has a garden overlooked by no one, means that he doesn't even have to think about being scrutinised or followed until he leaves the estate. Also, he refuses to apologise for how much he loves the weather here. 'I wake up,' he says, 'and it's sunny every day.'

Even so, there have been ups and downs. When he first arrived in town, he made a lot of friends very quickly – great friends for his great new life, it appeared – and he has been surprised and distressed to learn that many of them were not what they'd seemed. As he likes to put it, his dickhead radar was malfunctioning. 'They tell you about the people out here and how there's a lot of ulterior motives going on and networking and climbing,' he reflects. 'And I thought I could spot them all, I really did. And loads of them got underneath the radar. The last couple of weeks have just been a bit of a downer, because I got everything that I wanted as soon as I came out here – loads of mates, loads of things to do, and the ability to just walk around the street and really, really enjoy myself – and then ... ' He sighs. 'They're very fucking clever, because I normally spot people.'

The other thing that has got to him here is a growing paranoia that someone close to him is selling stories to the British tabloids. 'I only have to fucking *think* something at the minute and it's in the papers, and that's scaring the life out of me,' he says. 'I think all my phones are tapped. I can't trust *anybody*. It's fucking done my head in. Your mind goes and then you start to distrust absolutely everybody.'

He tells me that recently he's even planted false stories with people he suspects, to see if they turn up in the tabloids. Nothing, so far. He's had his phones checked but – and he knows this is funny, and he knows it is kind of crazy, but once your mind starts down this track it's hard to find its brakes – he's now even worried that the people asked to check his phones have actually tapped them.

* * *

After the first half-hour of driving, he pulls up in front of his own house. He gets out and pees in his front garden, and asks whether we should carry on. I encourage it. I have lots of questions.

He jumps back in and puts his foot down.

'Yeah, go on,' he says. 'Ask me another. Ask me one on sport. I know those.'

* * *

We drive on. He tells me that one consequence of getting settled here is that it has allowed him to realise that he wanted his father back in his life. 'The last time he saw me I was in a flat in Kensington, I wasn't too well, and I've moved up since then,' he says. 'And I want him to look and be proud.' The issues between him and his father are complicated, but one of the reasons he hasn't felt as though he wanted to see his father relates to his sobriety. Getting drunk together had been the cornerstone of their adult relationship. 'I loved drinking with my dad,' he says. 'I fucking *loved* drinking with my dad. We had the best laugh.' And for a long time he was scared that if he saw his dad drinking, he would.

He no longer feels that way, though his father is on the wagon for the trip. 'Getting on famously,' Rob says. 'We just slipped in like nothing had happened really ... When you go and do therapy and all that business, you can open up a whole can of worms that you don't really know how to deal with. Anger and resentment. It's just taken me a long time to accept. I mean, my dad's a great dad. He's a wonderful person. But once you delve so deeply into things: "This should have been like this … "'

The problem, he says, is that 'I needed a dad and I didn't need a friend. That's it. And I'd got a friend. A drinking buddy. Which is great … but I did need a dad.'

So do you now feel that he's more of a dad, or just that you're more accepting of him as a friend?

Rob stops the car so that we overlook a scrub-covered slope where the houses finish.

'Now I'm more accepting of him as a friend,' he says, and accelerates wildly up the hill, then brakes sharply. It's not clear how much he intends this as a conscious punctuation to our conversation. 'And it's great. I'm glad I am.'

* * *

A young and evidently attractive woman walks by.

'Hello!' he says. 'What's your name?'

She chats for a moment, from a distance. She says she's off to work.

'You know who you look like,' she says.

'Who?'

'Robbie Williams,' she says.

'Yeah?' he says. 'If only I had his money. And his good looks.'

* * *

Driving, still driving, he says it's weird to him when people think they own whatever talent they have. 'When people actually think it's them doing it,' he says. 'When it's not.'

What is it, then?

'God.'

You think that?

'Yeah. I'm not talking about a religious God. I call it God because that's how I can comprehend it.'

Earlier he had been expressing embarrassment about his number one single, 'Rock DJ', so, by way of clarification, I ask whether he believes that God wrote 'Rock DJ'.

'Yeah,' he says. 'He was having a bad day.' Then he reconsiders. 'No,' he corrects, 'I think *I* wrote the lyrics to "Rock DJ". I think God was working on somebody else's album at the time. I think he went and met Coldplay for a while.'

This isn't something he wants to talk about too much now – 'It's one of those theories that if it's down in black and white it's "Ooh, that's a bit weird"' – but it isn't something he takes lightly. He gets on his knees by his bed every evening to pray. Sometimes he sits in bed and talks, and he's sure someone's listening, just by the little signs he finds around him each day.

You can hear some of this within these new songs. 'Yeah,' he concedes, 'there's a lot of religion and death and rebirth in a lot of things that I do. It's always dodgy ground to step on because everybody thinks you're getting David Icke or something. You know, everything that I do, where I am, and my talent, is a gift from God. So every now and again he's going to pop up, isn't he?' He pauses. 'And I think he can give you all of this and take it away. I'm aware of that.'

* * *

He makes a declaration.

'I've got another five years,' he says. 'That's it, innit?'

Five years for what?

'In the business. This album's fucking amazing. If I can make one more like that and get to a greatest hits, and say thank you very much and then go off and raise kids. And then I'll see whether I like the attention or not.'

But do you really believe you'll do that?

He pauses, and starts laughing, as if amused that I've called him on it. 'No,' he concedes.

I don't, either.

'It's what I want to do,' he says, staring ahead through the windscreen.

* * *

He parks, and we go and sit at the mosaic table in his back garden as dusk falls. He talks about the new breed of pop stars. It's clear he doesn't think too much of what they've done, so far, but he still relates to them. 'Because I've *been* Hear'say, or I've been Steps or I've been any amount of Gareth or the other kid, Will,' he says. 'I've wanted what they've wanted. I've had the dreams that they've had. I've felt that small and wanted to prove myself. I've felt I had a gift and wanted to express it, just like them.'

And, like them, he didn't know where it would take him.

'I don't think you really know what you want when you're 16, heading into something full on. I'm really fucking pleased it happened to me but, just as much as some people have an allergy to alcohol, or an allergy to olives, I have an allergy to a lot of what comes with this.' Even though, he says, 'The result is, now I'm sat here and I have a life and it's fucking great.'

It took you a long time to get so that you could enjoy it, I say.

'Yeah,' he says. He hesitates for a moment, considering whether he is going to say this, then launches in. 'The truth is also that I've been a depressive.'

He describes a recent evening with his father, sitting out here, exactly where we are now.

'I get depressed in the evenings, Dad,' Rob said, trying to explain.

His father tried to brush it off. 'When you get depressed,' he suggested, motioning to the house, the pool, the view, 'just take a look around you, at what you've got.'

'It's like telling somebody that's got cancer not to have it,' Rob argued, but he's far from sure that his father understood. He knows that many people don't, and won't.

'People think that if you're depressed, you're depressed about *something*,' he explains to me. 'More often than not, I'm not. I just feel ... *terrible*. And it's not about record sales or media or family. That's stuff I can pin it on. The real root of it all is, actually, I suffer with an illness that's called depression.'

If that's the case, what does one do?

'Take medication,' he says.

And you do?

'Yeah.' Another long pause. He has never spoken out about this before today. 'And I say that only for the fact that, if that's written on paper, that somebody reading it goes "That's me, that is, and if that's what he's done, then I'm going to do it". The whole thing about therapy and about medication or treatment for anything like that in England is so hush-hush and so pooh-poohed. As a nation we've very "How are you?" and you don't expect anyone to tell you the truth.'

He had resisted taking antidepressants for a long time after he stopped drinking – 'Because I was determined one day I was going to wake up and it would have gone, and I could do it by myself' – but he has been on antidepressants for the last six months.

'That's why I'm happy today,' he says. 'It really genuinely is. That's why today's a good day. That's why I can appreciate what I've done in my career and can look at my old records and appreciate them now and like them, and value myself. You know, the fact that my father's here has got a lot to do with the medication that I'm on.'

He has a line worked out, one he's been waiting to use.

'Medication's what you need,' he says, 'if you want to be a record breaker.'

* * *

He doesn't like being alone. He doesn't trust his own company. 'I'm terrible in it,' he says. He always likes to have people around. 'Loads,' he emphasises. 'Loads and loads of people.'

Are you ever alone these days?

He shakes his head. 'No,' he says.

Never ever?

He shakes his head more emphatically.

Isn't that weird?

'Yeah,' he says, not meaning it. 'It's not weird, you know. It's what it is. I'm not good in my own company. I wish I was. Since I was 16, 17, I've travelled with a huge entourage.' He smiles. 'It's like technology advancing so much, you lose the ability by hand.'

This is the first real conversation we have when I reach Los Angeles that summer. After that, for the next 18 months we never really stop talking.

3

Rob doesn't like the lyrics he has written to a song called 'A Time To Die' and he wants to replace some of them. He and Guy sit in front of the mixing desk, agonising over it. After a while they start asking for ideas from anybody: his father, the programmer Richard Flack, me. For quite some time there is a search for a satisfactory rhyme with 'emotional', and, this being the type of pop music where imperfect rhymes presented with appropriate gusto and confidence are considered acceptable, amongst the suggestions are 'fall', 'crawl', 'ball', 'indestructible', 'cannonball', 'dismal', 'curtain call', 'fuck all', 'whore', 'casual' and 'wonderwall'. None of these work. I ask what the song is trying to communicate, hoping this might help.

'Basically,' Rob says, 'it's a vitriolic song about anybody that's been cynical towards me – don't hate the player, hate the game. Every album's sold more than the one before, I'm still here, and I've seen your measly little bands come in and go out, so I'm being a bit vitriolic. It was written when I didn't want to be Robbie Williams any more. The last 12 months.'

That comment hangs there, unexplained for now.

Guy begins to wonder whether this line really needs to rhyme anyway.

'Why are we thinking so much about it?' asks Rob, annoyed.

'You started it,' says Guy.

'Don't let me think too much about this shit,' says Rob.

'You started it,' Guy repeats.

'Well, don't *let* me,' says Rob. He says they'll just leave it as it is on the demo. 'I won't let you down,' he suddenly says, for no clear reason. 'I will not give you up. I've got to have faith in my sound. It's the one good thing that I've got.'

'Who's that?' asks Guy, his ears perking up at what sounds like a usable lyric.

'It's me,' says Rob. 'It's my first single. "Freedom".'

They try to think of other lines for ages. 'It's a bore when we get stuck,' says Guy. 'It doesn't happen often. Most of the songs on this album we wrote in two hours, tops. Some quicker.' Eventually Rob says, 'I'm just not in the mood, I don't think,' and scoots down the corridor. The song will remain unfinished.

* * *

Rob rarely mentions his first solo single, a cover of George Michael's 'Freedom 90'. It has been written out of his history. It appears on none of his albums and will not appear on his greatest hits album. He has never performed it in concert.

It marks the time when he was first a solo artist. So his contract said, anyway, and so he told everyone, but in reality he had yet to become one. He had no songs of his own, just a few poems. The first year since his messy parting of ways with Take That had been spent finding and then ridding himself of unsuitable managers, fighting in court and, most of all, getting off his head.

There is one story that he likes to tell, because it shows how uninvolved he was in his real career's mediocre beginnings; how hollow his claims to be an artist of any substance, rather than another piece of detritus from a manufactured boy band, might have turned out to be. For the video shoot for his first single in Miami he hadn't even got around to recording his own version of 'Freedom' yet, so he just mimed to George Michael's record instead.

* * *

Guy leaves the studio for a moment.

'Have you got the demo of "Come Undone"?' Rob asks. 'Quick. Lock the door before Guy comes back.'

There are a number of songs being recorded for consideration on the album that Guy did not co-write and 'Come Undone' is the best of these. The circumstances that led to its creation, and the arguments it has fostered, were right at the heart of the tensions during this album's genesis, and though everyone says those tensions are over, there are still the occasional echoes. Particularly involving 'Come Undone'. Guy is back through the unlocked door before 'Come Undone' is loaded into the computer. They listen to the song as it now is, and Rob tells Guy, in the way that you tell someone something you have told them many times before, that he wants it to sound more like the demo. This argument has been going on for weeks.

'It *is* like the demo,' Guy insists, a slightly despairing tone in his voice.

Guy tries to get Rob to come to the other studio down the corridor where Steve Power is mixing a song called 'Something Beautiful'. Rob says he will, but doesn't move, and starts talking about something else.

'Attention span of a gnat,' says Guy.

Eventually he does go next door with Guy, where the playback messes up. Guy sighs. It's that kind of day.

'Throw a strop, Guy,' goads Rob. 'Go on.'

Guy raises his eyebrows. 'I haven't thrown one in six years,' he says.

* * *

At the beginning of 2002, not long after our backgammon get-together, Rob and Guy went to the Bahamas together on a songwriting holiday. It was not a success. Rob was intensely critical of everything they came up with. Though later they would discover they had nonetheless written the basis of two songs they liked, 'Monsoon' and 'Love Somebody', at the time they both felt that little had been achieved. A second week of writing in Los Angeles was cancelled.

As far as Guy was concerned, they were just going through one of their occasional rough patches. But, in its wake, Rob made a dramatic decision. He wanted to kill off Robbie Williams. He'd made four albums with barely a break between them and he'd had enough. 'It's too much, really,' he explains. 'For the brain. Especially if you're me, can't handle much anyway. I'd come out hating everything that was Robbie Williams. I just wanted everything to stop that was Robbie Williams.'

His last album of original songs, *Sing When You're Winning*, in 2000 had been dedicated 'To Guy Chambers, who is as much Robbie as I am'. Rob says that, even when he wrote that, he knew it was a statement that cut in two directions. It was a public expression of thanks but also, for Rob, an indictment. It pointed out that, as he puts it, 'One of the main culprits for Robbie Williams was Guy Chambers.' That all this was as much Guy's fault as it was his. 'He had to go,' Rob explains, 'because I fucking hated anything to do with me.'

Effectively, he wanted to split Robbie Williams up. He would start a band instead. All the band members would write songs and he could lose himself within them. He planned to ask Dave Navarro to play guitar, and had some other people in mind to fill out the band. He did some songwriting in New York with a Norwegian called Boots Ottestad, and liked what they were coming up with.

Meanwhile Guy, spurred by how badly their time in Bahamas had gone and by their lack of future plans, started writing with other people. In March Rob met him at Guy's villa at the Sunset Marquis to tell him their partnership was over. 'I said,' Rob recounts, 'I need to reinvent myself completely, for my own sanity, and unfortunately we won't be able to work together any more.' They should finish off some new songs for a greatest hits album, after which he still wanted Guy to be musical director on the Robbie Williams farewell stadium tour, and that would be it.

'It went down like a shit sandwich,' says Rob. 'I could see, in his face, the arse fall out of his world ... I think he was fucking hideously sad and very worried, on many levels.' But he also agrees that Guy, on the surface, 'was brilliant about it'.

Over the next few months, this plot adjusted slightly. The two of them would now record a final whole new album, using up the backlog of songs they'd written, and some of Rob's other new songs, and release it, packaged with the greatest hits, as a double CD.

Along the way, there were other tense conversations. Rob thought Guy insufficiently keen on the songs Rob had written without him – Guy would tell him that he just didn't get them, that the chords were too obvious – and he was worried that Guy wouldn't do them justice. He also told Guy that he wasn't happy in retrospect with the polished sheen of *Sing When You're Winning*. When Guy argued, beseechingly, that until now they'd always agreed on everything, Rob's blunt retort was this: 'Look, I've been pissed and I haven't given a shit what the fucking records sounded like.' Before, he had always considered that his job ended when the songs were written, and – apart from the awkward period when he was forced to record his final vocals, usually with extreme reluctance – his job wouldn't start again until he had to promote the finished record. The actual record-making process he'd always found boring and lonely, and something to avoid. But while recording his swing album, in a room with a 60-piece orchestra, he had discovered that it could be fun. He was now sober, more interested, and more focused, and he wanted to be more involved.

In June, Chambers rehearsed a band playing these new songs for a week, and then they went into the studio with Rob to begin recording. The first day was a disaster. 'As it happens, we were just fucking both of us really bad at communicating,' says Rob. They ran through 'Something Beautiful', which sounded fine, though Rob was uneasy about how serious everyone was being. Then Guy suggested they try 'Come Undone'. One of the songs he hadn't written. Rob was thinking how mature and selfless this was on Guy's part, until the band started playing it and reached the chorus …

Guy had changed the chords without telling him. Whether the band finished playing the song, Rob has no idea. He had left the building long before. He didn't stay to listen, or to discuss. In his car he told Chris Briggs and David Enthoven that it was over between him and Guy. They told him that it would cost him quarter of a million dollars to cancel everything at this point. He told them that he didn't care. He wanted nothing more to do with any of it.

* * *

In the vocal booth, Rob sings 'Love Somebody'. I watch from the back of the studio. By the second verse he is raising his hands beside his head, testifying, gospel-style. At the end he says, 'I'm not sure about the lyrics in the middle eight.'

'We can't change that, mate,' says Guy. 'Fucking gospel choir.'

Rob sang the original guide vocal a couple of months back, after which Guy and Steve Power worked on the songs in London for a month. It was then that they added the gospel choir, mirroring the lyrics on Rob's guide vocal: *Help me feel the power, you just got to set me free, there's a love that lives forever in me.*

Rob insists that he wants to change them.

'We'll have to get a choir here, at great expense,' Guy explains.

'You should have asked me,' says Rob.

'Asked you what?' says Guy.

'"How are you?" more often,' mutters Rob. He means that they should have checked with him that the lyrics were the final ones before hiring a gospel choir in the first place. 'I'll just have to live with it, I guess,' he says. 'It's only my album. Only for the rest of time. Thinking we just should have talked some more.'

'I don't think it'll affect sales,' says Chambers, teasing.

'It affects me,' says Rob. 'I'm more important than sales.'

He goes back into the vocal booth, where he scribbles on a tablecloth. Later, when he goes to the bathroom, I pop in there and take a look. He has drawn a picture of a man in front of a house, his arm outstretched, the word balloon from his mouth containing the single word BOLLOCKS.

The track begins to play, and he burps loudly before the first line.

'That's nice,' murmurs Guy. '*That* might affect sales.'

They're used to editing these noises out. Rob has long had a tendency to punctuate his moments of greatest sensitivity in such ways. Even on the master vocal take for 'Angels' there is a loud and clearly audible fart.

* * *

In June, after announcing that it was all over with Guy, whatever the cost, Rob did agree to sleep on it. In the morning he had a change of heart.

'I was just being a diva, I suppose,' he now says. He went in to speak with Guy, who wasn't told how close everything had been to ending, and announced that they shouldn't even bother with the greatest hits idea. They should just make a new album. 'I said, "I love you and you're brilliant, you're a fucking genius and we're amazing together",' he remembers. 'And we've been swinging ever since, really.'

Despite writing the occasional song with Guy along the way, and those he had written with others, Rob believed that for the previous 18 months he had been suffering from writer's block. Now he and Guy quickly wrote three more songs from scratch and finished or radically overhauled several others. Everything is good between them, and the general opinion seems to be that the persistent sniping back and forth, and their frequent failures to communicate effectively with each other, indicate that their complicated, dysfunctional and productive relationship is as healthy as it has ever been. They have been through, everyone seems to agree, the kind of rocky phase that strengthens a marriage rather than signals its imminent collapse.

'We're back on board,' Rob tells me. 'We are the writing team again.'

* * *

An American session singer called Darlene arrives at the studio. She is to sing an operatic line in 'Feel', a song Rob and Guy wrote a while back. Guy was trying to play something that he thought sounded a bit like Moby, and Rob sang some words about how depressed he was, and how much he wanted to be rescued from that depression: a song about hope from a man with too little.

'It's not happy Robbie, it's sad Robbie,' Guy tells me. 'I like the fact that we can do five different types of song. A lot of artists can only do one. There's the ballad: "Sexed Up", "Nan's Song". You've got the dirty rocker: "Song 3", "Cursed". "Hot Fudge" is the party track. "Feel" is the introspective one. And we've got cheeky Robbie with "World's Most Handsome Man".'

Now they are trying to find an interesting way to fill some of the song's wide spaces, hence Darlene. She gives Rob and Guy some chocolates she has brought for them, and is given the Italian lyric translation, which has just arrived:

Voglio solo provare vero amore
Nella case in cui vivo
Perche ho troppa vita
Che mi scorre nella vene
E va sprecate

'Do you want to sing what you had in mind?' Guy asks Rob.

'Ad lib,' he mutters, unwilling to engage.

'You sang something the other day,' prompts Guy, and plays the instrumental passage where they want something to go, to which Rob suddenly starts singing, as though it was the most obvious and simple thing in the world, a beautiful and haunting opera-esque melody line.

Darlene goes into the vocal booth and sings what he has suggested a few times, in a few variations. It sounds great. Occasionally Rob offers a comment, or sings a new option for her to try, but always without looking up from the football pages of the newspaper he is reading. When she is asked to do an improvisation at the end, he explains a little more about the tone of the

song to help her: 'Very spiritual, very uplifting – there's definitely hope in this crazy world we call … Earth.' Guy mentions, out of her earshot, that there is another idea for this song. They have asked Ms Dynamite to do a rap, but haven't heard back yet.

Darlene rejoins them and says how much she likes the song. She compliments him on how emotional the vocal is.

'Well, it's before the medication,' he says, without explaining, and sings meaninglessly, under his breath, '*I just want to feel … your bum.*'

She leaves and Guy asks if he wants to do some harmonies.

'Do I fuck?' Rob replies. 'Do you think I am … *bothered?*' He's in a strange, silly mood. He rejects every idea Guy has – 'Fuck off! Fuck off! Fuck o-o-o-o-fff!!!' – then picks up an acoustic guitar and pretends to smash it.

'Did I tell you about the time I threw Guy's 12-string guitar into Lake Como?' he asks me.

Why did you do that?

'It was out of tune,' he smirks.

Why, really?

'Because I was drunk,' he says, more quietly.

'Latent hatred,' mutters Guy.

'Not for you, darling,' he says.

When Guy once more suggests that he sing some harmonies, he refuses again – 'Fuck *off*' – then goes into the vocal booth to do them.

'He's in a contrary mood today,' says Guy. 'I love it when he's in this kind of mood.'

In the vocal booth Rob takes his cigarette lighter and sets the tablecloth on fire, then does a few harmonies, which he finds and sings effortlessly, though he looks annoyed when Guy says that one of them is flat. When he misses another, he throws the microphone stand to the floor. A few minutes later he picks it up but says he doesn't want to do any more.

'It's your record,' says Guy.

Rob comes back into the control room and picks up some fruit.

'Have you seen me juggle?'

Guy rolls his eyes. 'Yes,' he says.

Rob wonders what he should do for the evening. 'I might go up to Les Deux,' he says. 'It's the Monday night hangout. For the vain and the beautiful.' He wanders back and forth. 'I feel so fucking strange,' he says. Soon afterwards he leaves.

* * *

He has Pompey, or a substitute, with him or nearby every hour of the day and night. He finds it hard to understand that people find it hard to understand. To him, it just makes sense. It's not about having a bodyguard. It is, quite literally, about *security*.

'I've always been paranoid,' he says. 'Even as a kid, you know. My grandma used to tell me the stories about the sandman – he'd come and take little children – and it petrified me. I always think there's somebody breaking in, you know. I couldn't sleep in this house alone; I'd be too scared.'

For a while, before he had live-in security, he would sleep with a hammer next to him. He also used to sleep with a starting gun. And a can of Lynx and a lighter. (Makeshift flame-throwers have got him out of scrapes before. Once when some blokes threatened to beat up the famous Robbie Williams on the forecourt of a Stoke-on-Trent garage he got them to back off by holding his lighter to the nozzle of his lighter fluid and threatening to ignite it.)

But even 24-hour security can't protect you from your dreams, and he has some of the worst. 'I'm always being chased, I'm always in prison,' he explains. 'They always find coke on me and I get arrested. Ghosts. Smack. I dream a lot about really embarrassing myself. I had a big one the other night when I was in church and I was off my face on smack and I just shit myself. I have dreams where I kill people. And I have a recurring dream where I've buried someone under the garage at the side of the first house I grew up in, and they're closing in on me. They know it's me. And then I add bodies. And all they've got to do is have a look under the brambles and they'll see them.'

4

Outside on the lawn the dogs cavort and fight over a giant horse bone. He'd always wanted dogs, and tried twice in England, but both times it went wrong. He had a Rottweiler for about three weeks. And two Great Danes for a night. 'A tiny flat and Rob waking up to 12 turds,' David explains.

Here, in Los Angeles, he has three dogs and adores them. He got the first, Sammy, a pit bull Labrador mix, from the pound. The original idea was that he was going to call the second dog Davis and the third Junior. 'But that was just silly,' he reflects. He named the German shepherd after the ska song 'A Message To You, Rudy' (though as his love for Manchester United's Ruud van Nistelrooy grows, he will begin to convince himself that Rudy was named after Ruud without Rob yet knowing it). And there's Sid, the wolf.

Sid Vicious? I enquire.

'Sid James,' he says.

* * *

Pompey drives him along the top of the Hollywood Hills to avoid the afternoon traffic, and then down the canyon into Hollywood and to the studio. I follow in my car. Rob walks in and sits at the studio computer, scanning the websites of Britain's most popular tabloids. Still no sign of his planted stories. Guy tells him that if they do get a choir back in to fix the 'Love Somebody' lyric, it will cost $20,000. 'Get them back in,' he says immediately. 'Cause for me it's a great song, and I wouldn't be able to stand that lyric in it.' He starts reading an old *News Of The World* he finds lying next to me on the sofa at the back of the control room, where I sit quietly most days, watching, taking notes.

'What are you going to change it to?' Guy asks.

'*Up your cunt, you silly fucks,*' he mutters, not looking up.

'That's *very* gospel,' says Guy.

They work on 'Come Undone' again. The mood is already a little edgy. Rob keeps saying, curtly, and accusingly, things like, 'Is that piano *you've* done?' and Guy will say, 'No, it's old piano.' The camera crew Josie booked the other day arrives and begins filming. Eventually Rob goes into the vocal booth.

When he finishes a run-through, Guy tells him he thinks he can do better. 'Put a few more down and we'll compile it and do the best we can,' Guy says.

This moment will later be replayed as a key one. It is immediately clear that Rob is really, *really* annoyed, though as he often does, he delivers the following rebuke in a semi-comedy voice: much of the serious business in Robbie Williams' life is done in the shadow of a not altogether innocent humour. 'I'm really sorry you have to do the best you can, you fucking cunt,' he says breezily. 'It must be tough, trying to polish a turd.' Laughter, edged with nervousness, rings out in the control room. 'Have you ever seen Jack Nicholson in *As Good As It Gets*?' Rob asks Guy. 'That's you, that is. A few levels down.'

'Sometimes it just comes out wrong,' sighs Guy, by way of apology. 'You've done the same thing.'

'Not as often as you,' Rob retorts. 'There's some great lines in *As Good As It Gets*. I watched it last night.'

'I'll watch it again,' says Guy. 'Take some notes, and try not to take too much offence.'

Rob tells a story of a group of men approaching them in Notting Hill once and asking Guy if he'd got their demo, and Guy dismissively saying, 'I don't think it's very good.'

'I don't deliberately hurt people,' Guy says.

'I know you don't do it on purpose,' says Rob. 'You've just got an OCD thing.'

'What?'

'Obsessive Compulsive Disorder.'

'And you don't?' says Guy.

'I have,' says Rob. 'Except I know it. It's not a river in Egypt, you know?'

* * *

Rob often takes Guy to task over his tactlessness. He has a store of favourite examples. One afternoon in the studio he brings up the time, for instance, when a German hotel manager told Guy there was no German word for 'depressed' and Guy retorted, 'Oh, that's right, because when you get depressed you invade Poland, don't you?'

'I've been better recently,' says Guy dryly.

Rob isn't finished. He moves straight on to the time when they were in the south of France with Guy's wife, Emma, and Geri Halliwell. Guy asked Rob if he had heard of Nick Drake, and Rob pointed out that he had a Nick Drake CD right there.

'Who gave it to you?' Guy asked.

'Amanda de Cadenet,' Rob told him.

And then Guy said, 'Did you ... ?' and made a graphic, hip-thrust shagging motion.

'No,' said Rob.

'So,' Guy persisted, 'you couldn't add her to your celebrity fuck-tree?'

Guy sits through these tales with reasonably good humour. 'Moments of madness,' he says. 'It's a creative thing.'

Another day, when Guy isn't around, Rob says, complaining about the lack of respect he considers Guy showed to Frank Sinatra's producer, Al Schmitt, 'He's just got as much social grace as Fred West. In fact, after this project he's writing the Fred West Side Story.'

* * *

He's only just heard that Coldplay are playing in Los Angeles tonight. It's nearly six o'clock. 'I definitely want to go to that,' he says. It's the hottest ticket in town, but Coldplay are also signed to EMI, the label desperately hoping to re-sign him. Phone calls are made; mountains are moved. He has some time to kill, so he agrees to come to dinner first with myself, David and Josie.

I drive him. On the way, he asks which women I've met in the celebrity world who seem like 'an all-round good egg'. It takes me a moment to realise that he's thinking about prospective Mrs Williamses. 'I don't know,' he says in the car. 'I always thought there was a fairytale ending to all of this, and naturally it was going to be love. You know, like in the songs and in the movies. And I thought the package came with "She's in Los Angeles ... and she's got her own career ... and understands my career ... and is not mad". But living here has demystified that myth to me.'

There's a lot of madness here, I say, as we slide down Santa Monica Boulevard.

'Yeah,' he says. 'It's a town run by children.'

The search for love is a recurrent one in his latest songs. Sometimes he talks as though it is a quest that may be over, and sometimes as though it is one that goes on. 'The last ten years have been spent most nights going out looking for Mrs Williams,' he says, 'and funnily enough I haven't found her in Stringfellows or Spearmint Rhino. The rest of the places I've been looking for her she hasn't turned up. I don't want to go out any more. I'd like to settle down. I've got three dogs – I'd like three kids. I'd just like to chill out. I wouldn't mind a pot belly, actually, and a tan. After a couple more records that's what I'm going to do – get a pot belly and a tan, play backgammon and smoke cigars. That's it. Get all Mediterranean on my own arse.'

Before we go to the restaurant he stops off in a posh clothes shop, H Lorenzo. He's decided he needs a jacket to wear to the Coldplay concert. He chooses a brown one with a long flap at the back and a white vest. Just over a thousand dollars in just under five minutes.

Then he decides he doesn't want to sit in the restaurant so he goes for coffee down the road and joins us briefly as we finish eating. Here he announces that he's changed his mind about seeing Coldplay. He and his new jacket are going home. 'I think where I was worried about staying in,' he explains, 'I'm now worried about going out.'

Pompey has recommended a movie, *Desperado*, so he has rented that to watch instead. He hates it.

* * *

Amongst the many contradictory truths about Robbie Williams confidently and repeatedly stated or implied by the British tabloids concerning the part of life they still have the nerve to call private – that he is an irrepressible lothario; that he is eternally lonely, alone and unloved; that he is obviously, secretly gay – is that he is going out with the model and former wife of Rod Stewart, Rachel Hunter. Things are rarely, if ever, that simple, though certainly she is sometimes round his house when I visit, and often when he is on the telephone it is her on the other end.

Over this period of time he tells me four things that relate to her.

First, 'We don't even know what's going on with each other – all I'd like to say is that we really, really enjoy each other's company.'

Second, after the tabloids suggest that whatever is going on between them is a sham: 'I will say this – I'm commitment-phobic. I get claustrophobic, and I run off for a little bit, and then, when I realise that she is the most amazing woman and we have really, really lovely times together, I really miss her. I don't know where that leaves us other than to say she's the most wonderful woman that I've ever had the pleasure of spending any time with.'

Third, his current favourite joke. 'The sex is nothing to write home about.' Pause. 'It's a shame, because my mum loves those letters.'

And the fourth is a long, messy cautionary tale.

* * *

In these first months in Los Angeles, he has twice tried to wrest control in the unbalanced relationship he has with the media, in ways that now seem less wise than they did at the time.

The first is the less important. Two of his Los Angeles friends, who until just recently have been living at his house, are a couple – Billy Morrison (most recently bass player in The Cult's touring band) and Jen Holliday. They were planning their wedding, and Billy suggested that Rob got ordained on the internet and marry them. 'I'm, let's fucking do it, that's brilliant,' he recounts. He became a reverend in the Church of the Universal Life and this March he married them in the grounds of the Sunset Marquis hotel to the sound of Aerosmith's 'Sweet Emotion' and Billy Idol's 'White Wedding'. It was beautiful. More surprisingly, he suggested that they supply the wedding photographs to *Hello* magazine, and that the proceeds would be his wedding present to the couple. He gained nothing from it himself, and was pleased to help them. At that moment it seemed a fun, innocent victory, conjuring a nest-egg for his friends from something so simple. It was only afterwards that it stuck in his throat. For the first time, he had accommodated one of the magazines he has so hated, the magazines who are also one of the primary markets for the paparazzi who endlessly distress him.

But it was his other attempt, the one that involved Rachel Hunter, that mattered far more.

You have to understand how crazy the Los Angeles paparazzi had been driving him this summer. (Though he is much less famous here, they all know how much money they can earn internationally with a hot Robbie Williams snap.) He would come out of an AA meeting and there would be four carloads of paparazzi shooting him on the steps. He was angry for himself, and furious on behalf of those around him dragged into this situation by his celebrity. 'There's a lot of people in that picture that wouldn't want it publicly known that they've had a drinking problem or a drug problem,' he says, 'but they've been lumped in a picture with me because unfortunately I'm one too.'

One day, driving to his therapist, he was followed by three cars. He couldn't lead them to his destination – 'She had other celebrity clients, she doesn't want anybody going through the dustbins, and I personally don't want them finding out this is the place I go and release all my deepest, innermost, darkest secrets' – so he went to Saks, the department store, instead. He didn't lose them there, so he went to Neiman Marcus and got the woman behind the cosmetics counter to call him a cab, left his own car where it was, ducked his head in the back seat of the cab, and managed to reach his therapist unfollowed.

For a while, they seemed to be everywhere. It really got to him, and more and more he wanted to find a way to get his own back. 'I'm a competitive person,' he says. 'Really fucking competitive, actually. And if I think that someone's got the upper hand on me in any way, I want to find a way to beat them. So all of this is going on, and I have always desperately wanted a way to win. A way to win the game they're playing with me. I am a *pawn* in the game they're playing with me, I'm not a human being, you know. They're not concerned about the ramifications of putting in a piece about me and my father, they're not concerned about writing about the contents of my mother's house when she's the only one who lives there, they're not concerned about printing where Geri Halliwell lives and then she gets burgled the next day. I mean, if I died, it'd make good copy, you know what I'm saying? And as fast as I can fall on my face won't be fast enough for them. So what you're actually dealing with is the devil, I believe. You're actually dealing with people who want to see you die. And to actually have that in your space 24 hours a day, like it was, it can be very frustrating if there's no way you can win. And, actually, the only way you can win is just to completely accept it, but that is so fucking difficult.'

This summer, that was not the path he chose.

He was just beginning to spend time with Rachel Hunter, though these were early days in learning whether this might become anything more than a friendship. She got tickets for them to see the Lakers one evening, and though the Lakers lost, he found the experience amazing, down close by the court. Leaving the Staples Center with 17,000 other people, they walked through a door and into what seemed about 15 paparazzi. 'Letting off all these flashes that pulsate,' he says. 'They call it strobe-fucking. The 17,000 people leaving the Staples Center are all going "Who's that?" and everybody wants to look, and it's claustrophobic as fuck and it's really really embarrassing, and on top of that you've got 15 blokes that are fucking taking liberties out of you. Pure liberties. They're treating me like scum, like they don't give a fuck about me. And they don't. And I can't do anything about it because if I hit any of them I'll get deported, and it'd be 500 grand and maybe a jail sentence.'

And a better photo for the other 14. He had his cap low so that they couldn't get a good picture of his face. 'Which they hate,' he says. 'And all of a sudden I get this clout on the back of my head.' One of them had darted past, whacking the back of his head, grabbing his cap and running away with it. Now he was so angry that he simply stopped. He just stood there, seething, defeated, but defiant. 'Right,' he said to them. 'Take your pictures.' He figured it just wasn't worth it; none of it. Eventually, he got in the car. He just wanted to cry.

As he stood there in front of the cameras, Rob was also measuring the ramifications. So far, he and Rachel had shared some innocent evenings, a little Scrabble and hand-holding. Now it was going to be in every paper, and everyone would be brought into it: her ex-husband, her kids.

It turned out that it was already too late, anyway. A photographer had snatched photos of the two of them the day before when they had gone bowling. Their supposed hot affair was all over the world's tabloids and photo magazines. He heard that the bowling alley shots earned £1 million worldwide. 'Have you ever been mugged for a million quid?' he asks. (David Enthoven says he believes the real bounty was more like £100,000: a lot of money anyway.)

That's when Rob had the idea. At the time it seemed like a wonderful plan – a way of getting the paparazzi off his back, and getting one over on them at the same time: 'I said, look, if we give them what they want – *exactly* what they want – then there'll be no call for them. If we give them everything, they won't hang out and there'll be no money for it.' He and Rachel talked about it, and it seemed so funny and satisfying as an idea. 'We got excited like schoolkids,' he says. The next day they did it.

They posed on a sunlounger by Rob's pool, Rachel topless, Rob caressing her and kissing her in various ways: the best, intimate, stolen paparazzi shots revealing a new affair you could imagine. 'We're pissing ourselves laughing,' he remembers. 'The whole thing is really giddy.'

From the start, some voices were counselling against this, Tim Clark's being the loudest. He warned Rob that he would be getting into bed with the devil, and suggested there could be unhappy consequences, but in the end he realised that Rob was intent on following this path, with or without IE's help. It was arranged for the poolside photos to be offered to the tabloids as genuine paparazzi photos and there was a bidding war. 'Everybody wanted them,' Rob says. '*Eeeeeeee*verybody.'

'It flew in the face of everything I've been brought up to do,' reflects Tim Clark. 'But ultimately Rob was going to do it, and we were concerned it should be done in as safe a way as possible. Of course I had a great deal of sympathy for his feelings of how the press had treated him, and that helped alleviate some of it, and I think it was me who suggested that the money go to charity, but I still felt, and feel, very uncomfortable about it, that whole thing of going down to their level.'

It was blazed over the *News Of The World*'s front page, and they simply wrote a story to accompany the photos, detailing what they imagined was happening, and describing the various stages of the two new lovers canoodling by a hotel pool – as they assumed – while guests came and went.

Whether or not that truly counted as a triumph in itself, it soon turned sour. The other outbid tabloids either smelt a rat or simply compensated for being scooped in the best way they could. 'It was all "sick stunt", "Robbie's sex shame", "publicity stunt",' he says. 'It just blew up in our faces.' The regrets began. 'I felt really dirty. I felt it was a huge, huge fucking mistake. I thought, what must people think of me?'

He had a torrid three days in his own mind with it, and then he decided he didn't care. But he did decide to cancel the sequels they had planned. They'd already shot the first one. If everyone was so convinced he was gay, he'd decided to give them that story too, and so he posed with a male friend holding hands coming out of Gay Mart. (They'd already thought of other follow-ups too. Maybe he could be having a row with Rachel and kissing her sister.) 'My thinking behind it all was,' he remembers, 'if I flood the market with loads of stuff, they won't know what to trust, therefore they'll stop taking pictures.' And to hell with them. 'Pretty much everybody thinks that everything I do is a publicity stunt anyway,' he says. 'If I'm supposedly dating Nicole Kidman, it's a publicity stunt. If I'm seeing Rachel Hunter, it's a publicity stunt. If I get up out of my bed in the morning and go and have a piss in the toilet, it's a publicity stunt.'

But the Gay Mart photos were destroyed, all similar plans were cancelled, and the matter never spoken of. He didn't keep any of the proceeds – well into six figures – for himself. 'It's a huge lesson learned on many levels,' he says.

Ironically, in one way it worked. Whatever the wider folly of what he had done, the market for snatched photos of his life had been torpedoed for a while. Nobody could hope to get anything as sensationalistic as what was already out there, and over the next few months he saw fewer paparazzi than he had for years.

5

We live in a psychotic time as far as fame is concerned, a strange and unstable period in the history of celebrity. A time where there's too much fame, and there's too much nonsense and hysteria surrounding it. A time in which too many people are too unsustainably and insincerely excited about fame and the famous.

Somewhere down the road, fame and success became uncoupled. When it was tethered to success, celebrity was somehow kept under control – the need for some collateral achievement anchored it and acted as a kind of reality check upon it. The link between celebrity and achievement may long have been an unsteady one – particularly as the high culture voices who traditionally controlled the judgement of achievement often saw little worth in those the public considered most famous (pop stars, and TV actors and actresses, for instance) – but there was still a reluctance to treat anyone as famous unless they had done something at least slightly substantial.

But in the last decade or so, the bond between achievement and celebrity has sundered. Suddenly a celebrity could now really be, in a circular way, someone who is *known*, and all they needed to be known for was for being a celebrity. (The fuss over Liz Hurley in the early nineties as this link began to disintegrate, and the professed outrage that she should be more famous for wearing not much of a dress than for a modest acting career, seems quaint and curious now.) Left to roam free and unchecked, celebrity has become ugly. It has become hateful and hated, both for its potency and for its pointlessness.

There are several consequences for those, like Rob, who wish that whatever fame they have can be of the old-fashioned kind. This era of overheated celebrity is not the easiest for someone of his disposition to be famous in. There are more magazines and associated media than ever before, covering the actions, movements and foibles of the famous, and more paparazzi and tittle-tattle merchants feeding each of them. Alongside this, more than ever before, there is a widespread scepticism in these shameless times towards anyone who professes to be uncomfortable with their celebrity. Also, even as there are more and more people who are treated as celebrities, each seems like devalued banknotes in a country that has tried to escape a recession by printing currency: in the process not only does each celebrity seem worth less but the whole world of celebrity seems devalued and tainted.

More unpleasantly, under the shadow of this runaway upsurge of interest in celebrities, there has been an upsurge of hatred for celebrities. At the same time as more and more people are consuming all of this stuff about fame – the magazines and the TV shows – they are increasingly full of loathing for fame and the famous. They buy the magazines and at the same time they all chorus that it's ridiculous how much endless, pointless nonsense about fame there is; blaming their desire on its object.

It is as though we, as a society, have become addicted to fame, and hate the subject and substance of our addiction. We hate the famous for demanding our attention, even if they haven't. We are angry that they made us drive a thousand miles to request an autograph, even when they didn't. We are always growling, 'How dare they treat us like that?' even if they haven't. And if any of this – the absurd attention itself, or the disdain it arouses within us

– somehow hurts or inconveniences the famous, what the hell? They have all the money and the fame and they shine in the dark and feel good all of the time, and they wanted all this anyway.

More and more, you can actually see the hate in the magazines. The latest craze is for photographs of celebrities looking at their worst: every sweat stain, every double chin, every spot, every wrinkle at the back of the thighs served up with delight as entertainment. There's a ragbag of excuses used to justify all this: that celebrities are celebrities, so they are immune to the hurt heaped upon them; that they are mostly useless, talentless and vain, so they deserve being taken down a peg or two; that these pictures show them to be, in the brilliantly cynical and insincere phrase used to justify a less savage version of this in America's *Us* magazine, 'just like us'. Beyond its intrinsic nastiness, this new fad has also created a new market and given a new impetus for the paparazzi: no longer do lingering photographers have to hope for a new haircut or a kiss or a fight to provide them with a big money photo. If they just keep their cameras trained on the famous long enough, hour after hour, they are only one weird facial expression or unguarded nose-pick away from a healthy payday.

It is not that Rob has always picked a perfectly judged, saintly path through all this. At times he may seem to be a needy, insecure, contradictory egomaniac who would like to be loved and prefer to be left alone exactly at the times and in the proportions that suit him. He knows that; he is the first person in line to spill that secret. But these are peculiar and difficult times in which to be famous, and to find a safe, sane and dignified path through its insatiable and inconsistent demands, particularly if you show any fragility in the face of its onslaught.

* * *

One day I arrive at his house, as arranged, for 2pm, but there is no one I know there – not even Pompey. The cook ushers me into the garden and offers me a cup of coffee. It later transpires that she has assumed I am a new bodyguard.

I sit and read, and watch a workman fiddle with the pump that sends water down a slide that winds through a rockscape into the pool. About an hour later, I hear a voice from above, calling me. Through the branches I see Rob standing on his balcony. He starts chatting. After a while it seems polite to remind him that he is completely naked.

'It's very liberating,' he explains.

He appears downstairs a few minutes later and asks whether I know how to play poker. We sit outside. His pack of cards have pictures of famous women from the cover of British *Esquire* magazine on them, which adds a weird frisson to the game: often $30 or $40 will hinge on a couple of Gwyneth Paltrows or three Nicole Kidmans.

He keeps going on about how calm it is. He seems thrilled by this, but also worried.

'Before the storm?' Pompey, who joins the game midway, asks.

'Probably,' he says.

Rob stares over towards the north hedge of his property, a few yards from us.

'What's that stone thing?' he asks.

'I don't know,' says Pompey.

'Have you ever seen it before?'

'No,' Pompey concedes.

The three of us put down our cards and together sneak up on it – we are acting like something out of a Peter Sellers movie – as if the weathered statue might, if it noticed us coming towards it, suddenly scarper. When we get there, we just stare at it. It carries on being a statue. It must have always been there, though neither Rob nor Pompey has ever noticed it before. When you have a big house and a busy life, it's hard to keep on top of these things. Rob shrugs. 'It's nice, isn't it?' he says.

Pompey is winning the poker game, but after a while Rob gets bored anyway and starts betting on his hands without looking at them. Soon he is cleaned out. Pompey and I continue until he gets the rest of my money. After a few minutes, I look over at Rob. He is sitting in a chair in the sun, out the back of his Hollywood mansion, by his swimming pool, fingering through an inch-thick wad of banknotes. (It's only a few hundred dollars, mostly $5 and $1 bills from the occasional blackjack nights he holds at the house, usually acting as dealer and bank.) I stare at him. He looks up and sees what I am seeing, and starts laughing: the pop star beside his swimming pool under the Los Angeles sun, counting his money.

* * *

The phone rings. It's Steve Jones, the Sex Pistol, who is someone he has hung out with here a little. One weekend Rob was invited to watch a Chelsea match at Jones's house. Jones answered the door completely naked and invited Rob in. Neither of them mentioned his lack of clothes. 'He sits by the pool, scratches his dick, and then we go and watch the football,' says Rob, then adds, as though he feels it is expected of him, 'I'd really love to be able to do that, but my cock isn't as big as Steve Jones's cock.'

Rob mentions that his last bad relapse happened after seeing the Sex Pistols film *The Filth And The Fury* at its London premiere. He'd been clean for eight or nine months. 'If it hadn't been that night it would have been the next week, because I couldn't be bothered,' he says. 'I probably got bored of feeling normal.' There's something about the spirit of punk that does that to him. He has to be careful with this big punk coffee-table book he's got; it kickstarts thought processes he doesn't trust. 'I feel reckless abandonment might be the key to all ailments,' he says. 'But I know it isn't. Sometimes I have to stop looking at things.' He used to play Ian Dury's 'Sex and Drugs and Rock and Roll' a lot simply because the lyric insisted '*sex and drugs and rock and roll are very good indeed*', and it would invariably inspire him to act accordingly. In those days, he used to consider many songs to be instruction manuals, direct orders to action. He was quite perplexed to later learn that Ian Dury, who he befriended when they both went to Mozambique for Unicef, didn't actually take many drugs at all.

* * *

After the cards, we sit in the sun and talk about when he was first on his own and famous; how angry and suspicious he seemed of his fame.

It was, I say, as though you loved it but didn't believe a minute of it …

He nods. 'No,' he agrees.

… but bought into it at the same time.

'Yeah. Of course. That's why I did it.' He sits silently for a moment. 'I'm trying to think of why I did it when I was a kid.' He thinks more. 'Because I was good at it.'

To make people love you?

'I can't say, because I'd been doing since I was in the pram. Apparently I smiled a lot in the pram because I knew I'd get an ice cream off strangers passing by in Guernsey where my dad was working on a summer season. I was always dancing in the pram. And then singing. And so I can't remember where I went, oh … this equals love.'

I ask him – I'm kind of being silly, but I also want to hear the answer – whether in some way he's still trying to get an ice cream off the stranger in Guernsey?

'Probably.' He laughs. 'I don't know.' He starts giggling. 'Probably five years ago I would have said that it's all been a desperate need for love.'

And would you have said that because it was sort of funny, because it was sort of true, or because it stopped anyone delving into unknowable or untellable things?

'I look at it … I was really loved by my mum, and I was totally loved by my grandmas, and when my dad was there I was loved too. I wasn't abused sexually. I wasn't molested. I was just – I know it looks like "stick your fingers down your throat" – I'm fucking sensitive. I was born sensitive.'

* * *

A helicopter comes over the brow of the hill, flying low.

'Noooooo … ' says Rob, and his face falls completely, all the humour with which he deals with nearly everything dropping out of it. He looks up. 'If it circles, it is,' he says.

If they've found him, everything changes.

It flies on. This time.

* * *

He shows me the tattoos he has on the inside of each wrist: 'Jack' on the right, 'Farrell' on the left. Jack Farrell, his mother's father.

'He died when I was about five,' says Rob. 'And he was fucking great. He was a lovely bloke. I think when my dad left and it was just my mum and my sister he was scared of me being a homosexual so he used to make me fight him all the time. You know, he was from Stoke-on-Trent. "Bounce up and down on the bed, son! Now, box! Box! Box!"'

* * *

Walking into the studio he suggests, 'Let's do "Nan's Song" before I start getting boisterous.' He tells Guy, 'Today is a good day in LA, man. The vibes are good.' He nails the song quickly, and movingly; when he finishes his vocal there is applause.

'So,' suggests Guy, 'from the sublime to the ridiculous.' It is time to sing the song, sung in the first person, called 'The World's Most Handsome Man'. 'It's just a pisstake on me,' Rob explains. 'People have this image of me that my persona is: I'm fucking arrogant and cocksure and overconfident and think I'm it.' So here, that's precisely how he presents himself, until the parts of the song where he lets some light shine through to the hollowness at the centre of all that bravado. '*If you don't see me, I don't exist,*' he sings at one point. '*It's not very complicated,*' he sings at another, '*I'm just young and overrated.*'

'That's just thrown in in case anybody completely misses the irony of what's being said,' he says. 'Because there's going to be a lot of people listening to it that are not listening to it properly going "Big-headed bastard".'

Do you really think of yourself, in your darker moments, as 'young and overrated'?

'Yeah. Yeah. I always have.'

He goes back into the vocal booth, with the light off, and his voice rings out of the darkness.

'*... it's hard to be humble when you're so fucking big ... did you ever meet a sexier male chauvinist pig ... ?*'

At the end of his vocal take, the studio assistant turns the lights back up without warning Rob. He is naked.

* * *

Back in the control room, he is offered some apricots and pumpkin seeds. The latter trigger memories.

'I used to eat pumpkin seeds all the time in Take That with Jason Orange,' he says. Here he sees the opportunity for some light melodrama to ease the afternoon through. 'That's all we had,' he sighs. 'Trill and water for breakfast. Bread and vinegar. That was it. They kept us all locked up in a lock-up in Salford.'

'I thought you all had tripe,' prompts his friend Max Beesley, who has popped in to visit.

'Tripe was when we had our first number one,' corrects Rob. 'Nigel Martin-Smith used to make us wash all his undies.'

* * *

'The first time Gary Barlow was on TV,' he declares, 'he was so unsexy they had to shoot him from the waist down.'

He's fond of this statement. He thought of it a while ago. The only thing is, he can't make up his mind whether he'd rather say it about Gary Barlow or Noel Gallagher.

Barlow ... Gallagher ... Barlow ... Gallagher ...

Noel Gallagher, he decides.

The first time Noel Gallagher was on TV he was so unsexy they had to shoot him from the waist down.

'It's really fucking funny,' he says. 'As opposed to "He's a fat dancer from Take That". So, I win again ... '

* * *

His brief friendship with Oasis began towards the end of his time with Take That. Originally, he was more friendly with Noel, though that soon changed. 'I went from Noel's mate, or hanging around with Noel and him ringing me up and knocking on my hotel door – "Come *Top Of The Pops* with us" – to him keeping his distance and me being mates with Liam.' For a while it felt great. 'Liam and I just used to do shitloads of charlie and sing Sgt Pepper to each other in the kitchen. But Liam was really fucking paranoid about everything, and I suppose I was just another person that he'd be paranoid about, even though we were mates. It's dreadful sad for him. He was the biggest icon in the world at the time, and he was definitely going through it, and I could see him going through it. It was just sad to watch him not trust anybody, and not be able to. You get your core group of the best leeches in London and they latched on to him.' He sighs. 'A really sad time, actually, because I was fucked up. I didn't know how not to do cocaine on Tuesday at five o'clock in the afternoon. I just lost the ability to say no.'

Soon the nastiness started. Hanging around with the messed-up one from Take That was no longer amusing. 'It wound me up the most,' says Rob, 'because I really loved them and admired them for a while.' The war escalated most visibly with Liam. They traded vicious insults via the press and Rob offered to fight him in the ring for a £100,000 charity purse. Then Rob's old girlfriend, Nicole Appleton, got pregnant with Liam's baby, and suddenly all the hostilities seemed silly. Rob and Liam spoke, and both agreed to knock it on the head.

Noel, however, has never stopped. He seems to be infuriated that Oasis were ever associated – and even, for one brief Glastonbury moment, shared a stage – with Robbie Williams. 'He's still intently putting the boot in,' says Rob. 'I'm in every interview. I find it amusing that I take up so much room in his head.'

And so, just occasionally, he likes to reciprocate.

* * *

In the studio control room, out of Rob's earshot, those present debate the pros and cons of new, hyperactive, all-present Robbie Williams.

'He was so much better when he was pissed.'

'He used to come in, shag the receptionist … '

' … and fuck off.'

'Mind his own business. He used to lie under the mixing desk.'

'Cans of Guinness.'

'They were the days. Now he's "We need a lyric change there … an extra string here … "'

'"The hi-hat's too loud … "'

* * *

At the end of the studio day Rob doesn't want to go home, so he leads us to the Coffee Bean on Sunset Boulevard – David, Pompey, Chris Briggs and me. Even before his four-shot espresso he's quite hyper. He leans back in the chair – we are sitting outside in the warm dark – and, in a silly voice, says, 'You see that cloud across the moon? You know, when you're creative you notice things other people don't. I see the world differently. I do. I notice strange *nuances* in the night … '

He suddenly declares that he wants a production credit on this album.

'Will that cause trouble?' he asks.

'How do you want to be credited?' asks David, carefully.

'I want to see my name in *Music Week*: "Power/Chambers/Williams",' he says. 'I've gone "Turn that down, turn that up, leave that in, leave that out". That's production, isn't it?' He notices the exchange of nervous glances around the table. 'Will that cause hassle?' he asks.

No one says yes, yet, but no one says no.

'Well,' says Rob, 'what passes for production?'

'Sitting in the studio all day, being bored rigid,' suggests Chris Briggs.

'I've done that!' he says.

'Production is what Guy and Steve have done,' Chris says. 'All the stuff with the engineer, how it should be recorded … '

'Well, I've done that,' he protests. He catches something in David's expression he interprets as a reproach. 'Don't fucking look at me!' he says to David. 'I've *done* that.' David's face still seems to suggest that this is an unrealistic demand. 'What do I have to do over the next two weeks to get a production credit?' Rob asks, but there is no answer, and after that the moment passes. (*Escapology* will be released with the usual Robbie Williams album credit 'Produced by Guy Chambers and Steve Power'.)

Rob sips his espresso. 'I miss Jonny,' he says, to murmurs of assent. He and Jonathan Wilkes have known each other since Rob was eight and Jonny was three, and have been best friends for nearly a decade; during most of his ups and downs of the past few years Jonny has been at his side. But Rob is in Los Angeles, and Jonny's career is keeping him mostly in Britain. A bid to become a pop star failed after Jonny's one single, 'Just Another Day', was a hit but not a big enough one; he was dropped and the album he had completed was never released. But now things are beginning to take off – he has spent much of the year touring Britain in *Godspell* and is preparing to appear as the lead in *The Rocky Horror Picture Show*.

Rob changes the subject. The record deal negotiations are proceeding, but each provisional date for concluding them keeps passing. Rob now explains to David Enthoven that he refuses to sign to EMI in America because they've done such a bad job for him in the past. Again, there are glances. No one contradicts him, but the silences clearly imply that to take the option of re-signing with EMI off the table might put them in a very awkward position.

'It's *my* deal,' he says, firmly.

The table goes silent.

'I'm winding you up, you tool,' he says to David.

* * *

His bedroom is the largest room in the house, a grand double bed in its centre, from where, when his retractable projection screen is raised, you can see over its private balcony to the valley and mountains beyond. He has been trying to sleep in there, because he feels as though it is the room in which he should want to sleep, but when he is in that bed on his own, he struggles. Too big. Too much peripheral vision. Too much room in the room to worry about. He grew up in a box room, and he is used to sleeping with a wall next to him, and a wall next to that wall. More and more often – as he does tonight – he gives up the fight sometime before dawn and sneaks into one of the smaller bedrooms, and only then does he feel secure enough to lose himself to sleep.

6

Today he walks into the studio fresh from a meeting at one of the world's big five record companies. Right now, Rob is in an unusual position for a successful artist. He is a free agent and everyone wants him. Most successful artists periodically renegotiate and extend their contracts, trading future freedom for greater immediate rewards. He has not done that. He has completed his initial contract with EMI records and is paying for this new album himself while he and his managers shop around for the best new deal. EMI would like to re-sign him, but all the other big record companies are also interested.

These other companies are mostly based in America, one of the few countries where he has had little success and where, as a consequence, not every record executive is automatically clued up about him. This has some wryly amusing upshots. In few other industries would someone be aggressively competing to commit an eight-figure sum while content to know so little about the object of their proposed investment, but the record business remains a weird, anachronistic blend of passion, flair and capability mixed with astonishing ignorance, inefficiency, bluff and bullshit. So during today's meeting, which until this point Rob had thought was going well, he mentions his idea that, as part of any attempt to break into the American market, he wants to record a new version of 'Angels'.

'Which one's that?' asks one of the most important figures in the American record industry.

It's his most famous song, of course, and the one that established his solo career. Far worse than them not knowing is their complete indifference at not knowing. They are selling him their grand plans for him, and yet they don't even seem to know what he does, or what he has done, or who he is. How can they begin to judge his value to them if they have no sense of any of this? Specifically, how can they gauge his prospects of American success without having an opinion of why his most obviously commercial song, 'Angels', failed to do in America what it did in so many other places? Today, they appear familiar with only one moment from his past – the video for 'Rock DJ', in which he strips naked and then continues undressing, tearing off his skin, flesh and muscle, in a hopeless attempt to impress a snooty female DJ. They seem interested in that. 'Very cathartic, ripping off skin,' they say.

'No,' he corrects them. 'I just wanted to make people sick.'

He plays them some rough mixes of songs from this new album. When he does this, the same thing happens as at previous meetings. Over here, people tend to find the stylistic diversity of the music and his confusing lyrical tone – is he being serious? – perplexing. He's still smarting from a comment at one of the other record companies, from the boss who said: 'I don't get that Robbie Williams whimsical stuff.' Robbie Williams' bloody-minded reaction: 'It's a lot of money to be putting a punt on for someone that's mainly whimsical, in that case.'

Today, they love the prospective first single, 'Feel', with its classic, sincere, sweeping melodrama, as everyone before them has, and then seem less engaged by what follows. At that point Rob tells them, as he has told others, that this is his best album and that if they can't hear three tracks they love right now, theirs isn't the label for him. As always, after he has said this, they really like the next two songs they hear.

These meetings have their moments of surreal entertainment. Last week Sony sent their jet to bring him to New York to meet with Tommy Mottola. Mottola, who is also Mariah Carey's ex-husband, has recently been in the news as the object of Michael Jackson's ire. Jackson has denounced him as a racist and appeared on top of a bus in Manhattan holding up a picture of Mottola with devil horns.

In his meeting with Rob, Mottola was about to listen to the new tunes when he suddenly turned away, did something Rob couldn't see, then said, 'But before we go any further ... ' and turned back.

'He'd got red horns and a white glove on,' describes Rob.

For now, Rob is happy to see them all and take in what they say while his managers stoke the bidding war. 'I'm just pleased,' he says, 'that they've all got massive egos and they want to outdo each other.'

* * *

As a general rule – and as the attitude that suits him best – Rob has an utter contempt for rock snobbery. He will rant about his mid-nineties drugged-up late nights with the rock-canon snobs: 'Sitting around wanking about *Pet Sounds*, and it all seemed more important that they knew a lot about the album than how the songs made them *feel*.' About what happened when he did try to get into Nick Drake. 'I thought he was a depressing fucker,' he says. 'I haven't given him a fair shot – I listened to it once – but, you know, I'm depressed enough, do you know what I mean?' About how he reluctantly sat down for an interview with the *NME* early in his solo career and almost the first thing they said was, 'So, Glastonbury ... ' – when, just before his exit from Take That, he paraded around the festival off his tits, with a blacked-up tooth, and briefly appeared onstage with Oasis – ' ... was when you became one of us,' and he was so incensed: 'I thought, I'm never *ever* going to become one of you ... ' About how he's 'listened to Dr Hook more times than I've listened to The Who, do you know what I mean? It's just a pile of incestuous wank.' (Not The Who, for whom he has an appropriate and reasonable regard, but the whole rulebook of pop cool, with its absurdly uptight taste tests and strictures.)

He has always enjoyed playing down the seriousness and the artistry of what he does. That is why, when his material is derided as whimsical by an American music bigwig, he will embrace the description rather than argue with it, even though he doesn't believe that his music is essentially whimsical at all. Certainly not in a straightforward, encompassing way – though there may be whimsical moments, he is more sincere and resolute about expressing and detailing his experience of life than most people who make pop records. But when the lights are turned on and everyone else scurries under the umbrella saying serious art, he has always enjoyed taking his place, with pride, under the parasol saying shallow entertainment.

Added to that has always been the severe love-hate relationship he has had with his own creations. (Though, as a rule, he doesn't appreciate other people sharing his doubts. If anyone makes the mistake of imagining that, because he criticises himself so readily and severely, he will understand if they take the same liberty, they are very much mistaken, and may be surprised at the fury they spark.)

And yet ... although most of Robbie Williams' triumphs have come by doing what the cool people think you shouldn't do, and a far greater part of him despises the in-crowd than hankers for membership of it, when you have conquered nearly everything else but cool, sometimes it is difficult not to wish. It's not that he would sacrifice any of what he has – his audience, his success – for their approval. But now he is proud enough of the records he makes himself in a fairly unconflicted way; proud enough to wonder, just occasionally, whether he couldn't have it all.

'I used to go round people's houses and see that they've got a fantastic record collection,' he tells me this afternoon, 'and I was never in them. That upset me. I'd like to be.'

He wonders whether this new album could be the one.

* * *

Steve Power is finishing the mix of a ballad, 'Sexed Up', that has been rescued from its initial unnoticed appearance in demo form as a b-side several years ago.

'Can I be credited for something I haven't done that isn't on there?' Rob asks Steve. 'Let's make up an instrument that doesn't exist. A melotonin. I want to be credited on every single song for playing something that doesn't exist. The variathon. The frumpy pony. I want to play the effexor, too.'

Effexor is the antidepressant he is taking.

In the other studio he plays songs from Richard Flack's iTunes. He puts on Ian Brown's 'If Dolphins Were Monkeys'. 'That's what the next album should sound like,' he announces. 'Like that, and Soft Cell.'

'I've wanted to do an electronic track for ages,' says Guy.

'A whole electronic album,' corrects Rob, insistently.

'And then you could have robots of yourself touring the world,' Guy suggests.

'Have you heard Rufus Wainwright's last album?' Rob asks Guy. 'It's really good. Track three made me cry yesterday.'

Pause.

When two paths lead onwards from a heartfelt comment, and one of those paths heads into the familiar comfortable land of the crass, self-deprecating joke, that is usually the path Rob will take. 'It's called "Robbie Williams Is A Cunt",' he explains.

* * *

There are few dirtier words in the entertainment business than *entertainment*. That is one of the quandaries that ensnarls him. In the modern era, to convey the trueness of your intentions it is generally considered obligatory to signal your indifference to the reaction of the audience.

It is comical how pervasive, and unquestioned, this is. The music industry, for instance, spends millions of pounds every year printing billboards and adverts of glum men trying to affect a look that suggests how little interested they are in being photographed (ideally, perhaps they are even *unaware*), while they and everyone involved knows that they are being photographed so that fortunes can spent showing the public photos such as these to persuade an audience that these are serious, glum artists who would never knowingly cooperate in the shame of marketing themselves, or acquiesce in offering themselves up as entertainment. Somewhere along the way an illogical principle was accepted: that to be seen to entertain is to admit a lack of depth. Entertainers trade in general, shiny, shallow truisms; artists deal in deep, heartfelt, individual truths.

Robbie Williams fits poorly in such a world. He is unashamed to entertain. (Though, ironically, he loathes being photographed.) Confusingly, he clearly has plenty of personal reflection and pain and demons squeezing out in every direction from the music that he makes, but is still unashamed to take all that mixed-up baggage and entertain with it. One of the reasons he annoys a lot of people is that he is breaking many of the aesthetic rules people use these days to separate what matters and what doesn't matter. He breaks the rules of sincerity, and he breaks the rules of insincerity too.

* * *

He has been told that David Beckham wants him to call. 'He won't phone me because he's scared and I won't phone him because I'm scared,' Rob explains. He thinks they're in awe of each other. 'I think he's brilliant. He handles it so well. It just washes over him. The media attention and being David Beckham. It looks like there isn't any cracks.' They met once at *Top Of The Pops*, but they just sort of half-waved at each other. David Beckham has since been in touch indirectly, to admire and ask about the jeans Rob has worn in a particular photo shoot, and the jeans have been sent over to him, but there has been no direct contact.

So are you going to call him?

Rob looks shocked. 'No.'

How did this message reach you?

'It's very showbusiness, darling. It's through Patsy Kensit.'

At the moment Beckham has the same kind of grown-out Mohican as Rob, so I suggest that maybe he's calling to ask for his hair back. Rob says that, in truth, he does indulge in some hair competition and when he saw that Beckham was growing his hair again, he realised that for once his was already longer and thought, 'I'm going to grow it fucking full speed and have long hair before he does.' But then Rob decided it made his face look like a football and had it cut. 'But,' he bluffs, 'I've got people I employ just to hair-watch David Beckham.'

Courtney Love is mentioned and he talks about the time he ended up hanging out with her in London. He remembers her floating the notion that she would like to have sex with him, except that she declared she had 'a problem with the pop thing'. He batted back the compliment with his own proviso: 'I have a problem with the ugly thing.'

He has a request for me. 'Can you ask me the question "Did you sleep with Courtney Love?"' he asks. 'And I can say, "Fuck off, I'm a good-looking lad."'

7

Rob and I are talking in the studio lounge when Guy walks in.

'Shut it,' snaps Rob. 'My interview.'

He is joking. Guy moves to leave anyway, but then Rob says, 'Come and sit down, ducky.'

'Are you sure?' he asks.

'Yeah,' says Rob.

This three-way conversation starts off badly. Rob says that he listened to his first album *Life Thru A Lens* at home last night because neither Rachel nor Max Beesley, who is staying with him, had ever heard it. Rob says he was surprised how much he enjoyed it. Guy agrees but insists that they've improved. 'We weren't anywhere near as good as we are now,' says Guy, 'especially you. Vocally.' Rob, who is forever gifted at being able to filter out a foghorn of compliments all the better to hear the whisper of criticism beneath, declares that Guy is insensitively insulting him again. Guy insists it was meant only as praise. Rob says the phrase 'especially you' was the offensive touch, and makes me rewind the tape on which I have been recording this conversation to prove to Guy that he really said it.

'I know he thinks I'm really critical,' Guy says.

'No, I think you have a … ' begins Rob.

' … a bad way of giving a compliment?' asks Guy.

'No,' says Rob. 'I think you can be taken wrong, because of your lack of sensitivity regarding how you talk.'

'Right,' says Guy. 'OK. Fair enough.'

I ask how the relationship has changed. Rob describes how they both used to party ('Guy not to the extent I did') but that now he's sober and Guy is a family man. 'And there is a difference in the dynamic between the two of us now,' says Rob, 'because he's very settled and I'm still not.'

'And obviously not seeing Rob as much as I used to,' says Guy. 'We've had quite a weird year, haven't we?'

'Mmmm,' says Rob.

'It's been very up and down, this year,' says Guy.

Do you spend much time together away from work?

'He lives in England, I live in LA, so no,' says Rob. 'And he likes going to restaurants and I don't.'

'That's right,' Guy agrees.

'You'd go to a restaurant every night, wouldn't you?' says Rob, unable to keep the tone of being quite mystified by this out of his voice.

'I *do* go to a restaurant every night,' says Guy. 'That's your idea of hell, isn't it?'

'It's not my idea of hell,' says Rob. 'It's just ... very grown up. It's probably something I will segue into very nicely at some point in my life, but for the time being I'll go and get a quadruple espresso from Coffee Bean and bounce off the walls.'

Why don't you like going to restaurants?

'Just in case I'm lumbered next to somebody that I don't want to talk to,' says Rob.

'Maybe me,' says Guy.

They talk about how nice it is to have no pressure to write any songs for a while, and enthusiastically discuss their plans to record future Robbie Williams albums of other people's songs.

What do the two of you have in common?

'Not a lot,' says Guy.

'Nothing, actually,' says Rob, and Guy laughs.

'We both like music,' says Guy. 'That's about it, isn't it?'

'Yeah.'

'I think the common ground stops there.'

Do you like each other?

'Yeah,' says Rob, almost indignantly.

'Yeah,' says Guy. 'Of course we do. There's no way we'd be sitting in a room right now if we didn't like each other, not after all this time. He doesn't need the grief and nor do I.'

'I love Guy,' says Rob quietly.

'I love Rob,' says Guy.

* * *

'My dad said, while he was here, "I never let him win anything when he was growing up – never",' says Rob. It's clear what his father was suggesting. That, through the kindness of never being allowed to win, Rob learned that achievements and results had to be worked for, and earned. Maybe there was even a hint of: *look where that kind of training has taken him.*

But that is not quite what Rob took from it. Not quite what he thought about when his father said it.

'You know, I suppose it served me well,' he says. 'But I wish he'd have just given me a few games when I was a kid. One game of pool, you know. One game of table tennis.'

* * *

Tonight Rob decides that he should go out to dinner. At Koi, one of the current hot restaurants in town, Rob sits with Pompey and Max. He seems a bit on edge. When I arrive, he insists on ordering me a glass of red wine and a saki cocktail, which seems weird. I've been operating a policy, based on what felt comfortable for me and polite to him, of avoiding drinking in his company, except when I had met him by chance in the bar of my hotel. Even that I found a little awkward. But he more or less forces these drinks down me. After a while, Guy and Steve Power turn up, and everything is friendly. While Rob is in the bathroom, Steve remarks on how everyone seems to be getting closer again. 'It's getting back to how it was on the first album,' he says.

Soon Rob wants to leave. There are now paparazzi out front, so we trail through the back to avoid them. One of the unmentioned truths about celebrity lives is that if you spend half your life in private jet cabins and posh hotel Jacuzzis, you spend the other half in kitchens and dirty service elevators and back alleys, waiting by the rubbish bins while someone finds your car.

His night isn't over. He heads to the Whiskey bar at the Sunset Marquis hotel, where I am staying. He stands away from the action. Matt Sorum, who used to drum for Guns N'Roses, says hello as he passes. Mickey Rourke is at the bar. Rob only looks comfortable when U2's 'Stuck In A Moment' starts playing. 'I want to be Bono,' he mutters, 'when I grow up.'

He notes the tics and comings and goings of those he diagnoses as disappearing to the bathroom to take cocaine. 'You know when I had my first line of charlie?' he says. 'Two minutes before we went on stage for the first Take That arena tour.'

They were in Manchester. He asked someone to get him some. 'I'd done speed and I'd taken a few Es.' He first took drugs when he was 14. 'Somebody was smoking speed,' he remembers. 'He was a very promising athlete, the guy, as well. He was fucking ace. He fucked his life up very quickly.' For Rob, pot followed the speed. He was tripping in the exam room as he took his Religious Education GCSE. By the time he was ready for arenas he reckoned he was ready for cocaine. 'I pretty much figured it'd be like speed,' he says. 'I just thought it would be a nice little upper to get me through the show.'

That night he was wrong.

'I came though the curtains and it was just like nine thousand people let flashlights off,' he remembers. 'It freaked the living daylights out of me. I was three steps behind everyone for the first number.'

* * *

I've been in Los Angeles for several weeks now. Some of the time I've been working on other stories, but in between I see Rob often. Whenever I am free I drop into the studio. Now and again we meet at his house for some combination of talk and cards and table tennis. Sometimes, late in the evening, I am about to go to bed in my hotel room when he calls from the house phone in the lobby, next to the Whiskey bar where he has come with Pompey to while away some time, and I'll slip on my shoes and join them. We both know that I've long had more than enough material to write an article about his new album (as eventually I will, in the Saturday *Telegraph* magazine), but I still bring my notebook and tape recorder each time we meet, and use them whenever it seems appropriate. I don't think either of us needs to pin down a reason for this, or questions it; if there is something interesting to be noted, it seems natural to both of us that I should note it. It doesn't feel like an imposition on our friendship, but rather is part of it, and for now I don't think either of us bothers to think much more about it.

8

This afternoon, Rob walks into the studio and asks Guy whether he fancies writing a song. In truth, Guy doesn't, but he knows that's not the appropriate response, so he goes and sits at the piano, still thinking that there's no inspiration in his fingers. Barely half an hour later, they have written a song called 'Blasphemy' and Guy is dictating the scribbled lyrics to the studio assistant.

No, it's not the heathen in me
It's just that I've been bleeding lately
Internally
So turn to me
But bite your tongue, your torrid weapon ...

'A lot of big words in this song,' Guy says. 'It's a grown-up song, not a pop song.'

I could learn a useful lesson
What's so great about the great depression?
Was it a blast for you?
Because it's blasphemy

'It's about making loads of friends and realising they're all cunts,' says Rob.

'Wish I was here'

Well, I wish you weren't
Your gift of anger's better burnt
If nothing's said then nothing's learnt
I thought I wasn't, but I'm really hurting
Our deaf and dumb dinners
There's gravy in the mud ...

They record it twice, and that's that.

'Yeah, man,' says Guy. He and Rob hug.

'I love you, motherfucker,' says Rob.

They listen back to it in the control room, all fired up.

'I reckon what we should really concentrate on now ... ' says Rob.

' ... is the musical,' says Guy.

'No,' says Rob. 'We should do an album that's songs from the shows. Songs from non-existent shows. Something I don't have to promote.'

They listen to 'Blasphemy' once more.

'It's a show-starter, isn't it?' says Rob, pleased as punch, and he wanders into the corridor, and away from the last song he and Guy Chambers may ever write.

* * *

I meet Guy for brunch by the pool at the Beverly Hills Hotel, where he is staying, to ask him a few questions. His perspective on this year so far very much seems to be, like Rob's, that the two of them have come through a difficult period, and that their relationship has had to adjust, but they are now back on track. We talk about their ups and downs writing together, and Guy says all the things a wise man would say. 'If somebody came up with a great song with Rob, it's for the whole album's benefit,' he says. 'I'm not an idiot. If he writes a smash hit with someone else that's going to sell the album, that helps our songs.'

I ask about their problems earlier in the year and at first Guy seems a little taken aback that I know all about them. He mentions that when Rob told him they weren't going to work together any more, Rob was two hours late for their meeting because he'd been watching the Oscars on TV. 'Very unlike him, actually,' Guy says. 'He's never been that rude. He's always been punctual and respectful.' He describes how Rob got straight to the point. 'Pretty much said: I don't want to work with you any more, I want to do this band. I want to kill Robbie Williams, I'm sick of him, I'm sick of my persona. But at the same time he wanted to do these stadium dates the following year. The farewell tour. Cash in his chips, I think was the expression he used.'

And what were you thinking as he said this?

'I thought, he's gone mad. I think that was what I was thinking.'

But what was your reaction?

'I encouraged him. I kind of wanted to be Mr Positive, so I said, great. Do the band. Do it. You'll learn a lot.' Pause. 'Which he did.'

And inside you were thinking ... ?

'That it was very sad that he'd got to this stage. I thought it was sad that the way he said it to me was quite aggressive and hurtful. But he was in a funny space. And I never forget that he's the famous one. I'm not famous. I can sit anywhere and have a cup of tea and be normal. And he can't. That whole fame was really doing his head in at that point. The problem with the hurtful things he did say was that he wanted to be in a band with mates. He didn't feel the band he had were mates. And I thought that was a bit sad because I do think that he's got some good friends in his band, and we've been through a hell of a lot as a band, and we're very loyal to him.'

He says that, after everything, making this album has been different. 'He's definitely been more opinionated, more interested in the process,' says Guy. 'Before, he wouldn't really comment at all on instrumentation or the feel of a track or anything really, just sing on and go. Literally. He'd be in the studio for an hour. He wouldn't turn up to the mix either.' Though Guy stops short of saying it, I very much get the sense that for Guy the new, more-involved Rob is a mixed blessing, and that Guy feels he has had to make compromises he'd rather not make, but he still talks with great excitement about their future together.

Before I drive Guy down to the studio, I mention that much of the tension while I've been around seems to have been triggered by Rob's feeling that Guy is not encouraging enough.

'Mmmm,' says Guy and laughs. 'Yeah. I can understand. It must be a bit boring looking at my face while he's singing. I think it's partly living out here as well. Everyone's so positive and everything's great here, isn't it? And I'm not so much like that. And normally when I'm not encouraging, what I'm actually doing is thinking about what he's doing, rather than saying "Everything's great". I'm not an "Everything's great" sort of person anyway. I'm pretty critical. But that's what's made our relationship good, I think. It's just sometimes painful for him because I'm not as effusive as maybe he'd like ... But every relationship has its difficult areas. You know, I'm trying to work on it, put it that way.'

* * *

Later in the week, Rob calls me and says he's realised that he is becoming increasingly concerned about the worsening situation in Iraq, and for entirely the wrong reasons. 'Always,' he says, 'before an album comes out I'm, "I hope the world doesn't end before this album comes out".' It's the same thing he told his therapist the other day when she asked him whether he was scared of dying. He told her he wasn't scared of it, but that he wanted just two things first. To fall in love. And to release his new album.

* * *

There are some further hurdles before the album, which is now called *Escapology*, can be released. For one thing, Rob still doesn't have a record deal. Some mornings I see his lawyers over the other side of the patio at my hotel, poring over long documents, but still nothing is settled. His managers are letting it be known that, if need be, they will release the record themselves and take venture capital from the City to fund the enterprise: they are having to staff a whole ghost record company that they hope they will never need.

Meanwhile, one Sunday, the schism between Guy and Rob blows wide open. That morning Josie is speaking to Guy about something else, and she happens to ask him about his plans for the day. She is astonished to hear him say that he is going into the studio, but not to work on Rob's album. He is planning to write a song with Natalie Imbruglia and to work on demos for the girl rock group he has put together, The Licks.

She knows this will be trouble. Sunday may notionally be a day off, but they are less than a week away from the end of a hectic scramble to finish Rob's album. What's more, it is only days since she endured a 20-minute rant from Guy's manager, his brother Dylan, about how Guy was being overworked and put under too much pressure. Rob had sent Guy home the previous Friday because he looked so shattered. It hardly seems appropriate that he is now slotting in extra work on other projects. And whether or not Guy has now decided he wasn't under pressure, he will be also using Richard Flack, who has been working extraordinarily long hours on Rob's album and has further long hours to go. Most importantly, she knows Rob will think it unprofessional and rude for Guy to divert attention from the album, especially without even talking to Rob about it and asking his blessing.

She tells Guy he needs to call Rob and tell him what he is doing. He says he doesn't want to and asks her to.

Rob is as annoyed as expected. He already has a bee in his bonnet about The Licks because he has found out that they are booked in to rehearse in the same building as his band in London later in the month; he's furious that Guy seems to imagine he can be musical director of the Robbie Williams band while intermittently popping in and checking up on his side project.

Knowing that Natalie Imbruglia is due in at four in the afternoon, Rob decides to torment Guy. He saunters into the studio at about a quarter to four and feigns ignorance, greeting Dylan warmly and telling Guy there's so much he wants to get done today: change the lyrics to 'Hot Fudge', record a song he has written last night, work on this, improve that …

He watches Guy's face drop. Rob walks out to the studio kitchen and after a moment Guy follows him.

'Great, man,' says Rob, breezily. 'What are you working on today?' Making it sound as though he means: which song off my album?

'I'm … not working on the album,' are the words Rob hears in response.

When Rob asks what he is working on, Guy tries to say but can't get Natalie Imbruglia's name out for an age.

Rob immediately changes his demeanour. 'Right,' he says, and summons Guy and Dylan upstairs for 'a chat'. He talks them through it from his point of view: that this is the most important of their albums, that he's been the most focused and attentive he's ever been, that there's seven days left. So why had Guy not told him about this? Guy says something about the fact he'd been having a massage, and asks whether Rob had known all this when he walked into the studio.

'Yes,' says Rob.

'Then why did you say all those things?'

At this point Natalie Imbruglia appears at the top of the stairs, sees something of what is happening, senses the tension, and turns straight round and walks back down again.

After that – the one bit of this Rob regrets, if only because he oversteps the mark and has to apologise – he lays into Dylan in a 'the more I hear about you, you fucking dickhead' kind of way. Nonetheless, they come to some kind of uneasy truce.

* * *

Rob takes the next day off, but after that they finish the album. The night before Guy goes home, Rob has a chat with him in the studio. He wants to square everything, so he explains again why he was so angry, though Guy doesn't apologise and he feels like Guy doesn't really get it. Rob also mentions about The Licks rehearsing in the same building and Guy denies even knowing about it. (Rob believes that.)

Guy also tells him that he has found him the most difficult to work with on this album; Rob responds that he finds that really scary, because everyone else, bar none, is finding him really easy to work with these days. He tells Guy that this makes him paranoid because maybe Guy's the only one telling the truth, but he doesn't mean it. He thinks Guy is talking nonsense, and that Guy is inconvenienced and threatened by his new involvement in his records, that Guy resents the fact that Rob has all kinds of opinions he didn't need to deal with before.

They talk about future plans. Rob gets the impression that Guy would like to cherry-pick which promotion he does, and not decide until Christmas how committed he wants to be next year. Rob says he can't wait until then and face being left in the lurch. Guy should stay at home with his kids and build up his company, or come away and MD Rob's band as always before. He tells Guy how weird it would be if he isn't there for Knebworth.

And in his heart he still imagines that Guy will be.

9

Before returning to London, Rob flies to Calgary in Canada to shoot the video for 'Feel', which has been confirmed as *Escapology*'s first single. The operatic passages have been abandoned, and Ms Dynamite's contribution is omitted too – although she has written and recorded a rap that everyone loves, it is decided that it is smarter for Robbie Williams' big comeback single to feature Robbie Williams alone. The single's release is only a few weeks away, but there is still no record contract, so for now Rob is footing the entire £700,000 bill himself. He plays a cocky but taciturn ranch hand who becomes involved with the female ranch owner. His fallback idea for most of his videos, whatever the storyline or scenario, is that he should end up kissing someone, preferably someone he might fancy in real life. He had no casting idea for his love interest in this video until he met Daryl Hannah out at dinner in Los Angeles and on the spur of the moment asked her to do it.

This brings its own problems. She is currently shooting Quentin Tarantino's *Kill Bill*, and plans to sneak up to Canada for the weekend. The arrangements are made, but at the last minute Quentin Tarantino gets wind of the plan and refuses to let her leave the set. It gets later and later on the day before the video shoot, and she still hasn't left Los Angeles. Soon she has missed the last commercial flight and they have to charter a private jet. (By then they are already considering casting a last-minute, on-the-spot Canadian replacement.)

Eventually, she arrives at two in the morning for a seven o'clock start. On set, for humour's sake, she tells the film crew documenting the video shoot, deadpan, that she had thought she was showing up to film with Robin Williams.

Rob, meanwhile, wakes up with a huge lump on the side of his face where he has picked at an ingrowing hair. He looks like the Elephant Man. Gina, his make-up artist, sends out for a doctor, but by the time the doctor arrives, Rob has cantankerously razored the lump off himself. There is blood all over the bathroom. 'I think I got rid of it,' he says, oblivious to the gash that remains. They cover it up and shoot around it as best they can.

* * *

Meanwhile, in England he is all over the newspapers due to the serialisation of the Appleton sisters' book, *Together*. Rob went out with Nicole Appleton on and off, for about a year when she and her sister Natalie were still half of All Saints; the longest relationship of his life so far. In the book, she discusses their times with each other in great detail, and reveals that she had aborted their baby – under pressure, she says, from her record company, band management and some band members. She explains that they had planned to call the baby Grace and that she was the unacknowledged subject of the song 'Grace' on Rob's second album. (As circumstances changed, its lyric was somewhat adjusted before it was recorded.)

Rob says that she telephoned him a long time ago, to explain that she was writing the book and would mention the baby. He just told her that she was brave. During the hullabaloo surrounding the book's publication, he speaks to her again, for the first time in over a year, to correct what the papers were claiming – that he was angry. 'Just to say, look, I'm not furious, this is what I think and good luck to you.' He doesn't read the whole book, just the excerpts printed in the British papers; he recognises these as pretty accurate. It reminds him of a lot that he has forgotten. 'I was really sad,' he says. 'I was really sad for both of us. Because there would be a child now, three or four years old, and I don't know where I sit on it. I understand completely why Nic had to do it, but I was really sad. I feel sad for her because she was going out with an idiot at the time. I wasn't the most peaceful person to be with. I was sad for everybody involved. I was sad for the All Saints. I was sad for me. I was sad for the unborn child. It made me question what that all means, what God thinks about that, and what my role in it was, and what I have to accept and what I have to make amends for.'

* * *

In London, other events are casting their shadows towards him.

Rob's managers, Tim and David, had met with Guy and his brother Dylan before *Escapology* was recorded, and Guy had suggested he wanted a royalty hike. They had told Guy that they should defer this discussion while they negotiated Rob's new record deal but that, while Guy and Steve shouldn't expect a higher percentage, they would benefit proportionately from all the other improvements in that deal.

When Guy gets back to London, the album completed, there is a further meeting at which he repeats his demands. As before, he is told it isn't going to happen. Tim points out to Guy that he is talking as though he has a partnership with Rob, when it comes to Rob's recording career, and he has no such thing. He has a songwriting partnership, in which he enjoys an equal share, but as a recording artist Robbie Williams has no partners. They suggest that he should feel very grateful, both as a songwriter and someone on a high producer royalty, that he has Rob going out and promoting his songs.

In response Guy makes three contentious statements. The first, by way of arguing why he should be further rewarded, is that he has 'saved the album'. His reasoning seems to be that Rob did some recording without him in New York that didn't work out, and that Guy came riding to the rescue. The second is that if 'Come Undone' is to be a single that he won't promote it; he doesn't like it. (He says, specifically, that he hates the lyrics and is 'shocked' by them.) The third is that he feels he should be further rewarded – on top of his regular percentages – as part of the forthcoming record deal. During the debate on whether he has been appropriately compensated, the managers mention the large cash gift Rob gave him in 2000 so that he could afford to get the house he wanted, and Guy seems upset that they should bring this up.

For a while after this meeting, as Tim and David try to sort all this out, they don't fill Rob in about any of this because they know he will go through the roof, and that there may be no way back from this. (Though Guy seems convinced that Tim and David have been deliberately trying to undermine his and Rob's relationship, there is little evidence of that, or reason for them to do so.) But at the end of the second day's shoot in Calgary, after Tim has had a further unproductive conversation in London, it's decided that the subject can be avoided no longer.

David and Josie go to see Rob in his hotel room. He can see they are really nervous about something, and he can tell that it's serious. 'Come on in,' he says. 'I love a drama.' They sit on the end of his bed, and it all comes out. As expected, Rob is furious. For lots of reasons, but I think in particular because any sign of what he sees as greed in his vicinity infuriates and upsets him. It's as though, just next to the place in his brain where he derives pleasure from those around him becoming enriched by working with him, there's a part of him forever scared and horrified of being treated as a commodity and a cash cow, and who resents the way one's riches can become just another route to being treated as less human. The moment he senses that anyone is more focused on the money than on what they are doing with him, he feels betrayed. He is often hugely generous, but he is also hugely sensitive to any hint that he's being taken advantage of. There is a story I will hear him repeat at least half a dozen times over many months. In the early days of his solo career, he would take the same £5 cab ride every day. One day, as he got out, a driver he had never had before asked him for £15. He challenged this. 'Well,' said the driver, 'you can afford it.'

He's still angry about that. Anyone who makes him feel like that taxi driver made him feel usually leaves his life soon afterwards.

And so the decision is made that night in Calgary. He relays a message via Tim to Guy that their relationship is over. Because Tim can't track Guy down over the weekend, he is only told when he turns up to band rehearsals on Monday morning, where it is explained that he is no longer needed.

When Tim speaks to him on the phone and explains the situation, Guy seems to receive the news calmly but then does something else that Rob will see as unforgivable. By now Rob's record deal has finally been concluded after weeks of brinkmanship; he is re-signing to EMI after all. The contract is due to be signed and announced the following day. Guy picks up the phone and calls EMI's chairman and CEO in the United Kingdom, Tony Wadsworth (a man, and company, with whom he has no direct contractual relationship at all) to tell him that his and Rob's collaboration has come to an end, and that he feels Tony should know this. Quite what he does he expect from this? That EMI will demand his reinstatement, or make the deal in some way contingent upon it, or decide that a Robbie Williams without Guy Chambers is worth less money? Certainly the anxious phone call Tim Clark receives on the way to the gym is the first of a flurry of such calls that day, but EMI are swiftly reassured and the deal goes ahead exactly as negotiated.

* * *

At the beginning of October Rob returns to London. He has many weeks of promotion ahead of him to launch 'Feel' and *Escapology*. His first public act after arriving home is to sign the record deal. The press conference is held at his management offices and he is asked how he feels. He raises his arms in part-ironic triumph.

'I'm rich beyond my wildest dreams ... ' he brays.

When they report this, the newspapers immediately characterise this as an '£80 million deal'. In truth, it's difficult to put a simple cash value on even simply structured record deals, and this agreement is far from simple. As well as committing to recording new albums for EMI a company has also been set up, called In Good Company, into which all his other income – song publishing, concert revenue, merchandise, endorsements and anything else – will now go, and EMI have agreed to purchase a 25 per cent share of that company from him. While it would be wrong to imagine that this week he is in receipt of an £80 million cheque, the figure offers a reasonable flavour both of what he receives now and is guaranteed in due course.

The advantage of telling people about such a deal (it lets people know that you are winning) is very similar to the disadvantage (it switches the focus away from what you have created and will create, and towards your financial victory). Still, it is a fine deal, and feels good. Two days afterwards he wakes up and discovers himself singing, to the tune of Abba's 'Thank You For The Music', the lines: *And I thank EMI for the money and giving it to me*. He will subsequently take to wandering around the house singing '*Have I told you lately about my lump sum?*' But he also discovers, in band rehearsals, that when he starts singing he has to shut out a distracting voice in his head going, 'Eighty million! Eighty million! Eighty million.' And he keeps thinking: how do you perform like an 80 million person? It knocks the wind out of his sails for a while. 'So,' he explains, 'I had to pretend that they'd given me two quid.'

The day after he signs the deal, he is told that *The Sun* is going to run a story that he had left the Groucho Club at one in the morning after celebrating, worse for wear, clearly implying that he was drunk. He wasn't even there then.

'The truth is,' he says, 'I was sat in front of the television watching highlights of the European football with a Selection Box to the right of me, chomping through Yorkies. Then I went to bed and watched a couple of episodes of *24*.'

* * *

Guy sends Rob a pained handwritten letter. Much of it is aimed at setting the record straight about something that Rob insists had never been an issue – that at the *Escapology* playback party Guy had thrown in London for his friends, he had skipped 'Come Undone' and 'Nan's Song', the two songs he didn't co-write. Guy explains that he had missed out the former as a joke, and that they had turned off the album before the end, omitting 'Cursed' as well, because the party was then in full swing and people were no longer listening. (Before receiving the letter, Rob only knew that he had skipped 'Come Undone'.) In Rob's eyes, the letter is mostly remarkable for the issues it fails to address, for the pennies he feels have failed to drop, so he asks for a final face-to-face meeting. 'I just thought he didn't understand why the relationship was coming to an end and that I need to tell him to his face,' says Rob. 'I wanted to tell him, look, it's not because you skipped the fucking tracks. It's because I think you're asking an extortionate amount of money from your friend that you're supposed to love, which you think you deserve, which scares the living daylights out of me. And the fact that you won't do "Come Undone".'

He goes round to Guy's on the day after the deal is announced. Guy's lawyer is at the meeting, at Guy and Dylan's insistence. When things get heated and Guy exclaims, 'We were expecting just a lighthearted chat,' he is reminded that he is the one with a lawyer there. (The lawyer does eventually go into the other room.) Rob is calm, on the outside anyway, though afterwards he says that on the inside he was 'so fucking angry and sad at the whole thing taking place'. When Guy alludes to the house money, then says he didn't want to go into that now, Rob insists that they do. He tells Guy that he didn't think it had been appreciated enough. He says that this was the first time Guy's card was marked.

Rob goes through the things he was annoyed with. When he mentions Guy's 'Come Undone' refusals, Guy objects. 'I told Tim and David not to tell you that.' After a while Guy protests, 'I can't deal with confrontation – I'm a writer,' and at one point pleads, 'Come on, Rob, you don't think I'm an egomaniac, do you?' Rob laughs but doesn't answer. Dylan suggests at one point that they adjourn the meeting but Rob disagrees. 'This is the last meeting you're ever going to have with me,' says Rob, 'so you might as well get everything out on the table.'

Later Guy sends an email saying he wants to give the house money back. They ask him to send it to Rob's charity.

Part one

1

Anyone subject to the madness and distortion fame brings with it is less likely to yearn for someone to write a controlled, sanitised account of their life than you might imagine. Why bother, if the result is planned from the start to be only one further twisting of their reality, another funhouse mirror, even when it is one constructed to flatter them? For most subjects, the appeal of being benevolently misrepresented quickly pales, because it offers no real antidote to the slush of nonsense, half-truths, carelessness, lies and misunderstanding that surrounds them. Often, after a while, they hanker instead for silence, or some truth.

It's not even necessarily that they want, or expect, most people to understand their life and its strange predicaments; it is perhaps just that it would be nice for there to be something reliable and honest from which anyone who truly cared to could form an accurate opinion. I think people who are famous and over-examined often also just want to see some truth about themselves simply for themselves so that for once, when they see or hear themselves reflected back in their own direction, they can at least recognise some of what they see or hear. In this respect, being famous is perhaps like being in a canyon that with an unreliable echo: whenever you shout, the echo you hear is of the same voice but different words, or the same words but a different voice. Sometimes it would be nice just to hear something you recognise as yourself.

People who encourage truthful accounts of their life and living also sometimes say that they want to set the record straight after all the lies and misjudgements they have faced. Sometimes they do, but I think that is rarely their main motivation. The big lies hurt, of course; they can hurt hugely. But you can point out a big lie; you can do battle with it, and perhaps you can rebut it. At least people will listen when you say: 'I didn't sleep with her/sleep with him/smash that/hit him/speak ill of them/buy that/betray anyone … '

I think that in the long run it's the little lies that somehow do more damage, because you're defenceless against them. These aren't the grand libels and slanders. They're the tiny untruths, the endless small misstatements of where you were and what you did and why you did it and what happened and who you are. If you try to point out a little lie, no one usually listens and, if they do, often they'll think you mad for making a fuss about something so unimportant. They are the grains of sand eroding a building; if you live inside its walls for a lifetime, you see the destruction they cause, but to everyone else they're just dust in the air. But these are the lies that tell the person being lied about that everything they believe to be true is subtly wrong; it is the little lies that can, in the long run, undermine your faith in reality and your relationship with the outside world.

To be famous in the twenty-first century is to be pelted with little lies, day after day. To be famous in the twenty-first century is to find yourself trapped as a character in a book with an unreliable narrator, forever trying to shout from the pages to explain how it really was. How could you not sometimes wish for it to be different?

* * *

Two days after he has signed his new record contract, I go round to Rob's west London house. The news of his split with Guy has just broken. In the street outside, the paparazzi wait. Soon they will take photographs of his new table tennis table being delivered. He drinks tea in his living room, picks up an acoustic guitar and begins playing a new song he has written today. On his own. Perhaps he feels spurred by the current turn of events. The song has an unusual, sad, insistent melody. It was sparked by the phrase 'soft corrosion' on a vintage Vivienne Westwood/Malcolm McLaren T-shirt framed in his downstairs toilet, but it has now turned into what sounds like an anti-war song.

Singing, we won't go to war
Lay down your guns
What are we fighting for?
I wouldn't know how to use 'em
I wouldn't know how to kill
I wouldn't want to anyway
And I never will

We go into the garden. He points at the flat across the way, which he says was recently advertised in *The Times*, accurately but creepily, as 'overlooking Robbie Williams' back garden'. A friend of his wanders out and Rob asks whether I mind an audience as we talk. Not as long as you don't, I say.

'Hey, it's me,' he scoffs. 'I'm Robbie Williams. Open the fridge door, light comes on, I do three hours … '

Mostly, we talk about Guy. 'We don't sing from the same hymnbook any more,' he says. He doesn't believe that Guy was ever happy working on others' songs. The counter-example Guy always gave to him – 'Come on, Rob, I'm not like that,' he'd say – was 'She's The One', written by Karl Wallinger, whose band, World Party, Guy was once in. 'I think he disliked

Karl Wallinger so much,' Rob suggests, 'he wanted to make "She's The One" a bigger hit than Karl Wallinger ever made it.'

For Rob, Guy's refusal to promote 'Come Undone' was the final straw. 'Which was just like, well, you can fuck right off.' As for Guy being shocked by the lyric, he feels it was just another excuse. 'In "Feel",' he points out, 'I say, *"I don't want to die but I'm not keen on living either"*. It's far more shocking than any of the lyrics on "Come Undone".'

He talks about their final meeting. 'I asked him point blank,' says Rob, 'does the money I'm earning irk you? And he went, "Absolutely not." But it absolutely did.' It's sad. 'You know, when we met I was on my arse – I had money but I was on my arse – and his roof leaked. And now he's in a multi-million-pound house and he's got a lovely lifestyle, and it's Robbie Williams that sells the records. It's not Guy Chambers that gets up in front of all those thousands of people and entertains them. And that's the fellow that can't go out because the paparazzis are outside his house or whatever ... ' Even so, without the other stuff that has been said, he thinks they could have got over the financial disagreements. 'I could have actually gone round to him and said, "You stupid fucking cunt – fancy asking for that much money – you're not going to get it, and this is going to happen, and that's going to happen ..." and we could have scraped something together.'

But not now.

'It got better on this album,' he says. 'We went up another level. And it does fuck me off. And I am sad, yes. It is really fucking sad because the last song we wrote is fucking amazing.' He's careful not to rule out ever working together again. 'We are an amazing songwriting partnership. And there is a musical to be written that I need to write with Guy. But it's going to have to be cap in hand. And there's going to have to be, point by point, "I'm sorry for this" and "I'm sorry for that" and he's going to have to mean it. Or else we're never going to write again.'

Much later, in the midst of revisiting all this fury, he will add this. 'And I love Guy. Whatever happens. I do. He's a fucking dickhead, but I love him.'

Now he is making other plans. 'I'm really excited about it,' he says, 'because now it actually forces me out of my safety zone, to go and change shit up.' He is already wound up by the suggestions in the media that he will be in trouble without Guy and that EMI will be very worried about how this bombshell affects their investment. He was particularly annoyed by a reference in the *Daily Mail* to how 'Chambers' melodies are instantly hummable', as though Rob just threw a few chirpy words on top of completed songs. 'They've got me as Bernie Taupin and Guy as Elton John,' he says. 'I would find it hugely disrespectful if anybody in my record company thought that a huge lion's share of the songs weren't done by me.'

Ostensibly, I am here to collect some final details and perspective for the article I have been writing, but it doesn't feel like we're wrapping up anything. It feels like we'll carry on. He mentions – as though it was an aside, as though it could be taken as seriously or as lightly as either of us wanted to take it – that maybe I should write a book. I say something about how I couldn't really think about that until I have finished my article. Inside I start thinking about the book I'm going to write.

After we have talked enough, we play on his new table tennis table with his new pink table tennis balls, and then he says he fancies getting some food. We wander up and down the streets near his house, chatting, as he keeps changing his mind about what and where to eat. Finally we stand outside the chosen restaurant, preparing to go in. Abruptly, he says that he has changed his mind. He wants to watch the new reality TV show, *Fame Academy*, instead. Off he walks.

* * *

He calls at the weekend, annoyed about a piece in the *News Of The World* in which they quote Guy as claiming that Rob had demanded an exclusivity deal, and asked Guy to guarantee that he wouldn't work with anyone else. Rob swears that this never happened. It's not clear that Guy has even truly suggested it did but, in the absence of more accurate information, it will become the enduring, official tabloid reason for why the split occurred.

The current tabloid stories all say that Guy will be concentrating on his girl band, The Licks. Meanwhile, the song Guy wrote back in Los Angeles with Natalie Imbruglia doesn't make the film soundtrack it was intended for. Perhaps just a little cruel pleasure is taken in some quarters that, when the film in question, *Johnny English*, is released, its theme tune, 'A Man For All Seasons', is instead sung, and co-written (with the film's composer Hans Zimmer), by Robbie Williams.

* * *

Halloween night. Before leaving his Holland Park house with Jonny, he puts on the same jacket and the same cap he always wears and a clear mask. The mask is moulded from his own face – it was made as a prop for the bank robber scenes in the 'Eternity'/'The Road To Mandalay' video – and when it covers his face he looks scary but featureless. It is for the paparazzi's benefit – outside all the time, sitting in their cars or loitering across the road. There is nothing Rob can do to stop them photographing him as he walks from the front door to the car, which is parked just outside the house, separated from the pavement only by some railings. But this way, by wearing the mask and always wearing the same jacket between front door and car, he can try to ensure that their photographs are worthless. His hope is that if all they can get, is a near-identical photograph of someone who is probably Robbie Williams in the same clothes, over and over, eventually they will tire of waiting here. And in the meantime, each time he does it feels like a small victory. Out he comes, they start snapping, but you can tell they know they don't have a shot they can sell.

'You're going to get fuck all as usual!' chants Rob, as he opens the car door. 'You're going to get fuck all as usual!'

Some kids in Halloween outfits go by.

'Trick or treat,' shouts Rob, merrily.

Only once he gets in the car does an awkward thought strike him.

'You know what their story will be now?' he sighs. '"Robbie Williams left the house with young kids trick or treating, shouting, 'You're going to get fuck all as usual'."'

That, at least, doesn't happen.

Sometimes he tries to make some kind of peace in his head with the paparazzi and the tabloid press, to try and find some kind of acceptance of them. But mostly his is a deep and fierce loathing. He is forever furious at how they are, and the manner they treat him, and the ways they jeopardised his recovery. Not even just by photographing him outside addiction recovery meetings. In London last year a recording device was found, taped under a table, at a similar meeting he attended. 'I wasn't left alone to get on with it and venture into this new world without chemical assistance or without alcohol being my crutch,' he says. 'I thought it was unfair. And it *is* unfair, you know, but the world isn't a fair place.' Even now, he argues it back around. 'If the world was actually fair, I wouldn't be getting eighty million. I wouldn't be a pop star. I would be in Stoke-on-Trent in some pub right now talking about how I used to sing when I was a kid. So thank God the world isn't fair.'

* * *

This weekend, the *News Of The World*'s front page crows that they have infiltrated and exposed a plot to kidnap Victoria Beckham. For many readers the story is an absurdity – a collision between the sillier, less plausible outer reaches of celebrity and criminality; an entertainment that has little relevance to their lives – but it really freaks Rob out. He thinks about the publicity given to the sums of money involved in his record deal and it makes him worry about those closest to him. It also forces him to reflect on how he has been virtually housebound, aside from work excursions, since he has been in Britain, and that he can only deal with it because he knows that soon he'll be back within his new freer life in America.

These two points of view have coalesced into one further thought, one that has been brewing for a while. The current plan is that, once *Escapology* has been successfully launched in the rest of the world, next spring it will be released in America and Rob will make a focused effort to charm the one continent that has so far been fairly immune to him. But he is already wondering whether it is worth it.

'What is the point of breaking the States?' he says. 'I was thinking, I want to have kids, and I don't want them to grow up living behind smokescreens and cars going to places and stuff, and having their own security.' He calls a meeting with David and tells him point blank that he doesn't want to go to America to promote his record. His life in England is no fun; why would he recreate that across the Atlantic? 'There's two ways that it could go,' he reasons. 'One is, massive. And the other way is, it falls flat on its arse. Which will be a dent to my ego. And I'll probably be constantly reminded of it throughout my career, you know. But if I do succeed there, what kind of life do I have then? Because it wouldn't be a half measure thing, I don't think.'

David responds that his only worry is whether Rob might have any regrets in ten years' time if his peers have broken there and he hasn't. Rob says he is sure he won't.

The next morning, when he wakes up, there are five paparazzi outside his house. One of them takes his photo the moment he peeks through the curtains, and, for today, the result is different. 'I thought, fuck you lot, I'm going to break the States and not be beholden to this country any more,' he says. 'When I say "this country", I mean "this media".'

He has also, in the wake of the Beckham kidnap plot, realised that there is at least one upside to having paparazzi constantly outside your house. Having several camera lenses permanently trained on your house may destroy your life, but it's also an effective, free way of increasing your security.

There is one more thing that happens this same week that he won't mention until months later. Two small bullet holes are found in one of the front windows.

2

There is one sentence that Rob never says to me, as I spend more and more time as a witness in his world, in the slipstream of all this luxury and intrusiveness and wonder and craziness and achievement and joy and pointlessness and privilege. It is the sentence that doesn't need saying, because if it needed to be said once it would need to be said dozens of times each day, and if it needed to be said at all it would mean that I was noticing nothing, realising nothing. It is the unsaid sentence implied in his every resigned shrug and exasperated silence and sly smile:

This is what it is like.

* * *

He reads aloud a letter that arrived at his house this morning.

Dear Robbie or whom reads this.

I think you R great. good luck in all you do. Love the look of your new video with horses. Can you let me have more infore on the horse you are ridding. My mum and dad are truing to sell there bungalow fro £130,000. Would U buy it as and invest-ment or to sell on as they have seen a house nearer two us that they want to buy. My dad is 70 my mum is 68 I think. It been a worrying time for them. I just don't no how to help them. Can you as U wont lose any money but it give them a chance to buy wat they want. I understand if you throug this in the bin but we all love our mums + dads and only want to help.

Yours faithfully …

The writer has thoughtfully included a photograph of the bungalow she expects him to buy. The saddest thing isn't how demented this letter is, it is how commonplace it seems to Rob. One of the many unexpected consequences of fame is that you become a magnet for indiscriminate dreams, hopes, madness and delusions. Its corollary is that you are always disappointing people. Once you become famous, you are always shattering dreams you never encouraged, withdrawing help you never volunteered, and breaking promises you never made.

* * *

Tonight's will be the second of two performances in front of an audience at Pinewood studios being filmed for a TV special, *The Robbie Williams Show*, its feel very loosely inspired by the Elvis 1968 Comeback Special. Beforehand, he plays me a recording of one new song he has written on his own last week, 'One Fine Day', and then sings me the latest version of the acoustic song he played me at his house. The lyrics have morphed slightly, and now it seems to be partly based on Muhammad Ali's experiences. '*No Viet Cong called me nigger, don't bother me,*' he sings. He wonders whether he needs to change that line. 'Do you think people will be offended?' he worries.

He strides on to the stage, standing on a giant RW, to the *Rocky* theme. Midway through the set he takes his guitar, for the first time in a show, to play 'One Fine Day'. 'There's been a redundancy in our firm recently,' he says. This has become his standard line on Guy's departure. 'So, yeah, I've had to start writing songs by myself. It's OK. I can do it. You only need three chords. People have built a career on it. I'm not saying any names.' Pause. 'Oasis.'

Most of this chat will be edited out for the TV broadcast. A while later, he asks the audience: 'Have you ever been really obsessed about somebody?' he says. They cheer crazily; silly question. 'Then you're a stalker,' he says, and continues, 'I wrote a song about a certain person who will remain nameless – only because if I fart it's in the papers – but I wrote this because every time I was near her I felt like a seven-year-old and I had nothing to say … ' He smiles. 'And in the end I just got my penis out. I've written about it in this song.'

He plays the opening song on his new album, 'How Peculiar'.

After the song he says, 'Thank you. Needless to say, I slept with her.'

* * *

He and his band convene at Townhouse Studios to record a song he wrote last night with Boots, 'Get A Little High'. First they need to work out an arrangement. Claire Worrall, his keyboard player, asks Rob what he wants her to play on the track.

'Breasts,' he suggests. 'You could just sit and cup them for a whole track. You know that Yoko Ono mic'd up a dead pigeon for a whole track. When I first heard that I was: she's dead mad. Now I'm: hmmm, I dig it. I want a dead mouse and three cockatoos.'

Claire patiently lets him finish, indulging him.

'So what do you want me to play?' she asks.

'Breasts,' he replies.

In between takes, he tells Chris Briggs about the Radio One interview he did this morning with Sara Cox.

'She's grown on me,' says Chris Briggs.

'She's grown on me too,' says Rob. 'I hadn't seen her since *The Girlie Show*. She was really sweet. Got a little bit of a crush, actually.'

'Married woman,' Chris points out.

'Doesn't stop me having a bit of a crush though,' says Rob. 'Doesn't mean I'm going to pursue it. I can put it in a box, say: lovely woman, great tits. She looks a bit like readers' wives as well. She's fucking great. She's like the girl next door that first showed you her fanny.' Pause. 'I got asked about Guy, obviously.'

'Everything you do now ... ' says Chris.

'I handled it very well,' says Rob. 'Said he was a cunt, I'm going to kill him. No, I was very dignified.'

He was also asked about something Westlife's manager Louis Walsh has been saying in the interviews he has been doing to promote the latest reality show, *Pop Rivals*. 'Louis Walsh said I was nothing more than a jumped-up karaoke singer and I wouldn't make it past the first round of *Pop Idol*,' he reports. (ROBBIE'S A FLOPSTAR was *The Sun*'s headline when Walsh spoke to them. 'He only had two things going for him – his brass neck and Guy Chambers, and now he hasn't got Chambers any more,' they quote Walsh as saying. 'Without Guy he is nothing.')

'So,' Rob continues, 'they said, do you want to say anything about the Louis Walsh thing? I said, he's right, he's got a very good knack of putting things together and making it stick. I often think I wouldn't get past the first round.' He smiles. 'I did it sincerely. It felt good, killing him with kindness. Twelve months ago, I'd have gone for a face-off with him, round his house in a tiger suit.'

He returns to Sara.Cox. 'I think she'd got a crush by the end too,' he says. 'She said, "I've got all embarrassed – I've gone the same colour as my mother at the checkout at Asda when she's 12p short ... "'

Before heading off, he shares with Chris Briggs a recent moment of self-discovery.

'I said to Rachel the other week: I've just realised I like drama,' he says. 'She looked at me like "Duh!". It was horrible. That dawning realisation that someone else knew before I knew.'

* * *

Outside his house this evening, the paparazzi have clocked off, but an Italian girl is waiting with a rose, which she thrusts at him through the railings as he gets out of the car. He accepts the rose, his face thunderous, but refuses to sign an autograph. This is his house, he tries to explain. 'It's about privacy,' he says.

She says that she's not coming again, as though this is the reason why he should give her what she wants.

He nods. 'But if you go, someone else will take your place.'

She beseeches him. He knows it will make no difference, but instead of going inside, he tells her what he is thinking.

'You think you know me,' he says, his voice somewhere between fury, exhaustion and despair, 'but you don't know me. I just want you to know that you're not welcome. I will shake your hand, but please go.'

She mutters something through the railings.

'Compliment received, please leave me alone,' he says darkly, and storms inside.

3

The other day Rob came across a home video made by Gary Barlow when they were in Take That together. 'I actually thought I'd watch it and have a bit of compassion,' he says. 'I didn't.' He laughs. 'What did strike me was how camp I was. Oh my God!'

The laughter soon fades. Even now, he can only joke about Take That so much before you can see the horror and fear welling up inside him. 'It took me forever to get over it,' he says. 'Even with success. It was always wrought with divide and conquer, lots of paranoia, 24 hours a day. Very formative years – I think there was a lot done psychologically then. The workload, and how insecure I felt, manifested itself a hundred-fold when I left. I knew I was insecure before, but I didn't have that intensified insecurity that it became. I think I just soaked everything up like a sponge – criticism – and I didn't react well to fame. When I went into Take That I thought I could do everything, and I left thinking I could do nothing.' Mostly, he blames their manager, Nigel Martin-Smith. 'He'd divide and conquer,' says Rob. 'He gave us all a bad time. Jason in particular, and me. But, you know, those stories of people fucking with your head, they're ten a penny. He was the person, I believe, in my life that fucked with my head, and made it impossible for me as a person because I just didn't have the facilities to deal with it. I just wasn't ready for it. Other people, it would have been water off a duck's back. It wasn't water off a duck's back to me. From the start of Take That I vanished into a void of trying to deal with life with an incomplete set of tools. And then as a 28-year-old I just started to come out of the hole.'

Josie asks about the other four. 'I wonder how it feels to them,' she says, 'to have been given it and then ... ' She doesn't need to finish.

'Exactly,' he says. 'On this video there's footage of his first home, the bungalow. Dreadful. Doing close-ups, zooming in and out of candlesticks. There's no footage of me, very, very little footage of me, I noticed. Lots of Howard, lots of Jason.'

'Just enough to notice you're camp?' notes Josie.

'I had a cigarette holder,' he says. 'I had a cigarette in my mouth all the time. Nothing changes.'

'Everything changes,' mutters Chris Sharrock, his drummer.

We are on a private jet, heading to the MTV awards in Barcelona. For now, he thinks about other things. Rob flicks through a French magazine, *Voici*, and finds an article headlined 'Las Ketchup Accusées de Satanisme!'. Odd. He says that he wants to make his next album in a month, and gathers his thoughts about The Prodigy performance he saw at the Coachella festival in the Californian desert. 'It's starting to look a bit Gary Glitter, a bit pantomime,' he says. Pause. 'And that's my job ... '

Josie tells him that Steve Coogan wants to do an Alan Partridge sketch with him for Comic Relief. Unsurprisingly, as on some days he uses Alan Partridge's voice almost as much as his own, he is enthusiastic about this. 'Can I do an impression of him and he can get pissed off?' he suggests.

* * *

A while later he hears the band laughing further down the plane, and looks up from the magazine he is reading. 'I know you're laughing at me,' he says, for comedy, and this in turn brings him back to the Take That days. 'Nigel Martin-Smith did that to me,' he says. '1993. Stopped the car on the hard shoulder: "I know you're all laughing at me. I put you here, and I can put you back down. It won't be difficult getting another bloke called Robbie from Stoke-on-Trent." No shit. And when you're 16 and you don't have 80 million quid in the bank ... '

He talks about when Take That were at a Radio One event in Derby and a girl asked him for his phone number. Nigel Martin-Smith didn't react until they were all on their way home together: 'He said, "We've all done very well today, boys. Apart from one boy. And we all know who that was. Robbie Williams. He gave his telephone number to a girl." I know he set it up. The night before, at the restaurant in Brighton, I said to this girl, "You're really pretty – what's your name?" and he said, "Who the fuck do you think you are? Go back to the hotel."'

'And did you?' asks Chris Sharrock.

'I did,' he says. 'I wasn't always this confident.'

Out gush the memories. Mostly of indignities from the two people he clearly considers responsible for much of the pain of his late teens, Nigel Martin-Smith and Gary Barlow. On a day like this, in a private jet floating across Spain, he tells these stories because they are entertaining – everyone gathers round as he picks up momentum – but also I think because he still can't believe some of the things that happened, and how they made him feel.

He begins with a list of Gary Barlow's eccentricities and cheapnesses. How Gary Barlow used to charge Take That something like a thousand pounds a week for the use of his keyboard on tour, forever telling them 'it's cheaper than A1 music'. How he bought a Mercedes 250 and had Mercedes 500 stickers put on it. How he would charge Rob a pound to use his mobile phone. How he would wear his duffle-coat indoors and say, 'Why heat the house? Wear a coat and boil the kettle twice.' How he wouldn't always indicate when driving and explained that it was a deliberate strategy to save the battery. How he once boasted to the band, whose pay cheques weren't yet very impressive, 'I don't believe it, lads! I've just been given a cheque for two and a half million pounds.' How, when you went round his house, he'd have his own special coffee and an economy-size tub of Nescafé for visitors. How he started out refusing all foreign food and being incredulous when anyone spent more than £30 on an article of clothing, then, after seeing how Elton John lived, changed it all – all of a sudden when you went round his house there'd be a butler in full uniform offering Baileys on ice in a cut-glass tumbler. How, after Rob did a rap on Take That's third single, 'Once You've Tasted Love' – 'I was just so chuffed that something I said was put on a song,' Rob remembers, 'and I didn't have a clue you could actually get paid for something like that' – Gary came up to him and told him that if he wanted 5 per cent of the publishing for the song, Gary would take off the rap instead 'because it doesn't enhance it'. 'That,' says Rob, 'was the end of wanting to write in Take That.' (Well, not quite. He and Mark Owen were eventually allowed to write the middle eight to the number one hit 'Sure', this time getting their 5 per cent each. And he once phoned Gary up to sing him his first composition down the phone. It was about a prostitute. When he finished there was silence. 'What d'ya think?' asked Rob, excitedly. 'It's alright if you're in a rock'n'roll group,' said Gary Barlow flatly.)

Rob explains – with such fresh hurt that it sounds as though he's worried it might happen again tonight – how when Take That returned from trips he was always dropped off at the Trust House Forte service station on the M6. His mother would have to drive out from Stoke to collect him or he'd have to call a taxi, even if it was three in the morning, and even though he'd explain how it would add only minutes to the journey if they cut through Stoke. 'I drew diagrams and everything,' he sighs. (He does add 'in fairness' that when the van reached Manchester, the other members were dropped at a central point and had to make their own ways from there.)

He remembers one time towards the end, when Take That were appearing on Germany's biggest entertainment TV show *Wetten Dass ...?*, Nigel Martin-Smith had a huge row with his ex-boyfriend, their make-up artist. There were tears and Nigel Martin-Smith stormed off in a huff. Back at the hotel the band got together and agreed that this wouldn't do. 'Everyone was moaning, and it was like the People's Popular Front of Judea – lots of talk and no action,' remembers Rob. 'Everybody was talking about how out of order it was, so I sat down and I went, "Right! Let's sack him, let's get another manager." Barlow turned to me and he said, quote unquote, "That's fine coming from you, isn't it? The worst member of the band. The one that only shines when the light's on him."'

'He knew,' says David.

'He must have known,' says Rob.

Rob describes how it ended for him. There was a meeting round Gary's house one day after tour rehearsals. 'I said I wanted to leave after the tour,' he remembers. 'And I sat on his swing, hanging from his tree, and had my feet on the ground, leaning back. And they all individually went through what I was doing wrong, what they thought of me ... '

'Did you call that meeting or they called it?' asks Josie.

'They called it,' says Rob.

'Because they were cross with you?' asks Josie.

'Yeah, because they were cross with me.'

'Were you pissed when you turned up?' asks David.

'Yeah, I was pissed ... ' He stops and corrects himself. 'I wasn't pissed when I turned up, no. I'd sort of cried myself to sleep staying at the Midland Hotel after rehearsals because I was just so fucked with it. They said, "You might be able to go on and do something, you'll be alright, but for our sakes can you just keep your head down for another two years, we can make two million each." And they'd all systematically gone through it all, and at the end of it I just lifted my feet up and went "Wheee". And that was when everybody just went "He's gone". We took a competition winner for a curry, and then afterwards I went back to the hotel, and unknown to me, they had a meeting about me having to go before the tour started. And they were really clever about it, how they worded it, because I came in as usual, did a half-arsed rehearsal in the morning for the tour – I was never going to get through it, never going to do it – but I rehearsed as normal, then they must have had word through from lawyers and all that sort of stuff, what would happen and how they'd have to go about it, and they all sat me down at lunch and they went, "Look, we've listened to what you've said, and we think that it's best that you leave now before the tour so we can prove we can do it as a four-piece – what do you think?" And I went, "Well, if that's the case, then I'll go."'

'Were you sad?' asks Josie.

'I was relieved.'

'And scared, I would think,' says David.

'Relieved and scared. I left and got in the car and the security guy Paul said, "I'll pick you up on Thursday." I'm: "I'm not coming in on Thursday." "Friday, then." I said, "Paul, I'm not coming back." And I got back and my mum was up in the loft in the new house. And I was just looking for someone to go "It'll be alright". And I said, "You're not going to believe this – I've been sacked." And she nearly dropped the pottery that was in her hand and said, basically, "Oh Christ, all the lawyers, all the fees, all the ... " And I was: *bmffffffff*. That moment, basically, I was: I think I'll get pissed ... I think I'll carry on getting pissed ... '

'Does it all seem a long time ago now?' asks Josie.

'It did do, until I watched that video the other night,' says Rob. 'In the early days, when I used to go to the toilet and we'd be out anywhere – the lads told me – Nigel used to go, "I fucking hate that Robbie – we should sack him."'

'But why?' asks Josie.

'Because I was from naff Stoke-on-Trent. And I was a naff straight,' he says. 'I think because the Force was strong in me. Bit of a maverick. "Don't know if I'm going to be able to hold his reins for too long."'

'In that van, going to all those men's clubs, was pretty grim, wasn't it?' says David. At the beginning, Nigel Martin-Smith's plan was to break them through gay clubs, and he deliberately avoided booking them at under-18 events.

Rob considers, and shakes his head. 'It was a load of fun. When we were doing the gay clubs we would actually, a lot of the time, five of us all travel up in Nigel Martin's XR3i. And then we got the yellow Salford Van Hire thing, and that was a load of fun.'

'Who was driving? Nigel?' asks David.

'No, they'd all take it in turns, apart from me who couldn't drive. So I had to pump the gas. But I refused. Along the terms of: "Because I'm not fucking doing it!" Quite a few times. Caused *mega* problems. And they'd have mega meetings about tours and stuff, with the choreographers and stuff, and I just wouldn't be there. Because I couldn't give a shit, basically. It wasn't my style of music. "Whatever you're going to do is fine by me."'

'That probably irked him more than anything else,' says David. 'You didn't see the dream. You didn't see his dream. Or didn't want his dream.'

'Yeah,' says Rob.

'Were you demanding lead vocals?' says David.

'No! God no. I can remember doing the vocal for "Everything Changes But You" and I smoked about 20 spliffs in about 12 hours I was in that vocal booth. And we did it again … and we did it again … and we did it again … and we did it again. And we didn't *need* to do it again … and do it again … and do it again.'

David asks if the others joined in his drug escapades, and he says that even Gary eased up a bit by the end. He stands up and imitates his old bandleader dancing on ecstasy, demonstrating the losing battle between a drug that tricks people into feeling free and a body suspicious of all freedoms.

Rob has a question for David, a question of amends.

'Are you supposed to apologise to someone like Gary Barlow?' he asks.

'Do you feel like you've done him harm?' says David.

'Probably,' says Rob.

'Would you feel better if you wrote him a letter?' asks David.

'No,' says Rob, abruptly. 'I'd feel better if I kicked his fucking head in.' It just surges out of him, and even he seems surprised by its force.

'Woah,' says David. 'Where did that come from?'

He considers this. 'Watching the video the other night,' he decides.

'We definitely need to work on that resentment,' advises David.

'Yeah,' says Rob, now calmly analysing it all. 'I do feel bad about saying really nasty things. Even though they were justified. Actually, when I said I'd like to kick his head in, that came from just being so unhappy. Just being so unhappy, really scared, and really having no one to talk to about it. I didn't start being an addict, full on. It sort of gathered speed the more miserable I got. It was always there. I think that the anger of the statement "I'd like to kick his head in" comes from the fact that I was really fucking sorry for everybody involved.'

David mentions the only time he met Gary Barlow, at a Princess Diana benefit in Battersea, when Gary Barlow's solo career was still the bigger deal, but in retrospect was beginning to teeter, and Rob's career had just begun to take off. 'He had no idea what was coming,' says David.

'I walked in and hugged him,' Rob recalls. 'Sang "Angels", "No Regrets", and then slagged him off when I left, which wasn't cool. I still wasn't brave enough to say anything to him. I was still pretty much … *scared* of him.'

That was the last time they spoke.

4

When he forces open his eyes on the thirtieth floor of the Hotel des Artes in Barcelona at around 11 o'clock in the morning, the Mediterranean stretching out below his window, he has no idea where he is. He doesn't even know who this man waking him up is. Slowly, it comes back.

Pompey. The MTV awards. Robbie Williams.

Oh.

Sometimes this happens. Once, in Milan with Take That, he woke up in a four-poster bed without a clue. He stood up, looked around the room. Still no idea even who he was. He felt so weird; he knew that. But he knew little else. He went towards the window and opened it.

From down below, five thousand girls screamed his name.

As he leapt back, he realised.

I'm *him* ...

* * *

'I feel so fucking tired,' he says. He pulls on his T Rex T-shirt, calls for sunglasses and is escorted downstairs to the waiting car. He still looks as if he's only halfway home from a long, arduous journey in a reality far from this one. 'No confidence this morning, everyone,' he mutters. 'No confidence.'

'It will return,' promises Josie. 'Your confidence isn't used to being up this early.'

'It isn't,' he agrees.

His mood is not being helped by the way the driver is treating the bends of the coast road, and the other cars, as some kind of slalom course. People who drive celebrities often assume that they value haste over safety. Maybe it is because some celebrities are always late and always impatient and always looking for someone to blame; I've been in a few of those cars too. But some drivers, even when they are told to go slowly and safely, as all those who drive Rob are pre-instructed, don't seem able to resist.

'I love it when they travel so close up to the next car at high speed,' mutters Rob sarcastically. 'Swerve in and out. It's *great* being thrown around. Pomp? Can we have Mika Hakkinen on the way back?'

This driver will not be seen again.

* * *

Walking into the MTV rehearsals, he spots Chris Martin, singer with Coldplay. They have never met. Rob goes over to say hello, and they get chatting. He tells Chris a little about his life in Los Angeles. 'Three doggies,' he says. Chris Martin plays the what's-a-serious-little-band-like-us-doing-at-a-celebrity-studded-event-like-this underdog role to the hilt. Coldplay's second album is just coming out, but it's too early to know just how big it will make them.

'It's over for us,' he says to Rob. 'One-hit wonder.'

'Yeah,' drawls Rob sarcastically. 'Shut up.' He suggests that they meet up for a coffee back at the hotel. 'Are you under your own name?' Rob asks.

'I'm under the name Bono,' says Martin, then gives Rob his actual pseudonym.

'It's the middle of the night for me,' Rob apologises.

'Is it?' says Chris. 'Where've you come from?'

'London,' says Rob, heading off to his dressing room. Chris Martin looks suitably confused.

In the dressing room, Rob considers this encounter.

'I like him,' he says.

'He's gentle, isn't he, Rob?' says David.

'Yeah,' says Rob. 'Really gentle.'

Rob explains to Gina, his make-up artist, how nice Chris Martin is. 'He reminds me of me,' he says. Pause. 'But not as muscular or as big cocked.'

He goes on to the stage and runs through 'Feel' a few times in a gruff voice. At the end of each take he introduces a new Europop-star of yesteryear – Dr Alban, Technotronic, 4 Non Blondes – until he notices Puff Daddy's actual scripted introduction for his performance on the autocue and starts reading without emotion from that instead: 'My next guest said that he wanted to thank MTV for his two houses, three cars, supermodel girlfriend ... 80 million deal ... really live the P Diddy dream ... '

In the corridor he walks straight back into Chris Martin.

'You seem to be doing alright,' he teases Chris. 'Mentioning no names.' (The hot, as-yet-unconfirmed rumour in the tabloids is that Martin has been seeing Gwyneth Paltrow.)

'Nah,' parries Chris. 'Me and Jon Bon Jovi are just good friends.'

Rob asks Chris whether he's having lunch at the hotel, but Chris says he's going to backstage catering here. 'Not good enough for you?' he asks.

'I've got a new record deal,' jousts Rob. 'Don't know if you've read about it. Can't do catering any more.'

'Yes,' says Chris. 'There's less for bands like us.' (Less money at the record companies, he means. Not food at catering. Presumably there's more of that.)

Rob goes to the bathroom and muses on this last sentence as he pees. By the time he comes out he is a little narked. 'What did he mean – "bands like us"?' he says. There are few men on earth more sensitive to a perceived slight. When I ask him exactly what he imagines Chris Martin might have intended to imply, he says: 'Cool, credible bands – not like you, you daft Take That reject.'

In the end, he does decide to go to catering, and so is, for the third time today, soon talking to Chris Martin. They chat some more. 'Medication's what you need,' Rob tells him.

'Medication is: you're a pop star and you're a good-looking guy and you shouldn't worry so much,' suggests Chris Martin. 'I worry a lot too,' he adds.

'Do you really?' asks Rob. 'Like you can't sleep at night and ... ?'

Chris Martin cuts him off. 'Let's not have a competition,' he suggests with a bashful smile.

'I'm suicidal, me,' says Rob, gleefully.

'I had a razor blade ... ' offers Chris Martin.

Rob is invited over to join the rest of Coldplay at their table. By the time he has talked and eaten with them, and is in a slower van on the way back to the hotel, he is nursing further slights. 'At the end, he went, "We just can't compete with you lot," and I said, "Who's 'you lot'?" and the whole table went ...' – he acts out an awkward, open-mouthed suspension of conversation – '... and I got him out of it.'

But it put him out of joint. 'It's definitely "our camp, and then there's Britney Spears and you lot",' he says. 'Which I felt a bit sad about. It's put me on my arse a little bit.'

I suggest that maybe these are just sloppy words.

'Probably,' he says, quite clearly not meaning this at all. 'It was less of a conversation and more of a battle. They're really, really lovely – don't get me wrong. But I found myself in a position where I'm nearly justifying my own existence. *Nearly.*'

'Well, that's progress,' says David.

'I suppose,' says Rob, 'if you talk about feelings and stuff and it's not met with a feeling back ... because I can only speak in feelings, otherwise a lot of what I say is panto. Especially in front of a band.'

He says that they talked some more about not being happy with aspects of what they were doing and Chris Martin said, 'We don't talk about it to sell records.' 'That's a bit savage, isn't it?' he says. They also talked about America. 'Even they do all the shaking hands, Dave,' he says.

* * *

In the lounge of his presidential suite he does an interview with Kyle and Jackie O from Sydney's 1041 Hot 30 countdown. They say that all the Australian tabloids are making a big thing out of the notion that his song 'How Precious' is about Nicole Kidman.

'"How Peculiar",' he corrects.

'Yes. Is it about Nicole?'

'No.'

'It's not?'

'No.'

The Australians say that last time he was on their radio show, he was kind enough to pluck one of his pubic hairs to give away, but one of their employees took it with him when he left the station. They request a replacement.

'I couldn't do it now,' he says. 'I feel a bit weird about it.'

* * *

He takes his backgammon board down to the hotel lobby. He wants to sit here, play backgammon, drink the Slimfast Pompey persuades the hesitant waiter to make up ('It's not drugs,' reassures Pompey), and watch the world go by. (Rob goes through crazes with games, then drops them completely. Backgammon is the latest, not for the first time. Once, not long after he had learned how to play and when he was just out of rehab, he entered a backgammon tournament at the Groucho Club and came third out of about 35 contestants. His prize: two bottles of champagne.)

Shiara, Nicole Appleton's old assistant, who now looks after the Sugababes, comes over and greets him. 'Did you read the book?' she asks.

'I read the extracts,' he says. 'Very painful. It is what it is. Fish'n'chip papers already.'

They talk some more.

'I sort of didn't see anybody for four years after Nic,' he says.

Puff Daddy spots him, comes over and they hug.

'Haven't seen you in a long time,' says Puff Daddy, and they exchange compliments. Puff Daddy then goes over to greet Chris Martin, who then comes over to us. 'It's like Madame Tussaud's in here,' he says. 'This place is absolutely bonkers.' Chris Martin goes shopping for clothes and Rob greets the Sugababes – 'Some words of wisdom on the youth,' he says after – then goes outside, undresses to his underwear and steps into the Jacuzzi. 'Oh,' he says. 'It's not warm enough. Bastards.' He gets dressed, chats with Kelis on the way to the hotel restaurant, where he studies the invitation to Puff Daddy's party – 'Please Join Sean "P Diddy" Combs As He Continues His Worldwide Crusade To Help Preserve The Sexy', it says, and instructs women to wax and men to have manicures if they want to attend – while a few yards away two teenage girls keep trying to record links for a TV camera. They're not very good at it, and they keep cracking up in a kind of sullen way. We slowly realise that these are the new Russian lesbian pop sensations, Tatu, who are just about to be launched on Western Europe. Rob laughs at their laughter and they laugh more.

On the way to the elevator he bumps into Marilyn Manson, who suggests he should paint Rob's portrait.

'With my cock out?' Rob asks.

'We like the same sort of girls,' Marilyn Manson tells him.

Sophie Ellis Bextor sits a few yards away, her back to him. Neither of them acknowledges the other.

* * *

The list of people Rob considers to have wronged him is not a lengthy one, but a few names are indelibly inked in. Sophie Ellis Bextor's is one. If it wasn't for what followed, he might not have held against her the first time she slighted him, but he would have remembered it just the same. She then fronted an indie rock group, The Audience. Rob liked their single 'If You Can't Do It When You're Young When Can You Do It?', particularly enjoying that she sang Stockard Channing's 'There Are Worse Things I Could Do' from *Grease* on the b-side, so he invited them to support him on his first solo tour. He heard back that the rest of the band had wanted to but that she had vetoed it. 'Because I was "crap", I think was the word I heard,' says Rob. 'So that was notched for future reference.'

In 1998, Rob's Nan, who had played an important role in his upbringing, died. The night before the funeral, he lay in his old bedroom in Stoke – 'In bits anyway,' he remembers – watching TV. He chanced upon Jo Whiley's music discussion programme, on which the 'Millennium' video was played and his worth debated by Whiley, Neil Hannon, James Lavelle and Sophie Ellis Bextor. Only Lavelle was supportive, saying that he didn't know what Rob had gone through but that he admired him for trying to come through it. Neil Hannon, who Rob had recently invited to sing on 'No Regrets', said he had done so just to tell his nieces. (That caused its own ructions. Hannon's group, The Divine Comedy, were about to support Rob on tour; after this Rob had him thrown off. When Hannon phoned up to apologise, and successfully petition for The Divine Comedy's reinstatement, Rob told him how he had been close to tears at Hannon's failure to stick up for him.)

But it was Sophie Ellis Bextor who hit the hardest. 'She tore into me bigger, deeper, harder and more nastily than any journalist's ever done,' he says. 'And there's me, sinking into my bed. I think she called me "the bastard son of Jimmy Tarbuck".' Pause. 'Which is both offensive to me and Jimmy Tarbuck.'

The next day, at the funeral, just as the coffin was about to be lowered, a local paparazzi wannabe was going *click click click click* about 15 yards away. 'Didn't have the decency to hide in the bushes or anything,' he remembers. 'Just stood there.' A wretched time, and for him Sophie Ellis Bextor's spitefulness would forever be associated with it.

Some time later, he saw her at a Capital Radio Awards Show. It seems that often, when he is at his angriest, his initial approach is a conciliatory one. He tapped her on the shoulder and said, 'Do you still hate me?' He remembers her as being nearly speechless, but saying that no, she didn't. 'Because,' he told her, 'what you said really upset me. Anyway, good luck with everything.'

After that, he received a letter from her. It wasn't exactly an apology, but it said that she now realised, having been in the business a while, that artists should stick together. That same morning, a Saturday morning, he saw her on a kids' TV show, slagging him off again.

'I think she's a poisonous witch,' he now says. 'I think she's malicious.' Pause. 'And I think she should get her hips sorted out.'

* * *

All day Rob has been saying that he won't go to the MTV party, but at the last moment he decides to drop by. It is in Gaudí's Casa Batlló. 'One of the most beautiful buildings in the world,' he announces as we draw up. Inside, he walks straight into Jon Bon Jovi, who compliments him on 'Feel' – 'It's really different,' he says – while someone from *Vanity Fair* unsuccessfully tries to persuade Rob to pose for a photo. 'I haven't got make-up on,' he argues. 'I only came out for a sausage.'

He stands with Chris Martin, yet again, and Anastasia.

'Do you know you look like my ex-girlfriend?' Rob tells Anastasia.

'Yeah,' she says, mock testily. 'Does that mean you want to jump my bones?'

Someone offers to show him the private areas of the house, and suddenly we are on a personal Gaudí guided tour with Moby and Tico Torres from Bon Jovi. As they walk, Rob tells Moby about how, while he and Guy were writing 'Feel', it was known as 'the Moby song'. When we return to the main party, Jon Bon Jovi talks to Rob about breaking America. 'You're such a great performer,' he says. 'You just have to go out. Even if you support a bigger performer.' Jon Bon Jovi says that they used to do 250 shows each tour, and that the shortest tour they've ever done is 60 shows. Rob, who hasn't played 250 shows in his solo career, looks horrified. 'Sixty shows?' he says. 'I do five weeks.' Jon Bon Jovi explains that they have to fly out right after the MTV show tomorrow, and the following morning must appear on a radio station in Miami. Rob is listening, thinking, I would never ever do that.

A woman is brought over and introduced to Jon Bon Jovi with the words 'You remember, you met at the White House', and this is the moment when Rob decides it is time for him to leave. We slip out of a side exit before the sit-down meal and speeches begin. He has been there no more than 30 minutes.

* * *

He takes up his place in the lobby and we play more backgammon. A while later Chris Martin returns from the party. Rob asks whether he would like a game. 'I'm mad for it, to be honest,' says Chris Martin. Rob immediately unilaterally abandons the game he and I have been having and sets up the pieces.

'What are we playing for?' Rob asks.

'Just for fun at the moment,' says Chris. He throws the dice.

Six and two.

For quite a long time he just stares at the board.

Rob, who doesn't hang around for anything, looks perplexed.

'I like to play patiently,' explains Chris.

Rob nods. 'You're the Steve Davis of backgammon.'

Abruptly, Rob puts his head right down and asks for us to feign deep conversation. He has just seen Nellee Hooper, he explains. I raise my eyebrows questioningly. A story for another time, he says.

Soon Rob is on the verge of winning the game.

'This is the first of a few?' Chris confirms.

'Yeah, of course,' says Rob. 'We'll start playing for money next.' Pause. 'Or just for honour.' He counts off his last piece. 'Shall we call that the warm-up?' he suggests.

'We'll call it your victory,' says Chris.

Game Two starts.

'Why do I keep throwing six and three?' asks Chris.

'The devil talking to you through the dice,' says Rob.

'It's no good,' says Chris.

The waiter comes. We order coffees; Chris Martin orders a water.

A few throws later, he surveys the board.

'This is shit,' he sighs.

'Your song's playing so loudly in my head it's unbelievable,' says Rob. He can hear the line *Oh yeah … how long must you wait for it?* repeating in a loop, but he doesn't explain this. 'Does that ever happen to you when you meet people?' he asks.

Chris gives a look that suggests it possibly doesn't, stares at the board, and says, 'I'm fucked.' He looks up. Around the table are Rob, Pompey, the local security person and myself.

'I can't handle this,' he says. 'All of you sitting and looking at me.' He laughs. 'It's a bit like playing with the Godfather. It puts pressure on your game. I can't win it. I'm shit. I used to be the don.'

He says he needs to go. The drinks haven't even come yet. He walks over to the lift, then comes all the way back over.

'Sorry about the water,' he says.

'It's alright,' says Rob. And then adds, when Martin is again out of earshot, 'World's most polite man.' He laughs. On one hand, it was a bit weird how seriously Chris Martin took the games. On the other hand, Rob only has the luxury of thinking that, and of being able to appear as though he was taking them casually, because he won. 'That,' he declares, 'was one giant strike for me as a people against the intellectual indie kid.'

* * *

Two girls try to persuade him to go to a club. 'I'm not a big club person,' he says. 'I'm a big eat-the-minibar, watch-television and go-to-bed person.' They soon give up. 'You know,' he says after they leave, 'I think I may have outgrown my shagging boots.' He realises that, if true, this has many implications. 'If it ain't about the sex,' he reasons, 'and it ain't about the money any more, it must be about the music.'

By the lifts he almost walks into Enrique Iglesias. 'Nice to meet you at last,' says Enrique.

A plan is hatched to go to the casino in the basement with some of Coldplay, for a little light gambling, and we go down but are refused entry because we don't have our passports. Rob tells the Coldplay contingent that he'll be back with his, but instead we return to the lobby. Pharrell Williams arrives. Rob shows him the tattoo on the inside of his left wrist. Farrell.

'Farrell Williams,' he says.

Pharrell Williams seems both utterly bemused and barely interested, almost as if he imagines that Rob has tried to tattoo his name but misspelt it. 'Went down like a shit sandwich,' mutters Rob afterwards.

Chris Martin phones from his room – Rob is supposed to be up there playing more backgammon but left because Chris was on a long personal phone call – and at the same time Kylie Minogue comes over. 'Just one second, call you back,' he says to Chris Martin, then says to Kylie, 'You're looking beautiful,' and takes her out on the balcony to chat away from the celebrity hubbub. (He is now standing up two different parts of Coldplay.)

A while later, he does head up to Chris Martin's room. Coincidentally, in the same elevator are Kylie and Pharrell Williams; Pharrell listens to this conversation without joining in.

'What are you giving me tomorrow night?' Rob asks Kylie.

'Top secret,' she says.

'Best Year Off?' he asks. They travel a few floors in silence. 'You've got a yellow bow on your knickers,' Rob observes.

'Oy!' says Kylie. 'Stop looking.'

'Just scoping,' says Rob.

The lift stops and Pharrell gets out, muttering 'Night' to Rob.

'What's the case?' Kylie asks Rob.

'Backgammon,' he says. 'Going to win some money.'

He does. By the time he leaves Chris Martin's room he is €100 ahead. He realises from Chris Martin's questions as they play that he seems worried as to whether Rob has proper friends. Rob tells him about Jonny but he doesn't feel Chris Martin believes that Jonny is his best mate.

But he likes the way Chris Martin saves him half of his tuna sandwich. He likes the sandwich, too.

5

On the day of the MTV awards, Rob and I are once more playing backgammon just inside the lounge, with a full view of the hotel lobby as usual, when Rob, who has been singing Spinal Tap's 'The Majesty Of

Rock' to himself as he concentrates on his game, is approached by Dominic Mohan, the pop columnist for *The Sun*.

'Good album,' says Dominic Mohan. '"Me And My Monkey". Great song. What's it about?' (All those short sentences he has to write at work have clearly infected his speech.)

'I don't know myself,' says Rob. We carry on playing.

'Having a good time?' Dominic asks.

'Yeah.'

'Not going to do a repeat of Stockholm?'

Stockholm was the site of the last MTV awards Rob attended as a drinking man. It was not a happy visit.

Rob says he won't be going to any parties. 'I'm going to vanquish my past and go home,' he says.

'I hope to see you soon, do that interview we've been talking about,' says Dominic.

'For one of the singles, maybe,' says Rob.

They shake hands. Dominic Mohan says that he's been playing 'Me And My Monkey' on his Virgin radio show; Rob says he knows because he heard it. Dominic Mohan takes his leave.

Presumably Dominic Mohan won't be needing that interview after all, as apparently he just got one. The story will dominate his page in tomorrow's *Sun*. ROBBIE: I'M HERE TO BEAT MY DEMONS. *Robbie Williams admitted to me last night he was determined to exorcise the demons that ruined his last MTV Europe appearance. In an exclusive interview in his Barcelona hotel, Robbie confessed he had been haunted by the shame of his booze-fuelled punch-up in Stockholm in 2000. He vowed to avoid the temptation of alcohol at this year's awards – by flying home immediately after his performance, without even waiting for the ceremony to finish. A reformed Robbie told me, 'I've come here to vanquish my demons'. He looked relaxed as I chatted to him during a game of backgammon in the lounge bar of the city's swanky Hotel Arts. He said, 'This year won't be a repeat of two years ago. I'm on my best behaviour and I'm not hanging around after I've done my bit tonight. I will be tucked up in bed by 3am while everyone's still out here partying.'*

And so on.

* * *

He goes to the bathroom. On the way he is approached by a man who asks him, 'Can I have a quote for the *NME*?'

'Yeah,' says Rob. 'Fuck off.'

The quote is faithfully reproduced on their website.

* * *

In the van to the show he says that he's not feeling well. 'Remember when you used to say,' he murmurs to himself, 'everything will be OK.' He stares out of the window. 'I've never seen a crane dismantled,' he says. 'How do they get them down?'

On the way into the backstage area he greets Jade Jagger and Patrick Kluivert. Chris Martin comes into his dressing room, his middle finger raised, holding €100 note. Eminem shuffles past in the corridor, surrounded by larger men, his head down. Rob goes to the bathroom and on the way back bumps into Mel C. He tells her how well she looks, and asks if the man nearby is her boyfriend.

'Yeah,' she says. 'Finally found someone who isn't a wanker.'

Then Marilyn Manson joins them. 'Melanie,' he says. Manson talks about the party last night – 'They had Parmesan ice cream; I kept the menu' – and says that he met Puff Daddy.

'Were you scared?' asks Rob.

'No, I took a picture with him,' he says and then elaborates, untruthfully: 'Jacked him off.' It is such a relief that, just when you think Marilyn Manson has forgotten who he is meant to be, he rediscovers the right level of inappropriateness.

Still, back in his dressing room, Rob admits that he found this whole encounter with Manson and Mel C embarrassing. Nothing that was said. Just that he had to leave a hand hovering over his groin throughout. 'I'd sprinkled,' he explains.

* * *

He plugs his computer into his dressing room's sound system and starts booming out his chosen songs: to begin with Eazy E's 'Nobody Move'. He lathers up, shirtless, and shaves in the mirror; asks Josie for a coffee; puts on Jay Z's 'Ain't No Love' really loud. The dressing rooms are actually all just thinly partitioned boxes, their walls about 9 feet high, clumped together in groups separated by corridors, and above them is maybe another 40 feet of communal space up to the ceiling. If someone lifted up all the partitions at once, you'd find many of the world's most famous entertainers, in various states of undress, humour and sobriety, packed close together on the floor of a huge warehouse. As a result, Rob's music is travelling far beyond his dressing room and insisting upon itself as the soundtrack for most of tonight's other guests. A bloke sticks his head round the door, and nods.

'Puff wanted to see who this was,' he says.

Rob plays more Jay Z, then 'Diddly' by P Diddy. Two of Christina Aguilera's dancers come by, also wanting to check out the source of the music. 'He is *jamming*,' says one. He plays something by L'il Rob; Ian Brown's 'Dolphins Are Monkeys'; 'Pump Up The Volume'. P Diddy appears at the door and has his photo taken with Rob, who then pops out to greet Ronan Keating. On returning, he selects The Stone Roses' 'Waterfall', some ZZ Top, 'Maggie May', 'No One Knows' by Queens Of The Stone Age.

Chris Martin dashes in. 'Quick game of backgammon,' he says, and sits down. He asks Rob when he's doing his walk-in. The artists are requested, long after they have actually arrived, to go back outside and pretend to arrive down the red carpet for the television cameras.

Rob looks at him as though he is insane.

'Are you not doing it?' Chris Martin asks.

'*You* gotta go and do the walk-in?' says Rob, equally incredulous. Chris Martin nods. (I can't help feeling there's a shadow battle here: Who's the pop sell-out now?) A few minutes later Chris Martin's security man collects him so that he can do his walking duty.

Jenson Button comes by to chat, nursing a Red Bull. 'I couldn't interest you in a Slimfast?' asks Rob.

'Lovely,' says Jenson, baffled, though not accepting it.

Rob puts on Guns N'Roses' 'Paradise City'.

'Miss Pink,' he declares, as she walks towards him in the corridor.

'Good song,' she says. 'Nice to meet you.'

I trail him as he flits back and forth, nervous and impatient. He retreats back into the dressing room, where he throws a chair with some violence against the wardrobe. Then he does the same thing again. Then again. Just because. Puts on Guns N'Roses 'It's So Easy', then goes into the corridor and talks to Rupert Everett. Marilyn Manson appears again. 'Keep the fucking noise down,' he says to Rob playfully. Taylor Hawkins, the Foo Fighters drummer, starts drumming on Rob's open dressing room door with his drumsticks. 'They want you to be their singer,' he says. (He means Queen, and this is somewhat true. After Rob sang 'We Are The Champions' with two of Queen as the theme to the film *A Knight's Tale*, they asked him to tour America as their frontman. He seriously considered it, too.)

'But they started doing duets with boy bands and stuff,' he says to Taylor.

Taylor nods. 'They need to chill out.'

In the arena, the show has started. We can watch it on a monitor in the corridor, just outside Marilyn Manson's dressing room. Rob bumps into Pierce Brosnan. Marilyn Manson reappears and relays the conversation he just had with Kylie. 'She said, "They made me stand on a box – I hope someone doesn't take away my box." I said, "Don't say that in America. I'll take away your box."'

'Robbie, I watched your Sinatra thing on the plane,' says Taylor. 'It was tight, man.'

'You did a *Truth Or Dare*,' notes Manson, referring to *Nobody Someday*.

'Yeah,' says Rob. 'I did a miserable-complaining-son-of-a-bitch.'

He goes into the arena area for a quick look, and a Spanish drag queen starts interviewing him. 'Very excited to be here and very pleased to be nominated for an award – I believe that's what you're supposed to say,' he tells her. By ten o'clock he is having his make-up done and starts making weird vocal warm-up noises. Gina complains that he has a toenail in his mouth. 'He just does it 'cause I hate it,' she says. Rob removes it and, slowly, he gets fully dressed, then sits for a final touch-up from Gina. 'Take it out!' she screeches, when she realises he has substituted a new toenail. 'You can't wear a suit and having a fucking toenail in your mouth.'

He tells Josie he wants to go round and see Ms Dynamite. He has written her a letter, apologising for not using her 'Feel' rap, but he wants to make sure she understands.

In the corridor he bumps into Dave Grohl, who says he wants a photo with him. 'You're so statesmanlike tonight,' Grohl tells him. 'You look really nice.' Rob poses with him. He thinks Grohl is slightly taking the piss, but he doesn't mind. He was in Nirvana. (Anyway, the bluffing and bragging and mock compliments all balance out. He met Grohl earlier in the year at the Coachella festival and told him, 'Apart from me, you're the best.' Grohl looked confused, then said, 'Thanks, man.')

Rob goes to the side of the stage and tries to run through the lyrics of 'Feel' under his breath. He doesn't really know them. He writes the first line '*Come on hold my hand*' on his hand, both to remind him and as a kind of tribute to Chris Martin's hand graffiti.

'My next guest said that he wanted to thank MTV for his two houses, three cars, supermodel girlfriend,' says P Diddy. 'He just ran into some paper, just negotiated a big record deal, £80 million – how much is that in American dollars? Can I hold some, baby boy? But now you can join the P Diddy club and really live the life, baby. Give it up for my boy ... Robbie Williams!'

Rob doesn't need to check his crib sheet.

Come on hold my hand ... I want to contact the living ...

In the song, these words are a sad and serious beginning to a serious and sad song. He will rarely explain that they come from an old comedian's exhortation when he's dying on stage – 'Come on, everybody! Let's join hands, let's see if we can contact the living!' – though there's something typically Robbie Williams about both the source and the use he has found for it.

The performance – the four minutes that are this whole trip's stated rationale – goes fine, though Rob can't hear properly and his pitching suffers as a result. When he squelches one big note, the camera catches a close-up of his disgusted grimace. Towards the end, he raises his hand above his head imperiously, in a manner consciously borrowed from Perry Farrell. As he leaves the stage, his place under the cameras is taken by the possibly satanic Las Ketchup.

* * *

On the way back to his dressing room he stops at Ms Dynamite's dressing room, still keen to see her before he leaves, but it is locked and there is no sign of her. He knocks and waits a moment. Nothing.

He is having his make-up taken off when he hears that Ms Dynamite is coming down the corridor, and so he rushes out to see her.

'Did you get my letter?' he asks her.

'No,' she says.

'I sent it to your office,' he says. 'Because I wanted you to know ... ' He offers the briefest of explanations. 'But I just wanted to say, you look fucking great.'

'Thank you,' she says.

It doesn't seem like a grand meeting of minds, and she does seem a little standoffish and suspicious, but there is nothing to suggest what will follow.

For now, the private jet is waiting. He finishes changing in the dressing room. At the last minute, just as we are leaving, he realises he needs to pee again. He could go down the corridor to the toilet, but he does not. There is a bin in the corner of the room behind the mirror so he pisses into that, instead.

'Oh!' says Gina despairingly. 'You animal.'

As we draw away in the van, he says, 'I always feel horrible in those places.'

By three o'clock in the morning, he is home.

* * *

The next day there is an article about his trip to Spain in the *Evening Standard*. ROBBIE GETS BLOWN OUT BY MS DYNAMITE is the headline. *Pride comes before a fall – well it certainly did for Robbie Williams last night ... he chanced his luck with Ms Dynamite at the MTV Europe awards in Barcelona ... and was promptly blown away ... he must be thanking his lucky stars today that the humiliation he suffered at the hand of the London rapping sensation was only witnessed by a handful of celebrities.*

It claims that he came offstage and made a beeline to her dressing room, hammered on the door, discovered it empty and said, 'Christ – she's gone! I don't believe it! Where are you Ms Dynamitee-hee? I must find you!' He then searched the maze of dressing rooms for 20 minutes before tracking her down, running up to her and saying: 'Thank God I found you! I've been waiting to chat to you for months.' It says that she grimaced as he hugged her and then demanded to know why she hadn't answered his letters: *'Didn't you get them?' he pleaded ... He added, 'I really love your work – I've really got the hots for you' ... At that point, Ms Dynamite turned bright red, flatly denied ever having received anything in the mail, did an about-turn and started chatting intently to Chris Martin from Coldplay. Robbie was left standing on his own. He then walked off, getting changed into a tracksuit, shunning the aftershow party completely.*

For the record, this is the exact text of the letter in question – there is only one – which the *Standard* clearly imagines as one of a series of overbearing flirtatious love letters. Rob handwrote it in block capitals on one sheet of paper, and it was sent some time before the MTV awards:

Dear Miss D.

First of all may I congratulate you on all your awards. I've been back in the country now for a few weeks and you're always on the telly ... video's great, you look beautiful, and the songs are wicked ... congrats, congrats, congrats.

Just wanted to drop you a line to explain what happened to your words of wisdom in my song Feel. I actually feel a bit gutted that it's not in and feel a bit embarrassed cos maybe no one's spoke to you about it.

Everyone loved it, and I thought it actually made the song better ... but there was a strong shout from my camp that said first single back should just be 'Robbie'. After many scratchy beard meetings and me throwing a few tea cups I had to concede.

I wanted to drop you this letter cos after our brief conversation and listening to your lyrics you sound as sensitive as I am! And I didn't want to piss you off! I really hope this hasn't fucked up a collaboration in the future ...

With much respect and admiration
Robbie Williams

✱ ✱ ✱

He goes to Radio Two, where he meets Alice Cooper in a corridor ('Hi, Mr Cooper,' he says, and is invited to play golf in Arizona sometime), has a strange encounter in a corridor with Steve Wright, who asks Rob to come on his programme and presses four pieces of chewing gum into his hand, and does an interview with Jonathan Ross in which Ross asks: 'What about that gay bloke you live with? I mean, does he miss you when you're away?'

Rob decides to just go with it. (If it is not clear from his inaccurate description, Jonathan Ross is talking about Jonny.) 'Every relationship that we seem to have are obviously beards,' he says. 'It's just a big cover-up and I might as well say that live on the Jonathan Ross show ... the thing is, that's going to be the news tomorrow. You know that, don't you? That's going to be it: Robbie finally admits he's gay.'

In fact, it doesn't end up in the papers at all. Quite possibly the tabloid press simply don't listen to Radio Two, but it may also be that they're much more comfortable in the land of insinuation and hidden secrets. Perhaps they're happier in a world where they can continue lazily implying those favourite three or four things (he's with Rachel Hunter, he's shagging all over the place, he's sad and lonely and unloved, he's secretly gay) without being the slightest bit concerned that these contradict each other, ready so that if any firm proof came up that any of each (firmer than somebody may be joking on a radio show), they can proudly hoot, 'We told you so.'

✱ ✱ ✱

At this point in the life of Robbie Williams, most days begin late, with a bowl of cereal and the post. Today, the following letter has somehow found its way to his house. It is written on both sides of a single sheet from a memo pad with a photo of an inquisitive lion cub peering towards the reader at the top. The stationery is personalised – it says 'This memo pad belongs to ... ' – but the writer has roughly scribbled over their name in dark biro to obliterate it, and neither signed the letter nor given an address. (They've done a poor job of it, though. If you hold the letter up to the light, you can still see the name.) The letter is written in eccentric, spindly handwriting, with shaky, wild, cursive capitals. What is remarkable is not so much what is said – people think these things – but that someone might bother to write it and send it:

This is only one report about you! an elderly couple, we sat up late one night, then a programme with you on! All you did was talk about you-you-you, 1½ hours! those young girl must be as bad as you to be interested, no wonder after a while they avoid you, arrogant, disgusting language, didn't, or rather can't seem to sing, they can't have any idea what real singing is, as you said "well, I'll be a popstar", can't be your looks!? money perhaps. Some Rich people are like you, why they're paying you £80,000,000 is beyond everybody beliefe, if we were your parents, you spoke about your grandmother, you must have got very bigheaded, we wouldn't want any son or grandson to behave like you, and your language? People who swear like you have no confidence, or respect. Still that sounds like you, no wonder some girls get away from you if you use language like this. Nic was wise girl. Whatever did Rachel Hunter see in you. We know you couldn't care less but had to tell you.

6

On the day of *Escapology*'s release he flies to Berlin by private jet for a press conference to announce next summer's tour. 'Apparently, I've been busy befriending Eminem and being blown out by Ms Dynamite,' he says, after briefly inspecting the tabloids during the journey. (As a rule, he doesn't seek out the tabloids. He tries to avoid having them in the house and will go for days without seeing one. But if one is nearby – lying on a table, or in a car or plane, or just its corner is sticking out of someone's bag – he will usually grab it.)

'I'm going to get a really deep voice for my next album,' he suddenly declares, 'and speak a lot of lyrics.' Then he reads Stuart Maconie's review of his album in Q. 'Wanker,' he says when he finishes it. 'He doesn't even review the album.' This sparks a thought. It has been a long time since he, too, has heard his album. He asks David whether he has a copy, which he does, and he spends the rest of the journey listening to himself.

After hearing a few of his songs, he makes a declaration: 'My album shits on anything out there – that's my review.' He shrugs. 'I don't think these songs will be respected for five years. I mean, it's so difficult not to get dragged down by the media image of Robbie Williams, because I do. Sometimes *I* can't get past it.'

'Hot Fudge' is next. *'I'm moving to LA! LA! LA! … '* he sings. I bring up one of most annoying things about the album reviews – the way most of them simply accept as gospel the idea that it is an album crafted to break America. They act as though this has been clearly and publicly stated by Rob, though in fact he has never said anything of the sort, it isn't true, and it doesn't make much sense when you listen to the record, even musically. If you were deliberately going to plan to seduce America, where a much narrower musical focus not only better fits in with the music business, but is seen, to a greater degree than elsewhere, as a sign of the artist's sincerity and authenticity, you wouldn't release an album as heterogeneous as *Escapology*.

But even that isn't the most idiotic aspect of their assumption. Almost every reviewer has quoted from the songs that actually mention Los Angeles and America, like 'Hot Fudge' and 'Song 3', as though this is clear evidence of his intent to woo America. Presumably, even their editors have blessed this as sensible commentary, and yet its logic is absurd. Think about it. Who on earth, if they could remove their Robbie-Williams-is-desperately-trying-to-break-America blinkers for a minute, could possibly imagine that the way to break America is *to write songs about how great America is*? Why would anyone imagine that what the American public hankers for is some English bloke singing at them about their country?

We discuss all this as the album plays on, until Rob turns to David.

'Have you heard from Guy?' he asks.

'Not a squeak,' David replies.

* * *

Perhaps there is something about lounging in comfort on a luxurious private plane that triggers reminiscence. As we fly into German airspace, Rob starts talking about his encounters with Bono. The first is one of his favourite anecdotes from the lost drug days. He had flown over to Bono's Dublin retreat for a party. Patsy and Liam had been on the plane and during the journey he had persuaded Liam that when Bono relaxes he likes calling the bingo. At the party, Rob got off his head on mushrooms and Bono found him staring at the wall. Rob had been staring at the same thing for ages, because he was quite sure it was the most beautiful picture he'd ever seen in his life.

'Bono,' he said, 'that picture's *amazing* … '

'Robbie,' pointed out Bono, patiently. 'That's the window.'

Rob stayed in the guest house. All the previous guests had written on the walls, and he was expected to do the same. Before leaving, he stood there for ages, looking at words from Salman Rushdie and Kofi Annan and all the others, intimidated by all the scrawled wisdom and poetry, trying to work out how he could match it. Finally, he raised his pen.

'To Bono,' he wrote. 'Love Robbie.'

He is besotted with Bono, and with U2. It was watching their April 2001 concert in Anaheim, California, that was one of the principal spurs to make him want to retire as a solo artist and form a band. In his prayers for some time afterwards he would literally implore: 'God, can I find the Edge, please? And can you help me to write really deep lyrics that touch my soul as much as Bono's touch mine?'

After the Anaheim show, he went backstage and told Bono: 'When I grow up, I want to be like you.' He received that look from Bono that suggested this was not the thought he should be thinking. Bono can make him feel like that quite easily.

There is one moment from his various encounters with Bono he regrets most of all. Bono has a way, now and then, of grabbing you and looking you in the eye and really talking to you. When Rob was around him, Rob would wish for Bono to do this, but be terrified of it too. One night, right at the start of Rob's solo career, Bono was talking to him like that, and said to him: 'If you want, you could be absolutely huge.'

And Rob replied, 'Yeah, I'm going to be the biggest celebrity ever.'

I'm going to be the biggest celebrity ever.

'The minute it went through my lips I knew it was wrong,' says Rob. 'And he looked at me like I'd stolen one of his children. And he said no, no, no … And I went no, no, no … '

* * *

Josie briefs him on what he can expect at the press conference, to be held in the British embassy: 269 media, an introduction from the ambassador, meetings with the tour sponsors Xbox and Smart. Rob walks out and stands in front of a large backdrop of himself leaping in the air. 'Thank you for letting us use your gaff,' he says to the ambassador, and sits on a stool, a microphone in his hand, like a seventies variety performer. He explains to the 269 media that he has the flu, he had two hours' sleep and he feels a bit intimidated. 'OK, any questions?' he asks.

He sets the tone immediately in the way he answers an innocuous opening enquiry about why he is playing open-air shows. Because they are big concerts, he begins. 'I love a big gig,' he explains and then adds, completely unbidden: 'And actually people should come and see this because I think that after this tour and after this album I think it's all downhill, I genuinely do, because I think this is the pinnacle of my career right now, and they should catch it while I'm hot. Or come to see the holiday shows that I will do each summer in England around Butlins camps in about five years. With Oasis.'

He's asked about America, and some of our conversation on the plane spills out. 'I've been very very interested to read an awful lot of stuff, especially with the album coming out. You know that this album, apparently from the media, is so obviously directed for an American audience. And the reason why I've spent a lot of time there is because I so obviously am desperate to break it Stateside. Which is actually an embellishment on a half-truth and a half-lie ... the absolute truth is, I'm completely not bothered. I've done an awful lot of hard work since I was 16 with Take That and my solo career ... the absolute truth is, I'm really not interested in breaking America. It's too much hard work, I'll be a new artist there, I can't be arsed. It's too much of a fight. I've got my money now. Thank you. For the record, I'm not bothered. I'm really not. I've got an amazing audience that listen to my albums over here and in Asia and other places. I don't need to go.'

Just like that. These words will be attributed in tomorrow's newspapers with causing a fall in the EMI share price.

He chats away, correcting stories – the Ms Dynamite rejection, the Guy Chambers exclusivity deal – and talking about his penis. The usual stuff.

'Thomas from *Bravo* – what do you do with all the money you got from EMI?'

'I'm going to have a room full of sweets,' he answers, 'and I'm going to eat my way out.'

There is some laughter, but more bafflement, at this answer.

'I really don't know,' he continues. 'I'm a celebrity. We have many divorces. A lot of it's going to go to future ex-wives, I'm sure. There's already a contingency plan put in for the tour in about 15 years when I really need to do it because two of my wives have got all of the dough.'

In a back room he is interviewed by two journalists from the German news magazine *Der Spiegel*. They ask about the *Escapology* CD booklet and say that he looks a little like Jesus. They point out that he hangs upside down from the tallest building in Los Angeles with his arms outstretched on the cover, as though in an inverted crucifix, and inside the booklet, when his body is encircled by several rings of light, one approximately level with his hairline, looks as though he has a halo. 'No,' he says, of both suggestions. 'Believe me.' This is the first time this interpretation has ever been suggested. They ask about the title, and he explains his plans to kill Robbie Williams, and how he changed his mind. 'The escape is just escaping from killing me off,' he says. 'I've actually managed to claw back, in my own mind, enjoyment for being me.'

'Escape can be a bad word, running away,' one of them says earnestly.

'Yeah, it just depends how you look at it,' he says. 'You could say it's an escape from things that really matter, you can say that it's an escape from responsibility. But you could also say that it's an escape from killing myself, which I would think would be the true meaning.'

They ask about his parents, and he talks first about his mother. 'She says, "I'm very proud of how you've handled yourself and what you've done," and that means the world to me,' he explains. 'That means more than an 80 million record deal.' He grins broadly and daftly. 'But you can't spend that.'

'Does your father give you any advice on entertaining?' they ask.

'Um, to watch my father is its own advice,' he answers. 'How he holds himself and his mannerisms. I've stolen a lot of everybody's act – Freddie Mercury ... Axl Rose, Tina Turner, Mick Jagger, David Bowie, Dean Martin, Sammy Davis Junior, Frank Sinatra, my dad, other comics that I know, Steve Coogan, Eddie Izzard ... I've just stole everybody's act and made it mine.'

They ask him what he does in a typical Los Angeles day. 'Nothing,' he insists. 'Absolutely nothing. And I'm very, very good at it. Occasionally I'll go and buy some clothes. But all my day is spent just sitting, doing nothing, maybe strum on the guitar, maybe take the dogs for a walk. After doing *loads* of things since I was 16, to actually just sit in a tracksuit and do nothing is a gift. And I've developed it as a fine art. I'm a man who does nothing all day.' He explains that this has been an important development in terms of his calm and happiness. 'Some people really suit fame, and deal with it really well,' he says. 'I don't.'

'You can't get used to fame?' one of them asks.

'No,' he says. 'I think what happens with fame is you spend the beginning bit striving to get there, and the rest of your career surviving it.'

* * *

In the car, David, making conversation, repeats part of a discussion he just had with their host. 'The ambassador said it's the pinnacle of his career ... ' he says.

'Me doing that?' says Rob seriously. 'That's nice.'

'No,' says David, 'being posted in Berlin.'

Amidst the laughter, some of it his, Rob wears one of those broad fixed smiles one adopts when the street you have confidently directed everyone down turns out to be a dead end, and there is nothing to do but walk back out the way you came. 'Can we go back to the beginning of that conversation?' he suggests.

* * *

At home, Rob wants to play blackjack, but we don't have any chips. He wants to go and get some new ones from Hamleys but it's shut, so we all sit round, cutting up bits of paper to use instead of chips. It doesn't work, so in the end we give up. Too late, Rob remembers that in America one time when they were also without chips they had used pills.

'Vitamins and antidepressants,' he says. 'Vitamins were five, anti-depressants were 50.'

7

As Rob eats breakfast, sings Coldplay songs under his breath and studies the *Escapology* CD booklet, Pompey wonders what to wear for today's day trip. 'It's too warm for a jumper,' he considers.

'I'll tell you what,' advises Rob. 'Cold in Stoke.'

We leave from Battersea heliport and sweep north. It's not like being in a plane; you feel as though the countryside is spread out just below, and is slowly reeled south beneath you. It takes about 40 minutes to reach Uttoxeter racecourse, a landing spot chosen for secrecy's sake, in the hope that this visit to Stoke can be kept from all but those involved.

'What a fucking pleasant journey that was,' says Rob as we land. 'Note to self: "Always be rich ... "'

* * *

When it comes to charity, the famous are routinely damned whatever they do. If they are seen to do nothing, they are cursed as rich, selfish and mean. But it is when they try to do something that the problems really start. Perhaps there was a time when the most innocent, obvious equation still worked: a person would become rich and famous; they would subsequently wish, out of some combination of gratitude and guilt, to 'give something back'; they would do something good for the benefit of others and maybe make themselves feel a little bit better in the process. It used to be a mark of selflessness and virtue not to draw attention to one's giving.

But for anyone famous who still wishes to do some quiet good in the world, all that has been spoiled, most markedly over the last two decades, as the divide between charity work and shameless self-publicity has weakened and, at times, shattered. These days, anyone prone to cynicism only has to hear the word 'charity' in the context of the entertainment world and they will start questioning the motives of the participants. Very often they will be right to do so. More and more, charity has become just another kind of promotion; the world of charity events and premieres and parties and fund-raisers and photo opportunities offers another way up the ladder, and another way to slow one's descent. The weekly celebrity magazines like *Hello* and *OK!* are packed with photographs from events where no one even seems to agonise about any of this any more or tries to unpick the selfish from the selfless; instead everyone just accepts a ghastly quid pro quo where both celebrities and institutional charities help each other get the exposure and attention they each need.

It's a dilemma for anyone who would like to do something without being sucked into that vortex. One way is simply to keep quiet about what you do, but do it anyway, and, when you occasionally offer yourself to publicise a particular event or situation, do so in a way that is as far removed as possible from the selling of what you do in your career. That is closer to what Rob has tried to do. Over the past few years it's clear that he has given away several million pounds, but the only time I hear him even allude to it (aside from a couple of exasperated outbursts in private when, because he doesn't trumpet any of this, people have implied he does nothing) is when he mentions earmarking the proceeds from various Robbie Williams projects for his charities. Some money has gone to Unicef, with whom he has an ongoing involvement, but most goes to his own charity, Give It Sum, which he started in 2000. Its work is entirely concentrated in the Stoke area where he grew up.

Today's visit to Stoke is to give him a chance to drop in on some of the projects Give It Sum works with: to keep him involved with what they have been up to, to show his support, and to pose for the odd photo that can be used to promote what they do locally at the appropriate, later date. This trip has had to be arranged with more secrecy than most of his professional arrangements because if even the local press or a single local photographer gets wind of what is happening, it will mess up the whole day. Everyone is also very mindful of the fact that the only day he could find to make this trip is during his new album's first week of release; it would be mortifying if word got out about the trip and it seemed as though the two were connected and he were doing the very thing he strenuously avoids – using charity as some kind of inappropriate promotional device. Still, aside from the car waiting to pick us up – whose driver, surreally, tries to direct the helicopter in to land – and a couple of women who work at Uttoxeter racecourse, the place is deserted when we arrive. So far, so good.

We drive to his mother Jan's house and gather in the kitchen. (Jan is on the Give It Sum committee, and heavily involved in disbursing its grants and monitoring their results.) Rob goes through the CDs in the rack and puts on a Mantronix mix of 'Millennium'. (It was unreleased, for technical reasons. 'It was crap,' he explains.) He dips fingers into the bowl of 'Angel' cards on his mother's dining room table. The first card he pulls out is blank. The second says 'forgiveness'.

* * *

The day's first stop is a children's hospice run by the Donna Louise Trust, for children who are not expected to live beyond their teenage years; it's still being built but nearing completion. The people there take Rob upstairs and tell him about their work, and show him a cutting from the local paper when his involvement was first announced. *Patron Saint Robbie set to haul in the cash*. The same cutting describes some 13-year-old girls who covered their mouths to raise money because he was involved. 'A sponsored silence,' he notes, smiling. He likes that. He tours the half-finished bedrooms and play areas, and asks quiet, concerned questions, and seems relieved when he comes across a builder's dog he can fuss over. Walking into another room, he meets a painter he used to know in his teenage years.

Outside the front door, he lines up for a photograph with the principals.

'Chins down, eyes up,' he says.

One of his hosts says she hates having her photo taken.

'It never gets any easier,' he sympathises.

In the van, he chats to Jan about Stoke's gay mayor. She said the mayor has asked her to thank Rob for sticking his neck out because he has given a grant to the local gay switchboard. 'I said he didn't stick his neck out, it came very naturally,' she says. Between destinations, Josie hands him fact sheets in the van to bring him up to speed. The next is the Old Blurton Community Centre. There is a collective gasp when he walks in.

'A real pop star!' one woman exclaims. 'I can't believe it.'

'I can't either,' Rob points out.

They make him a cup of coffee and tell him about what happens here, and how setting up this drop-in centre has helped them reclaim the area.

'It was like Beirut down here,' says one.

'You were frightened enough not to come out of the front door,' says another.

'What it means,' one says, 'to get some control back.'

'I'm not just saying this,' says Nina, the older woman in charge, who oozes spirit and determination, 'but it couldn't have stayed open the past two years without you.'

Rob says his mother told him all about it. 'My mum had a cry on the phone and then I had a cry on the phone,' he says.

They take him over to the playground across the road, built where the council had intended to build a car park before these residents intervened, and explain their plans for a community centre and sports court. Nina says that they'll have to raise over £100,000. 'We'll do it,' she declares.

'You will,' nods Rob. 'I think you're great ... and I'll sort that out for you.' This isn't said in a flashy way, or a demonstrative way, and I wonder how long before he said it he realised that he was going to say it. Certainly it takes a few moments before what these words seem to mean sink in.

'Seriously?' she says, in the kind of voice that is nervous to offend by misunderstanding, nervous to hope, but also spunkily scared to be silent when you could miss the world by not speaking up.

'Seriously,' he says. And she starts crying, and soon she is not the only one.

'I'm going to have to have a cigarette,' she eventually says.

'Me too,' he says, and they wander away together arm in arm to smoke and talk. When they return, she cries a little more and he says, 'Don't go too far, or I'll start and I won't stop all day.'

They go inside and she shows him the floor plans; he asks what happens in each of the rooms and she talks about yoga and martial arts, all practicalities and hope. Word is getting round and a crowd is forming. The reaction here is different from that in celebrity-spotted capital cities. There, people act awestruck, but they *expect*. Here, they simply seem astonished. Two teenage girls race over then just stand close to him, staring. 'It's nice meeting you,' Rob tells them. They look for words but they find none whatsoever, just carry on gawping. He raises his thumb. 'Wicked,' he says, grinning.

One of the older women sidles up to him and says, 'Can I ask you a personal question?'

'Yeah,' he says, and waits.

'How old are you?' she asks.

'Twenty-eight,' he says. 'That's not very personal! You can go deeper than that.'

He meets a six-month-old baby called Robbie. One of the teenagers' phones rings. Its ringtone is Nelly's 'Dilemma'. A middle-aged woman, who has risked being fired by shutting the local café and running down here, asks: 'Can I just have one hug? I know I smell of bacon and eggs.'

'I wish I smelled of bacon and eggs,' says Rob, hugging.

He says goodbye and there are more tears.

'I felt the love the second I came in,' he says. From the van window he shouts, 'Go get 'em, ladies,' and we drive away. 'They're ace, aren't they?' he says. 'Feisty little ladies ... I'll tell you what, it's much better to do something for those people there than buying a player for Port Vale.'

* * *

The next destination is a community centre, the Sutton Trust, on the Abbey Hulton council estate. 'The biggest council estate in Europe,' says Rob. 'And it's rough as.' (His father, who is staying with Rob in London, told a joke about Abbey Hulton just before we left this morning. 'In Abbey Hulton there was a pub quiz,' he said. 'The first question was, "Who are you looking at?" and the second was, "Who's the store detective in Marks & Spencer?"')

'Did you know you gave each house a fire alarm?' Jan asks her son.

'Did I?' he says.

'It was one pound something per house,' she says. 'It worked out at about ten thousand. They were having like a fire every month and the council wouldn't do it.'

At the Sutton Trust he is shown the computer centre upstairs filled with computer equipment Give It Sum has paid for. A newspaper cutting says: *Rock Megastar Robbie helps cyber centre*. He chats to everyone, and asks if things are getting better round here.

'The Abbey sorts itself out,' answers one woman proudly.

'Will you sign something for my daughter?' asks another.

'Yeah,' he says. 'It's a fair swap.'

He goes back upstairs to film an acceptance speech for a forthcoming local awards ceremony in which he will be given the award for 'the person who has raised the profile of Stoke most during the year'. I never see him prepare anything like this. I never see him even show any sign that he has thought about it until he faces the camera lens.

'Hello everybody,' he says. 'I'm Robbie Williams and I would like to thank you very, very much for my award this evening ... I'm sat at the Sutton Trust Community Group in Abbey Hulton and I haven't been to Stoke for a while because I've been out of the country doing things. When I was growing up it was instilled in me that Stoke-on-Trent people are the best – the most kind-hearted, the most giving, the most loving, the most capable of getting through hard times. And, I've got tell you, I've travelled around the world, and you're right – we are. We really are. And I've only noticed it because I've spent a lot of time out of Stoke-on-Trent, and you come back in – and I've travelled around a few places today and said hello to a few people – and I get nothing back but love and warmth and a sense of humour which Stoke-on-Trent has given me ... I'm very proud to be from Burslem, I'm very proud to be from Tunstall. I'll never forget my roots as long as I live, because it's shaped a great deal of who I am, and what I am. I'm very proud that I can raise awareness for my city, and I will carry on doing it, and I want to be more proactive and I want to be more active in and around Stoke-on-Trent, the place that I love, the place that I have come from, and the place that I will eventually return ... I really, really thank you. And I love where I'm from. Thanks a lot.'

He gets up and walks out of shot.

* * *

He is asked if he knows someone called Margaret.

'Rachel's mum,' the person prompts.

'Oh,' says Rob. 'Rachel.' He nods. A moment later he turns round to me and says, 'She was my first love.'

'So is Rachel courting then, Mum?' he asks his mother once we're in the car.

'She's still with that young man,' says Jan.

* * *

Of the girls he knew before he left Stoke, Rachel Gilson was the one he thinks most sweetly of. 'She was first, you know: "I'd ride six miles on my mountain bike to come and see you." Which I did,' he says. She taught him how to play two chords on the guitar – C major and A major – and how to play the beginning of Prince's 'The Cross', a song he'd never heard. They'd play tennis and hang out at her house. 'She had a short black haircut pretty much like mine now, but a bit longer,' he says. Though he had lost his virginity the previous year, they never had sex. One of his songs, 'Win Some, Lose Some', is largely about her. He joined Take That, and she started modelling in Manchester and somehow they drifted apart. Sometimes he still wonders.

'I'm still very fond of Rachel. I think there's still like a, we can possibly still get it on, kind of thing,' he says. 'She loves me,' he insists. He smiles. 'She's just the sweetest, unassuming, nice-natured, good-hearted, prettiest thing in Stoke-on-Trent.'

With a boyfriend, I remind him.

'Yeah,' he says, mock dismissively. 'She doesn't love him as much as me.'

* * *

We pass the turn to Fenton College, where he is registered as a student but never turned up. Becoming a pop star got in the way. 'I'll get a right bollocking if I turn up now.' Every few yards, there's a memory. He shouts out as we pass the pub where he sang 'Mack The Knife' on open mic night.

The final visit is to a youth project, the 7Cs, in Hanley Park, where he learns sewing, sees young DJs at work, watches a skipping demonstration and has a failed attempt at skipping himself. It's been a fine day, and successful in all aspects. (No media have got wind of it yet, and they don't.) It's been an inspiring day, too, amongst people trying to make lives better in real, sensible, unshowy ways. 'It makes me more centred as well,' he mutters.

He is home in London just in time to find Chris Sharrock and his father watching *Top Of The Pops*. Kylie Minogue is performing with Fischerspooner, and the contrast within a single day is perhaps too great to be comfortable.

'This,' he proclaims, 'is conceptual crap.'

8

He goes outside, into the BBC's circular inner courtyard, to smoke a cigarette. This evening he is to appear on *Later … With Jools Holland* at the BBC TV Centre studios, not to promote himself but to perform his vocal on the song 'My Culture' by 1 Giant Leap. The audience, queuing up for tonight's show, don't bother him. 'Notice how the record-buying public who are there for Coldplay and the Datsuns don't want my autograph,' he notes. Chris Martin wanders by, also unbothered, talking on the phone. When he spots Rob he simply says something to whoever he is speaking with then hands it to Rob. Rob wanders away with the phone; the last thing he says down the receiver when he returns it to Chris Martin is 'Thanks for not hating me'. It's obvious who it was. She has told him that the two of them like him, and afterwards he's not sure whether he should feel patronised by that.

Chris Martin goes inside, and a bloke comes up and greets Rob warmly. 'Like the shirt?' Rob asks. He is wearing his T Rex shirt with Marc Bolan's head on. The bloke is Marc Bolan's son, Rolan.

'My shagging boots,' he sighs, waiting in the dressing room. 'It was very

very difficult last night, but I was strong. There was a girl … but I knocked it on the head.'

No one asks what he means, and he offers no further explanation.

He performs on a stage with 1 Giant Leap, Baaba Maal, the Mahotella Queens and Maxi Jazz, and as he prepares to leave, Josie reminds him that he is still invited to join Kevin Spacey at the Sanderson Hotel tonight.

'I'm *literally* too busy,' he says, delighted. This message was already relayed to Spacey when Rob was first asked to attend. His delight is, of course, because life is slowly making real 'I Will Talk, Hollywood Will Listen', the one original song on his swing album. Its first verse:

I wouldn't be so alone
If they knew my name in every home
Kevin Spacey would call on the phone
But I'd be too busy
Come back to the old five and dime
Cameron Diaz give me a sign
I'd make you smile all the time
Your conversation would complement mine

I ask what he's doing instead tonight.

'My dad's at the house,' he concedes, 'and the football's on.'

* * *

Most of the tickets are already sold for Rob's tour next summer – 750,000 in the first few days after they went on sale last weekend – but plans for the actual tour itself are still in their infancy. There is a meeting round Rob's kitchen table for the principals to present their ideas to Rob. Lee Lodge, the creative director, does most of the talking.

It is a bravura performance, a torrent of ideas, images, phrases and attitudes: 'Darker, angrier side of the music that hasn't been registered recently … translate the energy of *Escapology* … bold images … opera … this connection between confrontation and disunity, both emotional and physical … go back to more of a punk mentality … this journey into maturity … people who think they're getting "Let Me Entertain You" are going to be confronted with a more aggressive, confrontational image … block colours … something a bit more subversive … that this isn't a tour, but something a bit more sinister … viral marketing … teaser ads … it's the majesty of the beast … when you look at an animal he can charm us by his grace, but he can kill you … anger and simplicity … this is not the Rob that you know … if Rob is a theme park, it's been fucked over, and this is what we build the show from.'

Rob is shown images from Terry Gilliam's *Twelve Monkeys*, works by the graffiti artist Banksy and a graphic for 'Angels' with words borrowed, with acknowledgement, from John Lydon: THIS IS NOT A LOVE SONG. 'Whenever we present an image, there's a twist but it's not what you think it is.

Just like your lyrics – you think it's a love song but then it isn't,' Lee explains.

Jason Mullings, one of the tour's art directors, shows him a panther image. 'The same idea of the untamed beast,' he says. 'A beautiful animal, but you don't know what it's going to do next.'

'You get the juxtaposition of the sweetness and the anger,' summarises David.

'At the same time,' says Lee, 'there's that little bit of fear. The same thing with a graceful anger.'

Jason holds up a graphic.

This

Is

Not

A

Con

Cert

Rob nods. 'You could separate "con" and "cert" a lot more,' he says.

'It's sold out,' says Jason, 'so we can send out a campaign: YOU ARE NOT GOING TO THIS SHOW. It can work both ways. Some people can think "I am". And THE CIRCUS COMES TO TOWN. I love the idea of buying a billboard and just keep changing it.'

'YOU ARE NOT A CELEBRITY – YOU ARE NOT COMING,' suggests Lee.

'THIS IS NOT A PHOTO OPPORTUNITY – DON'T TAKE MY PICTURE,' says Jason.

'We can distress it, decay it,' says Lee. 'People think they know what Rob is. And they have no idea what Rob is.'

'What do you think?' asks Josie. Rob has mostly just watched as all this is presented to him, without commenting.

He nods once more. 'I think it's amazing – go to town,' he says. 'It's exactly what I wanted. I didn't know what I wanted and this is what I want.' Pause. 'What I am more concerned about is what I say between songs. I think after the first three songs, which are all big rockers, "Let Me Entertain You", "Let Love Be Your Energy", "Monsoon" … ' – he says this as though anyone else here might have known that he had already thought this through, but it is news to everyone – ' … am I having one of those out into the crowd?'

Everyone waits to discover what 'one of those' is.

'A pulpit!' he declares. 'After the first three songs having a priest's garb and having a sermon about what's going to happen this evening: "Worshipping at the temple of light entertainment … "' Pause. 'I think we should phone Bono every night from the stage.' He stands up. 'I want the biggest karaoke thing ever assembled also,' he announces and wanders away from the table.

* * *

At the beginning of December he goes up to Stoke by helicopter again, and has an early Christmas dinner at his sister's house with both his mother and father, the first day in 25 years they have all sat down together like that.

Maybe he sometimes imagines this is how they could actually be. He once drafted a will – 'It was,' he explains, 'in my "distancing myself from you because you might stop me taking cocaine" phase' – which said that if anything happened to him, his parents had to spend a week together in the Arctic in a tent before they got the money.

'I think I've seen too many films,' he says. 'I thought it was sweet and funny. Didn't make my mum laugh, though.'

Over this year's early Christmas dinner, the gathered family listened to *Swing When You're Winning* in the background as they ate.

'It was fucking great,' Rob reports afterwards. 'I hadn't heard it.'

* * *

In the lounge at Northolt, waiting to board the jet for a ten-day promotional tour around Europe, Rob gleefully describes his latest plot to taunt Noel Gallagher. He has written a letter, which he plans to have delivered backstage with dancing shoes and pies just before Gallagher goes onstage for the first night of Oasis's British tour in Cardiff next week.

Dear Mr N Gallagher,

You said two nights at Knebworth is history. Well, I guess three is just greedy. Thought you might need these. Start with shuffle-ball, change and then progress. Do miss our chats.

Yours sincerely,

Rob

P.S. Finding it difficult to find adequate support for the show. What are you doing on the 1st and 2nd? Oh, and the 3rd.

'Because,' says Rob, 'he called me a fat dancer from Take That. Because it's funny. Because he absolutely hates me, and at every opportunity says how much he hates me. He said he'd rather be dead than Robbie Williams. I just want to let him know ... '

On the plane he stares out of the window, watching Holland arrive beneath us. 'Reclaimed land,' he exclaims. 'Always good to see. Man getting his own back on Mother Nature ... ' He turns to Josie. 'Not custard pies,' he clarifies. 'Meat and potato.'

He says he watched *The Entertainers* last night, the TV show that tracks the careers of a motley collection of faded stars: Leo Sayer, Bernie Clifton, Bernard Manning ...

'Every time I watch it I get so depressed,' he says.

Why?

'I don't know,' he says.

'You get depressed for them,' suggests Josie.

'They're all so lonely,' he says, 'and they're all still at it.' He found himself thinking dark thoughts about his own possible futures. 'I had to really have a talking to myself last night: none of these people did stadiums ... ' He stares into the space in front of him, his eyes unfocused. 'They're all so lonely,' he repeats.

* * *

He reads today's papers. In one, it says that the *Pop Rivals* band One True Voice are refusing to call themselves a boy band. They daftly insist that they are 'a vocal harmony group'.

'I'm a whole boy band in one,' Rob observes. 'There's cute, cheeky, the thinking one, the handsome one. When I'm on stage, I'm always multi-tasking it.'

I mention that for a whole boy band you always have to have The Other One – the one whose dolls don't sell.

He nods. 'That's me in America,' he says.

He cancelled America again last night. An hour and a half later – he hadn't called anyone, but inside his head the decision had been definite and final – he rebooked it. 'I went: who am I if I don't do it?' he says. 'You go because it's a place to go. I genuinely think I'd be a lot happier if I cracked it. A big thing is – it's ever so fucking small really – is what they'll say in the *NME*. "Robbie admits defeat in America". And I thought, nah ... '

* * *

The first stop is Amsterdam, where he is to play a concert to a couple of hundred fans. Amsterdam is one of the places that makes the sober him a little ill at ease. Once, with Take That, they all got stoned here and did a live radio interview: 'We couldn't stand up, so we all just laid down and passed the mic to each other.' Another time, he got freaked out because he thought the hotel was floating.

At the venue, he gets out a CD of the songs he recorded at the Townhouse Studios and puts on a song called 'Do Me Now'.

Prosecute Gandhi, persecute God, elevate Bono, eliminate Rod, I don't care ... World War 4, the Beatles touring, Chernobyl fallout, Global warming, I don't care ... oh, my head, I'm moving to the Med, those cats know how to boogie, this pill's done nothing to me ... I've got to catch a plane, you'd better do me now ... sings his voice from the hifi.

After a while he turns it off and starts writing something new on the guitar, murmuring words halfway between nonsense and meaning under his breath: '*It's time ... everyone knows ... everyone's so ... love you ... you get the feeling you're invisible ... radiation ... coming round ... listen to the radio ... all of the time ...*' 'Normally when I first write a song, the word "radio" is in it,' he says. 'And "pooh". "Pooh" rhymes with a lot of stuff.' Most of the songs written for *Escapology* originally included the word 'satellite' in their earliest lyrics, though the word doesn't appear once on the finished album.

He sings on, and as he does so, offers a windy off-key percussive accompaniment. Gina is appalled. 'How can you sing that beautiful song and fart so badly at the same time?' she asks.

David comes to chat. He mentions the performance on *Later* ... and they talk about Maxi Jazz.

'He's no spring chicken, is he?' says David.

'No,' Rob agrees. 'He's a black rapper.'

At the end of the evening, Rob decides to go for a walk into the Amsterdam night. 'We're going to look at some naked ladies, see if they're still there,' he announces. It's a bad idea. We walk along the canal outside the hotel, and he lasts less than five minutes. Everything about how this city makes him feel is not for him. He didn't even like it when he was young – he'd go to look at the prostitutes in the windows because that's what you did, and he'd just get upset for them. Tonight, everyone in the streets seems to be in the world of getting-off-their-heads. 'You know,' he says, turning back to the hotel, 'for many reasons I don't think it's good for me to walk around here.'

He goes to the hotel bar and orders a water, but he's not comfortable there either, so we go upstairs to watch the science documentary DVD he bought the other day at the BBC shop, *The Planets*, in his room.

'You know that Jupiter is bigger than all the other planets put together,' says Pompey.

'Really?' says Rob. 'Fuck. Imagine doing promotion on that.'

* * *

He wakes up in Amsterdam to the news that Mark Owen has won *Celebrity Big Brother*. 'It'll mean he'll get another stab at it,' Rob notes, 'which is great.' Rob will end today in Sweden, but first he must go to Italy. It has been planned as an in-and-out day trip because Italian visits aren't his favourites. He finds the fans just too mad, and in a disturbing way. Most of the people who stalk his doorstep in London are Italian. As we fly in he says, adapting a joke his father often uses, 'Italy, my second favourite place in the world. After everywhere else.'

He takes a copy of *New Woman* off the plane to cover his face as he walks past the paparazzi. Because it is in his hands, once he is in the van he starts flicking through it, and he chances upon an interview with Tess Daly, the co-presenter of *CD:UK*, with whom he had a nice chat when he was on the show the other week. In her *New Woman* interview she says, about Rob, 'He asked a friend for my number – he's a lovely bloke but he's not my type.' Rob is incensed. 'I didn't even really know who she was until a few weeks ago when Jonny started doing the show,' he fumes indignantly. 'I've been in America since she's been famous. I never asked for her number because I didn't know she existed.' So much of this stuff has been happening lately; it's such an easy way for people to get reflected publicity and try to elevate their importance, in some weird manner, by claiming that they have been propositioned by, but have knocked back, someone famous. '*I'm* going to start telling loads of people I've knocked people back,' he seethes. It's all absurd. 'J Lo, I've knocked back. Cameron Diaz, it got so bad I had to get a restraining order.' He sighs. 'Josie, why do people do that? Like Ms Dynamite.' He wonders whether it's often people's publicists and managers rather than the people themselves. 'I'm going to go round all these girls who say they've knocked me back when they've split up with their boyfriends,' he suggests, 'and go out with them. For three days.'

As we drive into Rome, this Tess Daly comment gnaws at him more and more, and eventually he decides to do something about it. He calls Jonny, who has been guest-hosting *CD:UK* with her, and explains the situation. Rob asks him to make enquiries. 'Of *course* I'm her fucking type,' he says with mock bravado. 'I'm everybody's fucking type.'

A few minutes late, Jonny calls back. Rob's body language visibly changes as he listens. 'Yeah ... ' he says. 'Yeah ... right ... oh ... yeah ... oh ... was that what she said? ... oh ... that girl ... '

His general point may stand, but it turns out that this is less of a good example than he had imagined. He has to admit that he does vaguely remember the scenario being described to him: 192 restaurant, some years ago; bumping into Mariella Frostrup, her sister and a third girl; asking for the girl's number.

Tess Daly.

* * *

'There used to be that joke going around,' he says on the plane back out. 'In 93, 94. "How does Robbie Williams chat up a girl?" "You'll do."'

I ask whether it was justified.

'Yeah,' he says.

So what was that about?

'I don't know. Cocaine, booze, sex was the staple diet.'

* * *

'Since I was 20 I've been chasing how I used to feel when I was 20,' he says. 'And I can say categorically that since 20 I have felt miserable every time I've drunk.' There was the briefest of good patches in there, or at least it seemed so at the time. 'It did the trick,' he remembers. 'It allowed me to hang out with Oasis when I felt like a fucking fat dancer from Take That. It allowed me to hang out with aristocracy, with the beautiful people in the south of France. Because without it – and I'm getting better – I'm socially inept.' He details the downward spiral in which depression and drugs chased each other's tails in his life. 'And then,' he smiles, 'you develop a hideous fucking twitch.' Or, rather, he did. Each time he took cocaine, it would bring on the same involuntary twitch, so that he didn't even have to tell the people around him what he'd done. But it didn't stop him doing it.

His drinking, meanwhile, was daft and extreme. He would sometimes drink a bottle of Sambuca in ten minutes, after which he would triumphantly declare, 'I'm pissed.' When he was still in Take That, he and the footballer Neil Ruddock – he knew quite a few footballers who could match him for drinking – would start the evening off at six o'clock with a bottle of peach schnapps each, to be swallowed in one. 'I drank 25 pints of Guinness once,' he says. 'That was at the height of it. I used to have a trick where I'd have five pints lined up and down them all in one. And then I spewed it all up over Liam Gallagher's curtains in New York. He wasn't too pleased.' He often tells these tales with a certain amount of laddish bravado, but it never takes the real emotion long to catch up. 'It was a really sad time,' he says. It wasn't as if he was ever the kind of person who was successful at drinking and drugging his problems away. There were years of trying, of stopping and starting. 'I don't know how you so easily forget, but at the start of the evening it might be great, but then very soon after there's a whole world of hell that you have to go through,' he says. 'How many horses were there in the Apocalypse? Were there four? There were about *fifty* when I came down. And it would last for longer than I'd been up. And I don't know how you forget so easily. The body apparently has no memory for pain.'

* * *

The evening ends in Sweden, where Rob is led into the hotel's grandest suite, of several rooms and many sculptures, and given the videos of today's English football he had asked for. He orders up some oysters and some lobster bisque – he doesn't even much like oysters, but it just seems right – and settles in with Chris Sharrock to watch Manchester United vs Liverpool. 'It's like fucking *Brewster's Millions*, isn't it?' he says.

Before bed, we chat a little about the past.

'I did look in the *FHM* Top 100 women list once,' he says, 'and there were 15 of them.'

Did that make you feel good or bad?

'At the time it actually made me feel bad. Now it's just funny. It was like Pokémon with me at one point. You've gotta catch 'em all.'

* * *

In the morning he records three songs for Swedish TV. When he is about to sing 'Come Undone', he thoughtfully checks something. 'Am I allowed to swear?' he asks. In English-speaking countries there are two lines – *so self-aware, so full of shit* and *so need your love, so fuck you all* – he usually has to censor on television.

'As long as it's not in Swedish,' says the director.

'Are you sure?' says Rob.

'Nothing about the devil,' adds the director.

'No,' Rob confirms, 'nothing about the devil.'

The director realises there is one further stipulation. 'And not about the mmmm-hmmmm,' he says.

'No,' confirms Rob. 'And especially no devils doing the mmm-hmmm.'

The director nods. This agreed, one primetime Swedish 'shit' and one 'fuck' later, Rob is done.

9

'Is this where you landed?' Rob asks Pompey.

'Yeah,' says Pompey. We are at Oslo airport. Pompey points over to the other side of some hangars. When he was in the marines and living in Norway, he jumped out of a plane 11,000 feet up. His parachute didn't open. He fell into a deep pile of snow on this airfield, and survived.

'You are a cat with nine lives,' says David, not entirely grasping how serious this was. 'Did it knock the wind out of you?'

'I should coco,' says Pompey, not explaining further.

'It broke his back,' says Rob. 'He was in hospital for 14 months. No shit, Pomp used to be my height.'

'I used to be over six foot,' Pompey nods. 'I went down to five foot ten before my last op.'

'How did you land?' asks David.

'Feet first,' he says.

'What is the best way?' asks Rob.

'Apparently if you stand up and cross your legs … ' begins Pompey. We all listen closely, as you do to words of wisdom and experience from a world you can barely imagine. ' … it makes it easier to unscrew you from the tarmac,' he says. He mentions that there is a Terminal Velocity club for those who have fallen and survived. 'I was conscious all the way through,' he says. 'I skied off and I went to the hangar and I collapsed. I was going to go up again.'

Our van drives off in the direction of the hangars.

'There might be a statue,' says Josie.

'To those that fell,' says Rob. 'And then got up.'

* * *

We have just heard about the Liam Gallagher incident: a drunken fight in a Munich hotel bar that has caused teeth to be lost and concerts to be cancelled. (And in whose wake Rob will eventually cancel Noel's pies, shoes and letter; it doesn't seem so funny now.)

'His natural instinct is to fight,' says Rob. 'To react to a reaction.'

He muses on the wonder of Oasis. 'Noel is a dismal lyricist,' he judges. 'But the emotion of brilliant songwriting can override it.' This sentence sits in the air, perhaps a little too seriously. 'Like "Don't Look Back In Anglia",' he says. 'It's about a whole TV region that can't address their past.'

He remembers the nights of Oasis excess he shared, in the brief moment he was a part of it. Sitting with Noel, 'when Noel was my mate', singing 'Ego A Go-Go' to him at T in the Park and being told 'You'd better put that in a song before I nick it,' munching a bag of Es. 'Then we got in the back of a removal van to go back to the hotel,' Rob says, 'and all the way there I sang the theme from *Tales Of The Unexpected* and danced around like the naked lady that looked a bit like Princess Diana. And we all laughed. But always always always around that time there was a real sense of not belonging. I slept with a girl that night and set the fire alarm off, and the whole hotel had to be evacuated, and I can remember going outside and The Prodigy being outside, Elastica, Noel, just everybody that was gigging.'

'Did you own up?' asks Josie.

'No. I just said to The Prodigy, "I was just in the middle of watching *Jobfinders*" because I'd just left Take That. And they laughed.'

How did you set it off?

'Lots of smoke.'

He remembers being in the toilet with Liam and Sean Ryder at the Brixton Academy. Taking drugs with Sean Ryder ... 'I thought I'd made it,' he says. Rob had taped the Happy Mondays concert at G-Mex off the TV and would watch it over and over. Once, in the Take That days, he had got Sean Ryder to sign his Toshini jacket at a train station.

'To Rob, get well soon, Sean,' he wrote.

More stories, more stories:

'Did I tell you about the time that I pulled that girl on the train on the way back down from the Oasis gig?' he asks. 'I went up with George Michael on this bus that he'd organised to go to an Oasis gig, and I'd been up for a couple of days and I must have stunk. I went up, watched the gig, went back to the hotel, got completely off my tits, didn't go to sleep, got on the train to go back to London. Oasis were all coming down to do The White Room or something, and I'd spoke to Liam in the morning and knew that he wasn't coming because he didn't fucking want to, so I pulled a journalist on the train, and I knew Liam's pseudonym at the time was Billy Shears, and I'd got a jacket on like this and did it up and I walked in with this journalist straight off the train and went "Billy Shears ... " "Mr Shears, please come this way." Went into his room, shagged her on his bed, drank the mini bar and left.' (When he found out about this, Liam passed on a rebuke via a third party: 'Tell that cheeky cunt he's been a right cheeky cunt.')

'Oh, I have been a naughty boy,' he sighs. 'I've done rock'n'roll.'

'Can't say you've missed out,' says Josie.

'Did it,' he says. 'I told you about the time I took George and Bono into the toilet?' Yes, he has. High on ecstasy and coke, he dragged them into a cubicle and sung 'Ego A Go-Go' and 'Life Thru A Lens' at them.

He laughs. 'Classic. Classic me.'

* * *

He stands on the balcony of his suite in the George V hotel, looking at the lights of Paris, eating an apple.

'What's weird,' he says, 'is I started to cry in the lift. I've been here before. I definitely think I've been French, I've definitely been Irish and definitely Egyptian.'

We play backgammon and watch MTV. Madonna's 'Die Another Day' comes on.

'I think I'd like to sleep with her,' he mutters.

Why?

'I don't know,' he laughs.

Have you ever met her?

'No. Well, I've been in her presence a couple of times. One time was in Italy when I'd been up all night and I was high as a fucking kite and it was half ten in the morning and I walked to the lift and she walked to the lift and I gestured for her to go in and I didn't follow. The other was in the gym and I caught her as she had just turned to her friend and said, "My God, it's Robbie Williams" ... ' He goes to the loo and when he returns he says, 'No, I take it back.' He doesn't really want to sleep with her. 'I was just more interested in causing a bit of controversy in the Ciccones. But I did go through a bit of a phase in 95, 96 where I slept with eighties' stars ... '

He doesn't elaborate.

A while later, he says, 'This book should be called *Bitchy About People, Apart From Eminem.*'

He starts shaking the dice for a long time with his eyes closed. 'I'm doing a very weird thing,' he says. 'I'll tell you at the end of the game.' He wins the game with a double four. 'I don't think it was working,' he nonetheless says. 'I was trying to drop my dice through my third eye.'

The Foo Fighters' 'All My Life' comes on MTV. Usually MTV just steers you from disappointment to disappointment but the good songs have stacked up one after another tonight. 'Let's go to bed when a bad one comes on,' he suggests. There are a few more easy winners and then Britney Spears' 'Boys', which only keeps us up because she fascinates us, less for what she has than what she hasn't – the way that, for all her Britney-ness, her personality doesn't come through at all. 'She looks like she hasn't really had enough sex yet,' says Rob. 'Do you know what I mean?'

A terrible mid-European rap-meets-techno record starts up.

'It'll be bedtime then,' he says.

* * *

At about 3.45am, maybe half an hour after I've gone to bed, Rob calls my room. Instead of falling asleep, he has written a bit of a song and he wants to record it on my tape recorder. He sits at the table, shirtless, plays and sings: '*What else can I say … about your daughter.*' He's excited. 'And I don't think it has to do much more than that. It's like a Lou Reed track … '

I leave him the tape recorder, just in case.

* * *

The next afternoon he rolls out of bed and straight into a Japanese interview in his hotel room. Sometimes he's at his best like this, too tired to say anything but what he really means. 'Robbie Williams is me, magnified by a hundred,' he clarifies. 'And I sort of invent a lot of stuff because I like to exaggerate to make me feel better about myself. In my songs it's me magnified. It's not me. But it comes from me. "The World's Most Handsome Man", for people who get the joke, people will laugh with me. For people who don't like me, they will hate that … and I like that. If you're angry, you don't get it. And it's understandable that people misunderstand me and misinterpret me because when I'm working I don't give them a real me. I do stuff to protect myself, to stop myself feeling boring. If Rob got up on stage, it would be a really boring show; if Robbie gets up on stage, people buy tickets and come back for the next one. So, yes, I'm misunderstood, and it's beautiful.'

Japanese interviews are very different from most others. For one thing, there is so much deference shown and the whole interaction is suffused with politeness. For another, few Japanese music journalists speak English well enough to conduct the interview directly, and so the whole process goes through a Japanese interpreter. Sometimes the interpreters translate the answers while the pop star sits there, and the interviewer and translator may debate and clarify the exact meaning in Japanese at some length while the subject waits for an invitation to rejoin the conversation. Sometimes, like today, only the questions are translated – presumably the journalist will be able to find out exactly what Rob said later, at their leisure.

'A lot of the album is about looking for love,' the translator translates. 'For you, what do you mean by love?'

'I think that I have quite a romantic version of what love is,' he says. 'I think that underneath all my songs about love what I'm really trying to say is: *will somebody come and fix me*. I think that in reality that's what the songs are about: if I find you, you'd fix me. But the romantic part of me thinks that love is the end of the game. You know, love is the victory. I don't know – I just want to find somebody I can go home to. I want to find somebody that is home –

wherever they are, or wherever we are together, we are home. Because I've been running for an awful long time, since I was 16. And I've always thought it was a sprint, but I want it to be more of a marathon. With somebody. You know, I'd rather walk it than keep on running. It takes too much out of you.'

He is asked why there no longer seem to be the kinds of entertainers around like those whose shoes he slipped into for *Swing When You're Winning*.

'Compared with Presley, Sinatra, Dean Martin, Freddie Mercury, people are really conscious about themselves these days, and they're scared to do anything that would make them look silly,' he says. 'I think that's why there are not many entertainers. Big showmen. And I am scared to make myself look silly, but I will do it in the name of light entertainment ... ' He laughs. 'There are no Elvises. There are no Frank Sinatras ... There's me that's stolen everybody's act. You know, I've tried to steal bits from everybody: Freddie Mercury, Tom Jones, Elvis Presley, Dean Martin, Sammy Davis Junior, Frank Sinatra, John Lydon, Liam Gallagher, David Bowie. Loads of people I watch and I go: I'll have that.' There is another aspect to this, too. 'There's this big saying that goes around, has been said for the last decade: "Keep it real",' he explains. 'Keep it real? No! *They* didn't. What they gave you was fantasy. What they gave you was romanticism. Was romantic. What they gave you was a place to escape. They didn't keep it real, you know. They kept it *unreal*. For the sake of entertaining and for the sake of their own lifestyles. And I love that. I plan to keep it unreal for as long as I can.'

* * *

In the car to a Paris TV studio, David tells Rob that Pat Leonard, Madonna's producer and collaborator in the 'Like A Prayer' era, would like to write with him. There has been a steady trickle of such offers and suggestions since his schism with Guy became public.

'No,' says Rob firmly. 'These are not the right names. I want to get something that's Primal Scream at their best, U2 at their best, Massive Attack at their best and The Prodigy at their breast, all suckling.' David nods. 'I want somebody who complements my ideas perfectly,' Rob continues. 'Who's got a bit more of an edge to them than Guy had. I mean, I don't want to do anything weird. I just want to do something beautiful. I want to write big, big pop songs and have them mean a great deal to people. Lots of people.'

At the studio he is more or less force-marched by the producer for a meeting with the French superstar Johnny Hallyday – 'I had no say in that, did I?' he says, baffled, after they have exchanged pleasantries – and is told by David that Charles Aznavour wants him to sing on his album of duets. Rob doesn't know what to think about that. He's flattered, but he doesn't really even know Charles Aznavour's songs and he worries he'd be doing it for the wrong reasons.

'If he sang "Thanks Heaven For Little Girls", I'll do that,' he says mischievously.

'That was Maurice Chevalier,' David points out.

* * *

As he waits in the dressing room, a chance mention of Jimmy Somerville releases a new cascade of reminiscence. The trigger is that once, in the early days of Take That, he was in the toilet of the Manchester gay club La Cage – the same club where the Take That auditions were held – and he heard a voice from one of the cubicles going, 'Can't get oot! Can't get oot!'. It was Jimmy Somerville, trapped.

'I let him out,' says Rob. 'That was my claim to fame for a while.'

And this leads him to thinking about the first two years of Take That when the gay clubs of Britain were their home. 'For me, when I was 16, stepping into that La Cage world, or New York New York next door, or the nights on Wednesdays at the Hacienda once every month – Storm I think they were called – it was fucking brilliant,' he remembers. 'Drinking in Stoke-on-Trent was often fraught with, "Am I going to get battered or not?" All of a sudden I was in a grown-up world where there was no threat of being battered and everybody was happy. It was a great time, really, other than being fraught with having to deal with the person I think is the spawn of Satan. That's Nigel Martin-Smith. Just to clear it up.'

'Did he ever try to make a pass at you?' asks David.

'No, never. Never,' says Rob. 'But he was definitely, definitely sure, because he told people, that I was gay. I was definitely gay.'

And why did he think you were?

'Probably because I found it so easy to get on with people in those clubs. Because I didn't walk in with any homophobia. It wasn't even a question. It was like the Japanese today – the Japanese came today and gave me a really nice interview, so I gave them one back from the heart. There was no question of any side to them. It was the same thing with gay clubs. There was no side. Nobody at all made a pass at me in those two years, like a "come on" come on. The big heterosexual thoughts about "Well, I'm not going down there, they're gonna try it on with me, try shag me" and all that business – which is really weird, especially when it comes from a really ugly bloke … nobody made a pass at me, everybody chatted to me and was nice … '

Did all your band mates slip as comfortably into that milieu?

'Yeah, I think they did. You'd have probably thought Gary out of anybody – you know, wouldn't eat foreign muck, wouldn't pay more than 20 quid for a shirt, didn't burp fart swear smoke drink or take drugs, you'd have thought he'd have had a problem with it in some way, but he didn't. Nobody did. We just really enjoyed it. I think you get lost in the escapism, because those clubs are escapism, aren't they?'

He says that the only money he can really remember them making in those days was £140 each after doing five clubs a night for three nights in Scotland. 'For the whole first two years I'd say that we made, and I'm not exaggerating, 400 quid,' he says. 'My mum had to pay the £8.50 train fare every day when we were rehearsing. And Nigel Martin-Smith actually, when we first did our first video of "Do What U Like", charged us a tenner to buy a copy of the video.'

He describes the Take That auditions to me. The first was in Nigel Martin-Smith's Manchester office. There were two other people there: a guy with loads of pimples and another wearing Dr Martens and short trousers who was also from Stoke. He looked a bit like Robert Smith from The Cure and couldn't dance. Rob and his mum had a brief chat with Nigel Martin-Smith, and he was called and asked to go to the final audition, the one at La Cage. The fiction maintained throughout Take That was that there were already the other four before Rob joined, but in fact, though the band was clearly being formed around Gary, all the others came on board at the same time as Rob did. He remembers when he arrived Mark was trying to get his mother to leave him to it, just as he was doing the same with his mother. Including Gary, there were only six of them there at the final audition – the five who became the band, and the Robert Smith clone. Rob remembers walking in and seeing this bloke in an alcove with a briefcase and spectacles and spiked hair. What he couldn't get past was this really uncool pair of Converse trainers the bloke was wearing. 'I've always been a trainer snob,' he says. 'So my first thoughts of Gary Barlow were: your trainers are shit, mate.'

He danced to a Jason Donovan song and clearly did just enough. In a way, he started as he would continue. 'I can just remember being shit-scared of Nigel,' he says, 'and thinking the whole thing was a bit embarrassing, actually.'

* * *

Every time he passes through the hotel lobby there is a girl with blonde hair waiting. For the most part, if she even draws a glimmer of acknowledgement from Rob, she seems to consider it a satisfactory encounter. Until next time.

There's a story behind her ever-presence. 'She's someone I slept with by mistake,' he says. 'Mistaking her for someone with a vestige of sanity.' It happened during the tour documented in *Nobody Someday*, and in that you can see him discussing their brief union afterwards. The one who, when he said to her in the morning 'I'm going now', after a night during which they had barely spoken, replied, 'Robbie, what about us?' She is consequently known by everyone in Rob's world as What About Us? She will turn up month after month, and she will email the office to announce when she is going round to Rob's house to see him, never deterred by his failure to keep any of these appointments. She always seems to know where he is staying, but once there she will just sit in reception all day, in the bar at night, seemingly just pleased that he is nearby. He will try ignoring her for months, and he also occasionally tries explaining, in a hope that she will give up this illusion, but whatever he does or doesn't do, she is there just the same. She seems to believe that they are actually going out together, and that if they don't spend the time together she would wish them to, it is because he is a little busy right now. She understands, and she will wait.

* * *

In the evening we go out for coffee and, strolling back down the Champs Elysées, we stop in the Virgin megastore. He buys CDs by Scott Walker, U2, Alison Moyet, Ronan Keating, Elton John, Jay Z and Kelly Osbourne. When he sees a listening post for *Escapology*, he puts on the big headphones and starts grooving to 'Something Beautiful'. (He looks like he's Craig David on the cover of his first album.) Robbie Williams is not yet a big deal in France and, perhaps thankfully, nobody notices.

Back at the hotel he skims through some of his purchases, playing a track here, a track there, then puts on Elton John's 'Tiny Dancer' to demonstrate how absurdly late the chorus arrives. '2.34!' he exclaims, when it finally gets here. He skips to 'Rocket Man'. 'This used to make me cry,' he says. 'Because of the lyrics.'

I miss the earth so much, I miss my wife, sings Elton John.

'Yeah,' he says. 'I do that.'

... it's lonely out in space ...

'Yeah,' he says, quietly. 'I was.'

... I'm not the man they think I am ...

'Yeah,' he says. He goes to the toilet; Elton keeps on singing.

Mars ain't the kind of place to raise the kids, sings Elton.

'That too,' he shouts from the toilet. 'My romantic notion of packing it all in and raising kids.' And Mars being this alien world in which he has found himself living his life.

He fetches his guitar and starts working on his new song. He can't work out what the lyric should be about until he focuses on the print behind the sofa in his suite. There is a young man on a horse, stopped to talk to an older man and a young woman. It is called *Love's Barrier*. Over the next few hours, he simply fills out what he sees as the story in front of him – the man on the horse asking a father for his daughter's hand before he goes to war, stating his case and staking his claim, offering every reassurance of his love he can find. Once he is finished, he plays it through twice, declares himself satisfied and goes to bed.

10

'Do you think God is angry?' Rob asks.

We are driving to another French TV show, for rehearsals.

'Why?' says David, a little taken aback.

'Do you think he gets angry?' says Rob.

A serious discussion begins, taking in war, famine, desertification and the essential nature of the human animal. After a while Rob nods, pleased. 'I'm going to start asking for more things to be discussed,' he announces. 'I like it.'

I ask him whether he thinks God is angry.

'Do *I* think God is angry?' he repeats, as though it is quite unreasonable to put someone on the spot with a question like that. He says he doesn't know, but he's been thinking about these things. That, and death.

'I plan to live forever,' he announces. 'So far, so good.'

When we get to the TV studio he asks Gina. 'Is God angry?' he says.

'What about?' she says. 'He's not angry with me. What have you been up to?'

* * *

He woke up this morning, listened to Dr Hook's *Greatest Hits* and played the guitar, and he now believes, after strumming it with the ridged plastic top of a French water bottle, that he may have stumbled upon an innovative, groundbreaking plectrum design. He calls Gary Nuttall, the quietly spoken guitarist who has been with him since the earliest days of his solo career, into the dressing room and shows him. Gary worries that these new bottle plectrums might be a bit heavy, and too cumbersome to be expressive. Rob is undeterred. 'I'm thinking of patenting them and making myself rich,' he explains.

Gary looks mystified. 'But you're already rich,' he points out.

Rob freezes for a second, nods and laughs. 'Perhaps I won't bother then,' he allows.

On the way back to the hotel, in line with Rob's new policy, we discuss the British firemen's strike, a conversation that yields one surprising fact. 'Even I went to the "Maggie! Maggie! Maggie! Out! Out! Out!" marches in London when I was little,' says Rob. 'With my auntie Jo, my uncle Don and my auntie Clare.'

In his room he plays CDs while the TV flickers in the background. CNN. 'That's sometimes why promotion gets a bit depressing,' he says. 'Because all you get on TV in English is the news, and the news is usually depressing.' He watches a news report about the solar eclipse in South Africa, and asks what the word 'landfall' means, then turns to Pompey and says, 'Did you know that?'

'Yeah,' says Pompey.

Rob scowls. 'You know that because you were in the marines,' he reasons. 'I was in Take That.'

Sometimes he seriously worries about this stuff.

'Arrested development,' he says to me. 'If you spend a lot of time just coping, you spend a lot of time not learning. Do you know what I'm saying? What's become more evident just recently is the lack of stuff that I've learned while I've been trying to cope.'

* * *

If there is a period of his life Rob romanticises above all others, it is his last years at school, just before Take That began and a vortex sucked him up. When everything was a laugh, and nobody treated him weirdly, and he was one of a bunch of mates. 'It was the last time I was genuinely happy,' he tells me tonight. 'During my depression, to think about my school made me even more depressed. It used to slaughter me, because I had loads of friends, and loads of fun, and genuine bellyache laughing. It was painful to think of it because I wanted to revisit it *so* much, and just go back school.'

Recently he has been looking on Friends Reunited and getting in touch with a few people. His two closest mates were Linno and Lee Hancock. 'Linno was very funny,' he says. 'He was a loner and I always wanted him to be my best mate. We'd drink Thunderbird and Blue Nun, and we'd all go for curries, which we thought was frightfully grown up, at El Sheeks. He lived on top of the bank, and I'd always have to go up to his house on my BMX, and we'd just hang out.' Rob emailed him recently, but both of their computers were acting up, and Linno wanted him to phone. He really wanted Linno to type something instead. 'I'd like to have heard him through a letter, instead of him speaking to Robbie Williams,' he explains. 'I wrote loads about what I remember about him and I wanted him to write loads about what he remembered about me back.'

Lee Hancock and Rob used to sell double-glazing together, and he was the person Rob was with the day he got into Take That. It's the story he's always told, but it's true. They'd both got their exam results, which were awful. ('Nothing higher than a D,' he says. 'A D in English, I think.') 'And we realised that we were going to get the biggest bollocking we'd ever had – and we'd had big bollockings.' So they did what any sensible 16-year-old does in that situation. Instead of going home, they went to the off-licence and bought six cans of bitter each. 'We sat on the bowling green in Tunstall Park,' he says, 'and got enough Dutch courage to go home.' When Rob walked in, his mother spoke first – he had been accepted into Take That after his audition four weeks earlier; he insists that he never even told her his results.

After leaving school, he tried to stay in contact with Lee Hancock. 'I do think our friendship in the end revolved around drinking,' he says. 'We had lots to say when we were drinking. And perhaps not a lot when we weren't.' He hadn't spoken to him for maybe a couple of years when he phoned Lee one day and said he was coming round. 'It was just really sad,' says Rob, 'because he went, "Well, I haven't got a suit on and I haven't tidied the house," and by that time I'd made the arrangement to go round. I was just: oh no ... you're about to meet Robbie Williams, aren't you?' Given that, maybe it made it even harder that he went round with Nicole Appleton. 'Conversation was stilted,' he remembers. 'It may have had a lot to do with the fact that I wasn't very well at the time. And we got drunk, and it didn't work. I just felt uncomfortable.'

He did recently strike up an email correspondence with another school friend, Matthew Cooper, who he used to play golf with. He remembered that one day when he was probably 15 they were in the school hallway, getting their blazers on to go home, and they had a bet about which one of them would become famous first. And Rob said, 'I bet you all the money I've got in my pocket.' It was about £1.70, and he can remember shitting himself, thinking, 'What if he gets there first?'

Not long back Rob sent him an email asking, 'Where's my £1.70?'

He's also corresponded with another guy, Clinton Cope, who was in the year above. These emails are on Pompey's computer, so he opens them up and reads them out loud. The first begins: *Dear Clinton, I was held against my wishes at a top London record company for the past 8 years. As you didn't pay the ransom I have been forced to escape and I now work alone as a soldier of fortune. Only you know my true identity and now you must die. Failing that, how are you, you old fucker?*

He asks a few questions about people from the old days, and drops in a few shared jokes, one about Clinton's deaf dog, so that he will know it really is from Rob.

Hello there, mr rock star. How the hell are you? begins the reply, which then warmly critiques his recent TV appearances. *What was Mr Diddy like?* he asks. In the next email, amidst chat about computer games and tattoos, Clinton tells Rob – who had enquired about his schoolboy crush, Lisa Parkes – that he has seen a sign in the oatcake shop for 'Lisa Parkes child-minding service'.

'It was actually kind of mad, sending those emails from a house in LA,' Rob reflects. 'It makes you think where you've come from, and now you're in a gated community in the hills in Los Angeles. It made me want to go "Guess what? Tom Jones lives next door!" During the writing of the email it kind of scared me a little bit. The realisation of exactly how far I've come.'

He knows, of course, that everything would have changed even if Take That hadn't happened.

'It's funny how, as soon as the school gates shut, your group just splinters off,' he says. 'You never think they will and inevitably it does. And to actually see in the space of a few short years instant cracks of maturity happening to your best friends that you laughed with so much, and now they've got babies and they can't get a job or they've stolen something from somewhere, he's in prison, he's got a drug problem. Or, he's Robbie Williams. It's so sad.'

* * *

He flicks through the new issue of *Heat*. He is mentioned in seven separate parts of the magazine: in a Mark Owen interview, in a letter about Rachel Hunter, in the album chart, in a piece about Clarin's moisturiser erroneously claiming that he uses it, in a full-page poster for an imaginary pop pantomime (he is cast as Cinders), in a review of 'Feel' ('full of cheek and poignancy'; five stars out of five), and in a quote on the inside back page, which has twisted its way here from the Berlin press conference: 'I'm a celebrity. And divorces get expensive. So most of the money will probably go to ex-wives.'

At midnight, David comes back into the room. Rob has now been sober for two years. He gives Rob a copy of Dr Seuss's *The Places You Will Go*, and Rob sits at the dining table and reads it aloud from beginning to end. A book in which things get better, then worse, and then better again, but not completely so. Parts of it that might work as metaphor for most readers speak more plainly to him.

'*… you'll be famous as famous can be, with the whole world watching you win on TV*,' he reads. '*Except when they don't, because sometimes they won't … I'm afraid that sometimes you'll play lonely games too, games you can't win because you'll play against you …*'

'Fucking … yeah,' he says when he has finished.

His eyes are moist. He says he needs to go to the bedroom to find some tracksuit bottoms.

* * *

He wakes up in his Paris hotel room bed saying the word 'Mogadishu' over and over under his breath, and he is still doing it as he plays the day's first game of backgammon. He's not sure why. He thinks he may have fallen asleep with the Fox News channel on. He remembers a story about how few Americans can even say where the different states of the USA are, let alone other countries. We both act appalled, but then I confess that I'd probably struggle to locate Wiltshire on a map.

'I know where Wiltshire is,' he says. 'Because I went to rehab there.'

* * *

In the van on the way to this evening's concert in Paris, he plays a trio of Scott Walker's interpretations of Jacques Brel songs – 'Jackie', 'Mathilde', 'Next' – on the CD player, and then his own 'One Fine Day'.

'*It'd break my heart to make things right*,' he slightly misquotes. (In 'Jackie',

Scott Walker sings '*and broke my heart to make things right*'.) 'I wish I'd written that,' he says.

Backstage, he keeps lifting his shirt and rubbing his stomach as he checks it in the mirror. In between, he does something different every minute: plays a Supergrass CD, eats some melon, air drums, (checks stomach again), plays a CD of his song 'Peace, Man', asks for a plectrum, gets an acoustic guitar, plays the song 'Mr James' he wrote the other night, gets Chris Sharrock to teach him The Who's 'I Can't Explain', (checks stomach again), heads towards the stage.

After the show he accepts congratulations backstage.

'Cool,' he says. 'Job done.'

The crowd can be heard from the dressing room.

'Robbie! Robbie! Robbie!' they chant.

'Me! Me! Me!' he shouts. 'I am him! This is me! I am him! That is me!'

They can't hear him, of course, and he doesn't return.

11

Once you're famous, any day, out of the blue, something like this can happen.

Back at the hotel, after the Paris concert, Rob is told about a strange message that has been left on one of his security people's phone. It is from someone he met out in London recently. 'She's saying she's being hounded for the story,' says Pompey.

'What story?' says Rob.

She says the press are trying to get the details of what happened between her and Rob, and that they're saying they'll print something anyway. Can he help?

He's bemused.

'Nothing happened,' he says. 'I got her telephone number. That's about it. Nothing happened at all. The only contact we had was having our picture taken, I had my arm around her, that's it.'

It's a bit weird, though. He asks Pompey to get Josie. Someone should call her back. There's something else, too. His face scrunches as though he's eaten something unpleasant. It's nearly as simple as he just said, but not quite. A few days after he'd met this girl, he did call her and ask her to come over late one evening. But while she was on the way he had a change of heart. He'd been telling himself that maybe they'd do no more than have a chat, but then he realised he was kidding himself; he recognised that what he would end up doing was not what he wanted to do. So he called her back and asked her not to come. And that was it. (This was the almost assignation he mentioned in the dressing room at *Later … With Jools Holland*.)

Josie arrives, and he explains. 'Somebody needs to speak to her, and to whoever's going to print it,' he says. 'That's not going to fucking happen. Because nothing happened.'

Here, in the room, Josie calls the girl. 'I was just calling to see if I could help you,' Josie says. 'Apparently you've got some problem with the press … how do they have your number? … and why would they be calling you? … what story? … how bizarre … do you know how they came just to ring you? … right … who's your agent? … and how did they know about you? … '

'Tell her we're going to sue them,' whispers Rob.

' … no, absolutely, I really apologise if it's causing you … ' continues Josie. ' … if they're trying to print things that are untrue we'll sue them … call me if they call you again … '

This is where things really tumble into a dark pit of ugly weirdness. Because during this conversation, while not really explaining what has been going on in a way that makes too much sense, the girl casually adds a new detail: she says to Josie that another girl has left her a message telling her that Rob raped her.

Rob shakes his head at the unreality of it. 'That's worth a fortune to me,' he says, imagining if someone were to print such a story. He says this with no joy, just to state how sensationally libellous it is. 'I mean, I've got no worries, because I haven't raped anyone. There's no story … ' But it begins to sink in just how awful it would be to be falsely accused. 'I'd love to take a million off those cunts,' he says. But not like that. 'I could do without somebody printing that,' he considers, 'and me having to sue them.'

Throughout all this, *Jackass* plays silently on the TV.

They need to know more. Josie calls the girl again.

'I'm just going through these various stories with Rob's lawyer,' she says. ' … that story's very bizarre … did she leave a number? … what did they say *exactly* because that's quite a bizarre message to leave … how absurd … OK, thank you very much … '

The girl says that this other girl left a message making this claim, saying, 'My story's bigger than your story,' and that she thinks the other girl did it to wind her up. And she says that immediately after that call, a tabloid called back and asked if she was ready to sell her story now.

'The plot thickens,' says Rob.

Pompey tells Rob that the soup he had ordered has arrived.

'I can't eat that now, mate,' he says.

He says he wants to speak with Tim, who is in the hotel. Josie calls and asks him to come up here. 'He's had a couple of really bizarre phone calls.' She tells Rob that Tim's in bed and offers Rob the phone.

'I'm not speaking about it on the phone,' he says.

They wait for Tim to come up.

Just imagine what this feels like. Twenty minutes ago, you are relaxing in your hotel suite after a successful Paris concert and, in every direction your life spreads before you, the view looks fine. And then, something like this. When things you have done catch up with you, there is at least some harsh justice in that, and you can somehow steel yourself for the occasional surfacing of past transgressions. But there is no way to anticipate, or prepare, for the fallout from things you haven't done.

Rob takes a turn for the maudlin. 'The thing is, stuff like this is going to happen,' he sighs, as he waits for Tim. 'And then you've got to question: is it all worth it? Seriously. Is it all worth it?' He answers himself. 'No,' he says. 'Because I don't think stuff like this is worth it. What's the point in having your name muddied that you're a fucking rapist? In all seriousness. If that was about you? I've got half a foot out already – I'd fuck off.'

'That is never going to be printed,' Josie points out.

'Yeah,' he says, 'but wicked whispers … '

'You can't insinuate that shit,' she says.

'You can,' he says. 'I'm not really worried about it, but if they did, it'd force my hand. I'd fuck off. If it doesn't happen, I'll carry on. But I'm a fucking paranoid person anyway. I'm scared a lot of the time. I'll fuck off. I'll make the albums, but you won't see me in any videos or any photos … '

Tim arrives.

'Hi, Rob, what's happened?' he asks. He is in his slippers.

Rob tells him the story, and Tim reassures Rob that all of this can be dealt with. 'There's so many weird people about,' he says. 'It's madness.'

Josie talks to their press agent in London and explains the situation: 'We're sitting here debating whether she had these calls, whether she made it up. Obviously Rob can deal with all the rest but these allegations are absurd.'

Rob goes to speak to Tim alone in the bedroom.

'I just hate it,' says Josie, 'because there's nothing you can do to make him feel better.'

Tim goes back to bed; Jonny calls. 'Are you ready for something that'll absolutely do your head in?' Rob asks, and recounts the night's developments. 'No, I'm not nervous, I just feel weird … I just feel really weird … it's preposterous … I'm completely alright, but I don't know how I'm supposed to feel … all you can do is just accept that it's unfair and this is my lot now and this is what's going to happen … '

We play backgammon, without any of the usual competitive jousting. There's nothing more that can be done tonight.

* * *

He goes to bed, but he's not happy. The same notion keeps going round his head, frustrating him and disturbing his calm. It's the thought, which he can't banish from his mind, that this movie he's watching, *Behind Enemy Lines*, starring Owen Wilson and Gene Hackman, is really useless.

* * *

In daylight, it just seems like nonsense. The tabloid implicated has denied that it is working on a story, which suggests either that the girl has invented her hounding, that an impostor is at work, or that the paper is swiftly backing away from the story. One of the most infuriating things about moments like this is that they often never get resolved. They just fade away, until you begin to wonder whether they ever really happened.

Rob has already decided to forget about it. 'It's all bollocks,' he declares. 'I can get on with being happy again.' He picks up his bottle of antidepressants off the dining table and tries to use them as an unwieldy plectrum to play his guitar. 'I reckon they were trying to drum up a story,' he says.

'It might just be desperation to get any kind of contact,' suggests Josie. 'Like that girl sitting downstairs for days. She'll sit there and then be happy when you shake her hand.'

He nods. 'She might be going away saying, "He wanted to see me but they wouldn't let him." It's like I get letters where they're *convinced* the song is about them.'

* * *

On the plane to Austria he reads in various newspapers that he is appearing in the play *One Night Only* ('Bollocks,' he points out), that he has 'made no secret of his desire to act' ('Bollocks'), that he has taken acting lessons at the Lee Strasberg Institute ('Bollocks') and that he was recently seen driving down the M1 with his father ('Bollocks'). He tosses them away. 'I'll have to tell you the Elton John kidnapping story,' he says.

'I've never seen anyone so pleased to see me,' says David.

'I got a pang of guilt not long ago,' says Rob. 'Elton tried to do a lot for me and I didn't thank him enough.' Pause. 'But what he did was really weird.'

* * *

To understand fully the Elton John kidnapping story, an earlier episode must first be described. Take That had split the year before, and Rob had just broken up with his girlfriend at the time, Jacqui Hamilton Smith. His first solo hit, 'Freedom', had been out, but he was yet to meet Guy, or Tim and David, or to find any stability or direction in his life. 'So I was in a right pickle anyway,' he remembers, 'and I'd just been through the worst year for drug intake that I ever had. 1995, 96. I woke up one afternoon after being up all nigh, and I knew I was fucked, you know. My bedroom was a pigsty and there was about four bowls of cornflakes dried up with cigarette butts in all of them, and that's how my head felt. And natural instinct kicked in to save myself and I opened my Filofax and went: right … '

He flicked through the pages and saw Elton John's number. They'd met when he was in Take That and Rob had been to stay a couple of times with Elton. (He went there, strange as it may now seem, with Gary Barlow.) 'Elton was very nice and a gracious host and very supportive of us and lovely,' Rob says. The visits also planted the idea in Rob's head that Elton might be a good man to call when you were in this kind of mess.

'I rang up and I just went, "I need help",' he says. 'And Elton was in Atlanta, and he said, "Go to my house." So I went to his house in Windsor. I'd sort of thought that I'd wanted to get clean, or stop drinking – little did I realise that I hadn't really had enough, and probably wouldn't have enough for another five years. God willing, anyway. And Elton made sure that I was alright at his house, and sent me a care package over – loads of Nike stuff in a box. I hadn't brought any clothes with, and I'd put weight on and I looked a dreadful mess and I felt awful.'

He spent two weeks there, 'drying out and pottering around, rattling around Elton's big house'. He had thought to bring his Playstation, so he messed around for hours on that, and he played tennis with the son of the people who ran the house for Elton. Elton called every day to see how he was. Elton also called Beechy Colclough, the therapist who has become semi-famous as a celebrity addiction specialist and media pundit. This, Rob would come to see as less of a gift. 'He came and made me his case for that two weeks,' says Rob. 'But he did an awful lot of weird things which I now know to be spiritually ... *wrong*.' One of the first things Beechy Colclough said to him was, 'You see this watch – Elton bought me that,' and for Rob that coloured everything.

But, that aside, he had reached out to Elton John when he was desperate, and Elton had been there for him. 'It was such a nice thing for him to do,' says Rob. 'Such an *amazing* thing for him to do. But I didn't feel good enough and I felt intimidated by it all. But the upshot of it is, Elton's really, really generous, really wanting me to be well, and I really, really thank him for it.'

Nonetheless, after two weeks, Rob left and stepped back on to the same merry-go-round. 'I must have decided that I was bored,' he says, 'and I decided that now I was well enough to go and batter myself over the head again, which I subsequently did.'

But that is only the beginning of this story.

* * *

'Anyway, so cut to, maybe eight months later, nine months later,' explains Rob. 'I've found Guy, we've written the album, I'm in the studio, I'm in a very, very bad way, you know. And I was supposed to hook up with Elton one afternoon to play him the tracks that we've been doing, and this was a week before I was going to rehab. I'd got a week to finish four vocals, I think it was. I know for a fact that one was "Lazy Days", I know one was "Angels", I can't remember the other two. I've already tried to sing "Lazy Days", I've already tried "Angels" and, frankly, it just wasn't good enough. You can see, there's video footage of me singing it and I'm drinking red wine out of the bottle as

I'm singing it – that's the reason why it wasn't good enough. So, I was supposed to go and play Elton these songs. I wake up in Notting Hill, and I'm on my way to the studio in Fulham Road, in a black cab, calling at maybe five pubs on the way, with the car waiting outside. Lager. Pints. In the end I pulled up at the pub opposite Chelsea's ground, and with the studio in eyeshot I just stayed in the pub and got pissed with some people that were working on the Chelsea Village – builders. We played pool and I got fucking hammered. And then I got to the studio, walked in and fell asleep under the mixing desk. Woke up, took the tape, after doing no work, and went to Elton's house. Five or six o'clock. Maybe later. It was in summer, it may have been seven or eight o'clock. So I walk through his door – not in Windsor, his pad in London – and I've got this tape in my hand and I'm pissed … ' – he acts out the wobbling and the slurring – ' … "I've got this to play you!" And he went, "Do you want a drink?" And I said, "I'll have a spritzer." Because spritzer at the time was the drink that I was drinking that wasn't alcohol. I'd drink spritzer because it's less fattening and there's no alcohol in it. Yeah, you figure it out. And Elton had a tear in his eye looking at me, and I saw his tear and I started to cry too. You know. And he went, "You've got to go to rehab right now." And I went, "I know." And I started to cry and he started to cry. And he said, "I'm going to organise it" and I went "OK", so he's off on the phone. As he's phoning I go in and go, "I've got to finish the album, I've *got* to finish the album." And he said, "You're going to die – you need to go now." So there was lots of to-ing and fro-ing with me going, "I can't go, nobody knows where I am, people'll be worried about me and I've got an album to finish." So after to-ing and fro-ing and crying every time that he said "You've got to go", I got in a car with David Furnish, Elton got in his car and we drove to Windsor. So I'm in this car, on my way to Windsor, one half of me's really happy because somebody's looking after me, the other half is really fucking petrified a) because I've got to finish an album, b) because I'm going to rehab anyway, and c) no one knows where I am. So we get to Elton's and I can remember really realising the situation that I was in as I was eating some food, realising that I was terribly pissed when I arrived at Elton's, it wasn't a good idea, and in the morning I'll wake up and I'll say: thank you very much for helping me – I've got a terrible hangover, but there's things that I need to do before I go to rehab. So I went to bed, and that's what I was thinking: in the morning I'll apologise profusely. Because I was already fucking full of guilt and embarrassment. So, I'm lying on the bed and I hear "Rob! Rob!" and I open one eye and I just see five sets of legs. I see riding boots, jodhpurs, and this is me hung over and I don't know where I am, and it's David Furnish and it's Elton and it's three men I don't know, and they're all looking at me. And I think: oh fuck, I've really done it now. I was told that this was Dr such-and-such, this is Mr such-and-such and this is Mr such-and-such. One was from the detox clinic – and I'm going to name them and fucking shame them as well – Churchill's detox clinic. So we all go downstairs and we're sat in Elton's main room on these two massive sofas facing each other – I'm on one sofa by myself and the rest are all sat opposite me, and Elton's perched on the side. And, bless him, to all intents and purposes there was a lot of sense in what he was doing and he thought he was doing me a favour. And in many ways he was. But I'm going: look, I can't go into detox today and I can't go to rehab – I've got vocals to finish. And I'm doing this and I'm going like that ... ' – he acts out how his arms are crossed, folded within each other, his fingers fiddling with the outside of his arms – ' ... and one of them went, "Well, you've got cocaine psychosis now – that's a symptom, what you're doing there." And reluctantly, because I could see the sense in going to rehab now, I went off to the detox clinic. It was a burgundy-coloured Citroen that we got in, and there was David and Elton at the door of his house, waving. There were two people in the back of the car sandwiching me in, the other was driving and the front seat was free. Presumably so that I wouldn't try to commit suicide or run off. So I'm looking out the back of this Citroen, waving to Elton, who's got one hand over his mouth, and David waving, God bless 'em. And off we went into London. I hadn't got a clue where we were going, I didn't know what a detox centre was. I didn't know particularly why I had to go there. And I didn't know what was happening to me. A thousand different I-don't-know-what's-happening-to-mes. So off we went into London, into the centre and then over the water. I found myself at this big private clinic opposite this war memorial with two cannons – that's all I can remember. I walked in and the receptionist looks up at me, and they were so snooty in there, you know, so very, very snooty. I can remember her looking at me like I was shit, and me having to sign my name, and off we went upstairs. And my room's got bars on the windows and outside the window is just a brick wall about four foot away from the window. I sit on my bed, and it's one of those beds with the plastic on so you don't piss yourself. And in reality I'd just got a massive hangover. That's what I was having. When I did eventually go to rehab I didn't detox, I didn't take any pills. I didn't get the DTs, they didn't have to wean me off anything, I'd just got a problem with my drinking. But here I'd just drank too much and I'd accumulated a massive hangover. So I sat down and this rather stern, big ... not a Hattie Jacques kind of character ... she comes in and I'm really treated like I'm a naughty, naughty boy. Really naughty. There's no love or care or "You're going to be cool, everything's cool, you're in the right place". There was none of that at all. They said, write down what you're addicted to, so I wrote it all down, everything that I'd ever taken – heroin, ecstasy, marijuana, cocaine, alcohol, amyl nitrate, speed, deh deh deh. There was only one other person on that ward and I went and chatted to him. And England were playing Poland that day and it was on Channel 5 and the hospital hadn't got Channel 5. Now there was no way I was going to stay after that – that was the straw that broke the camel's back. But in the meantime they'd given me a liquid cosh. So now I'm trying to get out of this detox centre … '

He turns to David, across the jet's aisle.

'Then what happened?' he asks.

'I did get a phone call – "Can you come and get me out?"' says David. 'And I wasn't sure how I was going to get him out.'

David went round, accompanied by Rob's therapist at the time, and she insisted that Rob was to be let out. So he was. Rob and David went and got some sushi and then he watched the football at David's house and fell asleep. 'And I felt so happy that I was with Dave, and I felt so happy that I could finish the album, not die, and go to rehab,' he remembers. And then, the following week, once he had finished recording the album and had one monumental final bender in the studio, he headed off to the rehab he wanted to be in, Clouds in Wiltshire.

'It was the first time I saw my mother as a seven-year-old,' he says. 'She knew that she was helpless and I knew that I was helpless.' Outside his house there were a few paparazzi and one film crew. 'I'm actually quite upset,' Rob told them. 'When Michael Barrymore went to rehab there was thousands of you outside his house.'

After a brief stop at Stonehenge, he checked into Clouds and started to get healthy. There were no TV or radio or tabloids there, but there were copies of the broadsheets, and one day he was astonished to pick one up and read, in an article about him, 'Robbie Williams, who lists his addictions as … ', and the list appeared just as he had written it going into the Churchill's centre.

'All's I can say is this, is that on the road to getting well and on the road to trying to sort my life out, there's an awful lot of fucking charlatans out there, and they're sick, and they are actually dealing with sick people that actually genuinely want to be well, and it boils my fucking blood,' summarises Rob. 'I'm sure that does happen to other people, and I'm sure they die.'

'They run away and die,' says David.

'So, from that,' he says, 'Elton sort of tried to do what he thought was best, and obviously came from a very loving place. But the whole thing for me is tarnished with the lack of professionalism, even though Elton came from a place of love.' They haven't really spoken since. About a year later Elton wanted him to do a duet on an album that already had the Backstreet Boys and Leann Rimes on it, and Rob declined. 'Anything near a boy band I didn't want to be associated with,' he says, 'because I was desperately trying to break away from it, so I said I didn't want to do it. And I think it really upset him.'

* * *

On arriving at the hotel in Vienna he goes to the loo – 'There's petals in the bog; that's *weird*,' he reports – then lies on his bed. 'Gwyneth Paltrow said something in an interview which I thought was pretty interesting,' he says.

'"People remain the same age as when they become famous." Which is pretty much what I was trying to say last night.'

So you're forever 16?

'Yeah. "Unless you've had to face adversity," she said. I think I'm about 18 right now.'

There is so much weirdness in the world. He mentions that the Duchess of York called the office the other day and asked if Rob could call her daughter Beatrice because she was ill. 'That's mad, isn't it?' he says. 'So I didn't call. I've got a pang of guilt for not doing it.'

An anti-smoking ad comes on. 'Be cool,' says Sophie Ellis Bextor. 'Don't smoke.'

'Fuck off,' says Rob.

A while later, he turns to Pompey.

'Has my food come yet?' he asks.

'Have you ordered any?' asks Pompey.

Rob looks at Josie.

'You didn't ask me to order it,' she points out.

He looks exasperated, both by the lack of food and the lack of anyone to blame. We all go down to the hotel restaurant instead, where he eats a steak then lets his body go floppy so that he slides on to the floor. 'I'm tired,' he says.

'You're like when you take a kid out to dinner,' says Josie.

He sits back up and falls asleep on David's shoulder.

* * *

When he wakes up he does an interview for German radio. He lies on the bed in the suite booked for his promotion, and the interviewer crouches on the floor holding his microphone. He talks about his career, his body ('I wish I was about 14 pounds lighter'), Oasis ('Noel hates me ... ') and the interviewer asks whether most pop stars don't think they're better than normal people. 'I don't know if that's necessarily true,' he rebuffs. 'I think that's propaganda started by the media. And I think that people like to believe that pop stars, rock stars, actors, models, musicians think they're better than people or think that they're nasty. It makes people feel better about themselves, thinking that there's something wrong with that guy. And it's kind of sad.'

The interviewer asks whether Rob does things to keep himself grounded and he replies: 'No – I don't believe that I am grounded. I'm from a council estate in Stoke-on-Trent, I'm from a working-class background, and in the space of a few short years I found myself travelling on private jets, staying in really nice hotels, meeting royalty and the government, and it's really weird. It's got to have an effect on you. And public opinion on you has got to have an effect on you in some way, until you sort it out and you realise that it doesn't mean anything. But I don't believe that I've got my feet on the ground. I've got my head in the clouds.'

His final question is whether Rob regrets anything, and Rob gives the answer, throwaway, as he is rising up from the bed.

'No, no, no, I don't regret anything really ... apart from a few people I slept with. Some right dogs ... Listen, man, I've got to get off.'

This interview will appear the following week over two pages in *The Sun*. ROBBIE UNCOVERED blares the headline. It is cynically passed off as an encounter – 'an exclusive interview' – between Dominic Mohan and Rob. Apparently he 'chatted before flying out to Los Angeles for Christmas with pal Jonathan Wilkes'. An accompanying photo shows Rob and Jonny at the airport, smiling at the camera, to further reinforce the dishonest impression of how and when the interview took place. Rob's words are reproduced with reasonable accuracy (which may either be a reflection of *The Sun*'s honour or their knowledge that there exists an independent record of what he said on a radio broadcast), but Vienna, and the words' context, are never mentioned. There are three separate, untruthful 'he told me' attributions in the piece, clearly presenting it as a conversation willingly undertaken by Rob with Dominic Mohan, though of course the last time Rob has seen him was when Dominic Mohan exclusively didn't interview him in Barcelona.

12

Backstage at *Wetten Dass ... ?*, the German TV institution that is, explains Rob, 'like *You Bet* mixed with *Parkinson*', he DJs to himself for hours from his computer's iTunes: a song by Gary Nuttall, Paul McCartney's 'Maybe I'm Amazed', Johnny Cash's 'A Boy Named Sue', The Smiths' 'Heaven Knows I'm Miserable Now', a jaunty folk-pop song by The Lilac Time, 'All Over Again' – 'Great lyric,' he says, and starts singing along: '*no one came so no one noticed, I shared a beer with the support band roadies ... tomorrow I'll be dropped by BMG ... girlfriend telephoned she said "don't come home," I know your muse is on some motel mattress, misery will always be your mistress ...* ' – Prince's 'Gett Off', REM's 'Nightswimming', then some of his: 'Phoenix From The Flames', 'Heaven From Here', 'It's Only Us', 'Karma Killer'. 'I've done some weird songs, haven't I?' he reflects. 'They've never been your run-of-the-mill archetypal straightforward pop song. Nobody can accuse me of that ... ' More songs follow: Badly Drawn Boy's 'Pissing In The Wind', Elvis's 'In The Ghetto', Joy Division's 'Love Will Tear Us Apart', Madonna's 'Don't Tell Me', The Divine Comedy's 'Something For The Weekend' and 'Frog Princess', two of his unreleased songs, 'Blasphemy' and 'Chemical Devotion', Crowded House's 'It's Only Natural', his 'Peace, Man' and 'Summertime', Dr Dre's 'California Love',

Air's 'Kelly Watch The Stars', The Beach Boys 'God Only Knows', The Ben Folds Five's 'Narcolepsy' and 'Army'. Then he starts on his b-sides.

'Have you heard "John's Gay"?' he asks, and sings along. '*Martin grew out of his A-team vest, and nicked the paddles off my BMX, and he says that he's had sex with a girl for effect, I lost my virginity, the year above us had discovered E, and I said it weren't for me, £12.50 … and we've written on the wall: John's gay. He's gay … what'll we grow up to be? … will you still be friends with me? … 14 … 15 … 16 … I know too much now to feel young.*'

It's as he said to the interviewer last night. His songs have always been personal. If the press really want to know about him, they could profitably spend fewer hours skulking in hedgerows and more listening to his b-sides. Every word here, for instance, is true. (The school mate wasn't called John, though. And maybe he wasn't even gay, because Rob has noticed from Friends Reunited that he is now married.) 'It's trying to capture what we were talking about the other night,' he says. 'The sadness of how lovely it was to be there, and how magical it all was, and how being grown up's kind of a responsibility and very real.'

We play backgammon and he finds some other songs too, unreleased ones I've never heard. There is a beautiful, stately ballad, "Snowblind", he wrote last year on tour in Australasia. '*While the world was looking at you,*' he sings, '*you came and wrapped yourself around me.*' He plays another, called 'If She Exists'. '*I know it will come in your own sweet time Lord and I don't like to ask but I'm lonely now,*' he sings. '*I don't want to make demands, but time and tide is in your hands, I never meant to ask for this, but God, send her now, if she exists.*'

'That's why Guy's brilliant,' he says when it finishes. 'And he's a fucking stupid cunt.' Rob throws the dice and moves his counters. 'And I miss him,' he says. He puts on a vitriolic, unreleased song called 'Big Beef' which he wrote on his own. '*I couldn't give a flying toss about the relatives you lost, I think that it's better that your bloodline stops from here on in …*' he skewers, jaunty and hateful. '*You got under my radar … you became my new best friend for a while. I should have guessed you were a psychopath …*'

'Somebody in LA who let me down,' he says.

He plays more b-sides: 'Come Take Me Over' ('probably the first song I wrote the music to, and then Guy did the end bit and it's not very good'), 'Happy Song' ('a very stoned song'), 'Talk To Me' ('fucking off my tits when I wrote this'); then another unreleased one, 'My Favourite American'. 'I've got to use that line again,' he mutters. '*Use my empty head, it's advertising space …*'

He says to Josie that he doesn't have a copy of his first album, *Life Thru A Lens,* and asks her to get one from the record company. He's always running out of his own records. Once, at home, he wanted a copy of *Life Thru A Lens* and couldn't find one, so he smashed open one of his *Life Thru A Lens* gold discs to play that. When he put it on he discovered that they had gold-plated someone else's CD.

There is a trouser crisis just before he goes onstage – they are too long, and he is due to appear live on television in minutes. As he stands in the wings, just off camera, four people are kneeling at his feet, frantically pinning up his trousers legs.

'... Robbie Williams! Mit "Feel"!'

He is ready just in time. He sings, then joins Michael Schumacher and the host on the sofa. He chats as required, and tells Michael Schumacher, 'I'm actually friends with Jenson Button ... and he's going to kick your arse ... ' Schumacher seems quite unsure how to take such disrespectful banter. When Rob loses a bet that a man cannot get undressed while balancing a tray of champagne glasses, he has to read out today's football scores. The crowd roars as he trips over each German name. When he reaches FC Shalke, who have drawn 1-1, he reads it as 'Shlake'.

'Shalke,' he is told.

He spots an easy joke. 'FC *Scheisse* ... ' he says. FC Shit. The audience erupts in mirth. Even the cameramen are laughing.

Backstage it is explained to him that there is only one unfortunate aspect to this joke. On July 13 and 14, he is playing two huge concerts in the German town of Gelsenkirchen, in the brand new home stadium of their local football team.

FC Shalke.

His tour manager Andy Franks has already been called by the promoter.

* * *

The next day his European promotional trip ends. He sinks into his plane seat, London-bound. 'Has Steven Spielberg rang yet?' he asks. (Steven Spielberg is the third famous person mentioned in 'I Will Talk, Hollywood Will Listen': '*Mr Spielberg, look just what you're missing*.') 'It'd be a shame to have all this charisma,' he smirks, 'and the Americans not know it, wouldn't it?'

He eats a plate of chicken and vegetables. He peers across the table at my pasta with curiosity, as though looking through a wormhole into another universe. 'I haven't eaten pasta for years,' he says.

We play backgammon, and he abruptly announces: 'The two things I learned in history was that the Renaissance started in Florence. And there was somebody called Isambard Kingdom Brunel and a weaving machine called the Spinning Jenny existed, and there was Luddites, and the three-field crop rotation was in use in the Industrial Revolution. That's it.'

What else did you learn at school?

'—— was a slag. But that's really nasty. She took my virginity. She told me that she was going to have sex with me when she arrived from Liverpool. She came from Liverpool to Stoke-on-Trent to go to my school, and made no bones about the fact that she was, in her words, going to fuck me.'

How old were you?

'Fifteen.'

What were your thoughts when she announced this plan of action?

'That I was going to let her.'

Had you been dating people and thinking about the loss of ...

'Virginity? The lack of commitment that I have sort of started early, and my going out with people would last maybe two weeks, maybe one date.'

What happened on the big night?

'Day. She said, "Right, this Friday I'm going to fuck you." She came round – my mum was at work – and I started kissing her. I nearly shit out actually. I was asking her to leave, and I just had visions of all my friends' faces laughing at me as she was walking out the door: "Ah, you shit out."'

What do you care to reminisce about the event?

'That it was kind of messy. Very, very quick. Smelly. She could probably say the same thing about me as well. General hygiene at that age is not ... you haven't washed your hair for ages because you know that it sticks in one place if you do a certain thing to it.'

What did you think afterwards?

'I thought I'd arrived.'

Did you see her again?

'No, it was definitely just a shag.'

Did you have your next one long afterwards?

'I think that would be a red coat,' he says. 'Zoe Callaghan always said that she was going to shag me, but she never. She was going to do it at Samantha Bannister's party. We used to kiss in the technical drawing department in the class because there used to be a bit where you could go and wash your brushes. We used to sneak in for a snog. A snog and a fumble.'

When were you first in love?

'I haven't been in love. Never.'

Ever thought you have been?

'No.'

Ever said you have been?

'Yeah. Yeah. Because I wanted to, desperately.'

Do you have any doubts you can feel like that?

'I used to, when I was going through my self-piteous decade. You know, it was just another one to go "oh woe is me" about. But no, not any more.'

So love will come when it chooses?

'Yeah. I'm pretty much of the opinion that God's got other plans for me for the time being. You know, I don't fear falling in love ... I fear, in the traditional sense of a relationship, being able to be faithful. You know, either I get through my twenties and a kinetic change happens, which it seems to do with people, or I have a very, very strong relationship with somebody ... It does scare me, because I do really want to be that bloke.'

He sits in silence for a moment.

'Perhaps I should call the next album something really serious.' Pause. 'It's a shit name though. *Something Really Serious.*' Then he says what he was going to suggest: *I'd Break My Heart To Make Things Right*.

* * *

Rob flies to Los Angeles for a Christmas break. On the way into the country he is quizzed by an immigration officer.

'What do you do?' he is asked.

'I'm a musician,' he replies.

These conversations can go in a number of different ways. Once he said this – 'I'm a musician' – and the immigration officer retorted, 'Well, where are your instruments?'

Today, the man surveys him, and his passport.

'You must be very good,' he observes. 'This is a very good visa. The last person who had this visa was Rod Stewart.'

* * *

By Christmas, I have cleared my diary to work on this book more or less full time. For some time now, I have almost always been there when he is working – whether performing, or having meetings, or doing interviews, or writing songs, or planning for the future – and I am there much of the rest of the time too. With some people that might be awkward, however friendly you are, but most people spend far more time behind closed doors, in their own company, than Rob does. As uncomfortable he is in many situations, he is a man who is comfortable with having those he is comfortable with around for a lot of the time.

We had a brief chat in his London house when we formally decided to do a book, just to make sure we vaguely assume the same parameters, but we never really discuss any of the deeper reasons for doing it, or the purpose behind it, and after that conversation the book is rarely mentioned between us. It is not that it is forgotten about in any way – I am often around from when he wakes to when he falls asleep, and for much of that time I am taking notes or placing a tape recorder on a nearby surface – it's just that there is nothing that needs to be said about it. Its only direct acknowledgment will come occasionally when he ushers me into a situation or a conversation I haven't been part of, implicitly because he thinks it would be useful or interesting. Even more occasionally he will deliberately ask me to step away, usually to honour the privacy of a third party needing to discuss something personal.

I don't think that the questions other people wonder about when they see or hear of what we are doing – to what extent am I a writer and to what extent am I a friend, and at any given moment do these roles not rub against or contradict each other? – bother or trouble either of us. What may seem eccentric, or conflicted, or confusing from the outside, seems perfectly natural day by day.

He never asks what I am writing, either because he knows, or he doesn't want to know, or isn't interested right now, or is content that he will know in due course. What is unsaid but understood is that it will be unvarnished and unembellished; the world as it happens, the words as they are said. That is not what most people are used to reading about others, especially about the famous, and I hope readers take that into account. For each occasional intemperate outburst or careless opinion or rough and cruel turn of phrase or misfired joke that I choose to note or record, imagine for a moment how your own life might appear, documented like this, if someone were with you all the time, encounter after encounter, day after day, as you mingle and deal with people you love and people you tolerate and people you dislike and people you fear, at your highest and at your lowest, at your most timid and your mostly carelessly, recklessly outspoken, at your drowsiest and at your most caffeinated, at your most thoughtful and when you couldn't care less about anything at all.

Part two

1

Over Christmas *Escapology* sells 3 million copies, and Steven Spielberg sends round a script for a movie, but as 2003 approaches Rob spends most of his time upstairs in the master bedroom of his Los Angeles house, playing his Tiger Woods computer game on the giant screen that folds down from the ceiling in front of the patio doors and blocks out the world outside. He hates Christmas anyway, with its forced jollity and expectations all set to someone else's schedule, and this isn't a good one. Some of his closest friendships now seem less than he had hoped them to be, and he becomes depressed and fearful that he is on his own in Los Angeles. He worries that fame fucks everything, and that he has messed up his life by becoming famous. Sometimes it seems as though, once you are famous, everyone you get to know goes weird in the end. 'It can bring out all of people's bad traits,' he says. 'It's like the Ring.' Meanwhile, the American paparazzi are bothering him more than usual. 'If I liked the way I looked,' he explains, 'it'd be OK.'

On New Year's Eve he briefly attends the Osbournes' party, where he has too many espressos too quickly from the machine set up outside and bumps into Justin Timberlake, though he leaves before midnight to go home and watch a movie. (He knew the Osbournes before their current media fame. He and Ozzy had exchanged compliments at the Sunset Marquis Hotel and one day he received a misdialled phone call in his hotel room that began with Sharon asking, 'Are you naked?' 'Yes,' he allowed, because he was. 'I'm coming up,' she announced. 'Sharon,' he pointed out, 'it's Robbie Williams.' After that they had a lovely chat.)

He and Justin speak on the phone a few days later. Rob has suggested that they duet at the Brits and this has now been arranged and scheduled, though Rob's choice of song has not been agreed. 'He was really hung over,' says Rob. 'I don't think he'd heard of "Under Pressure". I think there's something else we can do.' They eventually settled on Sam & Dave's 'Hold On, I'm Coming', but a few days later Rob's plans change. He has been asked to play a show in America for Rock The Vote the same week as the Brits, and while it would not be impossible to do both, it is decided that it offers a good excuse to avoid the Brits.

His Comic Relief plans have also fallen through. They are told that Steve Coogan doesn't want to do anything as Alan Partridge after the mixed reception for the latest series of *I'm Alan Partridge*. Instead, Rob is informed, Ricky Gervais is working on an *Office* sketch to include him. Rob refuses to have any part of it. Though he likes *The Office*, he heard Ricky Gervais on the radio a while back talking about him in a way he has no plans to forgive.

Meanwhile, he has been planning the video for *Escapology*'s second single, 'Come Undone', with the Swedish director Jonas Ackerlund. Rob thought most of the video treatments they received were useless; Jonas's was best but it was basically just a party scene, which Rob considered had been done too many times before. The idea came to Rob while watching *Fear Factor*. Bugs. Snakes. Frogs. Ants, maybe. 'I'm making out with a girl and then a snake comes up her mini-skirt, and then it just gets more and more,' he says, 'and in the end the whole place is just overrun with vermin.'

Slowly, this idea evolves. 'We're going to have a very fucking sick video,' he grins, after one productive conversation with Jonas, 'and we're going to have a lot of fun.' The latest idea is that he will be seen having sex with a girl in the video, and that as they are having sex she will change into a man, and then back into a woman. 'Not that I'm gay in any way,' he smirks.

He has also established a wider Biblical allegory within which the video will be framed. 'I'm going to this party,' he describes, 'and as I'm going up the road, on all of the doors is red blood. Lamb's blood. And I am a bit perturbed, as you would be, and I go up to the door, and you can hear the party's going on, and I knock on, and no one's answering for a bit, and there's lamb's blood smeared on the door, so I start to wipe it off, and I get a bit on my shirt. I open the door and it's Sodom and Gomorrah. It's like the most debauched party you've ever been to, and things start happening. I'll go for a vol-au-vent and it'll turn into lice, and then I'll start making out with this girl and a big fuck-off snake will appear from out of her mini-skirt. That's basically it.'

* * *

Marvin Jarrett, a friend of a friend who edits the magazine *Nylon*, comes round. Rob explains to him his half-hearted desire to conquer America – 'I want to do it because one guy wouldn't let me into a club one time, and I really don't think that's a good enough reason' – and we go out to Starbucks. He rolls the random-drink dice and gets a hazelnut latte. A good result. 'I should roll those dice more often,' he decides.

He discusses dating in Los Angeles and his desire for a wife. 'I don't think she's an actress, Mrs Williams,' he says. 'Actresses, models, musicians are mental. Actresses are in the relay team carrying the Mcbonkers torch to the stadium of mad.' He sighs. 'I'll marry one, I know I will,' he says.

There is some talk of strip bars, but Rob is not keen. 'The titty monster gets on my shoulder,' he says. 'I need to take her home and fuck her. Then I do. And then I talk to her, and then I feel genuinely sorry for her predicament.'

This triggers a story. About five years ago he flew into Los Angeles, his first visit here since the Take That days. He was staying at Shutters-on-the-beach in Santa Monica, and he realised that for the first time in ages he was somewhere where nobody knew who he was. He decided that he should call a hooker. He thought of it as a rite of passage. He looked up Escort Services in the Yellow Pages.

'What would you like?'

'A woman, Shutters-on-the-beach, please.'

'Do you want to know what she looks like?' he was asked.

'Oh, OK.'

'She's a Marilyn Monroe figure.'

'OK.'

A blunder, certainly. 'Not knowing that, for "Marilyn Monroe figure", see "beached whale",' he explains. He was already having anticipatory regrets. 'I'm waiting, thinking: this is karmically wrong … isn't this what you thought was wrong? But also: fuck off – it's a right laugh … you won't have to speak to her … it's as old as the Bible, it's as old as time … fuck it, she's coming … '

She arrived, and she may not have been the most attractive woman he had ever met, but she seemed sweet. In those days he wasn't at his best himself; he was 20 pounds heavier on a strict diet of vodka and cigarettes. She asked what he was doing in town and he gave a false name, saying that he played for an English football team, Liverpool; that a move to Barcelona had just fallen through because of a knee problem and so he was over here for corrective surgery.

'She gets her clothes off, and I'm not aroused,' he remembers. 'Not at all. And we're lying and chatting, and the video for "Millennium" came on the television … ' He thought she had noticed and he turned it off. But nothing of any purpose was happening, so he paid her $300 and she left.

The smart thing would have been to leave it there, but he didn't want to be smart: he felt as though he was $300 down and still without his hooker experience. 'So I've got a bee in my bonnet,' he explains. The next night he picked up a magazine and chose a new girl, with a picture this time, and called the number listed. The girl in the picture arrived, accompanied by a female friend. 'She's new, she wants to see,' the first girl explained. Rob handed over the agreed $400 and the first girl lay on top of him and then said that the $400 was for her agency and that if he wanted her to be a good girl he needed to give her some more money, just for her. He didn't have any more. Meanwhile, he could hear the other girl in the toilet, and he was quite sure he heard, from within there, a ckkk-ckkkk-ckkkk sound – the noise he had heard in thousands of movies of a gun being primed. 'I'm looking at this girl and thinking, I'm going to die,' he says.

But nothing happened, either with the gun or with the girl. When he could come up with no more money, both girls left.

'And that's my career with hookers,' he says. 'I thought: God's trying to tell me something, and listened.'

* * *

There is an article in the American magazine *Details* claiming that EMI have gambled £80 million on him succeeding in America. It will set the tone for much of the coverage here. It is clearly inconceivable to many people here that an artist could be worth that kind of money based on their earnings outside America.

In early January he does some interviews to begin the build-up for the American release of the album on April 1. One is for the cover of America's most prominent gay and lesbian magazine, *The Advocate*. It's less usual in America for entertainers to be playful when the subject of sexuality comes up, and often when they are it is interpreted, sometimes accurately, as a coy and discreet way of acknowledging something that they choose not to state explicitly. It would be understandable if a magazine like *The Advocate* took a dim view of someone fooling around with these ideas for fun and mischief, but instead they seem to rejoice in it. Though they quite accurately report his answer to their most blunt question 'So I'll just ask you directly: have you been "gotten"?' – Rob laughs and says, 'Not yet. It's certainly a possibility at some point in my life; I don't think too hard about it' – they revel in the repartee that surrounds it. It may just be that they enjoy the spectacle of a man who has no apparent qualms or anxieties about the way his sexuality is perceived, but I more get the sense that they still imagine that maybe he is gay.

ROBBIE WILLIAMS IS A BIG TEASE: 'Is He Or Isn't He?', it will say on the cover when the article is printed. That's a little disingenuous – he is a big tease, of course, but he is not this kind of tease. Just as onstage he will explain to the audience that he is doing some kind of manipulative entertainer's trick even as he woos them with it, he will tease but at the same time offer the answer that makes any riddle dissolve – that in his life so far, and as he anticipates the future, he is straight – as soon as he is asked. It's just that it doesn't stop him from moving from a discussion of Rupert Everett to declaring – not because he means it but to be funny – 'I quite fancy The Rock, actually. I'd love for him to throw me around a bit.'

There's more of that on the episode of MTV *Cribs* he films. *Cribs* is the MTV show where they offer a quick guide to the home decoration and lifestyle choices of the famous. Rob has been featured on it before, though the first time he fibbed and pretended that the country house he and the band were rehearsing in was his home. In fact it was rented off the actress Jane Seymour, who was furious to see Rob's keyboard player, Claire, simulating sex in her wedding dress (which had been offered by Seymour's housekeeper). This time Rob offers a guide to his real Los Angeles house, though he does so as one long self-deprecatory skit. When he leads the cameras into the TV room, there is a group of male friends watching *The Sound Of Music*. He shows MTV his huge dining table and insists that he ate Christmas dinner here alone because he has no friends. Outside, in the pool, his father is sitting in a rowing boat.

2

These days, in terms of hours spent on the job, Rob doesn't work as hard as most entertainers. He has found that there is only so much of what is expected of him he can comfortably bear to do, and when he does more than that he quickly starts feeling as though he wants to give everything up. Successful international albums usually require many months of intensive ongoing promotion; he does the very minimum. When he does work, he refuses the long days expected of most artists, packed with interviews and TV shows, one after the other, and as a rough rule of thumb, for every three or four weeks he works he will have a break of an equivalent length.

In mid-January he has to fly back to London. For most of this spring he is scheduled to promote *Escapology* at his own pace, building on its success around most of Europe, while also targeting the three principal territories that have so far resisted him: America, Japan and France. In the Los Angeles airport lounge, the mobile rings and Pompey chats enthusiastically to a man he has never spoken to before, who has been given the number by a car dealership they have both used. 'It's John Lydon here,' he introduces himself. 'Or Johnny Rotten. Have you heard of me?'

'I just thought that, from one Great Briton to another ... ' Lydon tells Rob. He is referring to the TV show of the 100 greatest Britons they were both featured on. They make a loose arrangement to get together when Rob returns.

As Rob is speaking to John Lydon, Andrew Lloyd Webber comes up to him, so he gets off the phone. Rob tells Andrew Lloyd Webber that he is thinking of writing a musical, and Andrew Lloyd Webber tells Rob that he must break America because that is where most of the money is. They are discussing private jets when Trudi Styler walks in.

* * *

Soon enough, he is in Sweden, for an awards show. This is the Swedish NRJ awards. There are now enough awards shows that artists having a successful year can spend months travelling from one to another, and some do. Ironically, the shows supposedly arranged to reward you for what you do often now offer the best promotion for what you do: they get high ratings, provide an opportunity for artists to be or seem appreciative to their audience, and also offer an easy way to build up goodwill in the complicated relationships between the artists and the radio or TV channels who usually set up such awards.

Rob plays a little guitar in the dressing room. 'I haven't sung for a month,' he says. He tells Gina that he got up at two in the morning and ate four Dime bars.

'Where did you find four?' she asks, puzzled.

'I've got three rooms,' he points out.

He looks into the mirror and tries to prepare himself for performance. 'For those about to pop,' he says, 'I salute you.'

As he waits behind the stage – standing by as Mariah Carey is steered through the hubbub by a man who has one arm around her and uses the other to push everybody aside – Rob decides to accept his award for Best International Male as though he were Eminem. Without explanation, he thanks his 'little baby Hailie', asks the audience to watch out for his movie *8 Mile* 'and my new rapper on Shady records, 50 Cent, blowing up real soon'. He thoughtfully also remembers to send a shout out to Obie Trice.

On the plane to France, he looks through *Heat* magazine and sulks over the discovery that Will Young has been voted second best-looking male. 'I came third,' he says. I ask who won. 'David Beckham,' he says. 'That's almost a given.' He starts shouting, in an Alan Partridge voice, 'On a jet plane! Flying over France! Don't be fooled by the rocks that I rock. I'm still Robbie from the block.' More quietly, he says that one of the things that really annoyed him for a long time after he got clean was that he had never taken cocaine on a private jet.

In the Paris hotel, he calls a meeting with David and Josie. He thinks they haven't been taking seriously enough his reluctance to promote himself in America. 'Why don't we just have a really easy life and not do it?' he suggests. 'If I break America, the pros are … I've broken America. That's it. I don't need the money. I've achieved more than almost anybody on the planet, musically, with my career. It brings the whole UK thing into America, which you know has made me feel ill, and makes me feel ill, and the only reason I can do it is because I can leave and go to the States where I'm reasonably anonymous, apart from the paparazzi … I shit myself about it being massive and I shit myself about it being small. You say we're in a win-win situation – I think I'm in a lose-lose situation.'

'Also to think about,' suggests David, 'is that'll offer up different avenues to you. If we don't do it in some form, I think the Hollywood thing, if you ever wanted to do that, might not … '

'I'm not interested,' says Rob. 'And I'm *really* not interested … '

'We're not going to put you through hoops over it,' says David.

'I'm really childish when it comes down to record sales,' he concedes. 'It's like a big game. I just want to see a few more zeros at the end of it. I don't know … yeah … it does get under my skin a little bit, I must admit. But it's just like, if I break the States, there's nowhere to hide. Ever. Again.'

'Listen, I don't know the answer to that, mate,' says David. 'I really don't know the answer. Because I don't have to sit in your shoes. I don't. I can't ever … I've seen what goes on for you and it's not easy … '

'I'm just a bit scared about Rock The Vote, to be honest,' he says. He laughs. 'Oh, well, a very conclusive blank drawn … ' Much laughter. 'With me heading to the States again. Go to bed … '

* * *

'Good morning, maestro,' says David as he enters the master bedroom.

'What time is it?' asks Rob.

'Ten past two,' says David. 'We've got to go in about 25 minutes. Do you want your breakfast here?'

Rob is lying on his front, his face pushed into the pillow, one half-open eye visible. He appears to be considering all this information that a new day has brought with it.

'Go away,' he answers.

Eventually he drags himself from bed. When his breakfast arrives, he stares at it suspiciously and then pushes it away. He asks for sunglasses and begins drowsily issuing demands that he sings to the tune of 'The Twelve Days Of Christmas'.

'Are we ready?' David asks Josie. She does an inventory.

'Bags? Yes,' she says. 'Security? Yes. One medicated pop star? Yes.'

Today the British newspapers say that he will be singing at the Superbowl in America. More pure fiction. Meanwhile, the Comic Relief issue splutters on. On his way to today's TV studio, Rob is relayed a message saying that he has got it wrong – that Ricky Gervais is a massive fan and has written a song for the two of them.

'No,' says Rob firmly. 'He was on the radio and they said, "What do you think about Robbie Williams?" and he said, "I just think he should go away, really." I'm not that *bothered* but, if he thinks that, we're not going to work together.'

The Office depresses him anyway, even though he appreciates it. 'Because I think I'm David Brent,' he says.

In the end he will do what he often does for filmed snippets when he can't think of anything else to do: be naked.

* * *

By the evening he is in Cannes, flicking with boredom through the TV channels – lingering on the lesbian porn, featuring three girls and a large pink dildo, but only for a second – as Josie explains that Dior have sent over a suit, unsolicited, in the hope that he will wear it at the awards ceremony. He says that they should get a plastic baby so that he can dangle it out of the hotel window tomorrow, in tribute to Michael Jackson's latest idiocy.

Downstairs he finds the band eating in the bar. It is called the Bar De Celebrity.

'Is everybody going out tonight?' he asks.

'Yeah,' says Chris. 'To rehearse.'

'Is it live?' he asks, surprised, about tomorrow's French NRJ awards show, the reason he is here. For most awards show performances he sings a live vocal but the band mime to a pre-recorded backing track.

'Mimed,' says Franksy.

'A *mimed* rehearsal?' says Rob, shaking his head, as if simultaneously marvelling at the madnesses of the world he is in and realising how many of its nuisances and absurdities he manages to avoid or subcontract.

* * *

Atomic Kitten are performing at a nearby club and Rob decides to go. We arrive during a ludicrous dancing competition set to Craig David's 'What's Your Flava?'; Rob goes to speak with Atomic Kitten in their roped-off cabana within the club, where he mingles, then sits at a table littered with Jack Daniels and champagne bottles and tiny French pastries. A bloke sits next to him and introduces himself as Jason. He claims a kinship with Rob and asks for a little of Rob's time and ear in a way that Rob is unlikely to refuse.

After a while, realising that Rob has not recognised who he is, he says his full name: Jason Fraser. It is still not a name Rob recognises. As he says afterwards, 'I don't think about who the paparazzi are.' Jason Fraser is perhaps the most famous of the modern breed, specialising in shots of the very famous in few clothes on beaches, royals on ski slopes, and also the strange modern category of photographs taken with a celebrity's covert cooperation, staged to look as though they have been snatched; a sale disguised as a robbery. He breezily identifies himself tonight by explaining that he took the photographs of Rob and Geri Halliwell in the south of France. He also says that he goes out with one of the *Mirror*'s 3am girls. 'You don't like them very much, do you?' he says. Rob answers through gritted teeth that he understands they have a job to do.

The most amazing and telltale thing about the conversation is not Jason Fraser's nerve in initiating it, but his blasé assumption that it would be alright. It's another sign of how deeply he, and huge parts of the modern entertainment world, have internalised a set of values in which all parts of the business – and in particular the artists, the tabloids and the paparazzi – have more in common with each other than with anyone outside their world, and in which, despite occasional tensions, they recognise their common interest. It is a world of *we're all in this together* and a world of *it's all just a game, isn't it?* A world of gloss and desperation where fame and money are the only lubricants, and the only goals. In this new pop world, the tabloids and paparazzi are no longer an ancillary nuisance that comes with success, they are your co-workers in the celebrity corporation, and you are expected to recognise and acknowledge them as such. I suspect that such people don't even really believe that the hostility Rob feels towards them, and the hurt he feels at what they do, is genuine. Nor that he feels he has something to protect – both in terms of the value of what he does artistically, and as a person – that exists outside their way of thinking. And if they did, I think they would find it eccentric, unrealistic and old-fashioned.

So perhaps that is what Jason Fraser thinks when Rob halts their conversation tonight.

'To tell you the truth,' Rob says calmly to Fraser, 'sitting here with you actually makes my skin crawl. Makes me sick to my stomach.'

Rob rejoins his band where they are getting drunk, post-miming, in another part of the club.

'I think I handled it very well,' he reflects. 'I now want to go and kick his face through the window.' Much later, he will elaborate on his exact feelings: 'I actually wanted to glass him. Really, really wanted to make him blind. Then what I wanted to do was get razorblades and cut his feet open and stick Tabasco sauce in and make him take acid, and hire a helicopter, blindfold him, and make him think that he was a mile up but really he was just two foot off the ground, and push him out and watch him shit himself.' He nods. 'That's what I wanted to do … '

* * *

'Do you know how lucky you are?' asks Josie.

In Rob's bedroom, the next afternoon, she is trying to wake him.

'No,' he sleepily responds. 'How lucky?'

'To be in show business,' she says.

'Oh,' he sighs through his pillow. 'I thought you were going to tell me I could sleep more. What time is it?'

'Two,' she says. 'And you've got a press conference at 2.30.'

'You're joking,' he says. 'What is it for?'

'The world's media,' she explains.

'You're joking,' he repeats.

'And then a photo,' she adds.

'No,' he sighs, feebly defiant, and beneath the sheets reports the first fart of the day.

Josie picks up the clothes scattered at the foot of his bed.

'Remember how we wanted to break France?' she reminds him.

He doesn't respond. He explains that he took 'a cheeky half' of Ambien at 5.30 in the morning. And the other half at seven.

'And you had a cheeky couple of these?' asks Josie, indicating the jelly babies scattered on a table by the window.

* * *

He browses through the *Mirror*. There is a small story about him. *Poor Robbie Williams. The singer boarded his Nice-bound private jet yesterday only to be escorted off minutes later because of technical problems* ... And so on. It is as harmless and inoffensive as such stories get, and consequently any regular reader could have no reason to suspect that it was not true, but it is complete fiction.

He shuffles towards the door. 'It's going to make an interesting press conference,' he says. 'I'll still be asleep.' He begins talking, as though addressing the world's media: 'Sorry, I'm going to be keeping my sunglasses on ...'

Before the press conference he has a French TV interview. They ask the things they are expected to ask, and whatever words seem closest to his tongue spill out in response. After the first few questions, to which he has explained that *Escapology* was recorded on crack and speedballs and that the title has many meanings but that five of them he neither knows nor understands, he realises from the interviewer's slightly desperate demeanour that she is hoping for something more serious and substantial. She asks what he wanted to express when he made the album.

'I don't know,' he says. 'The inner workings of my mind. I wanted to get them out, and have people listen to them and relate. Or not. I don't know really what I wanted to express. Just sometimes I'm sad, sometimes I'm happy, sometimes I'm indifferent, and sometimes I get confused and don't understand stuff. Like everyone else. Which is good. Because if I had problems that no one understood, that wouldn't sell records at all. "I've got these Martians, they land in my house and they make me dance in a Hawaiian way." Can you imagine if that was one of my problems?'

She is clearly struggling. Her next question is an enquiry, in strangled English, why he has 'an 'airdo like a punk'.

He nods. 'I am Urdu like a punk,' he agrees.

Behind his dark glasses, his eyes are shut for much of the interview. He is asked about America and explains that his only reasons for wanting success there is to get into clubs. 'That, and Cameron Diaz doesn't know who I am.' Pause. 'But she does now,' he says. 'Ever since the restraining order.'

'Is that why you went to LA, to escape from your celebrity in Europe?' she persists.

He nods. 'That,' he says, 'and donuts.'

* * *

'It's 25 minutes, this,' Josie tells him in the lift on the way to the press conference. 'We'll bail you out though if we need to.'

'Oh,' says Rob, feigning a carefree attitude, 'give them half an hour.'

He sits on a high stool facing a wall of interrogators. He apologises for his sunglasses, explaining that he had a late night, and waits for questions. None come. 'Wicked,' he says. 'Aquarius … 29 years old … ' Still no questions. 'Or we could just stare at each other for 25 minutes,' he says. Nervous laughter. 'I'd win,' he mutters.

Eventually there are some questions about where he lives, and about whether he has settled down in America. ('I'm Robbie Williams,' he parries. 'I never settle down.') Then he is asked his thoughts on piracy.

'Piracy?' he repeats. 'I don't own a boat.' He shakes his head. 'I haven't got a clue what you mean.' The questioner makes clear that they mean piracy involving music. 'Oh, downloading stuff?' he says. 'I think it's great.' Everyone laughs. 'I really do,' he says. What will be lost in the fuss caused by this, and what he says next, is that from now on he is purely referring to people illegally downloading music from the internet – one particular kind of problem for the music industry – and not the other, more organised problem of the illegal counterfeiting and sale of CDs. 'There's nothing anybody can do about it,' he says. 'I actually signed a deal last year – I don't know if you read – and I went and saw all the heads of the record companies, and each one in turn brought up the thing about piracy and downloads and all that business, and just out of interest I said, well, what are you going to do about it, and there was a lot of hot air blown … ' – he slips into an American accent – ' … "We're going to sit down and there's going to be this referendum and everybody's going to get in this room and figure out what we're going to do about this thing and then we're going to have meetings and deh deh deh deh." And I was going, "You don't really know, do you?" The heads of the record companies don't know what to do about it. And I'm cool, man. I'm cool.' He smiles. 'If you want my music, download it. You know, I'm sure my record company would hate me saying that. And my management. And my accountant. But the record did alright before Christmas – everybody else, have it free. I don't know, man. I don't know what you want me to say. Nobody knows what to do about it. It's there. I'm not going to be all Metallica about it and say don't. I probably should do … thank you.'

He is then asked whether his image of being arrogant is something he fakes. (You could spend months trying to work out whether that's a compliment or an insult.)

'Yeah, I'm really boring, actually,' he replies, deadpan. 'Really, really boring. I just project "interesting", I hope.'

He goes outside for a photo call that turns into a mob scene, and then retreats to his hotel room. There, he longingly eyes the window and thinks of the crowds below.

'This is a perfect opportunity to do the baby over the balcony thing,' he says.

'Yeah, I know,' says Josie, firmly, 'but you must not.'

'Would it raise a furore?' he asks. He is itchy, and in the mood to do something unwise.

'It'd be awful,' she says.

'Horrible,' says Gina.

He reluctantly agrees to be overruled.

* * *

Josie explains that the French are pleading with him to relax his policy and walk down the red carpet at tonight's awards. Though this is one of the many rituals expected of pop stars that he generally opts out of, he agrees to do it just this once. He gets dressed as he watches the TV, peering closer when he sees a woman holding a glass of orange juice in an advert for a bank. 'I think I may have slept with her,' he says. His accountant arrives from England with his tax return to sign, and Josie relays the French record company boss's extreme excitement at the red carpet thumbs-up. 'He says, "This is brilliant news – we will sell half a million records now",' she reports.

Backstage, the red carpet successfully traversed, Rob sees Mariah Carey making her way down the crowded hallway, a camera crew in tow. He ducks into his dressing room; he has no desire to become a part of whatever that is. He spots Jason Fraser across the room and wonders what kind of trouble he would get into if he punched him. Instead he goes over to talk to him, briefly, because there is something he has always wanted to know. It has always annoyed him that when he and Geri were photographed in the south of France it was treated as some kind of deliberate set-up to get press attention. For him it was never anything of the sort. But he has wondered for a while, and even more so since the other night, so he now asks Fraser whether Geri was involved in arranging for them to be photographed. 'Indirectly,' says Fraser, an answer that Rob believes and that infuriates him.

'... un star authentique ...' he is introduced, as he is lowered on a platform to the stage. 'L'inimitable Robbie Williams!'

As he sings, he goes wandering into the audience. When he puts his arms round a girl, the stiff seated audience buzzes. He strolls up the aisle, away from the stage, sits on a man's lap and winks at the camera. By now the crowd – those he is not sitting on – are on their feet. It is an obvious triumph. 'Je m'appelle Robbie Williams,' he says, taking his bow. 'Merci beaucoup. Bonsoir.' Two hours later he is back in London.

* * *

The *Guardian*, 20 January 2003: *Controversial culture minister Kim Howells today switched his anger from rap to pop music when he accused the singer*

Robbie Williams of assisting international vice gangs who use music piracy to launder profits by describing the copyright fraud industry as 'great'.

Mr Howells' attack on the former Take That star followed reports that Williams had told journalists at a music trade fair in Cannes: 'I think [music piracy is] great, really I do. There is nothing anyone can do about it.'

Notice the damage done by those square brackets.

In the rest of his comments, Howells seems as confused as anyone. At one moment he is quite reasonably – whether rightly or not – criticising Rob for defending (or at least accepting) illegal downloading; characterising it as theft; and defending 'all those singers, songwriters, musicians, and music publishers who depend entirely for a living on receiving honest revenue from sales of their product'.

Fair enough. But Howells slides from this to music theft of a completely different kind, and claims, completely without justification, that they are connected: *He should also realise that many of these pirate operations are linked to organised crime on a worldwide basis. In saying that piracy is a 'great idea', Williams is doing the work for international gangs involved in drugs and prostitution who find music piracy an excellent way of laundering their profits.*

It is, of course, preposterous. (To be clear, no one has yet suggested any mechanism for crime gangs to earn or launder money through music downloading. The main barrier to them doing so is the same one that has made record companies reluctant to transfer music in this manner, and which has made the record industry feel so threatened by this technology – the difficulty of collecting payment from consumers, particularly those now used to downloading for free.)

Rob, by refusing to condemn what millions of music-lovers are doing in their bedrooms around the world, in the vacuum created by the music industry's sluggish response to new technology, has found himself abruptly castigated by a sloppy-thinking government minister as an apologist for international crime, drug and prostitution syndicates. And such is the nonsense to which he has become accustomed, he is barely surprised or bothered at this turn of events. When I tell him what he has been accused of doing, he barely takes it in.

'Wicked,' he says. 'I did all that yesterday? Just watching the telly?'

* * *

This is not the only news he makes in Cannes. A couple of days afterwards, the tale of his big backstage kerfuffle with Mariah Carey is exposed by the *Sun*:

*Mariah Carey has had a vicious bust-up with Robbie Williams at a music awards show. Furious Robbie hurled abuse at the diva, telling her to 'f*** off' during the backstage spat before bouncers pulled him back.*

The only strange aspect to this is that none of us can remember it happening.

3

In the Heathrow departure lounge, on his way to Singapore where he is scheduled to perform and receive at the MTV Asia Awards, he speaks to Justin Timberlake on the phone, apologising for pulling out of their Brits duet, and hands me this morning's post: a woman from Worcester who sweetly recounts her journey to becoming one year sober and expects an exchange of empathy; a Dutch fan who encloses cash for an autograph (the £5 note is paperclipped to the letter 'as an allowance for costs … if you don't need the money then buy some bones for your dogs'); a synopsis of a screenplay about Norman Wisdom. 'If the film was ever developed and made,' says the writer, 'it would be hard-hitting drama – sad/funny and edgy and real … '

This film proposal sparks uncomfortable feelings; he well knows that he has a tendency to seem a little Norman Wisdom at times, and it is not the proudest part of his entertainment repertoire. 'That's all I need, really, isn't it, for my confidence,' he says. 'I read it with dismay. It's that thing in the back of my mind that goes: *you're Norman Wisdom you're Norman Wisdom you're Norman Wisdom,* and I go: no I'm not!' He restates this. 'I actually go: yeah I am, that's crap. Not to say Norman Wisdom's crap, because he's not – I love Norman Wisdom, but to be Norman Wisdom in 2003 I don't think is something one would put on a list of achievements.'

* * *

'If Missy Elliot's got my villa … ' he worries, almost angry already at the possibility he has just invented. We are driving in from the airport in Singapore and he is anticipating his hotel room, a villa he has stayed in before with its own individual pool, and worrying that he could have been gazumped.

Josie asks what he would do.

'What would I have done?' he repeats, as though the question is absurd. 'Gone home.'

Josie tells him that he doesn't need to worry – all the other artists are staying in town at the Fullerton.

When he arrives in the Bougainvillea suite he takes an apple from the fruit bowl, strips to his underwear and climbs straight into the pool as he takes his first bite. When he gets out he searches for the sports channel on the TV. He chances upon the video for The Rolling Stones' 'Angie', featuring Mick Jagger at his flounciest. 'Well, if I'm Norman Wisdom,' Rob observes, 'he's Charles Hawtrey.'

Will Smith's 'Summertime' comes on, and we discuss its genius; how it makes you nostalgic for the summers in the hood you never had, and never could have had, and maybe shouldn't even be able to dare imagine. 'It's like the Pet Shop Boys,' he says. 'They got a lot of heterosexuals singing, like me, *"a nervous boy* … ". I knew it was about another boy but it's a beautiful song … ' One, too, that conjures its own imaginary past. 'I'd be, yeah, that's about when I was gay … ,' he remembers.

Thinking about this triggers the memory of another who imagined they remembered when he was gay. Lounging on the sofa in his Singapore suite, he tells me about his first unhappy managerial relationship after leaving Take That, with a man called Kevin Kinsella, who his mother introduced him to. He remembers his mother calling him and giving him a bollocking as he sat round the pool in the south of France with Nellee Hooper, Lisa M, Michael Hutchence and Paula Yates. ('It was quite a big A-list celeb-fest,' he recalls. 'Also Elle McPherson and Kate Moss – they weren't round the pool but that was who we'd been hanging out with. And Dodi al-Fayed, who I called Sheik Myhandy all night.') His mother told him to get back to Manchester. 'So I turned up at the airport and I'm fucking all sorts of spinal fluids fucked, no serotonin in my head, raging alcohol problem, and now I'm meeting this big bear of a man.' Kinsella asked Rob to tell him everything. He stayed at Kinsella's wife's house for three or four weeks, and there was a lot of sleeping and a lot of vodka drinking and a lot of crying. Pretty soon Rob also realised that Kinsella was not the kind of person he wanted to be in business with, but not before a weird episode when Kinsella's wife phoned his mother and said they needed to meet and talk about Rob. 'So she comes up and she goes, "You do know Rob's gay, don't you?" My mum's, "I know my son, and my son's not gay." And she'd just go … ' Rob mimes the appropriate 'Well, if you won't believe me … ' expression. The only explanation he can even hazard for her belief is that they went out to a casino a couple of times with a gay male friend of hers who worked in TV with Jeremy Beadle and, Rob surmises, 'Because I wasn't being heterosexual northern male going, "Ho ho, I'll have to watch my arse around you," she thought I was gay.'

That has not been the only time. He was once in a gay club when someone came up to him and told Rob that he had slept with him. He was flummoxed.

'That's nice,' he said. 'Was it good? Hope you enjoyed it … '

It all amuses him.

'How do you prove you're not gay?' he says. And he is right – in terms of proving that he has never had a gay sexual experience, proof is a problem of science and logic more than sexuality. A thousand contrary examples will not prove he hasn't, any more than one can logically prove by induction that the sun will rise tomorrow just because it has risen every other day.

He nods. 'Unless you spend 24 hours with me for maybe 24 years and you'd get more and more confident that … ' – he smiles – ' … that the son rises with a woman.' He shrugs. 'You know, who gives a flying fuck? I'll say again, for the record, until I'm turned on enough by a man to do it … and I'm not saying that to be PC either. It's the truth.'

We talk about what it is about him that makes people wonder.

'I'm an entertainer,' he says. 'I'm vaudevillian. It's very camp. Every entertainer is camp, from an old school perspective. It's like, Mick Jagger: camp as you like. Jarvis Cocker: he's camp. If Mick Jagger was born in this day, there'd be a lot of people wondering whether he's gay or not.' He smirks. 'And Jarvis Cocker's not the best-looking man on earth, so nobody's really bothered. I mean, I think people would rather not think about Jarvis Cocker having sex, do you know what I mean?'

* * *

The buffet room overlooks the South China Sea, tankers and junks edging to and from the shore all around us. He remarks how nice it is here, but how depressed he was the last time they stayed at this hotel, and how it's hard to change that feeling. 'I've got a feel-bad factor about it,' he says. Vangelis's *Chariots of Fire* soundtrack is piped above our heads. He studies two old people sitting opposite each other across the room, never speaking.

'They've said it all, haven't they?' he says. 'She's thinking: I should have killed him when I had the chance.'

'They should die in an orgasmatron,' suggests Pompey.

'That's the name of Guy's company,' says Rob. 'Thanks for bringing that up and depressing me more. What are you going to do next? Suggest I have some Nigel Martin-Smith buffet? Some Mr Shropshire the Chemistry Teacher water?' Then he adds quietly, reflectively, 'I don't think there's been enough Guy-bashing. I've been very good about it, in all.'

'I think we're the devil,' David points out, meaning him and Tim. 'I think it's all our fault.'

'Nothing to do with me as well, I bet you,' says Rob.

'Nothing to do with you,' predicts David, relaying what he believes Guy is thinking. 'We've poisoned your mind.'

'Nobody gives me any credit,' sulks Rob. 'Always, always, it's never *me* that's made the decisions.' It's a final indignity. Rob felt at times as though people – maybe Guy included – never appreciated his role in the songwriting. And now even at the last, after splitting the partnership, it seems as though Guy may not be fully appreciating his role in doing that.

'I think it's easier to deal with,' suggests David. 'If they blame us, then he doesn't have to look at his responsibility for how he handled you, if you know what I mean.'

'Yeah,' says Rob.

Andy Franks comes over and says that the promoter has offered to bring some girls round during the day tomorrow.

Rob nods.

'Poolside,' says Josie.

'Poolside,' predicts David, 'and then dark side.'

* * *

The next day, when he wakes up in his villa, Josie explains that Matthew Vaughan has phoned, offering Rob a film role as a 30-year-old drug dealer who gives everything up and retires to the tropics. He says he'll read it in due course, but he's barely interested. She has more stuff for him to sign. In his Singapore villa, he signs his will, and she and I witness it.

The phone rings.

'There's a couple of girls in the foyer for you, from Michael,' reports Gary.

'That's weird, isn't it?' says Rob, even though he had vaguely encouraged the idea yesterday.

'You can always go and have a look,' says David.

'Yeah,' Rob decides, 'I'll go and have a look.'

He puts on his Momentary Lack Of Reason Pink Floyd T-shirt and takes his guitar with him. By the pool, he chats with the girls. They're both models. (They really seem to actually both be real models, and not anything seamier; and when he later half-heartedly invites one to join him for his afternoon nap she politely declines.) One is Croatian and shows a picture of her family and discusses how her sister is fat, and they discuss how strange weight can be for teenagers. 'I was a little tub of lard all the way through growing up,' Rob volunteers. He tells Pompey that last night he had a Kit-Kat and a big Toblerone from his own fridge, then raided the Toblerone from Pompey's.

He is invited to two concerts in town tonight. We arrive at the Avril Lavigne show just before the encores, as she launches into 'Complicated' in front of a very young audience play-acting a kind of comfortable, cosy hysteria.

'This'll do her head in, appealing to kids,' considers Rob. He has another observation too. 'I was right about the breasts.' After a while he says, 'If I was 13, I'd be in love with her. Instead of perving over her as a 29-year-old.'

Afterwards, he disappears for a quick chat with her in her dressing room. 'She did coy,' he reports, 'because she knew she was in the presence of the cock of justice.' (This is principally for our entertainment. It is a safe bet that he will have been far more respectful and less lascivious in person.) Within 15 minutes of leaving Avril Lavigne's concert we are across town at Norah Jones's; the two biggest new stars of 2003 in one Singapore evening. It is like a school recital, with her and her band set up halfway down a long room, faced by an audience on rows of chairs. We are led to four saved seats near the front, where Pompey has to elbow me and save my shame when the combination of her soothing jazz-tinged tone and jetlag coaxes me to sleep.

As Norah Jones shyly slides past into her dressing room, Rob chats with her manager, saying that he would like Norah and Diana Krall to sing on his next swing album, before he is invited in. 'I always think that people like Avril Lavigne and Norah Jones won't know who I am,' he says afterwards. Interactions like these often scare him, and he often avoids them, so he is pleased – proud, even – at how this evening's have gone. 'I charmed the pants off people this evening,' he says. 'It's at that good stage of jetlag that alleviates my shyness and awkwardness, leaving witty anecdote and charm in its place.'

He wakes up to the news that in France, following his appearance at the NRJ awards, *Escapology* has leapt to number two in the charts. 'Shows what walking into an audience will do,' he says. He flosses his teeth as he plays backgammon, and confesses that he likes the way everything is going. 'It's a new thing for me, excitement,' he says.

* * *

He reminisces about Take That's appearance on *Spitting Image*, the joke being the hysterical excitement they all displayed when their manager gave them 50 pence. He says that *Spitting Image* made a special Gary Barlow puppet, but for the rest of them they simply put masks on four puppets they already had.

'You ask me why I've got problems ... ' he says.

* * *

Organisers make a mistake when they insist that Rob turn up for events like tonight's awards show with plenty of time to spare. He gets bored very quickly. After sitting in his dressing room at the MTV awards for a brief moment, he looks in Blue's dressing room (empty), returns to his own, hurls an orange violently against the partition, wanders again, finds Atomic Kitten and says brief hellos, returns to his dressing room, lobs pieces of fruit over the partition hoping that they will land in Blue's dressing room several cubicles from his (he always wants to throw fruit as soon as he walks into a dressing room; a desire fuelled, if not created, by the time Gary Barlow told off the rest of Take That in Italy: 'Come on, lads, that's not right, look at the mess you've made ... we'll make a bad impression on people ... '), goes to the balcony from where you can see the stage, then after about eight seconds announces, 'Right, had enough of being out here,' returns to his dressing room, mutters unnecessarily that he is feeling 'very antsy', elaborates that he 'might just say or do something I'll regret – you know, when you go and get arrested?', throws some more fruit indiscriminately around his dressing room, upgrades his condition to 'bored shitless', re-wanders the corridors, returns to the dressing room and aimlessly strums his guitar, pulls his pants up over his stomach in the style of Simon Cowell then gets angry ('No! Fuck off!') when David tries to photograph this, puts on some different trousers, leaves the dressing room, finally finds Blue ...

'I threw a lot of fruit in your room,' he explains.

'Yeah,' says Lee. 'The melon ... '

'Are you the one who said ... ?' asks Rob. He means: is Lee the one who said after news broke of Rob's record deal that he should do something good with it, like give money to charity? Rob had Josie send a letter quietly informing him about Give It Sum and asking whether he would care to make a donation himself.

'Yeah,' says Lee. He may be thinking of this, or of other memorable things he has said.

'Did you get my letter?' Rob asks.

'No,' says Lee.

Nobody ever seems to get his letters.

'He's not even embarrassed,' laughs Rob, back in his dressing room. 'He's the one who said: fuck the World Trade Center when elephants are dying.'

His fellow nominees for the Best International Male award are Eminem (the only other to receive a huge roar when his name is mentioned), Enrique, Moby and Ronan Keating. But he already knows he has won. After receiving the award, he offers it to fans in the front row three times, then takes it back at the last moment. The fourth time, he actually gives it away and walks off empty-handed.

* * *

He goes to the bathroom, as he does more frequently than most humans, all day and much of the night, both because of the copious quantities of water he drinks and because he is built that way. I mention that this constant back-and-forth must have looked very suspicious and telltale during his drug-taking years.

'Yeah,' he says. 'But I'd usually have a line while I was in there anyway.'

* * *

After definitively announcing that he wouldn't attend, both because he was tired and because his shagging boots were again hung up, he decides to go to the after-show party, a glitzy, crowded affair at Indochine on the waterfront. As soon as he walks in he is accosted by a Patsy-from-*Absolutely-Fabulous* type who throws herself all over him, flirting at him and patronising him at the same time. She is drunk in that rather sad way of someone who has stayed at the party several years too long. She repeats several times, as though it demonstrated sincerity rather than rudeness, 'I'm not a fan of yours.' Rob tries to deflect her with politeness, but that doesn't work. Then he tries to ignore her, but that only stirs her to redouble her attentions. Finally, he cracks. He is much more patient in the face of this kind of irritation and adversity than he is given credit for, but when he cracks, he cracks wide open.

'You're absolutely shit,' he tells her, 'and you're embarrassing yourself. You're charmless. Go away.'

She splurts out a few empty slurred words of retaliation.

He nods. 'Now fuck off,' he says.

She stays put.

'Pompey,' he asks, 'can you move that?'

Twenty seconds later he is being introduced to the Prince of Brunei. The prince seems low key and nice enough, and Rob chats briefly but warmly with him. (The grace with which Western artists regularly treat all nobility from Brunei may also reflect his family's notorious largesse when booking the entertainment for private parties at home.)

We go upstairs and on to a balcony overlooking the river, where it's calmer. All's well. 'I used to pay a lot of money to feel like this,' says Rob. 'To feel just OK in my body.'

Pompey hands him the mobile. It is David, calling from the hotel, where he has been woken from his sleep. There is a problem.

* * *

'David, it'll be two pages in the paper on Sunday,' Rob says calmly. 'Let it roll ... bye.' He clicks off the call and explains. 'The *News Of The World* are running with a story that I've got a gambling addiction, and I've spent more than a million in the last year.' He has many addictions, but he does not have the full set, and this is not one that has ever troubled him. David is furious and wants to try and get the story stopped. Rob seems less concerned. His outrage that they would print something so untrue has been blunted by the constant drip-drip-drip of smaller untruths, and it is also tempered with a kind of relief too – that the *News Of The World* hasn't found out anything true that is worth two salacious pages of its attention.

It seems such a strange and off-the-mark story for them to be floating, but Michael Owen has recently been unveiled, to widespread astonishment, as one of football's high-stakes gamblers, the newspapers printing creepily specific records of bets he has made, and perhaps they imagine the scent of a sequel. Rob says that in the last year he has been to a casino once: when he took a coachload of friends to Las Vegas to see Jane's Addiction. A few hundred dollars have changed hands over blackjack games at his house. He and I have paid up the occasional cumulative $50 or $100 between us after dozens of games of backgammon. 'I lost two grand in the casino one night – Park Lane,' he says. 'I was up 1500 quid in all the time I'd been going, and I lost two grand in about an hour and a half, and it turned my stomach over, and I haven't really been since.'

Since then, on the rare occasions he has got involved, he has preferred to act as the house, a role he first took in his youth. 'I ran the book at school a couple of times,' he remembers. 'Port Vale vs Tottenham I creamed everybody. I probably won about 17 quid, 18 quid. And it was really comical because I couldn't add or subtract and I didn't know how to give odds, and I just gave ridiculous odds. What I was amazed by was that they thought I was going to pay out if they won.'

As he walks along the river to the van, he meets Shaggy coming the other way, fresh from presenting the show. Shaggy's female consort takes a picture of Rob and Shaggy together, at Shaggy's request. 'I think that's the first picture I've ever taken with fucking Robbie,' says Shaggy, surprised, as though he has lined up next to most of his contemporaries in the charts a dozen times. Possibly he has. It's the modern way.

The woman escorting us warns that if we head in this direction Rob will meet people on the way out.

'That's OK,' Rob consoles her. 'I've met people before.'

4

He has his first cigarette before he gets out of bed, and explains that he dreamt about Pamela Anderson. ('God help us if she comes on the scene,' mutters Josie.) He and Pamela were watching the Superbowl at his house, and I was there too, and the house was so big that I was staying in a room Rob had never seen before. I went off to interview a gang member and then Rob found himself in Stoke, on a road near where he used to live, and the wind was so strong that it blew him onto a tree, and he was trying to hold onto a fence to pull himself back up. But the wind was so strong.

He goes to the bathroom, then calls for all of us – Pompey, David, Josie and myself – to join him in there. In the centre of the floor is a gigantic cockroach on its back, still alive and wriggling its legs but unable to right itself, being eaten by rivers of ants. David takes the responsibility of putting it out of its misery.

Now Rob remembers something else about his dream. Gary Barlow was there, and he looked just as he looked in the early Take That videos.

'We hugged,' Rob says. 'I felt like such a hypocrite.'

* * *

After Singapore, Japan. At Narita airport he is mobbed by maybe 30 girls and women, all panicking and close to hyperventilating, and many of them thrust presents and packages at him. It is his first trip here since the release of his first solo album, *Life Thru A Lens*. Back then everybody seemed convinced it would continue Take That's Japanese success, but it didn't. After that, Japan was somewhat ignored.

As subsequent records were released, the idea of promoting them enthusiastically anywhere became less and less realistic. He reminisces on the long drive into Tokyo how this culminated in the fiasco of the European press interviews for *Sing When You're Winning*. Rob did turn up at the London hotel where the press were to meet him, but that was more or less the end of his cooperation. He flirted outrageously and disruptively with one interviewer, and for another he answered every question as though he were a character in a different film. 'For example,' he remembers, 'that I was raised in a big family, looked after by a nun, a singing nun, and she taught us all to sing and we put on a big show for the Nazis, and I went on for ages and ages and ages, for a good ten minutes, and then I went, that's *The Sound Of Music*, isn't it? I always get my life and that film mixed up – I'm sorry. And then she asked me another question and I went, well, that summer there was a spate of shark attacks ... And then *E.T.*' The interviewer left in tears. Halfway through the day, Josie and the EMI representative decided it would be better to cancel the rest of his press commitments.

Now, he says, it is different. 'I'm a man on a mission. On *Sing* I hated the record; I was a man on a mission of destruction.'

* * *

In his room at the Four Seasons Rob goes straight into the bedroom, gets on the phone and starts chatting. 'I'll come down in a bit,' he says. No one has any idea who he is talking to.

'Who the frig was that?' asks Pompey.

'That,' he grins, 'is my regular shag when I come to Tokyo.'

He has never mentioned her to anyone here, in the past or in anticipation of this Japanese trip, and he had no contact with her before arriving here, but she was at the airport – as I think he expected she would be – and in the crush handed him a note with her phone number on it.

We go downstairs to have a drink with her and her two friends. He knew these other girls in the Take That days too.

'What was I like then?' he asks.

'Very young,' one says, giggling.

'Was I nice?' he asks. He really wants to know. 'You can tell the truth,' he adds.

'Very nice,' she replies. 'You remember my name.'

His friend gets out her Hello Kitty notebook and shows him her photos of Rob and her through the years: on a plane, at concerts, in a bedroom: the floppy-haired Take That era, the shorn-head late Take That rebel era; the short hair and tattoos of his early solo career.

* * *

There have been heavy conversations between Rob's management and Rob's lawyers and the *News Of The World*. In the airport lounge on the way to Japan David had asked him to consider carefully the most he could possibly have gambled. 'Over the last two years, probably ten grand,' Rob told him. When he wakes up in Japan David tells him that, in the face of their clear denials, the *News Of The World* have decided not to run the story.

He goes sneaker shopping and then to Inter FM, where the woman known as DJ Snoopy suggests on air that he tries to hide his sensitive side. 'No, it's not that I try to hide it,' he says, 'because it's in quite a few of the songs. But as an artist I'm a showman, and I think if the real me got up on stage every night the show would be kind of boring. It really would. My art, if you like, is to project myself a hundred times bigger than I am, and have people believe me, and fortunately they do. But yeah, but underneath all that I'm far too sensitive a person, really. I really, really am. You know, I dent quite easily.'

I dent quite easily. He will never explain it more accurately than that.

DJ Snoopy nods. She wants to get into the real psychological nitty-gritty. He is asked if there's one place that feels most comfortable for him.

He nods. 'Starbucks,' he says.

At the end of the interview he is to sing an acoustic version of 'Feel' with his two guitarists, Gary Nuttall and Neil Taylor. It's quite a radically different arrangement, and a beautiful one, and the baffling thing about all of this – another example of, despite all the insecurities, Rob's extreme confidence in himself – is that the arrangement is one that Rob only hears for the first time as it unfolds around him, live on Japanese radio.

* * *

At J-Wave their DJ, Sasha (not *the* DJ Sasha) introduces himself in perfect English; his German father and Japanese mother used English as their common language. 'Is Japan the last great wall of China for you?' he asks without any evident irony. Sasha also asks Rob his advice for people who want to be successful, and Rob suddenly erupts with a full-blown version of the point of view he was edging towards in Paris at the end of last year.

'You know, it's as easy as this,' he says. 'Either God wants you to be or not. That's it. You know, and you can't stop that. I think you've just got to know when it's your time to give up. Don't follow your dreams.'

'Don't follow your dreams?' queries Sasha. Perhaps he has misheard.

'No, don't follow your dreams, follow somebody else's dreams,' says Rob. '*Always* give up, and *don't* stay true to yourself – and you'll be fine. It's what I did. It *literally* is what I did – I didn't follow my dreams, I wasn't true to myself, and I gave up really easy. And that's what I did and here I am at the top of the pile. So if anybody says any different, say it's rubbish.'

Sasha translates. Rob interrupts.

'And that's the *truth*. That is the truth. I didn't follow my dreams, I followed somebody else's. And I used to give up an awful lot, very easily. And I'm never, *never* true to myself; I make it a rule in life.' He laughs. 'No, don't follow your dream, man. Follow someone else's dream. I wanted to be an accountant; I did, I did. I always did, yeah. This was somebody else's dream. I sort of got given it.'

'What is your dream right now?' asks Sasha.

'I don't really have one right now. I'm staying untrue to myself. I'm keeping it unreal.'

'Really?' says Sasha.

'Yeah. There's that as well. All that keep-it-real crap that people say. "Keep it real." You're heard that, haven't you? Real's crap. Real's boring. Real's *real*. Why don't we all keep it unreal for a bit? What do you think? Keep it unreal … Look where real's got us … '

Amidst the silliness, and safely away from the judgements he is used to facing and the usual knowledge that anything he says may end up, secondhand and twisted, in a tabloid, these Japanese interviews find him at his most honest and self-reflective. He is asked why he has been so successful around the world.

'I don't know,' he says. 'Something caught their imagination. I think maybe it's because people are really afraid to make themselves look fools because the world is such a cool place right now. And I think the art of entertaining died, or is dying, with this new cool generation and I'm just pleased that if I can make myself look an idiot for other people's pleasure then I will. Entertainers are a dying breed because of not wanting to make themselves look silly. And I will actually risk and fulfil looking silly on many occasions for the high price of entertainment. I think nobody's really *acting* a song these days. I don't know. I'm a throwback to the eighties … the seventies … sixties, maybe.'

He explains that for him the point of being onstage is to be someone else. 'My job is to lie to people and have them believe it,' he says. But then he also says, 'Considering that I've just started to enjoy it and considering I've just started to believe in myself and believe in what I do, everything's just started for me – it's taken five albums for it to just start – and I feel a genuine excitement about the world again and I feel a genuine excitement about my job. I knew I would, but it took me quite a while to get it. Now I want to make one of the best albums written.'

* * *

In the van he had declared, 'It's a proper Sunday, isn't it? It's: "I've had some lunch and just watched the football and *Bullseye* isn't on yet but it is soon and Cousin Tony has fallen asleep and Auntie Clare has put some food on and is just about to give me a lamb chop." It's a really good state of mind to be in.'

He picks up this theme talking to Sasha, explaining how pleased he is to find that this particular Sunday feels like a Sunday. He talks as though he has reclaimed something. 'The week sort of lost its form as soon as I left school and became a pop star,' he explains. 'Pop stars don't have weeks or weekends. People normally get drunk on a Saturday and Sunday; pop stars and rock stars just get drunk. Whenever. "It's Tuesday morning – let's get drunk." Also, to be quite honest with you, I don't know what day it is a lot of the time – because I don't have to, really. People pick me up and take me to places and I get on planes, and I turn up – I didn't even know I was coming to Japan.' Pause. 'But it was lovely when I got off the plane.'

'We have a superstar here,' observes Sasha, baffled.

Rob explains how Sundays used to be depressing because there'd be school tomorrow. 'But guess what?' he says. 'No school for me tomorrow! Suckers! And I'm really rich. Yeah! Stick that in your pipe, Mr Bannon.'

Mr Bannon was his school headmaster.

Sasha translates; Rob continues.

'I still get excited on some Sundays knowing that I don't have to go to school the next day. It's the truth. And sometimes, I just stay up really late on purpose. That's how growned up I am. And if there's a cake in the fridge, I can eat it all – I can. It's my cake. I couldn't do that when I was at school. Yeah! You've got no control over me now, Mum ... '

Sasha translates.

'*And* I know girls ... *and* they want to kiss me ... *and* I kiss them back. Yeah. And we stay up really late. And my mum, she lives in England and I live in LA – I can do whatever I want ... '

Sasha starts asking a different question, but Rob interrupts him.

'Sometimes I don't brush my teeth,' he says. Pause. 'Or wipe my bottom.' Pause. 'Sorry. I've really realised how much I can get away with these days. Sorry.'

Sasha asks him to record some IDs for the radio station. In the middle of them Rob whispers, low, but still audibly, adding one more to the list.

'A girl's touched my willy ... ' he says.

* * *

Josie says that Kevin Spacey has phoned the office again. He wants Rob to appear with Elton John at a benefit he's arranging for, and at, the Old Vic next month. She knows what he will say.

'I'm busy,' Rob repeats. 'Tell him I'm busy.'

* * *

Another interview, some more personal philosophy shared with the people of Japan:

'You are in favour with women,' he is told. 'Do you have any secret to be sexy?'

'Yeah,' he answers. 'Get famous and rich. Yeah. If you're famous and rich, you become better-looking instantly. In fact, I'm quite an average guy but it's what people think I've got that makes me sexy, it's not what I actually have. You know rock'n'roll helps ugly people get laid, and long live rock'n'roll. I mean, look at Linkin Park ... ' he stops himself. 'No, I'm only joking – Linkin Park are good-looking men, I just couldn't think of a band quick enough.'

He elaborates and finesses this answer throughout the rest of his trip.

'It's 50 per cent of what you've got and 50 per cent of what people think you've got that makes you sexy ... Yeah, I'm rich. That makes me sexy. Sexy's in the eye of the beholder. I don't fancy me much. They've got the perception that I'm a bit of a wild one, and I think people like to think they can tame you. And I like people trying to tame me – it's fun. I'm always up for a good taming of an evening ... '

* * *

It is during his second day of interviews in Japan – talking to a show called *Space Shower TV* and being filmed by a cameraman whose T-shirt, to Rob's delight, bears the words OVERJOYED BY NEWS, and after a night dreaming about Heidi Klum – that he realises for the first time that the title of his album, *Escapology*, contains the word 'apology'. He had never noticed, and he seems both pleased and slightly spooked by this. 'That's me all over,' he says. 'Apology. Me apologising for my escape.' From now on it will become a regular part of his explanation. 'That's a big theme that runs through my life,' he will explain.

* * *

On his third night in Japan, he dreams of Gwyneth Paltrow. 'I'm having a right celeb-fest in my dreams at the moment,' he reflects. To bring himself down, he muses on the perplexing matter of the new dirrty Christina Aguilera. 'She looks like a cross between someone in Trade at six in the morning and someone who's trying to save trees,' he judges. 'She's like a rock eco warrior. She's like a cross between Swampy and the Village People.'

His workday begins. He is interviewed in the back of a limousine by a Japanese pop star, Fay Ray. After she has asked a few questions and they have flirted a little, he says: 'Now let me ask you a question. I've heard about these vending machines that sell used panties ... '

'That's true,' she concedes.

He arrives at a radio station. 'It's half-unbelievable that you're here,' the female DJ tells him.

'Well,' he says, 'here's the other half.'

He explains to her that he could never have imagined this kind of success. 'I think the word "surprise" would be an understatement,' he says. 'You can't dream of this ... ' He lists his shortcomings. 'I'm useless at everything else. I'm quite good at sport. I'm no good with mental arithmetic. I can't add up and I can't subtract; I can't write very well, and I'm not good with my hands. So I pretty much was absolutely relying on the fact that I'm a good show-off to get me through life. And so far, so good.'

He is asked what his ideal show would be. They mean concert performance.

'In the bedroom, trying to impress Cameron Diaz,' he says.

'What a great answer,' says the interviewer.

'It's the truth,' he says.

'She really will think you're stalking her,' laughs Josie.

'She will,' Rob concedes. 'It isn't the way to go about things at all. But I don't care. She's just a fantasy figure really. She can't live up to what I think she is.'

* * *

He is allowed the last morning off to go shopping. In the van, he starts talking about parties he attended in the old days. There was the Ab Fab party when he was 17 or 18, where he offended Ade Edmonson by saying, 'I thought the show was meant to take the piss out of all this,' and where he bottled it when Naomi Campbell came up and told him that Christy Turlington wanted to dance with him, absurdly claiming that it was impossible because he had broken his leg.

There was the time he came down to London to see a famous model – 'Not a date or anything, but just I'd been invited to go and have something to eat' – and Liam, by chance, was on the train when it pulled up at Stoke, hanging out of the window. 'So I got absolutely fucking hammered with him on the train going down and then carried on into the evening. Then she came round with one of the Clash … ' Soon the numbers filled out. 'There was one side doing smack and one side doing coke,' he remembers, 'and there was me in the middle, singing the songs from the shows. *When you see a guy, reach for stars in the sky, you can bet that he's doing it for some doll* … '

He acts out how one side were chirpily, manically joining in while the others nodded along slowly, in a befuddled kind of way.

After a while, he disappeared.

'I had this whole sketch where if there was a wardrobe in the room, it was Narnia,' he remembers, 'and I'd just go and sit in it for about half an hour and then come out giggling.'

* * *

After the seat-belt signs have gone off, Rob comes and visits me on the plane. 'I've taken my sleeping tablet,' he announces, 'and I'm trying to stay awake on them, see what it's like.' He is bending it. He will turn out to have taken two and a half Ambien. Already he seems pretty out of it. 'Weird things are happening to my eyes,' he explains, then says that he is going to start acting completely normal. 'Do I look normal now?' he demands, but his eyes are distant and so is his voice. It is a shock to see him off his head, and I find it quite disturbing.

I ask what he is looking forward to in Los Angeles.

'Dogs … swimming pool … nothing … '

He suddenly collapses into me, his muscles completely rigid. He is half on me, and half on the empty seat next to me, and is completely out. I have to use all my strength to lift him off me and settle him into the next seat. A few seconds later, he wakes, looking confused. I explain that he just nodded off. He looks as though he is trying to process this.

'I'll go downstairs,' he says. He finds his seat and sleeps for the rest of the flight.

5

During a week off in Los Angeles, Martin Bashir's Michael Jackson programme is shown, and Bashir gets in touch asking to make a programme about Rob. He doesn't even consider it. (He has already turned down slightly more palatable options. Louis Theroux came round his flat once; Rob wanted to meet him but it worried him that Theroux wanted to make a programme about him because so many of his subjects seem to be freaks.)

Instead, he relaxes and gets restless, turns down appearances on two big American TV shows (*Alias* and *Charmed*) and goes to Justin Timberlake's birthday party for ten minutes. One afternoon Linda Perry comes round. Linda Perry is the cool songwriter of the moment for her work with Pink and Christina Aguilera, and particularly for writing Aguilera's last hit 'Beautiful'. He would rather they had tried to write a song together there and then, but instead they talk for nearly two hours. 'Bonkers,' he reports afterwards, approvingly. 'Very strong-headed. I think she's got good morals. She didn't know anything about me. I think she thinks I'm the "Rock DJ" man.' He plays her 'One Fine Day' (she says the chords could be different, and the melody), 'Come Undone' (which she really likes) and 'Feel' (which she sort of likes). 'She was talking about "changes" and stuff,' he says. 'I don't know what a fucking "change" is. I'm just like: if it sounds like it's a song, it's a fucking song.'

'Did I pass my interview?' he says as she is leaving.

'That's normally what I say,' she replies.

* * *

'Do you want to ... ?' he asks. He doesn't finish the sentence, because he wants to anyway. 'I know it's me me me,' he says, 'but, fuck it, let's look at my websites ... '

Out of boredom and self-obsession, he has been searching for stuff about himself on the internet. 'I searched for "Robbie Williams Escapology review",' he says, 'which was fucking stupid because I felt great before I went in there. Basically what I found is either "Yeah, fucking great, Robbie's done it again" or that I'm Satan incarnate. Nothing surprised me. It was me going: let's go and see how many poisonous people there are in the world and how much I can upset myself today ... '

We sit in the office downstairs in his Los Angeles house and survey his fans' latest opinions. One says that the way he writes songs so that you want to listen right to the end is 'a clever marketing ploy'. Another describes 'Feel' as 'an Enrique wannabe song'. There is a long, evolving debate on one site about what he should do to break America. They build opinion upon opinion, and specious fact upon specious fact, and once they reach a conclusion they act as though Rob has also reached it; as though their debates were actually forming, or were at least an accurate reflection of, the reality they speak about. We scroll through these for maybe an hour. I point out to him that the weirdest thing about these postings is their absurd shared assumption that he is sitting somewhere reading and digesting them.

Um …

'Oh,' he says. 'That's weird.'

He types his name into eBay to see what Robbie Williams collectibles might be on the market. He finds a signed CD and photo for £100. 'That's not my signature,' he says. Then a signed photo of him and Oasis at Glastonbury: £75. 'That's not mine either,' he says. A signed photo of him and Nicole Appleton. '*Absolutely* not!' he says. 'My God, that's not even a good copy.' (This comes with a 'certificate of authenticity', the sort of brilliant flourish that defines internet chicanery. As though someone who would sell a photo with a fake autograph would have any qualms about providing a fake, meaningless 'certificate of authenticity'.) He becomes determined to find a genuine signature, and he clicks on item after item: 'Absolutely not … oh my God … absolutely not … no … no … no, absolutely not … '

He can't find a single real one, though he's signed plenty over the years. There's something very depressing about the whole business: the ridiculousness of autographs in the first place; the preying on people's willingness to believe; the tricking them out of the real pointless totems they desire.

* * *

He has a wardrobe fitting for the 'Come Undone' video. All the clothes have been brought up to the house and hang on rails in the main bedroom. He tries on a trashed tuxedo jacket from the morning after a debauched party, and lurches around, fake drunk. 'Is that good pissed?' he asks.

'Don't do pissed,' Josie beseeches. 'I hate it.'

B, the stylist, says that they need to talk about the bed scene and whether he wants to wear underwear in it. He points out that he doesn't have the usual misgivings about such scenes. 'Usually when people talk about sex scenes,' he says, 'they're, "Oh my God, it was so uncomfortable, like the whole set's looking at you – is it passionate? *No*!" Well, I'm really different. I've got a steaming fucking hard-on all the way through every passion scene I've ever done. So I think it's probably best if I wear underpants.'

His mother calls from his London flat, explaining that she is having problems ejecting a video cassette. He carefully tries to ensure that she only uses the video player downstairs, and not the one in his bedroom. He knows what video he left in there.

That night he dreams about Madonna.

'We were just chatting,' he reports. 'She had this coffee flask that recorded things.'

* * *

It is late on Saturday afternoon in Los Angeles, which is after midnight in Britain. Rob is upstairs having an afternoon nap, and I am in the office in his house. Since I started working on this book I have got in the habit of checking the British tabloids online every day, and as Rob sleeps, I idly click on to the *News Of The World*'s website, and see the front page headline: ROBBIE'S £2m GAMBLING ADDICTION.

After the denials and a week's breathing space, they have gone ahead anyway. Among the subheads is *He loses £50,000 on a single hand of poker* and *Robbie fought drugs, booze, sleazy sex with strangers … now he's hooked on gambling*. The article is full of specifics, and I don't even have to wake him to know that many of them are absurd. One of the many instances it highlights, for instance, is: 'RACED away from last year's MTV Music Awards in Barcelona to bet £10,000 at a flash casino'. I was with him all that evening, the one where he met Ms Dynamite and we went straight from the ceremony to the airport.

* * *

As soon as he wakes, Rob heads into Hollywood for a final meeting with Jonas Ackerlund about the 'Come Undone' video. In the foyer of the Chateau Marmont, David briefly tells him about the *News Of The World*, but first he must concentrate on the matter in hand. Jonas, who is wearing a Rolling Stones tongue pendant and a belt buckle that spells FUCK YOU, takes him up to a room on the fourth floor with piles of film-making equipment stacked everywhere and a storyboard pasted to the wall, and summarises his vision. 'The video is very much like an attitude,' he explains. 'I want it to be beautiful and weird and fucked up at the same time.' He shows Rob Polaroids of the house where they will shoot – 'I am so happy with this house; he don't want us there but he finally said yes' – and of various girls. 'This one's OK with snakes,' he says. 'This one's OK doing bugs. This one is also OK to making out. These are real porn girls and are willing to go all the way, especially for that last bedroom scene … '

'Wicked,' says Rob.

He hands over another Polaroid. 'That's just an extra one,' he says. 'We have a back-up one.'

'Back-up porno?' clarifies Rob.

'Yeah,' says Jonas. He shows Rob the two men.

'Are they gay?' Rob asks.

'I don't think so,' says Jonas, 'but they are OK with it. I mean, they should. It's a job.'

Jonas wants to talk some more, about second unit close-ups and lip-syncing, but Rob stops him. He says he needs to go downstairs and get a coffee. 'I'm fucked,' he explains.

In the foyer he sees B sitting with some people and joins them. Rob chats briefly with a good-looking man, who turns out to be French, and asks whether he is one of the models for the video. The man looks confused and maybe slightly put out. It is the actor Oliver Martinez.

Only now does he ask David about the *News Of The World*. 'Is it the front page?' he says.

'Yeah,' frowns David.

'Wicked,' he says. 'I have got an album out, you know. We'll see if the album goes up next week. If it does, I'll have a gambling problem every week. I'll come out of a club pretending to be sozzled. Assault a paparazzi who's an actor.'

* * *

It's only funny for as long as he can imagine it as a big, untrue headline. As soon as he gets back to the house and reads what has actually been written about him, his mood changes. He reads passages out, baffled and bewildered.

Robbie Williams stood under the glittering chandeliers of a gold-carpeted Las Vegas casino wearing jeans and trainers and craving yet another date with his latest obsession – cards ... Robbie, 28, has embraced cocaine, compulsive one night sex stands, tortured relationships with celeb stunners like Geri Halliwell ... and endless wild booze and junk food binges, but his latest all-consuming passion has cost him a hundred grand in a night, and has pals deeply worried.

It says that his 'secret three-year gambling binge' began while playing cards with Alcoholics Anonymous friends. He spent £60,000 'in a frantic three-day gambling frenzy in Monte Carlo' (he says he went to a casino once with Jonny and Geri Halliwell and lost maybe £500), lost £30,000 on a single card bet at the Sahara casino (fantasy), blew £5000 during a two-hour blackjack session at London's Victoria Casino ('I've never been there,' he says), begged 'showbiz pals' like Tom Jones and Kelly Jones to join him at his LA home 'for high stakes poker', borrowed money from Nicole Kidman after running out of £100 chips ('That happened,' he says. 'But they weren't £100 chips. I said, have you got 100 quid?') and then that he gambled £10,000 after the MTV awards. In the article, an unnamed 'friend' describes an evening at the Mandalay Bay Hotel in Vegas. It says that over the night he was down £100,000 and that he gambles every day now. 'Three weeks can see a million done,' says the friend. Then comes perhaps the most offensive insinuation:

His friend explained how gambling is a major form of relaxation for recovering alcoholics. He said, "You bet on anything ... Robbie loved the fact that a few of the guys had running bets on who would have a drink first."

For someone who treats addiction as seriously as Rob does, an obscene suggestion.

There's more.

... he treats gambling like most blokes treat going down the pub. Over two years £2 million is a conservative estimate of his losses.

Untrue.

Music bosses used to give Robbie a monthly allowance of £60,000 to control his spending.

Untrue.

He still appears to enjoy a drink and seemed the worse for wear after boozing with mates in LA Whisky bar on Thursday night.

Untrue.

'That's disgusting,' he says when he finishes reading. It is an astonishing, woefully inaccurate character smear. He's half amused, half furious. He says that he used to sometimes go to Aspinalls in London, but he stopped going when they put their minimum bet up to £25 because that was too big-time for him and didn't seem like a laugh any more. He studies the photos the *News Of The World* have used. One is a grainy picture of him and some gambling chums in a circle round a table, cards in hands, and the impression is of a surreptitious snap of a high stakes gambling den. In fact the faces shown are of Josie, Chris Sharrock, David, film director Brian Hill and Rob, and, as the tiny photo caption saying 'Robbie, in green, and workpals on DVD' acknowledges, without explaining or making clear, it is a still lifted from his own movie *Nobody Someday*. They are playing the children's card game Uno. On the night in question they were playing for the pure love of winning, though sometimes they would play for a fiver.

He knows all this. But he also knows that by tomorrow night several million people in Britain will be convinced by all the details here.

He calls David and discusses it. There are downsides to suing, even when you're confident of success. If it comes to court, he can expect the *News Of The World* to cast everything he's done in the poorest light. It may be particularly tough on someone who regularly deals with life by intertwining the least and most serious parts of their world together, and often hiding one within the other. He can expect every ironic sentence he's ever said thrown back at him as though it was completely earnest. But how can he let these slurs just sit there? If he doesn't challenge them, they will quickly become cemented as the truth.

'It's just completely principle,' he says. 'I don't care. But if they get away with that, what's the next one?'

It is decided.

'I think we should sue 'em,' he says. 'And if we win, put the money on black.'

6

'Oh dear,' he says. 'So it starts.'

He says hello to a pretty girl in few clothes who is dangling in a crucifixion pose. She is suspended in one corner of the bedroom where much of his new video will be filmed. On the surface of the swimming pool outside, an inflatable doll is floating face down. He looks round the house. There is a photograph of the house owner, an heir to the Dole pineapple fortune, with his father. They are smiling. Between them is George W. Bush.

He greets as many of the cast as he can find – 'Hello, I'm Rob, I'm singing today' – and then walks back up a hill to his trailer.

'It feels like we're doing something bad, doesn't it?' he says. 'A black woman on a cross.'

David steps up into the trailer and announces with excitement that 'Feel' has broken some kind of ten-year-old record in Holland for 'airplay call-up'.

'I don't know what that means,' says Rob.

'Neither do I,' giggles David, but nonetheless tries to elaborate. 'Nobody has gone higher than 7.5, and you have gone 7.9.'

'Cool,' says Rob, baffled, and they both laugh at this unintelligible good news.

* * *

His first scene to be shot is of the beginning of the morning after, waking up in bed with two girls. He gets into bed, between them, leans against the alligator skin headboard and chats. One already works as a porn star, and the other is doing her first porn movie next weekend. He asks this second girl what her parents think about it.

'They're not talking to me,' she says.

He acts out the scene for the camera: waking up, inspecting himself in the mirror and staggering drunkenly outside. David watches the monitor and worries that Rob is overdoing it, veering into Norman Wisdom mode. He has a quiet word. This will be a recurring issue throughout the day. 'Too drunk and too cokey,' Josie will observe after one particularly over-the-top take. His acting today seems to be a combination of remembering how he used to be, hamming it up for effect, and pretending to be Colin Farrell. ('I just got carried away,' he apologises after really overdoing it, though he does lay claim to a good excuse. 'I did ten years' prep,' he points out, 'just for this role.')

Between takes, Hamish Brown, his regular photographer on occasions like this, takes some stills of him with the two girls on the bed. They snuggle close on either side of him. 'How's my chin at this angle?' he asks Hamish earnestly. Hamish reassures him.

As Hamish shoots, Rob touches tongue-tips with the blonde girl, and then, as though he is concerned not to be showing any favouritism, does the same with the black-haired girl. Both of them have hands resting over his crotch. 'Just acting out my fantasy here,' he says, and puts his tongue in the black-haired girl's ear. He laughs. 'It's all gone very German seventies with me, hasn't it? "Ya! Ist goot. Ya, we do triple entry."' The girls now laugh, and he says, 'Why do I feel like Ron Jeremy?' Then he invites the girls to pull at his nipples. One each.

'He likes to have his nipples pulled,' observes the black-haired girl.

'No, I don't at all,' he says, and goes into Partridge voice. 'It's ... *strictly for art's sake*.' And he kisses the blonde girl, full on, just because.

'Hamish,' he says, 'instruct me to kiss them both.'

Hamish takes a moment to get the hint.

'What was that, Hamish?' Rob asks.

'Three-way tongue?' suggests Hamish, and his subjects helpfully comply.

'Let's be crazy now,' urges the blonde, and there is lots more kissing and some breast nuzzling, and rather less care is now being taken about posing for the camera.

'To me, Rob,' requests Hamish, still trying to maintain some professionalism.

'Nah,' says Rob, otherwise occupied.

Hamish snaps a little more, then says 'cool' to indicate he is finished. He knows that Rob has little patience for photo sessions that overstay their welcome.

'Nah,' says Rob again, resurfacing. 'Another roll.'

Eventually they do finish. 'Thanks, ladies,' he says. They get out of bed and go to have their make-up retouched. He stays put. 'I won't be getting out of bed for a while,' he says.

Out of diligence, I ask him what the two girls are called. He thinks for an instant, and then smiles in advance of his reply. 'Don't know,' he says, and laughs.

* * *

There is some concern in Rob's camp that Jonas Ackerlund seems to have jettisoned one of the aspects of the video that Rob was most keen on – the religious allegory; the blood on the doors. I overhear a discussion where they wonder whether they should raise this with Rob:

'As long as Rob's happy.'

'He's got his bugs.'

'The problem is that Rob saw the naked shagging and that was it. All thought of the Bible went out of the window.'

* * *

Back home for the evening after the first day's shooting, he reads about the forthcoming American pay-per-view TV programme during which they intend to contact Princess Di. He thinks it is sick but is still fascinated by it. He met her once, when Take That were invited round to Kensington Palace. She seemed lovely. 'Like a kind, warm-hearted person,' he remembers. He once said, on a webchat, somewhat flippantly, that there was something not right about the accounts of her death.

'The next day Mohamed al-Fayed sends me a letter: "Very interested to hear your thoughts ... we should do tea one time, let's discuss them".'

He didn't reply.

* * *

He is up at 7.30 the next morning, ready for his big day. 'Today,' he announces, as we drive through the Los Angeles drizzle, 'I have sex. I reckon it's going to get a bit kinky, Josie.'

At the house he sits in his robe and underwear and pink socks on the bed where he will later film his sex scene, and discusses the detailed legal response to the *News Of The World* article with David and Josie. They go through it point by point. Josie explains that they need his response to the allegation that he has 'a massive gambling addiction'.

'I most certainly do not,' he says.

'"I enjoy the occasional flutter?"' suggests David.

'Yes,' he agrees. '" ... just like everybody else". Yeah. "For modest stakes."'

The next allegation: 'Robbie's losses amount to £2 million.'

'Complete nonsense,' he says.

'"It is alleged that he has lost £50,000 on a single hand of poker and £30,000 on one bet during a high-rolling game ... "' says David.

'I've never ever come *near* to gambling in those figures ... ' says Rob. '"It's alleged that Robbie's cock has massive girth." Yes. Girth – big.'

'"It is alleged that previously Robbie was hooked on cocaine, booze and sex ... "' says David, and answers the charge himself. 'Yes. Not the sex.'

'Yeah,' says Rob. 'Not the sex. What shall I say to that?'

'Just say that,' says Josie. '"And this has been well documented ... which I have never hidden".'

'Yeah,' says Rob.

They go through the named venues and Rob details his small or non-existent history with each, and rebuts other slurs, particularly the article's most unpleasant allegation – that Rob places bets on addicts messing up. 'That's the bit I'm the most pissed off about,' he emphasises.

'"The most offensive allegation,"' writes David, '"is that I would gamble on someone's sobriety ... Alcohol is a life and death business and not to be gambled on." Yeah?'

'"And it's not to be taken frivolously,"' says Rob,

* * *

For one reason or another, David and I find ourselves standing in the hallway of this house discussing the potential curse of being born with too much money.

'That'll be the challenge for your children,' David points out to Rob.

'Yeah, well I aim on being poor by that point, for that very reason,' says Rob defiantly. That's one option. He also shares with us an alternative plan: 'I'm going to buy an island and create the world there, and everyone pretends they don't know who I am. Where I'm ignored, and so are my kids.'

* * *

He stands in the kitchen, bored between shots, hiding from the rain. CNN is broadcasting the first message believed to be from Osama Bin Laden since the invasion of Afghanistan. 'If I was really naughty, and I fancied some time off,' Rob says to Josie, 'I could go, oh, I'm really scared of getting on planes ... '

'Yes,' she acknowledges. 'You could.'

Instead, he decides to take the opportunity to tell her some things that are missing in his life, and that she should be kind enough to sort out forthwith. 'I want a masseuse,' he begins. 'And a dogwalker – not for the dogs, though. For me. To walk me around. And an Altoid man, because you're not doing your job. And I need somebody to point at trees, so I know where they are. I always want a man from the local tourist board, to point out places of interest and tell me about local attractions. But I don't want him to talk to me directly – he must do it through you. I must never see him. He must be invisible, but informative. I also want a Spiderman outfit and supernatural powers ... '

Josie nods.

* * *

The question of whether Rob truly intends to have sex on camera in this video has been floating in the air, and nobody has been addressing it directly. There has been a lot of joking about it, but at the same time it has not been treated a joke – nobody has been left in any doubt about the need to have some performers on set who are prepared to participate if required. But by what he says during the lunch break in the trailer, it seems that Rob is only now seriously working out how far he should go.

'David,' he says. 'I'm thinking in the sex stuff there should be some sex stuff performed.'

'Penetration?' asks David evenly.

'I was thinking of oral,' says Rob. 'And ... ' – he casts his eyes around the gathered entourage in the trailer – ' ... you're not watching.'

I ask him why he wants to do it for real.

He shrugs. 'It pushes the boundaries of taste. And it might go hideously wrong. It's the same thing as recording a swing album. And as far as I can remember, no one else has done it.'

Is there anything you won't do if she's up for it?

'Probably penetration. "I did not have sexual intercourse with that woman."'

He asks to see the blonde-haired girl during this lunch break. He wants to discuss their scene, and I'm not sure he has entirely ruled out a little bit of rehearsal. Word comes that she's still at lunch. By the time she reaches the trailer he is due back on set, but they have a chat in the street, she grins and they shake hands.

'Sorted,' he reports. 'As long as it's not with snakes.'

First he must do a lip-sync of the song. This will be the first time 'Come Undone' is heard on the set, a day and a half into the shoot. Usually, on a video shoot, everyone gets abominably sick of the song in question from hearing it in 20-second snippets over and over again as scenes are filmed, but this video has been filmed mostly in silence, except for the party scenes, where Jonas wanted more energetic up-tempo music than Rob's song offers. (AC/DC's 'You Shook Me All Night Long' has been a favourite.) Rob has greater reservations, and is more nervous about the lip-sync than anything else he will do today – he is not comfortable with this process at the best of times, but it's easier with his lighter lyrics. 'I'm good at the trivial throwaway thing,' he says. He points out that there's no lip-syncing at all in the 'Feel' video and that this is no coincidence. The lip-sync scene is to be filmed with Rob sitting against the wall in the house owner's 'secret pink room', which Jonas has just discovered. (It is not part of the agreed location and the owner negotiates another $5000 on the spot for its use.)

He sings the song beautifully (as he does so, he is thinking of Coldplay's 'Yellow' video), though at the end of the second take the camera pans down and catches him picking his toenails. When he walks into the kitchen after a third take full of passion and crushed hopes there is a smattering of applause.

'Don't,' he says. 'It won't be enough.'

On CNN they are talking about the prospect of removing Saddam Hussein. 'It's better the devil you know,' he says to me. 'Write down that I said that.' He is horrified to see me writing in my notebook, as though I had not understood he was being daft and had taken it as a serious instruction.

I explain that I am not writing down what he told me to write down, I am writing down that he told me to write it down.

'Oh,' he says.

* * *

'Rob, do you need anything?' Josie asks.

'The love of a good woman,' he answers.

'I think it can be arranged,' she points out.

'No, a *good* woman,' he says.

'Coffee in the meantime?' she suggests.

'Yeah.'

* * *

The blonde-haired girl comes up to him and tells him that her agent has told her not to do it.

'OK,' he says. He doesn't try to persuade her. As with many of his encounters away from video sets, it can take only one thing to make him lose interest, and once he has lost interest, it is over. Maybe it's for the best anyway. 'You'd like me to not do anything, wouldn't you, Josie?' he says.

'Well, we'd hardly be able to use it,' she says, not directly answering.

'Bummer,' he mutters, now getting a little more annoyed. He remembers why it appealed to him. 'Controversy,' he says. 'Controversy, controversy, controversy ... ' Most entertainers vehemently deny ever trying to stir up controversy; everything must be presented as the sincere product of an artistic impulse, and all collateral controversy must be presented as an accident. But it is much more the Robbie Williams way to brazenly declare that he is seeking to trigger controversy, advertising his shallowest motive while – as so often – hiding the fact that, in its shadows, he wants to communicate something pretty serious and heartfelt.

Anyway, perhaps he doesn't need to have sex.

'You've got bugs, bloody slashed wrists, drugs, a sex scene,' Josie points out. 'It won't be on *Blue Peter*.'

Whatever. He knows that if he asks, Jonas will make his co-star stick to what she agreed before the shoot, but now he has gone off both the act and the idea. 'I'm not bothered, genuinely,' he says. 'Just get it done and go home.'

He goes outside and stands on the lip of the lawn, perfectly horizontal and green in defiance of the scrubby slopes around it. He stretches his arms out and then curls them behind him.

'I'm touching Robbie Williams' bum,' he says.

* * *

The bed action is left until last. Rob asks for some deodorant and then a mint. 'I'm going in,' he says. While he is with the girls, I sit in the bathroom next door with Daniel, Rob's hairdresser friend, and the two guys waiting for their turn in the bed with Rob. They seem really drunk. From the bedroom I can hear Jonas shouting instructions and encouragement, and lots of laughter. After a while, one of the crew bursts out of the room and shouts with some urgency, 'Video snake!' (This is some piece of technical film-making equipment, it turns out, rather than the real snake, or the other snake.)

Time is running out. They have a strict curfew both for their filming permit and to get out of the house. Jonas won't even talk to his producer. The two guys are sent in. More laughter reverberates through the wall.

'Up!' shouts Jonas. 'I don't see a face! And down again. Up on your knees! Stand up on your knees!'

I can just hear Rob's voice. 'Everyone's trying to dominate,' he says. I'm not sure if it's a complaint, or a commentary, or a celebration.

* * *

The moment he leaves the room, there is no time for anything but the briefest goodbyes, and he explains nothing of what has happened until we are away in the dark of the van.

'Smelly fanny,' he says, and then leaves that remark for later explanation. He talks about the boys first. 'The one with the white hair was pissed as a fart,' he says. 'Just wanted to fucking shag. I was, brother, it's only a video and I'm not drunk.' He chuckles. 'That's going to cause so much trouble.'

'Had he had mints?' asks Josie.

'I didn't kiss the boys,' he says. 'I just shagged them from behind.'

'No tongue, just shagged them from behind ... ' Josie summarises, as though taking notes. (Before and during the shoot, and in this van, there has been no need to clarify that he has not done, and never intended to do, anything more than feign sexual acts with the men. But perhaps it needs stating.)

'The two girls are absolute fucking nutters,' he reports. 'So they're doing my head in, but it's cool, and we're rolling about and whatever. And then we stop rolling about and whatever, and the two lads come in and the one with the blonde hair seems pissed out of his fucking head and wants to shag me – he was just throwing me about a bit. But it was so funny because there's all three of us, and it was like everybody was trying to dominate.'

I ask him whether it was fun.

'Yeah. I suppose so. They were all giggly and really young and laughing about things that weren't funny. And I was just like professional in the end. No going down business or anything, but lots of naked breast touching, them two kissing, us three kissing each other. And then the lads.'

Did you keep your pants on?

'I did, yeah. They didn't. But it wasn't like difficult. It wasn't erotic or sexy, but it wasn't difficult either. Put it this way: erect with the ladies, real fucking tiny for the boys. I'd tell you if I found it sexy.'

He returns to how shocked he was by what he thought were most unprofessional female odours.

'You'd sort your fanny right out, wouldn't you?' says Rob.

'It's like a plumber not turning up with his spanners,' says Lee.

'I had a quick fiddle,' Rob mentions. 'Both of them. I didn't realise I was doing it, until I was, oh, I've got my finger on her clitoris … '

* * *

We go for a late-night snack at the Standard on Sunset strip. Rob says he's been up nearly 24 hours, in front of the waiter, and Josie chides him for exaggerating. 'He doesn't know,' Rob says. 'He thinks I'm really cool now.' Pause. 'He doesn't know I was in Take That.' Pause. 'He'll be in there now going, "Who's that really cool dude? He's a bit like Liam, but Norman Wisdom too."'

From this conversation it transpires that Daniel, who is English and lived in London at the time, has only a faint idea of who Take That were. It further turns out that there is a whole area of pop culture that has passed him by, so Rob gives him a helpful recap of boy bands over the last 15 years: 'New Kids on the Block. Break. Grunge music and techno and Take That. Break. N'Sync, Backstreet Boys.' (Daniel says that he is aware of the Backstreet Boys because he cut off Howie's hair.)

'Can you remember this?' he asks Daniel, and begins singing 'Pray' to him, here at the table.

'It's a lovely moment, isn't it, between two men,' says Lee.

'Number one for four weeks,' says Rob.

'What's another one?' asks Daniel.

Rob sings 'Everything Changes'.

'Yeah, I know that one,' Daniel agrees, then Rob sings 'Could It Be Magic?' and 'Back For Good'. Only now does Daniel remember that he was actually a steward when Take That played Wembley. But he liked house music and was oblivious.

'My ego's not hurt that you don't know who Take That were,' Rob clarifies. 'I'm just flabbergasted.'

Daniel has never discussed Rob's past with him, and suddenly he seems interested.

'And then you quit?' he asks.

'Yeah,' says Rob. 'It all got too heavy, man. Things got weird. Help centres were set up all over Germany. One girl committed suicide.'

'How many fans did you have?' asks Daniel.

'Put it this way,' says Rob. 'One Valentine's Day I got 80,000 cards.'

I ask him how many he sent that year.

'None,' he says.

* * *

This has started something off. All the way into the hills, Daniel keeps asking Rob questions, and they continue when we reach the house and sit around the counter. There is something both sweet and interesting hearing Rob explain this to someone who has no angle and who knows none of it.

'I mean, not everybody knew them, right?' says Daniel, about Take That.

'No,' Rob concedes. 'You and some old people.'

'How long was the band together?' he asks.

'Five years.'

'So were you like big straight away?'

'I think we were big for like three and a half years.'

'Were you excited when you started getting popular?'

'There were certain elements of it that was exciting, yeah. See the workload was so big that we were just too tired.'

'What were these guys like in the band?' Daniel asks.

'Great, man,' says Rob.

'Dicks?' says Daniel.

'No, they weren't dicks. They were young. And we had Satan as our manager, and he was divide and conquer and he played all kinds of fucked-up mind tricks with everybody, and it caused us all to be divided.' He laughs. 'That's the official line. Barlow was a bit of a dick.'

'So when you broke up in the band, then straight away you started doing your own stuff?'

'No, I sort of … I was drinking very heavily and taking lots of drugs, and I was quite fucked up … '

'That was the peak of it?'

'Yeah, well, towards the end … I mean, all the way through it I was, the occasional little dabble, and then towards the end I was just mullered every day. And then I left and I sort of *experimented with drugs* for a year, solid. And

I went through massive litigation, because of stuff, lost all my money, and signed a new record deal, and just fannied about in London with the celeb circuit, you know, wanting friends, wanting to be cool and all that business. And after about a year – after a whole year the record company went, look, we need to put a song out. I was like, alright then. So the record company said, we want you to put "Freedom" out by George Michael and I was like, alright, if this means this'll get you off me back for a bit, I'll do it. So I released "Freedom" by George Michael.'

'Really?'

'Yeah.'

'How was it?'

'It went to number two, but it's pretty much lost in the annals of history 'cause no one ever mentions it, ever. I was all like, I want to do something different, be somebody different, be myself … and then the first thing I do is release a cover.'

'So then what?'

'Then I got sent to write songs with Desmond Child, who wrote "Living On A Prayer" and a few other things in Miami.'

'That's a guy?'

'Yeah. And it was another one of those: get off my back, I'll go. And I spent a lot of money and a fair bit of time, writing wrong songs with him.'

'Whose money?'

'Mine.'

'Really?'

'Yeah.'

'But where did you get the money from?'

'Out of my record advance.'

'Right. And then they fuck you on it.'

'Yeah. And I found one half-decent tune, called "Old Before I Die", but I sort of fell out with Desmond and fell out with the head of the record company in a certain roundabout fashion, said I wasn't going to sing the songs. You ever hear that Ricky Martin song "Private Emotion"? "*It's a priiivate emotion* … " Well, they wanted me to sing that. So then I went home and I was given this sheet of paper and it had all these writers on for me to go and work with, and I saw this name, and it was Guy Chambers, and I went, that's him. And I went to his house to write with him, and the first day we wrote this song called "Angels", which made my career. And then we wrote the whole album in a week.'

'Did you like him?'

Rob pauses. 'Yeah. I thought he was strange, but I liked his weirdness.'

'And you were still drinking then, or not?'

'Yeah, I was fat then. I was a big guy. Because of so much … cocaine worked the reverse way for me. Instead of losing weight, it made me retain liquid. Plus I was eating a phenomenal amount of pies.'

'Wow. So what happened?'

'What happened was, the album was coming out and I realised that I was a dick, and that I was going to have to go to rehab, because I couldn't promote the album looking the way I looked, and I knew I couldn't stop drinking, and I pretty much went because of vanity. Not really to stop drinking. It was like, lose a bit of weight, make yourself look good and go out and promote this album. And that was ... while the album was being mixed I was in rehab. And also they let me out for the day to shoot the video.'

'And you got sober? That was it? That was the time?'

'For a bit, yeah.'

'And you never drunk after that?'

'Oh God, no. I was only sober for like two months.'

'Oh.'

'But I walked like ten to 15 miles a day in rehab, and ate nothing, and lost all my weight, and came out looking pretty lean and good. Then the album came out, and sold 23,000 copies in three months.'

'Is that good or bad?'

'No. Really bad. So what happened was, it was just about to be jacksed and we released "Angels" and it shot off from there.'

'What else did you write apart from "Angels"? What other songs did you do? "Let Me Entertain You" ... "Rock DJ" ... '

Rob lies on his back on the kitchen counter and recites a few: '"Old Before I Die", "Lazy Days", "South Of The Border", "Angels", "Let Me Entertain You", "Millennium", "No Regrets", "She's The One", "Strong", "Rock DJ", "Let Love Be Your Energy", "Supreme", "Kids" ... '

'You wrote these with Guy?'

'Yeah.'

'And now you don't even chat to him? You think he's a dick?'

Another pause. 'It ain't as cut and dried as that. I think he lost the plot ...'

* * *

The *Daily Mail* have jumped on the gambling story – ROBBIE'S £2m HABIT – but by the next evening that is not the newspaper article that is troubling him. At about five in the afternoon Los Angeles time – one o'clock in the morning in London – we are able to read online *The Sun*'s front page for the next day: RACHEL DUMPS ROBBIE. It's a nasty story, claiming that she has ended a relationship with Rob 'because she can no longer cope with his "paranoia"'. In it they state: 'The model-turned-actress, 33, told the mega-rich singer their romance was over last night, the eve of his 29th birthday.'

The only thing that is true about this is that they no longer see much of each other, but whatever has gone on bears very little relation to *The Sun*'s story or the reasons they attribute, and none of it has just happened. He shakes his head. 'It's a made-up story,' he says. 'I feel a bit weird about the potential Mrs Williams out there reading about my state of mind, do you know what I mean?' He thinks that because he has been honest about his depression, the papers now reach for it as their ready-made explanation for whatever it is they wish to explain whenever it suits them. 'It's sort of a self-perpetuating monster that they can pick up and run with at any time,' he says.

There is something else brilliantly dishonest about this story that few people in Britain will notice.

... told the mega-rich singer their romance was over last night, the eve of his 29th birthday ...

Not even just yesterday. *Last night.*

Both Rob and Rachel are in Los Angeles. We are reading the story now and it is still the late afternoon in Los Angeles of the day *The Sun* are referring to. Amongst *The Sun*'s other transgressions, they are challenging the fundamental scientific laws of the cosmos. They are describing the events of an evening that has *not yet happened.*

7

He is in New York to do promotional interviews and, at the end of this week, the Rock The Vote concert. He is uneasy about being here and he has been feeling lonely. Down in the Mercer Hotel lobby, he lingers over a cappuccino and gets chatting to a girl. As he talks to her, her boyfriend comes over and silently winds his arm around her. It is like watching a natural history film.

A little after nine Rob gives up on the day and goes to bed. I am still chatting with Pompey downstairs when he gets a call on his mobile. It is Rob. He needs some help. He can't find the remote control for his TV.

The next morning, as we drive away down Prince Street in the van, we are aware of a slight kerfuffle on the snow-covered pavement next to us. It is Kate Winslet, being pursued and snapped by the paparazzi as she walks down the street.

'Kate!' shouts Rob, banging on the van window to get her attention. She ignores this, obviously assuming it to be further unwanted attention.

'It's Robbie!' he shouts, and she stops and then comes over to the window. It only swings open a few inches, so they speak through this small crack.

'Hello darling,' he says. 'Where are you off to?'

'I'm going home,' she says. 'I'm here for four months, making a film.'

He invites her to pop round to the Mercer for a cup of tea any time, and tells her his pseudonym.

'Tell them bollocks,' he advises her, about the paparazzi.

She nods. 'I wish they'd fucking fuck off,' she says.

We drive off. Rob sips his coffee and smiles. 'It's the gift that keeps on giving, celebrity, isn't it?' he says. 'Oooh, she's made my tizzer go foo.'

'She's sweet, isn't she?' says Josie.

'Yes,' he replies. 'Tizzer. Foo.'

'In a proper relationship though,' Josie reminds him. 'Sam Mendes.'

'Oh,' he says, face falling. 'Great.' We chat about other things for a while and then, about 20 blocks further uptown, he suddenly says, 'Sam fucking Mendes.'

* * *

'I'm thinking of coming on in a straitjacket,' Rob announces. There is a meeting in Rob's room about the summer tour to discuss where they've got to so far and to pin down some more aspects of the production. Lee says that they need to agree how Rob will enter the stage. It's clear from the way Rob presents his straitjacket idea that he is open to better ones. 'What about coming on as an astronaut?' he suggests. No one responds. He shakes his head. 'The helmet will ruin my hair,' he decides. 'I think the straitjacket is the best.'

Lee nods. 'I think the astronaut could be complicated,' he says.

'What'd be funny is,' says Rob, 'if it was a straitjacket with a hook on the end of it. And there was a big crane, and I come up with my arms behind my back in a straitjacket, and I'm winched up.' He poses as he would, with his head down. 'So, in the intro of "Let Me Entertain You", I'm eight foot up in my straitjacket. I don't know how I'd get down.'

'You'd be on a safety wire,' says Lee. 'You have to be unhooked.'

Suddenly the idea is there. It is Wob Roberts, the production manager, who first makes the vital connection.

'You can start upside down, like the album cover,' he says, 'and then you can spin as you come down so you land on your feet rather than on your head.'

It is so obvious and such a logical show opening, mimicking his album sleeve, for which he was suspended upside down off the tallest skyscraper in downtown Los Angeles, that no one has thought of it.

'Escapology!' says Rob. 'Yeah. That would be cool. I don't even have to be in my straitjacket. Yeah!'

They start wondering about practicalities.

'It's just a bit unsexy getting out of that,' says Rob.

'You'd have to wear that harness for the rest of that number,' says Wob.

'I don't need a harness now, because it will be on the feet,' says Rob.

Wob suggests Rob should be on a hip harness so that he can pivot.

No, says Rob. He wants to be suspended by his feet, as he was for the photo shoot. Also, he can't be wearing a harness during 'Let Me Entertain You'. 'It's a big harness and it'll be difficult to dance and I want to dance,' he says.

'Are you going to be alright doing that every night,' says Josie.

'Yeah,' he says. 'Because it's a great entrance, isn't it?'

'You can't do that for more than five minutes,' says David. 'Five minutes was your max.'

They debate whether he should be winched up or whether he can launch himself from the stairs just before the screen opens, but the basic idea is agreed, and Rob has already moved on.

'Are there definite no-nos and definite things that you're thinking about song-wise?' asks Lee.

'Just think "singles" and you'll be right ... apart from "Eternity",' he says. 'I don't have to sing "Eternity" ever again. Unless it's to save someone I love from death. Or some sheik offers me a million quid.'

He reels off a long list of the songs he'd like to sing.

'"She's The One"?' suggests David.

'No, fuck off,' says Rob. He has disliked singing "She's The One" since its composer, World Party's Karl Wallinger, slagged off his version. 'Oh yeah, and what I want to cover is "99 Red Balloons" in Germany.' He bumped into Nena at an awards ceremony in Germany last week and asked her to sing her big hit with him this summer in Gelsenkirchen.

He kind of winces. 'I should put "She's The One" in,' he says. 'It was fucking huge for me, wasn't it?' He has a novel idea as to a way he can perform the song that might make it bearable. 'I should sing it with feeling,' he suggests.

* * *

He loses interest in the tour meeting after a while, lying on his stomach on his bed while the meeting continues across the room, reading about himself on his computer. I have made what may turn out to be a big mistake by showing him how, if you type the words 'Robbie Williams' into Google's news search engine, you can find nearly every recent English language news article that mentions him, worldwide. He is reading an Australian newspaper that says Rachel found someone else's knickers in his bed. 'We can sue for that, right?' he asks.

He finds other mentions of his name. A betting site is offering odds of 4/5 of him being named Best Male at the Brit awards. He is the favourite, but these are rather long odds considering he has already filmed his acceptance speech; he resists the temptation. He stumbles upon a reference to being voted Villain Of The Year in the *NME* readers' poll. Osama Bin Laden has come second. 'I've won it before, so I'm pretty blasé about it,' he says in an award-accepting voice. 'The first time I was really over the moon.' I note that competition must have been tougher this year, with Osama on the scene. 'Yeah,' he says, 'but when there's talent around like me, when there's *evil* around like me, there's just no competition.' Pause. 'And he's made a massive mistake by not releasing a ballad.'

He's stopped making videos too, I point out.

'Yeah,' says Rob. 'He thinks he's George Michael or someone'.

* * *

He does an interview with *Spin* magazine. Rob's suspicions are raised at the start when the interviewer, Chuck Klosterman, asks whether it is weird that since his record deal, money is now the crux of every interview he gives, and tells Rob that *Spin* certainly became interested partially for that reason. Rob responds, honestly, that apart from a couple of questions at press conferences he has barely been asked about it.

'Really?' says the interviewer sceptically.

They seem to have not just a clash of personalities and cultures, but a very different sense of who Robbie Williams is. As Rob *is* Robbie Williams (or as close as anyone gets) but knows that this other person will be writing an article, the situation gets increasingly uncomfortable. He faces a series of questions about whether he is a serious artist, the kind of thing that may be of interest to parts of the American culture industry, but is of no interest whatsoever to Rob. 'It's like,' Rob finally explains, increasingly exasperated, 'I don't take the *White Album* seriously. I fucking love it with a passion, but what's *serious* about it? The word "serious" – what is serious about the *White Album*? The emotions on it really touch me, the lyrics are amazing. But if they said Osama Bin Laden's on a plane now and he's going to crash into another building in New York, I'm going to treat *that* seriously. The *White Album*, I'm going to *listen* to. And then when I've stopped listening to it, I'm probably going to have a piss. Or go and eat some food, do you know what I mean?'

But Rob is far from sure that the interviewer does.

It is only after Rob has discussed all this, and much else, and is in a slightly defensive and angry mood, that he is asked his feelings about breaking America, and whether he thinks it will ever happen. Nothing he has said so far will be directly quoted in the finished article, but most of the following answer will, and it will echo far.

'I don't think it will, no,' he begins, honestly. Such honesty might be seen as slightly eccentric and wilful in an English interview; in America, a culture less tolerant of ambivalence about success and achievement, it is more likely to appear insanely counterproductive and almost insulting, as though it invites the response: *why are we wasting our time on your dream when you don't even believe in it yourself?* As Rob continues, he more or less pre-empts that reaction. 'Um ... and I don't know where I sit on it, to tell you the truth,' he says. 'I don't want it badly enough, which sort of defeats the object of our interview today, you know – I'm sat here saying I don't want it badly enough and I'm doing an interview. "So why are you doing an interview?" I don't know. I keep turning up. People put things in for me and I turn up and I do them, but I've been blowing hot and cold about it for the last eight months. I mean, basically my ego goes … ' – he whispers as though to himself – ' … "Break the States, break the States, go and do it, go and do it", and the fellow that wants to raise kids and have some of normality goes, "What are you fucking doing, you idiot? Why are you doing this over here? No one knows who you are. It's great. You love it." But the ego goes, "Break the States break the States break the States." Or try and break the States. But to tell you the absolute truth, it's not going to happen here for me.'

The aspect of this that perplexes the interviewer is the one Rob isn't even thinking of: the money. It turns out, once more, that he is someone convinced that Rob's new record contract must represent an outrageous gamble on EMI's behalf which can only pay off if he breaks America. Rob tries to explain it to him, in some detail, but he sounds sceptical. 'You've got to do some simple math, that's all I can say,' Rob finally tells him. He still doesn't get it, or anyway believe it, so Rob goes over it again. 'All that money there,' he explains, 'is about me never breaking America.'

But surely, Klosterman argues, it is predicated on …

'Absolutely not at all,' interrupts Rob. 'You know, now let's look at the track record. If EMI were giving me that much money because I was going to break America they'd be fucking stupid, because the track record says I'm not going to. And the track record says that really every other British act hasn't. So why the fuck would they do that?'

Some very rough maths might be useful and appropriate here. It is reasonable to assume that a record company could receive between £4 and £5 net on each copy of a current release. (This is before paying out any royalties, which they don't need to while an advance is being recouped, and taking into account their non-recoupable marketing and costs on one hand, but also the profits they may silently make through their share of production and distribution revenue on the other.)

Based on that, if his deal were as widely reported, for EMI to break even they might have to sell fewer than 20 million albums over its term. *Escapology* has already sold over 6 million copies outside America, as did the last album to pre-date this deal, *Swing When You're Winning*. So unless there is a severe collapse in his sales outside America – the only real risk to which EMI are exposing themselves – the deal seems a perfectly good one, without selling a single record in America. (This very rough analysis excludes EMI's share in his other income streams that, even just from this year's touring, stand to be substantial, though it also excludes the substantial cost of advancing the large cash advance Rob received.)

Towards the end of the interview, despairing at any of this being understood, Rob simply repeats and amplifies his prediction.

'I think what will probably happen is,' he says, 'I might sell 500,000 records here, with a bit of luck and a following wind. But it's not going to happen for me here because I'm not prepared to put the work in. I don't want it that badly.'

* * *

'That's not going to be a good piece, David,' says Rob afterwards, and he explains that all the questions seemed to be about money and whether he was or wasn't serious. He doesn't mention that he has predicted his imminent failure in America, but down at band rehearsals he mutters quietly to me, 'I'm about ready to jack it in.'

Jack what in? I ask.

'America,' he says. 'I really am.'

* * *

He invites round a model he met in the foyer last night to watch the latest Michael Jackson documentary in his room, and then we all head out to see a performance by Fil Eisler, Rob's old guitarist, who is playing at a nearby club. In the cab, Rob, the model and myself have a strange conversation about what the word 'demure' really means, and whether it could ever be applied to Rob.

The Living Room is uncomfortably crowded. When we arrive, another act is still playing; the singer is wearing an I'm In A Promising Local Band T-shirt. Fil soon replaces him, and by the end Rob is heckling and he is answering, and Rob is loudly singing along with the songs he knows. 'My Fuck You To You', for instance. Afterwards there's quite a bit of hugging.

'I got emotional in a little bit of that,' says Rob outside. He says there's about four of those songs he'd like to cover.

On the way back to the hotel, he and the model hold hands and compare nails.

'Mine are shit,' he says.

It's a nice night. The thing he likes most about her is that she quotes Steven Wright to him: 'You know that feeling that you get when you're on a chair and you're rocking and it's about to fall over – I feel like that the entire time.' When he comes down to the lobby the next morning, he hears about the Brit awards. The big news is the duet, and accompanying dirty dancing, Justin Timberlake did with his replacement partner, Kylie Minogue. *The Sun* has a cartoon of Justin grabbing Kylie's bum. The word balloon from her mouth says, 'I wish it was Robbie'; the word balloon from his mouth says, 'Yeah, I wish it was too'.

He tells his father, who is here for the week, that he noticed in the bathroom mirror how much grey hair he now has. 'Can you remember that perm I had when I came up to Scarborough?' he asks.

'Yes,' laughs Pete. 'It never moved, did it?'

'And I never washed it,' Rob says. 'It must have stank.'

'How old were you?' asks Josie.

'Fourteen,' he says. 'I had it permed for when we broke up for school holidays, and at the beginning of the next term I was the first one called into the headmaster's office and sent home.'

'Did you go the whole summer holiday?' asks Josie.

'Mmmm,' says Rob.

'Great, wasn't it?' says Pete. 'Four or five weeks.'

'Great Yarmouth was my favourite,' says Rob. 'Remember that night when I wouldn't come out of the dressing room because that girl was after me because I'd got off with someone else? Then she slapped me. She *slapped* me! I felt like James Bond.'

8

This week is Grammy week in New York. The Grammys are the American music industry's equivalent of the Oscars; Rock The Vote is just one of the events occurring in its shadow. This morning Rob is taken to Madison Square Garden where, on either side of one of the walkways outside the arena, tables are lined up, and on the far side of each table is a DJ from one of the most important local radio stations in America, one after another, just a few feet apart. Dozens of artists will be tugged and cajoled from table to table today; an endless babble of pop and promotion.

Rob's first station is Kiss 95 from Charlotte, and his first question is about breaking America.

'I always think that I'm a charlatan and I'm going to get found out,' he explains. 'Perhaps they just *know* in America.'

Each interview lasts maybe four minutes, and then he is dragged – always in a rush – to the next. 'We're going to San Francisco!' he will be told, as though he is actually on his way to a new city, and he will criss-cross the room, passing Art Garfunkel or George Clinton as they are dragged to some other city, each of them giants in seven-league boots striding over America, who will within seconds be in, or at least over the airwaves of, their latest destination.

In San Francisco, Rob is challenged to 'impress us with a piece of trivia'.

'My penis is not very long, but it's got amazing girth,' he says.

They applaud. 'Robbie Williams!' shouts the DJ. 'Hung like a tree stump!'

'Baby's arm,' corrects Rob.

He bumps into John Mayer on the carpet highway between cities, and tells him he'd love for them to work together. John Mayer seems keen.

'We'll get people to talk to people,' Rob promises.

As he goes round, people make comments to him that are meant to be encouraging but only emphasise how difficult it can be to conquer the American radio waves. DJs tell him that they love 'Feel', for instance, and that they hope soon their station will be able to play it, as though the actual mysterious process by which a record gets played is so much bigger than anybody's taste or enthusiasm.

A few stations later he finds himself at Tampa Star 95.7, live on the Florida airwaves.

'Do you know Michael Jackson's coming there today?' Rob says earnestly.

'To Tampa?' the DJ says. She has no idea where this is heading, or that it is anything other than hot celebrity information.

'Yeah. He's going on holiday. He's coming to Tampa with the kids,' says Rob.

She hasn't a clue what he has just said, though some of her listeners must certainly realise.

'So you talk to Michael Jackson?' she asks keenly.

* * *

There are great difficulties in conveying Rob's speech accurately on the written page because he will often slip from irony to sincerity – just as he will onstage – in the same sentence and then back again. Frequently he will, without drawing any attention to it or offering any kind of signposts to the listener, slide through a range of voices – most commonly his Alan Partridge voice for anything particularly pompous or idiotic or pretentious, or anything that needs protection from being accused as such, though there are plenty of others in his repertoire. He will sometimes do this while talking to someone young and British who might be expected to spot the reference and understand how to interpret it, but he will also do the same thing, without explanation, in the middle of a Japanese interview. I think these are all ways of indicating what he means and what he doesn't mean, and often of acknowledging the defeat he feels already over his chance of being understood. They are also simply ways of stopping himself feeling bored. He has a very short attention span, and I think that sometimes he just finds himself saying a sentence and is too bored to get all the way through it without twisting it or diverting it or somehow offering another perspective on it. In effect, talking with Rob, you often get the film and the director's commentary at the same time.

* * *

At the Roseland ballroom, he soundchecks with the band, messily running through 'Get A Little High'. ('Get A Little High' has been added to the American version of *Escapology*, along with 'One Fine Day', and is earmarked as a potential single here. 'Song 3', 'Hot Fudge' and 'I Tried Love' have consequently been edged off – the first two of these, ironically, are the songs highlighted by the British critics as those calculated to pander to America.) In the middle of a verse he climbs down off the stage to greet someone from one of the other bands on the bill whom he has spotted standing halfway back on the empty floor, watching him.

'I grew up listening to you,' Rob says. '*Really*. Really. I just thought I'd come to say hi.'

'It's a pleasure,' says Public Enemy's Professor Griff.

'No,' says Rob, trying to convey that he is not just exchanging insincere intra-celebrity flattery and that he means rather more than that he used to own a couple of Public Enemy CDs. 'It's a real pleasure,' he emphasises, and tries to explain that Public Enemy were almost a mythical group to him in his teenage years. He says how much he also like Professor Griff's solo album, *Pawn In The Game*, but the only impression he gets back from Professor Griff is that this is a very weird thing to have said. He jumps back on stage and runs through the set. Professor Griff nods his head along to the swirl of rap cacophony at the end of 'Millennium', then starts doing press-ups on the floor.

I have a hunch that there's a song Rob might be less keen on performing in front of one of Public Enemy. Perhaps I am right, because as the band launch into the beginning of 'Rock DJ', Rob jumps off the front of the stage and strides out towards the waiting van.

Back at the hotel he watches a stand-up comedian on Comedy Central. 'You should see me live,' the comedian says to the audience. 'I'm amazing.'

He returns in the same van a couple of hours before he is due onstage. On the way, Shelby, his American press agent, explains that people may ask political questions as he walks down the red carpet, and briefs him about Rock The Vote. 'They raise money to get kids out to vote,' she explains. 'Teens, to make a difference and make their voice count.'

'OK,' says Rob. 'But do you think it's important that people should get out there and vote?'

'Yes,' says Shelby.

'Yeah,' mutters Jason in the front seat. 'Vote for asshole number one or asshole number two.' Jason is the third of his three regular bodyguards; a Canadian ex-kick boxing champion.

'Your voice makes a difference,' Shelby argues.

'Well,' Rob points out, 'I'm not really bothered. I have never voted. See, that's my reality ... '

Shelby laughs nervously. This is perhaps not a debate she expected to have, and certainly not five minutes away from the venue.

'My reality is,' Rob continues, 'it only encourages them.' He considers. 'I could lie,' he suggests. In the end, it is not Shelby's words that he takes on board as wisdom, but Jason's. 'Yeah, that's it,' he says. 'It's really important: vote for asshole number one or asshole number two. And why it is important is because he's *your* asshole. There you go. That's the answer. I always thought, actually, that you shouldn't do because it only encourages them, but that's an ignorant viewpoint to have. I actually realise that I should vote at some point. And I will. But not just yet. When I find one I like. When I find an asshole that I like.'

'A likeable asshole,' suggests his father.

'A clean asshole,' says Rob. 'An asshole that's clean.'

* * *

The first ugly moment of the evening occurs before we're even out of the van. As we try to pull up outside the Roseland ballroom, a policeman waves the van on, precisely so he can keep clear the space intended for our van. The driver tries to explain, but the cop hollers over and over, repeatedly demanding that the driver move on, and won't listen to a word that the driver says. When the driver doesn't comply, he demands the driver's registration and says he's going to book him. Only Pompey, swiftly jumping out the passenger side and intervening with huge politeness, manages to calm the situation.

Rob walks down the carpet, doing brief interviews.

'It's one of those things where I've got to win people over,' he tells one camera. 'It's full of people that don't know who I am. And I'm quite scared.'

At the end of the line is *Liquid News*.

'Robbie, come and say hello to *Liquid News*, we've got Robbie Williams with us … '

'Is that England?' he says.

'Yes, it is,' she says, brightly.

Liquid News is a pop and celebrity gossip show on BBC's new cable channel. Their attitude, not miles away from *Heat* magazine's, could roughly be summed up as: *We're in the know and we know as well as the celebrities do how silly their lives are.*

'Your programme's shit,' he says. 'Quite frankly, I've watched it, and every celebrity bar none's a wanker, according to you. And personally I find it insulting.' He says some more, then abruptly states 'That's enough', and walks inside.

For about ten minutes he is pleased at having spoken his mind to *Liquid News*, but then regret seeps in.

'I wish I hadn't of said it,' he says, sitting in the dressing room. 'It's what I felt … but I shouldn't have said anything at all.'

Rob is led into a tent where Iann Robinson from MTV is conducting interviews.

'So what brings you to something like this tonight?' he is asked.

'My record company and my management. To be really honest with you.'

'Really? That's it?'

'Yeah.'

'Wow.'

'Yeah. They said it was a good thing to do. I went, "Alright then".'

He later says that he can't believe the question that follows, but he answers it without breaking his stride.

'Well,' says Iann Robinson, 'with a whole world kind of waiting to see whether or not a war breaks out, do you personally think you're going to be more active ... ?'

'Um, I don't know what's going to happen, to tell you the absolute. I'm really worried ... it just looks so up in the air. To me ... smoking gun, haven't seen one. And then the UN are going ... ' – his answer is turning strange – ' ... and America and England and Bush are going "Yes yes yes yes yes" and everywhere else is going "No no no no no" ... '

He is, unbelievably, talking to MTV news about the prospects of war in the style and tone of voice of an Eddie Izzard monologue.

' ... so I'm just really confused.'

He fields questions about Public Enemy and Peter Gabriel (who is here to accept an award), and then the interviewer asks him about the fire that has just happened at a Rhode Island club – the eventual death toll will be 100 – and whether he has ever personally felt he or a club or an audience was unsafe.

'No,' he says. 'The only danger I get is if people get too close, and I like that danger. Normally I'm a bit "Abracadabra, I want to reach out and grab you ... ".' He realises that he may not be hitting the appropriate tone. 'But this is a serious question. I saw the videotape. It's horrible, and it should never have happened ... '

'Now who do you think has got more to answer for in a situation like that?' the VJ persists. 'The artists who are performing or the club?'

'I don't know,' says Rob. 'God, probably.'

Iann Robinson turns to the camera.

'Well,' he says, 'you heard it here first ... '

* * *

Back in the dressing room, Josie lays out his dinner.

'Josie, I'm not going to be able to eat,' he says. 'I hate being here. I really do.' He says he's nervous and simply can't bear the thought of playing to a crowd who don't know his songs.

He is summoned to have his photo taken with some of the other people here tonight. Peter Gabriel greets him warmly. They share the same birthday. He shakes Lou Reed's hand and says, 'Pleased to meet you.' ('From the look in his eyes,' Rob reports, 'he was a bit, who are you? Or it could have been, what are you?') Alanis Morissette looks slightly bemused and shakes his hand with both of hers. Then he finally meets Chuck D. 'Robbie,' he says. 'Follow you around, man. I read about you everywhere.'

'I'm always misbehaving,' says Rob.

'You're here, ain't you?' says Chuck D.

They pose, from left to right: Lou Reed, Rob, Alanis Morissette and Peter Gabriel.

'I can imagine the *NME* having a field day with a photo of Lou Reed and me,' he says, back in the dressing room, and muses on Alanis Morissette's reaction. 'She had that look in her eyes of "completely no interest in you, whoever you are",' he says. 'Maybe I've said something.' Then it strikes him how often he used to go on in interviews about all the things in her most famous song that aren't ironic, and wonders whether that is it. 'I would have quite willingly got into a conversation with her about it,' he says. 'I mean, "a black fly in a Chardonnay" isn't ironic. It's a dead fly.'

I point out that I think it's because it's *white* wine ... *black* fly.

He thinks for a moment. 'I'm wrong,' he shrugs.

He meets Peter Gabriel's daughter in the hallway and mentions the shared birthday with her father. 'Is he incredibly complex and insecure?' he asks her.

'Yeah,' she says.

'Oh good. I'm glad it's not just me.'

A few minutes ago he was told that Public Enemy were planning to invite him onstage to perform with them, and he was momentarily excited. Now their tour manager comes round and says it can be on 'Motherfucking President' or 'Shut 'Em Down'.

'"Shut 'Em Down" then,' he says. 'It would be an honour.' But as soon as the tour manager goes, he says that those are two recent songs he doesn't really know. It's their early, most famous albums he knows by heart. 'I'm not going to do it anyway,' he says. 'I'm going straight off.' He already wants to be out of here, and once his work is done even Public Enemy won't delay him.

He goes into his band's dressing room, and there is a worried conversation amongst his management in his absence. This event is not as they had been promised it would be; they feel misled, and are quietly furious to have been put in this position. Not only does the crowd seem to be almost entirely a record industry one – never the easiest audience – but the ballroom is far from full.

'I'm scared,' he repeats, matter-of-factly.

In the corridor, he passes Vanessa Carlton, fresh from the stage.

'How was the audience?' he asks her.

'They were just talking,' she says.

'Oh, *great*,' he says.

'But they'll listen to you,' she says. 'I'm just a girl on a piano, you know.'

Round the back of the stage Wayne Coyne comes up. He is holding a plate of food. Rob says something complimentary to him about the Flaming Lips show, which he saw a little of from the balcony.

'We throw balloons to the crowd,' Wayne says.

'I know,' says Rob.

'Never throw anything they can throw back,' Wayne advises. 'A balloon comes back, it doesn't matter ... '

'I used to throw insults,' says Rob, 'but they used to throw them back ... '

At the end of the conversation, Wayne holds out his hand, balancing the plate with the other. 'Well, it's nice to meet you. I'm Wayne from the Flaming Lips.'

* * *

When he comes on to the stage, there is a little fevered excitement at the front, but only in modest amounts. Halfway back on the floor, where I'm standing, it's more like one of those movie scenes of a high school dance, when all but the desperate have gone home. There's a raised area at the side, where Peter Gabriel sits, nodding encouragingly, and a balcony all the way round lined by people oozing an attitude of 'OK, British hotshot, whoever you are, impress me if you can'. The other weird touch is provided by the service table about halfway down the floor on the side, from which thick, crumbly cookies are handed out, with a napkin half folded around them, as though at a village fête.

Rob frantically bounds around the stage for most of 'Let Me Entertain You' and then, towards its end, in the instrumental section, he halts. He stands upright, his arms folded, his body stock still, and slowly looks around the room, surveying defiantly. Then he shoots back into motion, sprays the front rows with water and, as the song ends, starts chatting madly. After a few manic non-sequiturs he says,'Thank you – it's really important that I come over to America every now and again just to do a show for my fan.' He is babbling, a touch of let's-win-them-over, a dab of hostility and plenty of I-wish-I-was-somewhere-else. Before the first chorus of the second song, 'Let Love Be Your Energy', he is simulating full-thrusting sex with the microphone stand. He introduces the third, 'Monsoon', by saying, 'This song is off my new album. It's called *Escapology*. And, funnily enough, it's going to be in the shops on April 1st. So *that* bodes well.' Before the fourth, 'Millennium': 'This next single was another non-massive hit for me here in America.' When he reaches the ' ... *so corporate suit* ... ' and ' ... *so damn ugly* ... ' lines in 'Come Undone' he points to the balcony. He drops 'Get A Little High' from the set. The last song is 'Angels'. By now five people in the balcony are holding candles and waving them along. The cheering has got louder with each song, and most people here probably consider it to have been a modest triumph. As he sings 'Angels', he offers a spoken commentary between the lyrics: ' ... *do they know the place where we go when we're grey and old* ... this should have been a hit here ... *cause I've been told that salvation lets their wings unfold* ... you should have seen me live – I'm amazing ... '

Backstage, Tim and David offer him their apologies.

'Hard work,' he mutters. 'I don't work right unless they're playing with me. And as it goes, it was an industry gig, it was very cold out there, but I did alright. I did the best I could without their help.'

'I almost died,' says Tim.
'Never again,' says David.
He is quickly into the van.
'That was painless, Rob,' says his father.
'Oooh, it wasn't,' he says.

* * *

The next evening he watches the Grammys on TV, only half paying attention. He was invited to the ceremony, but never even considered going. In one of the commercial breaks he says, 'It'd be great if we released a DVD of the Knebworth and called it *You Know What I Did Last Summer*.'

He has agreed, under considerable pressure, to attend the EMI post-Grammy party in Times Square. Arriving, he spots the *Liquid News* crew lined up behind the barrier and walks straight up to them.

'Hello, darling,' he says.

'Are you being sweet to me tonight?' she asks. 'Do you reckon you'll be here next year?'

'Do I reckon I'll be here next year? No, I don't think so. No ... '

'No? I have to say, last night was pretty impressive ... '

'What? My show?'

'Yeah. Did you notice, the crowd, they weren't really paying attention – by the end everyone was up front. Were you surprised by the reaction?'

'I thought it was the worst audience I have ever had.'

'Did you? Why?'

'I normally preach to the converted and last night was ... that's why I was so angry when I was coming in, because I was shitting myself ... ' – she laughs – ' ... and you got the brunt of my anger, so I apologise for being rude.'

'That's very, very sweet,' she says. She asks him a few questions about the Grammys and the Brits.

'You're just here for the piss-up, aren't you?' she says, about this party.

'No, I'm here because of the EMI thing,' he says, 'and they paid a lot of money for me, and I've got to shake hands or else I'd be in bed.'

'OK. At least you're honest. Have a good time. Thanks a lot.'

'I'm sorry about last night.'

'You're sweet.'

'I was really angry,' he says, and hugs and kisses her.

Another camera crew traps him: 'What are you doing to de-stress after the event?'

'I haven't been to the event,' he says. 'This is the event that I'm at.'

'After tonight?'

'I'll probably have a wank.'

They don't ask him any more questions.

The party is unpleasantly crowded. Waiters walk round offering sushi and coloured vitamin water. He lasts 25 minutes. Back in the foyer of the Mercer there are celebrities all over the place, but the atmosphere is strangely calm and nice. It's when celebrities are surrounded by people who want to be near celebrities, and who want to get ever nearer, that things get frantic. Here, where most people are already famous, and everybody is near the end of a long night, the mood is relaxed. No one is standing on ceremony; it's like the warm, friendly room you burst into out of the storm.

He chats to Lucy Liu, then bumps into Linda Perry. He asks whether they will write together and she says he's supposed to tell her that. '*You're* supposed to want *me*,' she says.

'Well,' he considers, 'I really fucking want you.'

'You're supposed to *call* me,' she explains, 'and tell me how much you like me and that you want to work with me.'

He nods. 'I'll call you and tell you.'

He gets a number off Gina Gershon as her boyfriend loiters, then chats to Mike Myers. Kylie comes to say goodbye.

'I'm over today,' he tells her.

'Today is actually over,' Kylie corrects him. 'It's tomorrow.'

'I've had enough of tomorrow too,' he says. 'Which is a bummer, because I've got to wake up in it.'

Justin Timberlake says a brief hello before disappearing, and he chats with Drew Barrymore and Fabrizio from The Strokes, and then with a woman he saw last night. (The model is gone. He was less keen on her after the second meeting, and has been evading her calls.)

'I've got such bad cottonmouth,' he says.

'Karma?' she says, mishearing.

'Cottonmouth,' he says.

'Oh,' she says. 'I thought you said karma.'

'That too,' he sighs.

* * *

A few minutes before one o'clock the next day, Rob reappears in the foyer and orders some breakfast: Shredded Wheat and All-bran. A few minutes later Cameron Diaz comes by.

'Thanks for the DVD,' she tells him. (She means the Royal Albert Hall DVD, which he had sent to her a year ago; the one that includes 'I Will Talk, Hollywood Will Listen'.) 'It's in that stack next to my bed. You know … that stack.'

He nods. 'That's where I keep all of my self-help books,' he says.

She pushes her bare stomach out under her short top, trying to look fat. She says she's just off to do an *FHM* photo shoot with the other two Charlie's Angels. 'What poses do you want to see?' she asks.

'It's good when you point at things,' says Rob, dryly.

'Is the labia majora really sexy?' she asks.

'I prefer the steak,' he replies.

With that, she goes out for a quick bit of shopping before the shoot. Rob's pleased with how this encounter has gone. 'I said something really funny,' he says. He greets Gwen Stefani, then sinks back into the sofa. 'How cute was Cameron?' he sighs.

'Which one's that?' says his father.

'That girl,' he says. 'That was Cameron Diaz.'

'Who's that?' says Pete.

'She commands over $20 million a movie,' says Rob.

'"*Cameron Diaz, give me a sign …* "' quotes Pompey.

'"I Will Talk … "' says Rob.

'Oh!' says Pete. 'That's her? I thought Cameron Diaz was a fellow who worked with Steven Spielberg.'

It is one of those days. Next Mike Myers comes by and joins us for a bit. He chats with Pete for a while, and asks where in England he is from, then says, 'I'm going to walk around. I like it here in SoHo because it reminds me of London. Los Angeles has no … *destinations.*'

'That's because you live on Crenshaw,' says Rob.

Mike Myers shrugs comedically, follows the fiction. 'I just do what the real estate lady tells me,' he says.

There is a certain familiarity to the conversation between Rob and Pete once Mike Myers has left for his walk. Rob mentions Mike Myers and his father asks who that is.

'Austin Powers,' says Rob.

'I've heard of him,' Pete says, still uncertain.

'Mike Myers!' Rob exclaims, though he obviously also loves how immune and removed his father is from all this. 'He's the most successful comedian in the world!'

'Wow,' says Pete. 'Good for him.' He says this in the way you might say it about a child who has just picked up a handful of conkers. 'I was the most successful comedian Stoke-on-Trent has ever had,' he says.

Tim comes over and tells Rob that the *News Of The World* have already made an offer of damages over the gambling story. It's inappropriately small and has been rejected, but it is a good start.

In a quiet moment I ask Rob how he is feeling about his great American adventure.

'I've found the last few days a bit mentally exhausting, emotionally exhausting,' he says. 'I don't know. It's the most uncomfortable I've felt working. It made me question why I was doing what I was doing again.'

The whole thing?

'Yeah. Yeah. But I knew that wasn't serious. I noted that as, oooh yeah, this is how you used to think. Just because I didn't enjoy it. Anything about it. But what I'm really pleased about is the fact that I didn't go, right, fuck

America. Do you know what I mean? It's like, well, I've done that bit, let's see what happens next.'

* * *

A few days later, there is an article in the *New York Times*, on the front page of the Business section: *Struggling EMI Pins U.S. Hopes On Over-the-Top British Singer*. In the article, after quoting EMI America's chairman and CEO David Munns' upbeat assessment of Rob's chances, the writer, Lynette Holloway, states: *He said he planned to ship four million copies of the album in the United States.*

Were this true, this would be extraordinary for an artist whose best-selling American CD, *The Ego Has Landed* (a compilation drawing from his first two British releases), has sold a little over half a million copies. It seems very unlikely that David Munns would even have projected such a sale, but if she literally means 'ship' – sending actual copies of the record to the shops – it could not be true, as anyone with any grasp of record business economics would know. CDs can be manufactured quickly and very few of even the biggest stars have ever sold two million copies in a month in America, let alone someone who is not yet established here. It conjures the image that, however many copies short of four million he does sell, the balance will be sloshing around in American warehouses, a cruel reminder of his relative failure.

Afterwards, the *New York Times* has to print a retraction, but it is too late: the original item will appear elsewhere time and time again as fact.

* * *

Rob watches Daniel Day-Lewis being interviewed on *BBC World*. 'I like him,' Rob says. 'How old was he when he decided to go on that five-year thing ... ?'

He is referring to Day-Lewis's unannounced five-year retirement, a retirement that ended only when he reappeared to act in *Gangs Of New York*. Some cogs are turning, and it is still not clear where they will stop.

9

One Friday in March, after midnight, Rob, Max, Jonny and Jonny's fiancée Nikki Wheeler go the Shamrock tattoo parlour on Sunset Boulevard to get tattoos. (After Max calls his father for his blessing, he decides against it.) Rob gets three. First he tells the tattooist that he wants 'Bertha' on his hand, in commemoration of his grandmother. The tattooist is sketching it when Rob remembers that she always hated her name. He can hear her voice saying to him: 'Well, if you've got to have it, don't have "Bertha", just have "B".' So he has a cursive 'B' tattooed behind his left ear.

His second tattoo is the numbers 1023 on the outside of his left wrist; a private testament to his friendship with Jonny. J and W are the tenth and twenty-third letters in the alphabet. (Jonny has the appropriate matching tattoo, 1823, hidden more discreetly on his body.)

The third, the largest, he asks to have on his neck. He has chosen the French phrase CHACUN À SON GOÛT – 'Each to his own' – that caught his attention as one of a list of French phrases in the book *Schott's Original Miscellany*. The tattooist argues that there are too many letters to fit on his neck, so Rob tells him to put it an arc across the top of his chest. The 'C' hurts plenty, but after that it is fine. He breaks half way, between the 'À' and the 'S', for a cigarette.

He considers having a fourth – the phrase 'It's your birthday' just above his penis – but thinks better of it, for now.

* * *

A while back he agreed that a song from his swing album, his version of 'Beyond The Sea', could be used as the theme song of a forthcoming Pixar movie called *Finding Nemo*. He has thought little about it since, but tonight he is invited to see a rough version of the nearly completed film, so about eight of us go to a screening set up on the Disney lot just for him.

At the Disney gate, Rob explains why we are here.

'Can I see your ID?' asks the guard.

'I don't have ID,' says Rob.

'Oh,' says the guard. He considers this. 'Well, seeing as you know about it, it must be you,' he reasons.

The screening room is just past a wooden sign announcing 'Pooh and Piglet corner'. At times the sea and the fish will unexpectedly reduce to moving grids of lines approximating their shape, but we're all completely sucked in by the film, though perhaps none of us quite realise what a big deal it will become.

'They're the best movies,' says Rob as the light comes on.

'I cried,' says a woman from Disney who has let us in here. 'Did you cry?'

'Yeah,' says Rob. 'Well, I'm on medication so that stuff's not going to affect me these days.'

* * *

A tour of American radio stations is upon him. Though sometimes it seems as though nobody really knows the most effective path to an American hit record, it is widely believed that you are unlikely to succeed here without intensively wooing regional radio stations in a way that has no parallel anywhere else in the world. It is something that even the biggest stars, if they are ambitious, cannot avoid.

To lessen the strain, his record company have agreed to provide a private jet, so for the first few days he can commute back and forth from Los Angeles. He still has to be up at six in the morning on the first day, and he is tired.

In the van to the airfield, Rob announces that he has an idea for the summer tour. 'It's not a big 'un,' he says. 'They never are.' It is a new elaboration on how to perform the troublesome 'She's The One'. He describes what he intends to do: 'Go offstage for a little bit, and I say from the side, "The next song I'm singing is going to be a beautiful song called 'She's The One' – thank you – now, when I've introduced this song before I've always said something bad about Karl Wallinger ... but I have no animosity and I'm going to sing the song the way Karl would want me to sing it." And I come on in one of those ostrich suits.' Legs flopping off to one side.

He also explains how he has been thinking of ways to embarrass Max when Max plays piano during the swing section, mostly through rude innuendo to do with The Spice Girls. (Until quite recently, Max went out with Melanie Brown, Scary Spice.) 'Ah!' he sighs contentedly. 'The lowest common denominator every time. Sex, smut and swearing ... ' He raises his eyebrows. '*Sex, Smut and Swearing* – good name for the book.'

We have been on the private jet about 20 minutes when Rob yawns, stretches and asks of the cabin, 'Where are we going?'

'San Francisco,' says Josie.

Driving into town – 'Do you know,' he says, 'by the time they've finished painting the Golden Gate bridge ... they're fucking knackered?' – Rob mentions that San Francisco is the town where that author lives who has about 20 parking spaces, in a city with few, because her house is so big. But he can't tell me who he means. He can't think of her name.

It's bad, I say, when you're more famous for your parking spaces than your books.

'Yeah,' he says, but indicates himself. 'Wrong demographic. I'm more interested in the parking space story than the books.'

The radio show is called *The Alice Lounge*. As soon as he is in the studio, he goes into flirtation autopilot.

'Aggy, be honest,' he says to one of the DJs, 'was the cleavage just for me today?'

She pauses. 'I can't say I did, sweetie,' she says. 'I dress like a hoochie all the time.'

On air, he lets them snip a little of his hair for a competition and they ask him when he last had sex with someone else.

'Two weeks ago,' he says.

'Last self love?' they ask.

'Not last night, the night before,' he says.

They inquire about his tattoos, so he takes his shirt off and gives them a guided tour. They ask whether they can have some chest hair to add to the collection.

'Take some nipple hair,' he suggests.

'You've got very inviting underarm hair as well,' the female DJ says, moving in with her scissors.

'Take some of that as well,' he invites.

'You smell of butterscotch,' she remarks.

The male DJ chats on and mentions that Rob is not yet quite as successful in America as elsewhere in the world.

'You don't have to sugarcoat it,' says Rob. 'No one knows who I am. That's OK. That's why I'm letting you take my hair, and I'm telling you my personal problems ... '

He steps next door and sings four songs acoustically with Gary, Neil, Claire and Chris. The contrast between the daft playful pointlessness of what has just happened and the way he can suddenly sing these songs seems absurd, though there are still moments when the two sides he is showing the people of San Francisco today come together. In 'Angels' he changes the chorus from '*I'm loving angels instead*' to '*this should have been a huge hit*', and in the instrumental section before its final crescendo, he starts talking, filling in some of the details: 'Yes, ladies and gentlemen, "Angels" was a song released in America about four years ago when I was on Capitol records – a huge hit everywhere else, but somehow they managed to really balls it up ... yeah! ... I should just let it go now but I can't seem to ... but I don't understand why this wasn't a hit here ... OK, let's do the chorus and get out ... '

Afterwards, he goes straight to a San Francisco hotel to sleep for a few hours and then the jet takes us to Sacramento. At the radio station, he glad-hands the people who work there and records some IDs. They ask him to sign a life-size cardboard cut-out of Sarah Michelle Gellar. Uncle Kracker has already inscribed the right breast, so Rob takes the left. He is here to perform some songs, not even to be broadcast, but just for the enjoyment of some radio station competition winners, and to foster some sense of goodwill. Wooing radio stations in America can be a slow and intensive business.

The stage is in a kind of high-ceilinged warehouse, with two trees placed on either side of the stage in a desperate attempt to convey intimacy. The ambience is that of a supermarket loading dock. There are maybe 50 people in the audience, scattered across the floor. Many of them look, at best, vaguely curious. There is a buffet at the side and when they feel the need they saunter over for snacks. (One thing is becoming uncomfortably clear. In some parts of America Robbie Williams is not yet at the level where he is considered a big enough draw on his own, without free food.)

And yet, whether because he is determined to win them all over, which he seems to do, or because the situation is so absurd that the pressure is off, it brings out the very best of him. He's funny and charming and friendly, and sings like a dream.

If he did this for month after month after month, to ever-increasing audiences, which I am sure is what the record company wish and hope for, and think he should want to do, it is hard to imagine America resisting him. But, for perfectly sensible reasons of his own, he won't. That's one of the problems his American campaign faces. Unless events like these are the magical catalyst for something much bigger, there is the danger that his best efforts at seducing America will never reach the mass of people who might be up for seduction.

* * *

The next afternoon, after a 28-minute flight, it is San Diego's turn. Pulling into the parking lot at Star 100.7 FM, we pass four girls holding up banners, begging for tickets to the performance he will be giving in the radio studio. Rob sends for them, and brings them into the tiny-back room office where the fruit plate and sandwich components have been laid out for his benefit as he waits.

'Would you like some cheese?' he asks them. They don't answer. 'Are you really scared?' he asks, and their failure to answer suggests that they may be, though they soon hit their stride.

'Is this a good radio station?' he asks.

'No,' says one firmly.

'They were knocking the shit out of you,' says another. 'Slagging you.' (She has an English accent; it will turn out that she runs San Diego's English shop, selling baked beans and Yorkie bars to homesick ex-pats.)

'Go on,' he urges. 'Tell me. It's OK, I can take it, I've got a thick skin.'

And they all start chipping in.

'Well, your sexuality, you're fat, you're not that cute, you just sing OK … '

' … how you blanked one of the DJs at the Ozzy Osbourne house. Jen said, "He totally looked straight through me".'

' … the guy said, "He likes his bacon – don't hold it against him because he's a porker".'

' … he goes, "He's kind of doughy, isn't he?"'

Rob's eyes light up. The downside of this – hearing the insults – is far outweighed by his joy at knowing what has been going on, and having some information he can use to his own ends. 'Let me write all this down,' he says. 'Jen said … ?'

'Jen says you blanked her at the Ozzy Osbourne party. That she went over to see you and you just looked straight through her like you couldn't be bothered, even though you were on your own with Jon Lovett … ' (Jon Lovitz, she means.)

'"Blanked at party",' he repeats, writing. 'OK, I'm "a porker" – who said that?'

'Jen'.

'They said, "It's not like he's *Robin* Williams or something".'

'"He's doughy" – that's what Greg said.'

'The fat guy?' says Rob, who has already briefly met the DJs. He laughs. 'OK, this is how you're guaranteed not to get any radio play, by what I'm about to do. OK, what else?'

'They said you couldn't really sing.'

He nods. '"Couldn't really sing … " Anything else?'

' … and that you're not that cute.'

Then they tell him that Jen is said to have made out with Johnny Rzeznik from the Goo Goo Dolls. (Apparently, the two of them disappeared into the bathrooms together at Sushi Roku, a chic Japanese restaurant in Los Angeles.)

'You know what?' he predicts. 'I bet they'll be really nice to me.' He pulls up his shirt and rubs his stomach. He shows his 10/23 tattoo. 'That's the time I had this done,' he lies.

One of them asks how his single is doing over here.

'I don't know,' he says. 'People blow hot air up you all the time. "It's doing really, really well." I don't know what that means.'

They chat for a while, and the girls start slagging off Ben Affleck and Jennifer Lopez, until he stops them. 'You don't *know* these people,' he says, and points out that people's cartoon images in the newspapers can be very different from the truth. 'I'm such a wanker, apparently,' he says. 'A really, really bad wanker. They get you as a certain thing and that's it, that's what you are.'

'If they said you ate children,' says the English woman, 'I'd still like you.'

'That's a bit weird,' he says. 'But thank you.'

* * *

At the beginning of the interview he lifts up his shirt and Jen goes, 'Hi, fox!' There are three hosts, Jen, Greg and Sarah. He goes straight into it.

'So great for you to be in here,' says Jen.

'Well, you know, do you know what, I've got to say, I've heard a few things that have made me quite upset,' he says.

'What's that?' says Jen.

'Jen – I blanked you at an Ozzy Osbourne party. Is that what I did? I'm a bit of a porker. It's not like I'm Robin Williams. Greg – I'm a bit doughy and I can't really sing, and I'm not that cute.'

There's a flurry of denial and justification. Jen says she was crushed when she went up to him at the Osbournes' house.

'Baby, baby, you've got to understand,' he says, 'I really, really suffer with social anxiety … it's the absolute truth … I'm on pills … really, really bad, honestly truth to God. And I'm at a party, I'm really, really scared, and if anybody comes up to me and they want to talk I go, mmmm … hello, I've got to leave now … so, sometimes Jen, it's not always about you.'

'That's what my therapist is trying to teach me … ' she concedes.

'Spend half an hour with the old love doctor here and we can get all of that sorted out,' says Rob.

Greg asks what someone should say at a party like that to get a conversation going with him.

'They'd probably say, let's cut all this crap, it's just about sex, let's go,' says Rob.

'OK,' says Jen. 'Well *hell*.'

'And it worked with you and Johnny Rzeznik,' he says.

Her mouth drops open. 'Who the hell have you been *talking* to?' she says.

'You know what I'm saying,' he bluffs. 'I was speaking to him last night – he says you're a damn good kisser, girl.'

'Oh, my *God*,' she says. 'Somebody's in trouble here.'

'Now I've met you face to face I can see the love you've got,' says Rob.

'Are we made up now?' she asks.

'We are – we're all made up,' he says. 'Because I was a bit … ' He makes a tearful face to convey how he felt when he heard what they'd been saying behind his back, but then confesses to them that he does the same thing – says stupid things about people and then meets them and has to apologise or run off. 'We're all guilty of it,' he says.

'So can we have a group hug and a group kiss,' says Jen.

'Yeah,' he says. 'God grant us the serenity to accept the things we cannot change … '

'You've heard about a great kisser she is, right?' says Sarah, the other female DJ.

'Yes indeedy,' he says.

'So if you want to find out for yourself … ' provokes Sarah.

'But, Jen, I'm coffee and cigarettes now – does that matter?' he asks.

She shakes her head.

'Shall we just have a big kiss?' he suggests.

She says that Johnny Rzeznik smoked cigarettes without filters.

'That's because he's rock'n'roll, man,' says Rob. 'Listen, though, did he kiss you live on air?'

'No,' laughs Jen. She still doesn't imagine what will happen.

'With tongues?' asks Rob.

'No!' she says, laughing.

'Can I kiss you with tongues live on air?' he asks.

And he does. Not just a little film kiss, but what turns into a full, extended tongue-twirling snog. There is astonishment and screaming from the other DJs and the listeners watching through the glass from next door.

During the traffic report, detailing an accident on southbound 67, Rob chucks Jen a stick of gum. They cut to some ads and, off air, she thanks him. 'I enjoyed it too, baby,' he says. 'It's the most action I've had in quite some time.' Someone from the radio stage suggests that they re-pose in their kissing positions for a photo, so they do, and their tongues get moving again. Rob looks at the digital photo. 'That's disgusting,' he says. 'We should do another one.' So they do that, too.

'He knows how to work a record, doesn't he?' says the man from Virgin, his American record company.

'If anyone else has a camera ... ' says Jen.

'Honestly,' Rob tells her, 'I got, like, a hard-on.'

'Me too,' she says, 'and I don't even have a dick.'

Still off air, the DJs quiz him how he knew about the things they'd been saying.

'It was those tramps you picked up on the corner with those signs,' suggests Sarah.

The listeners waiting next door, including those girls, are brought in to watch Rob sing some songs. As he does so, the three TV screens mounted on the wall behind him silently show the war.

* * *

In the van to the airport, he sings to himself: ' ... *I left from the station, with a haversack and some trepidation.*'

'What a bummer if I hadn't done this tour,' he says on the plane home. 'It's really enjoyable. Whether it works or not.' As we fly over the Los Angeles valley, he looks down. 'There's a driving range down there, and a golf club,' he notes. He used to play golf as a teenager, and he is always talking as though he will take it up again.

Josie says that the Matrix, the current hot songwriting team who worked on Avril Lavigne's biggest hits, have been in touch about writing with him. He shakes his head. 'I don't really want to write with them,' he says. He has also gone off the idea of writing with Linda Perry after her people sent over a legal document saying that she had to produce any of the songs he wrote. I don't think it's this stipulation itself that has put him off as much as the fact that someone he would write with would want any kind of business agreement to come before the songs.

Josie also tells him that there is a problem with 'Come Undone', his new single in Britain. The video has been completely banned, which was to be expected, but Radio Two aren't playing the song at all, which was not. It's not just the swear words, the 'fuck' and the 'shit', which they knew they had to obscure or replace for a radio version, it's the line '*such a saint, such a whore*'. Though it seems absurd that Radio Two would object to the word 'whore' – which is not being used literally and is being directed at no one but the singer of the song, just one more entry in a catalogue of self-laceration – they do. Chris Briggs is in the studio in London, Rob is told, trying out various fixes by editing and looping words. Ironically, the 'fuck' and 'shit' are relatively easy to fudge, but it is very difficult to remove the 'whore' without it being completely obvious which word is supposed to be there.

David mentions that Radio One will be broadcasting one of the Knebworth concerts live this summer.

'I can remember listening to the Oasis Knebworth thing,' he says. 'I was travelling down from Stoke-on-Trent to London.'

'Did you think to yourself, I wish it was me?' asks Josie.

'No, I didn't even dare think that big,' he says.

'Not that long ago, is it?' says David.

'No,' says Rob.

* * *

The American experiment continues another day. Just as the scrambled eggs are served on the private jet, flying east over the Rockies on its way from Los Angeles to Salt Lake City, David looks down and admires mile after mile of snow-capped mountains.

'I snorted that,' says Rob.

At the first Salt Lake City radio station, 107.5 The End, a man wearing a suit that says Disco Instructor on it introduces himself as 'Chunga the DJ'. 'My real name's Brett Smith, but who gives a shit,' he adds. Rob goes outside for a smoke, and we stand by the back door in the rain next to a large satellite dish on the bank of a rank, oblong pond below a freeway flyover. Some CDs are hanging in a nearby tree.

'I guess we had a CD-throwing contest,' Chunga the DJ explains, 'but the wildlife people came and told us not to do it again.' He asks Rob about his tattoos and Rob says: 'It's going to be, Daddy, why are you painted?' then adds, mostly joking, 'Because I didn't like myself ... because inside I hurt.'

Chunga sees me making notes and asks what I am doing.

'It's my parole officer,' Rob explains.

Even by the standards of this week, the setting of today's performance is extraordinary. This summer he is to sing these same songs to 375,000 people over three nights at Knebworth, and every ticket is sold. But this morning he will sing in a tiny, rectangular, windowless room to an audience of 14 fans, sitting on fold-up chairs. He greets each member of the audience as they come in and hands around the Krispy Kreme donuts. During 'Feel' he gets on his knees and feigns sleep, nuzzled between the breasts of a woman in the front row. By the time he reaches 'Angels', the station has stopped broadcasting from this room, but he sings it better than I have ever heard him sing it, maudlin but soaring, just for these 14 and himself and the joy of it. In the instrumental break he steps forward and shakes hands with each of them before letting loose on the chorus.

He sweeps into the second Salt Lake City station, Star 102.7, greeting people and shaking hands as he goes. After he has passed I hear the DJ explaining to one middle-aged man who Rob is. The man is taken aback.

'If I would have known,' he says, 'I would have shaked his hand better. I would have cared more.'

* * *

On the plane home, he battles to resist the confectionery basket. So far, so good. 'My nan used to be home every night when I came back from school – every night without fail – and she'd always have two packs of Maryland cookies, a Twix and two doughnuts,' he says. 'Every night. A Twix or a Wispa. For me. And then my sandwiches and stuff.' He says he used to just eat and eat. 'We used to have a little shop round the corner through the alley that put things on tick – Buttons, Dairy Milk, éclairs.' His trick was to demonstrate to the other kids that he had no money – 'Watch this' – and then he'd go into the shop and come out with lots of chocolate. His favourites were the little lollipops called Drumsticks.

David asks which pudding he most dreams of, and offers three choices of his own: chocolate semolina and rice pudding with a big lump of jam in it, custard with the skin on, and pannacotta and berries.

'I think the treacle pudding's in there,' says Rob, 'but I think it would have to be bread and butter pudding, with ice cream or custard. Banoffee pie's in there.' He talks about how he loved his mother's tuna toasties. 'What she'd do was she'd get tuna and mix it with salt, pepper, tomato ketchup and mayonnaise, and then butter the inside of the bread and the outside of the bread and then put it in the oven. They fucking *rocked*.' He hasn't eaten one for over ten years. 'I'm going to have my mum make me one,' he says.

He says that at school he would eat the same thing every day: 'chips, beans, gravy and tomato sauce'. In the morning he'd have Weetabix mixed with cornflakes. But at home there were always vegetables and loads of fruit, and his mother would cook something healthy in the evenings.

He remembers how frustrated he would sometimes get with his grandmother after school. 'She used to do my head in because she was old,' he says. '"Nan! I'm trying to explain what Pacman's about! And why it's interesting to me! And why I like Ice T! The rapper! He's a rapper! He's a gangsta rapper!" Trying to explain what a video was. She just wouldn't get any of it. And then she used to be mega-worried about me.' She came in once when he was sniffing a bottle of butane gas lighter fluid. 'Robert!' she chastised him. She didn't know quite what he was doing, but she knew it was wrong.

He was 24 when she died. 'I really took it for granted, too, my nan being there,' he says. 'You do, don't you?'

* * *

In even the most honourable and truthful account of someone's life and how they live it, there are choices made, and by necessity each choice must sidetrack or evade some small part of the experience the reader would have had if actually present. Many of the things left unsaid here are to do with the mundane and unremarkable moments that make up all lives: the dark matter of life as it quietly continues in predictable ways between the galaxies of incident. Other things are left unsaid for other reasons. It would be untenable, for instance – and distracting, and perplexing, and scarcely credible – to convey accurately in a book of this kind just how often and loudly Rob farts. When he was young his mother had the kindness to tell him that these gifts to the world smelt like primroses, and perhaps he still believes this to be true. Mostly this habit, and the joy he takes in it, is accepted as something that just is, but occasionally, as now, it is discussed.

'I wonder if I fart so much because I drink so much water,' says Rob.

'I think it's more to do with the speed you eat at,' suggests David.

Don't you think, I propose, you mostly fart so much because you don't care not to?

He smiles. 'Yeah.'

'I don't think Bryan Ferry has ever farted in his life,' David points out.

* * *

He tells me that he is trying not to read about himself on the internet. Over the past few weeks he has become a little obsessed. 'I think it did really mess with my head,' he says. 'A lot of it is because I'm genuinely just interested. Some of it is to see how much it hurts. Subconsciously. I think people like me are always looking for something to spoil their day. Or to confirm their worst fears about themselves.' But one day, on the treadmill, he realised that he was imagining himself standing behind someone writing an article about him, a piece of chicken wire in his hand, and he knew it had to stop.

He talks about his idea for the next Robbie Williams album. 'Air meets "Come Undone",' he says. 'Electronic rock. Like a modern-day album that sounds like "Cars". We'll get Daft Punk to produce it.'

He sings to himself. '*When I see you with your new man, something stirs inside of me. It's not that I want you back, it's how ugly love can be … How did I make "I love you" sound sincere, when you were just a one-night stand that lasted a year?*' It's a song of his called 'Ugly Love'. ('Has that been used on anything?' he asks. The answer is: barely. It was an audio track on a German Xbox game.) It reminds him of people he used to hang out with, and people he used to take drugs with. He mentions a group of musicians, and wonders how each of them is now. 'That was very messy, actually,' he reflects. 'That was when I dabbled in a little bit of heroin. I said, what does it feel like? Like being wrapped in cotton wool. Was it fuck. It was like smoking bad prawns and being sick a lot.'

Why did you do it?

'Because we ran out of coke,' he says. 'It's what normally happens, I suppose.

And it was phoning your mum up to say, "I'm not coming round to the house in London because I'm staying out tonight" and thinking, oh my God, I've done heroin. And being sick out the window as you're speaking to your mum.'

You were?

'Yeah.' Pause. 'Yeah.' Of course it was a blessing that it didn't take to him and he didn't take to it. 'Quite fortunate, really,' he says, 'because heroin, I thought, fuck that, and crack, I just thought, fuck that. I think if it didn't go up my nose, I couldn't get along with it.'

Did you try crack?

'Yeah, well I was really high and somebody gave me three rocks and I gave them 60 quid, they come back and put three rocks in my hand and I thought it was better than nothing, and went back to my house and proceeded to smoke it through one of those silver things that individual cigars come in. I think there's two sets of people – you're either opiate or you're not. You either want to sleep or you want to stay awake forever.' He shakes his head. 'I was: stay awake forever.'

* * *

Back at the Los Angeles house, the spring evening is a warm one, and Rob has the idea that we should all lie out under the stars on the trampoline in the back garden. He fetches some duvets and pillows, and the six of us – Rob, Max, his friend Milica, Chris Sharrock, Jason and I – arrange ourselves on our backs, fanned out in a semi-circle, our heads near the rim and our feet converging at the trampoline's centre. Sid jumps up to join us. It's lovely out here. We talk all kinds of nonsense for ages, about the past and the present, and then Max leads us into a series of lightning answers, one after other round the circle. Rob's answers are spliff ('what you call weed'), trampoline ('first word that comes into your head'), 'Tie Your Kangaroo Down' ('first song that comes into your head'), Halle Berry ('first woman you want to fuck right now'), chips ('food'), milk ('drink'), Smith ('people called John'), Duchovny ('people called David'), Neptune ('planet'), Australia ('country'), *Dog Day Afternoon* ('film'), Eddie Murphy ('comedian'), Man United ('football team'), Magaluf ('holiday'), cedar ('trees'), dog ('animal'), orange ('fruit'), Stealer's Wheel ('band'), roses ('flower'), Elvis Costello ('solo singer').

'Shall we stay out here dead late?' he suggests.

Chris Sharrock points to a shape being formed by the trees at the end of the garden as the wind bends them. 'It looks like Jimi Hendrix with an afro,' he says.

'I feel like we're in Tahiti, 1958, making *Mutiny On The Bounty*,' says Max.

'Can I be Brando?' asks Milica.

'No,' says Max, miffed. 'I'm Brando.'

We lie there, not talking.

'I've just figured out the meaning of life,' says Rob.
'What is it?' asks Max.
A long pause.
'It's to leave Take That,' says Rob.
More silence.
'I'd *love* to see a UFO,' he says.

* * *

It is too early to know whether this costly, swift promotional offensive will ultimately pay off, but if it is working, it is doing so slowly. Success at American radio is measured in 'adds'; the number of stations adding your current single to their playlist that week. The pattern seems to be that hit records develop a momentum, first finding small loci of regional support and then, as a song builds its audience and popularity on a few stations (they do constant research with listeners), and as programme directors talk to each other, and as the specialist music industry magazines identify and amplify what is happening, it gains adds by the dozen week after week, rolling out across the nation.

'Feel' is on a few playlists – some of the visits Rob has made so far have been both to shore up and thank early supporters rather than convert new ones – but it is not yet exploding. In fact, last week 'Feel' gained precisely one 'add', and that was in Kansas, a state that has not even been under our flight path.

In Britain, meanwhile, the 'Come Undone' problem has been solved, and the song can now be heard on Radio Two, albeit in a version that will never be released. '*So self aware so full of shit*' has become '*so self aware so full of it*', '*so need your love so fuck you all*' has become '*so need your love good luck you all*' and '*such a saint, such a whore*' has become '*such a saint, such a bore*'. Rob has not been available to re-sing the lines, and they could not all be edited from existing material, but it had been noted some time ago that a session singer called Paul Caitlin Birch, who used to be Paul McCartney in The Bootleg Beatles, could do a good approximation of Rob's tone. This spring, for the occasional anodyne word, it will be him that the oblivious listeners of Radio Two hear.

10

Rob has decided to go house-hunting. He likes where he lives – the house itself has plenty of space and luxury, and enough bedrooms for a constant stream of guests, but is cosy and compact enough to give him some feeling of security – but he wishes his dogs could run around in a bigger garden. Maybe he is also thinking of living in a bigger, more expensive house, just because other people seem to like to do so; he can afford it, and it would be something to do.

Today he has arranged to see some homes in one of the poshest estates in the Hollywood Hills.

'We're moving up, kids,' he says as we drive through the gates.

Everything here is immaculate, every tree, hedgerow and path – either beautifully so, or creepily so.

'Much better kept, isn't it?' says David.

'Yeah,' says Rob, 'but it's a bit of a soulless vibe, isn't it? Can you feel it? I don't know if it's me feeling a bit inferior.'

'Fucking hell fire, I'd live in the fucking lamppost,' says Max. 'Even that's lovely.'

We pull to a halt opposite the first house.

'Here comes the working class,' announces Max.

The 12,000-square-foot house belongs to a well-known movie producer. Rob is shown round by a realtor who doesn't do much for Rob's hopes that one could live a discreet life here – from the balcony he happily points out the homes of the nearby famous: 'That's Sylvester Stallone's ... Denzel Washington ... Rod Stewart ... ' As we go round the house he points out the features he hopes will attract Rob.

'The dining room can seat 30, 34,' he says.

'I've only got two friends,' Rob tells him.

The next house, which belongs to another famous movie executive who is shown in dozens of framed photos around the house standing next to his fellow famous, is on the market for $14 million. It is nestled in a dip in the hills and so it has no view, and is overlooked by several houses nearby. There is a whole children's wing, with hundreds of toys, and there is a letter from President Clinton framed on the wall, for the kids.

'It was great, growing up like this, wasn't it?' says Rob to Max, grinning.

'We had a book a year,' Max replies.

A couple of days later he looks at some more properties. The most memorable is a ludicrously manicured house owned by a motorbike champion. 'All the gardening,' says the earnest man showing Rob around, 'is done by botanists with scissors.'

The man has barely started. He points out every refined feature – 'everywhere it's Venetian plaster', 'the chandelier is Louis XV' – as we pass. The house is effectively a compilation of the best of a thousand years of top decorating ideas, in the Los Angeles way. In the bedroom a fifteenth-century tapestry rises electronically, as its makers must have wished would one day become possible, to reveal the Dream Vision plasma TV screen.

It's a little much. Walking into the kitchen Rob points to the stove and mutters to Max, in a serious voice, as though he has spotted a period feature he especially admires: 'Sandra the tenth foo foo valves ... '

Botanists with scissors.

He learns something very valuable from these outings: how much he likes the house he already has.

* * *

On a plane to Toronto – a commercial flight this time – Rob sits in the seat next to me. I read the newspaper. There is some mysterious disease called SARS they have just identified, and they think there may be some cases in Toronto, but it says that it is under control and there is no reason to be concerned. I don't mention it. No need to offer up fresh opportunities to worry.

Rob goes through The Great *FHM* Man Test, multiple choice questions to gauge one's manliness, in the magazine he is reading. Some of his answers:

Number of girls slept with: 21+. (The highest option offered.) Ever enjoyed a threesome: yes. Had anal sex: yes. Maximum number of girls ever 'on the go' without any of them knowing: 2. ('And that was before I was famous,' he says.) Number of races slept with – he ticks the 'pretty much all of them including the Inuit' category. (Though no actual Eskimo? 'No,' he says. 'But I'm having ten points for that.') Given women multiple orgasms: yes. Has a girl ever thrown a pint over his head for a misdemeanour: yes. ('Well, there's been several slaps. And pints. Starting when I was 13 ... ') Are there women in his past who'd take him back in a heartbeat if he asked? Yes. Has he ever convinced a girl to do any of the following: lapdance for you in your living room (yes), star in your amateur porn film (no), have sex in a public place ('I won't fill that in'), dress up in your fantasy costume (yes; he declines to elaborate), lick your brown eye (yes). He has bungee-jumped, surfed and fired a gun but hasn't parachute-jumped or whitewater-rafted. Has broken 'a minor appendage (nose, finger, rib, etc.)' and an ankle ('football'). Most extreme experiment with facial hair: he ticks 'huge mutton chop sideburns'. Number of mates you could list as 'good mates': 2 to 5. How many of these would take a bullet for you: 2 to 3. Fist-fighting rumbles in his life: 6 to 10. Number won: 'more than half'. Number of times arrested: 0. How much he earns: £40,001+. Why he left his last job: he ticks 'made redundant', 'headhunted', 'more money here' and 'sheer mindfucking boredom' (though not 'sacked' or 'moved house'). Perks of his job: he ticks 'company car', 'regular travelling to foreign climes', 'little actual work' and 'attractive female co-workers'. Worst bit of job: he ticks 'the stress' and 'not much really'. How many of his female colleagues has he bedded? He ticks the 'most of them – save the mingers, obviously' option. How long he sees himself in his current job: he ticks 'until something better comes along'.

FHM judges that the average score should be around 95, but a pop star's overheated life is packed with the manliest opportunities and obligations, in these respects anyway, and his aggregate score is 199.

* * *

He does a Canadian TV interview with a woman who is the right combination of motherly, smart and sympathetic to get him to open up.

'Do you find,' she asks, 'that you have sabotaged your own relationships?'

'No, I just find that I pick ones that I can leave. But I'm getting better.'

'What's easier for you?' she asks. 'To love or to allow yourself to be loved?'

'To love. Yeah. But it's always with an escape route. It's, like, listen, we're on the plane, there's one parachute, I've got it on ... But hopefully it will be different as I get older.'

At the end of the interview she asks what misconceptions there are about him.

'There's no misconceptions about me,' he says. 'I'm 100 per cent of what people think I am. And I'm 10 per cent of what people think I am. There's no misconceptions.'

Later, after he has watched a few more episodes of *The Sopranos* (HBO have kindly supplied videos of the whole fourth season), I hear him speak on the phone in the other room to someone he knows who is in trouble. Sometimes it's a surprise to be reminded of how grown-up he can be when he chooses or needs to be: the advice and encouragement he gives, in what is clearly a very difficult and volatile situation, is beautifully patient, supportive and undogmatic; the friend you would wish to have at a moment like that.

Then it is time to watch the final *Sopranos* episode of the season.

'I feel like saying grace,' he says as the tape is put in the video player.

David, who has missed the last few, asks, 'Is there anything I need to know?'

The opening credits roll.

'No,' says Rob. He reconsiders. 'That I plan to retire in two years,' he says.

* * *

We sit in silence at the end, stunned.

'I still don't think they should have killed off Pussy,' says Rob.

Rob, Pompey and I go down to the bar.

'So what does one do for shits and kicks in Toronto?' he asks the woman behind the bar.

'I like to club myself,' she says.

'That's very sadomasochistic,' he says, as though taken aback.

Various stories are shared across and along the bar counter, until Rob says, 'That'd make a good book – misconceptions about sex before you knew what it was about.' It sets him to thinking about the seven-year-old boy he was. He says that he can remember doing the primary school play. 'It was called *Sean, The Fool, The Devil and The Cats,*' he says. 'I was the Devil. And I never learned my lines, and I made them up for the three nights we were on. And I had a big soliloquy and everything. Because I really wasn't into learning stuff. Still not.'

How did you imagine you'd be able to do that?

'I didn't imagine that I'd be able to do that. Before I knew it the night was upon me.'

Did you just not give a fuck?

'No, I was tremendously scared about the fact that I didn't know my lines. And Mr Collis thought I'd stole the devil's hat. It was black, like a skullcap with two red horns. And I hadn't. It turned up a couple of months later in the school.' (At this moment, he is clearly just as annoyed, if more annoyed, about Mr Collis's false accusation than the Rock The Vote shambles. He wonders whether he should do a poster campaign around Britain, settling minor vendettas and grudges from his past. 'Name and shame Mr Collis,' he hoots. Then he reconsiders. 'I don't think we should name and shame Mr Collis,' he says to me. 'Put *that* in the book.')

'And he made me eat caterpillars,' Rob adds.

Pompey and I both look shocked.

'I made that up, the caterpillar bit,' he laughs.

I bet you ate one anyway, I say.

'No, I didn't,' Rob protests. 'I ate flies.'

'You *are* the devil's child,' laughs Pompey.

'Adrian Tams bet that I would,' says Rob. 'They were smeared in custard. I just swallowed. Like a good catholic boy.'

He remembers something else.

'I got thrown out of the choir,' he says.

I ask why.

'I can't remember,' he says. 'Thinking about it, it was my first bad review.'

Late in the evening, he lies on the sofa in his hotel room with his shirt off, thinking about the music he wants to emulate and the album he wants to make now.

'Do you know what?' he says, as though he has just come round to fully feeling what he has been telling himself he feels for a while. 'I don't miss Guy.'

* * *

Back in London, he phones one morning.

'Got some news,' he says. He's excited. 'Number 43 in America. 24,000 sold.'

His efforts seem like they are bearing some fruit. The British press has been acting as though it should be possible to put his celebrity and success on a plane and simply transfer it to another country, but he knows how hard it is to win over America, and this is an encouraging start.

A good day.

* * *

The paparazzi are driving him mad again. They arrived outside his London home within half an hour of his return, and have been following him wherever he goes. When one of them jumped out of his car in stationary traffic and started photographing Rob through the window, Rob shouts at him, 'I hope you die.'

'And I thought, I shouldn't think that,' he says. 'But I do.'

It's not just the paparazzi. Within a few days of his return, the whole dormant, uninvited circus that surrounds his London life has sprung back to life. The doorbell rings several times every night – pissed people coming back from the pub and amusing themselves by disturbing their local pop star. One night, after midnight, Pompey asks Rob whether he knows a girl called Becky. She is outside in the street, insistently ringing to be let in. He watches her on the TV cameras. He doesn't know her. 'It's Becky,' she says through the intercom. 'Are you not going to let one girl in for a pee?' There's a man behind her who she says is a cabbie, but Rob and Pompey immediately smell some kind of entrapment. Rob answers in a posh voice saying that it is not possible for her to come in, that it is private house and will she please leave. 'I can't believe you're not going to let one girl in for a pee,' she insists, and carries on buzzing. After a while of watching her he goes back to the intercom and, still in the posh voice, asks, 'Who's that man behind you?'

'It's my cabbie – let me in for a pee,' she says, and she sits down.

In the end they have to tell her they have called the police, and she would be best advised to leave before they arrive.

'Oh I don't think so,' she replies, oddly. 'I work for the police.'

'Well, let me try another tack,' Rob says, angry with her and with all these situations. 'Fuck off, you ugly fuckwit. You're going to have to piss yourself, aren't you?'

She stays, and the police come. When the police arrive another man shows himself on the corner across the road, so some kind of trap was being sprung.

'It's worked in the past,' Rob reflects. 'But not with new Robbie.'

* * *

He has a meeting at his house about the Cole Porter movie, *Just One Of Those Things*, in which he is to make brief appearance. The principals are already gathered around his kitchen table: the producer Rob Cowan, the director Irwin Winkler (best known as a legendary Hollywood producer: the Rocky movies, *Raging Bull*, *Goodfellas* and as far back as *They Shoot Horses, Don't They?*) and the musical coordinator Peter Asher (who became famous as part of the sixties duo Peter and Gordon, and who produced Rob's beloved early James Taylor records in the seventies).

'I'd like to apologise for the state of the house,' says Rob, though it's not very untidy, the only unusual touch being the bottle of Effexor that sits between everyone in the middle of the table and remains there throughout the meeting. To begin with they all break the ice by chatting about real estate in Malibu and Beverly Hills.

'How much time do you spend in LA?' asks Irwin Winkler.

'As much as I can,' says Rob. 'Nobody knows me there.'

'Well,' says Irwin Winkler, 'we may change that.'

Rob nods. 'With a little bit of help, maybe we can all ruin my life.'

There's more small talk and then Rob calls the meeting to order by saying, 'Well, what's going on?'

'We'd like you to do this movie,' says Irwin Winkler, and talks Rob through the story, describing its end in a way that is wonderfully moving even as he just sits here and says it.

'Stop!' says Rob. 'If I had a heart, I'd be crying.' He turns to Tim. 'Did you nearly have a tear in your eye? I wish I could sell a song like that.' He reconfirms his willingness to appear in the movie.

Once they leave, we rent *Donnie Darko* from the local video shop. When he sees the words They Made Me Do It written by the school statue in the film, he says to himself, 'Album title: *They Made Me Do It*.' He starts worrying towards the end of the film whether the ending's going to be any good. It is a very Rob kind of concern: he's anxious because he is enjoying it so much, and it has been so good so far, that he knows how annoyed and frustrated he will feel if it lets him down.

* * *

The modest American progress that has made Rob so pleased is interpreted rather differently by the British media. The weekend papers are full of their reports of what they consider Robbie Williams' American disaster. The same statistics that excited him earlier in the week are re-cast as humiliating and disastrous. ROBBIE'S LATEST ALBOMB judge *The People*, claiming that part of the problem is the way he is confused with Robin Williams. GIVE UP ROBBIE, YOU'LL NEVER CRACK THE U.S. is the *Sunday Mirror*'s headline. *Superstar at home – a superflop Stateside ... Once again the cheeky chappie from Stoke fell flat on his face with the Yanks as he tried to justify his £80 million record deal*, they write. Next to the main article is a sidebar from Louis Walsh, headlined HE'S NOT GOOD ENOUGH TO MAKE IT BIG IN AMERICA, in which Walsh offers some further considerate comment. '*I've never been a fan of his. I don't think he's very talented. He's not a great singer and he's not a brilliant songwriter either. The only song I have ever liked is* Angel *[sic] and that was written by his former songwriter Guy Chambers ... Robbie is just a cheeky chappie from a boyband who has been lucky.*'

'It's "bash Robbie Williams" at the minute, isn't it?' Rob reflects. 'It's such a massive thing for them, this America thing. It doesn't bother me as much as it bothers them. At all.'

Meanwhile, another media hullabaloo has abated. The *News Of The World* have made a suitably large payment to his charity and apologised. The first Rob knew of it was when he saw the apology in the newspaper, which spells out that he is not addicted to gambling, only ever gambles for relatively small stakes and has not had any alcohol or drugs for over two years. The other newspapers that subsequently splashed the story all over their pages – now in a hopeless position once the principal source for their story has caved – will soon all apologise and pay damages too. The *Observer* reports that the *News Of The World* journalist who wrote the original story has been moved to the obituary desk, with the suggestion that he should see how much trouble he can get into libelling the dead.

11

For years, everything Rob saved from the Take That era has been stored in the attic of his mother's house in Stoke. Recently he has decided that he wanted to see it, and asked his mother to send it all down to London. One day, when I am round, he starts randomly pulling things out of the row of cardboard boxes next to the pool table and showing them to me. A photo of the young him with Bruno Brookes. A photo of a girlfriend, Natasha: 'First grown-up girlfriend,' he says. A picture at the end of a Take That tour. (He can remember exactly what he was thinking at the specific moment the shutter clicked. 'I was really mortified that none of my friends had bought me drugs,' he says. 'I was fucking mortified.') A photo in which he has his arms around Nigel Martin-Smith on a sofa, Gary Barlow to his other side. 'I'd be absolutely pissed,' he says. 'I really wanted him to like me.'

'Who – Gary or Nigel?' asks Josie, leaning over for a look.

'Nigel,' says Rob. 'Really, really needed his approval. And never got it.'

I point out that he's already oozing *actually I'm not always going to be in a boy band* and *I have declared myself a separate universe*.

'Yeah,' he says. 'What I'm going to do is, take lots of drugs with this man.' He shows a photo of an old friend. 'We just took an amazing amount of drugs, really. I don't think there was one day that went by at that point where my mood wasn't altered with ... if it wasn't speed, coke, Es, then it'd be like slimming pills. So there was always something constantly in the system.'

His cuckoo clock, which his sister has just given him, goes off.

'I told you about the Peter Cunnah thing that happened where I was in bed with ... ?' he asks.

No, I say.

'There's a bit about it in this letter somewhere,' he says, handing me an envelope with a small stack of correspondence inside. 'I'll give you these if I can have them back.'

He takes me upstairs and shows me the Gary Barlow home video he found a while back. The part that haunts him is the footage of them arriving in New York. The teenage Rob looks into the camera at the airport and says, goofing around, 'I haven't been shot yet – I'm really depressed'. And a moment later you can see Nigel look at Rob furiously – Rob is oblivious – and nod his head in a kind of contemptuous way.

'Just a look of thunder,' says Rob, watching.

I ask him what he thinks Nigel Martin-Smith is thinking there.

'Just how much he hates me,' says Rob. 'He couldn't stand me having any attention.'

The tape rolls on and we watch Gary Barlow giving a tour round his house, zooming in on his candle-holders.

'Trying to be 80,' says Rob.

The boxes at home have set Rob thinking about the past even more than usual. He wonders aloud how much Take That earned. It is all a bit of a blur. 'I had a 500 grand cheque once,' he remembers. 'I snorted cocaine with it.'

* * *

Peter Cunnah was the gay lead singer for D:ream, a dance pop group now best remembered for Labour's use of their 'Things Can Only Get Better' in their 1997 campaign. At the time in question, Take That had just been on tour with them. An exhausted Rob had just returned to London and was in bed with Natasha.

'She was going down on me,' he explains, 'and I fell asleep, nine shows on the trot so I was knackered, and I was dreaming about him, because we'd just been on tour, and I was just chatting to him in my dreams, about whether they were a good crowd tonight and whether we went down well, and I went, oh Peter … '

Out loud.

As he says, she mentions it. The letters he has given me track the familiar stages of young love, and then young love getting complicated and young love going wrong. The Peter Cunnah incident is mentioned in a letter in the middle of 1994, after one of their splits. '*I know you won't write first so I figured I should,*' she begins.

There is also one letter written by Rob to her in the better times, five pages hand-written in turquoise, apparently on a plane; it's not clear whether it was ever sent. He says that he runs through his mind a scene where she calls him, her voice lowers, and she explains that she needs to split with him and find a steadier relationship with someone else. '*Jesus!*' he writes. '*I think this flight is on paranoid airlines!*' He shares lots of other fears – '*my paranoia is one of my downfalls unfortunately*' – and, in between, expressions of how much he feels for her. '*Me writing this letter is sort of cleansing in a way. I hope u understand that because I didn't.*'

* * *

Outside the house, a paparazzi snaps through the railings as Rob gets into the car. Rob scowls. He's not in the mood. 'Nice job,' he says sarcastically.

'I hate it just as much as you do,' the paparazzi says. 'I wish there were no celebrities left in the world and then I could get a proper job.'

We drive off.

'What a weird thing to say,' mutters Rob.

* * *

'It'd drive me mad if I was here for another week,' he says, after a few days in London. 'Fucking bonkers. I'm treating it like: my house is a hotel, this is a territory, it's work and I've got a single out.'

Today he is flying to Sweden anyway. Another TV show. When we land, Josie says that she has just had a message on her mobile from Mark Owen, saying that he'd heard Rob was in London and he'd love to have a cup of tea. It is a very long time since they have last spoken. Rob calls straight back and leaves a message, inviting Mark round.

Four hours later, Rob is back on the plane and is asking David what it was like when he used to disappear for 48 hours at a time.

'Not very nice,' says David, and they reminisce ruefully about some of the messier times.

'It's like three lives,' Rob eventually reflects. 'It's like I'm on my fourth, actually ... school, Take That, reckless abandon, trying to get sober and being sober. Fifth life.' Pause. 'Four more.'

What do you think they'll be?

'There'll be the greatest hits, the marriage, the children, the divorce and the boxed set ... ' he says.

'You've been planning for a divorce the last five years, you lunatic,' says Josie.

'Yeah, well it comes with the broken home thing, doesn't it, I suppose,' he says. 'You know, my view will change once I fall in love and be with the right person but right now it just seems inevitable that I'll fuck it up in some way.'

'It might not be you,' points out David.

'If you're with the right person, you know,' says Rob. 'There's been no one that I've wanted to work anything out with. I have doubts, I really do have doubts, that I'll go and be in love.'

'What?' says Josie.

'That I'll be in love,' he says.

'That's a very good state to be in,' says David. 'Something's going to catch you round the back the neck when you won't expect it.'

'I'm preparing for that,' he says. 'And I'm preparing for the possibility of me not being in love.'

* * *

Back at his house, he decides to go through the rest of his boxes. He pulls out his collection of 1994 *Smash Hits* awards: Best LP (*Take That And Party*), Best Group In The World, Best British Group, Best Single ('A Million Love Songs'), Best Video ('I Found Heaven'), and Best Haircut (Robbie Williams). 'The kids have spoken,' he says. Then he digs out his Best Haircut 1993 award; two years in a row. He finds a black-on-white My Drug Shame T-shirt ('that's what I wore towards the end of Take That'; when he wasn't allowed to wear it, he would put on his My Booze Hell shirt instead); a True Fucking Star shirt he was given by a fan and didn't wear; and a metal Versace chain-mail shirt, part of a whole outfit he was given when they would hang out with Gianni Versace.

'Shall I see if I can get it on?' he wonders. He can, and so he parades around the room in his teen-pop chain-mail.

He digs deeper. A Take That T-shirt with the four-man post-Robbie line-up on it, which he would enjoying wearing after he had left. A checked Pervert cap and leather waistcoat. A Howard Donald Take That doll. ('I don't know why I've got this,' he says.) A Take That calendar. He looks at their first promo shot: 'We were only a little bit gay,' he laughs. He is wearing a leather jacket open to the waist, boots and cycling shorts. 'I look so bloody young and I'm sucking my cheeks in even then,' he says.

He reads the text in the poster pack. 'This is it,' he says, discovering an account of Take That's official history, and reads it out. '*Meanwhile a young school leaver Mark Owen worked in a local bank. He quite liked it but decided to get an evening job where he made tea in a recording studio. That's where he met Gary. They started working together and in between cups of tea a friendship was formed. Meanwhile on the other side of town two tall lithe chaps were in rival breakdance groups. Howard Donald would watch Jason Orange dance and often wanted to go over and say how much he admired it. Jason remembers their first meeting clearly. "I have to give it to Howard – we were in rival groups but he was the one who eventually came over and was friendly to me first." One by one the group ended up at Nigel's agency and knew they'd get on well. A fifth member was auditioned. A cheeky lad just out of school turned up and sang "Nothing Can Divide Us", a Jason Donovan hit. His name was Robbie Williams. Says Mark, "I really admired him because we all knew each other and he didn't and he had the guts to sing and win us over. Take That were formed!"*

He shakes his head.

'This was Nigel's brilliant plan to make people think we weren't manufactured,' he says. 'What actually happened was, none of us knew each other and we all auditioned at the same time and we were all given "Nothing Can Divide Us" to sing.'

'Really?' says Josie, who also doesn't know this.

'Wow,' says Chris Sharrock likewise. (Chris is staying with Rob, as he often does when the band are working in London.) 'All my illusions.'

'It was actually said during this that I was put in because we were sure that one of us would drop out and I was there to make up the numbers,' says Rob. 'I was on the subs bench, basically.'

He hits a seam of Christmas cards. One from Elton and David. One from Frank Bruno ('To Robert, best wishes, Frank Bruno'). One from Nigel: 'Rob, Have a great Xmas. Love ya! Nigel.' This is written in the final Take That card, Christmas 1994, a few months before his departure. On the front it says – and this is the card that went to everybody on their list, including the media – '*We told Robbie to stay in this Christmas. We think it's for the best. Less of the party animal thing. We think he's come round to our way of thinking ...* '

When you open it, it says ' ... *just!*' opposite a photo of Rob, raging, in a straitjacket. 'It's kind of affectionate,' he says.

Rob reads out another piece about Gary Barlow: '*He's also very fond of Pilsbury dough croissants* – this is Guy – *You pop them out of* ... Gary, I mean ... *you pop them out of the tube and into the oven* ... '

I stop him. Did you just say Guy?

'Yeah.'

Does Dr Freud need a word with you?

'Mmmmm,' he says.

He finds some newspapers from the year he went solo. The *Daily Express*, 30 August 1995: TAKE THAT ROB IN TEARS AT REUNION. '*I feel so weird, he said,*' Rob reads out, '*but I know I've got to start a new life. It's just hard seeing them. I haven't spoken to them in words tonight, just a series of hand signals. But I suppose that's the way we've always communicated.*'

'Bless,' he says. It was the National Television Awards and he was really in tears. 'And Leslie Grantham was behind me,' he says, 'and he put his hand on my shoulder, and he went, "Don't let them see you cry, son."'

'It's all there in the boxes,' Rob reflects, 'but it's also like reading through a biography that Andrew Morton had pieced together.'

Does it really seem that remote?

'Yeah. The only feelings that I can remember is sadness, and being ostracised.'

When you look at some of those photos you don't remember any of the moments of sort of triumphant fun?

'No, because there was always a price to pay for it,' he says. Then he reconsiders. 'We laughed together,' he says. 'We did laugh together. Like that night in Madrid.'

* * *

That night in Madrid was the first time he ever took ecstasy. Take That had just appeared on their first TV show abroad, on a line-up that also included The Village People, performing 'Promises'. Afterwards they went to a club, and he was given a pink E.

'It was *phenomenal,*' he remembers, of that evening in Spain. 'Phenomenal. You know, there was only one thing missing – women. We were in a gay club. But I loved it. The first time I took coke … ' – this is the real first time; the time he told me about last year when he took it just before he went onstage with Take That was actually the second – ' … was at a nightclub. ——— was running the door and he went, "Do you want a bump up?" and I knew what it meant and I was like, yeah. I said I've never done it before, and he was like, yeah, really. So I took that and then went to the hotel, the Thistle next door, and we'd got to do some TV show in the morning, and I'd got some coke left over, and it was at the garden on the top of the hotel, Kensington Roof Gardens, so I just carried on snorting. And it did nothing.'

The effects of the ecstasy were wearing off by the time he got back to the Madrid hotel. 'Horny as a … ' he remembers, 'and alone, and no one to shag.' He wandered around the hotel, looking for someone awake, or in the bar, but there was no one. 'I mean, that comedown, the first comedown, is not that bad,' he says, 'but it's bad enough to go, fuck I wish I was asleep now.'

* * *

He has one last glance at the piles of his past.

'I'm glad I'm not him any more,' he says, and goes to bed.

12

One evening, Mark Owen comes round to his house and plays Rob some of his new songs. Rob's impressed. 'It's closer to Ryan Adams and Radiohead than me and Avril Lavigne,' he judges. He suggests to Mark that, for fun and old times' sake, he might want to come onstage at Knebworth one night to sing 'Back For Good'. They watch the Gary Barlow home video and chat for hours.

'He will not have a bad word said about anybody,' marvels Rob the next day. 'And I'll try. We were talking about someone and I said, oh, I don't like him, and he was, "It doesn't matter, does it?"'

And Rob realises that there is something to this. *It doesn't matter, does it?* From now on, for fun at light-hearted moments but also in times of adversity, Rob will sometimes call upon this philosophy as a check to his natural impulse towards stewing resentment and revenge. It will become known as The Tao Of Owen.

* * *

On a jet to Denmark, Claire hands Stephen Duffy's next album, which she plays and sings on, to Rob, and he listens to it on his headphones. 'Right up my street,' he says after four songs. 'He's depressed again.' Then he turns to David. 'I want to do a photo shoot where I'm Mickey Mouse,' he announces loudly. 'We should do a photo shoot that's interesting all the time.' David nods. 'And then we should go to bed,' Rob adds.

He asks Gary Nuttall to tune his acoustic guitar and gently strums quietly making up a song. 'Wouldn't it be great if I went to write a song with Stephen Duffy,' he suddenly says, 'and he just wrote the words?'

We land and the van drives into town. Today he is shooting an advert for the new Smart car; Smart are one of the sponsors of his summer tour. He looks out of the window with bemused interest.

'This is Denmark,' he notices. 'I was expecting Holland.'

We pass a cyclist who is lying on the ground next to his bicycle. He appears to have cycled straight into a pole.

The commercial is filmed on a blocked-off street in the centre of Copenhagen. A young man is singing 'Feel' badly next to the new Smart car, trying to get some money for the meter before an approaching parking warden reaches his car. Of course it is Rob walking by, who gives him the money and says, 'Nice car, mate.'

There are crowds at either end of the street trying to see what is happening – one girl keeps staring at Rob as though trying to get his attention, and he can't work out whether maybe he has slept with her – and there are paparazzi trying to get shots along the street, and hanging out of balconies in the distance. There's little that can be done while the camera is rolling, but as soon as the director yells cut, people run in holding large boards to block the paparazzi's shots. Not of Rob. They're fairly unconcerned about him. Of the car. Its exact design is still a commercial secret, and there is a huge market for photographs of the newest models. It is not yet in production, and this actual car that people will see in the adverts is a handmade prototype that cost around £1 million and is largely made of wood. (They are also worried about the weather, because if there's rain its surface will bubble up.)

After he is done, he must appear on a Danish TV show. In the dressing room, Rob plays 'One Fine Day' on the guitar.

'*Don't rewrite my history* … ' he sings, and then stops and explains that the line came from when he logged on to Friends Reunited and realised that there were four of five people pretending to log in as him and saying things like 'It's Robbie – you know what I've been up to'. 'It *pissed* me off,' he says. 'And that's "*Don't rewrite my history* … "'

He starts playing it again, but soon stops. He says the song's initial inspiration was an episode of *The Simpsons*, where Grandpa Simpson, falling in love, said something like, 'You remind me of a film that I never saw and a time I've never had.' And the beginning of the chorus – '*one fine day in the middle of the night*' – is the first line of the folk poem he learned when he was young.

There was a further impulse at work. 'I think my mum and dad were in the same room in the house,' he says, 'and subconsciously lyrics just flew out because they were there. It was weird seeing them together.'

'*Remember when we never struggled through a bad time we never had, a love we never fell into* ... my mum and dad ... *please don't remind me to forget, because forgiveness is a place I ain't got used to yet* ... and, you know, it's like as much as my mum says she's cool about it, I don't think she is, still ... It's probably what could have been, the relationship with my mum and my dad ... *You remind me of a place I've never been, and something no one said, when I was 17* ... That's probably from my perspective. You know, and at the end it's *please don't rewrite my history because you'll never really know how much you didn't mean to me* ... Sad.'

When he walks back into the dressing room after his performance, a woman is waiting there, and she is holding a present for him.

'Hello, darling,' he says.

'Hello,' she says.

'How's it going?' he says.

'I'm fine,' she says.

'What's your name?'

'Pia.'

'Pia? You've very beautiful, Pia.' He tells Josie to let her be. 'Don't throw out the beautiful ones,' he mutters quietly.

'Thank you. Can I give you something?'

'Yes, of course. Pleased to meet you, Pia. Very beautiful. Very beautiful indeed. It's a shame you weren't near the front or else I would have come and sung to you today. I'll look at it later,' he says. 'I'll see you in a little while.'

'You do?' she says.

She goes, leaving a Polaroid of herself and her number, and a 'soulmate' Angel card, and two interlocking rings in a jewel box.

'Dear me,' says David.

She was the one staring at him during the Smart shoot.

'She's beautiful – absolutely beautiful ... even some of the beautiful ones are bonkers,' Rob observes. He opens her note.

Please read this letter with an open heart and mind. I have written to you because my heart can't stand the loneliness anymore.

I am your lost angel, the one you sing about in all your songs. I know now that we simply has to meet and this is my way to get to you. I have fore a long time followed your way, life and this melancholi – the same feeling I have sometimes, because you're not in my life, spirit and universe.

Many people will certently make fun of me, by writing this, but I'll risk the embarrassment ... So if this has reach you, I will shortly tell this about myself.

My name is Pia, I am Danish and 24 years old. I work in a hospital at the emergency room ...

Let love be our energy ...

The angel

As we leave, Rob says to Gary Nuttall, with a certain pride, 'I've got my first mad obsessed stalker fan who's really beautiful. They're normally mingers.'

In the car, David looks at the photo. 'That is seriously tonto,' he says.

'Cuckoo for cocoa?' says Rob. 'If I was staying for the night, I'd have had to get my boots out for a kickabout.'

He says that the letters he has been getting recently have been becoming stranger and stranger. He mentions a completely hateful one from an Italian fan the other day that he promises to tell me about later. It's amazing how many of them reach his house. A few people know where he lives, but the British postal system does a remarkable job of helping out others. Sometimes the envelopes will just say 'Robbie Williams, England' as the address. Or, weirder still, just 'Robbie Williams, Pop Star'. 'Just outside Rock Star,' he notes.

Since his record contract was announced, there have been more and more begging letters. He reckons he now gets a request for about half a million pounds a month to the house. 'It's like the back of *Private Eye*. "I'm a painter and I need … " "I've just finished school and I need … " "I have an overdraft and I need … " "I, like you, have a … " "Come on, you must know what it was like in the early days", all that business. "Here's a picture of some of my work." The one yesterday was from the headmaster of a school: "You may see us from the back of your house … some of these kids have never seen the countryside … will you donate some money to make a trip possible for them to go and see cows?"'

Have you had any you've been minded to respond to?

'I nearly fell for this woman the other day whose daughter was at school and she'd sent like a *Smash Hits* thing, with likes, dislikes, music she's into, age she is, and then she'd sent every grade she'd got and the school report, and the grades for each autumn, spring … a file like that. And "she's not only my daughter but she's my best friend … "'

'Saying she couldn't afford to finish her daughter's private education and she didn't want to tell her daughter because it was too worrying,' says Josie.

So, the natural course of action is … to ask a pop star for help.

'I was searching for the mindset, I was trying to put myself in her place,' says Rob. 'But all roads lead to: "You're mad, you are." There was 30 per cent of me at one point going, oh, if I was in the predic— *No*. And what she started off with was this: "I was watching a news programme with you on the news, the one where you said I'm rich beyond my wildest dreams, and I was … " You know, "rich beyond my wildest dreams" was me being fucking *ironic*. I realise it was probably a mistake to say it but there was like a baying pack of journalists in front of me. "What do you want me to say? I'm rich beyond my wildest dreams?" Whatever I'd have said then wouldn't have gone down well, and that wasn't the best thing to say, but at the same time I was fucking joking, you cunts.'

And you've had wilder dreams than that, I'm sure.

'I have,' he says.

* * *

He adds lines to the song he began writing on the plane yesterday morning. By the afternoon, after a day bored in his Rotterdam hotel room, it has found what it is about, which is himself and the parts of his past that have been hovering close by, and he has a rough verse and chorus:

When I was a kid, I didn't want to be an astronaut
I wanted to live in Compton, because I heard on the records that I bought
I fell into a boy band, they weren't big on rapping
And I discovered that I could dance a little bit, so I stayed around to see what would happen
Oh we were a phenomenon
I was the cheeky one
Sent to fill the void
Now that the New Kids had gone
And when you've seen one screaming face you've seen them all
All the promises they make well they break them all
You said you'd love me forever
Now you dig the Strokes and you dress in leather
And you've forgotten all the words to our songs
Your world moved on
My work here is done

Backstage at the TMF awards, he reads some fan mail – '*I have seen you on MTV Cribs I have so laugh that I piss my pants because you have an elevator in your home, you are crazy man but fun crazy man*' – and does an MTV interview in which they ask whether he thinks he will win as Best Male tonight.

'Well, I know I will,' he says. 'I've been told.'

They look genuinely shocked and taken aback, as though they imagine that in some nearby back room voting slips are still being breathlessly tallied.

In the band dressing room, between his first and second awards, he works on the second verse.

' ... *They set up helplines ... when I left the band ... teenagers in crisis ... they wouldn't understand ... without the cheeky one ... no phenomenon ...* '

In the van to the plane, he writes the bridge: '*No more best haircut, now that Judas had gone ... when you've seen one screaming face you've seen them all ... well the promises they made I broke them all ...* '

The next section comes on the plane, and when it does he goes straight down the cabin to play it to the band.

' ... *We were never the Beatles, and I'm not Wings, but I've moved on to bigger better things ... and I've forgotten all the words to our songs ...* '

He dictates the words to Josie before we land, and wonders whether he could play it at Knebworth. For a week or two, it's a song he loves and one that he'll play on his guitar at any opportunity. (In that period he will write a middle eight for it that incorporates various Take That lyrics.) But, as with nearly all of the many songs I have seen him write in the last few months, he becomes disenchanted after a while. He moves on from them rather as he might move on from a fleeting relationship, as though the moment he decides they are only what they are and they are not everything he wants them to be, then they are of little further use to him. If you speak well of such songs after they have fallen out of favour he looks almost annoyed. And for all that he has built up a catalogue of songs since the split with Guy, it becomes more and more obvious that he is on a search for something else. I don't think he even knows what it is he is looking for; he just knows that it is there, inside him or outside him, and that he hasn't yet found it.

13

'Guess who phoned me?' he says. It is a few days after his return to Los Angeles. 'Guess who wants to apologise?'

Guy called him from the Beverly Hills Hotel. After avoiding the original call because he was just going out and he wanted to gather himself anyway, Rob called back.

He acts out the conversation that followed.

* * *

'Hello,' answers Guy.

'Hi ya.'

'Hi ya, mate, how are you?'

'I'm really good, man – how are you?'

'Good, yeah … uh …'

'What's going on?'

'I just wanted to phone, you know, and say hi and check in … and apologise really.'

'Oh … that's very brave of you – I really admire that.'

'Yeah, one of us had to do it … and because you know, my big mouth gets me into trouble and I just really wanted to apologise, because I think we've both been a bit silly.'

That is when it begins to derail.

' … *both* been a bit silly?' repeats Rob, and hears silence at the other end of the phone. 'Where have I been silly?'

'Uh … oh … you've put me on the spot – I wanted to do this face to face.'

'Well, so we know we're on the same hymn sheet, you know, I don't want to invest any emotional energy in coming down and possibly being upset by it all, so I'd like you to tell me where I've been silly so I know.'

'Uh … well … ' A long pause 'I can't actually think of anything.' Guy explains that he thought the lack of communication was bad, and says that they had a great chat in LA at the end of making the album and then it all went to shit when they got home. He apologises for 'Come Undone' and says that he doesn't know why he had a problem with it.

'I love you loads, Guy,' Rob tells him, 'and give my love to Emma, because I do miss her, but, bolt out of the blue a little bit, give me a couple of days to digest it and see what I want to do with it. Whether I want to come down or not.'

* * *

He's still thinking about it all.

'I don't know if I'm ready to invite that back into my life,' he says. 'My instant thought, because I'm a cynical bastard, is: Knebworth's coming up.' He's also not sure whether he'd want to work with Guy again because of Guy's recent collaborations. 'He's been writing with anybody now,' Rob frets. 'I don't want to be lumped in with that crew.' He told Guy that he had forgotten why they had fallen out, but once he put down the phone he began to remember. 'The only thing I'm ready to hear is an absolute 100 per cent meaningful apology,' he explains. 'I'm not in the business of taking a look at what I've done, because I've had a big look at it and I think I did great. Do you know what I mean? Apart from being an arsehole with him a couple of times when we were doing vocals, but that's out of frustration because he's not dealing with me very well.' He realises something else. 'I think he wants me to say sorry too. And I can't.' He doesn't mean that he incapable, just that he finds no reason for it. All these things considered, he's not sure he wants to see him.

'As much as finding him was a relief in the early days,' reflects Rob, 'not having him now is a relief … '

* * *

Since coming home to Los Angeles, he has been working out, walking the dogs and relaxing. He starts reading a script Steven Spielberg's people have sent over, *The Disassociate*, but only gets to page 60. The role is of a man in a boring job who God sends a postcard to and instructs him to start spreading the universal language he invented in college. Rob won't be doing it.

One lunchtime we go down to the local deli. Rod Stewart and his family are dining on the patio. Rob and Rod hug – they're outside, in public; one photo the tabloids would have gobbled up, but thankfully they miss it – and they briefly discuss the English football scores and whether West Ham will stay up. Inside, he sits under the photo of welders having their lunch sandwiches on a girder in the New York sky, one of the inspirations for the *Escapology* sleeve.

There's a table of Baldwins in the corner. As we leave, a woman comes up and says she is a massive fan and a close friend of Brian Wilson's wife, and asks whether he would like to sing on Brian Wilson's forthcoming duets album.

Later on, four of us go into town – Rob, Pompey, Daniel and me – and have coffee at Coffee Bean on Sunset, into the heart of Los Angeles' quiet madness. A choreographer comes up to him and explains that he has worked with Michael Jackson and Ricky Martin, and just worked on the German version of *Pop Idol*. 'It'd be an honour for me to show you my work,' he says.

Rob gets chatting with a blonde woman whose friend is snogging someone she has just met round the corner. They discuss God boxes, where you write down your problem in the evening, put it in the box and let God deal with it. 'I have a Desire List instead,' she says. She gets it out and he asks to read it. The first item: I Desire A Fulfilling Loving Relationship.

'So do I, the top one,' says Rob.

'You're the only person in the whole world who's seen it,' she says.

'Well, I'm perhaps the only person who's said, can I read it?' Rob points out.

They chat on.

'I like cars,' she says.

'What cars do you like?' he asks.

'I love Aston Martins,' she says.

'Got one of those,' he says.

The kissing friend has returned. She has curls cascading formlessly from her head. Daniel offers to sort these out for her, and when she accepts, he goes to his car, gets out his scissors and a white smock, and starts cutting her hair on the pavement of Sunset Boulevard.

'I work with kids, so you can't make it too crazy,' she says.

The first woman mentions that she has just been in the Hustler sex superstore down the street, doing research. She wants to manufacture pre- and post-orgasm wipes. 'Clean-ups,' she says. 'Sensual ones.'

'Sensual clean-ups,' repeats Rob.

A man comes up to speak to her. It turns out that he was talking to her before, but then he saw someone he has a restraining order against, so he went to call his lawyer.

A woman shouts from a passing jeep, 'I love you, Robbie!'

'Thank you,' he says.

The haircut is finished.

'You came as Chewbacca,' Rob tells her, 'and left as Audrey Hepburn.'

We meet Max at the Chateau Marmont hotel. There is an actress here, reasonably famous, who supposedly has a crush on Rob. She sent her CV to the office last week, offering to appear in any of his videos. Within five minutes of meeting The Actress he tells her, 'You do look very first wife.'

'First wife?' she queries, confused.

'My first wife,' he says.

She joins in the spirit of the conversation, and of the flirtation.

'Will it be more painful for me or for you?' she asks.

'Oh, for me,' he says, 'because I fall too hard.'

We have to go to another party, but he has enjoyed this encounter. 'She's gorgeous,' he says in the car. 'But she's an actress, so she must be fucking bonkers.' He nonetheless leaves her a message, suggesting a date tomorrow night.

We go to a Maxim party, where Rob dances and the DJ plays Barry White's 'Ecstasy' melded into 'Rock DJ', a song built around a sample from the Barry White classic. During The Rolling Stones' 'Emotional Rescue', Rob parades his Mick Jagger peacock strut around the dance floor. For Wham!'s 'Everything She Wants' he hands Pompey his Comme Des Garçons coat to free his movements. When the DJ drops out the music, his is the loudest voice shouting out the missing lyrics – '*and now you tell me that you're having my baby*!' – and he stays in motion for 'Let's Dance', 'Into The Groove', 'Kiss' and 'Groove Is In The Heart'.

'I've never heard "Rock DJ" at a club,' he says on the way home. 'I don't go to clubs.'

'Well, lap-dancing clubs,' Pompey points out.

'They play "Angels" at lap-dancing clubs,' says Rob. 'It's a bit disconcerting.'

* * *

In a few days' time Rob is scheduled to play in New York again, this time at a free concert in Battery Park connected with the Tribeca Film Festival, on a bill with Norah Jones, The Roots and Jewel. Last week he called Tim and David and said that he didn't want to do it. He explained that he couldn't afford to be insecure about performing, going into the summer tour, and another debacle like Rock The Vote might crack the thin veneer of self-confidence he has developed: 'I said, my greatest strength is also my biggest weakness and that's my insecurities. Rock The Vote made me feel really insecure about my performances.' They persuade him to press ahead; he agrees but says that it must be on their heads. 'If I do this and this is in any way, shape or form like the Rock The Vote,' he tells them, 'you will never *ever* get me to do anything that I ever don't want to do again. Ever.'

The other looming business issue is the greatest hits album. EMI would prefer to release it for this Christmas. Rob would rather wait another year. Anyway, he would need at least two new singles to put on a greatest hits album, and he doesn't consider that he has them. Soon he will be concentrating on the summer tour and the time to have written them, let alone record them, will have gone.

* * *

Rob has now decided that he should buy the large, well-situated plot of land at the end of his estate and build a house on it. We go down there with the realtor to inspect it. There is a small pipe running across it and Rob asks the realtor what it is, but the realtor doesn't know.

'It's all the gossip from the estate going to *E! News*,' Rob suggests.

He wanders around the empty grass lot, pointing to imaginary buildings. 'I want a treehouse there,' he says. 'And, Josie, I'd like a fairground. And monkeys. And are there any Culkin brothers left?'

Afterwards, back in his kitchen, there is a tour meeting. David gives him an email from his new musical director, Mark Plati, suggesting a way of arranging 'Mr Bojangles': recording it, cutting an acetate of it and then playing it until it is scratched, so that the backing track sounds like an old record being played. Rob says he should go ahead. They discuss costumes, and Rob says he wants 'as a side issue' to go down Sunset Boulevard in the ostrich outfits with Max. (Max demurs. 'Jonny'd do it,' Rob taunts.) Rob suggests that for 'Rock DJ' they should start off with some of Barry White's 'Ecstasy'.

That night he goes to Les Deux, the low-key bar with a large outdoor area where the chic and chilled-out still go on a Monday. There he chats with a Welsh actor he knows a little, and explains how his date last night (with The Actress, though he doesn't specify this) didn't really work out. 'I started thinking of what she'd be like at my funeral, going around to everyone,' he says. 'And she wasn't doing it well enough, so I decided to knock it on the head.'

About an hour later the Welsh actor comes back up to him.

'I was thinking about what you said,' he tells Rob. 'And maybe you should be thinking about what you'll be doing at *her* funeral.'

'Thanks for pointing out that I'm selfish,' Rob tells him. 'I *know* that ... '

In the parking lot Tatum O'Neal, who has been speaking with Vincent Gallo all night, comes up and says to Rob, 'I just want to know if the rumours are true.' Rob disappears elsewhere, with a woman he met earlier and without a bodyguard, and he doesn't return to his house until the following lunchtime. He has had fun, and has heard Marianne Faithfull's *Broken English* for the first time, though there was one strange moment. Before they went to sleep, she asked him how he was with guns. Alright, he said. Why?

'There's a loaded gun by the bed on your side,' she told him. 'First chamber's empty, second chamber's full, so if somebody breaks in you have to shoot twice.'

'It's great in LA, isn't it?' he sighs, as he relates this. He compares notes with Pompey, who had his own strange evening, and discovers that they suffer from different problems. 'You can't talk to them if you want to shag them, just if you want to go out with them,' he concludes. 'And I'm the complete opposite.'

* * *

One afternoon everyone is lounging around the house when Rob says to the assembled company, 'Do you want a coffee?'

Pompey goes to fetch the car keys. He assumes that we are going to the local Starbucks.

'No,' says Rob. 'I'm going to make one. With the kettle.'

This is unusual.

'Are you?' says Pompey.

'Yeah,' says Rob, and heads for the kitchen.

'I'll come,' Pompey decides, 'in case you go through trauma.'

A few minutes later Rob hands round perfectly good coffees.

'I'll make you another one in a couple of years,' he promises.

* * *

On the way to New York there are more radio stations to visit. He is up at dawn, eating cereal at the kitchen table in his underwear, when a thought strikes him. 'Josie,' he asks, 'if they want the greatest hits out this year, I was just thinking, what does that mean they think about America?'

Best not to think too hard about that today. Instead, by lunchtime he is sharing his thoughts with the people of Denver on how celebrity enhances your looks. 'I mean, Mick Jagger,' he says. '*Jesus*, you know what I'm saying? There's a case of celebrity really getting you laid. Rock'n'roll – getting ugly people laid since 1950.'

In the van he listens to a message on his phone from The Actress. He has called to say that he's not in the place for dating, but he still finds himself thinking about her. 'What a lovely message,' he says. 'I "couldn't be fun-der". It's not a word, but it's a nice thought.'

'Is she nice?' asks David.

'I don't know,' Rob replies. 'She's an actress. I wouldn't find out for eight months.'

On the jet he says, 'I thought about some ideas for songs the other day where I was actually talking about somebody else's experiences.' When he tried them out, he made a discovery. 'They still sound like my experiences when they're not.' Maybe there's another way round it. 'Next album,' he suggests, 'I'll still write it all about me, and just proclaim that none of this stuff ever happened to me.'

Late at night we descend into a storm just outside New York, and the flight gets bumpy. Rob suggests that we turn off all the lights. We ride down in darkness.

14

He decides to go shopping for clothes and art. In the Mercer Hotel foyer he bumps into Mike Myers, who tells him that they are on the *Tonight Show*, America's biggest chat show, together next week. Outside the front door, some fans are waiting on the New York sidewalk. One gives him Elvis Monopoly and the other shows Rob some photos of himself and asks whether he wants any. 'I'm alright,' he says. 'I know what I look like. But thank you.'

At Pop International Galleries he admires a Warhol of a small chicken rice box, but buys nothing. In Ralph Lauren he sees a vintage leather jacket that they say is from the forties. 'One of Mr Lauren's archive pieces,' they explain. It is $1295. 'I think I'll get a lot of use out of it,' he reasons, and buys it. For once, he is right. From now on, when faced with wardrobe insecurity and needing some clothing confidence, it is usually this jacket he will reach for.

Back in his room, he lies on his bed and Josie dials so that he can do a pre-interview on the phone for his appearance on the *Tonight Show*. This is the process that leads to the sometimes puzzling phenomenon when a chat show host will say something, often something bewilderingly specific like 'So your mother collected kettles, I believe', and the interviewee will miraculously have a medium-length and slightly funny anecdote to tell on this very subject. The pre-interview – which is usually much longer than the TV interview will be – is used to identify some of these areas of interest, and to pinpoint some of these stories.

He stares at the ceiling and rambles into the receiver:

' ... I just bumped into Mike Myers ... no, I'm not a fan of the way British teeth are portrayed ... mine are alright ... I actually have an E-type Shaguar ... but I don't drive ... I never learned ... I didn't drop out of school, no ... in England we finish school at 16 and there's only a small percentage of people that go on to college ... a boy band ... we made N'Sync look like Led Zeppelin ... I did it for five years ... no, a horrible time ... my father's a comedian and a singer and I've grown up around tremendously bad cabaret acts ... and some good ones – my dad's a good one ... why did I move here? ... it's sunny here ... I'm looking for Mrs Williams ... yeah, I can find Mrs One Night but not Mrs Forever ... I've got a wolf ... Pets of Bel Air ... yeah ... *Honestly* ... You'd have loved me to have said, "Well, I went into the Canadian outback and rescued a pack of wolves, and their mother" ... Actually I'll do one of those stories and then go, well, I actually got it from Pets of Bel Air ... no, they're just a ruse to disguise my homosexuality ... no, keep to dirt and gossip – don't ask me about music ... '

He has given them what they need. He has been on the *Tonight Show* before, with mixed results. He sang 'Have You Met Miss Jones?' and chatted with the host, Jay Leno. The song felt like a triumph – 'singing this swing song in their back garden, big eyes and everything, charisma overloading, the audience really lapping it up' – and as he walked over to the couch he was aware of a voice inside him saying: *This is where it could all unravel.* For a while it did. 'He said, "What was it like working with Queen?" and I said, "Very scary in the studio, actually singing Freddie's vocals with Brian and Roger – it was the first time I realised that the colour of adrenaline was brown..." They were stone-faced. Had this petrifying moment that I was on American television and I've just done a few gags and no one's got them and it's sort of like I've sent off a charm missile and it's been intercepted by the lack-of-irony gremlins in the air, and no one's laughing and people now just think I'm weird. It's scary.' Watching it back, he realised it wasn't as bad as it had felt at the time, but it unnerved him, and he has mixed feelings about repeating the process.

He goes downstairs, where he stands at reception and picks up a copy of *Spin* from the hotel magazine rack. He reads enough to know that he was right: it isn't good. The introduction refers to him as 'Britain's clown prince of pop' and the large pull-quote from him on the first page of text is: '*To tell you the absolute truth it's not going to happen for me here.*' The article itself says: '*In short, Williams is predicting his own failure. And no potential failure has ever cared less.*'

* * *

On the morning of the Battery Park concert, David Beckham is on the front cover of *USA Today*. The headline reads: *He's The Most Famous Athlete In The World (Except For The USA).*

'He's got Williams-itis,' diagnoses Rob.

Downstairs, he bumps into Lisa Stansfield and they chat about the repetitiveness of promotion.

'Yeah,' she says. '"How many times have you been around the world?" And it's that smile that you develop.'

'No,' says Rob. 'I just tell them to fuck off.'

He heads out to the shops for a while, then goes back to bed so that he doesn't have to think about tonight's concert any more. When he wakes, he runs through the lyrics to 'Millennium' under his breath and discovers that he can't remember them. Pompey finds a fan site on the internet and Rob scans their transcription. '*Run around in circles* ... ' he repeats, and nods.

'If only they knew,' says Pompey.

We drive downtown. There are yellow posters all over the place, advertising ROBBIE WILLIAMS FREE CONCERT, his record company cheekily passing off the Battery Park event as his own. He wanders anxiously around the backstage area. As he passes, I hear two New Yorkers discuss him.

'Who is that guy?' says one.

'He went out with Ginger Spice I know,' shrugs the other.

The woman from *Liquid News* is here, and asks about his 'attacking America thing ... the whole strategy' and for once he decides to try and explain how succeeding in America has never been that much of a big deal to him. 'But it's weird how England's treated my so-called onslaught into America: "Robbie will never do it, and stop it, don't even try", and all that business,' he points out. 'Come on, England. Get behind me.'

On the side of the stage, waiting to go on, he starts singing '*New York, New York, it's a wonderful town* ... ' and the actor Mario Cantone from *Sex And The City* joins in. There's a large crowd – he is told there are around 10,000 here – in the open air, and he seems nervous. In 'Come Undone' he messes up the end, singing a different part of the song from the band. Before 'Feel', just as he is settling in and the crowd is beginning to respond to him, he makes the speech that will be edited and reprinted over and over in Britain as a prime example of his desperation when it comes to American success. Here, in front of a big crowd warming to him, it doesn't seem desperate at all, just a little peculiar:

'This is the song that I've got out here at the minute, and I believe that you have to ring in your radio stations and request it for me to have a hit here,' he says. 'And even if you don't like me, can you just do it, please? Phone your fucking radio stations and request it! This is a song called "Feel".'

By the final song, 'Angels', the lighters are out and he looks properly pleased and, at last, slightly relaxed by the response.

In the van, David doesn't say anything. He has been terrified the whole way through the show; he knows it seems to have gone pretty well, but he knows that there is enough that is imperfect about the whole situation that if Rob chooses to, he can make good on his threat to heap blame upon David and Tim for an unpleasant ordeal. He is waiting for Rob's declaration, either way.

'I'm fine,' Rob finally says. 'I was knackered. But I nearly enjoyed it. I did John Travolta all the way through, and I did humble at the end.'

That established, relief spreading over David's face, they plot how to wind up Tim.

'Say "He's furious, he won't even speak to me",' Rob suggests. 'You should say, "Rob went off in the fourth song, smashed his guitar, didn't even do 'Angels' ..."'

* * *

Rob, Daniel and I are sitting on the bench outside the Mercer Hotel – Rob can't smoke inside – when Rachel Weisz pulls up in a cab with a friend she'd mentioned to Daniel earlier. Daniel greets them.

'I thought you'd be a woman,' Daniel says to the friend.

'I am,' Rachel Weisz's short-haired friend replies.

There being no easy way back from that, we all just go inside.

'Is it frantic tonight or is it just me?' Rob says to the friend. She is an artist.

'It's you,' she says.

She asks about the concert. Rob describes the crowd's evolution from apathy to engagement.

'Was it fun?' she asks.

'Sort of,' he says. 'It was full of anxiety because they don't know any of my stuff. I've been doing it since I was 16. I don't want to be winning people over when I'm 30.'

They go off to a party and we sit on a sofa, drinking coffee, watching the lobby ebb and flow, and discuss paths taken and not taken. 'I haven't got the brain that sits down, listens and receives information,' he says. 'I can only retain stuff that I'm interested about. Which just happens to be football. I know for a fact that going on to sixth form to retake my GCSEs I'd have just fucked them up again, and by that time I'd got into smoking draw and experimenting with speed and acid and stuff and I'd fell in with a bad lot, and I do genuinely think – thank the Lord, bless the Lord that I got the break that I got – that I'd have ended up probably in jail. And it's not me romanticising about that in any way. Who's to say? Hey, I became a fucking drug addict and an alcoholic. *That* was never going to happen. But seeing the route I went down, it would have happened anyway and I probably would have had to do bad stuff to get it. If that break hadn't come, I'd have probably been a drug dealer. But it hasn't happened – praise the Lord.'

Do you think your mum thought you'd come to good, or do you think she was scared that … ?

'It was really early on, so there was no real decision made whether I'd come to good or come to bad. I know she was worried when I used to drink when I was 17 and 18 – she turned up at a pub once and I was just coming up on ecstasy. I'd just started rushing and the car turns into the pub car park. I was 18 … '

So you sat in the pub with her?

'Yeah. Gurning.'

Did she have a clue?

'Yeah, she did.'

Not a good feeling.

'No, it's not. No. It's funny now but it wasn't at the time. Yeah, and then there was one time when she was away for the evening and I'd fucking wrecked the house – all kids do it though, don't they? She came in and I'd just passed out, and she came in and the table was on the floor and her flowers were all over the place, and mud in the house, and a girl in my bed … '

Did she express her disapproval?

'Oh yeah. She's good at that … she can be very scary. The power is dissipating slowly, but if she had a go at me now I'd still crumble … quite badly.'

* * *

Late the following evening, he walks into his Los Angeles kitchen and finds both his parents there.

'It doesn't half take it out of you,' he tells them, 'conquering places.'

15

Rob has been back in Los Angeles for a couple of days before his father remembers that someone called for him while he was away, and left a letter at the gate house. 'Somebody who lives near here,' Pete eventually explains, vaguely.

Dear Robbie, the letter begins.

This is kind of weird man, but I found out from a friend of my wife's that she approached you up at Starbucks, and asked if you might be interested in singing on my new CD. I dig your voice and thought it would be perfect for a song I have written called 'Gettin In Over My Head' … I am not sure if you know with who I am, but I was one of the Beach Boys, but since my brother Carl died in 1998 I have been doing solo work …

'Brian Wilson rang,' laughs Rob, 'and my dad forgot to tell me.'

* * *

One day in the van, towards the end of his visit, Pete mentions that when he gets home he has to do an interview with Radio Wales about the birth and heyday of the British cabaret club. He describes the small clubs, their capacity no more than 150, that you used to find in many British cities, and where he would share top billing with a singer for a week at a time, always from Sunday to Saturday.

'Cabaret clubs died in the latter seventies, early eighties,' he says.

'Alternative comedy came in 82, 83?' checks Rob.

'A little later,' says Pete.

'So that didn't kill cabaret?' asks Rob.

Pete shakes his head. 'The outlook on entertainment changed,' he says. 'Discos and nightclubs came up.' For him, something was lost. 'Most new acts don't know how to walk on or walk off,' he says. 'And nobody listens to them either.'

Rob asks him about the old clubs in the Stoke area: the Place, the Torch. Though many of their father–son exchanges involve re-running family lore or funny stories, bonding through repetition and familiarity, this conversation, about the nuts and bolts of his father's entertainment world, seems to be one they have never quite had before.

'Northern Soul got into the Torch,' says Pete. He says this as though Northern Soul was some kind of unfortunate infection.

'Did you not like Northern Soul?' asks Rob.

'I was more into the Place,' says Pete.

'What did they play at the Place?' asks Rob.

'It was more across the board,' Pete says, and talks about how his friend didn't let The Rolling Stones in there in the early sixties because they had jeans on. The Rolling Stones had just played the Gaumont in Hanley. It was when he was still a policeman. 'I was on duty that night at the nick,' he remembers, 'and we drove the van and brought them straight in, and I was security backstage. Remember Dave Berry? I was backstage security with Dusty Springfield and The Troggs and Dave Berry.'

'Did you like Dusty Springfield?' asks Rob.

'Yes,' he says. 'She was with Madeleine Bell then. I saw her without her wig on, her hair straight to her head. The wigs were on stands.'

'When you were a copper, right?' Rob confirms.

'How did you go from being a copper to an entertainer?' Josie asks.

'I always fancied it,' says Pete. 'I was knocking about with a comedian called Tony Braddock, who was a very good friend of mine, and he emigrated to Australia … '

'Was he from Stoke?' asks Rob.

'Yeah. And I used to watch him and think, I'm sure I could do that – I know I can do that. I had this thing in here that I could do that. Anyway, Tony emigrated to Australia and I knew Tony's act backwards, and I was in the pub one night and there was a talent competition on and everybody was singing "The Green Green Grass Of Home" and I went up and I did ten minutes of Tony's act, and everybody laughed and I thought, I like this, this is good. And I won two quid.'

He was 24 and working in an electrics factory at the time.

'Bear in mind wages were £17 a week then. I was with two other lads and that was like our night out on two quid, so there was a thing in the paper that said there was another talent competition at another place the following week. So I went to that one and I won that one. So now I'm in two finals.'

'Using your mate's act?' asks Rob.

'Yeah,' he says. 'Yeah.'

'Had you just memorised it?' asks Rob.

'Yeah, I'd remembered bits of it … I didn't know it all … '

'Oooh,' says Josie to Rob. 'That's where you get it from … '

Rob nods. 'I'm a little magpie,' he concedes.

'Yes, well, we all are,' says Pete. 'So the outcome was I won these two finals and won a fiver in each one, and that was going to be the end of that. I'd had my little bit of fun.' But he was offered some more bookings, and then more after that. For ages he still tried to hold down his day job. 'And then there came a time, it was just one morning, I hadn't made my mind up, I was at work and I thought, I can't do this any more.' He went to his boss and told him, 'I'm going to give this entertainment lark a bit of a bash.' And he left. 'I thought, well, if I get 12 months out of this entertaining nonsense … and 36 years later I'm still doing it.'

'My dad,' Rob tells the rest of us, 'used to have these cards: "Pete Conway, comedian …" – and the telephone number – " … don't call when *Star Trek*'s on".'

'No,' says Pete, 'it said, "call this number any time", and then in brackets, "except during *Star Trek*".'

'Where are all your trophies, Dad?' he asks.

'All wrapped up in a box, which needs pulling out,' he says.

'Because I just remember there being tons of them,' says Rob. 'Loads of football ones and golfing ones ...'

' ... and all the entertainment ones as well,' says Pete. 'Entertainer Of The Year awards.'

'I won best haircut in 1993,' says Rob.

'I know,' says Pete. 'You've got a few as well, haven't you? It'd be nice putting mine with yours. They're all a bit tarnished now. All the gold fell off them ... '

* * *

Outside the back of the building where the *Tonight Show* is filmed, Rob bumps into Simon Cowell, another guest, and they stand in the sun and compare notes: Californian real estate, pop music, success. Cowell offers his theory about himself: that every American show has a British villain and he has found a niche by embracing that tradition.

'I'm having the time now I should have done when I was 17, 18,' Rob tells him. 'I've only started enjoying it in the last 12 months, and now I'm fucking loving it.'

'Good for you,' says Cowell.

'Listen,' says Rob, 'I'm going to go and do my hair ... '

In the corridor, Rob meets Katie Couric, the host of this evening's show. The *Tonight Show* is usually hosted by Jay Leno, but this week is sweeps week. In a bafflingly antiquated system, on American TV 'sweeps' happen four times a year, and it is the audience the TV networks get on these weeks that determines the advertising rates they can charge throughout the year. Consequently, they reach for all manner of stunts to boost their viewing figures during these weeks. (Whenever you see a very famous film star appear in an American sitcom, for instance, the episode will usually first have been shown during sweeps.) One of NBC's stunts this spring is to have their most famous hosts swap jobs for a day. This morning Jay Leno filled Katie Couric's usual shoes co-presenting the morning news programme the *Today Show*; this evening she is to fill his.

'Is this too much?' she asks her entourage as she walks towards Rob. She is wearing a black evening dress offering rather more décolletage than her usual power woman morning outfits. They encourage her that it is not. She greets Rob and says how nervous she is.

'It's not brave unless you're shitting yourself,' he tells her.

'Shooting or shutting?' she asks, not quite catching it.

'Shitting,' he repeats.

'Oh,' she says, and smiles. 'The colour of adrenaline's brown, right?'

She is quoting him, the time he was on the show; the joke that seemed to bomb.

By the time Rob sings 'Feel', Simon Cowell and Mike Myers are already sitting in armchairs next to the desk Katie Couric sits behind. The performance area is off to the left, as the audience and cameras look at it. Before the first chorus Rob is wooing the front row, and soon he is over to the guests and host, first serenading Katie Couric by the desk. He moves on to Simon Cowell, turning away from him and lap-dancing, grinding his rear inches above Cowell's groin. Cowell seems both embarrassed and amused. Mike Myers, aware that he must be next, leaps behind the armchairs to avoid Rob, who follows him there.

Perhaps the audience at home imagine that this, too, is a sweeps stunt and that it has all been arranged. It hasn't, and to whatever degree Rob has thought any of this through beforehand, he hasn't discussed it with anyone, other than mentioning to the director on the floor during rehearsals that he might wander in Katie's direction and checking that this wouldn't be completely out of order.

* * *

Tomorrow he will learn that his episode of the *Tonight Show* is their highest-rated Monday night show for five years. His album, which had dropped off the Top 200 of the Billboard album chart three weeks earlier, will reappear at number 125, and all over the American media his appearance is noted with approval. For the next few weeks, people will come up to him in shops and car parks and Starbucks and compliment him on his performance. It is not enough on its own to make his record a hit, but it shows that, given the chance to see and hear him do what he can, the American public responds just as other audiences around the world do.

The performance is also noticed in Britain. If Rob is correct that his British public persona is a character cast in a soap opera, then their current plotline is that Robbie Williams is demeaning himself by throwing himself at an America that wants no part of him. Nothing will shake them from this conviction. '*The tedious bid by Robbie Williams to crack America continues apace,*' judges the *Daily Mirror*. '*Just how low will Robbie go?*' echoes *OK!* magazine, claiming that he '*humiliated himself* ... *by embarrassing guest host Katie Couric* ... *who, clearly embarrassed, was seen pushing his face away*'.

It depends, I suppose, what you wanted to see. And worse is to come.

* * *

One day some large, heavy cardboard boxes arrive in the forecourt of his Los Angeles home. They are from Austria. Last month, in a Chelsea gym, Rob had discovered a new fitness machine, called the Vacunaut, that seemed to work well for him, and he has bought one for himself, for the price of a medium-sized car. It is a full body suit with a series of pads around the stomach, connected to a pump. It is designed according to a theory that fat loss is difficult around the midriff because circulation is poor there, and so the body is less likely to convert and transport fat from there than elsewhere. The Vacunaut is intended to counteract that problem. Rob swears by it. Most days he appears in his suit, like an eccentric spaceman, asking either to be zipped up or unzipped.

* * *

Over dinner at Koi, Rob accuses Max of rearranging the candle on the table so that it provides Max with the most flattering light. Max denies it strenuously, but not convincingly. Neither of them disputes that it is something one might do. 'I must admit,' Rob confesses, 'I did it somewhere the other day.'

Two slightly overawed and giggly women approach, and ask to have their photo taken with Rob. One of them says, thrilled, that they like how rude he is. 'What do you say?' she asks.

'You say "fuck",' says the other before Rob can speak.

'You two girls have got lovely foo-foo flappers,' Rob tells them, as they snuggle either side of him, under his arms, for a photo.

'We love your work,' says one.

'Guess where my friend lives?' says the other. 'Guernsey.'

It takes a while to understand what is going on, especially as their confusion is multi-faceted. (They clearly imagine Guernsey is something to do with Ireland.)

Rob begins to realise. There is no point in doing anything but play along.

'You look very dapper tonight,' the first girl says to him.

'Thank you, Colin,' the other says.

They are all grins and giggles as they back away, believing that they have just had a satisfying, intimate encounter with Colin Farrell.

* * *

Rob wanders into the kitchen. It is time for his father to leave for his plane.

'I hate leaving anywhere,' says Pete. 'I don't like goodbyes.'

'You don't like goodbyes?' says Jan. 'I've noticed. "I'm just going for a drink across the Leopard." Thirty-seven years later … '

* * *

He's been worrying about dying, and he has come to see his concern as a good omen.

'Dying,' he argues, 'I think that's the last one you can possibly worry about, when you've got everything out of the way. The committee in the head, that's the last one they can throw over from the trenches – death.'

* * *

He decides to go shopping for some new pool cues and balls. In the car he listens to the demo Brian Wilson enclosed with his letter, 'Getting In Over My Head'.

'Really sweet,' he says. 'It sounds like the Beach Boys, doesn't it?' In the third verse he turns it off. 'It's too long,' he says.

I ask him whether he'll consider doing it.

'Today I wouldn't,' he says, 'because I don't want to do anything today.'

From the car, he calls a friend and discusses romantic possibilities.

'She's as cute as a button, yeah,' he concedes, 'but she's as cute as a boring button.'

He has been asking me how downloading music from the internet works – he may be castigated as a public apologist for the habit, but until today he has never done it. When we get home, once he has played with his new pool balls and watched the Lakers lose their final play-off game, I show him how to use Limewire. We lie on his bed, our computers facing each other between us, downloading songs and playing them to each other. His first illegal music search is for something by Boogie Down Productions; his first successful download is Dr Hook's 'Cover Of The Rolling Stone'.

There's a party tonight for *Nylon* magazine at a chic hotspot called White Lotus; many beautiful women are expected.

'We're going to Willi Wonka's Chocolate Factory now,' hoots Max, excited, 'and we're kids who love chocolate … '

'I've got diabetes,' murmurs Rob.

Max says he thinks it'll be mad for Rob at the party after this week's TV.

'And,' Rob points out, 'I'm wearing the same clothes.'

'Yeah,' says Max, 'actors do that.'

Hugh Hefner arrives at the same time as we do, flanked by a handful of security personnel. ('About Hef,' Rob, who has never met him, judges later, 'there's something gloriously right and hideously wrong.') Inside the party he is interviewed for the second time in a few days by *Us* magazine. The reporter asks him what the inspiration was for his new album. 'I have to do something with my time,' he says. His heart isn't in it. 'After the meeting today,' he says, once she has gone, 'I can't even be bothered to be funny or irreverent. I am wasted here. That's how I feel. I'm wasting my time.'

He sits at a table of unflashy English girls who work for Nintendo and are in town for a computer games conference. They've gone out for dinner and found themselves in the middle of a party. He gets them to order a coffee for him. They asked how America is going. Max wanders by.

'Do you know Max Beesley, from the film *Glitter*?' Rob asks the English girls.

'Oh fuck,' says Max. 'You better not do that out on the road.'

In Rob's head you can almost see the wheels turning.

Marvin Jarrett, *Nylon*'s editor, suggests to Rob that he comes over and meets L'il Kim, the party's nominal hostess. Eventually he agrees to, but he immediately regrets it. When he is led up to her table, he has to hover there for ages while someone gets her attention, and after they have their photo taken together Marvin says to him, 'Good exposure in America,' which infuriates him.

As Rob and L'il Kim have their brief, pleasant and meaningless interaction, a drunken English bloke harangues Pompey with a monologue about Rob's finest qualities.

' … he's just got a *wicked* sense of humour,' the man babbles. 'The best one-liner ever was when he got all that money and they asked him on TV how he was feeling and he said "fucking wealthy!". Know what I mean? … '

Rob returns and looks around. 'I think I'd rather be playing pool,' he says. Our party gathers in the parking lot across the road.

'Fucking horrible,' says Rob.

'Claustrophobic and rancid,' Max agrees.

'Everybody looking for a celebrity,' says Rob. 'Not realising I'm one.'

In the car he says, in full Alan Partridge mode, 'Ooh! I feel like a pastry that's been deflated. And the filling's America. I've had an American pie and it's gone flat.'

* * *

It goes flatter. Late that night, after he has already gone to bed, Rob shouts from his room; I'm staying just across the landing. He is in his bed, his computer next to him, and on the screen is a horrible piece about him from tomorrow's *Daily Mirror*, headlined ROBBIE'S A YAWN IN THE USA. He reads some of it out.

When he signed the biggest record deal in British pop history, the irrepressible Robbie Williams was £80 million richer and had the UK at his feet … But as he gyrated on Simon Cowell's knee during a desperate appearance on America's Tonight Show *this week, he looked more like a wannabe than an all-conquering superstar. The tragic performance … marked a new low in his seemingly futile attempt to crack the lucrative US market. It's a campaign that has taught him the hard way that American fans will never be won over by arrogance and greed …*

After a number of mistakes – they take literally, or pretend to, Daryl Hannah's deadpan joke that she thought she was going to be working with *Robin* Williams on the 'Feel' video – and an analysis linking Rob's American 'failure' with his lack of humility, they conclude that his British career may now be on the slide as well, finishing with:

As Westlife's manager Louis Walsh says: 'Robbie only had two things going for him – his brass neck and Guy Chambers. Now he hasn't got Guy.'

'Sick, isn't it?' he says. 'It shouldn't be allowed. There's nothing you can do about it really.'

Here in Los Angeles the public have been shouting 'Love what you did with Katie!' at him, and he has been feeling like Jim Carrey in *The Truman Show*. 'I think the one major thing about the American work I've done here is, obviously as much self-hatred as I've had myself in the past, I feel more self-contained and I feel as though I know my worth,' he says. 'You know, after the *Tonight Show*, which you know was a piece of magic television. It's one of those, for want of a better term, it was like Freddie Starr on fucking *Des O'Connor*. I'm not saying I'm Freddie Starr, but you know what I mean. Or like when the elephant shat on *Blue Peter*.'

I love the way you've chosen examples that somehow both elevate and demean you.

'Alright. So let me think of one ... ' He thinks for a moment. 'Well, the only ones you remember are where people are drunk or animals shit. Or Freddie Starr on Des O'Connor, great television. Either which way, what I'm saying is this: I've been a true fucking star, and I've felt, and I've really enjoyed being a true fucking star. And I've gone around, everything that I've done, with assurance, confidence – I've been loud, confident and right. Instead of believing myself to be loud, confident and wrong, you know. I do it a bit differently than everybody else does, and it's appealing to people. I know my worth. But, you know, it's another classic case of, I really shouldn't read that stuff. Because, actually, it doesn't matter. I think what I've started to realise as well, is that there's a selection of people that don't buy my records, and a majority of the journalists now in Britain that will attack and judge everything that I do, and I will always come out losing to these people, and then there's a huge selection of people, that has been proved throughout the five albums that I've done, that actually buy the records and connect. You know, connect with the lyric on every level. You know, Chris, I fucking mean everything I write.'

We chat until he falls asleep in front of me.

* * *

These last two weeks of Los Angeles calm, as the summer tour looms, pass quickly. He works on his fitness in the gym and on the basketball court near the house, and hiking round Runyon Canyon's steepest trails with his dogs, with only occasional disturbances. One Saturday a vintage 1956 military plane crashes into a ravine near the house, killing its pilot, and from the kitchen he can see the helicopters hovering over the wreckage. He writes to Brian Wilson, politely explaining that his schedule won't allow him to accept the honour of appearing on Wilson's album, but thanking him for everything he has done for Rob without him knowing it. (It may be that even Rob doesn't know everything Brian Wilson has done for Rob. While they were making *Escapology*, Steve Power mentioned to me that everyone thought there were sleigh bells on 'Angels' because it was being planned as a Christmas single, but that wasn't the case: 'Really they're just there because Guy and I love Brian Wilson.')

Rob also meets with a couple of songwriters. Chris Briggs had suggested he listened to a CD of songs by Dan Wilson, formerly of Semisonic, and Rob liked it enough to invite him round. Nothing much happens. They listen to records, and occasionally Dan Wilson plays a chord or two on a keyboard. Rob sits on the bed and smokes. 'It was really weird,' Rob says. 'He was a really nice bloke, but we sat around for three hours and he didn't come up with anything.' Rob also spends a few hours with the singer and songwriter Robin Thicke, but Thicke is filming his own video the following day, and has been out the night before. 'His heart wasn't it,' says Rob. 'So we just sat around for a little bit. That was just a little bit weird too.' He also makes plans to call the Pet Shop Boys to discuss the possibility of doing some writing, but doesn't get around to it yet.

And then there is Guy. Just as Rob seems to be entertaining the possibility that there could be a way for them to do some work together – he surprises everyone by suggesting that if he did need any new singles this year he could do them with Guy: 'If we went into the studio and worked for a week we could come up with three singles, and I would be quite excited to do that, to see what we would come up with.' – he hears that Guy has blanked David at the Ivor Novello luncheon. That, once again, is that. Rob isn't much bothered by any of this. Perhaps he doesn't even need someone to write songs with – one day he writes a new one he loves, and gets Max to play it on the keyboard in the basement while he sings. If he is to find someone, it will happen in its own good time.

By the time he returns to London, as ready as he can be for the weeks ahead, he also has new tattoos from Pompey's Devon friend, Glen: two swallows facing each other on his lower stomach, and two hearts on the inside of his wrists. The hearts scab up horrifyingly, so thick and irregular that you can barely see what shape the tattoo beneath them is supposed to be. He thinks he put the wrong lotion on them afterwards. But he won't check with a doctor; if he ends up with heart-shaped scars, that's what will be. He saves his worrying for more intangible things.

Part three

1

He prides himself on being able to fool anyone – the audience, of course, but also even his closest friends and colleagues – when he is onstage. He will present them with the evidence that he is a confident but emotional man performing at the peak of his powers and having the time of his life, and he will do this so well that even the doubters, even the people looking for the cracks in the vase, even those who have read paragraphs like these and swear that they will be able to spot any fakery, will believe him.

The truth is he dreads going on tour. 'I *hate* it,' he says. 'That's why my tours are so short. I'm not like U2 or the Rolling Stones. I hate it. I'm not like one of those artists. I *prefer* doing TV. It's too much responsibility. It takes me two, three months to get over doing a tour. It absolutely, categorically is as cut and dried as that.' In front of an audience, he is driven by fear, and many of his most extravagant, extrovert tropes are simply those he uses to cover this fear.

This is why the summer tour has been looming all year as an obstacle that must be overcome, and why he has been so determined to get in shape for it. He wants to prove himself once more – he is playing bigger shows in more places than ever before – but most of all he looks at it as something he needs to survive. His touring history is not a happy one. Some tours have been cancelled just before they were due to start, and most of the others have just been endured. And then, along the way, there have been the nightmare days.

In late October and early November of 2000, Rob played six nights at Docklands Arena in London. On the afternoon of the final night, he announced that he couldn't do the show. 'I'd just had enough,' he says. 'I'd just cracked. I'd gone over the edge. I was just unhappy. I just couldn't do it because I was so scared. I was just petrified of getting up onstage and looking like I was scared, looking like I was feeling. I'd convinced myself that that night was going to be the night I couldn't do it.'

The promoter was told, and the procedures to cancel it were put into action. David went round to Rob's house and sat on his bed, and explained one last time. He said it was Rob's decision and that they would support it, but that it would cost Rob £400,000. ('I did double it,' David concedes.) Rob had spent all day screaming so that the doctor would come round and say that his throat was destroyed. 'And it just wouldn't break,' he remembers. 'My voice just wouldn't fucking go.'

Finally Rob said he would do it, and David called to uncancel it.

'But I've been screaming for hours now,' he said. 'Bugger.'

He got through it. Then, in July 2001, there was his second night at Milton Keynes Bowl. He had decided to take some new antidepressants that morning. (Rob intermittently tried antidepressants in his drinking days, up until the disaster of this weekend.) 'When you're coming up on the tablets, when the tablets kick in, you go all nauseous and it's like coming up on an E,' he explains, 'so it makes you sort of anxious. And the anxiety of performing in front of this massive crowd at Milton Keynes, doubled with the anxiety that I was feeling because of the tablets, just sent me potty. And we came through on the tour bus and I looked out of the window and saw the crowd and I thought, I'm not going out there.'

He meant it. This time he was told it would have cost £1 million. 'I'd better get on then,' he said. Again, he agreed only at the last moment. 'Went on and did one of the best shows I've ever given,' he remembers. 'Sometimes it gets that scary that it's like a theme park ride that you just want to get on but it's got no seatbelts in, but you've heard that centrifugal force keeps you in. And in a weird way it can work in the exact opposite of how you feel.' ('He hammed it up all the way through,' David remembers. 'He was pretending to fall down the stairs, and I thought he was quite ill, and then halfway through he came over and gave me a kiss and I thought, you *fucker*.')

As painful as Docklands and Milton Keynes were, when they are mentioned Rob now seems amused, and slightly sheepish at how melodramatic they sound in retrospect. There is another, earlier such memory that is less readily discussed and in which he finds little humour at all. Few things can draw a darker expression over Rob's face than when anyone refers to Hull, and when they do so he usually asks them to change the subject. He will skirt around telling me what actually happened that night for months, and when he finally agrees to discuss it, it's quite obvious how painful he finds doing so. 'Let me just get through it really quickly,' he says at the most unbearable part, and rushes through it like someone holding their breath as they swim for their life down an underwater tunnel.

This, eventually, is how he describes it to me. It was 1999.

'OK,' he says. 'I won three Brit awards the night before. I was doing this tour that I felt a tremendous responsibility for. They were coming to see Robbie Williams, and I had little belief in myself, even though the evidence of people turning up every night in great numbers to see me suggested that I'd got something worthwhile to come and see. And the reviews suggested that too. But inside I didn't have any belief in myself. You know, I thought I was shit. So the pressure of the tour was getting to me, you know, of having to give them their money's worth. And then after the tour one night we flew down to London, did the rehearsal for the Brits, flew back, did a show, flew back the next day, did the Brit awards, got rat-arsed, won three awards, *hated* the entire evening. Which is kind of amazing. I was in rehab one year and you very often have nothing to do and I was planning my acceptance speech in rehab for the Brit Awards for the album *Life Thru A Lens*. And then a couple of years later I won three and I fucking hated it.'

At the time, he had just split with Nicole Appleton and she was at the ceremony with Huey from the Fun Lovin' Criminals, which didn't help his mood. He opened the show, abseiling in to sing 'Let Me Entertain You', and on his way down he hit his head. Later, he drunkenly tried to get off with Cher, though he kept calling her 'Chair' as he did so.

'Come here,' he told her. 'I really fancy you. You're alright for an older bird.'

She didn't say anything. (He was serious, though, and would have happily followed through. '*Absolutely*. Of course,' he insists, and laughs. 'It's very broad, my taste.')

The next night, he was scheduled to play in Hull. It should have been a triumphant post-triple-Brit-award-triumph celebration. 'I arrive at the hotel, I see this guy, I've seen him before in Hull, he's got drugs. He says he's got drugs, he gives me his drugs. I go up to my room, think: I'll just have a line, pep me up before I go onstage, because I was knackered. So I did – I just had a line. Then I had another. Then I had another. And the twitch came out. Then Jonny came and knocked on the door to say we've got to go. And I wouldn't let him in.'

Eventually he let Jonny in. Jonny asked if he was alright. Rob twitched. His involuntary cocaine twitch.

'You are joking, aren't you?' said Jonny.

'No, I'll be fine, I'll be fine in ten minutes – I'll sort myself out,' Rob promised. But he wasn't, and he didn't.

'I went to the gig, I was still twitching,' he says. 'I couldn't go on. Tim said there'd be a riot if I didn't go on. I'd put myself in a very, very bad situation, where I was just about to go on twitching in front of 7000 people. Anyway. It was awful backstage. It was the worst. It was just, not only had I got the pressure of the gig – which I always felt anyway – but now I was off my face.'

Andy Franks went back to the hotel and collected everyone's bags so that they could leave Hull that night, in case there was a riot.

'Anyway, I did 40 minutes. Got on, got off. Don't want to talk about the gig,' he says. There is something about the way his private mess got mixed up with his pride in his professionalism as a performer, and the way the worst of it had to be acted out in front of an audience, that he finds unbearable.

His eyes are moist.

'God, it's so painful,' he says. 'It's the worst.'

* * *

His band has been rehearsing for a couple of weeks at Music Bank studios in south-east London when Rob first joins them in mid-June. He wanders in late one morning, picks up a guitar, asks Josie for a coffee, and without even acknowledging that they are there to prepare for his summer tour, starts showing them the song he demoed with Max in his Los Angeles basement. As the arrangement slowly comes together, Rob's father practises his putting on the blue-grey carpet, apparently oblivious to everything happening around him.

Eventually they record a rough version of this new song as a reference, and it is suggested that Rob runs through the opening part of the show. Rob refuses – though he has been belting out his new song over and over, he now says that he shouldn't sing because he has flu. Instead, he listens. After hearing instrumental versions of the first two songs, 'Let Me Entertain You' and 'Let Love Be Your Energy', he applauds and says, 'That's fucking great, man – almost makes me want to do this tour.' He describes a speeded-up, hi-energy bootleg remix of 'Supreme' he found on the internet, and says they should make the live version more like that. 'Like what the kids are up to these days,' he says, 'with their amyl nitrates and their lubrications.' And with that thought, his first appearance at the 2003 tour rehearsals is over.

He returns the next day, but again is more concerned with working on his new song – he scrapped the middle eight last night and wrote a new one – than on his imminent tour. Finally, late into the afternoon, he agrees to sing a few of the songs he will be performing this summer, though when 'Something Beautiful' starts, he stops. He doesn't want to do it. Now or ever. 'It's the next single,' he reasons, 'but so fucking what? Just fuck it off. And then when they walk off they'll be, "Where was that?" And I'll be at the hotel. Because, to tell the truth, there's a few songs here every night I'm going to be a bit I-hate-this-one about. I can do a few of them.' 'Something Beautiful' will be one too many. He studies the set list, striking out 'Something Beautiful', and 'Sexed Up' as well for good measure, and puts 'Kids' back in. In an instant he has undone everything he has been persuaded to do over months of tour meetings.

He asks around the room for suggestions of a good cover version they can do. In the midst of this debate, Pompey tells Rob that David is on the phone for him.

'I'm busy – can you take a message?' he shouts, and Pompey does so.

Rob realises something. 'I've never said that before,' he points out. He smiles. 'I've never been busy,' he says.

* * *

In the eyes of the pop world's professional songwriters, where Guy once stood is now a hugely attractive vacancy, and one that would be extremely lucrative for anyone who would fill it. Messages come from potential collaborators most weeks, and usually Rob dismisses them out of hand, especially if they are in any way the kind of professional songwriting partners people might expect him to work with. Today's call from David is to relay another of these, but a rather more interesting one. Brian Eno, who knows David from when David used to manage Roxy Music in the early seventies, has been in touch to say that he has written a song for which he would love Rob to write the lyrics. That sounds very promising.

The CD is sent over to Rob's new flat, along with the sweet note Eno has written to David, decorated with five randomly distributed 'Xs', explaining the song: *It's called, modestly, 'Life', though it could equally well be called 'Wife' or 'Thick' or any other one syllable word. But it's 'Life' to me.*

Unfortunately, when Rob listens to it, it does nothing for him at all.

* * *

Life in his old Holland Park house had become unbearable, and in preparation for the summer here Rob has done something about this. He has a new London flat; as well as having remarkable views over the city and the river, it is located somewhere without public access from which he can come and go in complete privacy.

One evening Chris Briggs comes round to see the flat and hear Rob's new songs. After a while, we go to a nearby hotel for coffee: Rob, Chris Briggs, Pompey, his other British bodyguard Gary Marshall, and myself. Westlife are staying here. Yesterday evening Rob had coffee here too. Westlife weren't around, so he took two of their fans up to their room and slept with them.

'At the same time?' inquires Chris.

'Yeah,' he says.

I ask whether it was nice.

'It was,' he says, 'except one of them was on her period, so she got semi-naked, then left, and she couldn't kiss, and the other one instantly got guilty after it all – "I'm not normally like this." She got instant guilt. "Don't think that I am … a *slapper*." She was genuinely feeling …'

'Shame?' prompts Chris.

'Yeah,' he says. He says they're the kind of fans who follow the Westlife van on the motorway from Birmingham to London. They were slagging Westlife off to him for not speaking to them enough. 'And I was fighting Westlife's corner,' he says. '"Well, it's like this …"'

There's something really brilliantly bonkers about sleeping with their fans and then defending them, I say.

'It is, isn't it?' he says. 'It's weird in a load of ways, because Take That used to stay here. I've got to say that that corner over there, when I was 19, over there, was the first time I realised I've got a drink problem. Walking around there. It was that corner over there where I realised: oh, this isn't normal.'

This was Take That's regular London hotel, until the hotel management banned them. It wasn't anything they themselves did – it was the fans, who would wait outside day and night. It wasn't even just the regular noise the fans made, and the general nuisance they caused, that made Take That's residency impossible. It was because the girls were so determined not to miss a single Take That entrance or exit that, rather than leave their post, they would both piss and shit in the hotel's flower beds.

We sit outside on the balcony, chatting, watching the world go by. After we have been there about half an hour, a portly, grey-bearded man approaches our table.

'Sir, I'm from the States ... you're Robbie?'

'Yes, sir,' he says.

'Could we get a picture with you?' he asks. 'I was here for QVC England. Maybe you saw me last night.' Pause. 'Unlikely – it was a joke.' He says he is a chemist and was selling a new stain removal product on the shopping channel. Rob's ears pricks up at the word 'chemist'; perhaps he instinctively realises that a man who is a chemist but pitches stain remover on TV will be interested in the kind of a medicine on the edge of science he favours. He asks the man if he takes calcium.

The man nods enthusiastically. 'Oh, yeah, I love the stuff. Now, you've got to take coral calcium, Okinowa,' he says. 'I can tell you all about it ... ' and he relays a theory of how people live a long time in the high Himalayas, and how the Okinowans put it on their food and have their low cancer rates. He and Rob have a long and enthusiastic chat about various vitamins and dietary supplements. Rob asks me to note the names of some, and by the next week he will be regularly taking them.

Inside the bar, a few members of Westlife mill about. 'They've obviously got something good going, Westlife,' says Rob, 'but I think they're a bit lazy.' He means the way they perform, and the way they don't seem to take pride in what they can be as pop stars.

Chris Briggs nods. 'They can't even be bothered to shag their own fans.'

* * *

Rob's face clenches. He has spotted someone else, inside, by the bar. Louis Walsh, Westlife's manager. The man who has made a sport, over the last few months, of putting Rob down. 'I think I'll have a chat with him,' Rob says.

He stirs his cappuccino. It's not as though they don't know each other. They used to get drunk together when Rob went to Ireland. Walsh waves at Rob through the glass, and Rob beckons him outside. He strides out, grinning.

'The Robster!' he hoots.

'Who rattled your cage?' asks Rob, his voice low.

'Is this a Take That reunion?' he asks, not hearing what Rob has said.

'No,' says Rob. 'Who rattled your cage?'

'When?' he asks.

'A few things have been printed in *The Sun* and that ... ' says Rob.

I think that Louis Walsh has made the mistake, much as the paparazzi Jason Fraser did, of imagining that everybody else inhabits this new, shallow, dumb post-modern entertainment world, where everything is just a bit of fun and nothing matters enough to be deadly serious about, apart from not being able to get your photo in the papers and magazines. Louis Walsh has been flourishing in a land where you just say stuff, and it's all theatre, it's all without consequence. Now Rob is inviting him to discover that the other world, where things matter and people get hurt, still exists.

Walsh begins to squirm a little. He is still grinning, but his voice is getting higher. 'You say things, you know, you say things,' he says.

'They're not nice things,' says Rob calmly.

'It won't happen again, though,' he says. 'People just ask me things.'

'Really disgusting, nasty things,' continues Rob. 'And you're a manager. They shouldn't come out of your lips. Leave it to your boys to do it.'

'Why?' he shuffles.

'Because it's really unfair,' says Rob. 'I haven't said anything bad about you.'

'You haven't been misquoted?' asks Walsh.

He has tried evasion, he has tried an implied apology, and he has tried brushing it off lightly – all of these tactics having failed, he seems now to be plumping, rather late in the day, for denial of guilt.

'Well, you know, the three things that I've read you've said now can't have all been misquoted,' says Rob. Walsh says nothing. Rob quotes Walsh back at himself. '"Brass neck", "nothing without Guy Chambers", "useless karaoke singer".'

In Louis Walsh's face you can see that he is no longer enjoying this friendly pop-mates chat with the Robster.

'I was reading that,' Rob says, 'and I was like, what's rattled your cage about me?'

'Nothing,' says Walsh, half-swallowing the word. 'Nothing. People just ask me stuff.'

Throughout the conversation Walsh has been standing – he is a few feet from our table because he never managed to get much closer – and Rob has remained in his seat. Perhaps Walsh is wondering how he blundered into this position: standing like a pupil in the headmaster's office, being calmly reprimanded by a 29-year-old.

'Yeah, well, you know,' Rob continues, 'you want to be a bit careful what you say about people because people have feelings ... '

Walsh suddenly spots my tape recorder on the table.

'Is somebody taping ... ' he stutters, 'is somebody taping the conversation?'

'Yeah,' says Rob, barely breaking his flow. 'People have feelings and people have respect for other people and I have respect for you, and when I read things like that I'm just like, well, what is that all about?'

He's looking at Rob and at the tape recorder, and I think maybe he now thinks this is all a trick, a set-up. Maybe that's what he'd do, but in fact the tape recorder has been sitting on the table, taping our own conversations, for the last hour and a half, long before he was spotted.

'... so be careful what you say about people – people get upset. That's all I'm saying,' finishes Rob.

'OK,' he says.

'Alright, man. Have a good evening,' says Rob.

'Cool. Cool. Bye-bye,' he says, and scurries indoors.

Rob doesn't feel triumphant after all this, just a bit saddened and depressed. He stands up and lets his eyes arc around the hotel bar before turning.

'Right, shall we call it a night?' he suggests. 'I think I shagged the pretty ones.'

2

It is the unfortunate combination of how famous he has found himself and how approachable the public find him, and the endless chain that such encounters form, that makes life in Britain so uncomfortable for him. I am not now talking about the gross and grotesque invasions of the paparazzi, or the few members of the public who consider his presence in public an incitement to hostility, as difficult as he finds those. At least they offer an easy focus for his anger. I am talking about the general, gentle attention faced by the very famous when they step out into the world.

It may not seem much measured against all the favours that fame grants you, but imagine it like this. Imagine if, when you walked down the street, one person gently threw a small, light foam ball at you – not hard enough to hurt you, its impact barely enough for you to feel it. Who could possibly complain about that? But now, instead, imagine that, as you tried to get on with your life, every single person you met threw a foam ball at you. Imagine if, for nearly every moment you were outside the sanctuary of your home, these balls continuously cascaded upon you from all sides. Nothing that each ball-thrower was doing could possibly be said to be so bad (unless you expected them to empathise with your overall predicament and not just their part in it), but all together, the incessant soft pelting might seem unbearable. And if some people would have the temperament and constitution to ignore such a barrage, it's easy to imagine that others wouldn't.

But maybe even that doesn't quite capture it. Imagine that, instead of everyone you met throwing a foam ball at you, you could see a foam ball in every single one of their hands, but that only one person in five actually threw them. And you could never tell which of them it was going to be. So, almost worse than the impact of the balls themselves was the way you were always tensing for a shot that sometimes didn't come. Flinching at nothing as often as you failed to flinch at something. Forever trying not to jump the gun and blame those who didn't throw for the actions of those who did. Forever trying to pretend that none of it was happening, as each new incoming salvo reminds you that it always is.

Maybe it is just a little bit like that.

* * *

This description troubles Rob.

'I don't think that's annoying enough,' he argues. 'It's so difficult to explain. It's like everyone's trying to *take away* a moment with me. And every time they take away a moment with me, they take away something from me. Which leaves me at the end of the day with nothing to give. That sounds really corny and will probably end up in *Private Eye*'s Luvvies, but it's the truth.'

These are just the people whom everyday life throws him by chance into contact with; the background static that envelops him every time he steps into the public. There are others of course – the ones who seek him out, to impose themselves in ways far stranger and more severe.

* * *

... I really hope you got over all your problems. It seems so cos since you're back with "Escapology" you're quite different. You have always a smile on your face now and I really like it (I can remember some bad times years ago). You know, I even hated you cos I couldn't understand why a boy like you could throw him away in that way. But, that wasn't just "hate", when you love a person you suffer for him, you get angry to see that he's destroying himself with his own hands and you can do nothing to help him ... you understand that your rage and your hate are not against this person but against this feeling of someone told me that you were just arrogant and selfish. But sometimes it was like I could see inside of you, the fear and insecurity, but at the same time I could also see a lot of positive energy, because I went beyond the mask ...

As he reads the letter, thrust at him as he went through the private plane terminal outside Milan, his expressions rotate between puzzled, sad and exasperated. 'She can see the real me,' he reports.

They all can.

He is on one final promotional day-trip to Italy before he concentrates fully on his tour. We pass a poster on a wall with Sting's face on it. 'I've got a feeling that that Sting thing he does, when he thinks he's doing us all a favour, is for real,' Rob notes. 'Whereas I, on the other hand, am just arrogant and selfish on camera.'

He says he has been thinking about death again. 'I'm just enjoying life,' he says. 'I don't want it to be over.' He mentions that he has upped the dose of his Effexor and it has made his dreams even more vivid. He dreams that his toes are rotten and all falling off, and that the dogs have been kidnapped by gypsies who want to cut them up.

As he walks to the lift of the Principe Hotel in the centre of Milan, he spots four Italian fans sitting in the lobby. They don't get up to greet him, or to ask for autographs, though he knows that they are here for him. There is a history.

'Hang on,' he says. He walks away from the lift, strides over and makes a speech to one of them – the one who left him the most horrible letter a couple of months ago in London. The one he mentioned in Denmark. The one that went: '*Why you treat us like this? You are horrible man … You think because you star you can treat people like this way but you cannot treat people like this way because you do not know the meaning of friendship and love and trust. We try to help you and all you can do is … well, I hope you are happy … You will have no one … Jonny is not a friend, soon he will grow and leave you and you will have no one …* '

'Thank you for your letter,' he says. To begin with, the sarcasm only drips, but soon it is sloshing all over the place. 'It really, really got to me,' he says, 'and now I understand what an arsehole I've been. I thank you very much from the bottom of my heart. I really do. I read it all, both sides, and I appreciate what you had to say to me, and I'd like to say, I'm sorry. Thank you.'

Message conveyed, he turns on his heel.

He has a long history with the Italian fans, these and others. 'One I know as Why Robbie?' he tells me. '"Why Robbie? Why you hate us?" Because you're outside my house. Because you've moved to Notting Hill and you're an au pair and you've brought 40 of your friends to live in Notting Hill.'

Earlier in his solo career there would be a crowd of them outside his house in West London every day. He would tell them, over and over, to fuck off, but they never did; they were just as keen to share at close quarters their resentment and disdain for his lack of appreciation of their devotion as the devotion itself. One evening, by way of retribution and as a protest at how they felt he mistreated them, about three dozen of them ambushed him and Nicole Appleton as they left 192 restaurant in Notting Hill Gate. Nicole was on his shoulders when they turned a corner and were greeted by the fans simultaneously letting off all their camera flashes in their faces. He learned something then that he has seen again many times over. 'The more mad at them I got, the more they fed off it,' he says. 'It was like any sort of reaction they could get – if it was a positive one, it was really positive, if they got a really negative one, it was really positive.'

Upstairs, immediately he walks into the suite formed by rooms 907 and 908, he recognises it. 'I've done loads of drugs in this room,' he says. 'This very one. Me and Liam. And we just played "All Around The World" over and over again before it came out.'

There is a crowd down below, for his benefit. He leans out of the window and shouts down to them, half-heartedly trying to get the women to lift up their tops. He says he wants to make a baby out of something and do the Michael Jackson trick. Once again, Josie dissuades him. Instead, he tries to throw grapes into a rubbish bin on the street.

3

On the way to Air Studios in north London, Rob listens for the first time to the song he must record today for the Cole Porter movie, Porter's 'De-lovely'. It is a long, complicated and difficult song, and though he vaguely remembers it from his childhood, he doesn't really know it at all, and the traffic isn't bad enough to allow him much learning time. He also has a sore throat.

Unsurprisingly, on the first take he is all over the place, garbling some words and mispronouncing others, squabbling with the tune. But he hasn't managed to get away with winging things so outrageously in his career by being a slow learner. During the second take, the musical director and the producer are nodding at each other, recognising that this is going to work out after all. The plan is that he will record a few rough takes now, they will work on the track for the rest of the day and he will do his perfect final vocal later this evening.

Before he leaves the building, he remembers that Stephen Duffy has a small studio in the attic at Air. He knows Stephen slightly through Claire, his keyboard player, who also sometimes moonlights in The Lilac Time. Rob and Stephen Duffy have talked about writing something together several times in the past, but nothing has ever come of it. Rob has always imagined that by putting the two of them together he could get at least one good, weird, folky song from it.

He pops up to say hello. They chat for about ten minutes, and Stephen promises to put a couple of musical ideas together. 'What a lovely bloke,' says Rob as he walks down the stairs.

When he returns to the studio in the evening there is already a CD of two pieces of music and a note (*Rob. 2 instrumentals. 2nd maybe too strange … cheers, Stephen*) waiting for him.

He breezes through the Cole Porter song, adding the intro. He has a way of singing songs like these, layered with antiquated wordplay – ' … *this verse I've started seems to me, the Tin-Pan-tithesis of melody, so to spare you all the pain, I'll skip the darn thing and sing the refrain'* – as though they are neither period pieces nor absurd. Once he is finished, Rob chats with the producer, Rob Cowan. This movie is currently called *Just One Of Those Things*, but it had once been called *Delovely*, and Rob encourages them to re-adopt that title. Rob Cowan says that if they did, a lot more of the weight might fall on his shoulders. 'If it's called *Delovely*,' says Rob, 'I'll promote and promote. I'll be a little Gurkha for you.'

He isn't finished making music for the day. On the way back to the flat he drops in at a studio where Max is working with his music partner, Jerry Meehan, and stays five hours. Max played him a song several years ago that Rob said he would record if Max would let him change the lyric; back then, Max refused, but he has changed his mind. Over the evening it turns into a tune called 'The Appliance Of Science'. '*Don't believe in clever people, clever people dropped the bomb,*' he sings at one point. He and Max were in Coffee Bean in Los Angeles a few weeks back when a man came over and insisted on engaging them in conversation. 'One of those kind of homeless prophets,' says Rob. And that was his key advice to them: 'Don't believe in smart people. Smart made the bomb. Clever dropped it.'

* * *

He likes Stephen Duffy's sketches when he listens to them the next day. The first is electronic and not scared of monotony, but Rob can already feel the kind of thing he could do over the top of it, and starts singing melodic ideas as it plays. The second is a little more what might be expected for the man behind The Lilac Time's autumnal strummings: delicate, sweet, slightly maudlin and acoustic. Rob finds himself singing over that too. He leaves Stephen a message with his phone numbers and says he'll try to come into the studio one day next week. After that, he lies on the sofa and watches a DVD called *Out Of The Blue* about UFOs. He is gripped by it. 'It's one of the best things for a fantasist, a conspiracy theorist, to believe,' he says. 'Because you can't really be proved wrong.'

He sleeps for 45 minutes and when he wakes up asks me to zip him into the Vacunaut. By sunset he is sitting outside the nearby hotel with a group of people, including Max, David, David's wife Maren and their granddaughter Mia. A slightly drunk boy and girl come over and ask if they can have a photo with him.

'No, I don't want to do it,' he says politely. 'I want to sit here and not be Robbie Williams with my friends.'

* * *

For days at a time, the band rehearse at Music Bank without seeing the singer who provides the sense to what they are doing. He's aware that he doesn't even know the words to his old songs yet, but he's in no rush to get there. Take That used to rehearse their tours for a month, working on their dance steps all day, week after week. Often they'd stay at a farmhouse with a marquee erected in the garden for rehearsals. They'd have to be up at eight each morning. It made him hate everything about rehearsing.

One time, when they were at a band rehearsal studio, the kind of place with space for several bands at once, Status Quo came in to rehearse for their forthcoming tour.

'All they did,' he remembers, 'is go through their set once. I remember thinking: I want to do that when I'm older.'

* * *

His film career begins on what would have been Cole Porter's 112th birthday. His scenes are being shot over two days at a country manor house, Luton Hoo, just outside Luton. Driving up the M1, he turns on the radio and hears Sara Cox speculating about his 1023 tattoo – she suggests the correct explanation, but only amidst a long list of other possibilities. He calls Jonny. 'Keep your mouth shut,' he counsels. 'They should never find out.'

In his trailer, he listens to 'De-lovely'. He is playing the wedding singer at Cole Porter's wedding and he must mime to his performance today. He sings along, only getting some of it right, even with his recorded version to prompt him.

'I know it now,' he declares.

'Do you know it?' asks Josie.

'Well,' he laughs, 'not really, no.'

The Actress, whom he has not seen since their date, has left him a message to say that she is coming to London. He calls her back on location in Europe. '*I'm* on set for a film *I'm* doing,' he nonchalantly tells her. 'So there.'

He has his make-up done.

'I know this is a mental question,' begins the make-up artist, 'but ...'

'I'm not gay!' he interrupts. 'God!'

There was an extract from an unofficial biography in the newspapers the previous Sunday that concentrated on innuendo that he is 'struggling with his sexuality'. That afternoon he played football with some friends, including Ant and Dec, and at one point announced, 'Ooh, I'm really struggling with my sexuality right now,' and requested that no one pass him the ball for 30 seconds while he worked his way through it.

The make-up artist is actually trying to tell him that the film's leads, Ashley Judd and Kevin Kline, have a manicurist on set each Monday morning – she introduces her to Rob – and if he'd like his done too ...

'There's nothing to manicure,' he says, holding up his bitten, chewed and desiccated fingers.

'We can sort that out,' says the manicurist. Josie persuades him to have his first manicure.

Ashley Judd comes in to say hello.

'I'm feeling slightly effeminate,' he says.

She asks how he's finding his first manicure.

'It's a bit weird,' he says. 'It feels the same sort of way as when I had a colonic. It felt wrong; I won't do it again. I see how J-Lo could go all weird, with the flowers and the manicure and stuff.' He also worries that he is losing the hard guitar-player's skin on the tips of the fingers of his left hand. 'I mean, I bet you don't see The Boss do this?' he says facetiously.

On the contrary, says the manicurist. She herself has softened and tidied the Springsteen fingers.

'And done that at the end?' asks Rob.

'Yeah,' she confirms.

'On you go,' he declares. 'If it's good enough for The Boss … '

'We've been trying to keep him out of the movies,' Josie sighs. 'One day into it and he's gone all diva.'

Ashley Judd mentions that there is a lot of press watching today, presumably because of him. He fills her in on his current media profile. 'I'm struggling with my sexuality,' he explains, 'and I'm not big in America. I've got two elephants in the room, everywhere I go. One elephant called Struggle, the other one called Not Big In America.'

Finally, after several hours of hanging around, he is called to the set. The mansion is almost derelict, but one of the rooms has been set up as a grand wedding banquet from 85 years ago. Rob does his first take. It's immediately clear that he doesn't know the words, and it's affecting his whole performance. He's so used to charming and bluffing his way through these things, but there's no way of cheating through and bluffing a lip-sync when you aren't the star of the show and everything won't be edited to make allowances for you. Even though they're shooting him from behind, this isn't good enough. Already the producer, his expression dark, is having a very severe word to David and Josie about tomorrow.

They quickly wrap, not because they've got what they need but because they know they're not going to get it. They can't shoot anything else: the shots include Kevin Kline and Ashley Judd, and they're not going to ask them to act their hearts out and to give their best performance only to find out that it's unusable because the mouth of the singer in the background doesn't appear to fit the words he is singing.

He has barely been on set for half an hour. He knows. He gives a breezy, cheerful 'OK, folks, thanks for today' to everyone, but then says quietly to Irwin Winkler: 'I'll have the words by tomorrow.'

'No,' he says in the car, summing up his first taste of movie-making, 'I am right. I don't like it.'

'Rob, the one thing that was noticeable was … ' says David.

' … the fact that I didn't know the lyrics?' Rob interrupts. 'Mmm hmmm.' Pause. 'But when I did! Uh? The bits where I did?'

'Tomorrow they'll be head-on,' David points out. The camera shots.

'Yeah,' he says. 'They got what they needed, though, today, didn't they?' he says.

On the way into London, he speaks to Stephen Duffy.

'I've done this Cole Porter song for this Cole Porter movie … I've just left the set for it … I didn't know the words … fortunately it was shot from the back … I've got to learn the words tonight … it was interesting … I don't want to do it at all, acting … I was thinking Wednesday evening if it's alright with you … shall we do it at Air? … yeah, because I wouldn't mind sort of having a groove to do something to instead of sat with guitars … yeah, it's a great place … you know, I'm really into doing something electronic … I don't want to do anything that I've ever done before … yeah, you know, give us a hand here … yeah, no, I've done it … I've done it to death now, and I wouldn't mind something of substance … not saying that all of them haven't had it, but I wouldn't mind going: right, that was that and now this is a new chapter and this is what it sounds like … you're breaking up, mate, just one second … yeah yeah yeah back again … go on … I just wouldn't mind being someone else now … or some*thing* else … you know, I mean, I'm still up for the big song, but not the same way I've been doing it … OK … cool … '

He gets off the phone.

'I get on with him already,' he says.

* * *

He stays home tonight, trying to learn the words, but falls asleep by ten. In the morning he runs through them again and again. He's far from perfect. As he gets into the car, he says, 'Yesterday was the first time for ages I've felt short-changed by a day,' and maybe he just means that he was in bed too soon, or maybe he means that he let himself down on the film set, or maybe he means that he didn't like wasting a day in a world where he was neither allowed to be its centre nor to disengage from it. 'It was weird yesterday when the band struck up and the attention wasn't on me,' he says. 'I've never done anything like that. And then they plunged me into darkness. I'm not used to that. It was really weird.' He pauses. 'I mean, I was upset. I don't know. It's a bit like kryptonite – if you don't look at me, I can't do it.'

He sits in the front seat with his laptop on his knees and sings along to 'De-lovely'. '*It's de-bollocks, I'm de-bitch,*' he improvises when he can't remember the real words. There's not much time left for that now. He rewinds to find the real words. '*It's de-regal, it's de-royal …* ' Then he decides that he needs to relax to Radio One. When he switches on they're playing 'Rock DJ' and he takes this as a good omen.

This morning there is a line of actors in the trailer, facing the mirrors and having their make-up done, all bantering back and forth. They ask Rob how he's enjoying the world of acting.

'Now I'm sat *here,*' he says, 'I quite like it. Everybody comes in and says hello to each other. I like that bit. Perhaps I could just come and have my make-up done on other sets and then leave. This is the bit I like. "Doesn't want to act, but likes getting his make-up on and saying good morning."'

One of the actors asks whether there isn't this kind of camaraderie in Rob's business.

'Yeah,' Rob says, 'but it's just me. I'm not an ensemble piece, am I?'

He listens as the two make-up artists discuss whether one of them can claim to have invented the way of covering up tattoos she is using to hide the B behind his left ear. 'It's already been invented,' she eventually concedes.

'Reinvent it again!' interjects Rob. 'That's what I do with songs.'

There are more photographs in the newspapers today. Last Friday, when we left Nobu, he and Max decided to put on the most ridiculous grinning and laughing faces as they left. Strangely, the photographs have come out looking quite natural. *The Sun*'s latest pop columnist, Victoria Newton, prints some of them and writes: '*Memo to Robbie – keep it up, you look so much more handsome when you smile ...* ' (When Rob sees this, he immediately says, 'Memo to Victoria ... ' and continues in such a way that by far the nicest part is where he just says 'fuck off ... ')

Even during the three-minute drive from the trailers to the set, Rob uses the time to listen to the song once more on his laptop. 'Well,' he says, getting out of the car, 'I don't know it and that's that.' Nonetheless, even during the first take, you can see relieved glances being exchanged around the room by the film crew. He also knows it well enough now that it frees him up to do what he can do best, and when the song finishes he gets a round of applause.

'He's pretty loose,' smiles Irwin Winkler wryly. 'He's going to be a movie star.'

There is plenty of whispering – even right here on the set – that Hollywood is making plans for him to be one, almost irrespective of his wishes. The stories that have been in the papers over the last fortnight – that he has screen-tested for a new Superman movie and agreed a $3 million fee; that he has bought the right to the Village People's story and is putting together a movie with him as one of the camp leads – are complete fiction, but the word on the film set is that MGM, who are making this movie, are thinking of offering him the role of the villain in the Halle Berry Jinx movies. No one believes that he is not bothered and really doesn't fancy it; no one from Hollywood seems to seriously conceive that anyone would turn down such an opportunity if it were presented.

After a few run-throughs Rob goes out for a cigarette while they re-set the cameras.

'Do you like it better today?' Josie asks him.

'Yes,' he says. 'It's all about *me*. And that's why I like it. Yesterday it wasn't.'

* * *

At lunchtime he declares, 'I'm bored now.' He goes back into make-up. Even that isn't the same now. 'It's not as fun as this morning when we were all saying hello,' he complains. 'I want to say goodbye now.' When he chats to Ashley Judd she tells him that what makes it all worth it are those special moments in front of the camera where you really get to do what you do all this for; it makes him think that all he has to do, if he needs that buzz and release and self-expression, is book himself on a TV show. Much quicker and far less bother.

He goes back to the set for more shots, all variations of Rob singing the song while Kevin Kline and Ashley Judd come together on the dancefloor in front of him. This afternoon, the shot is wider and there are more extras.

'Settle, please,' says the first assistant director. 'Kill the fans.'

Soon he is wrapped.

In the evening, he sees The Actress; the next day he has a love bite on his neck. 'That,' he says, 'is "No one else is having him this week".' Once when he was in Take That he collected a huge love bite while straying, and he was due to see his girlfriend Natasha. So he called her and, in the guise of romance, asked her to wait for him in bed with the lights off. When he joined her there, he made her kiss his neck a lot in the dark, so that she would claim another's work as her own. He got away with it.

* * *

He cancels the first songwriting appointment he has made with Stephen Duffy because he has forgotten England are playing football tonight. He now has time to drop in on rehearsals. There he leads the band through another new song, sings more of the set than he has done so far, listens to the new hi-energy version of 'Supreme' – he asks for it to be re-done a little slower – and runs through '99 Red Balloons'. He gets really into it, pogoing through the choruses and then at the end acting out the denouement …

'If I could find a souvenir, just to prove the world was here, and here it is, a red balloon, I think of you and let it go.'

… actually releasing an invisible balloon – heartbreaking, even though he is quite clearly also taking the piss – and watching it float away into the distance, as if it carried every dream and hope with it.

The band loathe the song.

'Am I weird to like that?' he says.

They think he is.

Max sits at the piano and they try 'One For My Baby', which will be performed by just Rob and Max. The words take an unscripted detour.

'And I've got a little film,' he croons, *'I want you to see … I think it went straight to DVD … with Mariah Carey and Max Beesley … it's* Glitter *you see … took nowt at the box office, and zip on DVD … '*

'Don't do the *Glitter* thing,' says Max afterwards, pretending to joke about it. (Rob is extremely respectful and admiring of Max's acting talents when Max is not around, but when he is there Rob can rarely resist. Inevitably, the next time they rehearse it, Rob merely intensifies his attack: *'It's a quarter to three … I hear you can get* Glitter *on DVD … Remember* Ishtar *the film? … Well, neither will we … you'll try and find it hard … but it is on DVD … at the back with the porn … where the children don't go …* Glitter*'s a film … just in case you didn't know.'*

It is time for 'Mr Bojangles'. The scratchy distressed version Mark Plati has recorded, as discussed, comes through the speakers.

'What's that?' asks Rob after a few seconds. 'I don't like it. What is it?'

Mark Plati reminds him. Rob asks for it to stop. 'Why can't we do it properly?' he says. 'Is that what I've got to sing to? It's too fast and … it's not right. How do we get it right?' The band will play 'Mr Bojangles' instead. He never hears more than 30 seconds of what Mark Plati has done.

* * *

The Actress has called, but he's not going to call her back. 'She'll know what it is,' he says, meaning that he nipped any relationship in the bud once before and he doesn't feel as though he needs to do so again. 'I can't be arsed,' he explains.

4

On the afternoon of 12 June, he finally goes into Air Studios to work with Stephen Duffy. In his tiny attic, Stephen plays him something on the acoustic guitar but Rob says that it would be too like what people expect. He suggests they do something to a drum machine rhythm instead, so Stephen programmes a simple four-beats-to-the-bar bass drum and an equally simple pulsating 16-beats-to-the-bar bass sequence. Rob begins to sing:

'Don't let your eyes tell the brain ... you should feel ashamed ... everyone needs it babe ... I know you feel the same ... I didn't quite catch your name ... hush hush hush don't say a thing ... let's see what the night will bring ... it might be everything ...'

He is singing in a tone of voice he hasn't used before on record, and the song sounds like nothing he has ever done.

After a while they adjourn to Stephen's favourite Japanese restaurant, but there isn't a free table. Rob is left standing on the street, attracting too much attention, so he hides inside a nearby Chinese restaurant and they decide to eat there. With only half a song written, he is already mapping out a whole new future. After a while a Chinese Elvis impersonator appears to entertain the diners; on the way out he and Rob trade their best Elvises.

He goes to sleep excited by the day's achievements but as he wakes, he is aware that it is not his new song that is swimming around his head but the music of Take That, interspersed with an occasional Robbie Williams tune. A strange dream to be having, he thinks, but as he forces himself awake the music gets louder, not quieter. He can hear two voices singing these songs, neither of them inside his head and neither of them his. He tries to figure it out; as far as he knows Gary Marshall is the only other person in the flat. Why on earth would Gary be singing Take That songs?

'*... a million love songs later! ...*' goes one of the voices.

And then he realises that the sound is not coming from inside the flat, but from right outside the bedroom window. Which is stranger still, as his bedroom is high in the air above London.

He pulls the blind.

One of the window cleaners spots him immediately and tries to reach for the button to move the platform to another floor, but the other hasn't noticed and carries on singing. (Right now Rob is quite amused by all of this, though he is less so later when he discovers that Chris Sharrock, who slept in another bedroom round the other side of the building, heard one of them shout to the other, 'I'm rich beyond my wildest dreams!')

Eventually, as Rob stares, the second window cleaner realises that his partner has gone quiet, raises his head and discovers why. His face goes ashen.

'Look,' says Rob, 'if you're going to sing any songs, don't sing fucking Barlow songs and wake me up.'

* * *

At Music Bank he sits outside on the roof in the sun, smoking and laying out big plans. 'The song we've written,' he says, 'it doesn't sound like me. I don't want to do anything Robbie Williams would do. So what I'm thinking about doing is developing a character so thoroughly, with a prosthetic nose, a wig and everything, and do the best album I've ever done. And while the greatest hits is out, release an album as someone else. I've got him as an alcoholic. An alcoholic and an American. A Neil Diamond-esque kind of character. I think he's from Orange County, moved to West Hollywood and has not had a lot of luck – I don't know his story yet but I'm actually thinking of spending some time dressing like him, eating like him, living like him. At the moment he's called Pure Francis, and the album's called *Diamond*.' He turns to me. 'What do you think?'

What I think is that it's a fine attitude to use and get excited about, and an excellent, liberating mindset with which to write some songs, and that it's a tonic to see him so fired up and inspired, but that in its specifics it's probably a bonkers plan in the long run. But now is not the time for all of that opinion.

'It's really exciting,' he says. 'It doesn't have to be secret, just to be: I don't talk about him and he doesn't talk about Robbie Williams. The thing is, as well: the greatest hits comes out next year, this period of those albums is over for the foreseeable future. I've got to do something that I find really interesting. Because America's not going to happen because a) I don't want it to, b) it takes a lot of slog and c) I don't really want it, you know. So that leaves me going, so what do you do next? Because another Robbie Williams album would be really boring for me. So do something really interesting. We know that we're on to something that's shit hot. It sounds a bit like "Get The Message", which is what I want – electronic with big jingly jangle guitar chords, like Neil Diamond ... '

What is he going to sing songs about?

'Love. Love and heartache.'

And is he broken-hearted?

'Yeah. He's broken-hearted and he's failed. He's a failed musician. It's not going to be a Tony Ferrino figure. Also, for the writing of the songs, it gives you an instant mindset for somebody else. You haven't got to worry about people reading into your lyrics personally and all that business because you're writing from somebody else's perspective ... '

When the rehearsals start up again he briefly leads the band through this new song, finding new words as he goes: '*I might be your saviour baby, despite what you've heard ... I might be a believer baby, despite what you've heard.*' Everyone who comes near him this afternoon is told all about his new idea and his new future. If they think it is weird that he is saying this as they are working hard so that the old Robbie Williams can stride imperially across Europe this summer, they don't say so. But his enthusiasm and delight is infectious. He is so excited by the freedom of not being himself.

* * *

This evening he has arranged to have dinner at Nobu, exactly a week after the last dinner, this time in a larger group including Ant, Dec, Jonny and their respective partners, and Max and Jerry. Before they leave, knowing that there will be a bank of paparazzi outside, they decide to reprise the over-the-top laughing performance Rob and Max pioneered the previous Friday. Just outside the door, they stand and point at each other and work through a whole repertoire of ludicrous mirth under the incessant strobe of camera flash. It ends up with Rob falling to the floor and lying on his back, giggling for real at the absurdity.

Unfortunately, the cars coming round from the garage to pick them up are delayed, and even after they have laughed as long as they can, the transport is still not here. They are left standing there, like actors stranded on stage after the lights have come up, so they do the only sensible thing and retreat into the restaurant's lobby. This time they wait until the cars pull up, after which they make a second exit with less hilarity. The laughing photos will be printed everywhere, accompanied by photo captions and stories that simply accept this as evidence of some famous people out on the town, caught in a moment of grand, sincere hilarity.

On the way back to his flat Rob picks up four bottles of white wine for his drinking guests, and everyone plays Killer on the pool table. Rob wins, then plays songs from his computer and suggests it is time to throw fruit out of the window into the river. Plums, to begin with, and when they run out, apples and pears. When Jonny hits a moored barge the fruit basket is declared closed.

* * *

For several months there has been an event marked in Rob's diary for this Saturday: the North London College Ball. There is no such thing as the North London College Ball but everyone involved has different reasons for not wanting the truth to get out, which is that Robbie Williams will be appearing as the surprise headline act for 10,000 employees at Vodaphone's annual party. Vodaphone don't want anyone to know because they don't want the surprise spoiled, and it might also be a mixed blessing for them if too much attention were paid to quite how lavishly they are treating the people who work for them. On Rob's side, no one wants word to get out partly because he is using it as a warm-up for the tour, away from the press and wider public scrutiny, but also because there is a stigma about such corporate events. Often they are seen as signs that an artist is selling out his or her principles and cashing in their chips. Any argument that entertainers in the twenty-first century conduct their regular artistic work in bold opposition to the forces of business and multinational capitalism is, in most cases, already absurd and spurious, but nevertheless, if the press were to find out, they would be likely to question and scoff at his motives and wonder why someone so wealthy might be greedy enough to do this.

In fact, he would have a very good answer, but it is one he would rather not have to give.

It is over two years since he has played his songs at a concert in England, and he is quietly apprehensive. He leaves his flat just after nine in the evening and sits in the back of the van with Jonny, browsing through a newspaper. 'Not in the honours list again,' he sighs. 'It's getting to be a joke.' He asks for an Eddie Murphy comedy CD to put on; Jonny complains about the volume.

'Why don't you just fuck off and be a 70-year-old now?' teases Rob. 'Play golf every day.'

'One day I'll be like that,' Jonny confirms.

'You're like that now!' Rob exclaims.

'We'll live in a house next to each other … ' Jonny says, ignoring him.

'You'll have one of those pianos no one plays,' Rob predicts, 'and one of those double seats for you and Nikki. A mock Tudor house.'

'I like those mock Tudor houses,' Jonny says. 'The kids'll say, "Can we go and see Uncle Robbie, colour him in? Colour his tattoos." Youth, I bet in ten years we'll have houses next to each other. We've got to have a passage that takes you straight through to each other's house.'

Rob changes the subject and declares that his hotel pseudonym on tour will be William Wallace.

'William Wallace is shit,' says Jonny.

'No it isn't,' says Rob. 'Why is William Wallace shit?'

'Because it's been done.'

'It's hasn't.'

'You're not Scottish.'

'I am a bit.' Pause. 'I've been there.'

The two of them are masters of the repetitive stubborn argument. Sometimes a squabble will appear to be over and then, like fires that seem to be out and then flash up again, the squabble will return. Jonny argues that Rob should be called Captain Sid Rudy Duke, after his three dogs. (After various canine upheavals in Los Angeles – at one point he has four dogs – Sammy's place has been taken by a bull mastiff called Duke.) 'William Wallace is crap,' Jonny adds.

'Why is William Wallace crap?' repeats Rob.

'Because it is,' says Jonny.

'Why?'

'No one else can be Braveheart,' Jonny says. 'There's only one Braveheart. And that was Mel Gibson.'

'You're really fucking digging out a trench now, aren't you?' teases Rob.

'Not,' says Jonny. 'There can only ever be one William Wallace.'

'Jonny, I don't *think* I'm William Wallace,' says Rob, goaded now. 'It just gives you the steel to perform. When you don't feel like you can fucking do it. Do you know what I'm saying? He single-handedly took on the fucking English wankers. It's either that or Rob Roy. Or Michael Collins. It's all about the steel to perform. If you're Captain Sid Rudy Duke, you're like Hong Kong fucking Phooey. You might as well go on each night and go "jigabow jigabow ..."'

Jonny points out that before now Rob has used his porn name, Trixie Farrell (childhood dog and mother's maiden name). 'How's *that* giving you the steel?' says Jonny derisively.

'Times have changed,' says Rob. 'I've been A. Gabriel – the Archangel Gabriel. Jack Farrell – big Jack the Giantkiller, my granddad. And now I'm William Wallace.'

'You might as well be Jason Orange,' objects Jonny.

'I might as well be fucking Jason and the Argonauts,' retorts Rob.

Jonny makes a further futile argument for Captain Sid Rudy Duke, and Rob exclaims that Jonny is the only person who thinks this stupid name is a good idea. Jonny looks for support.

'It's a bit *Carry On,*' says Josie.

'We're not *Carry On* any more,' says Rob. 'This is a serious operation now. And the operation is to bring entertainment.'

Jonny asks Pompey what his on-tour pseudonym is.

'Willie Recover,' says Pompey.

'So you're telling me *that's* serious?' Jonny scoffs.

'He hasn't got to get onstage,' Rob points out. 'And he's already got strength of character. I haven't.'

Eventually, to keep the peace, Rob says he will be called Captain Sid Rudy Duke on his days off, though we all know full well that he won't.

This bickering has achieved its main purpose, which is to take Rob's mind off the forthcoming performance. We drive on to the site, a huge marquee near Highclere Castle, through country lanes and then across a field in the dark. Lulu, Liberty X and Bryan Adams, all unannounced, have already performed. Rob is listed on the running order as 'Hot Legs'. Before they go on, Rob gathers the band around on the grass: 'Right ... I was just thinking the other day, there's nobody doing it like we're doing it, at all, anywhere. There's nobody fucking doing it like we're doing it. Justin Timberlake, Beyoncé, Christina Aguilera, whoever, there's nobody doing it like we're going to do it on this fucking tour, and tonight this show has raised a million quid for charity, so we're going out there to kick arse, give the money and put it into a good place. But I just want to say that all the other tours have started with me not really wanting to do it. I'm fucking bang up for this one ... ' – the band cheer – ' ... really, really bang up for this one. I've got a really massive point to prove, I have and we all have, we'll just go out and be the best that there is in the world at the minute because we can do it.'

The band leave to take their places on stage.

'Your gigs,' says Jonny. 'I love 'em.' Rob doesn't say anything. He seems to be mentally preparing himself. 'This bit, now,' Jonny continues, 'Rob just getting himself focused, Josie and I not knowing what to say ... ' Rob still says nothing. 'It's funny,' Jonny goes on, 'I get really nervous for him. Babble. Because I think if I babble, it's good, takes his mind off it a bit. So that's what I do.'

'It's annoying,' says Rob deadpan. 'I've always found it annoying.'

* * *

One and a half songs after the ecstatic drunken roar that greets his appearance up through a trap at the front of the stage, he splits his trousers. He has to change into some replacements on the stage. 'For one night and one night only, the half Monty,' he says. 'I bet you didn't get this off Bryan fucking Adams. Or Liberty X.' Many of the crowd are, predictably, holding up mobile phones, broadcasting the performance to people elsewhere. He seems to be having fun from the start. He certainly tells the crowd often enough. 'I am having a fucking brilliant time,' he declares about halfway through, before 'Hot Fudge'. 'I am! And I bet you're going "I bet he says that everywhere".' Pause. 'Well, I didn't say it in fucking Iceland, I had a shit time there. Iceland … and Sweden. They're shit. But here's great.'

In 'One For My Baby' he doesn't mention *Glitter* and, instead, shamelessly croons '*one for my baby … and ten for Vodaphone …* ' 'Supreme' is unveiled in its manic new high-energy version, though Rob will decide that he doesn't really like it like this and this will be its only public performance. Before 'Kids', he goes, as though introducing her, 'Ladies and gentlemen! Miss Kylie Minogue! … ', lets the cheers ring out, then says, 'Nah, she ain't coming … Does anybody know the words to "Kids" … ?'

The man next to me in the audience turns, impressed, and says, 'He's really done his research. He knew about Kylie from last year … ' (He knew nothing, of course. It was just a lucky hit.)

It is difficult to imagine that the audience could have responded more enthusiastically but he nevertheless says at the end – speaking more, I think, to his fears about this event than to their reaction – 'I know that a lot of you probably don't have a Robbie Williams record and aren't probably really into me, so I just want to say thank you for putting up with me this evening, and I hope that somewhere in there I've entertained a little bit.' Fake modesty, real modesty, showmanship and a sizeable dollop of insecurity are all in there somewhere.

Backstage afterwards, it turns out that he had a dreadful time with his in-ear monitors and hated how far away the audience were from the stage, which spoiled his enjoyment. But he is thrilled to have felt fit enough.

Gary Marshall, who hasn't heard of this, walks in.

'You enjoyed that, didn't you?' he says, smiling.

Rob shakes his head in a when-you've-worked-with-me-a-while-longer-you'll-understand way.

'You'll think I'm enjoying it every night on tour,' he promises. 'But I won't be.'

5

A Sunday afternoon kickabout has been arranged near Jonny's house on a school football pitch. A man no one knows stands behind one of the goals. For a long while he just watches and then, as though it were the most natural and normal thing in the world, he starts taking photos. He is asked to stop but he won't. At half-time Rob explodes at him.

'Do what the fuck you want, take your photos and fuck off,' he shouts.

The man argues – as though this were some kind of argument that makes any logical or practical sense – that he is not paparazzi because he is from the *Daily Mail*. He offers his business card.

'Are you going to give the pictures to the *Daily Mail*?' Rob clarifies.

He nods. 'Yeah,' he says. He seems almost relieved that Rob has finally understood.

'Then you're a fucking paparazzi, you cunt,' says Rob.

'They rang me,' the man protests. 'If you don't want me to, I won't.'

'Then what are you *doing* here?' rages Rob, because it is perfectly obvious he doesn't want him to.

'I've asked you for a second time,' the man persists.

'And I'm saying *no* a second time,' says Rob.

The man protests that he was trying hard not to get Rob's friends in the shots because he thought that was what Rob was asking when he first objected to the man taking photographs. He just doesn't get it. (And he obviously thinks Rob just doesn't get it. They are miles apart: he lives in a world where the way he is behaving is the height of considerate gentlemanly behaviour.)

'Mate,' Rob suggests, 'why don't you take your stupid point of view and shove it up your arse and wipe your personality with it at the same time?'

'Just go, please,' urges Gary Marshall. 'Turn around and go.'

'That's so uncalled for, mate, honestly,' the man tells Rob.

'*You're* so uncalled for,' Rob tells him. 'You're spoiling it for everyone.'

'I've just given you my card,' he feebly protests, as though this has somehow proven both his honour and legitimacy.

'I don't *care* if you've given me your card,' says Rob, and mimes glancing at it in the palm of his hand and reading it. '"Saddam Hussein – here you are …"'

* * *

This weekend, the *News Of The World* carry another extract from the unofficial biography. Plenty of nonsense, again, mostly from the same cast of characters – mostly the same embittered old managers and occasional collaborators who turn up in all these accounts. This weekend sees the return of Raymond Heffernan, the man who claims he co-wrote 'Angels'. ('The verse was mine,' he is quoted as saying. 'It's hurtful that Robbie won't even acknowledge me. I was part of that song.')

The real story of Raymond Heffernan's brief intersection with Rob's life is, at least, an interesting one; another improbable adventure on the crooked path that led him here.

* * *

It is the Christmas of 1995, his first Christmas after Take That, in the period where he has made lots of brash, confident noises about his future but proved nothing aside from his dedication to losing the plot. He takes the ferry to Dublin for the Christmas holidays. With him are his mother, her boyfriend at the time, and his sister. When they arrive at the house they've rented in the middle of Dublin late in the afternoon, Rob doesn't even go in. He leaves them to unpack and goes straight to a pub, on his own, to start drinking. A guy with big ginger hair catches his eye and they start talking. This is Raymond Heffernan. They chat for the whole evening, and soon they're thick as thieves and spending all of every day together. Rob takes loads of E and drinks lots of Guinness. Sometimes they stay at Rob's rented house and sometimes they stagger out of town, to Raymond's parents' house on a council estate and sleep in the attic on a mattress on the floor. When they and their monumental hangovers awake, Raymond's mother will always offer a cup of tea and, even when Rob refuses, make him one anyway. To him, it feels like he has stumbled into this loving, welcoming Irish family and he finds it nicer here than with his own. Here, there is no mother who he feels looking at him, not without reason, as a drunkard wayward son who is throwing his life away and melting in front of her. He also realises that his mother doesn't think that Raymond is quite what Rob takes him to be, but he's not interested in taking any notice of that. Rob is thinking: *I just want somebody to like me. I just want 'the people' to like me.* And, this week, Raymond represents 'the people'.

Rob has been trying to write some of the songs for the solo career he has been telling people he is going to have. One evening he comes up with the verse to a new song as he is sitting outside one of the Dublin pubs he and Raymond have been frequenting, staring at the crappy little waterfall in the pub's patio. Not even a waterfall, really, just a little modern art structure with water coming off it.

And down the waterfall, he writes, *wherever it may take me.*

There are other things bubbling around his head. Raymond has told him about a distant ancestor who had been shot in St Stephen's Green raising the tricolour. He was called Bobby Williams. That feels like it means something to Rob. He believes in reincarnation, and recently he has been going round telling people that he will die when he is 32. 'I won't be here very long,' he tells them. He's also sure that someone is helping him. He can feel it. And he is sure that it is an angel.

There is a chorus to his new song that he comes up with that just repeats itself: *I'm loving angels and angels and angels, oh-oh woah angels.*

One day he and Raymond decide to go into a studio in Temple Bar to do some recording. Raymond writes some music underneath Rob's melody and his lyric about angels and waterfalls, and Rob takes a cassette of it away with him.

Around then, it starts going strange. When they were first hanging out –

it's only been a few days – it was always Rob, Raymond and Raymond's friends. For Rob he'd remember these as nights of drugs and laughs. At the far end of the evening, when the sun was coming up, he'd move on to amyl nitrate and the poetry recitals would begin. But now it always seems to be just Rob and Raymond. On New Year's Eve they go to the Pod, off their faces. Raymond says he has to go and see his friends for a moment and he comes back with cuts all over his face and a bruised eye and a ripped shirt. 'My friends,' he says, 'they're all beaten me up. I've got no one now, apart from you, Robbie.' And that is the first time that, in his head, Rob steps back and thinks: *True or not, I don't know if I want that.* As the day nears when Rob must leave, Raymond gets clingier, pestering Rob about whether Raymond will ever see him again. Rob gives him his big puffa Stussy jacket, a jacket he loves, as a reassurance.

He doesn't give Raymond his address, but two weeks later Raymond turns up on his doorstep in Stoke.

'Hey,' says Raymond when Rob opens the door.

'What are you doing?' asks Rob, and he sees Raymond deflate, realising that this is not going to be what he hoped it to be.

'I thought you'd be pleased to see me,' says Raymond.

Rob invites him in for a moment and explains that he can't stay. He gives him some money for a B&B and the ferry back to Ireland and calls a taxi. They chat until the taxi arrives then say goodbye. That is the last time Rob sees him.

A few months later, on his second day writing with Guy, he sings to Guy the melody and lyrics he had for a while for part of a song. Guy writes new music beneath it, and they quickly write its other sections. Immediately, they know it is special, but Guy is feeling sick and takes to bed as soon as they have finished it. It is snowing, and Rob walks for ages before a cab finally stops for him. He asks the driver to play the cassette he is carrying, and the driver becomes the third person in the world to hear 'Angels'. He tells Rob it will be a number one.

Some months later Raymond Hefferman tried to claim a co-writing credit on 'Angels'. It was a claim Rob always disputed but Hefferman was given a modest one-off payment. Ever since, he has been popping up in newspapers and books to share his version.

* * *

Full production rehearsals are taking place on a sound stage at Elstree Studios, about 30 yards from the compound where the latest series of *Big Brother* is being broadcast live. There has been much talk over the last fortnight of opening the rehearsal stage's doors and Rob simply performing his new single over and over, very loudly, so that it can be heard on the 24-hour-a-day live *Big Brother* coverage, but it doesn't happen. For one thing, his new single is no longer in the set. For another, he doesn't seem that likely to perform anything over and over. The first day he visits, he watches about half of the show from in front of the mixing desk without taking part, and vetoes a film of a black, extremely muscular male bodybuilder flexing to be projected at the back of the stage during 'Strong'. The main reason he has turned up is to try out being suspended upside down for the show's opening. He lies on a floor mat on his back in the middle of the stage and straps are folded round his ankles.

'The things you do to sell a tour,' observes Chris Sharrock.

'The things you have to do to remain imperial,' corrects Rob.

He is lifted up.

'How do you feel?' Josie asks him.

'Fine,' he says. He is lowered down. 'It's good, that,' he declares.

He tells Josie he wants to leave and to head Air to see Stephen Duffy. 'I really need to write,' he says. 'I've got a bee in my bonnet about it.' He still hasn't seen the whole show run through, and has barely responded to the parts he has seen. For him, this is probably the way he needs to do this – to engage slowly without getting too worried about it all – and, as he would see it, it is his show, and his responsibility, and his burden. But for the people who have been working like crazy for weeks to make all this special, not only out of pride and professionalism but to please him, the lack of engagement and feedback is frustrating and infuriating.

On the way into town, a sports car with a young, pretty woman in it passes us in the outside lane. Rob asks Gary to keep up. At first he thinks it's Jordan, but it's not. He sticks his head out the window.

'Hello!' he shouts. 'Come here ... where you going?'

She smiles when she recognises him. She points to a side road, indicating that this is her turnoff, and also, it seems, that he should follow. He doesn't. Today he has songs to write.

* * *

Stephen's attic studio at Air is in a tiny, cramped room that you get to by walking through an office. There is just room for four people to squeeze in, if only one of them stands up at a time. The walls are covered with dangling musical instruments and, between them, photos and postcards and pictures ripped from magazines: Jack Kerouac on the cover of the French magazine *Les Inrockuptibles*, a still from *Easy Rider*, an article about Patti Smith, a Lilac Time poster, a picture of the sixties' Rolling Stones on the cover of *Uncut* magazine. There is a copy of Joni Mitchell's *The Hissing Of Summer Lawns* standing on the desk, with annotated drawings over its scene of the view south through Central Park by Mitchell herself, done when she recorded downstairs a while back, detailing the significance of various landmarks. There is a line drawn through the World Trade Center towers at the back, and she has written next to them GONE.

Rob says he wants to work on the song they started the other day. He says that he thinks it's called 'Today'.

'It's called "Everyone Needs It",' Stephen tells Andy Strange, who operates the computers and records everything.

Before they start work, Rob shares his latest excitement about the Pure Francis character, and about how he plans to change his hair and his nose and his eye colour for it. 'It's Neil Diamond,' he explains, 'but with Kraftwerk – Depeche Mode that aren't scared to do a big chorus. What do you think?'

'Fine,' says Stephen. 'Let's do it.'

Rob sings through the verse several times, making up new lyrics and melodies each time, sitting next to the keyboard and using a hand-held microphone. Stephen suggests that maybe they should write the lyrics and proceed from there, but Rob simply ignores this suggestion. Stephen asks whether he knows what Pure Francis's story will be because presumably that will help map out what these songs will be about.

'None of the album's comedy,' Rob says. 'You want the audience to be emotionally affected by the songs.'

'Well,' Stephen points out, 'I'm not known for my comedy.' More, he says, for misery. He mentions that in the current issue of *Mojo* magazine he's Number 13 in a list of the most unlucky people in rock. 'It's some of the best press I've had for ages,' he says.

Rob fills in a little more about the character as he sees it today. 'He's been a session singer for all manner of people,' he says. 'I don't know how he's got from America to England and on the radio and on the telly, but that will come. I know he's been in a lot of pain. It's sort of "my last go" kind of territory. That kind of territory.'

'Do you think there's room for a song about the Imperial War Museum?' asks Stephen hopefully. 'The words sound nice.'

This odd idea meets with a surprisingly warm response. 'Neil Tennant always said "that was our imperial phase",' Rob explains. 'And I'm going through my imperial phase at the minute.' He nods. 'So the Imperial War Museum ... it could be the rock hall of fame.'

'Have you listened to Neil Diamond?' Stephen asks. They had both planned to listen to *The Jazz Singer* as Pure Francis research.

'No, I bought the CD but I didn't have the time to listen to it,' says Rob.

'Maybe we shouldn't,' says Stephen. 'We're doing quite well.'

'No, I don't think we should, actually,' Rob agrees. He says he does want Stephen to listen to Electronic's 'Get The Message'.

Stephen suggests Scott Walker might be useful.

'As a mindset?' asks Rob.

'Yeah, because Scott Walker had an interesting ... the way he disappeared ... and then he came back as the avant-garde artist,' says Stephen. 'And nobody actually knew what he was doing. They'd say "He's a painter" but nobody knew.'

'We should make a record,' suggests Rob, 'that, to somebody who doesn't know what avant-garde is, sounds like it's avant-garde. Do you know what I mean?'

* * *

They decide to begin a new song. Stephen starts programming some drums and Rob begins singing immediately.

'*Caught the last train to Paddington station, made my escape in the rain, still got your mascara in my bag ...*'

And then, only seconds after it has peeked into existence, this song is abandoned. Rob decides that the rhythm is too 'Girl From Ipanema' for him. Instead, he starts noodling around on the synthesiser. After a while he asks if they have any more beats.

'What do you want?' asks Andy.

'I won't know till I hear it,' he says. 'Have you got any that are really hard?'

Stephen reaches over to the CD rack mounted on the wall by the room's one small window and pulls out a Rolling Stones bootleg, *Taxile On Main Street*.

'A bit of Charlie Watts might do the trick,' he suggests.

Andy finds a clean section from a version of 'Tumbling Dice' and loops it. As he does so, Rob mentions to Stephen that he hasn't told his management yet about Pure Francis. (Josie obviously knows he is here, but he is being coy about what he is doing.) He says that when he explains they may not know whether to believe him. He once announced to them that he knew the best way to break America: to become a wrestler in the WWF. 'I said, "I know someone who's got steroids – it won't be a problem. And the way we break it is that my entrance music will always be one of my records." And they laughed, and I kept a straight face, and they got really worried.'

Rob mentions other people who could be an influence on Pure Francis. 'I've only just got into The Smiths,' he tells Stephen.

'Well, this is going to be a very dangerous album,' Stephen judges. 'EMI are going to try and assassinate me.'

'Well, this is what I'm thinking,' says Rob. 'How do you get an album out while the greatest hits is out? You become somebody else.'

Stephen checks with Rob about his plan for the rest of the year: after the summer tour, an American tour?

'I don't think I'm going to tour America,' says Rob. 'I'd better tell someone soon.'

'I'll tell Tony Wadsworth for you that we're doing Scott Walker goes electro,' Stephen offers, 'and it's far more important than breaking America.'

Andy plays back the looped drums – 'Yeah!' shouts Rob with enthusiasm – but at that moment Josie comes in and tells Rob it is time to do an Australian TV interview downstairs. Charlie Watts will have to wait.

* * *

'Josie,' says Rob, as he is being made up for his interview. 'You know I'm not doing America?'

'No,' she nods. 'We're not touring.' The current plan is that if they don't tour, they will visit radio stations during October, just as he did last month.

'I'm not doing radio stations,' he says.

'Right,' she says, thwarting him by agreeing. 'Whatever you want.'

'And I want more money,' he says, sulkily, determined to find some resistance somewhere.

'You can't possibly have any more money,' she says. 'You've had it all. There's no money left in the world.'

The Australian interviewer makes small talk beforehand, saying that he grew up with Nicole Kidman as his next-door neighbour. 'Grew up with her over the back fence,' he says.

'Like ivy?' asks Rob.

The interview is heavy on the melodrama, but Rob gives as good as he gets.

'Do you like fame?' the interviewer persists at one point. 'Do you like the trappings that go with it? Could you go and live back in industrial north of England happily?'

'Fame is like having a little baby,' Rob counters. 'It's really great and really lovely and it takes its first steps and you're there and you cry, and then it dances a little bit, and you're there and cry too ... and then it shits itself and it pukes everywhere and then it goes through the terrible twos when it pulls things off and it burns itself and all that sort of stuff, and you just want to go, "This is great, can I give it you back for a little bit while I do this?"'

He talks about the future, and as he does so his mind is obviously on what he has been doing upstairs. 'What I do next, I've to put my arse on the line,' he says. 'I've got to do something that might go right down the dunny. That could be the biggest disaster I've ever done. Or immensely well received and immensely well appreciated. And I think it's that sort of adrenaline rush that I'll need next. I've done Robbie Williams. It's done.'

'Well, Robbie, I reckon you're a beauty,' says the interviewer, wrapping things up. 'Love your openness, your honesty.'

'Cool,' says Rob. 'I'll go off and write the hits that make the young girls cry.'

* * *

Upstairs, Stephen has speeded Charlie Watts up to 130 beats per minute and put a bubbling Kraftwerk-like sequence over the top. Rob messes around on the keyboard himself for a few moments and then begins singing.

' *... fall fall fall into these arms, make me feel again, I can breathe again ...* '

He does it over and over, each time finding new melodies and scatting words off the top of his head. They veer from the completely incomprehensible to the semi-cogent.

' *... love is a bastard, love is the kind, love is the soul and driving me blind ... feel feel feel, feel free again, lost in the me again, taking over your heart ... love is a temple, love is a guide, love makes it through to the other side, it's like a passenger falling free from your heart and soul ... I love you like angels, I love you like strangers, I love you in parts ... I feel like a freak, feel like a freak, only don't speak, it tears me apart ...* '

Stephen worries that the song is beginning to sound too rock for Pure Francis.

Rob shrugs. 'I don't think we should be scared to rock,' he says.

Perhaps encouraged by this, Stephen starts playing along some scratchy, loose, anthemic chords on electric guitar.

'*Find a place to crash ...* ' sings Rob.

Stephen asks him if he wants to write a chorus for this song or to leave this until tomorrow and write something completely different.

'Write something completely different,' Rob says.

Stephen gets up a new drum rhythm and suggests to Rob that he should start the song off on the keyboard. After some doodling, he fairly quickly comes up with a descending three-note riff. Andy records and loops what he is playing, and he picks up the microphone. There is no sign of any aforethought. Whatever process goes into this, whatever calculation and consideration in his head, it isn't apparent even when you're in the room with him. He just does it. But the first words out of his mouth will become the song's title and centre. '*You see the trouble with me …* ' he begins. '*Is that I love the song … The trouble with me is, it's bound to go wrong … the trouble with you, it passes you by … the trouble with you is you love me, you love me …* '

Rob stops. 'I've never really written any love songs,' he points out. 'In fact I haven't written any love songs.' He corrects himself. 'One. But it's not out. "Snowblind"'.

'Well, I think I've only ever written love songs,' Stephen says.

He continues. '*You see the trouble with me,*' he sings. '*The other team's going to score … the trouble with us … you're in love with me …* '

'So should we do another bit for the chorus?' prompts Stephen.

'Yeah,' says Rob.

'So if we go into the chorus, I'll play the guitar and you fiddle around until you find something,' Stephen suggests.

'I admire your belief, Stephen,' says Rob.

'I've worked with Nick Rhodes,' he retorts. 'I know how it's done.'

And it is. Rob carefully works out a synthesiser bassline to go with the other section. 'I think they call it "experimenting", don't they?' Rob says in an affected Northern voice. 'I am actually in the process of reinventing myself.' He sings some ideas for the other section, comes up with a 'woah-woah-woah … yeah-eyeah-eyeah' structure, and they record a new run-through. '*You see the trouble with me, is I'm afraid to be bold, I'm afraid of getting old, and I'm afraid to be loved loved loved … so she makes her last mistake … woah oah yeah …* '

'Very nice,' says Stephen.

' … shall we make do with that today?' he says. This song has taken maybe 45 minutes. He grins. 'We'll have ten songs by the end of the week,' he announces.

'That's the beauty of Pure Francis,' Stephen agrees.

Walking downstairs, thrilled, he says, 'We're on to something.'

'Does that mean I can play my Gary Numan records now?' Pompey asks.

6

He had announced that he wouldn't go to rehearsals until the end of the week but he has been persuaded that he must. Apart from anything else, he needs to practise being suspended upside down a number of times for insurance purposes. Today he is to try the opening at the beginning of a rehearsal of the full set. His ankles are connected behind the screens, and he lies there on his back, his feet just slightly lifted by the cords that will hoist him. Then he is pulled up. He has asked the crew members responsible to stand underneath him for this rehearsal just in case – he is mindful of the tale of Owen Hart, the wrestler who recently fell to his death while supposedly suspended in the air – but when he looks down none of them are even looking at him. ('I thought, if this snaps now, I'm fucked,' he explains after. 'And then I thought, "Ehhhh – he who dares, Rodney. He who dares ... "')

Once he is lowered, he launches into the set. He performs the first few songs, and speaks to the near-empty hangar as though he is in front of the crowd at Knebworth. (The imaginary crowd is specifically Knebworth's, which he mentions several times by name; though he will play to half a million other people first, it's Knebworth he is mentally preparing himself for.) After a few songs, he gets more playful. At the end of 'Hot Fudge', he convincingly and passionately explains that Queen will not be splitting up and that the press can kiss his ass, a speech that makes slightly less sense here than on the *Queen Live At Wembley* DVD Lee recently bought him. Before the swing section he says, 'So, I know a few of you have probably seen my Albert Hall show ... ' He sighs. 'Really, really a big risk. A lot of people tried to do that and they couldn't pull it off.' He pauses. 'I won't name names.' Another pause. 'Diana Ross ... ' Pause. ' ... Robert Palmer ... ' Pause. ' ... Rod Stewart ... ' Pause. ' ... Sheena Easton ... ' Pause. ' ... Harry Connick Jnr ... ' Pause. 'But I won't name names.'

He still doesn't make it to the end of the set. He wanders off the stage during 'She's The One', and by the time the band are playing 'No Regrets', he is in the car, heading back into London.

In the car, he muses about dating and shagging and love. He has been going on dates, a new experience for him, and it has set him thinking about the expectations either party brings to the table and the bedroom. 'You know, I am sensitive and humble ... but also ruled by little Robbie a lot of the time. But that's what they all think anyway. I think that people think I'm doing that more than I am doing. I'm not doing that as much as people think I am. Do you know what I mean?'

It depends how much people think you are doing that.

'Well, they think that I can have any girl I want and I can shag any girl I want and I do it all the time,' he says. 'But a lot of the times, the interesting or nice ones don't want to. I grew up sleeping with uninteresting ones. That's why, I think, as you mature a little bit, get into big boy's shoes, you can't be arsed, really.' He laughs; he knows that as sincere as this is, it only conveys about a third of the truth. 'And then you can,' he concedes. He reprises his line about how, for him, 'it is like being in a fucking sweet shop, being diabetic'.

Since when, I object, are you diabetic?

'Well, it disagrees with me.'

When I suggest that his disenchantment with what is available to him might be more like someone going into a sweet shop after having had quite a large meal, he just laughs.

* * *

At Air Studios, Stephen plays back the rockier of the songs he had worked on two days earlier. Immediately he begins singing to it.

'I'm on a mission … to abuse my position … '

'I like the direction Pure Francis is taking,' says Stephen.

They work on a middle eight. Rob tries whistling in it, and making 'doo doo' noises, but is satisfied with neither. Andy runs the backing track one more time and Rob suddenly sings, '*kiss me … with your mouth … kiss me … with your brain*'. 'That'll do there, won't it?' he says to Stephen. Stephen nods and suggests a harmony. There is no discussion of what Rob has done – borrowed the words from the chorus of Stephen Duffy's one big eighties' pop hit, 'Kiss Me' – and nor need there be, as it probably seems suitable to each of them in a number of ways.

After a while Stephen mentions that he has brought in some records for Rob: potential lyrical inspiration for Pure Francis. The first is Bob Dylan's *Blood On The Tracks*. '"Tangled Up In Blue", the way he goes from one person to the next,' Stephen explains. 'It's a great song for writing not from the first person point of view.' He also hands over CDs of Joni Mitchell's *The Hissing Of Summer Lawns* and Harry Nilsson's *Nilsson Sings Newman*. Rob scans the latter's sleeve – it's an album of Randy Newman songs – and says, 'Oh, I know some of these songs.'

'It's the way he goes from one thing to another,' Stephen explains.

'I love "Love Story",' says Rob, and begins singing. '*You and me, you and me, babe … we'll have a kid, maybe we'll rent one … it'll have to be straight, we don't want a bent one … '*

'If we can get all those lyrical ideas over Scott-Walker-meets-into-Kraftwerk … ' strategises Stephen, ' … I think we've got … I mean the whole concept gets more and more interesting the more you think about it.'

'It could be a guy, it could be a band,' says Rob. 'Pure Francis could be a band.' (There seems to be a moment in each new project where Rob tries to divest as much responsibility and burden as possible, usually by declaring it a band. If he is sensible, he will never succeed.)

'That's another pair of very sensible shoes,' Stephen observes. Rob has been wearing Redwings, these soft ankle boots, into the studio each day.

'Yeah,' says Rob. 'Times are changing.' He explains that he saw Eric Clapton wearing them about four years ago and thought: 'They're nice, but they're really sensible.' Then he saw them again recently in a shop and realised 'It's time ... '

After a while Rob gets out his computer and plays Stephen some songs he thinks might be pertinent: Electronic's 'Disappointed', Kraftwerk's 'The Model', The Bee Gees' 'Massachusetts', Glen Campbell's 'Wichita Lineman', Bobbie Gentry's 'Ode To Billie Joe', Dusty Springfield's 'I Don't Want To Hear It Anymore', Randy Newman's 'Short People', The Breeders' 'Cannonball', The Velvet Underground's 'Venus In Furs', David Bowie's 'Can't Help Thinking About Me', The Lilac Time's 'The Family Coach'.

'We should do a really bonkers album,' resolves Rob.

'I think we're on the way,' states Stephen.

'Because, you know, no one's going to be in the position to do one, really,' says Rob, 'because no one'll sign anything bonkers.'

Over a break for sushi, which they eat in the office just outside the studio, they discuss Elton John. 'He kidnapped me once,' Rob reminisces. 'Took me to Windsor. Actually he's a really lovely bloke; his heart is in the right place. He just misfires sometimes.'

* * *

The next day he returns to Elstree where he chats in the catering tent with Chris Briggs.

'Is there a song in your head?' Chris asks him.

'There are many,' says Rob, though he doesn't let on that some of them have been finding their way out recently.

Gary Marshall wanders over.

'Are we going to Stephen Duffy's again?' he asks Rob, blowing his cover slightly.

Chris is supposed to know none of this. 'Stephen "Tintin" Duffy?' he asks.

'Yeah,' says Rob.

'Formerly The Lilac Time?' Chris asks.

'The Lilac Time are still going,' Rob points out.

'Good writer,' says Chris, fishing.

'Is he?' says Rob nonchalantly. When Chris is looking away he grins at me. The secrets that don't make you sick make you stronger.

Eventually he goes into the hangar where the stage is set up. He is still acting as though the tour is someone else's project in which he is a non-participant investor, popping in every now and again just to cast an eye over proceedings and make sure that his money isn't being wasted. Today Josie has to bring him back into the hangar twice to make sure that he watches and approves the dancers' choreography for 'Hot Fudge'. He does join in the show for a while during the swing section, if only to take the opportunity to wind up Max a little more. 'He's got six films coming out over the summer,' Rob says. 'Keeping Boots very busy.' When he discusses their Christmas

heartbreak, he says, 'We only date celebrities – have you noticed? Weird. But if you're in prison, you shag the inmates … '

He lasts until 'Kids', and even then he does his rap sitting on a chair at the back of the room.

'See you later,' he says to David as it finishes.

'Are you off, mate?' asks David.

'Yeah,' he says. 'I'm going to do some secret stuff.'

'You got a date?' asks David, intrigued.

'Yeah, Dave,' he says. 'I've got a date. With destiny.'

* * *

In the studio, Rob picks out a new riff on the keyboard, a repetitive motif based around two chords. Stephen follows him on guitar, and then finds a descending chord progression that turns the two chords to four. Rob sings a little.

'It's nice, isn't it?' he says to Stephen. 'You be my Pete Waterman, I'll be your Sonia.'

They talk about people they have known in wilder, unwiser days: the actor, for instance, who had a heart attack and just carried on as before. 'It wouldn't have stopped me,' Rob reflects. 'In fact it didn't. I didn't have a heart attack but I was severely ill. First MTV awards. Black bile coming up. I actually got some kind of venereal disease and phoned up my girlfriend and said I had to get away for a while, and ended up at Damien Hirst's doing speed with Hell's Angels.' He sighs. 'Fucking hell. There was one year when I just couldn't stop drinking. Every day, all day.'

'What year was that?' asks Stephen.

'95,' he says. 'I did an interview on the six o'clock news once. I didn't even know I'd been.'

What was it about?

'I don't know. It'd be interesting to see ... ' He stops himself. 'No, it wouldn't. It'd be horrible.'

He shakes his head. 'I started to take coke when I found out ecstasy wore off and after seven there's no point having an eighth, and with three grams of coke you could go through the day,' he reminisces. 'And I couldn't stand Tuesday. The day after's monged, and the next two days are the most depressed you've been ever. Whereas with coke you just felt monged the next day and not very good the day after.'

But then there was the paranoia.

'I was either going to be gang-raped, or there were gangsters I'd upset, or the Special Branch of police,' he says. 'The cat flap. And the clever bastards, they'd got in the sofa and opened it and sewed it up again. And I'd checked the house but I thought, oh no – they're in the sofa.'

Stephen mentions how he once snorted hot chocolate and then began to worry it would be the worst rock star death ever.

'Man,' says Rob. 'It just regurgitates a load of old shitty feelings.'

They get back to songwriting. Time for another. Rob starts singing against some drums. After a long while he sings some lines that seem to lead somewhere: '*Inside it's aching to be misunderstood ... be misunderstood ... that can only be good ... because while they're understanding things ... we find in many places ...* ' He stops. 'A song about how great it is to be misunderstood,' he declares. 'If they're talking about you, then it's great.' He sings this against some heavy organ chords. '*You're misunderstood for ages ... bless for all eternity ... you needed me ...* ' Stephen picks up an acoustic guitar from the wall, finds the appropriate chords on that, and the song begins to take off. ' *... She said I'm dreadfully misunderstood ... I said, well, that's good ...* ' 'How lucky we are to be misunderstood,' he says, and continues. '*I hear you're a mean keepy-upper ... but at least you've got your supper ... your Tupperware affair ... up your derrière ... by the beautiful and good, dear ... we will be misunderstood, dear ... by the beautiful and good, dear ... we're not all Robin Hoods here ... please don't look so austere when they to shake your hand ... they try to understand ... when they try to shake your hand ...* ' The idea is thrown around the room, and he grabs hold of the phrase '*please don't understand*'. He sings on. Only much later does he mention that one of the ideas in his head as he does so is of the relationship between Woody Allen and his adopted daughter Soon Yi. '*When you try to shake my hand,*' he sings, '*please don't understand ... I'm trying to be misunderstood here ... silent faces form your hands ... foreign faces understand ... isn't it funny how they don't speak the language of love? ... love the way they smiled at me ... held that face for eternity ... let them all fly out ...* '

It's suddenly sounding quite beautiful, though Rob and Stephen both seem confused about the song's structure, or lack of it. The evening breaks up in a slightly awkward way for the first time. Stephen stays to work on the song. Rob still has a spring in his step as he bounds downstairs. 'It already opens up another lyrical valve,' he says. 'It stops me worrying what they're thinking, do you know what I mean?'

* * *

He returns to Air late the next afternoon in another pair of sensible shoes – same make, different colour – after a day of financial meetings and having his hair dyed bluey-black. 'I hope you've got some free time in September,' Rob says to Stephen, 'because I've just cancelled America.' He's got it all planned – they can record at his Los Angeles house, and put the drums in the bathroom.

He made up his mind about not touring America after being bothered to distraction when he went out last night. 'I don't want to do that everywhere in the world, thanks,' he says.

'Is America worse?' Andy asks.

'No,' says Rob. 'This country's actually now on a par with Italy. Absolutely. But they do it with a lot more aggression over here.'

'They resent people,' notes Stephen.

'It's the man who lives in the big house on the hill,' says Rob. 'The Americans look at him and go, "One day I'll live in that house." And the English go, "One day I'll get that bastard."'

* * *

'Now,' he grins, 'all I've got to do is alienate the fans.' He sticks up two thumbs, to indicate how much he is joking, and maybe also how much he isn't.

Stephen plays him what he has done with 'Misunderstood', looping some of Rob's vocal and editing in a new transitional section that Stephen sings. Rob seems puzzled. 'I still don't get it,' he says. 'Which is the chorus and which is the verse?' He sings some new words, but can't shake his confusion. Eventually, and appropriately, he realises that it is quite alright that he doesn't grasp it. 'Well, *you* understand it,' he says to Stephen, 'and I soon will.' He sings some more. 'It sounds like a classic,' he says, still nonetheless perturbed. 'How many songs do we have all together now?'

'Six,' says Stephen. 'That's not bad.'

'It'd be nice to have ten, wouldn't it?' says Rob.

They return to 'The Trouble With Me', trying to work out what it needs in the place where a middle eight might go.

'Would harpsichords ruin it?' Rob wonders.

'I don't know,' says Stephen. 'We can try.'

Apart from the very genuine progress they are making in writing songs, I think it is these kinds of exchanges that Rob most relishes: to be somewhere that he can say 'Would harpsichords ruin it?' and no one either laughs or immediately tries to talk him out of it, just considers exactly how a harpsichord might fit into what they are doing. It doesn't matter at all that the specific idea is soon forgotten, because Rob is now expressing an enthusiasm for some 'hoo hoo' noises in the style of the breakdown section of U2's 'Discotheque', or some fast manic keyboard as heard in the weird middle movement of A-ha's 'Take On Me'. (Stephen has to confess that he's not too familiar with the works of A-ha.) Then Rob tries to play some low, farty keyboard noises; they laugh about how perturbed his band will be if they ever have to reproduce this, but he has soon gone off this idea too. He asks Andy to just run the drums bare, and picks up the microphone. He does a staccato vocal, half-whispering and half-barking the words: '*work with – computers – in angels – for sing – more than – the angels – for being – unclean* ... ' Then he immediately does a higher spoken vocal over the top, matching the rhythm and some, but not all of, the words. Then, immediately, another pass, speaking much faster. A fourth, fast. A fifth, also fast. Quite how he knows what this will create is a mystery, and it has only taken a few minutes, but when it is played back there is a lovely wash of chatter, its babble rising and falling.

Rob starts playing some simple guitar chords.

'That's nice,' says Stephen. 'Is that anything?'

Rob shakes his head. Stephen grabs an acoustic guitar and starts following the chords Rob is playing. Suddenly, a different song is forming. Stephen keeps playing these chords, and Rob comes up with a stabbing bass-sound keyboard melody, though he gets frustrated at his inability to play what he wants to without any mistakes and eventually sings the notes for Stephen to play instead so that they can record his riff. Now some free-form words cascade out. '*It shows in my attic, it's all asiatic ... it lives in my basement ... I can feel the rodents ... it's in my confusion ... it's always on my brain ... he falls on my Oscars ... it makes all my engines go up uh! uh! ... it loves in the ages ... and falling awake on the mismim line ... and do it for you ... do it for you heh heh ... it's like the fault in my reason ... summer's in the radio ... tune in to the songs you know ... make it effervescent here ... and you can bring the song from here* ... '

Stephen applauds. 'Another chord maybe,' he suggests.

'It's got to go somewhere else,' says Rob. They listen back and Rob sings a high counter-melody: '*Love's got the radio ... it falls in the things you know ... it moves me all the time ... tune into the darkness, it's the only way to find* ... '

They loop a good bit of the vocal – the Oscars bit – as the verse, under Rob's instructions, and Rob sings a lower octave: '*fall and jump and shout at something* ... ' Then he keeps a bit from later on – '*tune it to the radio and listen to the songs you know – make it effervescent here and you may have a job my dear*' – that has a spirit that transcends its lack of sense. 'I like that,' he says. He re-sings and slightly changes it, but he's had enough. He looks half asleep. He goes to the loo, then returns and says, 'Steve, I'm fucked.' He needs to go.

Stephen nods. 'This is good though,' Stephen points out. Over the next few days, he will edit and loop these vocals, and add some more parts, and list its title on the CD he sends Rob as 'Radio'.

* * *

Towards the end of the day Rob speaks with Josie on the phone.

'See you tomorrow,' she says.

'Why?' he asks.

'Your tour is starting,' she points out.

'Christ,' he says. 'I had no idea.'

* * *

It is not the full tour that begins in Paris this weekend, just a prequel of sorts. He is playing at the Olympia Theatre, which only holds 2500, whereas few of the dates on the actual tour are to audiences of under 40,000. They are not unveiling the full show production here – perhaps a good thing, as Rob is yet to see the full show production. Though he is thrilled by what he has been doing with Stephen Duffy for itself, certainly part of the attraction the attic at Air Studios has held for him over the past few days has been that it offered not only a sanctuary in which he could hide from his summer tour, but a place where he could create an alternative reality where the tour didn't matter. The few times I have heard him directly consider the tour recently, he has been wondering whether he will hate it as much as he has before, and whether the fact that he is generally so much happier will blunt the highs as well as the lows. 'That euphoria that sometimes you feel,' he says. 'I wonder if I'm going to feel that.' If, inside, there's less at risk, perhaps there's also less to gain. 'But I'd actually rather lose the euphoria,' he says, 'for the sake of getting through it and not wanting to die.'

The plane rises from Luton and we fly over Luton Hoo, where we can clearly see the *Delovely* film set down below, the actors and crew milling around the catering tables just outside the house's front door. It is the day when the tabloids first report that Cameron Diaz and Justin Timberlake have been seen kissing. Eminem is playing in Scotland this week, on tour. He is all over the papers after he pretends to dangle a baby from his hotel window; the tabloids play their part in the spectacle by responding with feigned, almost celebratory outrage.

On the plane, Rob lets David hear a Pure Francis song for the first time: 'The Trouble With Me', the only one he has a mix of on his computer. 'I said, it's going to sound avant-garde to people who don't know what avant-garde is,' he explains to David. 'Avant-garde for the masses.' He says that he wants Pure Francis to have horns and fangs.

'You've always wanted those bloody fangs,' sighs Josie.

'I think I'll grow my hair,' he says.

'No,' says Josie. 'Little horns with short hair.'

'Skinhead,' he suggests. 'Really fit with shaved head. Top off. Grown-up shoes, horns. No dancing, minimal movement, maybe sit down for the whole of the gig.'

'No, you're not sitting down,' says David. 'You couldn't sit down for the whole of the gig.'

'No playing to camera,' Rob tells him. 'No playing to the audience. No nothing. One of the things I don't like about touring is that I have to run round like a mental person.'

He wonders if, or how, Pure Francis should do interviews, or even talk. I suggest that he should sit in front of interviewers, listen and tell them that he will answer all their questions on his next album.

* * *

The show is low key but successful, though before the encores Rob frets that someone was bellowing abuse at him during the swing section.

'Did someone shout "knobhead" before "One For My Baby"?' he asks.

Chris Sharrock sets him straight.

'"Robbie!",' he says.

'Oh yeah,' concedes Rob. 'I often get the two confused.'

* * *

On the plane home Max tries to persuade Rob that they should play golf together when they get to Scotland next week. Rob isn't keen. He used to play golf when he was a teenager. He was junior golf captain of his club when he was 15. His best club was a five iron; he hated the way lady golfers always hassled the juniors for leaving divots. He'd sometimes play when he was in Take That, smoking joints with his friends as they made their way round. But in recent years he has mostly stayed away.

'I can't stand being bad at it,' says Rob. 'It upsets me.'

'That says more about you than the game,' Max argues.

'That's right, Max,' says Rob in his best and-why-bother-to-state-the-bleeding-obvious tone.

* * *

Backstage at the Queens Theatre on Shaftesbury Avenue, Jonny is in a dressing gown. He already has his transvestite make-up on: the corset, fishnet stockings and high heels are to come. It is his opening night in the West End as star of *The Rocky Horror Picture Show*.

'You're all looking at me, giving me nervous vibes,' Jonny complains.

'It's a bit weird, lad,' Rob points out. As Rob has always maintained, there is something very disturbing about seeing Jonny dressed like this.

Early on in the show, when Jonny's character shows off his slave and says, 'What do you think?', someone in the audience shouts out, 'He's no Robbie

Williams!' In the second half, when Jonny has to pretend to snort cocaine, he does a double twitch with his head. A private joke. Rob's coke twitch.

7

Three days before the first proper show of his tour he flies up to Edinburgh by private jet. He's tired. He says that he forgot to take his medication yesterday, and that he got cranky and his back cramped up as a consequence. From the airport, he goes straight to Murrayfield Stadium, where the band are rehearsing as the final construction of the stage goes on around them, and joins in the rehearsal for a couple of songs but refuses to practise the show opening.

The hotel is a few miles from the stadium, in the Scottish countryside. 'Look at the trees bending over,' he notes as we drive there. 'The cows are sitting down.' In his room, he turns on the television and sees Cleo Rocca interviewing someone. 'I fell asleep outside one of my flats once,' he mutters. 'She put me to bed.' After midnight, he asks the hotel if he can use the driving range, and they open it up just for him. We are there until past two in the morning, hitting golf balls into the darkness.

At around five, just before dawn, still restless, he leaves his room to go for a wander. The door slams behind him. He doesn't have the key so he has to wake up Jason to let him back in.

* * *

As a distraction, he has bought the new, fourth edition of the computer game Championship Manager. The last time he played Championship Manager, he was addicted for weeks. In the game, you choose one of the real teams in English football to manage and make all the decisions a manager would make: purchases, wages, tactics, team selection, training and so on, in the most minute detail, and then watch games play out on the computer – 22 dots moving around on the screen. He has decided to manage Cardiff, reckoning that they have plenty of potential and healthy prospects of promotion. He started playing last night and already seems more focused on it than his imminent tour, which is perhaps precisely the point.

He also has his mattress changed. This isn't the kind of thing he is generally fussy about, but his bed was preposterously hard and uncomfortable, as everyone else he had try it out confirmed. The hotel has brought in a replacement that isn't much better, but he can't face having it changed again. He predicts that news of this will reach the press anyway and be reported as prima donna pop star behaviour. 'It's: I'm going to need a really good rest,' he says, 'and if I don't, the shows will be shit.'

'I think that's the most decadent thing we've ever asked for,' says Josie.

Two days to go. There is another rehearsal today, so we head into town. On the street walls close to the stadium posters advertise the new unofficial biography. 'Can you imagine if I was that person who was in that book?' he says. 'Or if I was the person that the tabloids wrote about? I'd be some sort of Hitler-esque character.'

Josie comes into the dressing room while he is doing some stretching.

'I said to this guy in the gym,' he tells her, '"Can you teach me how to do the splits?" And he said, "How flexible are you?" And I said, "Well, I can't do Saturday ..."'

He lies on the floor and plays a snooker game on his Xbox. He says that he is feeling drained. 'When there's any sort of responsibility,' he says, 'my body goes ... ' and he demonstrates his body sagging, as if every ounce of will and fight is leaving it. He has a theory about this. 'It's my DNA fighting,' he says. He thinks it is his parents' bloodlines at war within him. 'There may be centuries of men on my dad's side that can't be arsed,' he suggests. 'In many ways it's a fine quality to have. But on my mother's side, there's definitely men and women who can be far too arsed. Which is also a great quality to have. But when you've got both of them struggling against each other ... '

That, of course, is part of Robbie Williams' allure: a great primal battle between arsed and can't-be-arsed played out as public spectacle, entertainment and melodrama.

* * *

He is on stage.

'When I say "eve", you say "ning"!' he shouts, and waits for the requested response. 'When I say "ha" you say "lo"!'

On recent tours he worried that his ability to speak between songs onstage had dried up, but the chat is flowing now.

'And you thought I was just a celebrity,' he announces. 'Well, no, I sing and dance ... ' Then, as though he senses doubt, he adds: 'I do! I entertain ...' He explains that what he is presenting tonight is a huge cake. 'And it's called Entertainment Pie,' he tells them. 'Just for you. I just want to offer you a bit of "Come Undone" crumble ... '

If there is something particularly strange about the way he is doing this, it is that, once again, there is no 'them' here. There is no 'you'. He is talking to, and interacting with, no one. In fact, an extra £8000 has been spent securing the stadium this evening so that no one might accidentally see or photograph him as he dangled upside down at the beginning, and aside from the few people working on the show, Murrayfield is completely empty. But as he rehearses, he still does so as though there is a full audience present. Maybe it's just sensible and realistic – this patter, as much as anything else, is what needs practising – but it is what he always does when he rehearses, whatever the circumstance. The simplest way of summarising it might be this: Robbie Williams always performs as though the audience is there, even when they are not there. And maybe that is it, though sometimes I wonder if the truth is closer to the absolute opposite – that he always tries to perform, with all the chat and stagecraft and interaction and tomfoolery that go along with performing, exactly as it makes sense to do so in the world inside his head. As though the audience is never really there at all.

* * *

The rehearsal continues.

Max appears on the piano and Rob introduces 'One For My Baby' at great length. He explains that they actually sang this song together in the lonely reverie of their Yuletide heartache. (Not that they ran through it together for the first time in his basement in the spring.) After the song, he shouts, 'Max Beesley! Between the two of us we've nearly got a perfect Spice Girls jigsaw ... complete apart from one piece. Oh yeah. I did say one piece missing. You do the math! You know about three of them but there's another one. You don't know that.'

Max looks horrified.

Rob starts singing 'She's The One' in the lispy voice of Mark Owen – now he is less performing to an imaginary crowd than entertaining the few of us he knows are watching. He interjects lines from the Take That song 'Babe'. 'Oh fuck it,' he says after a while, and walks off. He asks Josie the time, then back-announces the song once it has finished: '"She's The One". Otherwise unknown pop song, "She's The One" ... written by Karl Wallinger of World Party fame. Robbie Williams records it and makes it hugely popular. Karl Wallinger – is he happy? Is he fuck? The ungrateful bastard. Ungrateful fat bastard, eh? I bet he was fucking happy when the royalty cheque came in. Every fucking time I sing that song now I'm thinking of that cunt. Think about that. Put that in your fucking bastard ... "Karl Wallinger, do you like Robbie Williams' version?" "No, I think he's a cunt," I think the words were. Well, I think you're a cunt. Yeah. Can't think of anything funny to say. You're a cunt too. Who's the bigger cunt then? Him! The answer's him. If you're thinking about what the answer is, it's Karl Wallinger. He's the bigger cunt. Anyway, excuse my profanities, ladies and gentlemen, I know it's not like me, but ... it winds me up. That'll go on the greatest hits and everything, that will, and earn that bastard more money. Cunt. Anyway, on with the show. "Supreme."'

He walks offstage at the beginning of 'No Regrets' and does not return.

* * *

Most of the waking hours in the 48 before his first show, he spends playing Championship Manager 4. Back at the hotel, he searches on the internet for tips, looking for good players to buy cheap, and phones up Ant for advice. His other pastime, as he waits for the first concert, is to listen over and over to the half-finished Pure Francis songs, to his future away from this. Stephen has given him rough mixes of five songs. (All the other songs he has written over the past nine months are now forgotten, superseded.)

One day to go. In the van into town, for the final rehearsal, he calls Stephen to find out when he can have versions of the others.

'What a great bloke,' he says afterwards. 'I don't think he's going to go up his own arse either. But if he does it, he'll do it in a much classier way ... '

He then decides, in the interests of sharing and disgusting and entertaining, to show us his latest injury from the Vacunaut machine. 'My left bollock's massive,' he says. 'Look.' It is, as he advertises, unnaturally large, and also worryingly purple. 'They are an ugly fucking thing, men's bollocks, aren't they?' he reflects.

At Murrayfield, he soundchecks 'Let Me Entertain You' and that is it. He has still not properly rehearsed, or even seen what happens in, the last few songs of the set, or the encores, and he will not now do so until they happen around him in front of 65,000 people tomorrow night.

He sits in his dressing room and thinks about Pure Francis.

'I suppose he'll be somebody I want to be,' he says. 'Instead of me writing about who they think I am, and who I am. You know, "Handsome Man" is obviously who they think I think I am. And "How Peculiar" is who I'd like to be, but Pure Francis won't be as cocksure as that. He'll be more cultured in his self-appraisal. I think he'll just be all-knowing.' Pause. 'Instead of all-guessing.'

I ask him whether Pure Francis is damaged.

'Oh yeah,' he says, 'he's damaged. 'But instead of "I feel nothing – I know much smarter men never got this far", it'll be "I feel everything – and I know less smart men have got further than me". I think there'll be a lot of looking down at people from the gutter.'

* * *

Do you even know how your show finishes?

'No,' he says, and smiles.

Isn't that weird?

'Not really,' he says. 'I get to see it when they do too.'

8

The day of Robbie Williams' first show is, predictably, also a big day for Robbie Williams in the newspapers. Some of what is written is meaningless, harmless nonsense. THE BED BOY OF POP proclaims *The*

Sun; the kernel of truth that he has had his mattress changed has been blown up into a story of how 'Robbie stunned staff' at his Edinburgh hotel by demanding a specific Four Seasons bed at short notice.

Much more infuriating is a two-page article in the *Daily Mail* by Nicole Lampbert, their 'deputy showbusiness editor'. It is headlined ROBBIE'S ANGEL and illustrated by a photo of Jonny dressed as Frank N. Furter with his arm around Rob. '*They live together, travel together and are as close as any couple,*' says the subhead. '*So what's the truth about Robbie Williams and his companion, Jonathan?*'

Though it craftily tries to protect itself by insincerely backtracking at the very end, it is a masterpiece of sustained, slimy innuendo, and the message it intends to convey is perfectly clear: everyone knows; it's perfectly obvious – how much longer are these two gay lovers going to keep on pretending otherwise?

In truth, the weirdest thing about Rob and Jonny's relationship is how uncomplicated it seems; how simple, solid and deep it is. How all their history – of Rob being older, and more famous, and then of the two of them standing by each other through various lows – has given them a friendship that has a comfortable balance, and one that, between them, has the luxury of being unexamined. That is not how the *Daily Mail* sees it, of course. Rarely does an article like this use so many different points of attack, and perhaps it is worth unpicking in detail exactly what it does.

* * *

It begins by describing the scene earlier in the week as Rob applauded Jonny from the stalls at the *Rocky Horror Show* premiere. It details their matching tattoos, and then says that Jonny is never so open about his 'long-suffering fiancée' as about his friendship with Rob: '*Two years after they got engaged she is still waiting to be taken down the aisle.*' The innuendo gathers pace and the piece then abruptly turns, using a parade of Rob's own jokes and teasings as though they must only exist to camouflage the very subject they are about, quoting the banter when he and Jonny performed 'Me And My Shadow' at the Royal Albert Hall, revisiting the references to The Rock in *The Advocate*, and describing the three-men-in-a-bed scene in the 'Come Undone' video. (One of the male models is quoted as saying, 'Robbie was really into it.') She then turns to sources from his past. She quotes Kevin Kinsella – she misstates that he worked closely with Take That, though in fact he only knew and briefly managed Rob afterwards – as saying: '*His confusion with his sexuality was very upsetting for him … Rob broke down and cried when he explained it to me …*' Then her second witness, Ray Heffernan, appears.

Ray Heffernan, who helped Robbie write an early version of 'Angels', added: 'I believe that, at that time, Rob's problem with homosexuality was one of his big battles. We'd walk around Dublin all hours of the night just talking about his problems, and the sexuality thing was definitely there. He was very open about it. It was hard for him to discover exactly who he was.'

There's a third.

And an openly gay pop manager tells how he spent the night with Robbie in a Los Angeles hotel room around the time the star left Take That. 'We just kissed and cuddled,' said the manager last week. 'He was in a bad way, he'd been doing too many drugs, and he just wanted some comforting. I would say he likes both men and women. He can't choose and feels he should. He is a northern boy and can't understand why he fancies men. That is why he is so unhappy, in my opinion.'

Who, reading all this, paragraph after paragraph, could have any confusion about what they have just learned?

The article then turns to Rob's relationships with women. It states, carefully, that he clearly '*genuinely likes women*', but it then paints a provocative picture that somewhat works to undermine this, briefly mentioning times with Jacqui Hamilton Smith, Mel C, Nicole Appleton and Tania Strecker, as if they were cumulative evidence of an inability to form a lasting bond with a woman. She then turns to more recent entanglements and implies that these were of a different kind; marking, the reader is led to believe, the beginning of an era of deception and camouflage. With regards to Geri Halliwell, '*the whole thing was judged to have been a publicity stunt*'; '*his relationship with Nicole Kidman happily coincided with the release of their single 'Somethin' Stupid'*'; and as for Rachel Hunter: '*so keen were they to show the world that they had a real romance, they posed for some excruciating pictures while canoodling completely naked. These were made to look like snatched paparazzi pictures. "Let's face it – Robbie will do anything to look straight," Boy George remarked bitterly.*'

Once more the suggestion is clear.

The story returns at the end to him and Jonny. At the last moment, as is traditional in such innuendo-packed stories, having achieved its aim, it draws back to preserve deniability. Having left little doubt in its readers' minds as to what they are expected to think, the stories swiftly protect themselves by saying the opposite. She writes that her sources maintain that Rob and Jonny aren't actually together in that sense, because though '*Robbie may be confused*', Jonny is straight. In a brilliantly cynical final flourish, which attempts to transfer both the writer's ignorance and any blame for it on to her subject, she concludes: '*In this confused environment, nothing can be taken for granted – except that no one, perhaps not even Robbie Williams himself, really knows the true nature of his sexuality.*'

* * *

Rob, who is actually well enough convinced that he does know not to trouble himself with reading any of this article directly, only slowly learns how obnoxious it is as parts of it are quoted to him through the afternoon. There is an exhaustion in his reaction that comes from being so used to being lied about, but there is some exasperation too. When David mentions Boy George's 'Robbie will do anything to appear straight', he wearily retorts, 'What? By being completely heterosexual? And really not interested in blokes whatsoever?'

Likewise, he sees little point in trying to work out whether Kevin Kinsella and Ray Heffernan, two men who have spent far more time talking about him than knowing him, sincerely believe he was or is in anguish over his sexuality. Did they misunderstand something he communicated in drunken unhappiness or bluff playfulness? Have they somehow imagined what they are now quoted as saying based upon what they subsequently believed to be true? Have they been misquoted? Or have they simply lied for effect or attention or profit? All he can know is that, although his confusions have been many, this was not one of them.

The third story, about the night with the gay pop manager, is different, and it takes him some time today to realise what has been printed: that a man is seriously claiming to have spent a night in Los Angeles kissing and cuddling him. If true, it is a tale that might be expected to be more than smuggled away in the midst of an article like this. It is also a claim that completely flabbergasts him. He has no idea who even could be alleging such a thing.

'I didn't even *go* to Los Angeles until *I've Been Expecting You,*' he points out. 'Shit like that shouldn't be allowed. Jesus. "We just kissed and cuddled?"'

He asks to hear the quotes again. For once, he seems quite shocked.

'People shouldn't be allowed to say that shit,' he says. He exhales. 'I mean, at the end of the day the bisexual stuff never hurt David Bowie and Mick Jagger – it makes people more interesting – but also at the end of the day people shouldn't be allowed just to completely make shit up. I have never even been *close* to snogging a man with sexual intent.'

But what can you do but shrug and carry on? Particularly when it comes to a subject like this. If you loudly object, simply because the story isn't true and because it is annoying to be lied about, many people will assume that you are loudly objecting because you consider the story's suggestions shameful. It is the *Daily Mail* and not Rob who regularly act as though they believe homosexuality to be something disgraceful that invites deceit, but it is hard to challenge their story without their prejudices seeming to project on to you instead.

So he shrugs and returns to Championship Manager. Cardiff have been doing well overnight, but just recently have faltered. 'That's the way it goes in football management sometimes,' he says earnestly. By five in the afternoon, he is so engrossed that he cleans his teeth in front of the computer as he looks for new players to sign. In town, thousands of people are filtering towards Murrayfield Stadium, thinking of Robbie Williams. In his room at the Dalmahoy Hotel & Country Club, Robbie Williams is wondering whether Cardiff should sign Matty Warner from Wycombe Wanderers.

* * *

He has a police escort from the hotel to the stadium. As we drive into the city, we see more and more people, some crowding outside pubs but most making their way in the same direction. When they see the van and the police motorcyclists, many of them stop, wave and applaud.

He spots Edinburgh Castle on the skyline and is reminded of the first time he saw it. 'Take That did their first gigs in Edinburgh and Glasgow,' he says quietly. 'Played five clubs each night, sometimes having to go from Edinburgh to Glasgow and back to Edinburgh. We got £175 for the whole tour.'

As he gets out of the van backstage, he waves to some fans who have spotted him through the fence, and then holds his forearm under his mother's nose. 'Look at my hair standing on end, Mum,' he says. 'It's great, isn't it? I'd shed a tear.' Pause. 'If I had a heart I would.' He arches his head up towards the outside of the stadium. 'Fuck me,' he says. 'Look at that.'

Chris Briggs comes over to see how he's doing. 'Enjoying it?' he asks.

'Don't push the boat out,' Rob warns him. 'I'm at a town near enjoying. It's better than a town near rather-top-myself-than-go-onstage ... '

There is a sense of nervousness in those around him, triggered, ironically, by how calm Rob is. They are nervous because it has not always been like this. In fact, it has rarely been like this.

He paces up and down the corridors outside the dressing room.

'I'm in the mood to go and prove a few people right,' he says, 'and lots of people wrong.'

He shows Josie the fourth finger on his left hand. It is infected and very swollen. It looks awful. He asks if she can find someone to look at it. 'See if they can take the pain away,' he asks. As he waits, he reads the typed notes Lee has left for him, going through the set, encouraging him to repeat some parts of his performance from the few rehearsals Rob has attended and reminding him about other aspects of the staging. After browsing them for a few moments he puts them down and laughs. 'There's no notes after "Kids",' he says, 'because we haven't done it.'

The doctor arrives and drains away some of the pus from his finger. 'You've bitten your fingernails,' the doctor reprimands him, 'and infected the finger around it.' Rob says that he has tried to stop and failed. 'I got used to Stop'n'Grow,' he explains. 'You've got to really want to stop. And I don't want to stop.'

He chooses his outfit for tonight from the clothes on a rack. (For all the theatricality of his performance, he is not the kind of performer who has a uniform. Nor – aside from putting on a fresh T-shirt for the encores, and in

Scotland a kilt – is he the kind to indulge in costume changes.) About half an hour before he is due onstage he has a request for his mother.

'You better make yourself scarce now,' he requests, 'because I can't get rock'n'roll if you're here. I feel like someone's son otherwise.'

'Really?' says Jan, getting up. 'Dear, dear.'

'I've now got to become the myth,' he explains.

She nods. 'I'll see you onstage,' she says.

'Thanks, ducky head,' he says. 'Love you.'

The ankle bracelets are fitted. He starts singing U2's 'Elevation', then paces the corridor some more. In the band dressing room, Mark Plati plays an acoustic guitar and everyone sings the Beatles 'Blackbird' together as a final warm-up. 'Anyone else feel like they could slip into a coma?' Rob asks, but then fends off any concern. This feeling regularly comes over him in stressful situations.

It's time. He joins the band onstage behind the screens, which hide them from the audience, striding around, a stern expression on his face, offering final handshakes. Then he lies on his back and is connected to the wire that will hoist him upwards. He's there for a while, his ankles a few inches above the ground, until he is lifted up. As he rises, he twists himself, to stop himself spinning. The screens open in front of him. The screaming gets louder, and stays louder.

* * *

It's not obvious out front – none of tomorrow's reviews will note it – but disaster strikes immediately. For the first two songs there is complete panic as the monitors and the in-ear systems that supply sound to the musicians cut out completely. They can barely hear what they are playing, and Rob can barely hear what he is singing. He is totally thrown and somewhat terrified. But that is not what the audience sees. He always maintains that the more scared he is, the more confidence he shows, and by that measure his terror must be truly awful.

After about an hour, he starts racing around the stage shouting, 'I'm not scared any more! I'm not scared any more! It only took me ten songs not to get scared!' He may be trying to communicate something honest about his experience up there, but I'm sure that most people watching are baffled, struggling to square this information with the supremely cocky and self-assured performance they have been enjoying.

At the end of the show he runs offstage and straight into a waiting car, wiping off sweat as the car accelerates, so that he can be away from the stadium before the lights have even faded from the audience's eyes.

He sits there, sweaty, panting slightly.

'Did you enjoy it?' asks Josie.

'Finding my feet,' he says. 'Finding my feet.' He insists that he was really not sure until the end whether the audience were enjoying themselves. 'I thought, this is where it all goes pear-shaped for me in my life,' he says. He was shaken at the beginning of 'Me And My Monkey' when he saw people going to the bathroom and he knew he had seven more minutes of the song to sing. 'A lot of the time I'm onstage I just question what it is that they're liking,' he says. 'I mean, I just question: *what is entertainment*? Why are they looking at me like that? I'm not having a downer or anything like that, it's just, I look at me and think, what is it that I'm doing? I don't get it.'

Whatever conversation the people beginning to leave Murrayfield imagine Robbie Williams is having right now, I'm fairly sure it is not this one.

He asks the driver to open the back window and let in some air, and says that while he was onstage he had another thought. He knew that all the journalists were here, judging him, and suddenly he was no longer worried.

'I thought, well, I can do whatever the fuck I like on this tour because Francis is on his way,' he says. 'I can be whoever I want to be, as the moment takes me, and not worry about it.'

* * *

Back at the hotel there is a buffet and low-key party in a private lounge with a pool table that has been set aside for the touring group. Rob sits on a sofa and watches a little of Radiohead at Glastonbury on TV, but he doesn't stay long. He's having a moment of sadness about not having a girlfriend, and Championship Manager beckons. Later, in what the *Daily Mail* might consider a further desperate attempt to prove his heterosexuality, he may pop down to the bar and stumble back upstairs in company. (Back in his room, he will tell his new temporary companion, by way of conversation, 'My ears are ringing.' 'Who's calling?' she will reply.)

Eventually, when even girls and imaginary football teams and a mattress that is still too hard cannot stop him, he finally falls asleep. As he sleeps, he dreams.

He, Jonny and his mother are looking up at the night sky. And then – there it is! Just what he's always wanted to see – a UFO! And then *another*. Two huge wonderful UFOs.

And then – in the dream – he turns to his mother and says, slightly disappointed, 'Oh ... this is a dream, isn't it?'

'No,' she goes.

'No,' says Jonny.

And he's so pleased. It was *real*.

But ...

But ...

He asks one more time, just to be sure.

'It is a dream, isn't it?' he says to his mother. 'Tell the truth.'

'Yeah,' she admits.

9

Jonny arrives the following afternoon. Rob is just waking. He sits in his room, naked apart from a towel, tending to Cardiff, who are beating Blackpool 3–0. He watches the screen intently.

'Good review again, youth,' says Jonny. 'On your sex.'

A girl he had sex with in his new flat a couple of weeks back has sold her story to the *News Of The World*. It is told in the usual panting prose:

He gazed down at her thong and said, 'You've got a peach of a bottom' … 'He certainly didn't seem out of practice' … 'Believe me, Robbie is 100 per cent man. There's no way he's gay …'

Rob, who seems barely bothered, says that at the time she had asked him what he thought of girls who sold their stories and he had told her: 'I think they're prostitutes – to sleep with someone for money is to all intents and purposes being a prostitute.' He told her it made him sad: 'People talk about your genitals and comings and goings for all the world to read – it's disgusting.'

'Oh,' she said.

* * *

In the past he has felt sure that tabloid newspapers have sent girls round to sleep with him and sell their story. 'The amount of girls that have sold their story is absolutely phenomenal,' he says. 'It used to be nearly every Sunday. Two girls came round one night, strippers, and if they weren't sent from the papers they were definitely playing a game where they were setting themselves up to go straight to the fucking cash cow.'

It was at the end of 2001. They knocked on the door one night and he went down to see them. They made their intentions clear enough, he remembers: 'They showed me their tits outside, through the railings. And then grabbed my cock.' So he told them they'd better come in. They stayed for a little over an hour.

I ask what happened and he says, matter-of-factly, 'I slept with them … well, it was cold. It was winter.' Then he elaborates. 'It was funny because … my co-dependency … because I was concerned about the one that wasn't as good-looking I spent more time with her, and of course the one that was good-looking got the right hump.'

He says that while it was happening he felt phenomenal; immediately afterwards he felt disgusted. A version of what had taken place was in the papers the next weekend. He phoned up the good-looking one and told her that what she had done was prostitution and made her a whore. She was in the car with her father, and they both hit the roof, saying that the papers had said he was fine about it. He also told her that it was a shame because he'd liked her and had hoped to see her again, which he had.

He says that when he's told that another of these stories is in the papers, he always just asks: 'Did they give me a good report?'

'I'm not bothered otherwise,' he says.

That's really what you care about?

'Well, yeah.'

And what if they give you a bad report?

He shrugs.

'You're only as good as your last single,' he replies.

* * *

In his dressing room, he lies down and watches Sky Sports' football news channel. He can watch this for hours, even though most of the stories are on a loop, and are rarely about anything too important. He finds the repetition soothing. He claims that it is like re-watching episodes of *The Simpsons*: each time round you notice new things. 'I get a chance to hear what they're saying,' he explains, 'and then in the next half hour I get to see what they're wearing, and then what's going on in the background – how many keepy-ups is he doing?' He knows how monotonous and insubstantial it might seem, and sometimes he imagines that there can only be a few people watching – himself, Jonny, Ant, Dec and a few other kindred souls. But this channel is a great consolation for him – not just now, but even more so when he was at his most depressed. 'Without football it would have been very difficult to get through that period,' he says. 'Football saved my life.' He gestures towards the talking heads, and a news story about some minor transfer speculation. 'The people that read the news on that, I loved them,' he says. 'They nursed me through the bad time. That was my family for a while.'

* * *

'Did you read the reviews today?' he asks the Murrayfield audience. 'Neither did I,' he continues, 'but I presume they were excellent ... '

From the beginning of the second Murrayfield show, his performance is at another level on stage. Yesterday, you could often sense the effort behind the entertainment, but tonight he seems to be gliding. He is almost as chatty and indiscreet as he is when talking to an audience who isn't there. 'Christmas was a very difficult period for me and Max because we both split up with two very high-profile celebrities,' he says. 'And I don't know about you, but I'm *done* with celebrities.' (There is a huge roar from the crowd, partly perhaps because some of them feel encouraged to think they're now in with a chance, but I think also because in these mixed-up muddled-up times people enjoy hearing celebrities being slagged off, even when they're eagerly craning their necks to catch every word from a celebrity doing the slagging off.) 'Quite frankly,' he continues, 'I find them dull. And we've broken them all, anyway ... Joking aside though, we're human and we have emotions. And we were left alone at Christmas like two unwanted puppies ... ' He breaks off his train of thought for some front-row flirtation. 'And let me tell you, lady at the front, your puppies are definitely wanted ... ' He sighs. 'With Maxie being here it's very difficult not to do any Spice Girl jokes, it really is. But I'll say this – we've only got to do one more and we've had a pop on all of them between the two of us ... That's right, folks! I did say one more. You do the math ... Really let the cat out of the bag there, didn't I?'

This, said in any other context, would be all over the papers the next day. But all the journalists came to last night's show, and the other 65,000 people here, though many of them might phone a newspaper if they overheard this snippet in a café, will assume that if it is said in front of 65,000 people it must be common knowledge. '*So make it one for Rachel Hunter,*' he sings at the end of the song's first chorus, '*and five for Scary Spice.*' Bizarrely, one of the safest times there is for a celebrity to share their secrets without consequence is while they are onstage during the second night in the same city.

Someone like Rob gives very few interviews (except during his occasional charm offensives in places such as America and Japan, and by virtue of the fact he is still fighting for an audience in those countries, these interviews tend to make less news), but when he is onstage he talks a lot. Some of what he says becomes part of his semi-regular patter – there is no script, even informally in his head, but there are a few stories and routines that reappear most nights, and others that will disappear for a week, then return – but much of what he says appears at just that moment in his mind and races out of his mouth without looking back. Given this habit – and given the fact that the tabloids run stories several times a week about him, often with the flimsiest of substance, and the extraordinary efforts that they and those that sell stories to them go – it amazes me, and will continue to amaze me throughout this tour, that the tabloids don't make the simple effort of sending someone to each of his shows with a notepad. But they don't. Later tonight Rob will worry about what tonight's indiscretions will spawn. How will they twist them? Will they claim that he has accused Rachel Hunter of being dull? Or that he and Max are aiming to complete a full Spice Girls collection? But neither will happen.

Before he sings 'Feel' tonight, he offers a different perspective on his sobriety, which he has never shared with me, and nor will I hear him mention again. 'I want to dedicate this to my nephew,' he says. 'He's in the audience tonight; he's called Freddie Robert, and he'll probably be asleep. But he's two years and nine months old. I gave up drinking because of him. I didn't want him to have an idiot for an uncle. This is called "Feel".' In the chorus he shouts, 'Sing it for Freddie!'

I'm fairly sure he really is enjoying it. Instead of launching straight into the final encore, 'Angels', he starts singing a series of Take That hits – 'Babe', 'I Found Heaven', 'Everything Changes' – without the band and free-associating about his boy band days. Then he says for the first time something he will return to several times over the next few weeks, something that he is obviously saying to himself, with determination and joy and relief, just as much as to the audience.

'Thank you for making my job worthwhile – thank you for making everything mean something,' he says. 'And when you see me in the papers – and when you see me in the tabloids – and when you see me and what they write about me, remember: this is what I do for a living. This is the job that I do. I'm a singer. I'm a songwriter. And I am an entertainer ... '

As he is bundled into the van, he says, 'The best ever.'

'Why did you do one more?' Jonny asks. After 'Angels' he returned to do a completely unrehearsed version of 'Back For Good'.

'Because I was enjoying myself,' he says, as though this was a thoroughly unusual and surprising turn of events. He says he couldn't hear himself again, but tonight it was simply because the crowd were so loud. 'It was like a Take That concert,' he says, 'but with roaring rather than high-pitched screaming.'

He asks how long he was onstage.

'Two hours ten minutes,' says Josie.

'He's turning into Ken Dodd,' says Jonny.

'Bruce Springsteen,' corrects Rob.

'You could have done another hour,' says Jonny.

'Easy,' he says. 'Easy. I think that's the most elated I have ever felt in my life. It was like ecstasy. It's like being Elvis.' Pause. 'But thin.'

* * *

The jet is waiting on the runway to take us back to London tonight.

'It doesn't get any better than this,' says Jonny, chewing crudités as we taxi before take-off. He reconsiders, clearly having given the matter serious thought. 'The only way it could get any better,' he said, 'would be if Spiderman were on the plane.'

Once we are in the air, Jonny looks around the cabin and remarks how much it looks like a caravan. Rob says that he wouldn't know. 'I've always had a private jet, haven't I?' he bluffs. But it sets them off, and they spend most of the journey south reminiscing about childhood holidays.

'Remember that time caravanning?' says Jonny. 'Where did we go?'

'Rhyl,' says Rob.

'How old were you then?' Jonny asks. 'Because you used to strongly pick on me then. "Stop following us!"'

Rob insists that he didn't pick on him, but he does remember pretending to Jonny that he could command God to make it thunder and lightning. He got lucky, and it actually came when he beckoned it. Jonny was terrified. 'We ran off,' Jonny remembers. 'You were well faster than me and I was crying because I couldn't see you. I cried a lot, didn't I?'

They talk about other holidays. Rob driving to Wales with his auntie Mary when he was 11 and hearing Dr Hook and 'Ode To Billie Joe' for the first time. The holidays where the grown-ups would fall out over rounders ('I used to think that was so hideously not grown up and ridiculous,' says Rob, 'and now I can see myself falling out over it') and have tarts'n'vicars parties. Falling in nettles. Rob always being asked to do his impressions. ('Frank Spencer, Ronald Reagan, Margaret Thatcher, Norman Wisdom, Sean Connery … you know, the greatest hits,' he says.) Jonny talks about going round to Rob's bedroom at home and admiring all the stolen traffic cones and the badges from cars; a pilfered bus stop in the back garden.

Rob wonders whether Freddie Robert will remember today.

'Nah,' says Jonny. 'You don't remember stuff when you're two and a half.'

'I can remember pulling a pan off the oven and it scalding me,' says Rob. 'Boiling eggs. I was pulling it off to have a look, see if it was done. I can remember that being the logic.'

Jonny says he recently met someone who knew the director they both hated who worked on the local Stoke productions. He directed Rob as the Artful Dodger. 'I stole the show,' Rob remembers. 'The opening night was the first night I was really like, "Oh, this is what I do for a living then". I walked onstage, whistling, and people were laughing already.'

Jonny got bollocked by the same director when he was six after he ran across the stage and pulled up his nightgown in Hans Christian Andersen. 'It was your fault,' he reminds Rob, who concedes that he did tell Jonny to do it. 'If you'd have said back then, "Jump off that fucking cliff," I would have,' says Jonny.

'No,' says Rob. 'You did it because you wanted us to like you.' He laughs. 'And I admire that. It's worked.'

After *Oliver*, Rob auditioned for *The Sound Of Music* and was turned down. 'I was devastated,' he remembers. 'There were *seven* kids and I didn't get one of them.'

He grins. It would, of course, be *ridiculous* to still be settling scores like that in his head, but he won't pretend he isn't that petty.

'Hello!' he says. 'Private jet! I think you know what I'm saying!'

* * *

'I don't like going to sleep,' says Rob to Jonny, as the jet dips towards Luton. 'Do you like going to sleep?'

'Yeah,' says Jonny.

'You do?' says Rob. 'I don't. That's why I took coke. If I could stay awake all the time, I think I would.'

When he gets home tonight, sleep is out of the question. He has things to do. At 6am Cardiff win the second division championship. He discovers that there is a whole other level to the game, where you can find notes on individual players and act accordingly. (So the madness isn't over, I say when he tells me this. He shakes his head. 'The madness has only begun,' he replies.)

When he wakes up the next afternoon, fresh from a Scottish stadium concert hours before, his Portuguese cleaner, Paula, has a go at him for his bedroom being messy. She is the person who one time leaves him a note, in a sincere attempt to compliment him when he has been tidier, saying, 'Just a note to let you know what a DELIGHT it has been to have you come and stay in your house.' She also says to Pompey: 'Please tell Junior not to use the washing machine because it is leaking because he will slip and break something and we will all be fucked.'

* * *

To be young and rich is almost inevitably to find oneself in the position of having domestic staff of some kind. It should not be too difficult. I see no signs that Rob is a particularly finickety or demanding employer. The only attributes needed for such roles are to be competent, reliable, honest and sane. Paula has been a great success – she has followed him from home to home for the past six years – but, sadly, many have fallen at one hurdle or another. There was the cook who sent a text message to Rob – his employer – explaining that he couldn't get there that day because 'I need to get my head together' and asking: 'Can you cover for me?' There was the housekeeper who asked whether she could bring her son to work with her. Her son turned out to be 27. (She was also the one who interrupted a conversation about clothes to say, 'If you're throwing stuff out, my boy'll have it,' and told one of Rob's bodyguards that he should settle for her, 'Because you're no oil painting.') There was the cook who made racist jokes, forever explained that she used to get chauffeured round herself, and was convinced that it was often one of Rob's guests, rather than the dogs, who was shitting on the Los Angeles carpets. 'This happens in the best households,' she would explain. There was the cook who passed the interview, then died. There was the cook who was found in the kitchen naked apart from her knickers while everyone was in the pool – 'Sorry, I guess I should use the bathroom to change,' she said. There was the cleaner who turned out to have been breaking things and bleaching things that should not have been bleached – so far, only mildly troubling – and then hiding the evidence for months in the boot of Rob's E-type Jag.

10

He spends his one day off in London in the studio with Stephen Duffy. Two more songs. The following morning the main leg of the tour – travelling around Europe for nearly a month without returning home –

begins. There is a larger private tour plane to carry the whole band, dancers and entourage together for the next few weeks. Rob doesn't know about the huge RW logo on its tail until he arrives at Luton's private jet terminal. He doesn't say anything. For a moment even he wonders whether it is a bit much.

In the waiting room, he starts joking with the dancers and immediately it goes wrong. As he and Suzanne Mole stand by the coffee machine, he asks her whether she has seen the article in *The Sun* today about them having sex together. As it happens – though she doesn't yet know – there is a small piece about her in today's *Sun*, which is presumably the trigger for Rob's comment, though it is only an anodyne snippet questioning how comfortable her boyfriend, Gareth Gates, is about her dancing with Rob.

'You're not serious?' she says.

'Yeah,' he says offhand. 'You've said I was great in bed.'

What happens next is unexpected. She simply bursts into very real tears.

Rob is understandably mortified.

'I'm so sorry,' he says. 'I'm so sorry. I'm so sorry.' She starts laughing, but continues crying just the same.

'David Brent,' mutters one of the touring party.

She goes outside to speak to Gareth on her mobile, and another of the dancers, Djeneba, comes over. She wants to offer an apology to Rob. They haven't seen each other since being onstage in Edinburgh, and she is worried that one of her improvised dance moves went too far.

'I'm *so* sorry,' she says. She explains that she is 'a stage beast' and that she gets carried away when she's up there in front of an audience.

'Djeneba,' he says. 'Jesus, it's me.'

She says that she thought she'd be sacked.

'What?' he scoffs. 'When you touched my knob? Djeneba, it's *me*. There's not a lot you can do that will offend me, regarding touching my penis.'

* * *

We land at Le Bourget airport outside Paris. Rob picks up his guitar to carry it off the plane. This breaks with all his usual travel routines. Though he doesn't seem averse to it, as a rule he carries nothing.

'Can you manage that?' Andy Franks asks him.

'Of course I can,' he retorts. 'I've written songs.'

We drive through a back area of the airport where a mothballed Concorde sits, sadly parked on the tarmac. We discuss the practicalities of buying one and keeping it in the garden; Rob mentions that he was once round at Vic Reeves' house when Reeves buried a Morris Minor in his garden, with just the front sticking out above the ground.

Josie says that Teddy Sheringham has called for tickets for tomorrow's show. Rob decides to call him to invite him backstage to say hello. He calls the number Sheringham has left and has a confused conversation, which he puts down to Sheringham thinking that someone is messing about, pretending to be Robbie Williams. When he dials again, no one picks up, so he leaves a message. Soon he gets a return call and they have a good chat. 'Band are on form, I'm on form, we're all loving it,' he says. (Josie and David look at each other and grin with relief; they've not heard too much of this kind of talk on previous tours.) Rob listens as Sheringham, who has just moved from Tottenham to Portsmouth, talks a little about what he's been up to.

'Fucking hell, he speaks fast,' says Rob afterwards. 'I'll tell you what. It's amazing that stuff about the inner sanctum of football doesn't get out because they're so quick just to tell you information. "I fucking hate Glen Hoddle ... "'

Rob talks about his years partying with footballers. The time he nearly got barred from British Airways, away with the Liverpool squad. 'Just high-jinks, really. Going to Spain. Robbie Fowler attached a condom to the back of one of the stewardess's pinnies.' He remembers listening to two well-known footballers drunkenly arguing: 'This is how the conversation went. "He's just said six and seven equal 12." "It doesn't, you fucking tool, it equals 14."'

'When I was a footballer ... ' Rob sighs.

Just one of the many worlds he has sampled. One more role slipped into, embraced with gusto, then abandoned. 'I've been a footballer. And a drug-dealer. And a student. Without the playing, the dealing or the going to university. I was a student when I was in Take That from about 17 to 19. I just went and got stoned with them all the time. They were lovely lads. We would meet at the motorway services. They'd hire a white van for the proceedings. We'd neck a couple of Es ... ' He stops, corrects himself. 'No, we'd do a gram of whiz first. Then we'd go to Miss Moneypenny's and drop Es ... ' He was best friends with the students' de facto leader, until it all went wrong: 'I think he must have been harbouring some big resentment towards me because it all filtered out after a while. He said I'd turned all big-headed and I was lording it. And I know I was no different than when I first started hanging out with him. He just couldn't handle it.'

* * *

The next morning Teddy Sheringham calls Josie and says that he can't make the show after all, but that a friend of his with prostate cancer happens to be in town and will go instead. And would love to meet Rob.

The penny drops. A while back Josie was scammed by somebody claiming to represent Sadie Frost and Jude Law. She is in no mood to be scammed again. She tracks down Teddy Sheringham's real mobile number through some football contacts, and confirms that this one is an impostor. She wonders whether it is worth having him thrown out when he arrives.

Meanwhile, Rob plays Championship Manager in his usual suite at the

Paris George V hotel, experimenting with five at the back. Downstairs there are problems. There is a celebrity car war. The hotel want Rob's waiting cars to be moved out so that Hilary Clinton's can be moved in.

* * *

In a backstage corridor he runs into Kelly Osbourne. She is opening the show all summer. He shows her his tattoos and she shows him the heart tattoo on her finger. 'I need to get this removed,' she says. Her previous boyfriend. It ended badly. She says that he is currently trying to sue her, and she hates him.

'How are you handling it?' asks Rob.

'Oh, I'm fine,' she says.

'No, I mean, how are you *handling* it?' he says. 'Do you want me to hit him?' With Kelly, he slips very quickly into older brother mode.

'I want to do that myself,' she says.

'Anthrax is good,' he suggests, as he heads away towards his dressing room. 'And poo.'

* * *

At tonight's show, which cements his breakthrough in France even though he finds the audience hard work and skips a song near the end, he recognises a woman at the front of the audience. But he can't quite place her. He asks Jason to get her number. In the van he is still trying to work it out. 'I think I might have met her on holiday, when I was 14 or 15,' he says.

Calls are made and the girl joins us at the post-show buffet.

Rob was 16.

'Carmarthen Bay Holiday Centre, 1989,' says Rob.

'1990,' she corrects.

'My dad was compère,' he remembers. 'Best holiday I'll ever have. No drugs, lots of beer, lots of laughs, cheapest chips.'

Max interrupts to say that he and Rob should go on a nice holiday soon. A boat. 'Deep-sea fishing at night,' he says. 'Mauritius.'

'See?' says Rob to his old flame, making a joke of it. 'It's all different now, isn't it?' He and his old flame talk about the songs they used to dance to. 'The "900" Number'. New Kids On The Block's 'Tonight'. Sometime in the evening, she tells him that he hasn't changed since he was 16, and there's little she could say that he would rather hear.

Back at the hotel, they discover a Kylie Minogue night on TV, which is perfect. It takes some time to discover how far apart two people are, when one is hoping for a future and the other is just looking to recapture a brief, happy moment from the past.

* * *

That night, he dreams that he is at an AA meeting with Anthony Hopkins. Anthony Hopkins is really nice, but he's annoyed that it's a 90-minute meeting. He only wanted it to be an hour.

* * *

Vienna. The show is already evolving. By the end of the tour, the way that 'Monsoon' is preceded by a minute or two of Queen's 'We Will Rock You' will appear to have been carefully planned and strategised over weeks of rehearsals, but it actually appears from nowhere but inside Rob's head, onstage in Vienna tonight. After the second song, he starts stomping his foot, Chris Sharrock starts hitting his bass drum in time, and the Queen lyrics – or some vague approximation – shoot out of his mouth: '*Johnny you're a man you're a poor boy sitting in a place gonna be a man some day blood on your face big disgrace wiping your banner all over the place* ... ' he begins, and the crowd join in. A new part of the show has been created, and will return, less spontaneously, from now on.

At the end, he comes back on and sings 'Feel' a cappella, just him and the crowd; all emotion and no razzamatazz. He has never done this before either.

'I cried,' he announces, thrilled, as the convoy of vans revs up. 'That was beautiful.' We pull away. 'Do you know what's weird?' he says. 'Every night I think about dying. Towards the end of the show.'

'"What if this is my last big thing ... ?" sort of crying?' asks Josie.

'I don't know,' he says. 'It's really weird. I don't know.'

I mention how good the solo reprise of 'Feel' sounded.

He grins. 'I heard Radiohead do it at Glastonbury,' he says. 'Not "Feel", obviously. "*For a minute there, I lost myself, I lost myself, I lost myself* ... "'

'Karma Police.'

This is how it happens: notice, assimilate, claim, change, make your own. He saw something that was good and that worked and could work for him; he thought he would have that, and now he has. It, too, will become part of the show – just him and the crowd, alone together, singing a final echo of 'Feel', or 'Angels', or sometimes both.

By the time he is at the hotel, he is making a joke of how emotional he felt at the end. 'I *knew* there was a tear coming,' he tells the dancers as they eat their buffet, 'and thought of the cameras and I thought, they're really going to like this, and I was, "Come on! Come on! *Cry*, you bastard! Cry, you bastard! ... Oh! Here it is. Well done!"'

* * *

He enjoys the fact that when he is onstage it is difficult to separate the moments of deepest emotion from the moments of greatest artifice. His core entertainment values are those of the pre-rock'n'roll entertainment model infused into him in his youth – the Rat Pack records he heard at home, and the old-fashioned showmanship of his father's peers – so as a performer he has a relationship with sincerity that can be confusing to modern-day sensibilities. He intuitively sees what the rock snobs consider to be The Truth – all their affected, hackneyed ways of being authentic and sincere – as just rituals from a bigoted, fraudulent blip in time. They might think of themselves as rebels striking out for moody freedoms; he sees instead the ways in which they are trapped into insincere, dour habits and paralysed by rules, too blinkered even to appreciate the joy and wonder to be found in the canon they protect.

In the modern rock tradition, for instance, failure is often taken only as further proof of a work's authenticity – its roar was so real and radical that the world was not ready for it. There is another tradition, in which failure is just a way of describing something that didn't succeed, and where the place for sincerity and the deepest emotion is not as far away as possible from pizzazz and melodrama and fakery and bad rhymes and cheesy golden melodies as possible, but right slap bang in the middle of them. In fact, it is a tradition that suggests that slap bang in the middle of all this is the *only* honest place to put the deep and important stuff because that is where you find it in life: right in the middle of life's messy everyday maul. It is also the best place to deny that you are opening your heart, and anyone who really intends to bare himself needs that option, that failsafe.

Rob will tell you that he is a light entertainer, he will grin and prance and take the piss out of you and take the piss out of himself, and as he does all this he will tell you his whole raw, fragile, honest story, hidden in plain sight.

11

He is so tired when Josie phones him the next afternoon to ask whether he is ready for breakfast that he keeps looking round his Vienna hotel room, trying to work out where her voice is coming from. He doesn't realise he is on the phone.

I ask what he got up to last night.

'I had sex,' he says.

'Proper pop star behaviour,' notes Josie. 'We've got 40 minutes before we depart.'

'This mortal coil?' he asks. 'I'm going back to bed.'

'No, you're not,' she says in a tone that allows no argument.

In the van, still half asleep, he says, as David tells him about ticket sales for the autumn leg of his tour, 'I'm so glad I'm really big. I'd be really gutted if I wasn't. It's fucking great. It all feels like it means something. It didn't before.' He laughs, and asks himself the obvious question. 'What does it all mean? It just means it's great.' He watches Vienna go by through his dark glasses. 'There's another man with really big feet,' he says.

He says he needs to stop smoking. 'It's just been building up,' he says. 'I think I'll get to my thirtieth birthday.' He tells us about smoking weed in the back of a van with Take That as they travelled to an airport in Europe and watching helplessly as a car of fans passed them on the sloped bank of the motorway, the driver collapsed at the wheel. The driver's pacemaker had stopped. 'Girls screaming,' he remembers. The girls' car was heading towards a bridge, where the bank stopped and the car seemed sure to launch into mid-air, but somehow it followed the bank down on to the motorway, crossed every lane, missed every other car, hit the central barrier, spun three times and stopped. Take That's van pulled over. Incredibly, everyone was fine.

Other Take That fans, in other following vehicles, also stopped. Some of them took the opportunity to ask Rob for his autograph.

* * *

Pompey declares that he's happier in the Munich hotel, where his room connects to Rob's. In Vienna his room was through several fire doors and across a corridor because Rob's suite was the only room on that wing of the hotel – so far away that Pompey couldn't sleep.

Rob is surprised to hear this. He had thought the whole time we were in Vienna that Pompey was right door next to him.

'So what was that other door in my room?' he asks.

'That was a cupboard,' says Pompey.

'Oh,' says Rob. 'That's why no one answered when I knocked.'

* * *

In Munich, as midnight is left behind, Cardiff squeeze into the play-offs in sixth place despite losing 2–1 to Bradford on the last day of the season. Rob lies on the floor in the corner of the room and heads for the play-off semi-finals against West Brom. The home leg is a 1–1 draw. There is no score at half-time in the away leg. If it stays like this, West Brom will go through on away goals. He tries changing things throughout the second half, but the clock ticks on and Cardiff can't score. They must stay in the first division. This matters more than it should, whether for itself or as a symbol of a wider unease. He is still lying there, on his stomach, on the carpet, when I leave for bed, affecting the kind of nonchalantly disconsolate look that hides a hugely down moment deep inside.

After I leave, at around three in the morning, he starts exploring the summer transfer market. Manchester United mysteriously get a new manager, who is simply called 'f' and who tables an unexpected series of generous bids for minor Cardiff City players. Rob is paranoid that the game will suddenly tell him that he's cheating, but it doesn't. Eventually he starts the next season, winning three matches and losing one. He gets increasingly manic. When the morning light starts coming through the window, he up-ends the sofa and leans it against the window in an attempt to block the day out. He gets back in bed, then decides he can position the sofa better, and gets up to move it once more. At eight o'clock, as the church bells ring outside, he is still buying players.

He is about to wake David and ask him to sit by his bed until he falls asleep when he finally slips away on his own. His dreams offer little respite. He has killed somebody and the police are closing in and somebody has had his baby but he is a murderer and he is needed in Paris for a DNA test and the police are getting closer and …

The next afternoon, he lies in the wreckage of his bedclothes, smoking. The sofa is still over the window. 'I lost the plot,' he says. 'Went a bit mental. I'm going to have to stop playing that game. It's driving me mad.'

Tonight's show is at the Olympic stadium, where England beat Germany 5–1 in 2000. 'I'll be singing "She's The Hun" tonight,' he says. '"We Have Ways Of Entertaining You".' (He won't be.)

Just before he is due on, he needs a piss. This time he just walks to an empty area on the back of the stage and begins urinating. The liquid runs away through the joins.

'Is there anything under there?' Josie asks Wob.

'Just all the electricity supplies,' he says,

'No, really … ' she asks.

'I'm serious,' he says. 'Just all the electricity supplies.'

During the show, I walk up to the back edge of the stadium. There are hilltops in the park behind the stadium and on top of each one are thousands more Germans sitting in the dusk, listening to Robbie Williams.

'I've never been this famous,' he says as he comes offstage.

* * *

He is determined not to touch the computer tonight, so at the end of the evening we sit in his room, talking. He says how different it feels to sing his songs and not hate them.

'I fucking hated going on tour,' he reflects. 'You wouldn't believe the person I am to the person I was.'

Even the last tour?

'Yeah. Oh yeah. Ask anyone. I fucking *detested* it. Detested it. Fraught with nerves all day, anxiety and depression. Was going onstage to perform songs that were meaningless and meant nothing and were shit. It was a state of mind of what I thought about myself. A lot of times I'd be onstage and I'd have complete disrespect for my audience. I'd perform my bollocks off because it's a natural instinct to perform like my life depends on it, but in my mind I'd be a bit: what have you lot come and see this cunt for? I completely didn't value me at all. At all.'

'Even the fact that there were 60,000 people there to watch you?' asks Gary Marshall, bemused. 'That didn't have any effect?'

He shakes his head. 'I can remember the night that it went,' he says. 'I started off doing the little club gigs, which were really sweaty, really loud, and, you know, finding my feet as a solo performer, and kind of enjoyed it, really loved the response that I was getting, just for me. And it felt as though it was rough and ready, and rock'n'roll in a way. And then I was backstage at the Roskilde festival. We were doing a warm-up for an arena tour, I think, and I slipped backstage playing football, and for the first time in my life I felt real embarrassment for falling over in front of people. You know like when you're a kid and you break some cutlery and you know you're going to get told off? I felt that.'

That dread of: I can't bear this to be found out but I want it to be over?

'Yeah. Exactly. And it was an emotion I hadn't had since I was a kid. And from then on in, something triggered. I don't think it was that moment that triggered it, I just think that it was about to happen. And from then on in every tour I've ever done I've hated.'

But, I put to him, take the bit of tour documented in *Nobody Someday*. The arc of that movie is: you start off hating it and supposedly by the end of it you love it. Is that bollocks too?

'Yeah. Pretty much. I genuinely felt that when I came off stage that night, yes. But if you're asking for a percentage of how much I felt like that, it would be 5 per cent.'

And what's the percentage now?

'100 per cent. Well, I'd say it's 95.'

But what's the possibility that in two years' time you'll look back at this and say, I was saying that then but now I look at it I wasn't that happy?

'Absolutely not. Absolutely not.'

So from that perspective can you put a finger on when the change happened?

'The studio. *Escapology*. And every piece of work that I've done for this album has just been a real joy to do.' Pause. 'Apart from Rock The Vote and Battery Park.'

On the way to the airport the next morning, Rob mentions to David that there is someone on the periphery of the tour he doesn't want on the next leg. 'He's a wrong 'un,' says Rob. David argues the person's cause a little, but agrees that if this is what Rob wants, it is what shall be.

Rob nods. 'And I don't like Josie,' he adds. 'And I don't like you. Can you not be on the next bit of the tour, please?'

All of this, both the serious bit and the joke, marks how well things are going. Usually at this stage in a tour Rob has decided that the one person he doesn't want on tour is himself.

* * *

'Please, Robbie,' pleads a man in a rather terrifying tone. 'I have tried so many times.'

Walking through the Munich airport, Rob has to deal with the aggressive and creepy autograph hunter who has been chasing him for the last couple of days.

'You're really weird, man,' mutters Rob.

'I'm driving more than a thousand kilometres,' he says.

This, of course, is the basis of so many interactions between the famous and those that follow them, unbidden. The followers make a sacrifice that has never been asked for, and that is often unwelcome, and then hold the famous responsible and in their debt for what they have done.

'You're freaking me out,' says Rob.

'Please, Robbie. Why are you so unfriendly always?' he shouts, and then adds, accusingly, 'To the guys?'

Rob walks through the X-ray machine.

'It's all just for me!' the autograph man shouts, answering an accusation that has not been voiced. As he realises that Rob really will not be stopping for him, he gets more hysterical. 'It's unbelievable!' he shouts. 'This is not correct.' He is freaking us all out now. 'We buy your stuff,' he moans. 'And you are so unfriendly to your customer … '

'Yeah, well, don't,' says Rob.

'Then don't buy it!' snaps David, louder.

'But I like the music!' he says hysterically. 'I like the concerts. They are so great.' He offers one final, desperate, futile argument. 'We give you the money!' he pleads.

On the plane, he reads about the 20-year-old skydiver, Stephen Hilder, who appears to have had the cords on both his main and reserve parachute deliberately cut and fallen 13,000 feet to his death in a cornfield.

Soon we are in Berlin.

* * *

Tonight is a night off, and an evening's competitive racing has been booked in at a Berlin go-kart track. When I check into my room, I find a message from Cameron Diaz, whom I know from other escapades. The German premiere of the new *Charlie's Angels* movie is in Berlin tomorrow and she has just arrived at our hotel from Florida. The other Angels are stranded on the runway in Italy because of a faulty jet, so I suggest she comes go-karting with us.

We head off to the track in convoy: Rob and Max in one of the two vans, Cameron, her assistant Jesse and myself in the back of their car, the two of them singing a song from *Ferris Bueller's Day Off* over and over. Paparazzi follow. At one traffic light one of them parks his Jeep diagonally in front of our car so that he can get out and try to shoot Rob through the windshield of his van. Cameron declares that if he does the same trick again she'll get out and throw his car keys away.

At the track, we rush indoors, away from the chaos.

'Fame,' says Rob, with an exaggerated shrug and grin to the guests, 'what is it like?'

'It's a bubble,' says Cameron, playing along. She admires his pink Adidas top. 'Did you get that for free?' she asks. (Which she knows he did. He has just been to Adidas's flagship shop and left with eight bags of free merchandise.) She points to her red-and-black striped top. 'I got this at H&M for 20 bucks,' she says. (Which, this afternoon, she also did.)

We split up into eight teams of three. Rob immediately picks Max for his team, and as a third, Adam Birch, the guitar tech, who he knows is good. Cameron is with Jessie and me, and is easily our best driver.

We take turns. At one point I can see Rob catching up with Cameron, lap after lap, until, on the lap he would have been alongside her, his car cuts out completely. He fumes as a new car is started up; he was looking forward to whatever kind of moment that would have been. But mostly he is quite low key. Whether because his crush persists or because it doesn't, he makes no move to advertise it or act upon it.

Rob's team wins; he makes a brief speech and accepts a trophy that will remain in his hotel room when he checks out. By the time we leave the go-kart track, there is a mad throng of paparazzi outside. The first plan is that everyone should leave wearing crash helmets so that Rob and Cameron can't be spotted, but the logistics seem a little fussy. Instead, Cameron's carload leaves first, while Rob and Max swap outfits, so that Max is wearing Rob's new pink Adidas shirt. They and two others put balaclavas over their heads. Max walks out surrounded by Rob's security, and the cameras go crazy.

'He's in the pink!' they shout. 'He's in the pink!'

Getting into the van, Max pulls down his trousers and moons. His arse will be shown as Rob's in several German newspapers. Meanwhile, Rob simply strolls out last, for once outside the hurricane, and quietly gets into a van.

'It was really weird,' he says after. 'I was by myself. And it was, "I'm walking … I'm walking … "'

Set free of your shackles?

'Yeah.'

* * *

Downstairs, at lunchtime the next day, I watch the three Charlie's Angels do a photo-call in front of 200 people, meet a competition winner on the move as they walk down a corridor, then sit down for more interviews. They have been working since eight in the morning, and aside from a break this weekend, have been travelling across Europe doing this day after day after day. It's the kind of life Rob has neither the will, desire nor constitution for; one of the triumphs of his career is how much success he has while sidestepping all this.

Today he wakes at three. He talks to Jonny on the phone. 'She looks a bit like Zippy,' he says. 'Crush is over. I can get on with the rest of my life.' He also speaks to his father. 'Me and Cameron, last night, go-karting … yeah, but you know, it's not happening … no, she's fucking great, she's really, really lovely but the crush has gone … great girl … looks a bit like Zippy … '

In the van Josie says that Guy has called and wants to come and see the show in Stockholm. Maybe, unlike Rob, he has read Rob's recent *Q* interview and has been encouraged by the part where Rob says he is sure that they will collaborate again. ('We'll get back together, but it won't be the same,' Rob is quoted as saying.) He has no way of knowing that that sentiment may well be a little out of date now. For one thing, when Rob said that, Pure Francis did not exist. For another, he is annoyed with Guy all over again. 'I don't think he should come,' he says to Josie. 'I'm really upset with him.' For blanking David at the Ivor Novello awards, and for the phone conversation they had. 'And for just being a tit,' he says. 'Because there's no excuses for what he said and did. You know, I'd rather not see him. He can come, by all means, but I don't want him to be anywhere near me. Or in my view when I get on stage.'

* * *

There is no usable stadium in Berlin at the moment, so Rob's booking agent, Ian Huffam, has come up with a different strategy for this visit. Rob is, apparently, to be the first artist to do major concerts on consecutive nights in the former West Berlin and the former East Berlin.

Tonight is the West's turn. Rob is not particularly in a performing mood.

Before the show he announces, 'This is the one I get paid for.' As usual, it is difficult to tell, though there are some strange moments. In the middle of the set a hefty bound document is thrown on to the stage. He only looks at it briefly. 'You really think I'm going to read this onstage?' he says. 'Jeeee-sus. You're mental.'

I retrieve it. It is a thesis by an Anne Schumann at the Institute of Music Science, Faculty of Philosophy in Dresden: 'I Did It My Way – De- and Re-Construction of Robbie Williams's Image In The Concert Swing When You're Winning'. There are about 100 pages of writing (all in German), and charts and tables and footnotes and appendices and a bibiliography, probably the only one in history to include both 'Morgan, Piers: *Take That – Unsere Story*' and 'Kriese, Konstanze: *Rock'n'Ritual – Der Starkult als Kommunikationsstereotyp moderner Musikkulturen*'.

* * *

In the van afterwards he says that he had a panic attack during the swing section. He put his hand over his chest and he could feel it going 'boom boom boom'. He remembers aloud the best advice he has ever been given about getting through shows that seem a struggle. It was from an elderly British actor, Dudley Sutton, who he called just before he went onstage in Dublin for his first stadium tour. He told Sutton that he felt like shit and that he didn't want to perform.

Sutton told him two things that he remembered and has quoted back, to himself and others, many times since. '*You're* not there to be entertained,' Sutton pointed out. Also that: 'It wouldn't be brave if you weren't scared.' Those two thoughts have helped him through a lot.

He was given one other piece of advice from Sutton, which he has taken longer to appreciate. 'Learn to love your audience,' Sutton advised him. 'I thought, bollocks,' he says. But over time he has begun to realise that this is not a luvvie exhortation but a piece of solid, wise, practical counsel. 'I'm starting to know what he means,' says Rob. 'I mean, I really appreciated them tonight.'

He sighs.

'Oh, I really don't want to die,' he says.

'Babe, you're not going to die,' says Josie.

'Cool,' he says. 'Thanks, Josie. Can you pencil it in that I don't?'

* * *

There's a party in an underground disco where he dances a bit to rave classics, then returns to the hotel and mulls over things in his room with Stephen and me. A chatline ad comes on the TV, and he is reminded about the time in his boozy days when he phoned one from a hotel and spent a pointless hour trying to convince the girl that he was Robbie Williams. Not even sexy chat. 'Just bollocks talk,' he says. 'I was off my tits and really lonely.'

Though both he and the girl were in England, the call was being routed via New Zealand. The hotel phone bill was £900.

He goes back down to the bar where a promoter, Jack Utsick – who is tangentially involved in tonight's concert, not as promoter but as owner of the venue, but who seems to be hanging around in hope of deepening his relationship with Rob – presents him with a mounted ticket from the show Elvis Presley would have done on 17 August 1977 at the Cumberland County Civic Centre in Portland had he not died shortly beforehand. 'To Robbie Williams. Elvis Has Left The Building. From Jack Utsick,' reads the plaque.

This is not the oddest thing that will happen before the night is over.

* * *

First – it is now the next afternoon – Rob recounts his dream. It is an unusual, vivid and brutal one, even by his standards.

He went to the toilet in a club. There was a gang in the toilet and he stood with his back to them; he was trying to pick up the vibe. They knew Robbie Williams was having a piss, and he wasn't sure if they liked that fact, or just hated him. As he urinated, he realised it was the latter. He turned, and one of the gang forced him to stand still, asked him some questions, and then rapped his hand with a crowbar. Somehow he got control of the crowbar and put it through the man's shoulder, and then yanked it out so that it tore his flesh open. As he did so, he was thinking: we're all fucked – this is where I die.

Then he turned to his gang – suddenly he realised he had a gang of his own – and told them: 'Go on, we've got to kill them all.' And maybe they do or maybe they don't, but all of a sudden his gang go off to rob a bank ... and a voice in his head is telling him *this doesn't make any sense*. Just the bit about there being any reason to rob a bank. *I've just done a tour and I've made loads of money*, the voice says. *I don't need to rob a bank.*

He tries to step back and assess what has happened. He wants to work out whether he has passed the point of no return or whether it is still not too late to turn back. Because if he has already done something that will put him in prison, he might as well go through with all of it.

Meanwhile, they continue the preparation for the bank job. For some reason, this involves ripping up loads of trees. And there's babies popping up all over the place. His babies.

* * *

He waits for Josie to go next door before telling Jason, Gary and me – and, when he comes in halfway through, David – what happened before the sleep and before the dreams. It seems to him to be amusing enough, and baffling enough, and infuriating enough, and telltale enough, to act out in detail. It is a snapshot of one random night in the sexual life of a modern celebrity. This part was not a dream.

A woman in a white dress is brought up to his room by a married woman he knows slightly, who then makes her excuses. The woman who remains sits on the sofa where Rob is now sitting. (He imitates her – the way she stared directly forward rather than at him as she smoked and spoke, her slightly cold, clipped, Germanic accent – and recites both sides of the conversation.)

'It is crazy, because there are so many people downstairs, and I do not want to be a groupie, and I know you are tired. I should go, I should go.'

'No, no, it's OK.'

'Yes, but my mother is a model and my father is an actor and I know how these things go. And you know, I don't want to be … if you are looking for fuck, we cannot fuck.'

'That's a shame. If we're laying it out on the line like that. That's a shame. I find you very attractive and … '

' … but we can talk. And watch the television.'

'Oh, alright then. Would you like some water?'

'Yes. I drink it out of the bottle.' (He imitates her as she fidgets.) 'I haven't taken drugs.'

'What? You're just hyperactive like that all the time?'

'Yes. I must go. I must go because you need your sleep.'

'I asked if you could come up … '

'Yes, but I must leave because I know you are tired … ' (He imitates her pulling her short skirt down as far as it will go and her top up as far as it will go, while he just watches her.) 'I will not fuck you, you know.' (Pause.) 'Can I kiss you?'

He says that he answered 'alright then' and describes how she kisses for a while – 'going all *Guns of Navarone*', as he puts it, perhaps unsuitably – and then says, 'Stop! Stop! … I have a mother! She is a model! … You will not fuck me! … And I must go, you are tired … '

There is a knock on the door. It is the married woman, and with her is a different girl. He still has the woman in the white dress in the living room. If he invites the new girl in, she will see the other girl leaving and it will spoil everything. So he goes to the bathroom to think about it, and when he returns the first girl is in his bedroom.

'Do you want me to stay?' she purrs.

'I don't know,' he says.

'But you can't fuck me,' she says.

'Well, you'd better go then,' he says, and she does.

The married woman and the other girl, a beautiful Swiss-Israeli, are now in the living room. The married woman soon departs for a second time, explaining that her husband might not like her being here, leaving the girl sat in exactly the same place on the sofa as the previous girl had been, jewellery and diamonds dripping off her, her arms and legs crossed, her cigarette in her mouth, her whole body language suggesting that she is set on ignoring him.

She tells him she is a singer.

'You're really beautiful,' he says.

'You say this to all the girls,' she says. (There is laughter in the room at this point, and shouts of 'Fair cop', and when he explains that he retorted 'But you are' and draws further jeers, he is obliged to add: 'It's one of those "You're the best audience" things. I've only said that when they've been the best audience so far on the tour.')

They chat about nothing. She does a lot more staring away from him. He asks why she doesn't have a boyfriend, and she says that she had one but it went wrong.

'So are there no men where you are that you like?' he asks.

She shakes her head. 'Just fuck,' she says.

'Can I kiss you?' he asks.

She nods, barely interested, and they start. She seems to him to be giving off as much sexual passion as the table leg. At one point she stops and commentates, without any emotion: 'Oh. I am kissing Robbie Williams.' And then carries on. Just as he is thinking that this would be it for the night, she simply stands up and takes her dress off in one motion, so he picks her up and carries her into the bedroom. The sex feels like surgery. As though his semen is being removed by an automated procedure. It is horrible. When they have finished, she says to him:

'Why you lie? What is your problem?'

'What?'

'Why you lie?' she repeats, loudly.

He has no idea what she means.

'I haven't lied since you've been here,' he says.

She stands up and puts her dress on.

'It's just a fuck,' she says, and walks into the living room. 'I want a picture,' she says.

'Have you got a camera?' he asks.

'No.'

He picks up his camera and takes a photo of them and asks her to write her address down so that he can send her the photo. He has thought it through. He'll send it. Why not? So what if she goes to the papers? Whatever.

'Why you lie?' she asks again

'I've not *lied,*' he retorts, but she is getting ratty. She leaves, announcing that she will be back today for a photograph.

Afterwards, before sleep, he opens a numerology book he was given downstairs in the bar, *The Life You Were Born To Live: A Guide To Finding Your Life Purpose* by Dan Miliman, which claims to analyse your personality based on a number generated by your birthdate. (His is 27/9.) He figures that his purpose in life couldn't be what he had just done, so he hopes maybe this book will offer some clues. It says that, as a 27/9 like Elvis Presley and

Robin Williams, the biggest lesson he has to learn is to trust himself; that people like him can get lost in addiction; that they need to realise that they are only taking things to make them feel what they already possess inside them. It also says that 27/9s shouldn't take opinions too seriously, theirs and others, and that they do tend to get misled by following spiritual beliefs and other people's belief systems. Which, it struck him as he fell towards the gang warfare of sleep, was a strangely contradictory thing to be reading in a book like this.

* * *

A problem has been brewing for the past few days over Nena. Rob's suggestion that they sing '99 Red Balloons' together had been intended as a bit of fun, and he'd been quite looking forward to it. (He has told me that it will remind him of being young. 'That, and shagging all of Bananarama,' he oddly explains.) But this prospective duet has spurred a series of increasingly unrealistic demands and suggestions from Nena's camp. She must do at least three songs because otherwise her fans will riot. The collaboration must be filmed, recorded, added to her album, added to his album. All of these demands have been rebuffed, but now they have further, unreasonable practical requirements. Nena needs first-class plane tickets for an entourage of eight, hotel rooms for each of them, her own van, her own limo, her own sound engineer, her own monitor engineer, her own security, her own hair and make-up, her manager, her tour manager and her assistant. For what was suggested as a fun singsong.

David explains these demands to Rob. David suggests that they send an email saying that if the duet can be kept in the spirit it was originally intended, they can go ahead, but David must know that there's no way Rob will want to do it now. He has huge enthusiasm for all kinds of things – musical ideas, collaborations, friendships, love affairs – but once something is soiled or spoiled for him, he usually turns away and doesn't look back. As he now does with this.

'Bye-bye, Nena,' he says. 'Fuck it. Fuck her. It means me learning the words as well, and I'd rather do something more constructive in my day.' Pause. 'Like have a wank.' He shakes his head. It's over. 'Fuck her. Great, man. It's good news. One less thing to think about.'

David decides to tell Nena's people that the duet is no longer possible for production reasons. Rob has a massage and listens to his Pure Francis songs with Stephen Duffy, who suggests arrangements and declares, to Rob's puzzlement, that he thinks Pure Francis's middle name should be Albert.

'I don't think my karma's very good today,' says Rob.

Why not?

'I don't know,' he says. 'Sex makes you feel a bit ... not very Pure Francis.'

* * *

Tonight's show is in the former East, at the Waldbühne, an auditorium in a natural bowl in the woods most famously used by Hitler to deliver inspirational speeches to the Nazi faithful.

'Have you seen the tunnel?' Pompey asks.

Hitler's tunnel. To get from the backstage area to the stage, the quickest way is through a long tunnel. It is curved, we are told, so that no assassin could take a shot from distance. There is a locked door near the stage end behind which, we are assured, is Hitler's personal toilet.

It is down this tunnel that Rob walks the band and dancers before the show. He leads them in a chant of 'If you're happy and you know it, clap your hands' and then, as they head towards the light, they all sing together the theme to *The Great Escape*.

* * *

In the hotel bar, Rob sits with some musician friends of Max's. One of them, Dominic, tells Rob that he knows Miss Legge, Rob's old music teacher, through his ex-wife.

'That's put the wind up you, hasn't it?' he says.

'She was *frightening,*' says Rob. 'And I wasn't very good because I didn't want to join in classes. I think she actually snapped my recorder.'

The two men fire questions at Rob, the kind of simple, direct questions that most people don't ask. And because the questions don't seem as though they are being asked with any edge, Rob answers.

'How did you used to write with Guy?'

'Most of the time it would be: he sits, I sing.'

'Do you talk with him at all?'

'Not really, no.'

'Good partnership, though.'

'Fucking amazing,' Rob says. 'Absolutely amazing partnership.'

'What song are you proudest of? Sorry. We're sounding like bloody rock journalists, aren't we?'

'No no no no, it's cool. "Feel". "Angels". "No Regrets". I don't know really. I used to hate them all. I'd just got that depression that you go through when you think you're shit.'

'Do you still care about sales?'

'It's like the Olympics. If you sell 5 million you want to do 6.'

He tells them about his next record. 'I'm already getting something together now that is going to be another seat of the pants stuff. Change the music. It's different. And it'll either do one of two things – sell bucketloads, or sell enough that I'll be happy with it and the celebrity will die.'

One of their partners is a police officer and mentions that she was involved in the Fred and Rose West case. This sparks a memory.

'I was ten,' says Rob. 'I got followed round the park, and I must have picked up the vibe. And he followed me all the way to the police station and then fucked off.' Pause. 'The next night he killed someone.'

* * *

He fancies an early, quiet night. As he walks towards the lift, a slightly nutty girl won't let him be. She keeps saying that he must come and play backgammon with her; she is clearly fixated on this happening and is confused by the way reality is refusing to fit in with her plan. She gets increasingly hysterical as he steps into the lift without showing any sign of accepting her invitation. Just before the door closes, she decides to scale down her ambition.

'Just let me touch him!' she pleads.

'Sorry,' says Jason. 'He's going to bed.'

'Robbie, can you give me a kiss?' she begs. 'I cancelled my plans for two days for you.'

That again. He decides that the most painless option is to step forward and allow her a brief hug and a peck on the cheek. Unfortunately, it just revitalises her greater ambitions.

'A backgammon game!' she says, almost barking the words.

'No, darling,' he says wearily.

'Room 103!' she shouts hopelessly. 'One second! Hold the lift! I won't touch him. I'll stand here.'

'Darling, I'm really tired, I'm going to bed,' he says.

'Don't do that to me,' she beseeches, wilting, but also blocking the lift door. It isn't pleasant to see people humiliate themselves like this. To see them crumble.

'No, darling, please,' he says. 'Move. Please. I really need to go to bed.'

Gary and Jason gently prise her free and push her out of the lift. As the door finally closes, she whimpers a little, defeated.

We ride up. 'She could have redeemed some sanity points,' sighs Rob. If only she had just taken her hug with grace. Instead, she is one more person bitter that her unsolicited sacrifice has not been rewarded as she would have wished. Rob goes to bed without even learning the greatest of this particular insanity: the delightful charm and logic with which, down in the bar before all of this, she had argued her case for meeting Rob to Gary.

'Can I speak to him?' she asked. 'I'm not a groupie and I don't even like his music.'

* * *

In his dream that night he meets Simon le Bon. Simon le Bon is really polite and friendly, and not much else happens, which is quite a relief.

* * *

On a bus in Germany, Rob and Max sit with the dancers and they go round the circle, one by one, detailing their first kiss.

'There was a spate of doctors and nurses, me taking my clothes off and them taking their clothes off, when I was about five or six,' says Rob. '————, who lived up on the estate – this is no shit – when we were about seven, I was round her house playing, she took me in the bushes, the back of her little garden and pulled her pants down and pulled mine down and went "Put that in here".'

'Noooo!' chorus the girls.

'Truth to God,' he says. 'As God is my witness.'

'What did you do – rub it a little bit?' asks Max.

'I didn't know,' he says. 'I hadn't got a clue it was a sexual thing. And … ' – he lowers his voice – ' … she'd got skids. I wanted to play football.'

'Right, virginity!' insists Max. 'Where and who with and what was the story. Go!'

The girls share details of varying specificity. Rob recounts the tale of his first time, and when he gets to the smelliness, the dancers squeal in sympathy and disgust.

'What did you do?' asks one of the dancers.

'Stuck it in,' says Rob. More sighs and laughter.

'With a bag?' asks Max.

'No,' says Rob, and goes into mock-ironic semi-Partridge voice. 'Aids hadn't been invented. Properly. So anyway it lasted all of half a minute, and as soon as I finished it – I thought I was being really cool at the time, I really thought I was being dead cool, I went, "Come again" … ' – much laughter – ' … and I thought that was really James Bond of me. And I went out to the landing of the house and I went …'

He demonstrates how he pumped his arm, his fist clenched; with the bravado he'd gained from what he now knew and, swamping it, the bravado he needed to hide everything he still didn't know.

* * *

At the next hotel, in a small town outside Cologne, the band party has a couple of days off. Rob has mixed feelings about days off on tour. He doesn't have to face the stress of a show in the evening, but he is effectively trapped in the hotel. This particular hotel is a 300-year-old baroque palace built on a hilltop as a hunting retreat, and in the information guide left in the rooms, the building's long history is recounted. 'Now,' it says, 'the Grandhotel Schloss Bensberg is operated as an exclusive five-star property by Althoff Hotels for pretentious guests'.

He sinks deeper into Championship Manager 4. As soon as he reaches his room, Rob immediately switches on his computer and turns his mind to Cardiff. He plays until half past five that morning, and when he wakes up the next afternoon he immediately carries on without even getting out of bed. He doesn't rise until just before dusk, when he not only leaves his room but the hotel grounds too, and walks a couple of hundred yards into town to buy an ice cream and some sweets. The paparazzi who has been waiting all day snatches some photos as he returns.

He goes back to his room, jumps on to his bed and opens his computer.

'I've been outside,' he says. 'It's horrible.'

Cardiff are 16th in the first division.

The next afternoon, waking, he looks shattered. But he has come to a decision. He walks towards me in his dressing gown and raises his hands. In his fingers is the Championship Manager 4 disc.

It won't break, but he bends it back and forth, again and again, until it is bent at a right angle across its diameter and he is sure it cannot trouble him any more, then tosses it on to one of the many occasional tables in his suite.

'I don't want to talk about it,' he says. 'Kids should read books.'

• • •

Jason looks at the front page of *Sonntag Express*, one of the German newspapers. Which momentous event dominates today's news?

'20.45 Uhr, mitten in der Bensberger City,' it announces in large letters.

'So,' Jason tells Rob, 'the most exciting thing in the country yesterday was you eating ice cream at 8.45.' This bombshell is illustrated with a photograph of Rob holding a choc ice, a further piece of it still visible between his lips. His mouth open, his eyes shut.

One of the other German papers has a different story. Nena and her people have gone public with what they see as her snub, complaining that Rob has time to go-kart with Cameron Diaz but didn't have the courtesy to call her himself. There are all kinds of suggestions of retaliation – that Tessa Niles, one of his backing singers, should sing the duet in a Nena wig, and so on – but Rob vetoes them. He has little interest left in the whole business.

In his dressing room, Rob puts on Eurosport and watches some diving.

'Breaking that Championship Manager 4 today is the equivalent of throwing coke down the toilet,' he says. 'I threw three big bagfuls of coke, really strong, down the loo on holiday once. Ten o'clock in the morning and I'd still got three big bags left.'

• • •

Max pays him a visit.

'When are we going to go on holiday?' he asks Rob.

'I'm not going on holiday, man,' says Rob. 'I will do, next year.'

'Where do you want to go?' Max asks.

'Skiing,' says Rob.

'No, you do that with a group,' says Max. 'Let's go to the Maldives.'

'What will I do all day?' Rob scoffs. 'Sit in the sun?'

'He'll go mad,' Josie points out.

'I'm like a little child,' Rob reminds Max. 'I have to be entertained at all times.'

'I've got some tricks,' argues Max.

'I've seen them all,' counters Rob.

'All I want is fucking nothingness in the mind,' says Max.

'I want to be able to jump off some rocks high up,' says Rob

* * *

After the concert, it is an hour's drive back to the castle hotel. On the way, Rob says that he wants to make a list of the people who matter to him, and have influenced him, and to get a photo of each and put them up in the hallway of his Los Angeles house. So, sitting in the dark as we slide up the autobahn, he does. This is his list:

'Mork ... The Fonz ... Homer ... Starsky and Hutch ... Norman Whiteside, from the 1985 FA Cup Final, because that's the first FA Cup final and the first proper football game I watched ... not at the game, with my dad, and he scored the winning goal ... Terry Butcher covered in blood ... I've got Muhammad Ali ... Port Vale 1988 ... John Travolta, *Grease* ... Wonderwoman ... and Batman, that one where he's walking up the side ... Spike Milligan ... Dr Hook ... Pet Shop Boys ... Public Enemy ... NWA ... and one of Eazy E ... De La Soul ... Dr Dre ... Eminem can go up there, yeah ... Jay Z ... Dusty Springfield ... Bono ... Bowie, *Hunky Dory* ... any Bowie actually ... Elvis ... and Tom Jones ... not together ... Freddie Mercury ... put a picture of Stephen Duffy up there ... Fred Astaire, Frank Sinatra, Gene Kelly, Norman Wisdom, George Formby ... Grace Kelly ... Lauren Bacall, Humphrey Bogart ... Dean, Sammy and Frank ... Brigitte Bardot ... Raquel Welch ... Sean Connery and Roger Moore ... Chewbacca, Han Solo, Boba Fett, because he always looks wicked, the Millennium Falcon ... Michael Jordan ... David Beckham ... Kobe Bryant and Shaq ... Zidane ... Bob Hope ... and Bing – I've got a great one of Bing already ... the Krays ... Peter O'Toole ... Richard Harris ... Oliver Reed ... Keith Moon ... Paul Gascoigne ... the cast of *Auf Wiedersehen, Pet*, the original ... Alan Partridge ... James Taylor ... Ian Botham ... Sid Vicious ... Johnny Rotten ... well, the Pistols ... Barry McGuigan ... de la Hoya ... Roy Jones Jnr ... Daley Thompson ... Vic and Bob ... the Blackpool Tower ... Bridlington ... Big Ron Atkinson, 1985 ... Brian Clough ... and who used to wear the fedora? He used to look fucking great. Malcolm Allison ... Michael Caine from *Get Carter* ... Daniel Day Lewis as Bill the Butcher ... you'd better put Elton up there as well ... I haven't got a really good one of Ringo, and I'll put my George Harrison up ... David Niven, the great picture of him diving into a swimming pool with a bow and arrow ... my nan ... Tupac and Snoop ... Dave Allen ... Dan Aykroyd and Eddie Murphy in *Trading Places* ... I'm steering clear of putting de Niro and

Al Pacino in because everybody has them ... Man United treble-winning side ... Wayne Rooney ... Jenson Button ... Goldie Hawn in *Private Benjamin* ... Kris Kristofferson in *Convoy* ... I like Ron Wood, he looks cool ... *Moonlighting*, the two of them ... Woody in *Cheers* ... Barry Sheen ... Kevin Keegan, with the perm, yeah ... Ozzy ... Slash ... the Banana Splits ... Showaddywaddy; that's the first gig I ever went to ... Scott Walker and Morrissey ... I want to put Oasis up ... Wembley, the twin towers ... JFK ... Lee Harvey Oswald ... Jacqueline Bisset, in the elevator – I knocked one out over that quite a few times ... ... Kermit, Miss Piggy ... Peter Sellers, Clouseau ... the Artful Dodger, Jack Wild ... Monkey ... Kirk Douglas as Spartacus ... Sid James ... That'll do for getting on with ... .'

* * *

Rob flits around the hotel bar, has a good look, returns to his room, and then sends one of his bodyguards back down. On a night like this, they may be asked to explain to a girl that Rob has spotted her earlier, and that it is difficult for him to chat in the bar, but that he would very much like some female company if she would like to come up to his room.

Usually she would.

But after that events often do not follow the course you might expect. More and more on this tour he is dealing with a phenomenon that each particular girl who follows him wants to be different from *the girls who follow him*. One of his bodyguards was given a long lecture from one the other night about the difference between followers (who were good – this particular girl who was speaking, for instance) and fans (bad). Followers don't bother the artist. (This from someone who has arranged to stay in the same hotel as the artist and is hanging around the hotel bar, waiting and hoping.)

'How I interpreted it was,' Rob says, 'followers are really fucking weird and might kill you, and fans just leave you alone and buy your records and listen to them at home. I think I'd rather be a fan. God, they're weird. And each of them's having a relationship with me. That I don't know about.'

If they do come to his room, there is a further extension of this way of thinking that he is finding something of a frustration. Rob is increasingly convinced that girls who will sleep with the crew or the band because of their proximity to him will not sleep with him. They each want to be different from those girls who do that. They hang around for days in their sexiest clothes, waiting for a moment alone with him, until at last they are spread-eagled on a bed with the object of their obsession and desire, and can finally say the special magical words they have been dying to share with him: 'I am not a groupie.' Nobody's a groupie any more.

He finds himself listening to these same lines over and over. They're convinced that what he wants is a soulmate; he's quite sure that what he actually wants is a shag. It is quietly driving him mad.

* * *

'Tonight,' he declares in the afternoon before his second show at the Shalke Stadium, on the day when the *Daily Mirror* anoint him Britain's 37th Least Influential Person, 'I'm going to have a lie-down with a really cute girl, I think.' He explains no more than this, but during the show, after 'Monsoon', he points at a girl in the crowd near the end of the thrust – the long walkway that heads out from the centre of the stage into the crowd – and asks for her to be lifted on to the stage. They have a long hug and then sit down together. 'Come Undone' begins and he tells her that she looks beautiful, then he lies down with her, hugging her as he sings. He gets up for the first chorus, they slow dance and she leaves. He tells her she has lovely breasts and lips, but asks whether she was here last night and is wearing the same clothes.

This has not happened before, but it is the start of something.

* * *

'She stunk,' he explains in the van. (This seems to be a perennial problem for him.) But that aside, and his tiredness, the show was a triumph. The audience was even more wildly enthusiastic that the previous night's. In some cases too enthusiastic. During the show, one girl tried to get to the pitch by jumping from the seats on to the top of a portable loo, which toppled under her weight. She ended up with a broken leg, covered in the toilet's contents.

'The great thing about these crowds,' says David, 'is that they'll stay loyal until the day you … ' And he stops, realising that he has driven this sentence down a cul-de-sac and that there is no happy way of continuing it. Rob steps in anyway.

'Until the day I tell them what I really think?' he says.

* * *

In America, the world of journalism has been shaken by the Jayson Blair scandal: a *New York Times* reporter caught systematically fabricating stories over a long period of time. During the investigations and recriminations that follow, which eventually cost the editor of the *New York Times* his job, other journalists fall under the spotlight. The latest to reach the public domain, while we are in our palace near Cologne, is the media reporter Lynette Holloway. One of the principal examples quoted of her sloppy or shoddy work is a story that ran in March, the one in which she stated that 4 million copies of Robbie Williams' *Escapology* were being shipped in the USA. This 'fact' has been endlessly cited as an empirical measure of his humiliating American failure: 4 million shipped, 100,000 sold.

It never was true, and it never could have been true, and there is some small satisfaction in this belated acknowledgement of how stupid and serious a mistake it was. In the wake of an investigation into a pattern of such mistakes, she subsequently quietly resigns. Of course, it is too late now to really matter; the damage has been done, and is still spreading.

12

Midway through the flight to Amsterdam he gets up and walks down the aisle with his naked bum showing. On the last flight it was his testicles. He has further escalation in mind.

The lift at the Amstel Intercontinental Hotel is lined with wood and has paintings and lamps in it. Rob decides that he should redecorate the lift in his Los Angeles house just like this.

'I want *The Laughing Cavalier* and Constable's *The Haywain,*' he announces.

'And Turner's *The Fighting Temeraire,*' suggests Pompey.

'No,' says Rob. 'It's what was up at my nan's house. She didn't have *The Fighting Temeraire.*'

Upon arriving at his canal-side attic suite, he sits down and says: 'Josie, can I play golf tomorrow?'

'What time do you want to go?' she asks.

He thinks a moment.

'I don't really,' he says. 'Josie, stop pushing things on me.'

* * *

That evening we watch some of a TV programme about Jeff Buckley until Rob can bear no more – 'I mean, God bless him,' he says, 'but to me it just sounds like a load of wailing' – and then a video of the recent documentary *The Importance Of Being Morrissey.* Rob is perplexed by the wound-up madness of Noel Gallagher, gets excited when he spots Runyon Canyon behind a speaking Morrissey, and takes some delight in the moment when an Australian woman, who won a competition to meet him ten years earlier, finally gets to do so.

'You've made me and so many people so happy,' she tells him.

'I didn't mean to,' Morrissey replies, but sweetly.

'He's just amazing,' Rob says afterwards. 'I'm so glad that the Pure Francis stuff is coming up, because I can take a bit of Morrissey and put it into that and see if I've actually got something to say, you know? You know, with my stuff it's always very A-B-C emotions, with a little bit of irony thrown in. But end-of-the-pier irony. With his stuff it sort of goes from A to F back to A to S, to N, you know. I was listening to the lyrics and thinking, I really wish I'd got into him when I was depressed. I was thinking, fuck, there would have been a kindred soul for me to listen to.'

In some ways, I point out, they're so similar – even walking their dogs in the same place, living a very similar Los Angeles life – but in other ways they're so incredibly different.

'Yeah,' says Rob. 'He likes to be alone, I don't. And where I would go out of my way to listen intently to a load of garbage that somebody would say, he just goes, "No, not having it." And it's a genuine "Don't care".'

He stands up. 'I'm going to turn on my computer and listen to him,' he says. '*I was happy in the haze of a drunken hour ...*' he sings, disappearing into the bedroom. '*In my life, why must I waste valuable time ... ?*'

When he wakes the following afternoon, he looks out of his window at the café across the street, six floors below. At the tables outside he sees Josie and Lee and Gary enjoying a quiet afternoon coffee. He opens the window and shouts down at them.

'That's great!' he hollers. 'You all have a great time. I'll be in here. Alone. On my day off.'

He says that the next time he is besieged by paparazzi he wants to put speakers out of the windows and blast Morrissey's 'Suedehead' at them over and over.

Why do you come here when you know it makes me sad?

* * *

The next morning I check my email and find a message that has been sent to me via *Rolling Stone* in America. (In the past month, it has been in the papers that I am working on some kind of book about Rob, which presumably is why the writer thinks to communicate via me.) At first I dismiss the email as madness, and am about to ignore it completely when I realise that, madness or not, it is a specific warning and will have to be considered. (Also, what it warns of is an act of madness, so why should I assume there are only mad messages and not mad acts?)

It reads as follows. (If, as it suggests, a previous message was sent, I never received it.)

CHRIS HEATH REALLY URGENT DANGER FOR ROBBIE WILLIAMS AGAIN

Dear Mr Heath,

I never got any message of you. I send the information to you that there will be great danger on 11th June for Mr. Williams. I really was wrong, cause in German June and July are nearly the same words. Juni and Juli, so it happened on 11th July, but not in London, it happend yesterday in the evening in Mannheim. But someone who's born in London is responsible for it. Maybe a guy of the Roadie-crew, not 30 years old yet. With shaved baldness. Not the people who made the installation are responsible for the damaged spotlight it was this gay man.

So you see I got messages that he would be shot. But it was in German the word SPOT for this light which should have been fallen on Robbie. I am not able to concentrate in this manner cause I got three children disturbing me and a lot of trouble, and so they know me and I get bad waves of energy from all his enemies, because the science world is not sleeping, if you are able to understand me.

He had great luck, cause his Angel was watching him. 'And through it all she offers me protection, a lot of love ... ' He's always singing songs of pictures he has forseen. He also got the second sight.

But now it's really your turn to be responsible for his health and live, because the next problem would happen on the 22nd in Antwerpen, the bungie rope will be manipulated. Really dangerous. He should have a special guard or detective to watch the scene and catch the criminals on acting.

Now if you would not send this message to Robbie Williams I will send it to BILD ZEITUNG or CNN or MTV or Radio 7 and you will be called a journalist who is interested to make his money in the biography of a already died STAR. It's your turn. GOD will bless you all.

The writer gives her name and email address in Germany. I forward this letter to Josie, who discusses it with Pompey, and they resolve to have extra security in Antwerp. Obviously, every rational bone in one's body says that it is delusional nonsense – and hateful nonsense, too, given the upset and worry such madness can spread – but on the other hand Rob often encourages the world that surrounds him to be one in which portents and predictions and auguries are taken seriously. With what kind of a conscience, then, can one casually dismiss this?

* * *

The woman who visited his room in Vienna has sold her story.

He hears a summary of her account.

'So,' he says, 'she actually didn't say: "What I did was, I went in his room, I couldn't speak very good English, so I just took all my clothes off and sucked his cock and then put my clothes on and left." Did she not say that?'

'No,' says Josie.

It says in the article that Rob pretended to be a Scottish football manager, as though he had genuinely been trying to pretend not to be the pop star Robbie Williams (and as though she had not propositioned him as such; she had been so full on in the hotel bar that he had thought she was possibly a hooker). In fact, he had just been explaining Championship Manager to her. (She had also obviously confused Welsh with Scottish.) Somehow this supposed fact becomes unhinged from the kiss'n'tell and gets further interpreted, until it is widely accepted that he has been going around Europe passing himself off as the manager of Falkirk.

* * *

Things arrive all the time: presents, messages, invitations. Some gratefully received, some less so. Today he has had an Arsenal shirt from the last FA

Cup Final hand-delivered to the hotel by Dennis Bergkamp, and a package with a handwritten note from Tommy Hilfiger. At the venue Skin, who has been support act on the last few days, shyly gives him a leather Yohji Yamamato bag. Josie says that she has had a call inviting him to Billy Connolly's house in August. That's just today.

In the dressing room before the show, he strums his guitar for a while, playing 'Better Man' and 'Nan's Song', then puts on lots of U2 records. The line he sings out loudest, from 'Who's Gonna Ride Your Wild Horses', is '*you're an accident, waiting to happen*'. (It reminds me of the creepy email, and I get a chill, but I keep it to myself.)

'I'm really shitting it tonight, for some reason,' he tells the band before the huddle. 'Really double scared. 60,000 people ... want to go to bed.'

Onstage, all this is less obvious than ever. He hauls up another girl during 'Monsoon' and this time they're soon going full at it, kissing properly and deeply. This lying-down-on-stage-with-a-girl concept is one he has purloined from Bono, but when Bono pulls girls up to lie with him there is a chasteness about it all, as if they assume and expect a certain respectability will be maintained. With Rob they seem to assume, not completely without reason, that he may be up for almost anything.

Tonight, at the end of the song, the girl grabs the microphone, says her name is Sabine and announces 'I'm the future Mrs Williams'. Rob gives her the weird glance this deserves but nonetheless instructs the band to start 'Come Undone', lies down with her and kisses her neck. She pushes up his shirt and rubs his back, then gets on top of him and pulls up the front of his shirt. Word has spread backstage and the dancers are now all on the side of the stage, watching. When she sits up, astride him, he ruffles her hair – partly, I think, to regain some control over the situation – but, undeterred, she starts gyrating on him.

For the second verse, he manages to get her to stand and they dance. She is wearing a homemade Chacun À Son Goût T-shirt – which is either sweet and devoted or a bit creepy and stalkerish. As they dance, she rubs up and down with her hand on the front of his stomach, lower and lower.

I run into David in the pit and we compare notes. We have absolutely no idea if Rob is enjoying any of this. Towards the end, he asks for his acoustic guitar. 'Here's something I wouldn't normally do,' he says, and on his own sings the two songs he played earlier in the dressing room. After that he will do this nearly every night.

Then it's 'Feel' and a heartfelt version of the introduction that has been evolving over the past few concerts: 'This is a song that I wrote when I was feeling a bit depressed. I didn't feel as though I deserved to be where I am. I didn't feel as though I deserved to be onstage in front of you lot. I didn't think that I deserved the life that I've got. I felt like shit. I wrote this next song. But right now, as I said before, I'm the happiest man on the planet and I've got you to thank. Thank you.'

I see him backstage as he changes for the encores.

'What a great night,' he beams. The only bit that freaked him out was when he lost control of his kissing partner. 'She started to writhe against the COJ,' he says. 'I had a bit of an Alan Partridge: "Right – that's enough. Get off. Thank you." I didn't know what to do.'

* * *

Sara Cox, who is in town to interview him for Radio One, comes round the next afternoon with her producer and soundman. (He dedicated 'Angels' to her at last night's show, but she had already left, and refused to believe him at the hotel buffet when he told her what he had done.) He is in his room, watching the golf. Just before she arrives, he goes to the bathroom to pee and while he is in there he stares at his tattoos. For a moment, he wonders how he would feel if his body were clean again, and it makes him feel so sad: all the pain he would have to go through to get his body redecorated the way he loves it. Like this.

They do the interview lying on a bed in his suite, though it is actually the bed Pompey sleeps in rather than his, and there are six other people in the near vicinity. She keeps pulling down her short skirt. 'Why don't you put a pillow there,' he says, handing her one, 'so you're not conscious about your knickers showing?' He makes gentle fun of her surprisingly sturdy feet. 'How long have you left The Shire?' he enquires. 'I'm being interviewed by Bilbo Baggins.'

Before the tape rolls, they chat about love and crushes. She says she won't watch *Moulin Rouge* with her husband because it has Kylie Minogue in it. 'I haven't had a girlfriend for a long time,' he says. 'I have no crushes at the moment. Apart from present company … ' (She later tells him that in advance of this trip she has had her first massage from her husband, three meals cooked in a week and a couple of 'you look nice's.) Rob mentions how, towards the end of bad relationships in the past, he would try to sidestep the guilt by steering girlfriends elsewhere. 'I was literally trying to pimp her to anybody,' he remembers. 'People would come on telly and I'd go, he's really cool and good-looking, isn't he? And I've heard he's really funny too … I think it's actually that if she's going to go, I'd rather have her go out with him than go out with somebody that would make me jealous.'

'Yeah,' agrees Sara. 'If you love them, let them go, but not to someone … '

'If you love them let them leave,' he says. 'But not to Liam Gallagher.'

Everyone laughs.

'Diddly did dee dee,' he says.

She has come at a good time. For all the flirting and joking, he is in the mood to talk seriously. They speak at length about addiction and touring and kissing girls onstage.

'Can I ask you, by the way, about the happy pills, as you call them?' she asks. 'Are you still taking the happy pills now or is this … ?'

'Well, yeah, yeah,' he says. 'It seems to be cropping up an awful lot and I think that the reason why it is, is because nobody actually mentions in it in everyday living in Great Britain, or in anywhere really, and I think it's a really honest thing to say and it sort of does make me curl my toes a little bit every time somebody mentions it … but, yeah, I take these things that stop me from not wanting to be on the planet, you know.'

'Sorry,' she says. 'I've not upset you, have I?

'No, not at all, but you mention one thing that's kind of, it is a bit I feel a bit ooh talking about that. But you know, and the reason why I do talk about it is there's an awful lot of people out there that probably have felt the same way or are feeling the same way and don't know what to do with it or about it. And I often think that, you know, I won't be on them for the rest of my life or anything, but I do think that it's a case of – you know when a kid gets knocked over outside a school and they put the speed bumps in? And I'm just putting the speed bumps in before the kid gets knocked over. That's it.'

'That's a brilliant way of putting it,' she says.

'I think there's that … the stigma of "Oh, he's weird – that's weird". And also people go, "What have you got to be depressed about?" … Depression isn't about anything. It's not about "Woe is me, my life is this, that and the other". It's like having the worst flu all day that you just can't kick. It's not about situations, places or things. It's about a chemical thing in your body that goes … hey, do you know what? I think it's 'cause I did too much ecstasy, to tell you the truth. When you take ecstasy your brain releases an awful amount of this thing called serotonin … '

'Serotonin, yeah,' she nods.

' … and it makes you go "Great!",' he continues, 'and the reason you're going "Great!" is because the serotonin in your head's going, "Hey hey hey, loads of it!" And then you use it all up and your brain's got nothing to bathe in. And that's what happens when you batter yourself.'

Much of this exchange will be broadcast on Radio One during the week before Knebworth, and the tabloids will also latch on to it and assume, understandably, that Rob now attributes his depression principally to ecstasy abuse. That's not the case. 'I'm sure it didn't help,' he'll later reflect, 'but, thinking about it, no. I was depressed when I was 14, 15, 16, and I hadn't taken E then.' The connection may be that ecstasy, while masquerading as a way out of depression, further depletes the resources to deal with it. It is a little like suffering from poverty and imagining that the solution to all your problems is a really big overdraft.

* * *

Soon the interview is over, Sara Cox is gone, and the rest of the day awaits. It is getting to him more and more, being trapped in the hotel day after day by circumstance and celebrity. And he's bored. Just before dusk, he decides that he needs to get out for a while. Go for a walk.

A dozen or so fans swarm around as he goes down the hotel steps, as he knew they would.

'Girls,' he pleads. 'I'm going for a walk, so please let me go. I'm bored and I want a walk.'

But of course they will follow. They always do.

He heads off down the street away from the canal, and we have gone about a hundred yards when he realises something very strange. Something wonderfully missing. I think he goes through the theatre of asking them not to follow each time, even though he knows they will, because it is through expressing such sensible desires, even when they are always thwarted, that you remain human. He has no realistic expectation of being heard or of being heeded. But this evening, here we are down the street, and not a single one of these fans is trailing behind us. To understand how much this simple small courtesy means to him, and how much better it makes the day, you have to imagine the drip-drip drag on his well-being every one of the thousands of times it hasn't happened.

Which is why what he does next – though it seems the action of a man, finally free, marching back into his prison – makes perfect sense.

'Fuck it,' he says, turning on his heel. He walks back to where the fans are loitering.

'Seeing as no one has *ever* said they won't follow me and they don't,' he explains, 'I want to take you all for a drink.'

There are 13 of them. He leads them to the bar-café across from the hotel and we all sit outside in the seats he had shouted down to yesterday.

Gingerly to begin with, they ask questions. They want to know about the girls who got on stage. He orders them drinks and food. They ask what he has been doing all day.

'Nothing,' he says. 'I watched the golf and then I had an interview with a radio station in England.'

'Is there a swimming pool?' one girl asks.

'Yeah,' he says, puzzled. 'But I haven't been in there.'

'How was your photo shoot?' another asks.

'I didn't do a photo shoot,' he says.

'We saw a flash light,' another says.

'That was a wedding,' he points out.

They have been doing what fans do: sitting outside a hotel all day, taking the meagre evidence available to them and embroidering it into the life they imagine a pop star would be living. Usually it's a far busier and more glamorous life than the reality. They rarely imagine the boredom, or the hanging around, or the endless cups of coffee, or even the object of their attention contentedly lying on a hotel bed watching cable TV.

They ask about Los Angeles; the dogs; Justin Timberlake; Take That; how once he sang 'Mack The Knife' as karaoke here; getting his first tattoo in

Amsterdam on his leg when he was 18. He spots someone across the road he thinks may be paparazzi and slips off his chair for a moment, hiding with his head level with his fans' knees.

When he gets back up, they ask why Kelly Osbourne is on the tour. It doesn't seem to make sense to some of them.

'She's an interesting pop star,' he says. 'Give me an interesting girl pop star. Christina Aguilera, she's not *interesting*.' One of them suggests Jewel. 'She's *musical*,' Rob says. 'She's great and she's beautiful but she's not interesting. Kelly Osbourne is really, really interesting. And we need people like that that go "Fuck off" to everything.'

'Britney Spears?' suggests another.

'I like Britney Spears,' he says, 'but she's not interesting.'

'Björk,' says a girl firmly.

'Björk's interesting,' he concedes, 'but she's not a pop star. She's an alien. I mean that in a nice way.'

He says he's going up to read his book. (It's one I've given him: Jon Ronson's *Us: Adventures With Extremists*.) 'Conspiracy theories, UFOs, stuff to get paranoid about,' he explains to them. 'Like I haven't got enough.'

When he gets to his room, he sees that they're still outside the café and waves down to them before shutting the curtains for the night. He will be up until six in the morning, coming to the conclusion that the scariest character in a book otherwise peopled by Islamic extremists, Ku Klux Klan members and those who believe that the world is run by a secret cabal of lizards is the Reverend Ian Paisley.

* * *

Just after one in the afternoon, Josie tries to cajole Rob into consciousness. 'You are a tired little thing, aren't you?' she says.

'Yeah,' he grunts weakly.

He staggers into the living room, stares at the bowl of cereal in front of him, then picks the pieces of papaya from amongst the pineapple and kiwi fruit and drops them on to a newspaper. 'I can't get out of my dream,' he says. 'About children in limbo. They can't get to the other side.' Slowly he explains more. 'I was in the old house in Tunstall. They didn't know they were in limbo. They started making things move. They stayed in my bed. There was Max, Chris Sharrock and these two spirits in my bed. I'd got to figure out a way of getting them home … '

I ask him whether he told the spirits that they were actually in limbo.

'Well,' he says, 'when I mentioned it to them they got really sheepish about it.'

* * *

Sara Cox is on the plane to do the final part of her interview. First, Rob looks at the British papers. There's a sad story about Paul Gascoigne's ongoing woes. 'I hope he's alright,' he mutters. 'He used to phone me up. I used to play for a football team on Sunday morning and he used to phone me up pissed as a newt at about half past nine, just as I was about to kick off.'

After take-off, he disappears to the bathroom. At his request, Josie has been shopping for him. Sara Cox talks into her microphone, setting the scene for her listeners, describing plane travel Robbie Williams-style: 'None of this duty-free shenanigans ... none of consorting with the scum ... none of this customs malarkey ... ' Rob appears in the aisle. He is wearing a curly black wig, a frilly black bra, fishnet tights open at the back to expose his rear, and a shiny red G-string into which his manhood is crammed. He parades down the plane.

'Does Robbie often do this sort of thing?' Sara Cox asks the stewardess.

'He normally gets his bottom out,' the stewardess helpfully explains.

Rob returns and sits down. 'Shall we do the interview then?'

'Do you like it?' says Max, laughing.

He looks appalled at the suggestion. This is entertainment, not fun. 'Not at *all,*' he says. 'It feels a bit weird.' He asks Josie to fetch his real clothes from the toilet. 'I've got fishnet tights on,' he says. 'It's really weird. I've got a bra on.'

'Do you like it a bit?' presses Max.

'No, not at all,' he says indignantly. 'It felt really weird in the toilet, but I felt like I'd got to follow it through.' He pulls on his black trousers and breaks the G-string so that he can remove it decently. Sara Cox asks whether they can give away the fishnet tights to the listeners of Radio One.

'I don't think that's a good idea,' he says.

* * *

He dreams about dogs and having to go to court in Italy. There is an arcade machine and a lift, and it's all muddled up, and he and Josie can't decide what he should wear for his Italian court appearance.

'It's all about image,' he tells her. He figured they should change his suit because everyone can see all his tattoos. 'I'll go and get my other suit on,' he declares. 'How long have we got?'

'We had two minutes,' Josie tells him in his dream, 'two minutes ago.'

13

For those around Rob on tour, their lives adapt to his shifting rhythms. As the tour goes on, he wakes later and later, until he is living exactly the same routine he hated at the end of his last Asian tour – rising in the mid-afternoon, preparing for the concert, performing, and then searching for some kind of entertainment, love or distraction long into the night. As the weeks pass, he seems less and less happy with what he is doing, until it seems he is gritting his teeth and hanging on, day to day. You can feel the effort those around him are putting into keeping him going, into helping him pass the time and make it through – less for pragmatic reasons (because there would be no tour without him) or professional ones (because he is their employer) than because they empathise with how, more and more, the tour seems to him like slow water torture. There is something about him that makes people around him try to look after him, and desire to make things better for him.

Once he has woken, and after the show, much of the time is spent moving between his hotel room and the public rooms in any given hotel – the bar, the restaurant, the lobby – where something interesting or distracting might happen. He moves in a peculiar, individual manner between these places, in a way that seems strange to anyone not yet used to it. For instance, he never waits to leave a room. Perhaps this has developed from a necessity, of not wanting to deal with either the rituals or requests that polite leave-taking can involve. (Leave-takings can be pretty gruesome when you are famous: what would just be goodbye for most people can often be taken as the-last-chance-to-get-what-I-really-want from the person you are talking to.) Or perhaps it is simply a luxury he has assumed into his life, along with the cigarettes that someone nearly always has on hand whenever he wants one.

Whichever, when he is ready to go he simply goes, usually without even a nod, and generally at some speed. Like many charismatic entertainers, he knows how to enter a room when he so chooses so that everyone notices, but he has also learned what may be a more useful art: how to leave a room without anyone noticing. If you want to follow, you have to be ready to catch and cover every movement and to instantly break any other conversation you are in. To begin with, I wonder about the etiquette of this: does the fact that he has left the room, without any invitation that I should also come, suggest that I am uninvited? Or should I find it somehow rude and presumptive? But it is not done in a disrespectful way: his bodyguards aside, he certainly doesn't usually convey from this that he expects anyone else to follow him and to live their lives at his pace, at his beck and call. His attitude is more: *I am going, because I want to go, and in doing so I understand that you may come too or you may stay ... I, however, have already gone.*

The most awkward, and occasionally embarrassing, aspect of this, particularly on tour in public places like hotel bars, is that there is often no way of distinguishing between a final exit and one of his frequent visits to the toilets. If one wants to stay with him, often one finds oneself trailing him, only to end up standing outside a toilet with Pompey or Gary or Jason, and then seconds later walking back with them into the bar.

* * *

Backstage in Antwerp, he watches Queen Day on VH1, then puts on Nancy Sinatra's 'These Boots Are Made For Walking' and mentions that Britney

Spears wanted to sing this with him on *Swing When You're Winning*. It didn't happen because he wanted them to duet on the much darker 'Some Velvet Morning' (which was subsequently revived by Primal Scream with Kate Moss), and Britney wasn't into that.

Before he goes onstage, he revs up the band. He says they owe it to this audience to deliver. 'In all seriousness, they live in Antwerp, they're bored as fuck. They're the most bored people in possibly the world. They are. Let's go out and give them some fucking fun, excitement, entertainment, some laughter, some tears. And possibly some arse cheeks.'

Though I have been weirdly worried about the hanging opening for each performance since passing on that email threat, oddly I forget about it tonight – the night for which the threat was made. A good thing, as the opening is a bit of a fiasco. There isn't room for the screens to come to the front of the stage in this venue, so Rob is suspended behind two giant sheets that are supposed to drop down, but they refuse to do so. For several long seconds the crew desperately tug at them, harder and harder, as Rob – half-revealed to the crowd in a triangular gap opened by the frantic pulling – dangles there.

The shows have been getting odder as his boredom and frustration have slowly increased, and tonight's is the most eccentric so far: there are plenty of snatches of other people's songs, a rant at those who insist on sitting down, about how this isn't a Sting concert, an exhortation to get 'On the good foot! On the bad foot! On the in-between foot!' At the end of the night, after 'Rock DJ', he gives probably the single most peculiar speech of the tour. It begins with an impromptu rendition of Nelly's 'Hot In Here'. 'This is the last song,' he says. 'Yeah. I know. I know. I said I wanted to do more and they said ... *no*. Bugger them. Bugger them all. The powers that control us all. Ah. Secret powers! Twelve-foot lizards!' Pause. 'Tiny men with moustaches!' A longer pause. 'Medium-sized women with large breasts. They control me. I don't know about you. I would be nowhere without this next song. And you'd be staring at an empty stage. And I'd be ... somewhere else, I suppose.' Pause. 'Uh, I've really lost my mind this evening, Antwerp, I really have. Yes. And it's not coming back!'

He does return, to sing 'Back For Good'. He usually mangles its lyric, out of playfulness and disrespect, but not like this. 'Sing it for Barlow!' he shouts.

'I got lipstick marks a dingy dingy-bingy plinky-plonky-plinky-plonk plinky-plonk

I got a fist of pure emotion, I've got a head of battered beans ...'

The last words the less bored but more puzzled people of Antwerp hear him sing tonight are:

'I want you back! I want you back! I want you back! I want you back-a! I want you-back-a! I want Chewbacca! I want Chewbacca! And R2D2!'

There is no sign that the people of Antwerp find any of this at all odd. One of his gifts is that he makes at least two contradictory kinds of triumphant pop music – music with great grace ('Feel' and 'Angels', for instance – the stuff I instinctively like the best) and music that is gloriously and marvellously graceless ('Rock DJ', 'Monsoon', for instance) – in the same way that he can ask for people to get their tits out and bring an audience to tears within seconds of each other. Somehow these two contradictory forces, which surely should barge uncomfortably against each other and demand some kind of resolution or compromise, float like religion and science through and past each other, unperturbed, and most of his audience seem able to take as much of either as they wish.

* * *

At the hotel buffet, he lights another cigarette. All his Silk Cut packets have been customised with new safer, sicker health warnings from a site Andy Franks discovered on the internet. 'Nicotine Protects You From AIDS.' 'Smoking Makes You Look Hard And Cool.' 'Jesus Smokes.' 'Cigarettes Make You Run Faster.' 'Smoking Helps You Fight International Terrorism.' 'Leave In Mouth Between Puffs For Extra Panache.'

Rob holds up today's packet. 'Smoking When Pregnant Makes Your Baby Cool.' 'I think that's my favourite,' he says.

Over the dinner table, he mentions to Max that he wants to cut one of the two swing songs, 'One For My Baby', from the set.

'Why?' says Max, immediately ashen, and Rob explains it is to do with the show's tempo. Max is crestfallen. A combination of ego and bluff tightly knitted to insecurity and hypersensitivity is not an unusual one, but within Max it is particularly extreme.

'Are you making it about you?' Rob asks him.

'Do you really mean that?' says Max, not believing that Rob would really drop the song.

'Yeah, I really do,' says Rob.

'"One For My Baby" is great,' says Max.

'Look at him,' says Rob, backtracking. 'It was only a thought.'

'It's fucking absolutely wonderful, you knobskin,' says Max. 'You're winding me up, aren't you?'

Rob doesn't say anything. He's not winding Max up at all, but Max takes his silence as confirmation.

'Wicked,' says Max. 'Well done.'

Rob decides to go with it. 'Did I get you?' he says.

'Good acting,' congratulates Max.

'Thank you,' says Rob.

'I want to throw up,' says Max, relieved.

The awkward moment has passed. Except for one small detail: that Rob still needs to tell Max at some point that he plans to drop 'One For My Baby' from the set.

* * *

The next morning, Josie finds an olive green bra hanging on an office chair in the living room of Rob's suite, abandoned in the course of some undisclosed event. She picks it up and looks enquiringly at Rob.

He shrugs.

'Sometimes I like to put on a bra,' he lies.

* * *

'That was a cruel trick about "One For My Baby" last night,' Max tells Rob on the plane. 'You acted so well. You had me. I was really not happy.'

Rob draws his breath. He has a decision to make.

'No ... ' he begins.

'What?' scoffs Max. 'You really meant it?' He thinks that Rob is trying the same wind-up a second time. 'Sloppy, son,' he says.

'No,' says Rob. 'I totally meant it.'

'But ... ' says Max incredulously. 'The cheers when you sing the opening line ... '

'Then they get bored,' says Rob.

Max realises that Rob means it, and now that he does, he quickly accepts it, unhappily but with dignity.

* * *

At the Hotel d'Angleterre in Copenhagen, he is ushered into the Karen Blixen suite. Blixen, who wrote under the name Isak Dinesen, is one of Denmark's most famous writers, and is best known for her book *Out Of Africa*, which probably explains the immense antler head in the living room. Rob looks a little perturbed by it, but hangs his RW baseball cap on the left antler. The photograph of a dead lion on the wall disturbs him more.

But he doesn't worry too much about any of that right now. On his way into the hotel he has spotted Pia, the girl who came up to him as he was leaving the Danish TV studio the last time he was in the country and gave him a box with a 'soulmate' card in. He goes to find her. In her room she immediately gets her Angel cards out. (She points out that there is one missing. The soulmate card, of course.) She explains that she had a feeling in her head: *Go and book a room in the hotel and he will come.* They chat for ages, and he doesn't mention that he is finding a lot of what she is saying somewhat barking mad. They end up lying on the bed and things start happening, and their tops are off, but then she stops him. So he says he has to go.

'We're coming from two different places,' he explains.

'What do you mean?' she asks.

'Well, you know all that stuff at the beginning?' he says. 'The soulmate card. It's scary, that. To be told that this is your future wife and soulmate.'

'What do you mean?' she repeats.

'You know,' he says, 'that I've met five girls on this tour that all think that they're my soulmate ... '

He sees the penny drop in her eyes; she is gutted. She says she doesn't want to be like everybody else, and he explains that everyone tells him that they don't want to be like everybody else. And then they have a long, good chat about sex, and the judgements he makes and the judgements she makes. He says that he has every right to suggest what he has been suggesting, and she has every right to say no. But he says that it is just sex. And the other stuff is scary.

'Put yourself in my position,' she says to him. 'You be me and I be Robert. You tell me what I'm supposed to do.' She explains that she lives out in the country and she is sure he is meant to be with her. 'What am I supposed to say?' she says.

It is a surprisingly thoughtful conversation, given the situation. In the end, they have managed to communicate and form any kind of bond only by beginning to understanding how very far apart they are, and how different their hopes and desires and expectations of this moment were.

* * *

After all this, he comes back to his room, and talks it over.

I point out that the ideas that girls like her have may not be as surprising, or as insane, as they seem to him. They are a predictable product of the era we live in and the dreams that are sold to us all every day. Half of the movies released each year dare us to believe in destiny and impossible romance. Often they encourage us to sacrifice everything – all sense and sanity and practicality – in their quest.

And, just as the seemingly-impossible-love-that-comes-true between the commoner and the prince, or the human and the god, is a staple of mythology, the seemingly-impossible-love-that-comes-true between the commoner and the celebrity is a staple of our modern myths and entertainments. So, whereas Rob thinks that each of these fans should notice, when they are standing with 120 other people outside a hotel or 60,000 in a crowd, that they are one of many who think the same thing, if you subscribe to those myths then that doesn't matter: the myth tells you that you should expect to be but one of many in a crowd, and that your cause will seem hopeless, but that you will eventually be pulled out from the mob, that you will find your pedestal or prince or impossible love, because it is destined.

He considers this, interested, deliberates over it a little, and acknowledges that it may all be so.

'Anyway,' he says, when he sees that I have exhausted my thoughts on this subject, 'then we had a shag.'

* * *

He has a bad night. I don't think that it is any of the day's residues torturing him. It is just this hotel. Maybe it is the dead lions and the antlers and the high roofs, but he detects something more specific. He can hear ghosts. There are two of them walking around his living room, and then he hears a bang and they open the door to the bedroom.

That's it. The ghosts have won. They can stay; he is leaving.

He phones Gary Marshall, the bodyguard on duty, who misses the call. When Gary doesn't answer Rob goes down to reception on his own at five in the morning. Gary, meanwhile, realises that Rob has phoned, rushes to the room and is alarmed to discover it empty. Eventually they find each other. Rob asks the hotel for their smallest room, which has a single bed up against a wall at the back of the hotel. There he puts in some earplugs, pushes them deep to shut out every sound, and eventually finds some peace at around seven o'clock in the morning.

* * *

In the afternoon, when he wakes, he discovers that his problems are not over. It is not now the ghosts. It is the earplugs. He has inadvertently pushed one of them so far into his ear that you can only just see its top by shining a torch into the cavity. Even Rob realises that this is potentially too serious to mess about with, and a doctor is called.

While he waits, Jason tells him that when he was three he shoved a crayon up his nose. For two months, before it was discovered, his parents just thought he had a really bad cold.

Max also pays a visit.

'Guess what I've done?' says Rob.

'Shit in your pants?' guesses Max.

The doctor comes, examines him and says he needs to fetch the proper instrument. While Rob goes next door, he grins and asks, shamelessly, 'Two spare tickets for the concert?'

'We can sort something out, I've no doubt,' says Pompey through gritted teeth. Doctors and dentists almost always ask for something. You might imagine these would be jobs in which professional pride and principle, and the desire to set people at ease when they are feeling vulnerable and need care, would counteract any daftness in the face of celebrity, but it does not. Rob has become used to doctors coming round to give him a medical with their doctor equipment and a stack of calendars for him to sign, or to be sitting in a dentist's chair and be asked whether the dentist can use his name in promotion of a particular mouthwash.

The doctor returns, pulls out the crushed, waxy earplug, and leaves. Rob is pleased to have lost the earplug but has some disappointing news for someone planning to sing for thousands tonight. 'I still can't hear anything,' he explains.

A different doctor is summoned to the stadium to syringe his ears. Hot water is injected inwards. A huge lump of wax is ejected from one ear; a small chunk from the other.

* * *

Ozzy Osbourne's tour manager, whom Kelly has been close to all her life, has been found dead in his hotel room in America. She must fly home, and will miss the concert in Sweden. David and Ian Huffam explain to Rob that they need a replacement support act.

'Phone Noel up,' says Rob mischievously, 'and ask him if he wants to do an acoustic set.' Even as he says it, he warms to this idea. 'Go on,' he urges. 'Go on. Ask.'

'There's no harm in asking, is there?' Ian concedes.

'Go on,' says Rob, excited. 'Please ask. Please do that for me.'

'He could pop over on Easyjet, couldn't he?' laughs Ian.

'Say I'll send him a jet,' says Rob seriously, upping the stakes. 'Please do it.'

'You want me to do that?' Ian checks.

'Yes,' says Rob firmly. 'I just want to wind him up the week before Knebworth. And the jet thing is to make it sound real. And if he says yes, we'll send the jet.' He goes to tell Max, thrilled by the no-lose joy of it all. 'It'll go two ways,' he says. 'It's 98 per cent definite that he'll hit the fucking roof and get really wound up by it. Perfect fodder for Knebworth. And the other 2 per cent, he might do it. You never know.'

Ian reports back a few minutes later that Noel Gallagher's agent has received the request seriously and is looking into it.

* * *

Rob has been getting noticeably more tired before, and weirder during, the last few shows, as though he is now only just managing to get through them. Tonight he reports he is the most scared he has yet been, hanging upside down. 'Because I was the most tired,' he explains, 'and psychosis had set in.' By the third song tonight he has thrown his black shirt and white tie into the crowd; no doubt they imagine that this is a regular part of the show and he has many such outfits, but neither is true. His voice is going, too.

Between songs he keeps saying that this is 'the best crowd in the Europe'; I think he may mean that he needs them to be that good for him to keep going. During the swing interlude he tells the Danes, 'I'll tell you why I'm sad tonight – because I've got to go to Sweden next.' There is a huge roar. 'Last time I went they were shit,' he says. In the acoustic section he returns to this fame, making up a song about it. '*I'll go to Sweden,*' he sings. '*I don't know what for. When in Denmark. I should have done one more.*'

It is amazing how often he gets away with these outbursts, playing off rival countries against each other for a cheer. It is much safer, of course, when you slag off somewhere you have just visited rather than somewhere you are just about to visit. This time, his luck will run out.

* * *

He asks Max to sleep in his double bed with him tonight, to offer some protection against the hotel ghosts.

'The undead,' he sighs. 'It's a ruddy nightmare.'

'Like two gay lads?' asks Max. 'Can I get a nosh?'

'Yeah, of course you can,' bluffs Rob, deadpan.

Perhaps it would delight the *Daily Mail* to discover that he is very relaxed about sleeping with his best male friends. He likes the company, and the comfort of not being alone. He and Max would sometimes sleep together when they were first in the Los Angeles house together, just chatting and watching telly until they'd fall asleep on the same bed, and they both give good accounts of the funnier moments. Max waking up with Rob entwined around him; Rob opening his eyes from sleep to see Max's paralysed, terrified expression.

14

There are echoes and reminders of Rob's past all round Stockholm's Grand Hotel. 'That is the balcony I punched Nellee Hooper on,' he'll say as we walk downstairs. Or, in his suite, 'I can remember pissing in that corner.' Or, down one corridor, the door he was forbidden to go through but did. And down another corridor, Victoria Beckham's room, where he kept pounding and demanding 'the wife of the England captain'.

Rob doesn't want to hear it, or think about it.

'We'll all grow from this experience,' he says.

* * *

It is weeks later, during a quiet afternoon in London, Jonny sitting nearby, that he agrees to talk about what happened in Stockholm when he visited for the MTV awards in November 2000. It was not long before he gave up drinking and he had been advised by his doctors not to go to Sweden. He had just completed a tour, and on tour he had drunk only on evenings before a day off. On the plane there, he and Jonny had two beers – to prove, as Jonny remembers, that it was possible for him to have just a couple of beers.

'Yeah,' remembers Rob, 'but it was no good for me, a social drink. You know, it didn't make any sense. I don't like the taste of it. So why just have a social drink? The whole thing regarding alcohol was that I drank to get drunk – I didn't drink because I enjoyed it.'

He got up the next day and performed 'Kids' with Kylie Minogue on the show. He wasn't in the greatest of moods. He remembers this fellow saying to him while he was having a piss, 'So, we meet at last,' and he had no idea who it was, and he found it all annoying. (It was one of Dolce and Gabbana.) He was bored and depressed. Bono pulled him into his dressing room for a chat, but even that didn't help: 'He was very complimentary and he was really, really lovely, but I couldn't handle talking to Bono. And all I'd got to tell people or say was, "How fucking depressed am I?"'

Then there was Nellee Hooper. He'd hung round with Nellee Hooper a little in times past but had concluded that he didn't consider Nellee a nice person. The last time Rob had seen him, in the south of France, Rob had shouted 'You fucking cunt' at him. Now Rob was tired and drunk and was charging around to stay awake – 'I'd just walk forward because my body weight was carrying me,' he remembers. He saw Nellee and slurred at him, in a kind of hostile apology: 'Do you know what? It's not good to have bad things going on with people … let's just stop that … I'm sorry for calling you a cunt in the south of France – I don't want to have a problem with you.' Inside, he still felt just the same about Nellee Hooper, and if there is a pattern to these encounters it is that Rob is never closer to fury and violence than when he is offering an apology, and if he considers that such an apology is received ungraciously, things get messy.

'Well, Rob, it's just not good, you know,' he remembers Nellee Hooper saying. 'I thought I was your friend; all I've ever done for you is good things and wished you good stuff and … '

By then Rob wasn't listening.

'I'm going downstairs,' he told Nellee Hooper. 'When I come back I'll be very different.'

He went downstairs and drank six sambucas, one after the other, and charged back up. He was followed up the stairs by Mel B and Emma Bunton, who had decided that everyone else was boring and that Rob seemed to be the centre of fun and they wanted to hang out with him. Within seconds, they would be retreating, saying that this was all a bit much for them.

'I wasn't going to hit him, you know, but … actually I was,' Rob realises. 'Actually, saying that, I would have hit him if I hadn't heard everything that I wanted to hear.' Rob didn't. Anyway, Nellee Hooper hit him first, in the solar plexus.

That was the worst thing he could have done. Years before, when Rob used to get off his head with Hooper, late at night Hooper had a habit of hitting him. For fun, sort of, though Rob hated it. He would get in a little ball and Hooper would punch him. Maybe like a mate would. Maybe like a bully would.

And now Hooper's new punch sent Rob straight back to those strange nights in Hooper's house, so Rob hit him in the face. Rob thinks he got one more shot in before it was broken up. 'Never hit my solar plexus!' Rob kept shouting, and he still had a hold on Hooper's shirt, which he ripped off. Then, while everyone was trying to calm everyone else down, Rob tried to sneak away on his hands and knees. A few minutes later, he bumped into Kevin from the Backstreet Boys. It was around that time that he blacked out, and he has to rely on others' memories for everything that followed.

After the fight, Rob went on a manic search for cocaine. Jonny remembers thinking that if they could just get Rob into bed before he found coke, then he would pass out and everything would be fine. They got him into the hotel elevator.

'Rob, calm down a bit now,' he was urged.

He looked at Jonny and at Josie and exclaimed, drunkenly reassuring, as though they had really misunderstood something, 'I'm on your *side*'.

It was after that that he started banging on Victoria Beckham's door.

'Let me in! Let me in! I want to speak to Mrs England Captain Man.'

She came to the door.

'Go to bed, Robbie,' she advised sweetly.

Down the corridor was a door that led to the ballroom where the MTV aftershow party and the world's press were. They told him that, whatever he did, he shouldn't go through there. So, of course, he made a run for it, and the cameras started flashing as soon as he opened the door. His shirt was ripped from the earlier fight and there were trails of drink down his white vest and he literally roared at the photographers as they snapped. Onstage, Wyclef was rapping, and Richard Blackwood was up there too, so it made perfect sense to Rob for him to jump up and join them. The crowd went bonkers. Someone in the audience handed him up a pint and he necked it in three gulps, Chubby Brown style. Wyclef looked bemused. Rob grabbed the microphone off Richard Blackwood and started to rap: bits of 'Rock DJ' and whatever came into his head. Jonny and Josie tried to get his attention, to get him off.

'We got Robbie Williams!' shouted Wyclef.

'Wyclef!' shouted Rob.

The one bit Rob remembers is being onstage and suddenly seeing Josie and Jonny, and going, 'What am I doing here?' Then he blacked out again.

They got him out of the party and tricked him. They said there was another party and that there might be coke there. Instead they led him into his room and shut him in. He tried to uncage himself. He would be docile for a while, then suddenly roar and make a futile dash for it. After one attempt, his bodyguard Jonah swept away his legs with a rugby tackle. At one point Rob started fighting Josie, doing really drunk wrestling, but he was so out of it and weak that she was easily his match, though he did bite her in the process. Then he gave up, tipped his bed over and took all his clothes off, throwing his trainers round the room, and pissed against the hotel wall in protest. He fell asleep on the floor with Jonah sitting over him on a chair, watching. When he woke up, Jonah had been replaced by Marv, his other bodyguard at the time. Rob was completely naked, lying crouched on his front with his knees beneath him, and he opened his eyes, felt hideous, shifted enough to discover the carpet burn on his forehead, looked in front of him at his upturned, empty bed then looked round and discovered Marv sitting just past his arse, looking at him.

'Hi,' said Rob.

* * *

Jonny has flown over to Stockholm, and goes to greet Rob as he is waking. 'Guess who was sat behind me on the plane?' says Jonny. 'Guy Chambers.'

I have already bumped into Guy in the lobby, where he seemed a little surprised that I would come over and greet him. When I said that I would see him later, he had wryly remarked that he was unlikely to be where I was.

'I didn't know he was coming,' Rob says to Josie, with a hint of accusation, when she walks into his bedroom.

'I told you,' she points out.

David backs her up.

'I'm not seeing him,' says Rob defiantly.

'I know,' says Josie. 'He doesn't want to see you either.'

Rob makes a theatrically miffed expression. 'He does,' he insists.

Everyone drifts into the living room while Rob supposedly gets dressed. A few seconds later he appears in the bedroom doorway, completely naked apart from a hand towel wrapped around his penis and held in place by his left hand, and poses for photographs.

In the van he says that he's not feeling good. 'People are not going to be bothered after a while when I tell them I'm not feeling very well,' he realises.

'Why?' asks Jonny.

'Because I keep saying I'm really bad and I'm really ill,' he says, 'and then I get up and do really fucking good gigs.'

* * *

Frida from Abba, and her two step-daughters (who are the princesses of Lichtenstein), arrive backstage to say hello. 'You look fantastic,' he says to Frida. She is, against all Abba logic, newly blonde. Rob became friends with them when they met skiing in Switzerland. (He says they're lovely. The hardest part of the skiing trip was that he couldn't get Abba songs out of his head, and he was forever on the verge of bursting into 'Super Trouper' when he was sitting next to Frida on the chair-lift.)

'Now,' he tells the Swedish audience about halfway thought the show, 'you may have read something in your paper today.' His derogatory comments in Denmark have been widely reported. The crowd are split: some roaring, some booing. 'I was very, very wrong … ' he begins. He doesn't need to say any more than that, though he does. He redoubles his apology with an acoustic lullaby that begins, '*Stockholm you are lovely, you really are very nice, sorry if I said something in the papers … chicken and fried rice …* '

'It was the only thing I could find to rhyme,' he apologises, then also apologises for not being able to play guitar very well. 'But it isn't really the point,' he says. 'The point is, expressing yourself, and expressing yourself from the heart, and I mean everything that I've ever written. I mean all my sad songs, I mean all my happy songs, and I mean all my love songs, you know.'

Guy Chambers is watching from the sound desk in the middle of the stadium. He texts Andy Franks during the show, saying how great it is, and Josie passes this on to Rob before the encores. I wonder whether, when he reaches 'Angels', he will at least acknowledge Guy, and somehow nod to the fact that, whatever else is now true, most of these songs are their songs. But he says nothing.

15

The local Stoke paper the *Sentinel* has not made his life easy over the years. Though not everything it writes about him has a mean edge – it documents his Give It Sum work respectfully, for instance – often it seems to cover him with the same ignorance, inaccuracy and derision as many of its national competitors, but with a little bonus hometown spite thrown in. It is as if everyone knows that he needs taking down a peg or two, and they feel they are in a privileged position to do it; it is also as though any sense of pride that he is from Stoke is, for them, every day outweighed by the greater snub that he is not in Stoke.

For months the *Sentinel* has been trying to connect three facts: the severe financial woes at Port Vale football club, Rob's support of the team and his wealth. They have whipped up local feeling: how easy would it be for the club's most famous fan, Mr £80 Million Boy, to throw them a few million? For some weeks Rob has been planning to write a letter to explain his feelings: that he loves the club, and his home, and that he has been tempted to get involved, but that it is not the sensible thing for him to do at this time in his life, and it is not reasonable for people to expect him to do so. (These expectations have sometimes trickled through to him at the oddest moments. One day this winter he was out in Malibu, enjoying the Pacific air and his relative anonymity, when a bloke walked up to him. 'Robbie,' he says by way of hello, 'are you going to buy the Vale then?')

This week, things come to a head. On the day after the Stockholm concert, Rob and Jonny are given a tour of Chelsea and the box Rob has bought there for the year as David's birthday present. Someone leaks a skewed version of this visit to the tabloids, and it is printed that Rob was so impressed by the set-up at Chelsea that he committed to a ten-year-lease on a £1 million-a-year box, and whipped out his cheque book to pay for the first million on the spot. (Complete nonsense on many levels, not the least of which is that he doesn't even own a cheque book.) The story was picked up by the *Sentinel* and characterised as 'a kick in the teeth'.

'Fuck this,' he thinks, and picks up the phone. Seconds later Samantha Lawton, a reporter at her desk in Stoke, finds herself doing one of the two proper British press interviews he will give this year.

* * *

He explains about the Chelsea box: how much it really cost and how it wasn't for him but for his manager, a lifelong Chelsea fan. She says that people up there are so upset with what the football club's financial woes are doing to local businesses that they just want him to come and have a look. He points out that he has put £3 million of his own money into a charity. 'Go down to the Donna Louise Trust,' he suggests, 'and take the people down from the local businesses, and have a look at the kids who are dying. What do you want? Do you want me to help save somebody's life or do you want a new left back?'

He feels she isn't getting it, and he gets increasingly angry and upset. He tells her that what has been happening at Port Vale is heartbreaking and has been pulling at his heartstrings, but what is more heartbreaking is spending your childhood being given £5 from your grandmother's pension money so you can stand in the Railway Paddock on Saturday afternoons, and then making it into the directors' box once you're famous and realising that while the club is funded by grandmothers and their pension money fivers, very different, more self-interested principles are operating up here. He says that they should be asking the people who ran the club in recent years, and not him, about Port Vale's money problems: 'I feel like I'm being villainised for something that isn't my fault. You're asking me to give loads of money, and then give another load of money in another 12 months because of something that isn't my fault.' He might get involved in the future, but not now.

She says that part of the problem is that they don't have a number where they can call him to check these things. As though his ideal solution to anything would be to open a hot line to the *Sentinel's* news desk.

'To be honest,' he tells her, 'I don't trust you as far as I could throw you, and I don't give a toss about anything else. Slander my name about all and sundry, whatever you want. But don't mess with Port Vale.'

The story comes out on the day before the first Knebworth show and he reads it online before he leaves his flat. It is a fair account of their conversation that begins by saying that he was 'close to tears' as he discussed it all. He seems most relieved that she hasn't quoted him as using the word 'villainised', as it has since struck him that it doesn't exist. (She has changed it to 'made to look like the villain'.)

'I'm from Tunstall,' he says in the story. 'People in Tunstall aren't stupid with their money and I'm not either.'

* * *

Another story in the papers has annoyed Rob. It is in the local Hertfordshire paper, the *Comet*; he has stumbled on to it via Google news. The article states that local businesses in Knebworth village are furious at the way Rob's concerts will affect their weekend's trade due to the traffic congestion and parking restrictions. The sternest complaints are made by a Paul Elleston, owner of Trussells the butchers in the High Street. 'All this just for a pop star is ludicrous,' he moans. 'We will be suffering but nobody will be compensating me for my losses.'

Something about this has really wound Rob up. Overall, his concerts will bring a windfall to many people in Knebworth's vicinity. He says that he has considered sending the butcher a couple of thousand pounds, which I think in Rob's mind would be less to compensate him than to dramatise how stupid he is being.

As it happens, our route today takes us through the village.

'That's it!' shouts Rob, when he spots it. 'Trussells butchers! Silly cunts.'

The concert site looks strange without the 125,000 people who will fill it – a huge stage set in the dip of a slight natural bowl, with grass stretching away into the distance. Rob wanders around. 'I can make this seem really intimate,' he says. Onstage, he runs through a couple of songs. People working on the site and at the concession stands gather at a barrier some way back in the field.

'Thank you for letting us play in your town,' he says. 'And I'd like to make a personal apology to Trussells the butchers in the High Street, who seem to be very upset about the fact that we're here.' He sings a snippet of 'Hot Fudge', all of 'Come Undone' but much of it in an unusual register and messing around with the melody, all of 'Kids', a bit of 'Better Man' with invented lyrics about the people of Knebworth, and one verse and chorus of 'Nan's Song'. That is the full extent of his rehearsal for the biggest engagement of his life.

'I'm trying not to take it in,' he says in the van to the hotel. 'I think that's the best thing to do.' Instead, he and Jonny start arguing about whether R. Kelly's 'Ignition' (Rob's choice) or Beyoncé's 'Crazy In Love' (Jonny's) is the better song. It gets heated, and eventually I foolishly intervene to suggest that perhaps it is an argument that doesn't need to be resolved. Jonny puts me in my place. 'Yes, it does,' he snaps. 'Or we die.'

The two of them start singing the songs they would sing when they were young. Terrifyingly, they have a perfect recall of Black Lace's 'Agadoo' – not just the chorus but the verses and all the accompanying movements. Likewise Black Lace's 'Superman'.

'Nobody was worried about looking a dick then, were they?' sighs Rob. He says that the first time he even noticed fashion and what people looked like was in Madness videos. He would see them round Zak Bentley's house because the Bentleys had MTV. Rob would study Madness and think that was how he and his friends looked. 'You know,' he says, 'the Fred Perry shirt and the bottoms, ruddy-faced eight-year-olds with unkempt hair. A real late seventies, early eighties type of little oiks.'

They talk about the places they used to go, in their turn, for underage drinking. Jonny says that he used to be so scared that the police were going to arrest him and put him in prison.

'I can remember when I was about nine,' says Rob. 'All the lads were drinking cider, a big bottle of Scrumpy Jack, and I just didn't want to do it because it was *wrong*. I was dead against *everything* until I was about 13 and then – it must have been overnight – I just went: *Go on then! Let's have what you've got!*' He sits in silence for a moment. 'I reckon it had something to do with my Auntie Jo's death,' he says. 'I went to my Auntie Jo's funeral, and everybody left from the graveside and went to the pub, and I was there by myself. And I sobbed, the longest and hardest I've ever sobbed. And then I went to the pub. And since then, nothing. No more emotion about Auntie Jo.'

I ask him what he thinks he was crying about.

He gives me a weird look. 'My Auntie Jo was dead,' he says.

* * *

Late that night, in the hotel grounds, Rob leads a small party stalking their prey in the dark. We crouch like bad commandos, and hide behind bushes, and crawl across the grass, and try not to crunch the gravel. Jonny's phone keeps beeping.

Perhaps because it has not struck them that they are in any danger of an ambush while enjoying a post-dinner stroll in the gardens of a posh Hertfordshire hotel, Kelly Osbourne and the female bass player in her band are oblivious to all this action in the surrounding shadows. Finally, Rob leads the surprise charge. There is some whooping, a little screaming, a 'You bastard!' from Kelly, a bit of laughter, and then quite a bit more laughter at the lovely daftness of the whole manoeuvre. Kelly explains that they have just seen two people through the glass of the locked greenhouse who could not possibly have been there, and as we wander back towards the hotel, she and Rob discover that they have both consulted the same psychic and compare notes.

Kelly doesn't want to go indoors. She has an idea: let's steal the hotel's golf carts and drive them around in the dark. She has already been refused the keys by the hotel. 'Does anyone have a pocket knife?' she asks.

'Not a good idea, stealing golf carts, the first night in a hotel,' advises Pompey.

'The voice of maturity,' teases Rob. 'I'm not kidding you, it's like having Dad about.' He complains about the way Pompey has curtailed the plum-throwing sessions from the balcony of his London flat.

'We should go to the front desk,' says Kelly, who figures that a Robbie Williams request might achieve what a Kelly Osbourne request has not.

'No,' says Rob. 'It's more fun to be vandals.'

'Shall I go to get a knife from the kitchen?' she suggests. Rob says this is a fine idea and she scurries off.

'She's fucking great,' he says.

Kelly returns with a penknife borrowed from one of the bar staff, but it turns out that the carts' ignitions are more complicated than she had imagined. Simply turning them does nothing. Undeterred, she prises out the whole ignition mechanism and examines it. Pompey, who I suspect could work out how to get it started in seconds, is careful to offer no encouragement or help at all. Soon there are wires all over the place.

'We're a bit fucked here, aren't we?' laughs Rob.

'I'll close it,' Kelly declares, tucking all the wires back inside and replacing the ignition, 'so they don't know we've done this.'

Rob says that he'll work out how they can steal some carts tomorrow night. Pompey gives him a severe stare.

'That's what I'm *supposed* to do!' Rob exclaims. 'I can't drink, I can't take drugs ... let's drive a golf cart into the lake! Do you know what I mean?'

* * *

Late on the night before his first show at Knebworth, Rob sits in his hotel room with Jonny and me. He and Jonny start chatting about the messy old days, like the night of Rob's grand bender in Newcastle. At seven o'clock in the morning the hotel woke David up and asked if he could come downstairs. 'I think Mr Williams is in need of some assistance,' they told him. Rob had gone down to the golf course in his pyjamas and slippers as the sun was coming up, and had stood there for a while, having sambuca shots brought to him three at a time.

'Hi, Dave,' he said when David arrived to find him on a bench. 'Are you alright?'

And then Rob sobbed his heart out. Eventually David led him up to his room, expecting that they would have some kind of soothing spiritual chat before Rob slipped away to sleep, but when Rob opened the door, he was surprised and delighted to discover there was a girl in his bed. He had completely forgotten that he had pulled. In one motion he shut the door on David and bounded under the sheets.

He offers one more tale of madness and excess before he goes to bed. He was in Jamaica, writing songs with Guy for what would become *I've Been Expecting You*, and on this night he was already pissed and Guy was already in bed, so he walked out of the compound they were staying in and wandered to the rough fisherman's bar down the road where it was really dark and crowded inside and the clientele were shouting *bo bo bo* over the manic staccato music.

'Anybody got any coke?' he asked.

'You want cocaine, rock star?' someone replied, and he was diverted to a man called Blacker. ('He was called Blacker,' Rob explains, 'because he was blacker than any of the rest of them. And he had this amazing physique. I don't know why that's part of the story.')

'What d'you want?' Blacker asked.

'Coke,' he said.

'What you got?' Blacker asked.

'I haven't got any money,' he explained, 'but I've got this traveller's cheque.'

Blacker got him to sign the $100 traveller's cheque and handed over some silver foil. ('They keep it in silver foil because they all work on jet skis and stuff,' Rob explains. 'I don't know why that's part of the story either.') He went back to his hut, chopped out a huge line and snorted it, and realised it was doing nothing whatsoever. Chalk. He was outraged. So he marched back to the fisherman's bar.

'Oi, Blacker!' he said. 'You sold me fucking chalk.'

Blacker took him outside, pulled out a machete and held it up against Rob's throat.

'And,' concludes Rob, 'I went: can I have some more, please? Signed another traveller's cheque for $100, took it, went back, knew it was chalk, and snorted the lot. *That's* drug logic.'

* * *

He says that he won't be able to get to sleep. Instead he opens up a packet of cards called Déjà Vu that fell out of a package sent by a fan, and spreads them face down over the white carpet. He lets his hand hover over them, shouting at Jonny to shut up so that he can concentrate. Jonny is reading a copy of the football magazine *4-4-2*. Rob asks the cards for guidance in love. The first he turns over reads: 'Wealth is on the horizon, bringing respite from your money worries ... ' The next two don't seem much more relevant.

He keeps dealing and turning over cards until he finds one that he believes applies; though, even now, only obliquely.

'You had a choice of 15 goes,' says Jonny. 'I just think all this is ... we're not proper psychics, you know.'

'I am,' says Rob.

'No, you're not, youth,' says Jonny. 'You think you are, but you're not.'

They start bickering.

'Youth, I am.'

'You're not, youth. You're really not.'

'I am.'

'Bless you for thinking you are ... but you're not.'

'I fucking am,' says Rob, firmly.

'You're not,' shouts Jonny.

'No, I am, youth,' insists Rob.

'Youth, you're not,' says Jonny. 'You're a singer. Songwriter.'

'I'm also psychic,' says Rob stubbornly. This has been a real row at some points, but now he's also just trying to wind Jonny up.

'I'm slightly worried,' says Jonny, 'because you think you're Mystic Meg now. You're not psychic ... '

'Alright, youth,' says Rob, brandishing the cards, 'how about this: will you and me know each other, be in each other's lives, in five years?'

'That's a *horrible* question,' objects Jonny. 'That's horrible. That's a horrible question.'

'Why are you bothered what the card would say?' asks Rob.

'Because you shouldn't question friendship,' says Jonny.

Rob picks up three cards. They don't seem to comment on the matter either way.

'I can't be psychic when I'm tired,' Rob says.

And they're off again.

'You're not psychic,' says Jonny.

'Fuck you, I am!' says Rob.

'You're not, you *dick*! You're not psychic.'

'You really mean that, don't you?' says Rob, amused.

'Yes. You are *not* psychic,' says Jonny. 'You're a lot of things, youth, but you're not psychic. What makes you think that you're psychic? Tell me.'

'I just know I am.'

'You're not. What have you ever done that's proved you're psychic?'

'I just know I am.' Smile. 'I'm the Son of God.'

That last bit was a joke. But I interject and ask him myself whether he really thinks he's psychic. He says, quite seriously, 'Yeah. Yeah. Really.'

'I think them drugs and alcohol have messed up your head,' says Jonny.

'There's a whole thing waiting to be tapped into and I just need to plug into it, that's all,' says Rob.

'You're not,' says Jonny. 'Next you'll be doing Scientology.'

'I can't believe that,' says Rob. 'That's so disrespectful.'

'What?' says Jonny.

'Telling me I'm not psychic.'

'You're not psychic.'

'Well, it's not disrespectful, really,' considers Rob. 'I'm just sad that you don't think I am.'

'It's alright, youth,' Jonny consoles him. 'You haven't *got* to be psychic. You're a lot more better things than that. You're *spiritual*, but you're not psychic. I believe all the spiritual things you do, big time, but you're not psychic.'

'It's very difficult to prove a positive,' says Rob. 'You can prove a negative.'

'Fate's the biggest thing,' says Jonny. 'I'm a great believer in fate. And karma.' Pause. 'But you're not psychic.'

'YOU ARE NOT PSYCHIC is a good T-shirt,' Rob says. 'It's a good album title. *You Are Not Psychic*. It's a good album title. Like *The Man Who Suddenly Fell Over* ... '

'Youth,' says Jonny seriously. 'Do you think you're psychic?'

'No,' he says.

'Seriously?' asks Jonny.

'Seriously, I don't,' says Rob.

'Be honest with me,' says Jonny.

'OK, I don't,' he says.

'Good,' says Jonny. 'I thought you'd gone a bit mad.'

Jonny looks up, catches Rob mouthing 'I am' to me, and hits him.

'Define the term "psychic",' says Rob.

'That person who can see other people's futures,' says Jonny.

'I don't want to see other people's futures,' says Rob.

'See your own future,' says Jonny.

'I don't want to see my future,' says Rob.

'So what kind of psychic do you think you are?' asks Jonny.

'I can move shit,' he says, joking. 'No, I think I'll be able to talk to the dead.'

'That's spiritual,' says Jonny.

'That's a psychic,' says Rob.

'Yeah, alright, but I'm looking at a full psychic,' says Jonny. 'A hundred per cent psychic. Where you're predicting the future.'

And then Rob simply changes the subject. 'Don't girls cry a lot?' he says.

Just after three in the morning, he announces that he is going to try and sleep. 'I've completely forgotten I'm doing a show tomorrow,' he says, 'and then every now and then it seeps through.'

'I'm really looking forward to it,' says Jonny.

Rob smiles grimly at him. 'I know you are,' he says.

16

By the time he awakes, around four in the afternoon, a helicopter with RW on its tail is already parked on the hotel putting green, not far from his bedroom window. He hears it arrive in his sleep, and wonders who on earth is flying around here in a helicopter. It takes him a while to realise that it's for him.

He eats cereal, milk dribbling from his chin, and says he's not sure if he's ill and he's not sure if he's bothered. Jonny tells Josie and David about last night's argument over Rob's lack or otherwise of psychic ability.

'He had a real go at me,' Rob complains.

'He starts saying, "I'm psychic",' says Jonny, defending himself.

'I didn't say I was psychic,' argues Rob, 'up until you said, "You're not psychic, you know," and then I said, "I fucking am."'

'He's not psychic,' says Jonny.

'I'm not having this discussion with you,' says Rob. 'I think it's rude.'

* * *

We have been told that traffic is at a standstill for 40 miles around Knebworth, but when the helicopter first takes off, there is a little evidence of this. Rob gestures to the golf course below, on which the golfers are enjoying a typical summer Friday stroll. 'I've brought the golf course to a *standstill*,' says Rob. He points to an empty field. 'I've brought that field to a standstill. I've brought those cows to a standstill.'

Then the site appears – a mind-bendingly huge city spread beneath us.

'Oh my God,' says Josie.

Jonny hits Rob's knee. 'Oh, Jesus,' he exclaims.

Rob doesn't say anything for some time, and whatever wonder and delight he feels for what he is seeing is buried beneath more troubling emotions.

'It's alright for you,' he says to the rest of us in the cabin. 'You haven't got to get up in front of the fuckers.'

* * *

In his dressing room he opens the fan mail waiting on the sofa. Two women have written because they'll now be arriving later than they hoped to on Sunday and wonder if he could save them a good car parking space.

Chris Briggs arrives. Rob has kept very quiet about the Pure Francis songs until now, but today he wanted Chris to hear them for the first time. Rob sits him on the dressing room sofa and chooses, song by song from his computer, what he wants him to hear: 'Misunderstood', 'Everyone Needs It', 'Boom Boom', 'The Trouble With Me'. By the second tune, Chris Briggs is beaming, quite obviously very happy and slightly surprised at what has suddenly been achieved.

'The melodies,' he says. 'Fuck me. It's unbelievable ... you've done very, very well.'

With excitement, Rob starts describing all the ways they've written songs: 'He's very trusting and non-judgemental and very patient and he'll go, "Get on the keyboard" ... and I've been writing the guitar melodies for different things ... it's like my first solo album.'

Chris nods. 'From listening to a Lilac Time record and listening to a Robbie Williams record,' he observes quite reasonably, 'I wouldn't have expected this.' He asks how many songs there are.

'Twelve,' says Rob. 'Seven days.'

'Where were they?' asks Chris with bewilderment.

This distraction aside, Rob is feeling scared and queasy. There has been a concerted effort from everyone involved to act like Knebworth is just another date on the tour. No big deal at all. Care has been taken to make sure that his before-show schedule, apart from the helicopter here, is exactly the same as on any date on the tour: to relax and listen to music (most nights it's been his own new music), watch TV, have a massage, eat the same meal every show day (tuna or steak, potato, baked beans), run on the treadmill to get revved up, limbers up (today in his dressing room doorway), change into his stage clothes while listening to some old favourites pumped out from his computer.

But Knebworth isn't just another date, and he knows it. 'I think with these three gigs the pressure's really on for me just to get through them,' he says. 'Because you know all these gigs are being filmed and stuff. And, you know, there's a possibility that after Knebworth I might not be able to do that sort of thing ever again. There's a possibility, you know. So this is going to be like that piece of film that you associate Robbie Williams with. You know, like when you see Freddie Mercury you associate him in Wembley Stadium doing that, or when you see Bob Marley you see him with his three backing dancers at that gig ... this is going to be that gig that you associate me with.'

* * *

Aside from a glimpse as the helicopter descended hours earlier, his first view of the Knebworth crowd is upside down, a sky of screaming faces and dangling arms above his horizon. Once he has righted himself, he appears awestruck. It's a remarkable sight. The field that had seemed manageably small when it was empty now seems to go on forever. When everyone in the audience puts their hands over their heads to clap out the rhythm of 'We Will Rock You', each hears the sound from the stage a tiny fraction later than the person in front of them, so their hands come together the same fraction of a second later. From the stage, each collective handclap looks like a perfectly formed ripple sweeping away into the distance. It's a wonderful thing.

'Knebworth, for the first time in my life I'm speechless,' he tells them the first time he takes a breath, and it feels less like stagecraft than a reflection of what he is feeling. As ever, he immediately welcomes them into his world where humble, grandiose and arrogant happily co-exist in the same sentence. 'I really hope I can do a show tonight that will make you all proud,' he says. 'Because so far you've been better than me. It's going to take me a couple of numbers, because when I saw you lot tonight, I've never seen anything like this in my life. Ever. And after these three nights I don't think Britain will see anything like it for a long time to come either.'

It is also a world, of course, where at the biggest concert of his career he may loftily express grand emotions and ideas, or he may just talk about the local tradesmen. 'I'd like to take this opportunity to apologise to Trussells the butchers in the High Street of Knebworth for the inconvenience that I've caused to their sales of pork chops this weekend,' he says. 'It's *very* important. And just a bit of advice for Mr Trussell of High Street, Knebworth – why don't you stand outside and serve hot dogs to the lovely people that have come to my show this evening. Uh? It's not about losing, it's about *new thinking*, isn't it? Ahhh … .'

By this time, he has hit his stride. He works his way through many of the tricks he has used on the tour, and a few new ones. At the end of a particularly focused and impassioned 'No Regrets', something unusual happens. The intensity of the crowd's roar seems to halt him for a moment, and his halting only intensifies the crowd's roaring. He lowers his head, standing still, either to prolong the moment or to gather himself, and the cheering just builds and builds. He looks up, his expression suggesting that he is bewildered and on the verge of tears. It gets louder still. Eventually, he speaks.

'You know, during tonight's show, every now and then I get quite used to it,' he says, 'and, you know, I've got my confidence with me and I can see you all and it's beautiful and I'm enjoying myself … and then I just look at you lot, and I look all the way over to the back … and I don't know what I've done.'

* * *

From the stage he goes straight into a waiting jeep that takes him the few hundred yards to the waiting helicopter. We are in the air before the crowd is even sure it is all over, and we are back in his hotel room before 11 o'clock.

'Did you enjoy that?' asks David, uncertainly.

'Yeah, of course I did,' he says. 'I'm just really chilled.'

It was, he explains, fun once he got used to it, but he only allowed himself to enjoy it a certain amount because inside he knew he had to save some of himself for the next two nights. 'My body put its own cap on itself,' he says.

He runs a bath with the door open, singing Take That's 'Babe' to himself. '*Then a voice I once knew* ... ARGHHHH!'

More cold water needed.

* * *

He sits out on the hotel patio in the dark with Jonny and Jonny's friends, Brian and Julie. They mention their son's difficulties sleeping, and how scared he is.

'I was like that when I was growing up,' says Rob. 'It's self-perpetuating, though. It may just be a fear of fear. He's got a creative mind as well. I mean, even now at 29 my mind goes all over the place and if I don't put tabs on it and go: "You're being creative and daft ..." Which is nearly impossible to do. For an 11-year-old it's more difficult.'

He muses about whether it relates to knockbacks suffered earlier in that particular day. 'When I was a kid,' he says, 'you wouldn't be able to tell that I'd be absolutely fucking gutted. I wouldn't show it to my dad for fear of letting my dad down. And that's just, your kid wants to do really good for you. When I used to play football as a kid I used to have *crippling* insecurity. I didn't want the ball to come to me. You know, I wanted to be amongst the lads and everything, but, yeah, fear of failure. People'd pass the ball to me and I wouldn't want it. It used to do my fucking head in. It was horrible. And I only recently got rid of it. Really. Honestly. 27.'

Julie says that if Brian wasn't at home and her parents weren't around, she'd check into a hotel. 'Isn't that silly?' she says.

'No,' says Rob. 'It's not silly. I'm completely that. I haven't slept one night alone for the last three or four years. No, I haven't slept one night alone ... ever. Since I was a kid.' Without someone nearby. 'I stay up because ... I think I stay up now more because there's a sense of *calm* when everyone's gone to sleep. There's a sense of calm. And also, when I'm awake I don't want to go to sleep. And also, to let you in really deeply, I don't want the hassle of turning the light off, putting my head down and then all the thoughts. I don't want all those thoughts. If I'm going to be up ... thoughts feed on thoughts feed on thoughts feed on thoughts feed on thoughts and I'm: "I don't want this." And literally I have to knock myself out to go to sleep.'

He says that he wishes he could go to bed early and get up early. If he was with someone, he thinks he could do it. 'I'm like, get me a wife now, because I want to go to bed early,' he says.

I suggest to him that when he meets a potential wife he maybe shouldn't go too big on *I really want to marry you because I want to go to sleep early*.

'Yeah,' he concedes. 'But I tell you what happens with me. I feel like the day goes too quick if I get up early. Because like from seven to 12 doesn't really count. I think there's also a bit of, when I had my first flat when I moved away from my mum there was this massive Barn Cake of Mr Kipling's that I used to get, and I used to think, I can fucking eat all of that. So I did. And then I used to get another one. And the sleeping thing has got to be a bit naughty. "Oooh, it's four in the morning." It's the most rock'n'roll thing I get up to these days.'

Rob goes and pisses in the hedge. While he's there he gets a weird feeling, like there's someone in the undergrowth, listening. He sends Gary to have a search around, but nothing and no one is found.

* * *

Max joins us and people start sharing embarrassing tales.

'Do the spitting one,' suggests Max to Rob, 'or is that too rude?'

'No,' he says. 'So, I was a little inexperienced in bed … '

He was in his late teens, and his girlfriend invited him round. He was going down on her.

'Spit on me,' she suggested.

And he didn't know.

So – and he acts it out – he stood up and spat on her face.

'Obviously another lovely story for Parky,' he comments as the laughter slowly dies.

* * *

As the helicopter lands for his second Knebworth show the next day, he spots a lake behind the backstage area, and resolves to go and find it. He's annoyed that the papers are only concerned with how much money he is earning (*The Sun*) and in digging up his past problems (*Daily Mail*) and seem oblivious to what is being achieved this weekend, and he's anyway finding everything too much. Searching for the lakeside, he passes Justin from The Darkness, who are playing at the bottom of the bill.

'It's saying we're friends in the papers,' says Justin, 'so it's wonderful to finally meet you – we've been so close.'

They quickly have their photo taken together at Justin's urging. Rob assumes that it is for Justin, but it is for *Word* magazine.

We can't get to the lake – the same fencing that protects the concert site prevents such expeditions – so Rob, Jonny and I sit down in the middle of a small copse, next to a small, stagnant pond.

'Do you remember when we went to Las Vegas and we were going to run off to Mexico?' says Jonny.

'I was going to go to the bank, get a couple of grand of cash out and then fuck off to Mexico,' says Rob. 'Without telling anyone.'

'Just me and him,' says Jonny.

'And then just keep on moving on cash,' says Rob.

Have you got a cash card?

Pause.

'I think so,' Rob says.

Do you know its number?

Pause.

'No,' he says. 'I'd got my passport and my card – I could go into a bank.'

How seriously did you think about it?

'Quite seriously. I just wanted to get away.'

What would you have done in Mexico?

'I don't know. It'd have been a bit of an adventure. It'd have been naughty.'

Who would you have been running away from?

'No one,' he says. 'It would have just been naughty. And everybody would have had to find us.'

'We would have got a bollocking,' says Jonny. 'The night before we went, how are we going to do it? We were going to get up at four or five in the morning when everybody's asleep … '

' … and get on the train,' says Rob.

Why didn't you do it?

Pause.

'Couldn't be arsed, could we?' says Rob.

* * *

In his dressing room he listens to music, watches the TV and stews in his own anxiety. His mother asks him, as though it was the most incidental favour, whether he could dedicate 'Nan's Song' to some kids she knows in Stoke who are going through a hard time. He doesn't answer. I don't think he can believe he is being asked this. She says she'll mention it to Josie.

'Mum,' he finally says. 'I'm a bit stressed.'

He cheers up with the arrival of his cousin Richard and associated family and friends from Stoke. They all go to catering, where he asks for a smaller portion than usual of his tuna, baked beans and potato, and mashes it all together with a fork, as a kid might. He and the Stoke contingent reminisce about old friends. Some have fallen by the wayside. One name comes up and Rob talks about being at a party with him; the friend necked 30 Es in two hours. Later he found Rob upstairs. 'Have you seen Rob?' he asked Rob. 'He's downstairs,' Rob told him. 'Cheers, mate,' his friend said, and that was the last time Rob ever saw him.

He tries to persuade the Stoke contingent to come back to the hotel for tonight's school disco after the concert, and after some demurring – Richard has an important golf engagement tomorrow – they agree. 'Please come,' Rob emphasises.

Tonight's show is to be broadcast as live on Channel 4. (In truth, they broadcast it with an unadvertised time lag, which allows them to run adverts and edit the occasional piece of between-song speech. Trussells the butchers will be castigated again, for instance, but the TV audience will never know it.) Still, towards the end of the show, there is a certain amount of panic backstage. Perhaps because he's a little on edge, Rob is racing through the set, and the show is going to under-run its contracted TV slot. A plan is hatched. As he changes for the encores in a cubby-hole directly beneath the middle of the stage, Rob is asked by Lee if he will consent to adding 'Millennium', which has made intermittent appearances over the past month, to the encores. Lee explains the situation. 'Can we put it in?' he asks.

'To tell you the truth,' says Rob, 'no.' He explains why. 'I lost my balls,' he says. 'Lost my bollocks.'

'It's looking great, honestly,' Lee tells him.

'Yeah, I know, I know,' he says, 'but I'm suffering. I just lost my balls. I've been shitting it since "Monkey".'

'Well,' says David, 'then you've been … '

' … acting like somebody that's … ' says Rob, and doesn't need to finish the sentence. *Acting like somebody that doesn't feel the way he feels*. The twin, contradictory gifts of this kind required by great entertainers are the ability to show the way you feel and the ability to hide the way you feel – a Robbie Williams show is a masterful, perilous, unpredictable juggling of the two.

'On camera it's looking great, mate,' Lee further reassures him.

'Yeah, no, I'm sure,' he says. 'I'm just so scared.'

'I thought you were loving it,' says Jonny.

'It's one of your best gigs,' says Josie.

'Not a fucking clue, mate,' admits David.

I say that I also had no idea.

'Good,' he says, and asks for a Gatorade. 'I think it's probably the live telly thing. And there's 125,000 people there. I'm alright, but it's not comfortable. But don't worry. I'll go out and act my bollocks off.'

He lies face down on the trolley that will carry him down the tunnel to the end of the thrust, where he will suddenly rise up and appear amongst the dancers in "Rock DJ". As he is pulled into the darkness, he flaps his legs up and down at the knees, his feet held together, like a beached fish.

* * *

'That,' says Rob, as he takes his seat in the helicopter, 'was will over want. What I wanted was to disappear with the piano after "Bojangles".'

Because of the TV broadcast's time lag and the speed of the helicopter, when he walks into the hotel Rob is greeted by the extraordinary sight of himself performing live on the television. He is in the deserted lounge of a country hotel but, as far as British TV watchers are concerned, he is, right now, on stage in front of 125,000 adoring fans at Knebworth, singing 'Kids'.

'I don't want to watch it,' he says, but he doesn't move. He watches the rap in 'Kids', then goes up to his room and changes while Josie tells him about an awful misunderstanding backstage during the encores. Gareth Gates was told by his security, who had heard something on their headsets, which they had misinterpreted, that he was expected on stage – something that had never been discussed or considered – and Josie had to stand there explaining that this wasn't the case to a polite and apologetic Gates while the security guard kept trying to overrule both of them. 'It was so embarrassing,' she says.

'Bless him,' says Rob. 'He's a handsome lad, isn't he?'

Rob decides he'll watch the acoustic section on the TV in his room.

'I am getting older,' says the Rob on TV to the crowd, 'and I want you to get old with me.' David applauds the screen. The camera pans over the crowd up to the Knebworth stately home. 'Wow,' says the Rob in the hotel room. 'That looks amazing. Wow.' He grins and turns to Jonny. 'You know we were thinking of going to Mexico, youth … ?'

The Rob on TV says that he is 'the happiest man on the planet'.

The Rob in the hotel room nods.

'Didn't say *which* planet,' he says.

* * *

Tonight there is a school disco in some of the hotel function rooms and a specially erected marquee. There are pea-shooters for all those who care to use them, the food is traditional school canteen fare and Rob is dressed in his old school uniform. He takes Jack Osbourne into a quiet corner for a chat, by the look of it offering some solidarity and encouragement, and meets Gareth Gates for the first time. When the Stoke contingent leave, he goes out into the drive to see them off. He seems more moved by the time he's spent with them today than almost anything else, as though they offer a chance to reconnect to something he mislaid. He says to me, wistfully, about Richard, 'He's like me before drugs.'

Back inside, he hits the dance floor and whirls around to 'No Diggity' with Jonny and Kelly Osbourne, a St Trinians video playing in the background.

A while later, I wander past Sharon Osbourne in the doorway telling her daughter that she needs to dress up properly when she goes onstage, and find Rob and Jonny sitting outside in the dark, away from the party, chatting. High in the dark above the makeshift helipad, we see a shooting star.

* * *

When he wakes, he peers carefully through the curtains without revealing himself. There is a woman standing on the grass outside, staring up at his windows, waiting for a sight of him. She doesn't move. 'She looks like she's just grown from the soil,' he notes.

A while later, a larger crowd has gathered down there and he opens the window and chats for a while, telling them about last night's show and how scary it all was. 'Listen, have a great day,' he concludes, and they all applaud.

'You're a man of the people,' Josie tells Rob, slightly teasing.

'Yeah,' Jonny agrees. 'Now let's piss off in your chopper.'

* * *

'How are you feeling today, Mr Williams?' asks the helicopter pilot over the intercom.

'Stiff but excited,' Rob says. Pause. 'But not excited and stiff. You know what I mean.'

'I do,' confirms the pilot.

Rob starts singing David Essex's 'Hold Me Close' and looks down at the golf course below us. 'I've got to develop a Dean Martin-esque lifestyle,' he announces.

'Did Dino play golf?' asks Jonny hopefully.

'*Every* day,' says Rob. 'Every day. And he never rehearsed. And he went in, one take, bye!, and then fucked off and got on the golf course. And that's what I'm going to do.'

Dean Martin is the one of the rat pack he has always admired, and related to, the most. After *Swing When You're Winning* came out, he was thrilled to receive a letter from Sammy Cahn's wife, Tita, saying that she and Dean Martin's widow Jeanne had listened to it together and loved it. 'Frank's got the best voice, he's got the most *amazing* voice,' he judges. 'Dean is more relaxed. He was more laidback. He made it look easy. I think to him it was easy. And he was the funniest. I love Sinatra, but I *adore* Dean Martin.'

* * *

'I think I'll check myself into a mental ward by next Tuesday,' he tells Mark Owen backstage. 'The whole tour's been great and at times a stroll in the park. I've got here and I'm all kind of ... broken biscuits.'

'I'm shitting my pants,' says Mark. He leans forward to Rob. 'Does it go when you're up there?'

'No,' says Rob.

They rehearse for the first and only time sitting on the plastic chairs on the grass outside Rob's dressing room. Mark Plati strums an acoustic guitar, which they try to hear above Moby's set, and they sing a little of 'Back For Good' together for the first time since Rob left Take That. Rob sings the first verse, Mark sings the second, they sing the middle eight together – suddenly rather moving, as you watch them comfortably, unconsciously slip back into old habits and old roles – and Rob says that Mark can do what he wants in the chorus.

That is the full rehearsal.

'I did my harmony,' Rob realises. 'And it just came, like a natural reaction. How weird's that?'

'Once there was another Take That boy in the room,' Mark laughs, 'you just couldn't help going back into the old harmony.'

Wayne Rooney comes backstage to say hello. (Rob has been quietly thrilled for weeks that Wayne Rooney was coming; he is the only other person they have allowed to use their makeshift helipad.) They share a little small talk and Rob is given two signed ROONEY shirts. He thinks for a second. 'Let me go and get you something,' he says, and disappears into his dressing room, but he can't find anything suitable. He brings out a pillow. 'I've got you a pillow,' he says.

* * *

Mark Owen rises up from the hole in the stage used for Max's piano at the beginning of the second verse of 'Back For Good'. There's a wonderful joy in the way they pogo together in the chorus, then sing-speak the middle eight lines at each other, and there's an amazing roar from the crowd throughout.

'They didn't get *that* last night,' Rob shouts at its end. 'The memory of

TT lives on.'

In the acoustic section he starts strumming some chords, but he doesn't sing any of the accompanying words and I'm not sure that many people in the audience understand the significance of his next comment.

'Well, that's the only way they'll hear it on the third night, isn't it?' he says.

He was playing Oasis's 'Wonderwall'; another low-key salvo in the cold war that never ends.

* * *

Before 'Angels' he repeats what he said last night but expands upon it. 'I'm getting older,' he says. 'I want you to come with me. You've watched me grow up, I want to get old with you lot.'

And then, just as the song begins, he says one more line, perhaps the most unexpected he has said all weekend. Maybe he is just trying to milk the emotion of the moment and pushes it a bit far, or maybe its quietly desperate, insecure plea is more honest than he means it to be.

'Please, please, don't leave me,' he asks everyone.

* * *

As the helicopter rises over the crowd, Rob waves for the waving's sake.

'They're never going to see you,' Jonny says.

'I'm waving anyway,' he says. 'Waving indiscriminately. It's like a Cup Final, you know.'

We fly away.

'I'm going to stay up all night,' Rob announces.

'Oh, don't,' sighs Jonny. 'Why? To do what?'

'Because I do every night,' says Rob. 'You don't have to stay up.'

Pause.

Rob grins.

'But you'll miss out,' he says.

* * *

After the show, as ever, the hotel buffet. He sits with Mark Owen for a while, and soon they are discussing the excellence of Agas, until Rob pulls himself up for talking nonsense. 'Me talking Agas,' he scoffs. 'I don't even know where the knives are in my house.'

They take the conversation outside, and laugh about some pranks they played in Take That. When it goes quiet for a moment Rob says, 'Come on, come on – more stuff, more stuff. Can you remember everything? Can you remember how everything *felt*?'

Mark smiles.

'Do you remember the Isle of Wight?' Rob asks. He tells a long, involved tale of trying to get together with a girl at a B&B, which includes Nigel Martin-Smith granting then revoking permission for the tryst, Mark hiding in a cupboard, Rob gouging his leg climbing through a window, plenty of fear and panic, and no sex.

As they piece together more stories from those days, the most remarkable thing is how few of them they share in common. Rob spent five years of his life in Take That, but this is pretty much the first time since then that he has compared notes. The five of them left with their own shattered pieces of what they had been through and have never glued them together; after living through it, they never chatted their way into a shared common history. But the memories are in there somewhere, and tonight they start to roll out.

'Remember when Kurt Cobain died and we sat on the roof in Denmark?' says Mark.

'Yeah,' says Rob.

'Remember that?' says Mark. 'The day he died. I always remember that, whenever that's mentioned. I always remember me and you went and sat on the roof.'

'Yeah,' says Rob.

'Was it your birthday when you got your scar?' says Mark. 'Do you remember your scar? It was Howard's birthday. And we were pulling the plants over for his present, we kept giving him more plants as his birthday presents … '

'And Howard pushed me into the pool,' says Rob. 'Well, he didn't push me – he just knocked me and I just went straight in and bumped my head … '

' … and got your scar … ' says Mark.

'Then I went and got the stitches … ' says Rob.

' … we were all laughing,' says Mark.

' … then we went back out, all blood pouring down here,' says Rob.

They reminisce about the outfits and the different stage shows.

'There was one time we came up and we had those tin hats on,' says Rob.

'That's what I'm talking about,' says Mark. 'The tin hats and the glasses.'

'There was one night, though, that we came up and I was so tired,' says Rob, 'it was tired logic. We had to cramp down, didn't we, and I just thought, I'll have a little kip. And the band had started and everything but I was that knackered that in my mind I went, I'll just have a little kip before we go through this. We're in position to come through the stage. Just have a little kip. Ahhh … fell asleep. The riser comes and I go … ' He acts himself being startled, and jerking awake. 'It was horrible. I didn't know where I was and then all of a sudden there was like loads of screaming … '

'Oh dear,' Mark laughs.

'Can you remember your favourite bits in the show?' asks Rob.

'I liked that tour when we did "Pray" in the black coats,' says Mark. 'Can you remember when we did it in rehearsal once and we had nothing on underneath … ? And we got to the bit and we all dropped our coats and we're all naked. And Nigel was like that … ' He does a furious, exasperated sigh.

'I think the bits I enjoyed were the ballads,' says Rob. 'Sitting down.'

They talk about old acquaintances, about whom Mark is invariably generous.

'The Tao of Owen,' says Rob.

'What's that?' asks Mark a little suspiciously.

Rob explains it. 'Loads of things on this tour have just been The Tao of Owen. *It doesn't matter*. It really made me think. It *really* made me think. Because you can spend a lot of time just digging up people and going: don't like them because x y z and z and z … what do you think? Don't like 'em, don't like 'em. And then you go, it don't matter. The Tao of Owen.'

'I like that,' says Mark.

'There was this one time that I went "Fuck off!" to Nigel,' says Rob. 'Can you remember?'

'Yes!' says Mark. 'Yes!'

'But this is what happened,' says Rob. 'We were in the van and we were all giggly giggly and Nigel said something and I went "Fuck off!" and the van went … ' Complete silence. 'And I went, *huuu* …' He couldn't believe he'd said it. 'And Gaz went … ' – he seems surprised to himself for a second to have called him Gaz, but this was when Gary Barlow was Gaz and Rob is about to express gratitude to him – ' … and Gary got me out of it. He went, "Well, Nige, Rob's developed a sense of humour since you've been away …" And he got me out of it.'

Rob goes and pees into the hedge.

'Mark, can you remember … ?' he shouts back to the table.

'Don't say the wanking on the tour bus,' warns Mark.

'Oh, I'd forgotten that,' says Rob. 'I won.' Pause. 'And sort of lost at the same time.'

* * *

Mark asks if Rob remembers meeting Princess Diana.

'That was a good night, wasn't it?' says Rob. 'How lovely was she? We went round Di's. She was really nice. Did you go home thinking, "She fancied me"?'

'She was a bit tall for me,' says Mark. 'Too tall.'

'She was great,' says Rob.

'She was lovely,' says Mark.

Did you think she fancied you a bit, I ask?

'No, not really,' says Rob. 'I'd have thought she fancied J.'

Jason.

'Yeah, it was always like that, wasn't it?' says Mark.

* * *

Mark has a question.

'What would you do if you saw Nigel?' Mark asks Rob.

Pause.

'Am I allowed to ask that?' says Mark.

'Yeah,' says Rob, and considers for a second. 'I'd probably cry.'

'Would you?' says Mark.

'I'd probably really break down,' says Rob.

Mark and Jonathan saw him a couple of years back at his club in Manchester.

'It's his club and he plays you all the time,' says Mark.

'He's a changed man,' says Jonathan. 'Honestly.'

'I think he is,' says Mark. 'I think he is a different man.'

'How does he look these days?' asks Rob.

'He can't look at you,' says Jonathan. 'He talks away … '

'The thing is about Nigel as well,' says Rob, 'is that I just wanted him to love me. Because as much as I hated him, I loved him as much as well. Which was really weird. I just wanted … '

'You wanted to be accepted, didn't you?' says Mark. 'That was all it was. It was about being accepted.'

They say that he has a funeral company as well.

'Well,' sighs Rob, 'there'll always be people dying.'

* * *

'It was mad,' says Mark. 'It was … '

'It was what it was,' says Rob.

' … what it was, yeah,' says Mark. 'And, I mean, I look back on it now, there's so many things … I don't know how I … '

There's obviously something important that he wants to say.

'I don't know how I should have kind of dealt with it, but I didn't even ever … I didn't even actually … ' Mark hesitates. 'I don't ever remember saying, "Are you alright?"' he says.

It's a very heavy, sweet, sad moment.

'Yeah, but because you couldn't, because … ' says Rob.

'Why?' says Mark. 'Why couldn't I? I don't remember why I couldn't … '

'Because everybody at that time … ' begins Rob. 'It wasn't anybody's fault.'

'Was everybody just scared or … ?' asks Mark.

'Everybody was just scared shitless … ' says Rob.

'Yeah?' says Mark.

' … because, you know, it's like, I was past the point of no return,' says Rob. 'I couldn't have got through that tour at all. I was *fucked* … '

'No, but I said it on your show the other day,' says Mark. 'Looking back now, we were all going home, and you were going to a hotel … '

'Yeah,' says Rob.

' … and how fucking ridiculous is that?' says Mark. 'Why were you left on your own in a hotel? I don't know.'

'It was at that point in the band, I think, where I think we'd all become so *scared* about … there was not a lot of communication,' says Rob. 'And I never said what I was really thinking anyway, because what I was really thinking would have just *destroyed* everything. It was nobody's fault, at all. Everybody had to look after themselves, cause that's … you know, when there's a situation where somebody's doing divide and conquer … '

'Was it just water boiling and boiling and eventually it has to … ?' asks Mark.

'You know, Nigel did do divide and conquer – say a bit over here, say that little bit over there,' says Rob.

'Yeah, we all saw that,' says Mark.

'And I think that puts everyone on the back foot and makes everybody retreat like that,' says Rob. 'It was no one's fault. There was nothing anybody could do.'

'What had to be … ?' wonders Mark.

'I was going … somewhere loony.' Rob chuckles. 'People deal with it in different ways.'

'Yeah, but I'm not just talking about where you were going,' says Mark, 'I'm talking about the whole thing, the fact that we were together for a long time … the first couple of years we were really quite close. Me and you, especially. But the last couple of years, I don't … it just became a bit mad, didn't it? It just became mad.'

'Because, it's like, there was no after-care,' says Rob.

'Yeah, that was it,' says Mark.

'But, at the same time, nobody knew how to do it,' says Rob. 'Nigel didn't. And home life was weird, and you get a weird perception of the world. And then there's a hundred fucking girls outside your house, you know. And all of that stuff mixed with the insane promotion that we did. Because we worked our fucking bollocks off. All of that mixed together ... we were tired and scared. *I* was tired and scared ... '

'That's it,' says Mark.

* * *

'That was nice, wasn't it?' says Rob, back in his room, preparing for bed.

'I think at one point Mark really wanted to get deep,' says Jonny.

Rob nods. 'I wasn't ready for the ... ' he says. 'I could have ended up crying then. I didn't want to go there. It's like, I'm emotional as it is, the last three days. I just didn't want to go there. But nothing was his fault.'

17

It takes 12 minutes to fly back to London by helicopter on the Monday after the three Knebworth concerts, on a flight path that takes us over Buckingham Palace and Rob's flat. We can see the chairs on his balcony as we pass.

In the waiting car he finds *The Sun*. HE'S THE ONE – ROBBIE'S KING OF POP, FANS INSIST is the headline, and the *Sun*'s main pop writer refers to the concert as 'without any doubt the best live show I've ever seen'.

Almost as soon as he gets home, after a few minutes of restlessly sitting about, he calls Stephen Duffy and asks whether he can come over to the studio. Off we go. At some traffic lights he buys an *Evening Standard* with his photo on the front page. ROBBIE – THE BEST EVER? is their headline. *Star weeps after singing to 375,000.*

He reads aloud some of the article – '*He seemed desperate for adulation yet unsure whether he was deserving of it. He is unable to reconcile his certainty that he's a failure with the evidence in front of his eyes*' – and laughs. I ask him what he makes of their analysis of his psyche.

'I'm a showman,' he says, dismissively. 'And as far as " ... *that he's a failure with the evidence in front of his eyes* ...", that was two years ago. I know my worth now.'

And the 'desperate for adulation yet unsure whether he was deserving of it'? That's part of the show now, isn't it?

'Yeah,' he says.

There's another passage of analysis that draws the eye: *Just as Oasis were never the same after their weekend here, so complacency looks inevitable for Robbie after he has pulled off a stunt as huge as this …*

Complacency looks inevitable. That seems pretty funny to Rob when, the day after these three concerts, he is already on his way to the recording studio and will, before he goes to bed tonight, have stacked away yet another song for his future.

* * *

He has been in the studio about half an hour when the phone rings. Stephen answers. George Michael is working in the studio downstairs and wants to come up for a chat. A few minutes later there is a knock on the door and George Michael comes in carrying a Starbucks cup. (It is the Starbucks cup that first gets Rob's attention. He had no idea there was a Starbucks nearby. He asks for directions and sends Pompey out immediately for supplies. A mocha frappuccino for George Michael, coconut for Rob.)

George Michael sits on Andy's chair and turns it so that he faces Rob and Stephen and me. He tells Rob about his new album, and how hard he always finds it to write. 'You've had an entire career since my last album, haven't you?' he laughs.

'I think with me putting out so many albums one after another one after another,' Rob explains, 'is because I always go, I think this is the one. And then it comes out and I go, no, it isn't … it's not that one. Quick! Let's do another … And now what we're doing here sounds like my first solo album.'

'You must have loved this weekend, right?' says George.

'Yeah,' replies Rob, but without any gusto. 'I don't think I will until about a year's time. Right now I'm just a bit: "We're going to take your personality and everything out of you for a while and just put it over here, and then you can have it back next weekend after you've finished Ireland." I'm just a bit washed out.'

He asks George why he doesn't tour.

'Because I can't bear it,' George says. He doesn't like the sycophancy; being surrounded by people whose day depends on him; the worrying about his voice. He says that even back in Wham!, while everybody else went out and had a great time, he sat in his hotel room with his humidifier, eating lemons.

'Do you know how I get through being self-critical?' says Rob. 'Never listen to it, ever. If I listen to it, perhaps my deepest, darkest fears will be proved right, and then I wouldn't get onstage again.'

They compare notes about fame. 'It gets weirder,' George promises him. 'The longer you've been on the front of papers and on the telly and in people's lives. You're at about ten years now. Once it gets to 20 years it gets really weird.' The way he describes it, it evolves so that over time people become more shocked rather than excited to see you, and he has found that difficult. He says it must be different for Rob because he is half an old-fashioned star, presenting himself as special, but he also gives people the idea that he is winking and being self-deprecating, and that must make him much more approachable.

'I'm going to go all left field and weird,' Rob laughs. George Michael asks about Rob's new music and Rob mentions Scott Walker and David Bowie, and says that at moments he's singing like Morrissey and Neil Young. The two of them then enthuse about The Smiths for a while, and discuss the fascinating conundrum of Morrissey. (His next album comes up and I mention that it is said to be called *Irish Blood, English Heart*. There is no indication at the time that Rob has even taken this in.)

'You're at the stage where you could take as long as you like on an album,' George advises Rob. 'I mean, what's going to happen? Who's going to come up and bite you on the arse?'

'I've got a record contract I want to get through,' Rob tells him.

'Oh, you should never do that,' George advises. 'Make 'em wait.'

'This album,' Rob tells him, 'I've enjoyed the promotion, I've enjoyed the touring, I've enjoyed everything about it.'

'And what was the difference?' George asks him.

'Effexor,' he says.

'So do you think you were always depressed before?' George asks.

'*Absolutely*,' says Rob.

'Just always kind of mild chronic depression?' asks George.

'Yeah,' says Rob. 'Not actually "take a gun and shoot your brains out" but could see it from there. Do you know what I mean?' He explains how, when he moved to Los Angeles, he thought he'd escaped all the specific things that caused this but realised he still didn't feel right. 'Everything I thought I was depressed about wasn't really there,' he says. 'And you go, well, what is it then? I'd run out of things to blame. I'd stopped drinking and doing drugs and I battled with not taking them for a good 13, 14 months until I got to the point where I felt worse than I did when I was doing drugs. And I thought, well, this is it – it's either do drugs again or I go and see a shrink and get him to give me some tablets. And I did, and ever since then it's been really cool.' He smiles. 'Socially, still a bit shit.'

Afterwards, he reflects on the friendly but distant and slightly odd relationship George Michael and he have had on their different trajectories. It was George Michael who chided him when Rob, in a deliberate embracing of the conventional wisdom at the end of Take That that Gary Barlow was to be the new George Michael, announced that he was actually going to be the new Andrew Ridgeley. 'Don't take the piss out of Andrew,' rebuked George. As Rob's success grew, George Michael would sometimes call Rob before awards shows to tell him that he'd won. 'It always started off with, "Well done, you bitch",' says Rob. 'And I couldn't understand why he did it because I didn't even know I was going to an awards show that day.'

* * *

Three weeks ago, *Escapology* finally fell out of the Top 75 in the British album charts. Since then, driven by the success of Rob's current single 'Something Beautiful' and the Knebworth build-up, it has rallied slightly, but no one had quite anticipated what 375,000 people at a concert over one weekend, and live broadcasts on both TV and radio, might do. By Tuesday, it is already clear.

Rob phones me, quite chuffed, with the news. In next week's chart *Escapology* will be at number one. Not only that, but for much of the week there seems some possibility that every one of his albums will re-enter the Top 75. (In the end, a couple will fall just short.)

* * *

By Wednesday, he is back in the studio. He is making up words for a song, written around a bass line he has just come up with and played.

... white 74 ... white 74 ... when she waited, they said 'What for?' ... you want some more ... white 74 ... into Dusty, into fame ... into working your silly games ... Friday's your payday ... white 74 ... talking on the phone ... sleeping all day ... getting it wrong ... the way it should be done ... white 74 ... white 74 ... ice cream in sand dunes ... magnifying ants ... white 74 ...

'I've got to do some music that suits my tattoos,' he announces.

He picks up the 1986 *Smash Hits Yearbook* that Stephen has brought in. Amused, he reads out a quote from Simon le Bon: 'I don't love myself to death. I just don't think I've got any bad points.' He sighs. 'Pop stars were so much more interesting,' he says. He reads more. (Along the way he discovers that he shares a birthday with Peter Hook and Peter Tork. And Peter Gabriel, which he knew. All the Peters. 'I was going to be called "Pete",' he notes.)

'God!' he exclaims. 'Pop stars were *great* then. It almost makes me cry.' He shakes his head, looking into this window to a past when pop music and its stars were such a broader collision of richness and weirdness and stupidity and smartness. For teenagers looking to articulate their dreams and their place in the world, as they come to terms and make sense of the wonder and crap that surrounds them, the pop stars then seemed to offer a much more varied and provocative inspiration. For years, critics and cultural commentators who weren't actually paying close attention derided the pop music teenagers liked as being vapid and meaningless production-line nonsense. It wasn't. The sadness is that more and more, in recent years, that is what much of it is becoming: its dumbest critics' ugliest version of itself.

'Because pop stars had all these ideas about stuff, it made people think they also should have ideas about stuff,' says Stephen, who enjoyed his own pop moment as Stephen 'Tintin' Duffy in the mid-eighties. 'And now nobody thinks that they should have any ideas about anything apart from going on *Pop Idol*.'

Rob turns page after page after page. 'I keep expecting to see me,' he says. 'And I'm quite disappointed when I'm not there. Can we do anything about me not being famous in 1986?'

* * *

George Michael calls from downstairs and asks if Rob can come down to see him. He plays Rob one of his new songs, 'Through', his retirement statement, and asks whether Rob would interview him on TV when his album comes out. Rob agrees to consider it, and likes the song, though he is a bit narked at George Michael saying to him: 'You're going through your rock phase, are you? Well, you should go and check out Joy Division's *Closer*, an album – the second half's really beautiful.' It seems more than a little condescending. ('Are you going through your "not selling any records" phase?' mutters Rob afterwards. 'What you should do is "write a hit".')

This evening, Rob goes to play football on a pitch underneath the Westway: £3 each for the pitch rental. It's mostly TV people – Jonny, Ant, Michael Greco, who used to play Bepe on *EastEnders*. But it's Rob who gets heckled. To begin with, it comes from people playing on one of the smaller adjoining pitches.

'Poof … '

'Shithead … '

'Robbie, you tit … '

'Fat cunt … '

'Robbie, you fat cunt … '

He has been playing on the left but starts drifting over to the right side of midfield. The hecklers have finished their game and they start getting into the sport they really enjoy.

'Poof … '

'Tit … '

'Show us your tits … '

He snaps, and moves towards them.

'Just a bit of banter, Robbie, just a bit of banter,' one of them says.

'Oh yeah,' he says. 'I've got a bit of banter for you. Your little brother was telling me about what it's like to suck your dad's cock.'

'Oooooh,' go the others.

'Poof,' retorts the one Rob has just insulted.

Rob tells him that he could buy this place and throw him off.

'What you saying that for?' they say. 'Why do you have to come buying things? What's that all about?'

'Poof,' they shout.

'Yeah, I'm fucking gay,' he explodes. 'I'm the fucking gayest person here. Why don't you come down to the gate down there and come and suck my dick?' He strides swiftly to the gate, intending to come round to where they are and have it out with them. (Gary and Jason are here, but they are on the other side of the pitch and, for once, have missed this looming confrontation completely.)

The hecklers start walking away. Meanwhile, the game breaks up for a moment as everyone realises what is going on. Now Jason runs over, goes through the gate and follows them.

'Can he not take a joke?' shouts one.

'He's got to be able to take it, he's famous,' shouts another.

* * *

He goes into the studio to do more writing the next day, and the one after. These are all songs sparked by bass lines he has come up with.

'This is fun,' he says on the Friday afternoon. 'This is what fun is shaped like.'

He is thrilled to find songs developing in a way that he can still see his skewed and sometimes off-kilter ambitions and intentions remain within them. In some ways it may have been a great blessing that so often with Guy Chambers whatever they started out doing would end up as the poppiest of pop music, but it also frustrated him. What Rob was trying to make using a sample from Barry White's 'Ecstasy' was a weird dance record, but it turned into 'Rock DJ'. When he played Guy 'Still Dre' by Dr Dre and Snoop Doggy Dogg and said he wanted to do a record like that, they ended up with 'Something Beautiful'. He seems relieved that nothing of that kind seems to be happening now.

This afternoon, when Stephen isn't watching, Rob points at the photo of a man exuding bohemian Frenchness on the wall and mouths at me, 'Who is it?'

'Serge Gainsbourg,' I mouth back.

A couple of minutes later he nonchalantly says to Stephen, as though he has noticed the photo for the first time, 'Is that Serge Gainsbourg?'

'Yes,' says Stephen.

* * *

Something else has been happening for the past two weeks or so, something that has drawn much of Rob's attention and emotional energy over the last days of the tour. A romance, or at least the stirrings of one. It is with someone reasonably famous, and begins with a note and a brief meeting, and some exchanged compliments but nothing more, aside from a feeling that something may have started. From then on, they start talking on the telephone, and he finds that these conversations are both enjoyable and encouraging. 'She's either a really nice person or she fancies me,' he concludes at this early stage, and is persuaded that possibly both could be true.

At home in London before Knebworth, he sees her, an evening that ends in a long hug and more intimate words, but nothing beyond that. He is fairly taken with her. 'She is Real Madrid,' he firmly declares. 'She is Zinédine Zidane.' After the meeting, there are further phone calls, which also go well, though he frets as always about his social skills. 'The only thing I worry about are the conversations,' he says one day, as the relationship develops. 'The bits between songs. Do you know what I mean?' One day I remind him that the other person can't hear the panic in his head; he seems quite surprised and taken aback by this notion, and repeats it several times in the days that follow.

Roses are sent, and he finds himself thinking about her more than he might have expected while he's onstage at Knebworth. Plans are made, planes are reserved, and a rendezvous is arranged for the week between Knebworth and Phoenix Park. But then the complications start to arrive. There's a text message that he finds too weird, cancelling their meeting. He works hard on a text reply that won't display his disappointment. 'The fickle hand of fate is a cruel mistress,' he'll write, in part. But then there's an encouraging message and a good phone call, and one day he walks back into the room and declares: 'I'm handsome again. I don't know if you've noticed. I walked out a fat 13-year-old boy from Stoke-on-Trent and I've come back in and I've just conquered Knebworth.'

It goes up, it goes down – all without them having met again – and he begins to feel messed around by all the mixed signals. She suggests he should just get on a commercial flight on his own and visit her, and he thinks that she doesn't get it. It's as if she imagines all that is some kind of paranoia and grandstanding on his part, not grounded in well-tested necessity. It's on again, off again and finally he calls it off himself.

'Look, darling,' he tells her as he closes the door on something that for a moment seemed to mean so much, but that never even really started, 'to tell you the truth I really don't think my ego can take another battering again. Look – I hold the cards to everything except romance. And if I get close to it, and it doesn't come off, it reminds me how lonely I am … '

Even that feeling doesn't linger for too long.

'I had some ice cream sadness, glazed with anger, and one of those Flakes with lack of self-worth in it,' he declares on the day after the final day, 'but then I woke up the next day and everything was cool.'

* * *

In the studio, he picks up Stephen's copy of this week's *NME*. Keith Richards is on the cover, but also the words ROBBIE CROWNED. 'Let's see how much they hate me this week,' he says, and browses through their schizophrenic double-page reaction to the weekend. He reads out some of the digs:

… naff Britain in microcosm …

... like last year's Jubilee, the celebration of another overpaid old Queen ...

... as he mugs into the camera, it's like you can finally see the darkness and depression he goes on about in interviews, giving his performance an edge of thrilling desperation. He really needs *the love of 135,000 people a night – how fucked up is that?*

Rob laughs at all of these, especially the last one. 'That's very, very funny,' he says. He reads their list of reasons why America has remained indifferent to him. The final stab in the heart is this: *'And, shorn of context, they recognise that he's only got about eight really great songs.'*

He reads this bit out again and again. He can't believe that they've said this.

'Eight!' he says. '*Eight!*' If life were a cowboy movie, he would be throwing his hat high in the sky and firing his gun into the air. 'That's great, man,' he says. 'Fucking hell.' It is, accidentally, one of the nicest things he has ever read about himself. 'In my head,' he says, 'I've got two or three. Fucking hell. Eight. That's great. Cor. That's the best back-handed compliment I've ever had.' He keeps returning to it. 'That's cheered me up no end,' he says.

18

For the final concert of his summer tour, and the largest, Rob has chosen to fly in and out of Dublin on the same day. Dublin is a town he likes, but not one he feels too comfortable hanging around in. It has too many associations with forms of relaxation he has renounced.

A police escort guides us into Phoenix Park. As we pull into the backstage area, Rob's face falls.

'I thought it was a stadium,' he says. 'It's a ruddy big field, isn't it?'

It is indeed. As subtly hinted at by its name, it is a giant park.

'Oh no,' he frets, thoroughly unsettled by this surprise. 'It's going to be scary. I can cope with them all up and around me. Big fields just scare the fuck out of me.'

* * *

'Good evening, Ireland!' he shouts in the middle of 'Let Me Entertain You'. 'I am Robbie Williams. This is my band. I've got English blood, but I've got an Irish heart.' It seems that the Morrissey album title did sink in after all.

He never seems like he's faking anything tonight. In private it is the Irish audiences he raves the most about, and it's quite obvious how much he cherishes the way they respond to him. Halfway through he gets all 130,000 of them to shout 'piss off' to a hovering helicopter. 'Magnum PI, you bastard,' he mutters. A while later, he advertises to everyone the presence of his old schoolmaster Mr

Bannon. 'You were always firm but, God bless you, you were always fair,' he says. 'And I'll never forget you, and I'll never forget my school. Thank you ... '

Towards the end of the set it begins to rain, lightly at first, but then harder. When he picks up his acoustic guitar, he asks for his microphone stand to be taken down to the end of the thrust, out amongst the crowd and under the sky. 'If you're getting wet,' he tells them, 'I better come down there with you.' This goes down as well as you would expect.

Before he goes off he tells them that they have the best band in the world here. 'And Bono, you happen to be God in my eyes,' he says. 'I think you're the most beautiful, wonderful man and the best front man there has ever been. And if I could be half as good ... ' (This, he hopes, is clear enough. The last time he was onstage in Ireland he sang 'Beautiful Day' and dedicated it to U2, 'the fucking best rock'n'roll band in the world'. In *The Sun* next day they reported that he'd said 'this is for Bono and the boys, the worst rock'n'roll band in the world'. He immediately got his office to call theirs and explain.)

As he sings 'Feel', he wraps an Irish scarf around his head.

'Best ever,' says Jonny, as Rob changes for the encores.

'Best show ever,' Rob agrees, and when he comes back on he makes Jonny come out and tell the crowd what he has just said.

* * *

Though he is flying back to England tonight, first he must show his face and say his goodbyes at the end of tour party at the Four Seasons hotel. He has a room booked upstairs to change in. He showers, then sits on the bed, naked apart from a towel around his waist, watching a *Have I Got News For You?* repeat and farting. 'It's the gift that keeps giving,' he reports gleefully.

We are the first at the party. At the buffet table Rob passes over the finest food the Four Seasons has to offer and makes himself what he really wants: a chip butty. He orders a double espresso and a regular coffee at the same time. Perhaps it's being in Dublin, but he suddenly says: 'It's a fucking horrible thing to be an alcoholic. A horrible thing. Fucking horrible.' Pause. 'And then sometimes it's the best thing ever. And it really is.'

'But you don't often think that way, do you?' says Josie. 'That this is a horrible thing?'

'No,' he says. 'The end of the tour. I can't explain it. I'm not going to drink, but I feel *drinky* ... ' He shakes his head. 'I mean, the tour is giving yourself completely to them for the whole five weeks. As is the fact that I haven't been out of the hotel. And now's all a bit ... I'm not comfortable with the end of this feeling.' All that stress was hard enough. But now it's the end of that stress, and how do you cope with that when you can't wash it away with too many drinks, as most people here will do tonight?

I ask him whether he feels some satisfaction at having done what he set out to do.

'I'd like to feel that now,' he says, 'but I'll probably feel it next week.' He bites into his butty. 'The girlfriend thing's played a lot on my mind this week. It's like that bottle with the silt at the bottom of it that never goes away, that's always there, and then when somebody comes along and shakes it, the silt … '

A while later I watch him walk over to the window with his nephew Freddie Robert on his shoulder and stand there for a long time in the shadows, somewhere between thoughtful and maudlin, staring into the darkness. When he sits back down, Freddie Robert, still on his shoulder, is fast asleep.

* * *

The party quickly gets too chaotic for him. A drunken Keith Duffy keeps trying to pull him into another room, he feels intimidated by Ray Winstone's very presence, and when he goes to the bathroom one man tries to take a photograph of his penis and another objects to the crown motif on the back of Rob's jacket because he interprets it as a symbol of the British monarchy and an affront to Republicanism.

'What a nightmare,' he sighs, as he sinks with relief into his seat in the car.

We drive for a while before he speaks again, and when he does it is to say something that he has not even hinted at but that he has clearly been waiting to say for some time.

'You know, I don't want to do the upside down thing ever again,' he says to Josie.

'That's fine,' she says. 'Has it been scaring you?'

'Oh, *absolutely*,' he says.

'You've done really well,' she says.

He says it's been worrying him more and more as the tour went on.

'I'd got it in my head about the guy that cut that parachute thing,' he says, 'and Owen Hart falling out of the ceiling … '

'Well,' says Josie, 'you've done it now, haven't you?'

After

1

The day after Phoenix Park he flies back to Los Angeles. He has been talking about how much he has been looking forward to doing nothing, and he has been talking about taking golf up again, but he does neither. Within a couple of weeks, Stephen and Andy are in residence, and the master bedroom has been converted into a makeshift studio, the drums next to the bed. They work late into the night, every night. When Mia, David's granddaughter, visits, she is asked to name their workplace and christens it Rock Band Studios. From then on, whenever the phone rings it is always answered with a crisp 'Rock Band Studios!'. One day Rob picks up and it's the woman with whom things never really started at the end of the tour. He pretends to be someone else and takes a message, another message he will never pass on to himself.

When he first returns to Los Angeles he also goes on a car-buying spree: a new Ferrari, a new Porsche, a new Mercedes. He now owns seven cars parked at his Los Angeles house, though he still has no licence. He bought these new cars to treat himself, and as a fulfilment of a childhood fantasy – he compares it to playing for Port Vale – but perhaps the joy is more in the thrill of buying them, and in being able to buy them, than in actually owning or using them. Though he has moments when these new cars delight him, within a week he is beginning to wish he hadn't bought them at all.

In London, the *Live At Knebworth* CD is quickly compiled. David brings him a test copy and he shakes it next to his ear so that it rattles a little. 'Sounds great,' he says. One day, far into the future, long after his fans have done so, he will listen to it, but not yet.

One day in late August it is reported in *The Sun* – though as a small enough story to suggest that they have only the flimsiest belief in their own reporting – that he has retired. A couple of days earlier the paparazzi had really been getting to him. 'You know that day when you just don't want you going to the coffee shop being a national event, and you haven't been out of the house and they've been waiting for you all day?' he explains, as though I might. That day, a guy with a camera came over to chat with them. He announced himself as an ex-marine, which particularly wound up Pompey, and shared his point of view about what he was doing, stalking the famous with his camera. It only seemed fair that Rob should counter with his own perspective. 'It's really sad,' Rob told him, 'because it's people like you that makes me not want to make records'. And for about half an hour he did think that it all wasn't worth it, and for those few minutes he did retire.

* * *

One of the most common criticisms he faces is that he is forever moaning. The real accusation here is, I think, one of ungratefulness, and it once more reflects the strange way in which people today consider fame and the famous. At the same time as it has become fashionable almost to pity the famous – to patronise them as those poor village idiots who are daft enough to stand in the middle of the town square while everyone stares at them – fame is still widely believed, almost as an act of faith, to make everything alright. And so, as much as people despise the famous for flaunting how happy their talents and success and riches have made them, the one thing people hate even more is when they detect someone famous flaunting unhappiness. (All you need to do to be accused of flaunting it, in this context, is to be heard whispering it out of the side of your mouth.) No matter that, if you find yourself famous, you very well may have many of the same problems as the rest of us, and some extra ones created by this extraordinary situation you are in – if, with everything that you have, you are heard to complain, you are seen to be somehow taking the piss. To have everything that people believe would make them happy, and then have the nerve to claim that you are still not satisfied ...

Likewise, and I think the two things are related, few people are judged more harshly in the modern world than someone famous or privileged who is caught contradicting himself. When you are seen to be doing this, you face being derided as either stupid or insincere. But it is not in the nature of lives to be neat, and all lives, when examined close up, are crammed with contradictions. Often, when lives are written about, these are smoothed away in a cosmetic, fake narrative, but there are plenty of such contradictions scattered across these pages, most of them as obvious to the book's subject as to the reader.

To be held accountable for those may be harsh, though at least it is also, in its way, fair. What is much harder is the way that, when you are famous, you may also be judged and skewered for things that feel or seem like contradictions only as long as they're not considered too deeply or carefully. For instance, is it really contradictory to desire to be left alone in the general sense – away from the constant, repetitive requests that can disrupt the flow of everyday life – while having a fear of being alone? Is it really contradictory to have a great need and desire for attention in some areas of your life, while recoiling in fear from the generalised unstoppable attention the world throws at you? As a matter of pure logic, not at all, but people's reaction to these questions seems more emotional than logical. For instance, people seem annoyed when they think they detect mixed messages toying with their affections – *love me, love me, love me, go away, go away, love me*. Their gut reaction to anyone who trawls for attention on a stage and then tries to avoid it in their life, however much logical sense it may make, is that the person is doing something insincere, tricksy and annoyingly have-cake-and-eat-it.

These are judgements Rob has to face persistently.

* * *

In August, Josie and Lee are married in a beautiful Malibu beach house, waves splashing on to the priest as they exchange their marriage vows. Two days later, a photograph appears in *The Sun* of the two of them and Rob, taken from a house further down the beach, and the wedding is described.

He performed a medley of songs – including his hit 'Angels' ... Robbie – whose albums include the hit Sing When You're Winning *– belted out songs throughout Saturday evening. ... Guests then made their way to the beach. They took turns to have pictures taken with the bride and the singer. Robbie stayed until late into the night, repeatedly taking to the mini-stage to perform for his pals.*

This is an act of pure imagination – presumably of what someone who has possibly observed a little from a distance might fancifully believe would happen at a wedding attended by a famous singer. His only singing, accompanied by Stephen on acoustic guitar, is of a hastily rehearsed version of U2's 'All I Want Is You' during the ceremony, and while he was photographed with the bride and groom, those were the only photos he posed for.

That night, after the wedding and the dinner and the party, he returns to his house and writes another song. At the end of the night, Rob, Max, Stephen Duffy and Chris Sharrock are all sitting cross-legged on the carpet at the foot of Rob's bed around a single microphone, strumming acoustic guitars.

'I'm either sharp,' announces Max after a while, 'or everyone's flat.'

* * *

The writing and recording at Rock Band Studios is often very different from the speed and focus of the writing sessions in the claustrophobic attic of Air. For much of the time Rob is playing the bass, as he tended to right at the end of the London sessions, but now he starts enjoying jamming, with Chris on the drums, Stephen usually on a guitar and Max generally on the keyboard. The late evenings are fired by 24-pack cans of Starbucks double-shot coffees, and Rob seems to be relishing the process of feeling like he is in a band, in his own house with the people he likes, as much as what they are trying to produce. Sometimes it seems as though, now that he has some songs he knows are good, he is indulging in the luxury of trying out every musical style he can think of, a luxury most musicians explore in their teens, when their band is yet to find an audience and is still in a small rehearsal room or basement. He never did that, but now he can. Plenty of music is made in this room that is unlikely ever to appear on an album. Max leads several songs off on unexpected funk-jazz detours of the kind he favours; on one evening Rob's occasional trainer, Paul, can be heard toasting over a reggae song they have just written.

One afternoon in August, Rob sits on the Rock Band Studios double bed with Stephen and they listen back to all the songs they have written since they came to Los Angeles, then they go through a list of all their songs and put a tick next to the ones that should be on the Pure Francis album. (The idea of the Pure Francis character seems to have receded, and there is little doubt that what are being written and made into records here are the next songs in Robbie Williams' career, but the name Pure Francis sticks – not necessarily as the name of a character or a band or an album or a songwriting partnership, but still as the overarching name by which everyone involved refers to this project.) Today, when they count the ticks, there are 13, though Rob is momentarily discouraged that so many of them are from the original batch written in London.

Perhaps it is this that encourages the rich vein they will hit over the next few weeks, or perhaps it is just the focus that comes as Rob's time runs out before he has to go back on tour. He is dreading his return to Europe. There is a further month of concerts to perform, playing indoor arenas across Europe in the places he didn't visit over the summer, and then, after a short break, some final stadium shows in New Zealand and Australia. He would rather stay in Los Angeles and obsess about his new songs. 'I'm really over-thinking them,' he says, less confessing to a sin than to a luxury. 'The way I look at it now is that everything I've done has got me to this point, and that's why I'm able to do what I'm doing now.'

The music he has been making here is still supposed to be a secret and a surprise, and though there has been the odd printed rumour that he has been working with Stephen Duffy, this information has been lost in the general chatter and cacophony of half-truths and nonsense about him. Which is why, at the beginning of October when he flies back to London to appear at the Royal Albert Hall at an event called Fashion Rocks, it is surprising that when Vernon Kay interviews him backstage on camera for T4 he says that he has written 42 songs with Stephen 'Tintin' Duffy. Purely by chance, they edit this comment out of their broadcast.

* * *

This month, Rufus Wainwright is interviewed in *Rolling Stone*. Here is a brief extract:

What musicians are in denial about their homosexuality?

'Like Robbie Williams? [laughs] I don't know. Part of me thinks that it may have been better if I had hidden that I was gay, in terms of record sales. If anything, I admire people who stay in the closet.'

'That's weird, isn't it?' says Rob. 'It just made me giggle. I think I was just quietly chuffed that I'm in his psyche.'

* * *

In the late summer I withdraw somewhat from his orbit. Though Rob and I still speak constantly and periodically meet up, for much of the time I hide away, surrounded by the dozens of notebooks and hundreds of tapes that have built up over the past year or so, and start to find this book within them.

In the middle of October 2003, Rob goes back on tour. Standing behind a red curtain as the intro tape plays for the first night of this new tour, in Lisbon, Rob realises that he hasn't mentally prepared for this. 18,000 people are waiting to see him, and he isn't at all ready to see them. 'It was a bit like I'd literally been, say, flicking through the TV channels watching what was on the television,' he explains afterwards, 'and then all of a sudden somebody had just plopped me on the top of the stage with the cane and a nice new suit and a big haircut, and I was just about to do two hours.'

On the surface both nights in Lisbon go fine, but he realises something that worries him. He simply isn't bothered. In the middle of 'Nan's Song', towards the end of the first night, alone on the stage with his acoustic guitar in his hand, he suddenly becomes aware of a voice in his head going: 'I'm going to walk off – how weird is that?' He is certain, as though watching from the outside, that in the middle of his concert he is simply going to remove his guitar, stride off the side of the stage, and keep going until he reaches home. He believes that he will do it in a very calm way, but he will do it nonetheless. It's such a strange feeling.

Somehow he stops himself. For now.

The day after the second Lisbon show, and on the way to the airport to fly to Madrid, he tells David that he doesn't want to do the planned South American and South African tour next February. Five days earlier, he had confirmed that he wanted to go, and tickets are on the verge of being put on sale. He now insists that the whole visit is cancelled.

2

I drive down to Madrid from where I've been hiding away, and find Rob shirtless and stretching in his hotel room. 'I'm so close to that point where my whole career's just too much and all that business again,' he says. 'I think if I'd done February, that'd have been game over for me for quite some time. I'm just putting the speed bumps in again.'

He asks about the book. At one point I mention that, over a year, there are some subjects (Gary Barlow, Noel Gallagher) and actions (principally farting) that, were each such incident retained in the condensed form of a book, would make him seem obsessed, and very windy. He takes this to heart. Over the next few months, whenever I haven't spoken to him for a while, and ask how things have been, he will usually say something like, 'You know – fart, Gary Barlow, Noel Gallagher.'

Josie comes in and reminds him that he has two New Zealand radio interviews to do. He sits on the sofa in his suite and she passes the phone to him. He chats with the DJs about his tour and Take That and his Maori tattoo, and then they ask him about something Sheryl Crow was quoted as saying after Fashion Rocks – that Rob was too camp to make it in America.

'Well,' he says, in his campest voice. 'I don't understand what they're talking about, really. I mean, you suck a few cocks ... '

He is being broadcast live over the New Zealand airwaves at breakfast time.

'Oh,' he tells them. 'I'll pay the fine. I'm sorry ... is this live? ... I'm very sorry ... '

They do repeat the question about Sheryl Crow.

'I don't know, she's probably right,' he says. 'She's been around a bit, so she's wizened with information ... '

Within Rob's world, America is rarely mentioned now. After the failure of 'Feel' to explode, it seems as though very little else was done by the American record company. If any real effort was made to promote 'Come Undone', Rob doesn't know about it, and it certainly didn't succeed. It is as if the whole experience never really happened. He only reflects on it when I ask him to.

'I think sometimes you can force yourself into the ambition,' he considers. 'My deepest feeling was "Fuck that" and it always was. And I'm not bothered about not breaking it. I am bothered about snidey comments about me not breaking it; I'm not bothered about the fact that I haven't, I'm bothered about the fact that they think it means a great deal to me. And also there is plenty of time for me to regret it, and there is plenty of time for me to have it mean something. But right now I don't regret it and it means fucking nothing. Also, there's not a bit in me that thinks it's not because I'm not good enough. I think that America ... ' – he pauses a second – ' ... would – I'm looking to put it in a better way than "would be lucky to have me". I think America, the entertainment industry, would benefit from having me there.'

* * *

On this tour, he has discovered the world of iChat, whereby, using the hotel's broadband connection and a small camera attached to his laptop, he can establish a two-way video link with Rock Band Studios in his Los Angeles house, where Stephen and Andy remain. Every night the three of them work on songs together, Rob listening to mixes in his hotel room and offering comments, and sometimes even playing ideas to them on his guitar. In breaks, Andy or Stephen will point the camera to the valley so that Rob can see the weather; when some of his possessions arrive from Britain, they walk the camera around the house so that he can see those too.

We listen to all his newest songs on the computer. Some of the ones he likes the best are very fine, and some of the ones he seems to have overlooked are also wonderful. My favourite is a sparse song called 'Cake', whose vocal he sang just once, off the top of his head, in his Los Angeles bedroom while playing Ms Pacman and eating a lollipop. He doesn't say, but I presume it is something to do with that time he has mentioned when he first had his own place to live and was free to indulge himself.

... And I'm drowning slowly
You'll be at home
And I'll be here wired
Because this is what we get
For having our own
Sense of identity
When we leave our homes
We get to do drugs
We get to eat cake ...

It sounds very honest; full of despair, but also of the comfort that comes from confronting it in a song.

* * *

As we listen to the songs, he opens the desk drawer in his hotel bedroom and discovers a pencil and a pencil sharpener. The pencil is already sharp, but he sharpens it with the pencil sharpener nonetheless.

He looks at the resharpened pencil with delight.

'I haven't done that for 15 years,' he says.

* * *

David comes by and they talk about this morning's cancellations.

'We love a drama, don't we?' laughs David.

'Alls I'm thinking,' says Rob, 'is it's apparent that from where I'm stood right now, I can see myself having a breakdown again.'

'I hear that,' says David. 'I hear that.'

'Do you know what I'm saying?' Rob presses.

'Yeah, I do hear that,' says David.

They talk about possible track listings for next year's greatest hits.

'I've an idea for a hidden track,' Rob announces. 'It's hidden in Swindon.'

* * *

Rob wakes to a note and some football boots sent over to the hotel from Luis Figo. Real Madrid have a Champions League game in town tonight, but even so, several of the players have been trying to work out how to get to Rob's concert. (At one point, it was suggested by one of their representatives that

Rob could delay his concert for them. The reply was sent back that maybe they could bring forward the football match.)

'Where are my antidepressants?' Rob asks as he stumbles from bed. 'I fucking need them today.'

In the dressing room, another gift arrives. A signed shirt for Rob, and one for Freddie, from David Beckham. Rob's reads:

Best wishes
'Amigo'
besos
David x

He agonises for ages about what he should write on the Robbie Williams shirt he is sending in return, and casts around for ideas.

'*I've scored in this – mind the wet spot*?' he suggests. '*I've scored in this and she was lovely*?'

'All he's done is "best wishes",' Lee points out.

'Yeah,' says Rob, 'but he's put Spanish. How about *Hola, patatas fritas, all the best, Robbie Williams*? It's the only Spanish I know.'

The debate goes on for quite a while, and Rob gets increasingly anxious about it. Eventually he writes: *To Mr David Beckham, love and admiration from Stoke-on-Trent.*

* * *

On this leg of the tour, the show no longer starts with the upside-down danglings. It is a streamlined production and there is no screen at the front of the stage for him to have hung behind anyway. Instead, as 'Let Me Entertain You' begins, he appears at the top of the stage, near its back edge, stock still. During this evening's performance he mentions both David Beckham and Figo in 'Me And My Monkey', and when he is told that Figo, who must have more or less walked off the pitch after Real Madrid's 1–0 win and jumped into a car, has just arrived in the audience he promises, backstage, 'I'll knock it up a few levels now then,' and does. He dedicates 'Rock DJ' to him and then, after 'Angels', decides to play 'Come Undone' for a second time 'for the friends who couldn't be here at the beginning of the show'.

In the van, Josie speaks to David Beckham's new right-hand man, Terry, and Rob asks for the phone. 'It's Rob,' he says. Clearly Terry is standing next to David Beckham, as without any further discussion the two of them are having their first proper conversation.

'Hi ya, mate … I'm alright, I'm alright … how did your game go? … you won? … do you know what, that's exactly how my concert's gone. I've played better but I won 1–0 … it was weird, it was really, really weird – the first five numbers, I thought they'd paid to come to see somebody else … honestly … I won them over in the end but it was really hard work … how you doing? … really? … '

He loses the connection. 'He said, "The same with me really – the feeling wasn't there at the beginning",' Rob explains. David Beckham calls back and Rob agrees to pop down to the party he's going to, for his teammate Michel Salgado, to say hello in the flesh.

Rob dashes back to the hotel to change, have a quick espresso and to burn on to a CD for David Beckham a copy of his unreleased song 'Blasphemy' as a gift. The club, Calle Serrano 41, is packed. I can see Ronaldo's bald head a few yards away. We wait by the bar while David Beckham is located. When he comes over, other people circle round and I find myself as the unofficial fourth member of a security cordon round the two of them, our backs to them, while they chat in the middle, their heads close together. The only bit that I hear, rising up out of the party noise, is Rob explaining to David Beckham about iChat, but from the little Rob will say afterwards, they didn't bother with small talk – they both seem to recognise in each other one of the few people they can share certain experiences with and have a chance of being understood.

Back in the hotel bar, Figo is waiting with his wife and his friends. (As a matter of footballer etiquette, Rob has had to sneak out to see David Beckham without Figo knowing and feeling snubbed, and now he appears as though coming down from his room.) He tells Figo about the difficulties of tonight's show, the weirdest moment being when a truly gigantic insect appeared on the middle of the stage, buzzing him, and wouldn't leave for ages, then eventually, its point made, flew in a long parabola over the audience to the back of the bullring.

'I have no skills to combat locusts onstage,' he explains. 'I can deal with fans, not locusts.'

Back in his room, he calls Jonny, and slowly winds him up by just telling him about Figo at first, then nonchalantly dropping in David Beckham's name. 'How good's that?' he says. 'We had a big, deep personal chat, and he was really, really nice. And I said it won't go any further than me, and it won't ... '

He puts on a video of Manchester United's game tonight; a friend of Figo's has kindly taped it for Rob and then driven into town with it.

'What a great night,' he sighs. 'From wanting to retire in the first five numbers to being the international spokesman for pop stars. I broke down the barriers of social ineptitude.'

* * *

The tour winds its way through Eastern Europe and Russia. Rob starts growing his hair, takes down his website's chatroom after being spooked by its weirdness (one night he finds someone claiming he has just died in a car crash), takes up Scrabble, and, week by week, drops more songs from the set list. We keep in touch via text iChats.

One night he's playing Morrissey songs as he types. 'Right now,' he says,

'I'm Morrissey for naff Britain.' A few days later he writes: 'I'm in semi-retirement mode again. I've got a bit of a bummer on … about my whole career so far. I'm having a melodramatic few days … about being a bit shit and fake. It makes me sad that there's so much stuff out there that doesn't represent me. My music.' After I ask some questions he clarifies that he isn't feeling down. 'I'm not having an Elliott Smith moment. I'm really quite chilled. Just want to make right what I think is wrong, that's all.'

* * *

In the middle of November I fly out to Oslo for the final two European dates. The evening I arrive, we play Scrabble and, as we do so, have a long talk about his thoughts on the last few months, and what he should and shouldn't do next. He has reached some unexpected conclusions.

'Knebworth was unenjoyable,' he begins. 'It was just stressful. I've never enjoyed any part of the touring, really, other than the two hours before I go onstage where everybody's in the same place. I enjoy that. I cancelled America because it's the final piece of the jigsaw, and it doesn't irk me, and Justin Timberlake wins three awards at the MTV awards and I'm completely not bothered … I think it's all adding up to me not being bothered. I've got my money, thank you very much. As far as I can see, how much proof do I want? How much proof that I'll be alright?'

'Do you reckon Elton John's like that?' interjects Pompey.

'No, Elton John likes performing, and Elton John likes making money, and he likes spending money,' says Rob. 'He actually enjoys touring – he actually goes on for three hours, just him and a piano, and enjoys it. I pretty much figure that if I needed to make some money, then I could tour again in the future. At some sort of standard, whether it be a few arenas or whatever. Alls I do is I look at what I really enjoy, and what I really enjoy is creating songs.'

The only question, I say, is whether you'll get annoyed if you make the records you're most proud of and, because you've withdrawn from the whole circus, you get less success and less attention.

'You know, let's look at it,' he argues. 'If I haven't got a passion for touring, and I don't enjoy it – which I don't – and I don't have to do it, then I shouldn't do it if I don't want to. Like, with the whole America thing: "Right, you knew at the beginning of it that you didn't really want it but you went anyway just to see if you did.' Well, I didn't, you know. The only thing that I would feel bad about, if I didn't promote the next album, would be Stephen Duffy not getting the recognition that he deserves. That would be the only thing that would bother me.'

But, playing devil's advocate, if you make the record you love to bits and it did well but it didn't do as well because it hadn't had the big hoopla surrounding it, would you really be chilled out about it? Or would you panic a bit?

'All that this has ever made me,' he says with passion and force, as though these are words he has been waiting to get out, 'is miserable and rich. What it's done is, it's fucked up my family life, it's made it difficult for me to make friends. What fame has done: it's made me fucking miserable and loaded, and in the last year and a half I've seen another way to live my life, which I can afford to do now. I genuinely believe that as an entertainer I'm gifted. I don't question it any more, what it is – I just do it, and they turn up and they enjoy it and then they clap at the end. But I also genuinely believe that I wasn't born *hard* enough to do this. I mean, mentally I've really suffered because I just wasn't hard enough. And all I know is that everything involved when a record goes out and I have to go and do stuff with it, it makes me sad. That's the be-all and end-all. You know? I've been around the world now. I've not seen much other than hotels.'

What about the part of you that seems to thrive on it? You've got a big ego and a lot of pride too, and that side of success has mattered to you a lot, the validation that that brings. And winning the game too. You like winning.

'Yeah,' he says. 'But I've won. To me it's like ... it's like the decathlon, and I'm on the 1500 metres and I'm Daley Thompson and I've pissed it anyway, so I'm going to have a look behind me. What I'd like to think is, I'd be happy making music, putting records out, and if somebody gets them and buys them, then great. In the meantime, my public persona doesn't vanish, but it goes down a hundredfold – whether that be over a period of 18 months, five years or six years – and during that time I enjoy my life, write a musical, write songs for other people, play fucking golf, have a life. Have a *real* life. 'Cause it isn't that fucking long, without getting into any corny ... it really isn't. I'd fucking hate to be 35, 36, having put out another two and a half records or three records or four records and still be going "I fucking hate this". You know, every part of my being, everything about me, is always, always screaming out "You hate this ..."'

Are you waking up every day right now thinking that?

'I'm not depressed about it. The reason why I'm not depressed about it is because I know ... before it was: *You hate this and you're not rich enough to stop*. Now it's: *You hate this and you're rich enough to stop*.'

Did you hate it as much before you got back on the road?

He pauses, and thinks before answering. 'I mean, if you look at it, where did we go?' he says. 'We went to Japan, which was interesting, but with the interest comes loneliness and boredom. Who knows? I might do an album and go and promote it because I'm married and I want to get away from the wife and the kids for three or four weeks. But with Japan came ... mild interest. And where else did we go? America, we got up early to get on a plane to go to radio stations, and the reason why it was alright was because I wasn't in pain with it. It was only alright.'

Pompey says that maybe he could become like other people who have become mostly known as songwriters, like the Bee Gees. I suggest that the conundrum with Rob is that his audience loves his songs, but everyone talks about his greatest talent being as a performer. And that, fundamentally, when they see him do what he does – whether they see it for three minutes on telly or whether they go to Knebworth – they *can't believe*, faced with the evidence in front of their eyes, that he's not getting fulfilment from that. They simply cannot believe it.

'Yeah,' Rob nods, 'but it's like, last night we had a phenomenal gig. We storm it. And they love it. And I *recognise* that this is a good gig. I don't get *joy* from it. Alls I'm saying is this: every part of me says no. And nothing about me says yes.' He smiles to himself. 'I think I'd be playing a semi-dangerous game to find out if I'm happy without it. Because what if they don't want me back? But I've got to find out.'

* * *

Josie is in her room the following morning when her mobile rings. When the caller says his name, she is cagey. She thinks maybe it's the Teddy Sheringham scamster, trying a new angle. She apologises, warily, and explains that they've had a lot of impostors calling this year. The caller says that he quite understands, but would like to get in touch with Rob.

'I don't want another Christmas to go by without speaking to him,' he says.

She takes his phone number. Her next move is to call Mark Owen and leave a message explaining the situation. He calls back. Yes. The number she was checking is the one that belongs to the man he claimed to be.

She really was just called by Gary Barlow.

* * *

Rob appears in the living room of his suite in the middle of the afternoon. A girl he found wandering the hotel corridors last night is still in his bedroom. Josie shows Rob the invitation to lunch Donny Osmond has sent – it's some kind of event with some kind of agenda, of course, rather than at a table for two to have a natter. Rob doesn't say much. He eats his cereal. Then she tells him about Gary Barlow. His expression suggests only that he thinks this is preposterous, and also that he thinks people are expecting some kind of reaction and so he's not going to give them the satisfaction of one. He doesn't say a word about it.

'What time is it now?' he eventually asks. It is half past four.

Rob says there are too many people in this room to make the girl walk past them all, and suggests letting her find her own way out once they've all gone. He's advised against this, and Jason stays to chaperone her. Pompey asks whether he should get her a ticket for the show. Rob nods. He stares at himself in the window. 'In the reflection,' he murmurs wearily, 'I look like Jack White from the Red Stripes.' He thinks about this for a moment. 'The White Stripes,' he corrects.

* * *

'I'm just pissed off,' says Rob in the van.

'What about?' asks David, concerned.

'That I'm still on tour,' he says.

David looks relieved that it is nothing more unexpected.

'Nearly there,' says Josie.

'No, I just had loads of nightmares,' says Rob. 'Really vivid. And then I woke up and you said Gary Barlow had phoned.'

'Sorry,' she says.

'I'm sure there's an ulterior motive,' says David.

'Yeah, I'm sure there is,' says Rob.

'It'd be interesting to find out,' says David.

'No, it wouldn't,' says Rob.

'No?' says David.

'No,' confirms Rob. 'Is that what he said? "Before another Christmas goes by"?'

'He rang and said ... ' begins Josie.

'That's very brave of him,' says Rob. 'The thing is I have no want to get in contact with him. I do not really want to do any reminiscing. There's nothing I want to say to him ... '

'You're not carrying any resentment any more, are you?' checks David.

'No,' says Rob, then sees my expression. 'Piss off, Chris.'

'If you are carrying resentment, it would be the perfect opportunity to get rid of it all,' says David.

'The thing is,' says Rob, 'I've forgotten what I'm resentful about.' He looks at me again. 'Will you remind me?'

A while later he returns to the subject. 'I was thinking, do I want to do that? And the answer's no. That's it. I was seeing if there's anything about him that makes me want to, "Yeah, it'd be nice to get in contact with him, just say hello ... you know, how you doing, how's life ... ?" But I've no interest in knowing what his life's become or who he is these days. I've just ... no interest.' He shrugs. 'You know. Fart. Noel Gallagher.'

* * *

'It's a shame she's married,' Rob tells the Oslo crowd. 'Imagine that! Robbie Williams, Prince of Norway!'

He performs for two nights in Oslo. The first is attended by the Princess of Norway and he talks to her briefly at the party thrown afterwards in his name. The following night, he talks about her.

'It's going to last, though, that marriage, is it?' he tells the audience. 'It's not. I want to be Prince of Norway ... '

A couple of songs later he returns to his theme:

'Oh yeah. Prince Robbie. I can see it now. When I am king, you will be freed! No more taxes! Free beer and vodka! What else could I do? Yeah! Plastic tits compulsory! Or if they're big enough, fine. This is the new law.'

A few songs further on:

'She's a really good-looking princess, as well, she really is,' he says. 'I mean in England, in England we have royalty as well but they all look like bulldogs chewing wasps ... "I'm nine hundred and eighty-seven ..."' Pause. 'I won't get my knighthood now,' he says.

The end of tour demob spirit doesn't really kick in until the encores, when he starts singing 'We Will Rock You' for the second time tonight, veers into 'Bohemian Rhapsody' and then leads the bemused band into a completely unpremeditated and shambling medley of 'Another One Bites The Dust', 'I Still Haven't Found What I'm Looking For' and 'Suspicious Minds', careering and collapsing from one to the next. After 'Angels' he apologises – 'Listen, tonight I have been so fucking tired it's unbelievable' – and says he's adding a song he hasn't played in a while. 'Do it for Gary Barlow!' he shouts in the chorus of 'Back For Good', and then, in the middle eight, starts discussing the lyrics. '*We will never be uncovered again* ... ' he sings. 'What the *fuck* does that mean? What does that *mean*?'

* * *

Usually there is a separate back route out of these venues for the vans to take, but here we have to drive through the car park, and we are caught amongst the departing crowd and the bootleg merchandise sellers as we slowly edge away from the arena. Only the darkened windows stop Rob from being spotted. He sits in the dark and sings to himself a song of Randy Newman's; a satirical song about fame written when Newman had little, which – whether Rob intends it to, or is just singing to himself a song he likes to sing – gathers new, messier layers in the voice of Robbie Williams, as he escapes, unseen, through a car park of his satisfied fans.

Listen, all you fools out there
Go ahead, love me, I don't care
Woah ... it's lonely at the top

* * *

His tour, anyway, isn't quite over. Immediately after the show, he goes to the airport where a plane is waiting to fly him to Berlin; tomorrow he is to sing a short swing set at an after-party for the German premiere of *Finding Nemo*.

It is two nights since he laid out with care, logic and sincerity the reasons and feelings that explain why he doesn't want to do any of this any more. By the time we are in the van on the outskirts of Berlin, he is excitedly discussing with David the logistics of fitting a swing tour into his schedule. 'I know what I said ... ' he says to me unprompted; sometimes it can be an infuriating burden, being held accountable for previous testimony.

'Do you think doing a swing tour would be less stressful?' asks Josie.

He nods. 'Because I just stand. It's laidback. No running. I could go to sleep after.'

We near the hotel.

'I'll tell you what, though, about this touring lark. It's quite addictive,' he says. 'Just always going somewhere, always doing something. I mean, if we did go again, with stadiums and stuff, four weeks on and two weeks off, four weeks on and two weeks off?'

'Yeah,' says David.

'Do you reckon we could go back to Prague and do a stadium?' he asks.

He is now booking a swing tour and another stadium tour.

There's more.

'We should promote the Pure Francis album a lot,' he says. 'Around the world, 'cause it's brilliant. We should then do a swing album, because that works. We get another studio album out; we're out of the contract by then ... '

He stops himself.

'Anyway, I'm not doing it,' he declares unconvincingly. 'I'm semi-retiring.' He laughs. 'The great thing about being me is I can always change my mind,' he says. 'Isn't it funny how I can absolutely mean that it's all over, and I can absolutely mean it's not?'

3

He can see the end of the year from here – and, now that he has cancelled South America and South Africa, the end of the cycle that *Escapology* started. There are four more stadium dates to play in Australia and New Zealand, and before that a short breather in Los Angeles. First, he must linger in London a while to honour a few final promotional commitments, and find a house in the country for next year. He plans to bring the dogs over and spend a few months here. Josie arranges a scouting trip by helicopter and he finds a property he likes.

A red carpet premiere for the Knebworth DVD, *What We Did Last Summer*, is held at the Odeon in Leicester Square. It is the evening when news breaks of Michael Jackson's forthcoming arrest on suspicion of child abuse, and consequently some of the news cameras are diverted from the premiere at the last moment.

The only other time he has been at the centre of an event like this, the premiere for the *Nobody Someday* documentary, his part in it was a disaster. The first question he faced, at the end of the red carpet, was: 'An hour and 45 minutes – that's a bit self-obsessed, isn't it?'

'I don't know,' he said.

More questions followed from the same interviewer. He replied 'I don't know' to every single one. After four such interviews – and after he had told the press 'I don't want to be here' – he was pulled away.

Tonight Rob patiently signs dozens of autographs on the way in and does a series of brief TV interviews. 'I haven't actually watched the DVD,' he explains to one. Then he is led into a small screening room full of seated journalists for a press conference. He is asked by a woman from Austria whether he still thinks about quitting.

'Yeah,' he says. 'Every day. Every day I do. And then ... I'm schizophrenic. You know, there was one night on the tour that I never wanted to tour again, and then the next day on the way to the venue I wanted to put three more tours in – a swing tour, this and that tour. So, you know, I can never trust myself really.' The first part of this – *Robbie Williams: I Think Of Quitting Every Day* – is the quote from this evening that will make the most news.

Time for some questions from the British tabloids.

'Hi, it's Nadia from the *Star* – I just wanted to ask, what do you think of George Bush and his visit to England at the moment?'

'What do I think of George Bush and his visit?' Rob repeats. 'From the *Star*? You're joking? *Really?*' She nods. 'Alright. Um ... I just hope that he arrived safely and leaves safely, and while he's here nobody gets hurt.' Pause. 'And I love tits and beer.'

At this, there is laughter and some applause.

His next job is to show his face inside the cinema to the audience. He stands with Ralph Fiennes on the side of the stage; Fiennes introduces a Unicef film about child exploitation Rob presented back in April, and then introduces Rob, who in turn introduces the Knebworth film. By the time the Robbie Williams on the screen has been lowered on to the stage, Rob is walking out the front door of the cinema, now deserted, and making plans for dinner.

* * *

As we eat, we discuss the strangeness of autographs. 'It's been going on for years,' says Jan. Rob says that once, when a woman approached him in a park, he asked her why. 'So I can show my friends I met you,' she said. He asked why she wanted to do that. 'Because it's nice,' she said. He kept asking her why to each new answer, until she seemed to get his point and walked off without his signature, neither annoyed nor disappointed.

He concedes that he got Bryan Robson's and Paul Gascoigne's when he was young, but that it is different when you are a kid. It's currency between children, and children will actually show each other autographs. Adults rarely do so, though they may say 'I got so-and-so's autograph', so why would it not just be enough to say that they had seen them, or greeted them, or whatever? 'There's something else when you're young,' he argues. 'You just want some of it to rub off on you,' he says.

He points out that he doesn't always react badly to autograph requests. 'If I haven't been asked 30 times that day, then I will,' he says. 'It's just that you want to save some of yourself for yourself, and a lot of people think they're the only person that's asked you that day. And they're not. Any other person's job, when they clock off, they clock off and go home. When I leave my house, if you're coming up and wanting a minute with, I'm working for the minute. You know, the first response, when people see me, they look at me and they go straight to their bag for a pen and paper.' If you are famous enough, these minutes simply join together until you are spending every hour or day or month or a whole lifetime being gently bothered to death. 'And however I say it and whatever I do,' he reflects, 'this will be perceived as me moaning.'

I ask him what he thinks when he reads – and it's almost a staple line in *Hello*-style celebrity interviews these days – of celebrities being asked about autographs and each of them saying, 'It's an absolute pleasure to be asked.' I ask whether, when he sees that, he thinks 'You're lying', 'You're different than me', or 'You're mad'.

'I think,' he answers, frankly and bluntly, '"You're not as famous as me".'

After a while, Jan relates her own unexpected history as an autograph-hunter.

'I collected one,' she says. 'Michael Holiday. I don't know if anybody knew him. Back in the fifties he was a singer. He was at the Theatre Royal in Hanley. And I went to see him and I was so delighted and I got his autograph.'

I think it is safe to say that none of us – even Rob – have a clue where this story is going, and that when it does go where it goes we are all gobsmacked.

'And the next day,' she explains matter-of-factly, 'he committed suicide at the Grand Hotel.'

29 October 1962. A drug overdose.

'And I haven't collected an autograph since,' she says.

* * *

One afternoon, several days before he is due to go back to Los Angeles he refuses to get up when Pompey tries to wake him but says in a tone of voice that makes clear he is serious and that he expects this to have been sorted out before he resurfaces from under his pillow, that he wants to be booked on a flight back to Los Angeles the following day. As plans are rearranged and planes are rebooked, he sleeps.

When he eventually rises we talk for a long time about the past. Jonny comes in with some new DVDs and, after making a spirited defence of his Muppets purchases, takes a seat, listening and occasionally joining in. After about an hour of discussing difficult experiences, Rob announces that now he's really happy. 'Perhaps there's more happy than this,' he says. 'But if I've got anything to go on, this is really happy. If I compare it to how I've been, you know. All I get now is tired – I don't get tired and depressed. I could do this feeling for the rest of my life. You know, I'm quite happy with this ...

I was in bed last night at half four and I was thinking, "Oh – didn't you normally used to lie in bed wishing you had somebody here with you that loved you?" "Yeah, you did, didn't you?" "Do you want to just go to sleep now?" "Yeah." "You alright?" "Yeah."'

* * *

It's really complicated, I say, what you think about your fans.

'Mmmm,' he says. 'I don't like the word "fans". When I write songs I've always been really excited about them, no matter what I say, and it sort of trebles my excitement that people are going to get enjoyment from it. I genuinely feel that way. And I'm very thankful that I have an audience, for many reasons. In a perfect world, for me, people would get that excitement, read into the lyrics, feel the same way. Perhaps people that buy my albums can't express themselves in the way they'd like to, and I express myself for them in a song. So in a perfect world they'd listen to the lyrics, they'd come to see the shows, they'd appreciate it and go home, listen to it a week after, and get that feeling that you get.'

But not all fans are like that, unfortunately.

'What comes with all this is these people that, you know … ' he begins, and then rewinds a moment. 'My lyrics are alcoholic lyrics. They're the -ism that alcohol is. They are the agoraphobic, they are the words of a man that's unsure about himself, unsure about his place in life, doesn't believe in himself. You know, alcoholism is a mental problem. No matter how you look at it, if you've got a problem, and you drink because you've got a problem, that's a mental illness because you're not well if you do that. So I have a mental illness. So I attract people with mental illnesses. If they understand me completely, a percentage of them are going to be ill.'

He goes to the bathroom, and as he walks back across the room he says: 'Let's not forget that the word "fan" is short for the word "fanatic". And let's not forget that I'm a man who hasn't liked himself very much. And Groucho Marx said I wouldn't be a member of any club that would have me as a member – hence, for a while I didn't enjoy people enjoying me, because I hated me.'

And so I imagine you were particularly suspicious of people who were really keen on you?

'Yeah. "Well, I hate me – you must be an idiot." Do you know what I mean? I don't feel that way now. I feel different. But there is a tiny percentage of people … I'd say that everybody that follows us from hotel to hotel that sits in the lobby has a life problem. It's my finding that those people that are in hotel lobbies weren't loved enough in areas of their life. Or have mental illnesses. Where they don't know they're mad either. That scares me. And also, you know, the term "fan" was applied to the hundred girls that were outside my mother's house. I hated them. I hated them for being there. I hated them for the fact that they had no concept that what they were doing could possibly be hurting me, and hurting my family. The fact that 24 hours a day we were being watched. Or 24 hours a day I was being wanted. Or the person that they thought I was was being wanted. And it wasn't me. I knew that early on.'

Some people have the attitude – because obviously you love the fact that millions of people want to buy your records and want to come to your concerts …

He nods. 'But I've said that.'

… but some people have the attitude of: well, obviously you have to put up with a bit of this as part of that.

'Yeah, obviously I do,' he agrees. 'But that scares me. Because these people, a lot of them can't believe that I'm not going to be their husband. I'd like to call everyone else something other than fans, because what I term to be fans are these incessant pests. Not the people that buy my records, that enjoy my records. I provide a service, I say, "This is my thing," and people go, "I like your thing, I think I'll get that," and then they get it, and if they do I'm really chuffed that I have the ability to put a thing out there that people like. But there is a fraction of people who are: "Don't forget who put you where you are." No. I said, "This is me – do you like it?" And you said, "Yeah," and you bought it. You only come back because you like it. How many people do you see outside John Sainsbury's house asking for free apples because they like his apples? This might sound completely ungrateful, but I provide a service. If you don't like that service, you can stop buying it. At any time. I don't owe anybody anything.'

Though of course you would be fairly miffed if they did stop liking it.

'The only reason that they'd stop liking it would be because it was something that they didn't enjoy any more. And I'd say fair enough.'

As regards the ones who hang around and follow you, is there any contradiction in the fact that every now and again you'll have the odd bored moment or lonely moment or weak moment and shag the odd one of them?

'Um … no. There's no contradiction. Where's the contradiction?'

I guess if you're criticising them very reasonably for having the delusion that they can be your wife, and are suggesting that most of them have problems, there would be an argument that it's not the best-selected pool of people to get involved with …

'I think that perhaps callously, on my behalf and as a human, the rock'n'roll myth is: get drunk, have sex. Right? You know. Well, I don't get drunk any more. And perhaps intrinsically in my make-up as a person I am flawed there. Perhaps there is … no, there's definitely a flaw there. 'Cause me as a sane person would go: let's not do that.'

Whether it's right or wrong it's certainly leaping into the lion's den …

'Yeah, but don't I do that all the time though?'

Your whole career?

'Yeah. It's not something I feel great about. My conclusion about who these people are as people is something that it's taken me a great length of time to come to, and has actually only been cemented in the last three months. In the last three, four, five months. I'm a young man still, and I'm single – I'm allowed to have sex. There's no law against two consenting individuals. If I'm stuck in a hotel room for five weeks, because I can't go out, then I'm going to go down to the bar and if there's somebody that takes my fancy ... you know. I will more than likely try to have my wicked way with them. Like any other single male in the world. You know. And hey, they're here to see me – why not? So you get them up to the room and you have a chat with them and then they end up with the same patter. They all want to be the different girl that doesn't sleep with me, so you're constantly on the chase for somebody that doesn't want to be like them. It's weird, and I have no divine right to get laid. I know that. I'm not saying that it is my right as a pop star. I'm just saying that it is very, very interesting, bizarre and kind of scary.'

* * *

As the dusk gathers round, here above the Thames, we talk about sincerity. He explains that the other moment when he nearly walked offstage in Portugal was during 'Come Undone'.

'If I stopped lying, I'd just disappoint you,' he sang.

'And,' he says, 'I thought: I'm lying. I'm going to stop. I don't feel this song. I don't feel you out there.' He heard Bob Geldof on the radio the other day, talking about when he performs 'I Don't Like Mondays', saying that as naff as it sounds he still gets a feeling in his soul every time he sings '*the lesson today is on how to die*'. Bob Geldof insisted with some passion that this was why he still did it, and that he wouldn't otherwise – if he didn't feel it, it would just be cabaret, and he doesn't do cabaret. And Rob decided that he was very different. 'I do cabaret,' he says. 'I do cabaret quite often.' He says that when he asked Bono in California how he did what he seems to do every night, Bono told him: 'I see my job as being an actor some nights.' Rob was pleased to hear that. He thought, 'So it's not just me, then.'

I wonder whether that doesn't describe most performers – it's just characteristic of Rob to be troubled by it and confess to it.

'The thing is,' he says, 'it's because I'm theatrical. A lot of people won't be questioned about it, or accused of it. Bono's not accused of insincerity when he performs.'

But, I point out, Rob nearly always does the opposite of what most people do in these situations – he draws attention to and dramatises any potential insincerities. He's always playing up whatever might seem insincere, and smuggling away the fundamental sincerity of most of what he does. Whereas most entertainers are constantly trying to make what they do seem more sincere than it is, he is usually trying to disguise what he does as less sincere than it is.

'Yeah,' he says. 'It's a coping mechanism. Because if you sing it every night with the sincerity that it was written with and somebody accuses it of … whatever, it hurts you. So by defusing it, if you can't beat them, join them. Do you know what I mean? It's like – if I behave in a way that you accuse me of, then you can't hurt me, ha ha ha.'

Which you do in a number of different ways …

'Yeah, you know, it's like somebody coming over to you: "I'm going to punch you in the nose," and me going, "Bang."' He punches himself and laughs disdainfully. 'And it's all because emotionally in lots of departments I'm still very young. I won't say it's immature, it's just something that I've not grown in yet, of having what people think about me not mean so much. And it means a lot less than it did 12 months ago, so I'm getting better. But somebody in Mis-teeq said. "I like Robbie Williams because he genuinely doesn't give a fuck." And I laughed about it because I give the biggest fuck. Like, Noel Gallagher, deep down, gives a fuck. *Tremendously* gives a fuck. It's all a façade.'

* * *

It's dark now in his London flat, and there are just three of us here: Rob, Jonny and me. By this time tomorrow he will be on his way to Los Angeles. I ask him whether he thought as a kid that if he became famous it would make everything alright.

'I thought, if you're famous – I didn't even *think* this, it was just this thing – if you're famous, everything is OK,' he answers. 'You know, everything's OK.'

What part in wanting it and not wanting it was played by your father's kind of semi-fame while you were growing up?

'I liked all aspects of it, actually. I can remember at a very early age when I was at Perrenporth holiday camp. My dad would perform and then there'd be cabaret on in the evening and they made me laugh, and I listened to the singers and I'd enjoy them singing, and then I saw the magicians and I enjoyed them. I'd be able to walk backstage, and walk out, and walk backstage and walk back out again. And I remember just saying to myself: I never ever want to be out front. I always want to be able to walk back. Because it made me feel important.'

'You were *expecting* to be famous,' Jonny points out. 'It was weird. I always looked at Rob as he was famous anyway, from the age of 11. He was the local boy who was in the *Sentinel* all the time.'

'I think the thing is,' says Rob, 'if you're found to have a talent for swinging a golf club as a five-year-old, you would have been encouraged to play as much golf as you could until you were on the tour. I found I had a natural talent for … making people watch me.'

4

One looming, unaddressed issue for these final four stadium shows in Australia and New Zealand, which will feature the full summer tour production, is whether, after his declaration in Dublin, he will agree to be suspended upside down for a final four times. In the end, he agrees without any fuss. Onstage, he even begins to perform 'Sexed Up', a song he refused to do all summer. Offstage, there are some ultimately unfruitful but diverting auditions for the role of his wife, and he finally takes up golf again, playing with the kind of hyper-focused mania he often brings to his latest enthusiasm. Most days he plays 36 holes; some days he still isn't satisfied, and goes out for nine more.

But within himself, he isn't as settled as he might seem. 'It's not an excuse,' he will say afterwards. 'It's just what happened. I was coming towards the end of a tour, a year where, as much as there were massive crowds and awesome experiences, it's a pressure cooker. It just got to a point … it was the straw that broke the camel's back.'

There is one particularly bad day in New Zealand. He is on the golf course, and word has clearly got out that he would be there today because on the balconies of some of the houses bordering the course the owners have draped Union Jacks, and they are expecting some attention in return. 'Come on!' they shout. 'You could just *talk* to us.' Kids are following on bikes from hole to hole. On the tenth tee, the kids and some associated adults all go 'Hurray!' when he tees off, and are whooping through his father's swing. 'Please, if you don't mind … ' Rob beseeches. Pete's shot goes into the lake, and Pete turns to the unwanted cheerleaders. 'You can't do that on a golf course,' he tells them.

'We put you where you are today,' one of the adults tells Rob. 'You could just say hello or something.'

'I'm on a golf course – you'll have to excuse me,' Rob explains. 'This is downtime for me.'

'Remember who put you where you are,' one of them repeats, and they walk off. They're dissatisfied; he's seething.

Back at the hotel, knackered, he lies on his bed and hears a knock on his living room door, and the sound of Gary Marshall answering it. When Gary opens the door, a group of people announces, 'We've come to see him,' and start barging past Gary, who stops them. He explains that they can't do this, and eventually they leave. Rob has a kip, and when he awakes there is an envelope for him, left by the same group of people, who are staying in a room down the corridor. Inside it are five of his CDs, four tickets for tomorrow's show – returned as a protest against his unfriendly behaviour – and a letter of complaint: '*We are the people who put you where you are … we knocked on your door to come and see you and you didn't even have the courtesy to come and say hello ... one of your monkeys told us to ... '*

And so on. They sarcastically quote what he said onstage at Knebworth, and on the live Knebworth CD – 'grow old with me' – and suggest that he is insincere and full of shit.

He's not in the mood to brush this off today. He removes the CDs from the envelope, pisses into it and leaves it outside their door. Later on he can hear them complaining to the hotel security about what has happened, but the hotel security think they are joking. *... and then Robbie Williams pissed in the envelope and returned it ...* ? It's obviously an absurd suggestion.

* * *

In Los Angeles, as 2003 drifts into 2004, he starts growing his hair and still plays golf every single day. When he is not on the course, he is on the driving range. 'I'm consumed by golf, but it's great,' he says. 'I go to bed early, the only thing that's on the television is the golf channel, I wake up early, I go and play golf, I buy golfing equipment and golfing clothes, play golf, and then I either have a good game or a bad game. I'm its bitch right now. But I'm not going to let it beat me.' His best round in Los Angeles has been 14 over. 'I'm just going to do it till my handicap's single figures,' he reasons, 'and then give up.'

His monomania does throw up a potential problem. Stephen Duffy and Andy Strange are scheduled to arrive at his house in early January to continue work on the Pure Francis project. This month has primarily been earmarked for writing lyrics – the vocals on the existing demos are generally just whatever Stephen has selected from the words Rob sang and scatted off the top of his head while the songs were being written. Some of it is beautifully formed already, but there is a lot of nonsense, sometimes quite literally.

The last thing Rob is interested in right now is dealing with any of this. 'I don't know where Steve's going to fit in, actually,' he frets. 'I genuinely don't. I'm slightly worried. Seriously. I play golf every day and then I go to bed.' Right now, he feels no desire to work on music.

It's fairly obviously that the practical hurdle – golf – disguises a more fundamental one. All through the summer and autumn, when he was supposed to be concentrating on his tours, Pure Francis was his freedom and his escape from all of that. It was the thing nobody was telling him to do, his precious secret from the wider world, and his freedom from Robbie Williams.

Now the situation has changed. In his absence, Robbie Williams' previous career is doing just fine – the live album is exceeding expectations, and the Knebworth DVD has sold more than any British music DVD has ever sold – but finishing some of these songs is now supposed to be his main focus. At least two songs are needed as singles for the greatest hits album this autumn and, as enthusiastic as he may remain in theory about this music, in practice it has now become the latest thing he feels compelled to escape from. It's not just the Pure Francis songs. Often he talks as though he will never again release another record, or leave this new life he has found.

* * *

As predicted, when Rock Band Studios is re-established in his master bedroom, its principal client shows very little interest in visiting. Very occasionally he wanders in, but it is tacitly agreed that little of the lyric-writing they had expected to do now will happen. Instead, Stephen and Andy will themselves work on some of the many songs that have been orphaned along the way, in the expectation that perhaps a few may work their way back into contention, and that in the meantime a few potential b-sides will approach completion. Mostly, this seems to work fine for everybody, though as Stephen comments one day over lunch, 'It is a bit strange, working on 80 songs for a retired golfer.'

By late January Rob is anyway reassessing the overwhelming role golf has taken up in his life. He is realising that, rather than being the solution to life's problems, it might just be another way of making himself busy enough to avoid the issue. Also, he's getting exhausted, as much from all the thinking that walking around a golf course allows you as from the golf itself. 'After the tour,' he recognises, 'I don't think I gave myself the opportunity to sit down and go: I'm going to do nothing for two weeks. Instead, after the tour, I went: I'm going to play golf like a mad person every day ...'

After a few weeks, he also shows a little more interest in sometimes drifting down the first floor hallway into the studio. Stephen gives him Brian Eno and Peter Schmidt's box of provocative creative instructions, Oblique Strategies. The first card Rob pulls out says, 'Use "unqualified" people.' One day he strolls in, sits down and announces to Stephen, 'It's only taken me a month to want to compete with the whole of the music industry,' though he doesn't stay long. Another evening he comes in, a little spaced-out, and starts playing a loping melodic riff on the electric guitar, around which very quickly he and Stephen write a new song. For all of January he has been insisting that if any of these songs are released, it should be under the name of a band, but now he relents. 'I'm going to be Robbie Williams again,' he says.

A few nights later, he walks in and asks Stephen and Andy to stop what they are doing. He writes a lyric and sings a vocal for the new song, now called 'Ghosts'. 'On the theory,' he explains, 'that all of your past relationships are now ghosts. Relationships that were so much pain or meant so much then, now they're just ghosts.' He works through the idea, line by line, taking and adapting occasional suggestions from anyone in the room, and arrives upon the line: *I did what I could for one of us, I always thought it would be you.* He likes this, but it also bothers him. 'Do you ever write songs that are the complete opposite of who you are?' he asks Stephen, then explains why he is asking. 'I've never been in a relationship where I've been selfless,' he says. At the song's end there is a haphazard list of locations where such ghosts may happen to haunt us.

... ghosts! ... in the restaurants and the cinemas! ... ghosts! ... in the library and the coffee shop! ... ghosts!

'I just like "libraries" being in a song I sing,' he grins.

* * *

One day in Los Angeles Rob reads that he has been voted Eighth Sexiest Man in a poll. Only eighth. He is affronted, and he expresses his affront in a familiar way. He pretends that he is annoyed to a comically inappropriate extent, the comedy of which is supposed to convey that he is not the slightest bit bothered about such daft and superficial matters, under which he is hiding the fact – as he is well aware, and as he is aware that those around him also realise – that he is genuinely a little miffed and hurt at this uncharacteristically low placing. The funnier part of his response is that, to address his shortfall, he decides to 'do sexy' around the house for the rest of the day. Often, one will look up from what one is doing to find Rob standing in the doorway, often with his shirt off, his head lowered and eyes up, his body tense, his mouth halfway between a smile and a snarl, one hand raised and leaning against the door frame, doing the kind of hammy sexy-male-in-front-of-a-camera acting he perfected in Take That calendar shoots.

* * *

I move into the attic flat of his Los Angeles house, working on this book. Sometimes he comes up to play Scrabble. He reads through some opening chapters. 'God, I don't half talk some crap,' he says. 'It's the can't-stand-the-silence-in-my-head-I'll-say-something ... '

5

Over a year ago Rob first recorded the dialogue as Dougal for a film version of the animated children's programme *The Magic Roundabout*. Since then, the director has been changed, some of the parts have been recast and much of the dialogue has been rewritten. Rob has been stalling this second session for months. He was supposed to do it in London just after the final Norway show, and he cancelled at the last moment. The session is now scheduled over two days at the record producer Trevor Horn's studio at his Bel Air home; he is not there, but his wife and manager, Jill Sinclair, is.

Rob stands in the vocal booth, watching each piece of action on a screen in front of him and speaking the appropriate dialogue. (Most of the animation is far from completed, so what he can see are animatics, rudimentary line-drawn animated versions of the characters, though already with expressions and mouths that move in time with the dialogue.) His Dougal voice is like his own, but more northern, higher and more plaintive:

'Oh, I see, the silent treatment, is it? ... Me gobstoppers? Oh no! There's only one left! ... nothing short of a sea of boiling lava would stop me from getting that diamond ... '

In between, Clive, the director speaks into his headphones, offering suggestions and making requests.

'If you can do three "*Zebedee!*"s with mounting alarm ... ' he asks. 'Why don't you just give me a few wild "*sugar*"s? ... '

As Rob does his lines, he moves a large file clip around his face, clamping it against any loose flesh, creating new temporary disfigurements. Hour by hour, his voice becomes more affected until he has to be asked to tone down what is becoming an Eric Morecambe impression.

They break for sushi.

'This is really the best food, isn't it?' says the director.

'Yeah,' Rob agrees. 'Apart from sweets. Bread and butter pudding pisses on this.'

He returns the next afternoon for more voice work. On the way there, he talks about an article on the nineties he has just read in *Word* magazine that referred to him as having 'the thinnest veneer of an edge'.

'I thought, yes!' he hoots. 'Get in! I've got an edge and eight great songs! How great's that? However thin it is, it's still an edge. That's not bad for the junior captain of Burslem golf club and amateur dramatic society member.'

Josie asks him whether yesterday's session has reinvigorated his desire to act.

'That desire died when I was about 22, 23,' he says. 'And, let's see ... no. What a piss-poor profession.'

'I think we should start on the hard stuff,' says the director when Rob arrives.

'The hard stuff is sounding panicked, because I'm on pills,' Rob explains.

He starts performing today's lines:

'I can't sleep! ... I'm too worried about Florence ... it's where the Renaissance started ... '

When all the dialogue has been done, he is asked to record a long list of wild sounds as Dougal, to be used in the film whenever and wherever needed. I can't see the list, but from what he does, and realising that they are alphabetical, I can work them out: alarmed, angry, balancing, catching, cheering, chuckling, confused, dazed, frightened ...

He stops at 'giggling.' He reckons he's done that already. 'What's a chuckle if it's not a giggle?' he argues. 'Fuck that.'

Next is 'grinning'.

'What am I supposed to do for "grinning"?' he asks. It's hardly a sound. He refuses.

'"Hopping" we don't need,' Clive says helpfully.

'"Jump"?' says Rob. 'Fuck that.'

Then there's Ohs. Ooops. Ouch. Puzzled. Running. Shocked. Ssshhhhh. Surprise. Teeth-chattering. (He tries. 'Can't do that,' he says.) Thinking. ('A deeper one,' encourages Clive.) Throwing. Yawning. Wows.

* * *

In the car home, he says, 'I was just thinking, there's nothing I've done for a while where I've proved I'm good at something that nobody knows I'm good at.'

'Yeah,' says Josie, 'until now.'

'No, no, that's not going to be it,' he says dismissively. He explains what he means. 'When the tours were first happening and I was winning over festival audiences and things like that, there was all that … '

So what do you want to prove now?

'I don't know.'

Do you need one?

'Yes.'

Why?

'To prove to myself again. And because it's fun. Swing was one.'

Was doing the Knebworths and all that slightly one?

'No. No.'

Is Pure Francis one?

'No.'

Why not?

'Um … ' he says, not changing his mind but not finding an answer.

'Do you mean more things that you actually feel scared about?' asks Josie.

'Yeah.'

'And you're really confident about Pure Francis and therefore it's not one,' she says.

'Yeah,' he says, and yawns. 'It might have to be a film.'

'It's almost, although you say never, never,' says Josie, 'you almost kind of know that if something really brilliant crossed your path … it might tempt you.'

He says no more about this now, but a few days later when we are chatting as he searches for clothes in his closet, I ask him to elaborate. He has poured scorn upon every interviewer over the last year who has brought up the possibility, but he now says, 'Well, James Bond would be one, wouldn't it?'

* * *

'Since I've been 23 I've been looking forward to being 30,' he told me many months ago. 'I sort of think it's that mythical age where, if you've been suffering in your twenties, then you start to even out. I kind of got the feeling that my twenties were a massive period of growth – growth that I didn't want, necessarily, but I just got the feeling inside me that I was learning a huge lesson, and at 30 I would learn what that lesson was, and start to mellow out a little bit.'

As the actual day approaches, he seems keen to play it down. It has been agreed that his thirtieth birthday will not be celebrated properly until he gets back to England, where most of his friends and family are, but his mother, sister, her boyfriend and nephew fly over to Los Angeles anyway as a surprise. On the morning itself, he refuses to get out of bed until he has some caffeine, then, a Starbucks coffee in his hand, sleepily opens presents on the kitchen counter. This is not the day he gives up smoking, and his resolutions much earlier to do so on this day are never mentioned. He later says that, inside, the principal realisation in his head was that he would now never be a professional footballer.

That evening, he has a birthday dinner at Nobu in Malibu. Over dinner he suggests to his sister and her boyfriend that they should get married soon. They agree. Two days later they all fly by private plane to Las Vegas for the wedding.

A few days afterwards, he comes into the room where I am writing and flicks through the latest *NME*. He scans the results of this year's readers' poll. He has slipped down their rankings: only the third greatest Villain of the Year. Nonetheless, still impressive in its way. He looks at the others in the top ten.

'So,' he says, 'George Bush went to war with a country under false pretences, Pete Doherty is a heroin addict who broke into his friend's flat, Michael Jackson has been accused of paedophilia, Tony Blair has been accused of the same thing as George Bush and ignoring the UN and about 10 million people marched all over the world against the war … I played Knebworth.'

* * *

He goes clothes shopping and really gets into it, choosing outfit after outfit after outfit at one of Los Angeles' most upscale stores. When he goes to pay, his credit card is refused. He has to phone Josie.

'How much is it?' she asks.

He makes a nonsense noise down the phone. She understands perfectly. He doesn't want to say.

'I'll be right down,' she says.

When she gets there she sorts out the $20,000 bill. Much of it is from the designers Libertine. Such news obviously travels fast. That afternoon, she receives a call inviting Rob to their New York fashion show. (He won't go, of course.)

* * *

Rob, his mother and Lee Lodge see Mel Gibson's *The Passion* on the opening day. 'It made me think how much dumb shit I worry about,' he says. 'And it made me think how bizarre it must have been to sit next to Jesus at the canteen while they were filming the film.' In his head, as Jesus is put up on the cross, the thought that goes through his head is: 'And so a couple of thousand years of guilt began.' During the brief instant where the resurrection is shown, he wishes he had shouted out 'Go on, Jesus!' He vows to see the film again just so he can do this.

The movie did make him think about when he got confirmed. 'How as a child you're given a version of what happens,' he explains, 'and it doesn't actually compute that it's actually fucking terrifying.' As his confirmation name, he chose Maximillian Colby. 'Because it was the coolest saint name I could find,' he says. 'He was the last ordained saint.' Maximillian Colby offered himself to be shot in the war in place of the real culprit so that the guilty man would not be lost to his wife and children.

After the movie, shopping at Book Soup, his mother buys some spiritual books and Rob buys some comedy – the complete Peter Cook and the new *Onion* anthology – and some photo books. 'To get some idea of what Francis is going to look like,' he explains. He particularly admires an old photo of Humphrey Bogart. 'I do like the braces,' he notes.

* * *

One evening Rachel Hunter comes over and we all sit round, putting our fingers at random in the dictionary and seeing whatever it will say about the subject we have nominated. Though there seem to be a strange preponderance of answers about the Koran, we decide not to heed those. That aside, no grand truths are revealed.

* * *

On the day of the Oscars, he sits with some friends on the patio at the deli near his house. He announces that he has just seen Demi Moore and Ashton Kutcher over our shoulders. Jack White walks out from the deli and takes photos of his friends in front of the shop window next to us. Rob eats his regular, improvised low-calorie, low-carb plate: a burger, cottage cheese and tomato sauce. 'I have it every day,' he says.

'Don't you ever get sick of it?' asks Alex, a sharp 15-year-old girl who has been brought along by one of his friends. Her question elicits an answer that is not only honest but that expresses some larger truths about the way he approaches life.

'I will, eventually,' he explains. 'And then I'll never have it again.'

* * *

Another night Rob decides he'd like to go bowling, so we head down to the valley – Rob, his mother, Pompey, Greg the actor and myself – to Pinz Bowl. There's usually room there but every lane is taken – it is a leagues night. It takes us a moment to realise more than this.

Rob works it out first, and points at the words on the back of the shirt of the man queuing at the desk.

Gutter Queens.

We are at gay bowling night. These lanes are where Rob was first surreptitiously photographed with Rachel Hunter; perhaps it is for the best that no one snaps him here tonight.

Meanwhile, occasionally girls do come and do go, without Rob finding anything close to whatever he is after. One calls him every day for two weeks, leaving increasingly hostile messages. He operates on a rough but fairly strict rule of thumb that if anyone calls more than twice without being called back, that is out of kilter enough to make him lose interest. Anyway, this winter his mobile carries the following message: 'Hey, you're through to Rob. As a person I'm incredibly flaky. Please leave a message 'cause they're always entertaining but, I'm being honest, I might not call you back.'

6

In March, he moves to England for a while. Before he has even moved in, photographs of the property he is renting – not just of the exterior, but of each of the rooms, taken by a photographer who tricked his way inside – have already been all over the newspapers. Typically, the truth is soon left far behind – the consensus seems to be that his new home has 22 bedrooms; in fact it has seven, at a stretch – but enough details are given of its location that letters pour in. One is simply addressed to 'Robbie Williams, Eighteenth Century Castle'. (It isn't an eighteenth-century castle – in fact, it is brand new – but that is how one publication has described it.) Another is simply addressed to 'Robbie Williams, singing superstar'.

In his first week there, he leafs through some of this correspondence, none of which will be acknowledged. Many of the writers want something, of course. One suggests, as though it were the most normal thing in the world, that Rob might like to buy a 27-pound dinosaur's tooth to bail out their museum. A man in Poland expects Rob's autograph for a charity exhibition of celebrity autographs. An 18-year-old girl methodically adds up the money she will need for the three years of her dance teaching degree and explains that she will require £27,000. A 66-year-old housewife in West Malaysia, who has stapled a copy of her passport photo and details to her dense four-page letter, takes a while to get to her point. After speaking presumptuously about his mental state, happiness and family (*'paradise lies at the feet of mothers'*, she notes), she drifts as though by accident to the subject of her £13,000 debt. She never comes out and directly asks him, just paints a picture of what her life would be like without this burden, and sends him her blessings. An 80-year-old woman from Sussex – *'I should be a shame writing to you,'* she suggests at the start – is less subtle. She notes that he is a big spender. *'I see as an opportunity of you liking old places, I've got a 54 year old Dressing Table maybe you would like to buy this, I need a helping hand to help out with my pension, if you like walnut-furnished … this could fit in any of your 22 bedrooms and it's now when I need cash, not when I'm dead … my friend thinks this will go in the waste paper basket, well, maybe they are right … '*

There are other letters, with less obvious agendas. Many share long specific details of alcoholism and depression. There are a few from people in the nearby village, most of these chatty and friendly, which usually begin by expressing a sentiment such as 'I hope you get some peace and quiet during your stay', then invite him for dinner, or to sponsor the local football team, or, in one instance, to come to their wedding reception at the local pub. He also hears from a man who needs Rob to know that he once had a telescope that would somehow use coordinates to project UFOs on to the wall of his house. ('He says,' Rob reads, '"*Don't be messing with homo sapiens, the most dangerous creatures on the planet.*" And he wants me to carry on doing the swing stuff.')

Others address problems they feel he has, real or imagined. Many of these are triggered by two articles around the time of his birthday, one in the *Daily Mail* and one in *Hello*, both of which paint him as a tragic character – rich and unhappy and lonely. It shouldn't be necessary to point out here, although it may be, that while he is undeniably rich, and while he is intermittently unhappy in the way that many if not most people are, and while, though he has many friends, he does sometimes feel the loneliness that those who wish to find a partner to spend their life and time with and have not yet done so feel, his day-to-day life, whatever its ups and downs, is almost comically far from the picture they paint of it. Still, these articles have planted the idea that he is a sad man in crisis who needs saving, and there are plenty of strangers with advice and proposals.

Many of those who have written spend several sentences offering reassurance, either to Rob or themselves, that they aren't crazy. *'The last time I wrote to someone after seeing a sad article,'* explains one correspondent, making sure Rob knows that she isn't randomly given to such behaviour, *'was to Lord Brocket when he was in prison.'* Often they float the notion that they may be the person he needs in these dark hours. As a rule, they feel that they understand the person inside and not just the pop star, and would be happy just to be there for him to talk to. (Some of them are so insistent that they are interested in the real, normal non-celebrity they spot within him that it's a wonder they haven't managed to find any other real, normal non-celebrities out in the world who might be more appreciative of their attentions.) A strangely high proportion of these letters are from single mothers. Some of them include pictures of themselves and their children. '*I am not a model like stunner but I am an attractive woman with a decent figure … I am sociable, well-liked … if you fancy a chat on the phone …*' they'll say. One baldly states: '*My 4-year old daughter wants you as her daddy …*' (It is amazing how quickly the letters that start out wanting to save him end up asking him to save them.)

One is from a mother in Northern Ireland, who has enclosed a photo of her daughter standing next to the sink in the kitchen (on the back she has written '*this photo doesn't really do her justice as she is making a funny face with her mouth and not smiling properly – she has a beautiful smile*'). The mother explains that he really shouldn't take the risk of not meeting someone who may be his soulmate: '*Go on, forget about Geri Halliwell, Rachel Hunter and Samantha Mumba and try dating my beautiful daughter,*' she urges, and shows that she has already been sensibly thinking through some of the practicalities: '*You know, if you come over here to stay at Angie's flat (in the spare room, of course) I'm sure you'd be fine, because nobody would believe it was actually you.*'

Just to be clear, in case you imagine this is not a true picture of how the writing public represent themselves to celebrities in this era: these are not examples of extraordinary weirdness sifted from thousands of typical fan letters. These *are* the typical ones.

* * *

iChat, March 2004, while struggling with lyrics for the song 'Tripping Underwater':

There's no soul to the story right now. Something about violence and silence. Neither I care too much for … Jet lag kicked my arse today. Got up at 5. Or, as I like to call it, *You've Been Framed* o'clock. Oh, the joy of being jet set … Lyric writing's hard. Can't seem to be brilliant. And I want it to be so badly. It's doing my head in. Being in England makes everything seem very claustrophobic for me. Makes the road seem very narrow. There's not much to write about when your world gets smaller … just tired and ungrateful, s'pose.

* * *

In promotion of his new album *Patience*, George Michael gives an interview to the *Telegraph* magazine, in which he criticises Rob's record deal. (This is someone, it seems fair to mention here, who told Rob that he was seriously considering the option of not using a traditional record company and doing a deal with one of the big supermarket chains instead.)

'That Robbie Williams deal fucks every artist, because it says "OK guys, you're not making enough money on the records you're screwing me on, come and take some of my merchandise, come and take my book publishing, take this, take

that …" It's like, you fucker. The point is, he has – and he told me – no, I'm not even going to say what he told me …'

The interviewer encourages him to do so.

'No, I can't say. At the end of the day I think it's a huge betrayal of any sense of community. But then there isn't a community any more, so I suppose it's understandable …'

'Ooooh,' says Rob when he hears this, in an isn't-*he*-tetchy-today? tone. 'What I make of it is, I must have been a huge thorn in his side for a long time. And he hasn't been able to deal with it. But I'll bring it up at the next community meeting.'

* * *

The main drawing room on the first floor has been converted into the studio. Various weird old paintings are on the walls – there is one of a particularly sinister girl over the couch where Rob lounges to write lyrics, and one of cattle drinking at a country pond over by the computer. Above the fireplace, on mantelpiece far too high to reach without a stepladder, leans a vinyl copy of Patti Smith's *Horses*; Stephen's doing, quite obviously, as are all the Rolling Stones books littered around. I count 19 electric and three acoustic guitars. There is also a grand piano with some broken keys and, amongst the other instruments, a melodica with a blow-tube.

At last, he is taking an interest in finishing the lyrics. Today, after finishing off a song called 'Please Please' that is earmarked as a b-side – and explaining to Stephen that he simply refuses to sing a word like 'hullabaloo' – it's 'Misunderstood'. Many songs will be considered as the first single off the greatest hits – at various times this spring it will definitely be 'Tripping Underwater', 'Radio', 'Boom Boom' and 'Ghosts' – but 'Misunderstood' seems secure in its position as the second.

Before he can complete the lyric to 'Misunderstood', he tries to decide what it is he wants to say with it. For this moment, it seems to be something rather different than it meant in the summer. 'I'm trying to think along the context of, I'm trying to be misunderstood … the joke's backfired,' he explains. 'It's like presenting yourself in a way that you know is not you, thinking that's going to be good enough, and then it all falls to shit. It's thinking that you're above it all, condescendingly taking the piss – *I'm trying to be misunderstood* – and then realising the piss is being taken out of you.'

'So *why* are you trying to be misunderstood?' Stephen clarifies.

'Well,' he says, 'it's a double bluff really.'

For a while he suggests a second line – '*we can't all be Robin Hood*' – half-remembered from the summer. '*I can't say it's gone as planned,*' he then offers. 'It didn't look like this in the brochure,' he explains. It's a slightly more haphazard process than people might expect when he's struggling to find a song's centre. After an hour or so of this, bouncing ideas off the rest of us here, one step forward, one step back, he stands up. 'I'm going to go to bed, I think,' he says, as though he isn't even quite sure of this line. 'But I think this will come in the morning.'

* * *

iChat, March 2004:

D12 single playing right now. Great, in an Outkast's younger dickhead brother kind of way … 'Ghosts' turned out to be a corker. Not a b-side. Hoorah. Like 'Louise'. Same nostalgic feeling, but with a bit more majesty. Not saying it's better, just like Bono writing 'Louise' instead. The words all make sense. Who knew? … I'm listening to *After The Goldrush*. Fuck yes. Amazingly beautiful … music's ace … The Shins are really good. I'm already planning on seeing them in Brighton … I got 'The Harper Valley PTA' on Limewire … and 'World In Motion' … Candi Staton 'You Got The Love'. A Robert top 10, easy … even Roxette sounded good. 'It Must Have Been Love', on the telly. Either it sounds good or something nice was going on in my life at the time … Anyway, I searched for Roxette on Limewire then couldn't bring myself to download. The shame, if this computer was stolen. 'Not only was he downloading Eminem but …' You can imagine. 'Someone who likes Eminem and British porn.' 'Robbie Williams, then …'

* * *

He listens back to one of the other songs they have finished, '1974', which is earmarked as a b-side. 1974 is the year of his birth. He sings along.

Child of the eighties, the Hillsborough crush
That girl in the fourth year that was up the duff
Lisa Parkes, I loved you, but you never saw
A year below you, 1974

He punches the air as he sings 'I loved you'.

He had such a crush on Lisa Parkes. Every time he saw her, he would start rapping because he thought that she'd think he was cool. 'She probably thought I was an idiot,' he sighs.

* * *

Over the months, other snapshots of the boy he was sometimes tumble out. How, when he was tiny and they lived in the pub, his sister Sally would phone him in the bar from upstairs and say she was either Wonderwoman or one of Charlie's Angels, and Rob would believe her and go to nursery and tell the other children who he had spoken to. How, when he was two and a half, he was playing with a friend down the road but he decided he didn't like his friend's mum, so he put a bin by the back gate, climbed on to it, jumped over and walked home. How he arranged to run away with two schoolfriends, but when they came round to pick him up and his mother, having answered the door, asked him what he was up to, he explained, 'Oh, I was going to run away but I don't fancy it tonight.' How he always imagined himself as one of the kids who wouldn't take drugs, but then one day saw a flyer for a rave in Blackpool that a girl had brought to school: 'I literally looked at it and thought: mmmmm, must take drugs.' How he would deliver flowers for his mother's florist, Bloomers, when he was 13: 'It was like performing. If it was a bereavement, I would be fucking terrified with embarrassment.' How, when he lost interest in school, it became an exercise in extended daydreaming for him, the challenge being to sit through the next 90 minutes of lessons undisturbed so that he could play with his mates. 'I did "look interested" for three years,' he remembers. How, going to see Port Vale, the evening matches were the best: 'Half past seven kick-off, and you'd all be huddled into the ground, slightly drunk, lots of jumping, when people weren't afraid to sing – I think men were less conscious of themselves standing up. We used to sing through every game whether we won or lost. Of course at that point you think you're rock hard as well. You think you're ten men. So I enjoyed the feeling of being ten men, but I was the first to run.' How, when he was about 17, he cycled from Manchester to Stoke and halfway back with a friend; they only got on the train for the last bit because it was getting dark and he was bored. How Jonny's dad got him a job standing outside Tesco's in a bowler hat and a big striped suit, 50 quid a day, signing people up for dividend cards. How he worked briefly as a diamond driller's mate, carrying pipes around before everyone adjourned to the pub. How, when Take That took off, his Uncle Danny was still so convinced that Rob was making a terrible mistake. 'Bricks and mortar, lad,' he would tell Rob out of concern for his waywardness. 'All of this will come and go. Learn a trade … '

It was only recently, after the Royal Albert Hall show, that Uncle Danny told his nephew, 'I've got to admit, Robert, I was wrong … '

* * *

iChat, March 2004:

It's weird having the country know what you're doing for your birthday, and you don't.

* * *

His postponed 30th birthday party takes place in March at Skibo Castle, the grand Scottish private members' residence where Madonna was married. He is supposed to have no idea where he is going. The tabloids find out and print details the day before, but he is warned and promises not to read them, and may even genuinely avoid doing so. On the way to the waiting private jet at Farnborough, his car gets lost in the countryside and he wonders whether it is all part of some clever birthday diversion.

I think part of him dreads any event like this and partly doesn't want to go

– if there's one thing in common with the things he avoids, it is that they involve situations and places where things are expected of him – but once he is through the bagpiper's greeting at the front door, he seems to relax into it. He lounges around in his kilt (which Pompey has secretly brought back from America and packed for him), and plays some golf (firing balls at the paparazzi who are shooting him and his friends from the public road). On the second of the two evenings, a set has been built in the library for a private episode of *Family Fortunes*, hosted hilariously, with real questions and the real *nnnn-uhhh* buzzer, by Ant and Dec. He and his family are pitted against a team of his friends: Jonny, Max, Milica, Pompey, Greg. At the beginning everyone sings the theme.

'We asked 100 people to name a great invention ... ' begins Ant.

'The wheel!' shouts Rob with great excitement.

'It's the top answer,' reveals Dec.

After a big quiz, everyone retires to the lounge, where some of the other castle guests are already in residence and where people relax with after-dinner drinks and sing to the house pianist. Despite what the tabloids insisted – based, as usual, just on how they expect him to do these things – he has not booked out the whole castle. Nor, for that matter, is everyone here for five days. Nor has he banned alcohol – those who wish to drink, do so, and by the evenings' ends some are sniffing at ludicrously expensive malts. The legend that persists afterwards, based on an offhand comment of Max's when deflecting questions at the airport, is that everyone has been on milkshakes, though of course there is not a single milkshake to be seen.

Rob says that he would like to sing 'One For My Baby', which sends Max into a small panic; Max is used to having the sheet music in front of him, and he silently sits at the organ built into the reception area, fingering chords and writing them down. After that, other people do turns – amongst them, his father offers his jaunty conversational take on 'I've Got You Under My Skin' and 'King Of The Road', Jonny reprises his Neil Diamond impersonation on 'Hello', which won him *Celebrity Stars In Their Eyes*, and after Rob urges her to, saying that she's been dying to get up there, his mother shimmies through 'Sentimental Journey'. Rob stands back up and sings 'Mr Bojangles'. 'It was probably my favourite song,' he explains, 'until we murdered it every night on tour last year.'

At 2.30 in the morning, the revellers who are still awake go outside to look at the stars, then return to the lounge, where Rob discusses *Pop Idol* in some depth with Ant and Dec. Pete mentions his experiences on the previous generation's TV talent shows. His career took off when he was on *New Faces*. He says that the group who won the finals of the first series in 1973 had a week at the Palladium; Les Dennis was second and he was third. He returned at the beginning of the next series. 'That was the first time he was mentioned on the telly,' he says, indicating Rob. He had been born between the first and second series, and Pete had mentioned it before the show, and so his introduction on his return was: 'Since the last time you saw him, he's had a son, Robert ... !'

As it gets later, they discuss different ways fame can change as time passes. Rob suggests that if he stopped everything right now, then in ten years' time he would no longer be famous. No one agrees with him. The truth is, I think, that once you have a certain level of fame, you can't disown it or disavow it or give it up or walk away from it. It may fade and tarnish and dwindle, with or without your encouragement, but its core remains. You can sabotage it, of course, but all that leaves you with is an uglier, broken fame – no less burden, fewer compensations.

* * *

iChat, April 2004:

Very weepy. Just depressed. No particular reason. It's OK. Nothing's different from two weeks ago, except now it all bothers and worries me. It's that feeling of alone with everybody. I know, it's 'woe is me'. Sorry ... Anyway, back to the drawing board. Life's fucking brilliant. I just want to be in my skin to enjoy it. It's like someone's squeezing my brain. This feeling's the one that didn't shift day after day for a decade. No brake and no respite. ... I'm gonna watch *The Sopranos*.

* * *

'I'm bored shitless,' he says after a few weeks in the country. 'It's going to drive me mad.' For a while he loved it here, him and the dogs and the countryside and the studio set up in the drawing room; he spoke enthusiastically about buying this property or one like it, and Los Angeles seems to recede in his mind, as though it was no longer his principal home, just a winter retreat. But as the weeks pass in England, the repetition of the days begins to grind him down. Mostly it's the fact that as soon as he leaves the grounds, the madness starts. It really gets to him. He wishes there was somewhere nearby he could go, where he could drink a good coffee and watch the world go by without it watching him, but there is nowhere here like that. He plays golf most days at the local course, rides quad bikes day and night through the fields and bluebell woods ('I'm always scared on them,' he explains, 'but the faster I go, the more scared I get, and the happier I am'), travels to town for football matches and parties, works on his music, and plays endless games of *Fawlty Towers* darts on Sky Interactive. He forgot to take his medication to Skibo, and feels fine without it, so tells himself that he can come off it. Two weeks later, he goes back on.

He seems uncomfortable with life like this, lived between extremes, rolling on day after day after day. For him, most days are quickly identified as either one of the best days or one of the worst days, and he finds it difficult to accept the days in between. He is easily and often bored; he has little patience in his own boredom, and he has little patience in pretending to have patience. If he doesn't want to do something or he doesn't want to be somewhere, he will remove himself from the situation. I think he would see this not as an intolerance with other people or the world so much as an intolerance with himself and his inability to endure boredom.

The issue of how and when he is interested in the wider world, in all its mess and glory, is a complicated one. Even though he is habitually self-obsessed and he is the first to draw attention to how self-obsessed he is (when he does this you could say that it is both a way of defusing any criticism and, I suppose, a way of bringing himself back into the conversation), he is not nearly as self-obsessed as a book like this makes him seem, distilling as it does a lifetime of self-obsession into a long day's worth of concentrated highlights. He is perfectly curious and inquisitive – he is forever peppering questions at me and others around him about all kinds of things – but he is curious and inquisitive about whatever he is curious and inquisitive about at that moment, and not yet about anything and everything else that might come before him. It could seem, on first impressions, as though he always likes to be the centre of attention, but I think it's actually more subtle and convoluted than that: he likes to be the centre of his own attention, and is uncomfortable when this fails to happen.

* * *

There are good days, of course. One evening when I'm back in London he iChats me. 'About to get with into bed with a six foot blonde ... where did it all go wrong?' (Of course, at times like this there are some comments he will never be able to resist. 'He's a lovely lad,' he types.) Another night I am staying out in the country – I have been writing in a belvedere on the rooftop – and four of us go for a long night-time walk through the forest, making our way through the mud. The torch gives out. Only a few stars force a little light through the clouds, but we can see the castle in the distance, across the lake. When we are at our furthest from home, Rob patiently explains to David's granddaughter, Mia, where the elves live.

7

iChat, April 2004:

I've never been more gay than this week in my entire life, don't you think?

* * *

As should be quite clear by now, though he has long enjoyed making mischief and playing around with other people's hang-ups about sexuality, and considers that to do so is part of his armoury as a pop star, Rob is always slightly mystified, living his life as he lives it, when he realises that anyone truly believes him to be gay. But this spring there seems to be a sudden sea change in the way he is written about, as though large areas of the media have decided that this must really be the great Robbie Williams secret. The catalyst for this is a TV documentary about Take That, in which Howard Donald says that he wouldn't be surprised if Rob was bisexual, and in which Kevin Kinsella reappears and bluntly ups the stakes even further by stating 'I don't think he is bisexual – I think he is totally gay' and claiming to remember a conversation in which Rob addressed the subject. 'He said, "I don't know if I'm straight or gay,"' Kinsella asserts. 'I said, "Well, it sounds like you are leaning towards gay, but do you enjoy it?" He said, "Well, yeah."'

I am away in London but I call him once the programme has finished.

'Gay helpline,' he answers. He seems bemused rather than annoyed by it all, and doesn't realise how much it will seem to some people as a credible confirmation. Even though the show was shoddy, inaccurate and mean-spirited, and its viewpoint seemed to be that Nigel Martin-Smith was the unappreciated, mistreated hero of those times, mostly it just made him feel nostalgic about Take That: 'I genuinely laughed and found it very funny. I thought I was going to be really angry by the end of it, that I was going to want to sue people and phone people up and tell them what pricks they are. I just enjoyed it.' The only bits he really minded were those where he was speaking like Liam Gallagher because he thought he sounded like such an idiot.

But, as his subsequent iChat acknowledges, his perceived gayness swells over the days to come. The Kevin Kinsella quotes travel around the world. The gossip website Popbitch repeats a story claiming that George Michael has told the editor of a national newspaper that both he and his boyfriend Kenny have separately enjoyed the pleasure of Rob's company. One of the tabloids writes about a gardener – Rob doesn't even know who they mean, but he was apparently someone who has worked in the grounds once – who they say is his new pal now that Jonny is not around so much and is regularly invited into the house. Nudge nudge.

He's not that bothered, but we discuss the familiar conundrum: how the offensive part of all this is not the suggestion that he is gay but the implication that he is living some kind of lie, and how weird it is to know that, if he were bothered, there is almost nothing he could do about it.

* * *

He eventually sets his heart on 'Ghosts' being the first single off the greatest hits, though he believes everyone else is pushing him towards the shouty swagger of 'Boom Boom'. That Saturday, when he sees David Enthoven in the box at Chelsea as they watch a dull 0–0 draw, David tells him that he thinks the only one of the songs they are working on that sounds like a first single is not 'Ghosts' but the one they wrote last summer called 'Radio'. David says he doesn't like what has happened to 'Boom Boom', finds the backing vocals on 'Ghosts' cheesy, and is unsettled by its lack of a conventional chorus.

Rob is thoroughly put out by this point of view, and he broods about it all weekend. Though he doesn't want 'Boom Boom' as the single any more himself, that is partly because he thinks it is too obvious, because he thinks it would be such a huge, predictable hit. He is taken aback by any suggestion that it might not be. As for 'Ghosts', 'I just think it's really nostalgic and beautiful,' he tells me. 'I like the fact that there's no chorus.' He tries to call Chris Briggs to discuss it, but he isn't home, so he sits there late on Saturday night, becoming increasingly fed up, while at the same time researching on the internet which are the strongest espressos. (Jolt Espresso seems to be the premium pick. 'Fuck me, I bet that's good,' he says. 'I bet that rocks. Got to get some of that.')

He realises that he may have reached a fork in the road with the choice he now has to make. 'It's as simple as this, basically,' he reflects. 'It's either private jets for the rest of my life, or first class. Do you know what I mean? In regards where I go now.'

If this is his dilemma, it is not one that is as straightforward as it might at first seem. It is not that the record company or his management will always push him in one direction, towards the more commercial choices that will maintain the private-jet lifestyle (though sometimes they might), and that he will always pull for the less commercial, more artistically pure choice (though sometimes he might). The real battle is within him: between the part of him that wants to entertain at all costs, to please and dazzle the most people in the most captivating way he knows how, and the part of him that doesn't like some of the choices this first instinct has led him to make, and imagines there is another way. Even within him, it is not some simple tug-of-war between art and commerce: many of his most passionate impulses are his most commercial, and he is just as suspicious of wilful indulgence as craven crowd-pleasing.

This debate rages during the trip he makes to Monaco – with Jonny, Pompey, Gary and me – to see the Champions League semi-final first leg between Chelsea and Monaco. We fly in two days before. No first class yet; a private jet to Cannes and a helicopter across the bay to the heliport squeezed on to the Monaco waterfront.

In his room he listens to 'Radio'. 'I never saw this as a single,' he says, shaking his head.

'I always thought this was struggling to get on the album,' says Jonny.

'I've always seen "Radio" as an album track that's weird and great,' says Rob.

He and Jonny throw golf balls at each other; they are each supposed to take the blow without moving. They continually criticise each other for flinching.

'Don't go for me nuts, Rob,' pleads Jonny.

'I'm going for your nuts,' says Rob. 'That's what you did.'

'Yeah, but you've got tracky bottoms on,' says Jonny.

After a while of this, they listen to 'Ghosts'. 'And I can sing the arse off this,' says Rob, picking up the conversation from before the golf ball violence took over. 'It's my "Vienna". I mean, it's not as big as "Vienna" … it's like I said the other night, it's the difference between private jets and first class. It's like private jets – unhappy, first class – happy.'

I point out to him that if this is the choice as he sees it in his head, it is not one he has been communicating recently to anyone else.

He nods. 'I always mean to not compromise, and then I forget,' he says. 'If I had a sign over my mirror in the morning that said NO COMPROMISE, then I'd remember not to compromise, but as it stands, I just forget. To not compromise. Because it's easier to go: oh … But I *can't*. I've just done so much of it. I've done *so* much of it. And having a compromised album like *Escapology* and thinking that I could promote it – "Well, I'll just do this one" – I don't want to do that again. No compromise!'

He has made up his mind.

* * *

He spends a little time in the hotel's casino. Mostly he enjoys playing this horse-racing game, where you sit around while six plastic horses race each other and bet on the outcome. The betting is done in increments of one euro, so it's difficult to raise the stakes too high, and he does fairly well anyway. The blackjack table is less kind to him, and during a couple of sessions he is separated from €1000 with frustrating ease. Between games, he innocently chats to one of the Chelsea players' wives, until the player's father asks, quite seriously, 'Does he want a stabbing?'

One evening we go out with Jenson Button. (The other day, after a race, Jenson tried to phone Rob on Pompey's phone and left a message – he, Michael Schumacher, Pablo Montoya and David Coulthard all singing 'Rock DJ' down the phone.) Jenson lives in Monaco but comes across as very far from the playboy he has been portrayed. He takes us to a quiet bar by the sea for soft drinks, then he and Rob gamble modestly on the horse races, though he barely seems familiar with the inside of the casino. Walking down the road – our hotel is on one of the twisting streets that make up the Grand Prix circuit – Rob points out the spot where he always crashes on his Playstation Monaco game. Jenson smiles and points over at the tunnel, towards where he crashed in reality last year, at 160 miles per hour, and was knocked unconscious.

Back in his room Rob hands me one of the chocolates the hotel have left for him.

I take a small bite, but I don't like it.

'Too rich,' I apologise.

'Yeah, I know,' he says, 'but I got us here, didn't I?'

* * *

David flies in on match day to find Rob fired up to discuss his single and where he is heading. 'I really like "Ghosts",' he presses. 'It's what I'm about. It's where I'm at.' David nods, acknowledging Rob's point of view and preparing his counter-arguments. 'I was just thinking,' says Rob, as though throwing in one further eccentric thought, 'of not compromising myself, for what I like.'

'Right,' says David. 'It's a great song but, hand on heart, I don't think it's a big hit single.'

'Well, then the conversation turns to … ' begins Rob.

'Other tracks?' says David.

'No,' says Rob. 'To: how happy has making big hit singles made me? When, if I went and had a look back at all of my singles, I prefer "Ghosts" to most of them. As something creatively that fits me, I prefer "Ghosts" to … *all* of them. It might not be a hit single – that's what I'm saying. All I'm saying is: how happy has making hit singles made me?'

They debate it back and forth. Rob sings a new chorus line over 'Ghosts', and David admits it gives him a shiver down his neck and begins to waver a little. In the meantime, Rob has to recognise that the song David is arguing for – 'Radio' – is not some cheesy, safe, obvious crowd-pleaser. In fact, it's a thoroughly eccentric and unusual song. David argues that it is the perfect way to introduce Rob and Stephen as the new songwriting partnership. 'To me, "Radio" says more about the future,' he says. 'And, I will agree with you, "Ghosts" does too, but it doesn't feel like a hit single.'

'I'm just a bit lost and I don't know which one to go with,' says Rob, yawning.

The match is thrilling, but Chelsea lose 3–1 against a ten-man Monaco after a disastrous last half-hour that leaves us feeling shattered. In the van to the airport, it leads him to think of his own solo career in the same context. 'I've got to say,' he reflects, 'that for eight years solid it's been like being in the Champions League and not getting knocked out.' He laughs. 'And going to the Copa America and getting stuffed. And thinking that I've got too many fixtures and I don't want to go again.'

On the plane, he tries to think of possible girlfriends and tells David he's going to have a gold tooth put in. He doesn't. The next night, back out in the country, he is so bored that he gets driven halfway to Guildford and then gets driven back again. Two days later, there is a summit meeting at the house about the single. Rob repeats, and expands, his new favourite metaphor. 'So we're on the same page about everything, so you know where I'm coming from,' he begins, 'I've got a choice to make, and my choice is: private planes or first class. Private planes – compromise, and be fucking miserable, and have another huge selection of songs that I'm singing live that I don't like, or do things like "Ghosts" and "Radio" and be quite happy and content.' (Notice that 'Radio' is now on the side of good.) 'In the process,' he continues, 'the best thing that could happen is that everybody comes with us. The worst thing that could happen is that it would just take a little bit of pressure off me. What I'm saying is, we could have it different. It could be *different*. Although it's nice to do like three nights at Knebworth and make all that money and stuff ... why don't we just chill out?'

Everyone laughs.

He talks passionately about 'Ghosts' and then they listen to 'Radio' and he says, 'You know, I'm quite happy for that to be the single. Because it's ... fucking mental.' It is almost as though, satisfied that he has stood his ground and prevailed and that people have accepted his argument that 'Ghosts' should be the single, he now feels free to change his mind. 'So that's the single then,' he says, of 'Radio'. 'I think kids will fucking love that as well. Not only is it just dark, mental, but kids are going to fucking buy that in droves. I just think they're going to go, "This is ace." And you could play that song to anyone and they wouldn't say "Robbie Williams".'

* * *

At a wine bar and restaurant in the small Sussex town of Billingshurst, they struggle to hide how surprised they are that one of the few diners on this quiet April Friday is Robbie Williams. Unbearable light jazz-soul plays in the background, and he strikes up a conversation with the young couple at the next table.

'I'm a bit bored,' he tells them cheerily. 'I might poison myself.'

On the drive back, he mentions the story in the papers that Britney Spears is moving in nearby, and then says, 'Do you know what I'd really like to be doing tomorrow – go on a promotional trip. Denmark. Then France. I'd like to wake up and do a press conference, then sing three songs that I really love. "Ghosts", "Misunderstood" and one we hadn't written yet.'

We stop off at the local pub. (He is chatting to Jonny on the phone as he walks in: 'I'm in a pub ... In the country ... I might be killed ... ') At first he sits quietly in the back room, then a lesbian couple invite him into the front lounge to play pool. Everyone here is sensationally drunk – tequila shots are flying down at a terrifying rate – and friendly in a kind of scary way. Each time they talk to you they lean towards you as though about to fall into you.

He starts playing pool. The agreed stakes are £10 for the game.

One of the women asks if he has a lighter.

'I have,' he says.

'Have you?' says one of the other women, astonished.

'Yeah,' he says, mystified.

'I'm surprised,' she says.

'That I smoke?' he says, confused.

'No, that you have a lighter,' she says.

They repeatedly encourage him to have a tequila.

'No,' he says, 'you wouldn't like me when I drink.'

He goes to the bathroom. One of the slightly creepy older men – this one looks a little like Pete Waterman – follows him there. He wants to know whether it does Rob's head in when people just want to get to know him because he's Robbie Williams. ('This,' Rob describes afterwards, 'is with my dick in my hand.')

Starship's 'Nothing's Gonna Stop Us' comes on.

'Never sounded so good,' says Rob as he sinks the black. He leaves, after '45 minutes of complete madness', £10 richer.

* * *

He has been growing his hair for months, but now he gets it cut off.

'I thought it'd be "new hair, new danger",' he explains, 'but it was just "new hair, look like a football player".'

* * *

There is a story in the *Daily Mirror* claiming that Gary Barlow told people at a party this week that Take That will be re-forming at the end of the year for a special event, and that even Rob is up for it. It is the first he has even heard of it. In fact, before he even hears of it, his management office supply a quote from him for the newspapers: 'I'm afraid there's more chance of hell freezing over.'

Rob endorses the sentiment attributed to him, but he might have chosen to express it differently, knowing as he does the most famous precedent associated with that phrase in pop music. After The Eagles acrimoniously fell apart, there was so much insurmountable rancour amongst the former members that, annoyed to be asked for the hundredth time whether they could ever re-form, one of them said that hell would freeze over first. That was why, several years later, The Eagles had the wit to name their reunion tour and album *Hell Freezes Over*.

* * *

One night I am on the verge of sleep at Rob's country retreat when I hear something familiar. Rob's bedroom is directly above the one I am staying in, and when his TV is turned up loud I can hear it rumble through the ceiling. Tonight I recognise the rumble. I am mystified by what I am hearing, though not mystified enough to stay awake for more than a few seconds of wondering why on earth Rob is lying in bed listening to 'Angels'.

The next morning Rob has just appeared from his bed, shirtless and yawning, and is yet to speak, when he is told that Mark Owen is on the telephone. Before he picks up, I tell him what he may need to know – that in this morning's *Sun* it announces that Take That are getting back together without him for a one-off performance this Christmas as part of a promotional campaign for the release of some Take That DVDs. He briefly says hello to Mark, learns enough to know that Mark has no plans to join a re-formed Take That, says he'll call him back when he has properly woken up, and sits down to read the story. He smiles.

'I quite fancy it,' he says.

Really? I ask.

'Yeah. If I wasn't doing anything this Christmas, I'd do that.'

Even if Nigel was involved? (*The Sun* say that Nigel Martin-Smith is negotiating the deals for the re-forming foursome.)

'Yes,' he says. 'I saw "Everything Changes" last night on the telly.'

It's only now I remember about hearing 'Angels'.

'That was on,' he nods, 'and so I watched some of that and then I turned over and there was "Everything Changes". I was just flicking through the channels.' He smiles. 'It'd be really weird to release "Radio" and then do a Take That gig ... I don't know if that's good.'

Why would you do it? I ask.

Sometimes he ignores questions or simply doesn't answer them, but he now sits there at the dining room table, looking away, pursing his lips. He is clearly pondering the issue deeply. For 78 seconds he says nothing at all. 'I don't know,' he eventually answers. 'I was thinking: why would I do it? I don't know. I just quite liked seeing the documentary the other week, and the songs. Just really innocent. I really enjoyed "Everything Changes" last night ... ' (The other thing he noticed about the video was that he used to have a Franz Ferdinand haircut.)

He says he'd most like to sing 'Why Can't I Wake Up With You' and right now he feels as though he'd really like to rehearse his socks off to prepare for something like that.

How would you feel, I ask, rehearsing with Gary?

Pause. 'Alright,' he says.

And the first time you felt he'd said something really patronising ... ?

'I'd be: I know why I'm doing this and you're a prat,' he says. 'He's one of those people that hasn't got a fucking clue what you're on about when you call him on stuff. He probably really feels really hurt by everything that I've said.'

He does worry, though, that however calm he feels about Nigel Martin-Smith's involvement, when he saw him he might kill him.

He eats some fish and rice, then calls Josie. 'See, I'm quite interested in doing something ... I am ... yeah ... yeah ... ' I can hear her astonishment. 'Yeah, completely for fun, no ulterior motives other than there was something beautiful there and I'd like to celebrate that ... ' he says.

'I'll have to get my hell-freezing equipment out,' she tells him.

He calls Mark. 'Hiya, dude … I've woken up now … ' he says. They exchange pleasantries and then he says, 'I'm quite interested in doing something … with Take That … yeah … ' It is Mark's turn to be astonished. He had told Gary he would only do it if Rob did, but he had no expectation at all that Rob would be interested. 'I just, I think personally in some way I would just like to acknowledge something that I've slagged off as being good, actually – do you know what I mean?' says Rob. 'I'll probably have David and Tim going … '

I tell him that David has just called on the other line. He calls David back. David is not happy.

'I don't think you need to go and revisit it … ' says David sternly, panicking a little. 'I think it should be left alone … you can never re-create what you did then.'

Rob says he will think about it.

* * *

He has been approached about the lead role of *Boys From Oz* on Broadway, replacing Hugh Jackman. Three months. Eight shows a week.

'How much?' asks Rob. He thinks. 'Three months in New York. It'd have to be next year. I won't say no … '

* * *

One Friday morning he sits at the dining room table and makes a CD for Matt Lucas, whose thirtieth birthday party he will be attending that evening. He cuts out figures from *Attitude* magazine to customise the CD case and cover. For the rest, he simply uses George Michael's *Patience* CD case. He titles the compilation 'Lonely At The Top'.

In town, he pops into Air Studios, where strings are being recorded, primarily for 'Misunderstood'. He chats with Chris Martin – Coldplay are also recording here – then tells Stephen, minutes before the session is about to start, that he intends to sing a vocal but that he wants to change the third and fourth lines of the song: *Love the way they smiled at me, held their face for eternity*. He knows what he would like the new fourth line to be – *I'd break my heart to make things right* – his mishearing of Scott Walker that he has been reminded of while reading a draft of this book. He wants a third line, right now. He leads Stephen into a back room, waiting for his sushi to arrive, and demands ideas.

'It could be *you do* … something bad,' suggests Rob, '*and I'll break my heart to make things right*.' Not that. '*I'll do the same again tonight*,' he suggests. '*I'll be the same again tonight*?'

'It's difficult getting away from the lines that didn't make any sense but felt big,' says Stephen. 'Everything else seems to be making it smaller, doesn't it?'

'I always thought that you were right ...' he sings. *'I always knew that you were right? ... I'm committed to the fight? ...'*

He settles on *'I always seem to start a fight.'*

'That's good,' he says. 'Yeah? Done. Yeah?'

He zips up his black coat. This is the right attire for such a vocal. 'Just straight lines,' he declares. 'Black. Cap on. Statesmanlike.'

He sings alone in the vocal booth.

I'm trying to be misunderstood. But it doesn't do me any good. I always seem to start a fight. I'd break my heart to make things right.

His coat is buttoned up and his hands are in his pockets.

I'll be misunderstood by the beautiful and good in this city. None of it was planned. Take me by the hand. Just don't try and understand.

In the main studio room, the string section runs through Claire's orchestration.

Still I find myself outside. You can't say I haven't tried. Perhaps I tried too hard. No excuses. I won't apologise. Or justify your lies.

Towards the end, he withdraws his hands and cups them in front of him.

Can't forgive, sorry to say. You don't know you're guilty anyway. Isn't it funny how we don't speak the language of love?

While the song is being mixed, Stephen persuades Rob that the old *'face for eternity'* couplet works better, after all.

* * *

It's usually not fun being an accidental magnet for strangers' attention, and sometimes it is not the slightest bit funny.

One afternoon, a woman in a yellow mini arrives at the house, already having made her way through gates and across acres of private land, and explains that she is expected: she has been speaking to Rob. She gives Gary her name, and a photo of herself and her kids, as though this were the normal way to identify oneself when turning up at a famous friend's house. He takes these to Rob, who is feeling low and having an afternoon nap. Rob doesn't know her. When Gary goes back out, she clarifies what she meant. She is psychic, she explains, and she has actually been speaking to Rob psychically. They've been speaking rather a lot over the past month, she calmly relates, and in fact she has been helping him.

Eventually Gary has to explain that his phone has a very real mechanism in it by which he can actually speak to the police, and she agrees to leave. Later she is seen down a nearby public road, parked up. Gary is woken at five the next morning by the dogs' barking; she has driven up by the house, waiting. Even when he calls the police, she won't leave. Eventually the police come and, in tears, she agrees to go, but by the afternoon she is back, her car hidden behind a hedge on the property. Rob cancels his golf game and stays home while it is dealt with. The police come and eventually have to arrest her.

She tells them that she slept with Rob last night. And this afternoon. 'Listen to the God in your head,' she screams.

Eventually, when the police cannot calm or reason with her, she is sectioned.

* * *

A week after his conversation with Mark Owen, I ask how the prospective Take That reunion stands. His answer is not a huge surprise.

'I can't be arsed,' he laughs sheepishly.

* * *

'Misunderstood' has been edging towards its meaning for months, but in the last few weeks it has found it.

'I think it's what this book's about really,' says Rob. 'Having something documented that tells the proper story.'

He bites into an apple.

'Basically, if two people watch a crime being committed and you take them away to be interviewed separately, they give two different accounts ... ' he begins. He thumps the table. 'It's autobiographical *again*,' he says, as though this admission is a cause of some frustration. 'I think there's some unfair shit written about me, and I think it causes people who meet me to think that I'm somebody else, and I'm not. And it upsets me and pisses me off. "Misunderstood" is like the older brother of "Strong", really, with a little bit more growth, I think.'

He sighs.

'It's a bit futile, anyway, because people that choose to perceive me that way don't want to see me in any other way. They'd rather have me pinned down as a wanker, rather than somebody that's not as premeditated or as cynical as people think I am. I've only learned how to be cynical because people point out what the cynical bits are. I think the second verse is more defiant. I always like Bono and Morrissey when they say lines like "*I'm not afraid of anyone in this world, there's nothing you can throw at me that I haven't already heard*". If they really mean that, that's brilliant, but I quite regularly am afraid of people and what they can do to me with words. It's quite nice to see some growth in me in the second verse – *I won't justify your lies*. There's so much stuff that you've just got to let it wash over you. You've got a two-million-pound gambling addiction and you've been seen pissed coming out of some bar ... documentary that said I'm definitely gay. There's no need for me to say or do anything. I won't justify anything. If you're thinking like that, then fuck off. *I'll be misunderstood by the beautiful and good in this city ... none of it was planned*. You know, none of it was my plan to create this monster that wins the worst evil villain of the year award. I just wanted to do some pop songs and sing them.'

* * *

On the morning after Chelsea's unsuccessful second leg against Monaco, he joins Jonny and Dec – who both came back after the match – at the breakfast table. In today's newspapers Britney Spears has given an interview in which she describes Rob as 'hot and very sexy'.

'She means fat and socially inept,' he scowls, but he's quietly pleased.

* * *

'Radio' now seems certain to be the first single, and Rob decides that it needs a second verse. As it stands, the first verse is simply repeated twice; many of these are just words Rob spouted off the top of his head when the song was being written last summer in the Air attic. (He has since tidied them up a little and added the word 'ouch' over the descending instrumental interlude before the song's climax.)

Today, he sits down with Stephen on the sofa in the studio, perhaps expecting one of those long, agonising evenings that have been needed to extract other new lyrics, but after a few minutes Stephen, who has been busy sorting the complete works of Belle & Sebastian on his iPod, mentions that he did already have a go himself. Rob reads it and declares that it is perfect. The new words don't exactly help the song to make sense, but they do help to suggest that its random madness is the singer's deliberate intention. As for what the song does now mean, Rob says, a little unwilling to engage in the conversation, 'It was just a train of thought. I haven't bothered thinking about it. It's like "... Monkey" – I don't want to get forced to look on the backstreets of "... Monkey" to see what that's about.' I do at least get some insight into the line in the chorus that never seemed as though it could possibly make it into the finished song – *'make it effervescent, dear'* – but which had done.

Why 'effervescent'? I ask.

'Because they were number one that week,' he says.

It was all a wonderful mistake. It turns out that he is thinking of Evanescence, who he has always thought were called Effervescence.

He sings the vocal again. In keeping with his recent habit of choosing appropriate clothing for each new song he sings, he says that he isn't happy with his footwear for these vocals. He's wearing brown Nikes, and they don't go with his blue tracksuit bottoms. He wishes he was in his white Nikes without laces, but they're in the car. Never mind. He will rise above it.

He sings, and as he sings, he starts to dance, beginning to inhabit his new persona.

'Ouch!' he says.

'Ouch!' he croons.

'Ouch!' he shouts.

* * *

iChat, spring 2004.

Does it just end suddenly? 'And then Robbie went to bed ... ?'

* * *

Sometimes over the past months there has been talk between us of how a book like this will stop. Depending on his mood, he might wish it to end on any one of the many snapshots of triumph, retirement, resignation, despair, contentment, daftness, focus, aimlessness, hope or inspiration that populate his life now, and echo those that have come before.

He will be about to leave for the golf course, and he will declare to me 'The end', as though that is the moment that should be frozen at the end of the reel: a man in golf clothes, walking away. Or he will do so after he shouts 'No compromise' in a Monaco hotel room, and promises not to forget it. Or, at an instance of little significance at all, he will declare: 'How about the end of the book is just I pour vinaigrette on my head?' Or, as he dictates one day with mock solemnity, he will suggest it should end: '*"Thank God I got in Take That," he says, sitting round eating food with his mates in his castle.*' Or maybe just ... 'Ouch.'

But when they are honest, books like this don't end so neatly; not with a pat, rounded conclusion, or with an apposite moral, or with a crowning moment, or with a final resonant incident presented as the satisfying culmination of an arc. They just finish where and when they finish, and in that instant they and their subject part company. They stop, having said all they can say for now, and their subject carries on, to fulfil and defy all that this history has suggested. And, with luck and providence, plenty more that it and he have never even imagined.

99 Red Balloons
English words by Kevin McAlea and
Music by Joern-Uwe
Fahrenkrog-Peteresen and Carlo Karges
© 1983 Edition Hate, Germany
Reproduced by Permission of EMI Songs Ltd,
London WC2H 0QY

All Over Again
Words and Music by Stephen Duffy
© 1999 Sony Music Publishing UK
All Rights Reserved. International Copyright Secured

Babe
Words And Music By Gary Barlow
© EMI Virgin Music Ltd

Back For Good
Words and Music by Gary Barlow
© EMI Virgin Music Ltd

Being Boring
Words and Music by Chris Lowe and Neil Tennant
© 1990 Cage Music Limited. Sony/ATV Music
Publishing Ltd
All Rights Reserved. International Copyright Secured

Freedom '90
Words and Music by George Michael
© Robobuild Limited
C/O Russells, Regency House, 1/4 Warwick Street,
London, W1B 5LJ
Used with Kind Permission of the Publisher

Guys And Dolls
Words and Music by Frank Loesser
© MPL Communications Ltd

Heaven Knows I'm Miserable Now
Words and Music by Morrissey/Marr
© Morrissey/Copyright Control/Sanctuary

In My Place
Words and Music by Berryman/ Buckland/
Champion/ Martin
© BMG Music Publishing Ltd
All Rights Reserved. Used by Permission

I Don't Like Mondays
Words and Music by Bob Geldof
© Sherlock Holmes Music Ltd

It's De-lovely
Words and Music by Cole Porter
© Buxton Hill Music Corp, USA
Chappell Music Ltd, London W6 8BS
Reproduced by Permission of International Music
Publications Ltd
All Rights Reserved

Karma Police
Words and Music by Thomas Yorke, Jonathan
Greenwood, Colin Greenwood,
Edward O'Brien and Philip Selway
© 1997 Warner/Chappell Music Ltd,
London W6 8BS
Reproduced by Permission of International Music
Publications Ltd
All Rights Reserved

Lonely At The Top
Words and Music by Randy Newman
© 1970 January Music Corp and Unichappell
Music Inc, USA
Warner/Chappell North America Ltd,
London W6 8BS
Reproduced by Permission of International Music
Publications Ltd
All Rights Reserved

Love Story
Words and Music by Randy Newman
© January Music Corporation

Rocket Man
Words and Music by Elton John/Bernie Taupin
© 1972 Dick James Music Ltd
Universal/Dick James Music Ltd
All Rights Reserved. International Copyright Secured.

Sex And Drugs And Rock And Roll
Words and Music by Ian Dury and Chas Jankel
© 1977 Templemill Music Ltd
Warner/Chappell Music Ltd, London W6 8BS
Reproduced by Permission of International
Music Publications Ltd

Stuck In A Moment
Words and Music by U2
© Blue Mountain Music Ltd

Suedehead
Words and Music by Stephen Street and
Steven Morrissey
© 1988 EMI Virgin Music Ltd/Sanctuary
Reproduced by Permission of EMI Virgin Music Ltd,
London WC2H 0QY

We Will Rock You
© Queen Music Ltd

Who's Gonna Ride Your Wild Horses
Words and Music by Bono/U2
© Blue Mountain Music Ltd

Chorus
G

Jack